Pro Android with Kotlin

Developing Modern Mobile Apps
with Kotlin and Jetpack

Second Edition

Peter Späth

Apress®

Pro Android with Kotlin: Developing Modern Mobile Apps with Kotlin and Jetpack

Peter Späth
Leipzig, Germany

ISBN-13 (pbk): 978-1-4842-8744-6   ISBN-13 (electronic): 978-1-4842-8745-3
https://doi.org/10.1007/978-1-4842-8745-3

Managing Director, Apress Media LLC: Welmoed Spahr
Acquisitions Editor: Steve Anglin
Development Editor: James Markham
Coordinating Editor: Mark Powers

Cover designed by eStudioCalamar

Cover image by Shutterstock (shutterstock.com)

Distributed to the book trade worldwide by Springer Science+Business Media New York, Plaza, New York, NY 10004, U.S.A. Phone 1-800-SPRINGER, fax (201) 348-4505, e-mail orders-ny@springer-sbm.com, or visit www.springeronline.com. Apress Media, LLC is a California LLC and the sole member (owner) is Springer Science + Business Media Finance Inc (SSBM Finance Inc). SSBM Finance Inc is a **Delaware** corporation.

For information on translations, please e-mail booktranslations@springernature.com; for reprint, paperback, or audio rights, please e-mail bookpermissions@springernature.com.

Apress titles may be purchased in bulk for academic, corporate, or promotional use. eBook versions and licenses are also available for most titles. For more information, reference our Print and eBook Bulk Sales web page at www.apress.com/bulk-sales.

Any source code or other supplementary material referenced by the author in this book is available to readers on GitHub (github.com/apress). For more detailed information, please visit www.apress.com/source-code.

Printed on acid-free paper

To Margret.

Table of Contents

About the Author

Peter Späth, **PhD,** graduated in 2002 as a physicist and soon afterward became an IT consultant, mainly for Java-related projects. In 2016 he decided to concentrate on writing books on various aspects, but with the main focus set on software development. With a lot of experience in Java-related languages, the upcoming of Kotlin for building Android apps made him enthusiastic about writing books for Kotlin development in the Android environment.

About the Technical Reviewer

 **Massimo Nardone** has more than 25 years of experience in security, web/mobile development, cloud, and IT architecture. His true IT passions are security and Android. He has been programming and teaching how to program with Android, Perl, PHP, Java, VB, Python, C/C++, and MySQL for more than 20 years. He holds a Master of Science degree in Computing Science from the University of Salerno, Italy.

He has worked as a CISO, CSO, security executive, IoT executive, project manager, software engineer, research engineer, chief security architect, PCI/SCADA auditor, and senior lead IT security/cloud/SCADA architect for many years. His technical skills include security, Android, cloud, Java, MySQL, Drupal, Cobol, Perl, web and mobile development, MongoDB, D3, Joomla, Couchbase, C/C++, WebGL, Python, Pro Rails, Django CMS, Jekyll, Scratch, and more.

He worked as a visiting lecturer and supervisor for exercises at the Networking Laboratory of the Helsinki University of Technology (Aalto University). He holds four international patents (PKI, SIP, SAML, and Proxy areas). He is currently working for Cognizant as the head of cybersecurity and CISO to help both internally and externally with clients in areas of information and cybersecurity, like strategy, planning, processes, policies, procedures, governance, awareness, and so forth. In June 2017 he became a permanent member of the ISACA Finland Board.

Massimo has reviewed more than 45 IT books for different publishing companies and is the coauthor of *Pro Spring Security: Securing Spring Framework 5 and Boot 2-based Java Applications* (Apress, 2019), *Beginning EJB in Java EE 8* (Apress, 2018), *Pro JPA 2 in Java EE 8* (Apress, 2018), and *Pro Android Games* (Apress, 2015)

Preface

Pro Android with Kotlin is a successor of the famous Apress series for Android development targeting the Java platform. With Kotlin as an official language in the Android environment, allowing for more elegant programs compared with the Java standard, the new book deals with advanced aspects of a modern Android app. With a thorough description of important parts of Android system internals and professional-level APIs, advanced user interface topics, advanced development topics, in-depth communication surveys, professional-level hardware topics including looking at devices other than the smartphone, a troubleshooting part with guidance on how to fix memory and performance problems, and an introduction to app monetizing, the book is supposed to be an invaluable source for developers willing to build state-of-the-art professional apps for modern Android devices.

This book is not meant to be an introduction to the Kotlin language. For this aim please have a look at the Kotlin website or any introductory-level book about Kotlin. What you will find here however is an attempt to use as many features of Kotlin as necessary to write elegant and stable apps using less code compared with Java.

In 2021 and 2022, Android versions 12 and 12.1 have been introduced. In a professional environment, writing apps that require a corresponding API level of 31 is a bad idea, since the worldwide distribution of devices running a 12.x version is below 10% as of the writing of this book. But you can write code targeting version 12.x and also version 6.0 all the way up to 12.1, thus covering approximately 95% of all Android devices, by introducing branches in your code or by using special compatibility-aware classes, and this is what we will be doing in this book. We still concentrate on modern 12.x development, but if we use modern features not available to lower versions, we will be telling you.

Note that this book does not pay much attention to Android versions below 6.0, which corresponds to an API level of 23. If you look into online tutorials, you will find a lot of constructs targeting API levels below 23. Especially when it comes to support libraries that were introduced to improve backward compatibility, development gets unnecessarily complicated if you look at API versions below 23, for the distribution of such devices is neglectable nowadays. The book will just assume you are not interested in such old versions, making it unnecessary to look at such support libraries in many cases and simplifying development considerably.

Introduction

A couple of years have passed since the first edition of this book. For the first edition, Android 8, and API level 26, was the current version, but since then Android versions 9, 10, 11, and 12 have been published. Also, Android Studio has migrated from versions 3.1 to 4.2 (June 2021) and later to Arctic Fox, Bumblebee, Chipmunk, and Dolphin (all mid-2021 till now). At the same time, the Android Gradle plugin migrated from versions 3.0 to 7.2 and Kotlin from versions 1.2 to 1.5. In addition, android.support packages, which help ensure version compatibility across different API levels, are now deprecated and replaced by Jetpack (`https://developer.android.com/jetpack`).

With respect to sophisticated graphics rendering and game development, while in 2018 the new 3D graphics rendering engine Vulkan was in its infancy and therefore not included in the first edition, it gained more and more influence, and adding a section on it in Chapter 9 today makes a lot of sense.

In mid-2019 Google announced *Android Automotive*, a variant of the Android OS capable of managing infotainment systems of selected cars.

With Jetpack Compose a simplified UI development technology entered the Android world, considerably reducing the amount of code by providing sophisticated APIs and applying an elegant declarative builder-like programming pattern. Jetpack was introduced in 2018.

All these changes reflect in the second edition of the book, making sure you as a developer are up to date with the current Android development APIs and tools.

Brevity vs. Expressiveness

The programs we will be explaining in this book, despite their strong affinity to the Kotlin way of thinking, however are not totally mysterious to a Java developer or developer of any other modern computer language. One of the design goals of Kotlin is expressiveness, so to understand Kotlin programs, you need less effort, even when the programs get shorter. But you have to understand that at some point you have to pay for maximum brevity with a loss of expressiveness and a loss of readability.

When it comes to deciding what is better, the author favors expressiveness over brevity, but be assured that a loquacious programming style is considered a no-go. In the end a professional developer wants to write a concise app, because less code means lower costs when it comes to maintenance.

The Transition from Java to Kotlin

Just to whet your appetite, we will have a look at a really simple app lacking lots of features you will want to see in a more complex and professional app and then compare its Java and Kotlin variants.

If you start *Android Studio* and enter the project creation wizard, you will be asked for a template. Select "Basic Activity," choose 23 as the minimum SDK, and have both legacy support libraries and Kotlin support disabled. After the creation, a MainActivity class shows up. Its Java code reads (comments removed)

```java
package book.andrkotlpro.frontjava;

import android.os.Bundle;
import com.google.android.material.snackbar.Snackbar;
import androidx.appcompat.app.AppCompatActivity;
import android.view.View;
import androidx.navigation.NavController;
import androidx.navigation.Navigation;
import androidx.navigation.ui.AppBarConfiguration;
import androidx.navigation.ui.NavigationUI;
import book.andrkotlpro.frontjava.databinding.
    ActivityMainBinding;
import android.view.Menu;
import android.view.MenuItem;

public class MainActivity extends AppCompatActivity {
    private AppBarConfiguration appBarConfiguration;
    private ActivityMainBinding binding;

    @Override
    protected void onCreate(Bundle savedInstanceState) {
```

```java
        super.onCreate(savedInstanceState);

        binding = ActivityMainBinding.inflate(
            getLayoutInflater());
        setContentView(binding.getRoot());

        setSupportActionBar(binding.toolbar);

        NavController navController =
            Navigation.findNavController(this,
                R.id.nav_host_fragment_content_main);
        appBarConfiguration =
            new AppBarConfiguration.Builder(
                navController.getGraph()).build();
        NavigationUI.setupActionBarWithNavController(
            this, navController, appBarConfiguration);

        binding.fab.setOnClickListener(
                new View.OnClickListener() {
            @Override
            public void onClick(View view) {
                Snackbar.make(view,
                    "Replace with your own action",
                    Snackbar.LENGTH_LONG)
                .setAction("Action", null).show();
            }
        });
    }

    @Override
    public boolean onCreateOptionsMenu(Menu menu) {
        getMenuInflater().inflate(R.menu.menu_main, menu);
        return true;
    }

    @Override
    public boolean onOptionsItemSelected(MenuItem item) {
        int id = item.getItemId();
```

```
        if (id == R.id.action_settings) {
            return true;
        }

        return super.onOptionsItemSelected(item);
    }

    @Override
    public boolean onSupportNavigateUp() {
        NavController navController =
            Navigation.findNavController(this,
                R.id.nav_host_fragment_content_main);
        return NavigationUI.navigateUp(navController,
            appBarConfiguration)
        || super.onSupportNavigateUp();
    }
}
```

A few notes about that Java code: The public in front of the class and almost all methods tells that they are visible from everywhere. It cannot be omitted here since otherwise the framework and the rest of the application could not use the class and the methods. The setContentView() is, by virtue of the "set," such a common construct that one could think of allowing contentView = s.th. to be written for it instead. A couple of competitor languages allow for such a syntax. Also for the setOnClickListener(), one might wish to use a .onClickListener = s.th. instead. The argument to setOnClickListener() is an object of an anonymous inner class – it is already an abbreviation of first declaring and then instantiating and using it. It can even be further shortened to

```
    binding.fab.setOnClickListener(
        view -> {
                Snackbar.make(view,
                    "Replace with your own action",
                    Snackbar.LENGTH_LONG)
                .setAction("Action", null).show();
            }
    );
```

This is because the interface has just a single method. The wizard just kind of forgot this abbreviation.

For the various `.getSomething()`, we could just as well write something like `.something`, which would express the same, but shorter.

A sister project doing the same, but *with* Kotlin support, leads to a transposed code in the Kotlin language as follows:

```
package book.andrkotlpro.frontkotlin

import android.os.Bundle
import com.google.android.material.snackbar.Snackbar
import androidx.appcompat.app.AppCompatActivity
import androidx.navigation.findNavController
import androidx.navigation.ui.AppBarConfiguration
import androidx.navigation.ui.navigateUp
import androidx.navigation.ui.
    setupActionBarWithNavController
import android.view.Menu
import android.view.MenuItem
import book.andrkotlpro.frontkotlin.databinding.
    ActivityMainBinding

class MainActivity : AppCompatActivity() {
    private lateinit var appBarConfiguration:
        AppBarConfiguration
    private lateinit var binding:
        ActivityMainBinding

    override fun onCreate(savedInstanceState: Bundle?) {
        super.onCreate(savedInstanceState)

        binding = ActivityMainBinding.inflate(
            layoutInflater)
        setContentView(binding.root)

        setSupportActionBar(binding.toolbar)
```

```kotlin
        val navController = findNavController(
            R.id.nav_host_fragment_content_main)
        appBarConfiguration = AppBarConfiguration(
            navController.graph)
        setupActionBarWithNavController(navController,
            appBarConfiguration)

        binding.fab.setOnClickListener { view ->
            Snackbar.make(view,
                "Replace with your own action",
                Snackbar.LENGTH_LONG)
            .setAction("Action", null).show()
        }
    }

    override fun onCreateOptionsMenu(menu: Menu): Boolean {
        menuInflater.inflate(R.menu.menu_main, menu)
        return true
    }

    override fun onOptionsItemSelected(item: MenuItem):
            Boolean {
        return when (item.itemId) {
            R.id.action_settings -> true
            else -> super.onOptionsItemSelected(item)
        }
    }

    override fun onSupportNavigateUp(): Boolean {
        val navController = findNavController(
            R.id.nav_host_fragment_content_main)
        return navController.navigateUp(
            appBarConfiguration)
        || super.onSupportNavigateUp()
    }
}
```

Looking at the Kotlin code more thoroughly, a couple of observations emerge:

- We don't need the ";" delimiters – Kotlin checks at line breaks whether the statement is finished or whether the following line needs to be included.

- We don't need that `public` in front of the class and the methods – "public" is standard in Kotlin.

- Instead of `extends` we just write ":", improving the readability a little bit.

We don't need to specify a `void` as return type if a function doesn't return anything. Kotlin can infer that.

- Unfortunately, we cannot write `contentView = s.th.` as suggested previously – the Groovy language, for example, allowed for that. The reason this can't be done in Kotlin is that the construct `contentView = s.th.` implies that there must be a class field named `contentView`, which is not the case. The compiler could check for appropriately named methods and then allow for that syntax, but the Kotlin developers decided to impose this restriction and to prohibit the construct if the field doesn't exist. The same holds for the `setOnClickListener`, because a field `onClickListener` doesn't exist either.

- Instead of an anonymous inner class, we can use the functional construct `view -> ....` This is always possible if the addressed class, the listener in that case, just contains a single method, like `void onClick( View v )` in the base interface used here. The Kotlin compiler knows that it must use that particular single method of the listener class. While for Java such lambda expressions were not available before JDK 8, in Kotlin they were available from the very beginning.

As a résumé of that comparison, the Kotlin code with 1117 characters (imports and spaces omitted) does the same as the Java code with 1329 characters. This is a savings of 17%. Usually, 20–30% is a savings rate you can expect for more complex classes.

Despite the syntax being different from Java, the Kotlin compiler translates its source code to the same virtual machine bytecode as Java, so Kotlin can use the plethora of Java libraries that are out there in the wild, and Java developers switching to or also using Kotlin won't miss them.

The Book's Target Audience

The book is for intermediate to experienced Android developers wishing to use the new Kotlin features to address current Android versions and devices.

The readers will in the end be able to use Android Studio and Kotlin as a language for building advanced and elaborated apps targeting the Android platform.

Being a Kotlin expert is not absolutely necessary for using this book, but having read introductory-level books or studied online resources is surely helpful. The online documentation of Kotlin also provides valuable resources you can use as a reference while reading this book.

Source Code

All source code shown or referred to in this book can be found at `github.com/Apress/ pro-android-with-kotlin-2e`.

Online Text Companion

Some lists and tables, as well as some class and interface details, are available to the public as a *text companion* at `github.com/Apress/pro-android-with-kotlin-2e`. References to such online resources are marked appropriately.

How to Read This Book

This book can be read sequentially if you want to get an impression of what can be done on the Android platform. Or you can read chapters independently when need arises while working on your Android projects. Besides, you can use parts of the book as a reference for both finding solutions with respect to particular problems that come up and determining how things can be done using Kotlin instead of Java. This includes the description of special Kotlin language constructs helping you make your code concise and reliable.

The book is split up in chapters. Chapter 1 gives a very short bird's-eye view of the Android system. If you already have some experience with Android, you can skip it or just shortly scan over it.

Chapters 2–6 talk about the Android architecture's corner blocks: an application as a whole, activities, services, broadcasts, and content providers. Talking to you as a pro-level developer, some of the information provided there may seem to be a little bit basic and may be easy to find in the official Android developer documentation or elsewhere on the Web. The reason I nevertheless added them can be seen if looking more thoroughly at it: the information you can find looking at other sources is of varying qualities, sometimes because of historical reasons, sometimes just because it is outdated. So I tried to rectify some of the peculiarities you find there and also provide you a consolidated, fresh, and new view on things, hoping I can save you some time when you try to find out how the deeper-level nuts and bolts of Android work. You can also see them as a reference just to keep under your pillow in case you are in doubt about some development issues coming up while your Android project advances.

Chapter 7 briefly talks about the permission system, something you must of course be acquainted with if you develop pro-level Android apps.

Chapters 8 and 9 deal with APIs you can use in your app, and user interface issues. Because both of them are big issues, it is just not possible to mention everything that refers to these topics. I however tried to give you a selection of useful and interesting solutions for various tasks in that area.

Chapter 10 introduces Firebase, which is a cloud based app development platform providing storage and messaging services.

Chapters 11–12 take a deeper look at development and building strategies and also describe how things can best be done inside Kotlin. While in the previous chapters Kotlin code was presented in a more empirical way, in Chapter 11 I describe how to use Kotlin constructs to produce more elegant and more readable application code.

Chapter 13 on communication describes some methods you can use to communicate between components inside your app or between your app and other apps or the outside world.

Chapter 14 handles different devices from a hardware perspective, including smartphones, wearables like smartwatches, Android TV, and Android Auto. Here we also talk about ways to access the camera and the sensors and how we can interfere with phone calls.

In Chapters 15–18, we deal with testing, troubleshooting, and publishing your app, and the final chapter, Chapter 19, explains how to use the tools provided with the SDK installation (part of Android Studio).

Some Notes About the Code

While in general for all the code presented in this book, I try to follow a *clean code* approach, for brevity and simplicity, I use two anti-patterns you shouldn't follow in your production code:

- I do not use localized string resources, so whenever you see something like

  ```
  android:text = "Some message"
  ```

  inside XML resources, what instead you should do is create a string resource and let the attribute refer to it like in

  ```
  android:text = "@string/message"
  ```

- For logging statements, I always use "LOG" as a tag like in

  ```
  Log.e("LOG", "The message")
  ```

  In your code you instead should create a tag based on the class name

  ```
  companion object {
    val TAG="The class name"
    ...
  }
  ```

  and then use that one:

  ```
  Log.e(TAG, "The message")
  ```

CHAPTER 1

System

The Android OS was born as the child of the Android Inc. company back in 2003 and later acquired by Google LLC in 2005. The first device running Android came into the market in 2008. Since then it ran through numerous updates, with the latest version number by mid-2022 reading 12.1.

Ever since its first build, the market share of the Android OS has been constantly increasing, and by 2021 it is said to stay above 72%. Even though the numbers vary with the sources you use, the success of the Android OS is surely undeniable. This victory partly has its roots in Google LLC being a clever player in the worldwide smartphone market, but it also comes from the Android OS carefully being tailored to match the needs for smartphones and other handheld or handheld-like devices.

Having said that, the majority of computer developers formerly or still working in the PC environment would do a bad job utterly disregarding handheld device development, and this book is the result of giving to you as a developer an aid to understanding the Android OS and mastering the development of programs herein. The book also concentrates on using Kotlin as a language to achieve development demands, but first we will be looking at the Android OS and auxiliary development-related systems to give you an idea about the inner functioning of Android.

The Android Operating System

Android is based on a specially tailored Linux kernel. This kernel provides all the low-level drivers needed to address the hardware and the program execution environment and low-level communication channels.

On top of the kernel, you will find the *Android Runtime (ART)* and a couple of low-level libraries written in C. The latter serve as a glue between application-related libraries and the kernel. The Android Runtime is the execution engine where Android programs run.

1

© Peter Späth 2022
P. Späth, *Pro Android with Kotlin*, https://doi.org/10.1007/978-1-4842-8745-3_1

You as a developer hardly ever need to know about the details of how these low-level libraries and the Android Runtime do their work, but you will be using them for basic programming tasks like addressing the audio subsystem or databases.

Above the low-level libraries and the Android Runtime sits the *Application Framework*, which defines the outer structure of any app you build for Android. It deals with activities, GUI widgets, notifications, resources, and so on. While understanding the low-level libraries certainly helps you write good programs, knowing the Application Framework is essential to write any Android app at all.

On top of all that, you will find the apps your users launch for tasks they have to accomplish. See Figure 1-1.

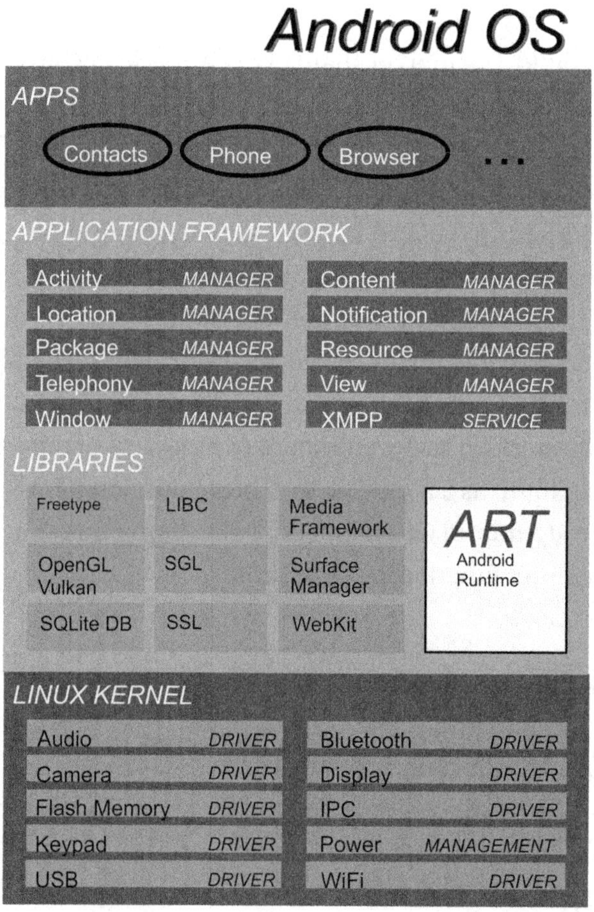

Figure 1-1. *The Android OS*

You as a developer will create Android apps using Kotlin, Java, or C++ as a programming language or a combination of them. And you will be using the Application Framework and the libraries to talk to the Android OS and the hardware. Using C++ as a programming language on a lower level, addressing target architecture peculiarities, leads to incorporating the *Native Development Kit* (NDK), which is an optional part of the Android SDK. While for special purposes it might be necessary to use the NDK, in most cases the extra effort to deal with yet another language and the special challenges it bears does not pay off. So in this book, we mostly will be talking about Kotlin and Java where appropriate.

The Development System

The operating system running on handhelds is one part of the story – you as a developer also need a system for creating Android apps. The latter happens on a PC or laptop, and the software suite you use for it is *Android Studio*.

Android Studio itself is the IDE you use for development, but while you install and operate it, the SDK gets installed as well, and we will be talking about both in the following sections. We will also treat virtual devices, which provide an invaluable aid for testing your app on various target devices.

Android Studio

The Android Studio IDE is the dedicated development environment for creating and running Android apps. Its main window together with an emulator view is shown in Figure 1-2.

Android Studio provides the following:

- Managing program sources for Kotlin, Java, and C++ (NDK)

- Managing program resources

- Allowing to test-run apps inside emulators or connected real devices

- More testing tools

- A debugging facility

- Performance and memory profilers

- Code inspection

- Tools for building local or publishable apps

3

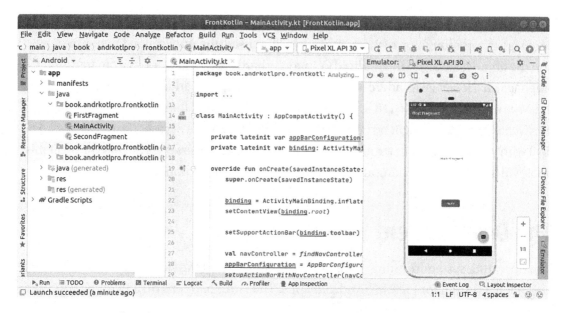

Figure 1-2. *Android Studio*

The help included in the studio and online resources provide enough information to master Android Studio – in this book we will be talking about it once in a while and in dedicated chapters.

Virtual Devices

Developing software for computers always includes the challenge to create one program that is able to handle all possible target systems. With handheld devices coming in so many different forms nowadays, this aspect has become more critical than ever before. You have smartphone devices with sizes between 3.9" and 5.4" and more, tablets from 7" to 14" and more, wearables, TVs at different sizes, and so on, all running with the Android OS.

Of course you as a developer cannot possibly buy all devices that are needed to cover all possible sizes. This is where emulators come in handy. With emulators you don't have to buy hardware, and you still can develop Android apps.

Android Studio makes it easy for you to use emulators for developing and testing apps, and using the tools from the SDK (see the following section " The SDK"), you can even operate the emulators from outside Android Studio.

> **Caution**   You *can* develop apps without owning a single real device. This is however not recommended. You should have at least one smartphone from the latest generation and maybe also a tablet if you can afford it. The reason is that operating real devices feels different compared with emulators, the physical handling is not 100% the same, and the performance differs as well.

To manage virtual devices from inside Android Studio, open the Android Virtual Device (AVD) Manager via *Tools* ➤ *Device Manager*. From here you can investigate, alter, create or delete, and start virtual devices. See Figure 1-3.

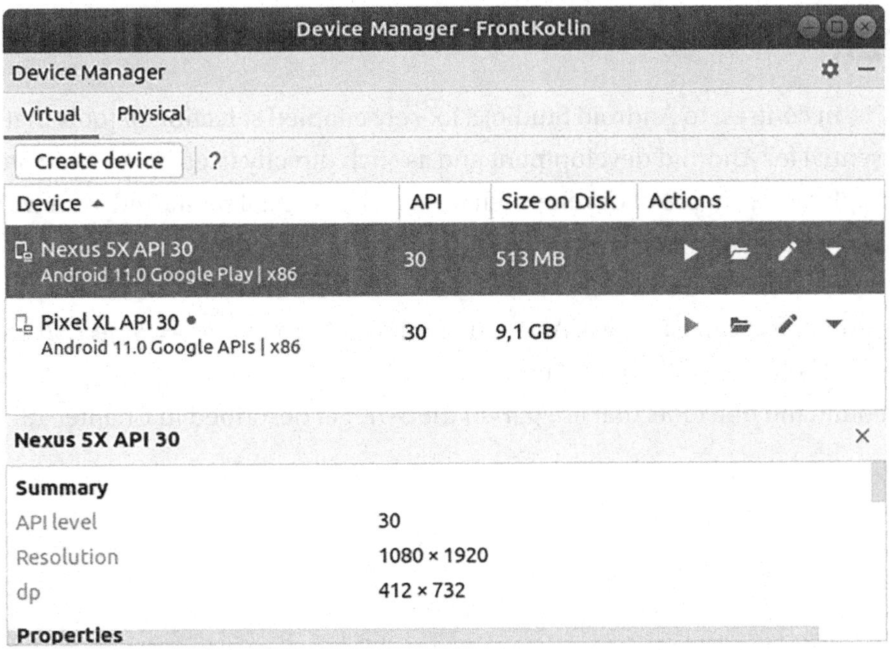

Figure 1-3. *AVD Manager*

When creating a new virtual device, you will be able to choose among a "TV," "Wear," "Phone," "Automotive," or "Tablet" device, you can select the API level to use (and download new API levels), and in the settings you can specify various things like graphics performance, camera mode, and more. For details about managing AVDs (Android Virtual Devices), see the online documentation at `https://developer.android.com/studio/run/managing-avds`.

The virtual device base images and skins used for creating virtual images can be found in

```
SDK_INST/system-images
SDK_INST/skins
```

and the actual virtual devices with installed apps and user data in

```
~/.android/avd
```

Handling running virtual devices can also be done by various command line tools. See sections "The SDK Tools" and "The SDK Platform Tools" in Chapter 19.

The SDK

The SDK is, in contrast to Android Studio, a loosely coupled selection of tools that are either essential for Android development and as such directly used by Android Studio or at least helpful for a couple of development tasks. They can all be started from within a shell and come with or without an own GUI.

In case you don't know where the SDK was installed during the installation of Android Studio, you can easily ask Android Studio itself: go to *File* ➤ *Project Structure* and select "SDK location" from the menu.

The command line tools that are part of the SDK get described in Chapter 19.

CHAPTER 2

Application

An Android app consists of components like *activities, services, broadcast receivers*, and *content providers*. See Figure 2-1. Activities are for interacting with device users, services are for program parts that run without a dedicated user interface, broadcast receivers listen for standardized messages from other apps and components, and content providers allow other apps and components to access a certain amount and kind of data provided by a component.

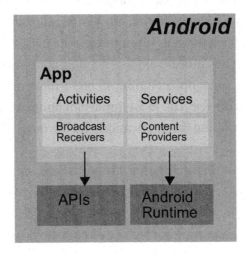

Figure 2-1. *An App in the Android OS*

Components get started by the *Android Runtime*, or execution engine if you like, either by itself or on behalf of other components creating start triggers. Under which circumstances a component gets started depends on its type and the meta-information given to it. At the other side of their lifecycle, all running components are subject to removal from the process execution list either because they have finished their work or the Android OS has decided that a component can be removed because it is no longer needed or must be removed because of a device resource shortage.

© Peter Späth 2022
P. Späth, *Pro Android with Kotlin*, https://doi.org/10.1007/978-1-4842-8745-3_2

In order to make your app or component run as stable as possible and give your users a good feeling about its reliability, a deeper knowledge of the lifecycle of Android components is helpful. We will be looking at system characteristics of components and their lifecycles inside this chapter.

An app or Android component is easy to build – just take one of the tutorials you can find on the official Android website, the templates and examples provided by Android Studio, or one of the thousand other tutorials you can find elsewhere on the Web. A simple app is not necessarily a professional-level stable app though, because Android state handling as far as the app is concerned is not the same as for a desktop application. The reason for this is that your Android device easily might decide to kill your app to save system resources, especially when you temporarily suspend the app in question because you use one or more other apps for some time.

Of course Android will most likely never kill apps you are currently working with, but you have to take precautions. Any app that was killed by Android can be restarted in a defined data and processing state, including most currently entered data by the user and possibly interfering in the least possible amount with the user's current workflow.

From a file perspective, an Android app is a single zip archive file with the suffix .apk. It contains your complete app, including all meta-information that is necessary to run the app on an Android device. The most important control artifact inside is the file AndroidManifest.xml describing the application and the components an application consists of.

We do not in detail cover this archive file structure here, since in most cases Android Studio will be taking care of creating the archive correctly for you, so you usually don't need to know about its intrinsic functioning. But you can easily look inside. Just take any *.apk file, for example, a sample app you've already built using Android Studio, from inside

```
AndroidStudioProject/[YOUR-APP]/release/app-release.apk
```

and unzip it – APK files are just normal zip files. Maybe you have to temporarily change the suffix to .zip so your unzip program can recognize it. Such an unzipped APK file, for example, looks as shown in Figure 2-2.

Figure 2-2. *An APK File Unzipped*

The `.dex` file you can see there contains the compiled classes in *Dalvik Executable* format, something that is similar to a JAR file in Java.

We will be talking about app-related artifacts shortly, but first we will be looking at the more conceptual idea of what *tasks* are.

Tasks

A *task* is a group of activities interacting with each other in such a way that the end user considers them as the elements of an application. A user starts an app and will see the main activity, does some work there, opens and closes sub-activities, maybe switches to another app, comes back, and eventually closes the app.

Looking a little more thorough at it, the main structure a *task* exhibits is its *back stack* or simply *stack*, where activities of an app pile up. The standard behavior for simple apps concerning this stack is the first activity when you launch an app building the *root* of this stack, the next activity launched from inside the app landing on top of it, another sub-activity landing on top of both, and so on. Whenever an activity gets closed because you navigate back (that is where the name *back stack* comes from), the activity gets removed from the stack. And when the root activity gets removed, the stack gets closed as a whole, and your app is considered shut down.

Inside the `<application>` element of the `AndroidManifest.xml,` we see several settings altering the standard behavior of the task stack, and we will see more in Chapter 3 covering activities. This way a tailored task stack can become a powerful means to help your end users understand and fluently use your app. But have in mind that a complicated stack behavior might be hard to understand for users beginning to use your app, so it should be your aim to find a good balance between power and easiness.

> **Note**   More insight into the functioning of tasks and the back stack can be found
> at `https://developer.android.com/guide/components/activities/`
> `tasks-and-back-stack.html`.

The Application Manifest

A very important central app configuration file you can see in any Android app is the file
`AndroidManifest.xml`. It describes the app and declares all the components that are part
of the app. The outline of such a manifest file, for example, might look like

```
<manifest xmlns:android=
            "http://schemas.android.com/apk/res/android"
        xmlns:tools=
            "http://schemas.android.com/tools"
        package="de.pspaeth.tinqly">
    ...
    <application
        android:allowBackup="true"
        android:icon="@mipmap/my_icon"
        android:label="@string/app_name"
        android:roundIcon="@mipmap/my_round_icon"
        android:supportsRtl="true"
        android:theme="@style/AppTheme">
        <activity ... />
    </application>
</manifest>
```

The most important attribute of the root entry <manifest> is called package.
It declares the ID of your app, and if you plan to publish your app, this must be a
worldwide unique ID for it. A good idea is to use your or your company's domain
reversed and then a unique application identifier as shown here.

All possible attributes of <manifest> are described in Table 2-1. Note that
for the most simple apps, all you need is the package attribute and a single
<application> child.

Table 2-1. *Manifest Main Attributes*

Name	Description
android:installLocation	Defines the installation location: use "internalOnly" for installing ever only in the internal storage, "auto" for letting the OS decide with affinity toward using the internal storage (the user can switch later in the system settings), or "preferExternal" for letting the OS decide with affinity toward using the external storage. Default is "internalOnly". Note that a couple of restrictions apply to using external storage for that aim, see the online document "<manifest>", and for modern devices usually having lots of free internal storage, you should never need to specify "preferExternal" here.
package	The worldwide unique ID of your app. A string like "abc.def.ghi. [...]" where the non-dot characters may contain letters A–Z and a–z, numbers 0–9, and underscores. Don't use a number after a dot! This is also the default process name and the default task affinity. See the text companion for what those mean. Note that once your app is published, you cannot change this package name in the Google Play Store. There is no default; you must set this attribute.
android:sharedUserId	Deprecated since API level 29. The name of the Android OS's user ID assigned to the app.
android:sharedUserLabel	Deprecated since API level 29. Only if you also set "sharedUserId", you can set a user-readable label for the shared user ID here.
android:targetSandboxVersion	One of "1" and "2". Serves as a security level. Starting with Android 8.0 or API level 26, you *must* set it to "2" for instant apps. With "2" in contrast to "1", the user ID can no longer be shared between different apps, and the default value for usesClearTextTraffic (see the text companion) is set to false.
android:versionCode	An internal version number of your app. This is not shown to users and only used for comparison of versions. Use an integer number greater than one here. Defaults to undefined.
android:versionName	A user-visible version string. Either the string itself or a pointer to a string resource ("@string/..."). This is not used for anything else but informing the user.

All elements possible as children to the `<manifest>` element are listed in section "Manifest Top-Level Entries" of the online text companion. The most important one, `<application>`, describes the application and gets treated in detail in section "The Application Declaration" of the online text companion.

CHAPTER 3

Activities

Activities represent user interface entry points of your app. Any app you need to interact functionally with the user in a direct way, by letting the user enter things or telling the user graphically about the functional state of an app, will expose at least one *activity* to the system. We say *functionally* because telling the user in a notifying way about events can also happen by notifications via *Toasts* or the *status bar*, for which an activity is not needed.

Apps can have zero, one, or more activities, and they get started in one of two ways:

1. The *main activity*, as declared inside `AndroidManifest.xml`, gets started by launching the app. This is kind of similar to the `main()` function of traditional applications.

2. All activities can be configured to be started by an explicit or implicit *Intent*, as configured inside `AndroidManifest.xml`. Intents are both objects of a class and an outstanding concept in Android. For explicit Intents, by triggering an Intent, a component tells that it needs something to be done by a dedicated component of a dedicated app. For implicit Intents, the component just tells what needs to be done without specifying which component is supposed to do it – the Android OS or the user decides which app or component is capable of fulfilling such an implicit request.

From a user perspective, activities show up as screens that can be started from inside an application launcher, be it the standard launcher or a specialized third-party launcher app. And, as soon as they are running, they get listed in a task stack as well, and users will see them when using the back button.

© Peter Späth 2022
P. Späth, *Pro Android with Kotlin*, https://doi.org/10.1007/978-1-4842-8745-3_3

> **Note**   Activities are such an important concept that it is advisable to see also the online documentation at `https://developer.android.com/guide/components/activities/intro-activities` and `https://developer.android.com/reference/android/app/Activity`. This chapter can only show an excerpt of that huge topic.

Declaring Activities

To declare an activity, inside `AndroidManifest.xml`, write, for example

```xml
<?xml version="1.0" encoding="utf-8"?>
<manifest ...
    package="com.example.myapp">
  <application ... >
      <activity android:name=".ExampleActivity" />
      ...
  </application ... >
  ...
</manifest >
```

As seen in this particular example, you can start the name with a dot, which leads to prepending the app's package name. In this case the full name of the activity reads "com.example.myapp.ExampleActivity". Or you can write the full name here:

```xml
<?xml version="1.0" encoding="utf-8"?>
<manifest ... package="com.example.myapp" ...>
  <application ... >
      <activity android:name=
          "com.example.myapp.ExampleActivity" />
      ...
  </application ... >
  ...
</manifest>
```

All attributes you can add to the `<activity>` element are listed in section "Activity-Related Manifest Entries" in the online text companion.

Elements that can go as child elements inside the `activity` element are as follows:

- **intent-filter**

  An intent filter. For details see section "Intent Filters." You can specify zero, one, or many intent filters.

- **layout**

  Starting with Android 7.0, you can specify layout attributes in multi-window modes here like

  ```
  <layout android:defaultHeight="500dp"
          android:defaultWidth="600dp"
          android:gravity="top|end"
          android:minHeight="450dp"
          android:minWidth="300dp" />
  ```

  where you of course can use your own numbers. The attributes `defaultWidth` and `defaultHeight` specify the default dimensions, `gravity` defines the initial placement of the activity in freeform modes, and `minHeight` and `maxHeight` signify minimum dimensions.

- **meta-data**

  An arbitrary name-value pair in the form `<meta-data android:name = "..." android:resource = "..." android:value = "..." />`. You can have several of them, and they go into an `android.os.Bundle` element available as `PackageItemInfo.metaData`.

Caution   Writing an app without any activity is possible – the app can still provide services, broadcast receivers, and data content as a content provider. One thing you as an app developer need to bear in mind is that users do not necessarily understand what such user interface–less components actually do. In most cases, providing a very simple main activity just to give information is recommended and improves user experience. In a corporate environment though, providing apps without activities is acceptable.

Starting Activities

Activities can be started in one of two ways. First, if the activity is marked as the launchable main activity of an app, the activity can be started from the app launcher. To declare an activity as a launchable main activity, inside the `AndroidManifest.xml` you'd write

```
<activity android:name=
    "com.example.myapp.ExampleActivity">
  <intent-filter>
    <action android:name=
        "android.intent.action.MAIN" />
    <category android:name=
        "android.intent.category.LAUNCHER" />
  </intent-filter>
</activity>
```

The "android.intent.action.MAIN" tells Android that it is the main activity and will go to the bottom of a task. The "android.intent.category.LAUNCHER" tells it must be listed inside the launcher.

Second, an activity can be started by an Intent from the same app or any other app. For this to be possible, inside the manifest you declare an intent filter:

```
<activity android:name=
    "com.example.myapp.ExampleActivity">
  <intent-filter>
    <action android:name=
        "com.example.myapp.ExampleActivity.START_ME" />
    <category android:name=
        "android.intent.category.DEFAULT"/>
  </intent-filter>
</activity>
```

The corresponding code to address this intent filter and actually launch the activity now looks like

```
val intent = Intent()
intent.action =
```

```
        "com.example.myapp.ExampleActivity.START_ME"
startActivity(intent)
```

The flag `exported="false"` must not have been set for calls from other apps. The category specification "android.intent.category.DEFAULT" inside the filter takes care of the activity being launchable even with no category set in the launching code.

In the example shown previously, we used an *explicit* Intent to call an activity. We precisely told Android which activity to call, and we expected there to be precisely one activity that got addressed this way through its intent filter. The other type of Intent is called *implicit* Intent, and what it does contrary to calling precisely one activity is to tell the system what we actually *want* to do without specifying *which* app or which component is capable of doing it. Such implicit calls, for example, look like

```
val intent = Intent(Intent.ACTION_SEND)
intent.type = "text/plain"
intent.putExtra(Intent.EXTRA_TEXT, "Give me a Quote")
startActivity(intent)
```

and what this snippet does is "Call an activity that is able to handle Intent.ACTION_SEND actions, receive texts in MIME type "text/plain", and pass over the text 'Give me a quote." The Android OS will then present the user a list of activities from this or other apps that are capable of receiving this kind of Intent.

Activities can have data associated with them. Just use one of the overloaded `putExtra(...)` methods of the `Intent` class.

Activities and Tasks

What actually happens with a launched activity concerning the task stack gets determined by the attributes

- taskAffinity
- launchMode
- allowTaskReparenting
- clearTaskOnLaunch
- alwaysRetainTaskState

- finishOnTaskLaunch

as given in the `<activity>` element's attributes and the Intent calling flags

- FLAG_ACTIVITY_NEW_TASK

- FLAG_ACTIVITY_CLEAR_TOP

- FLAG_ACTIVITY_SINGLE_TOP

you can specify in `Intent.flags = Intent.<FLAG>` where "`<FLAG>`" is one from the list. In case activity attributes and caller flags contradict, the latter win.

The name of an attribute or flag already gives you a hint what it is supposed to do. For more details about them, please see the online documentation.

Activities Returning Data

If you start an activity by

```
startActivityForResult(intent:Intent, requestCode:Int)
```

it means you expect the called activity to give something back while it returns. The construct you use in the called activity reads

```
val intent = Intent()
intent.putExtra(...)
intent.putExtra(...)
setResult(Activity.RESULT_OK, intent)
finish()
```

where inside the `.putExtra(...)` method calls you can add whatever data is to be returned from the activity. You can, for example, add these lines to the `onBackPressed()` event handler method.

For the `setResult()`'s first argument, you can use either of

- **Activity.RESULT_OK**, if you want to tell the caller the called activity successfully finished its job.

- **Activity.RESULT_CANCELED**, if you want to tell the caller the called activity did not successfully finish its job. You still can put extra information via `.putExtra(...)` to tell what went wrong.

- **Activity.RESULT_FIRST_USER + N**, with N any number from 0, 1, 2, … for any custom result code you want to define. There is practically no limit for N (the maximum value reads $2^{31} - 1$).

Note that you need to take care of also handling back-press events if you have a toolbar. One possibility is to add to the onCreate() method lines as follows:

```
setSupportActionBar(toolbar)
supportActionBar!!.setDisplayHomeAsUpEnabled(true)
// The navigation button from the toolbar does not
// do the same as the BACK button, more precisely
// it does not call the onBackPressed() method.
// We add a listener to do it ourselves
toolbar.setNavigationOnClickListener { onBackPressed() }
```

When the called Intent returns the way described previously, the calling component needs to be informed of that event. This is done asynchronously, since the startActivityForResult() immediately returns and does not wait for the called activity to finish. The way this event gets caught nevertheless is by overriding the onActivityResult() method:

```
override
fun onActivityResult(requestCode:Int, resultCode:Int,
      data:Intent) {
  // do something with 'requestCode' and 'resultCode'
  // returned data is inside 'data'
}
```

The requestCode is whatever you set inside the startActivityForResult() as requestCode, and the resultCode is what you wrote as first argument in setResult() in the called activity.

Caution   On some devices the requestCode has its most significant bit set to 1, no matter what was set before. To be on the safe side, you can use the Kotlin construct
```
val requestCodeFixed = requestCode and 0xFFFF
```
inside onActivityResult().

Intent Filters

Intents are objects to tell Android that something needs to be done, and they can be *explicit* by exactly specifying which component needs to be called or *implicit* if we don't precisely specify the called component but let Android decide which app and which component can answer the request. In case there is an ambiguity and Android cannot decide which component to call for implicit Intents, Android will ask the user.

For implicit Intents to work, a possible intent receiver needs to declare which Intents it is able to receive. For example, an activity might be able to show the contents of a text file, and a caller saying "I need an activity that can show me text files" possibly connects to exactly this activity. Now the way the intent receiver declares its ability to answer to intent requests is by specifying one or more *intent filters* in its app's `AndroidManifest.xml` file. The syntax of such a declaration is

```
<intent-filter android:icon="drawable resource"

            android:label="string resource"
            android:priority="integer" ➤

    ...
</intent-filter>
```

where `icon` points to a drawable resource ID for an icon and `label` points to a string resource ID for a label. If unspecified, the icon or label from the parent element will be used. The `priority` attribute is a number between -999 and 999 and for Intents specifies their ability to handle such intent requests and for receivers specifies the execution order for several receivers. Higher priorities come before lower priorities.

Caution   The `priority` attribute should be used with caution – a component cannot possibly know what priorities other components from other apps can have. So you introduce some kind of dependency between apps, which is not intended by design.

This `<intent-filter>` element can be a child of

- `<activity>` and `<activity-alias>`
- `<service>`
- `<receiver>`

So Intents can be used to launch activities and services and to fire broadcast messages.

And the element must or can have children elements as follows:

- `<action>` is obligatory.

- `<category>`.

- `<data>`.

Note   See also the online documentation at `https://developer.android.com/reference/android/content/Intent`.

Intent Action

The `<action>` child of the filter, or children – you can have more than one – specifies the action to perform. The syntax is

```
<action android:name="string" />
```

This will be something expressing actions like "View," "Pick," "Edit," "Dial," and so on. The complete list of generic actions is specified by the constants whose names have `ACTION_*` inside the class `android.content.Intent` and shown in section "Intent Constituent Parts" in the online text companion. Besides those generic actions, you can also define your own actions.

Note   Using any of the standard actions does not necessarily mean there is any app on your device being able to respond to a corresponding Intent.

Intent Category

The `<category>` child of the filter specifies a category for the filter. The syntax is

```
<category android:name="string" />
```

This attribute may be used to specify the type of component that an Intent should address. You can specify several categories, but the category is not used for all Intents, and you can omit it as well though. The filter will match the Intent only if *all* required categories are present.

When an Intent is used on the invoker side, you can add categories by writing, for example

```
val intent:Intent = Intent(...)
intent.addCategory("android.intent.category.ALTERNATIVE")
```

Standard categories correspond to the constants whose names have `CATEGORY_*` inside the `android.content.Intent` class. We list them in section "Intent Constituent Parts" in the online text companion.

Caution   For implicit Intents, you *must* use the `DEFAULT` category inside the filter. This is because the methods `startActivity()` and `startActivityForResult()` use this category by default.

Intent Data

The `<data>` child of the filter is a data type specification for the filter. The syntax is

```
<data android:scheme="string"
      android:host="string"
      android:port="string"
      android:path="string"
      android:pathPattern="string"
      android:pathPrefix="string"
      android:mimeType="string" />
```

You can specify either

- A data type specified by only the `mimeType` element, for example, "text/plain" or "text/html". So you can write

  ```
  <data android:mimeType="text/html" />
  ```

- A data type specified by scheme, host, port, and some path specification: <scheme>://<host>:<port>[<path>|<pathPrefix>|<pathPattern>]. Here <path> means the full path, <pathPrefix> is the start of a path, and <pathPattern> is like path but with wildcards: "X*" is 0 or more occurrences of character "X," and ".*" is 0 or more occurrences of any character. Due to escaping rules, write \\for a literal "*" and \\\\ for a literal "\".

Or you can specify both of the preceding options.

On the caller side, you can use setType(), setData(), and setDataAndType() to set any data type combination.

Caution   For implicit intent filters, if the caller specifies a URI *data* part as in intent.data = <some URI>, it might not be sufficient to specify just scheme/host/port/path inside the filter declaration. Under these circumstances you also have to specify the MIME type like in mimeType="*/*"; otherwise, the filter possibly won't match. This generally happens in a *content provider* environment, since the content provider's getType() method gets called for the specified URI and the result gets set as the Intent's MIME type.

Intent Extra Data

Any Intent can have extra data added to it, which you can use to send data with it other than that specified by the <data> sub-element.

While you can use one of the various putExtra(...) methods to add any kind of extra data, there are also a couple of standard extra data sent by putExtra(String,Bundle), with the keys given in the list shown in section "Intent Constituent Parts" in the online text companion.

Intent Flags

You can set special intent handling flags by invoking

```
intent.flags = Intent.<FLAG1> or Intent.<FLAG2> or ...
```

Most of these flags specify how the Intent gets handled by the Android OS. Specifically, flags of the form `FLAG_ACTIVITY_` aim at activities called by `Context.startActivity(..)`, and flags like `FLAG_RECEIVER_` are for use with `Context.sendBroadCast(...)`. The tables in section "Intent Constituent Parts" in the online text companion show the details.

System Intent Filters

The system apps, that is, the apps you have installed after you bought a smartphone, have intent filters you can use to call them from your app. Unfortunately, it is not always that easy to guess how to call the activities from system apps, and relevant documentation is hard to find. A remedy is to extract this information from their APK files. This is done for you for API level 26, and the result is listed in the online text companion in section "The System Intent Filters."

As an example, suppose you want to send an email. Looking at the system intent table in the online text companion, you can find a lot of actions inside the table for "PrebuiltGmail". Which one to use? Well, first, a general-purpose interface should not have too many input parameters. Second, we can also look at the action name to find something that seems appropriate. A promising candidate is the "SEND_TO" action: all that it apparently needs is a "mailto:" data specification. And as it happens to be, this is the action we actually need. Using an elaborated "mailto:..." URL allows to specify more recipients, CC and BCC recipients, a subject, and even the mail body. However, you can also just use "mailto:master@universe.com" and add recipients, the body, and so on by using extra fields. See section "Intent Extra Data." So to send an email, possibly with letting the user choose among several email apps installed on their device, write

```
val emailIntent:Intent = Intent(Intent.ACTION_SENDTO,
    Uri.fromParts("mailto","abc@gmail.com", null))
emailIntent.putExtra(Intent.EXTRA_SUBJECT, "Subject")
emailIntent.putExtra(Intent.EXTRA_TEXT, "Body")
startActivity(Intent.createChooser(
    emailIntent, "Send email..."))
// or startActivity(emailIntent) if you want to use
// the standard chooser (or none, if there is only
// one possible receiver).
```

Caution   It is at the receiving app's discretion how to exactly handle intent URIs and extra data. A poorly designed emailer might not allow to specify email header data at all. To be on the safe side, you may want to add all header data both in the "mailto:" URI *and* as extra data.

Activities Lifecycle

Activities have a lifecycle, and contrary to traditional desktop applications, they are intentionally subject to being killed whenever the Android OS decides to do so. So you as a developer need to take special precautions to make an app stable. More precisely, an activity finds itself in one of the following states:

- **Shut down**: The activity is not visible and not processing anything. Still the app containing the activity might be alive because it has some other components running.

- **Created**: Either the activity is the main activity and was started by the user or some other component, or it is an activity regardless of whether "main" or not and was started by some other component, from inside the same app or another app if security considerations permit it. Also, an activity creation happens when you, for example, flip the screen and the app needs to be built up with different screen characteristics. During the creation process, the callback method onCreate() gets called. You must implement this method, since there the GUI needs to be built up. You can also use this callback method to start or connect to services or provide content provider data. And you can use the APIs to *prepare* playing music, operating the camera, or doing anything else the app is made for. This is also a good place to initially set up a database or other data storage your app needs.

- **Started**: Once done with creation, and also in case of a restart after a stop – see in the following – the activity goes into the *started* state. Here the activity is about to become visible to the user. During the start process, the callback method onStart() gets called. This is a good place to start broadcast receivers, start services, and rebuild internal state and processes you quitted while the activity went to the stopped state – see in the following.

- **Resumed**: Shortly before actually becoming visible to the user, the activity goes through the resuming process. During that process the callback onResume() gets called.

- **Running**: The activity is fully visible, and the user can interact with it. This state immediately follows after the resuming process.

- **Paused**: The activity loses focus, but is still at least partly visible. Losing the focus, for example, happens when the user taps the Back or Recents button. The activity may continue to send updates to the UI or continue to produce sound, but in the majority of cases, the activity will proceed to the stopped state – see in the following. During the pausing the onPause() callback gets called. The paused state is followed by the stopped state or the resumed state.

- **Stopped**: The activity is going to be invisible to the user. It later might be restarted or destroyed and expunged from the active process list. During stopping, the onStop() callback gets called. After a stopping either a destruction or a starting happens. Here you can, for example, stop services you started in onStart().

- **Destroyed**: The activity is removed. The callback onDestroy() gets called, and you should implement it and do everything there to release resources and do other cleanup actions.

The possible transitions between an activity's states get listed in Table 3-1 and illustrated in Figure 3-1.

Table 3-1. *Activity State Transitions*

From	To	Description	Implement
Shut down	Created	An activity gets called the first time or after a destruction.	**onCreate()**: Call super. onCreate(), prepare the UI, and start services.
Created	Started	An activity starts after creation.	**onStart()**: You can start services here that are needed only while the activity is visible.
Started	Resumed	The resumed state automatically follows a started state.	**onResume**
Resumed	Running	The running state automatically follows a resumed state.	The activity's functioning including UI activity happens here.
Running	Paused	The activity loses focus, because the user tapped the Back or Recents button.	**onPause**
Paused	Resumed	The activity was not stopped yet, and the user navigates back to the activity.	**onResume()**
Paused	Stopped	The activity is going to be invisible to the user, for example, because another activity gets started.	**onStop()**; You can stop services here that are needed only while the activity is visible.
Stopped	Started	A stopped activity gets started again.	**onStart()**: You can start services here that are needed only while the activity is visible.
Stopped	Destroyed	A stopped activity gets removed.	**onDestroy()**: Release all resources, do a cleanup, and stop services that were started in onCreate.

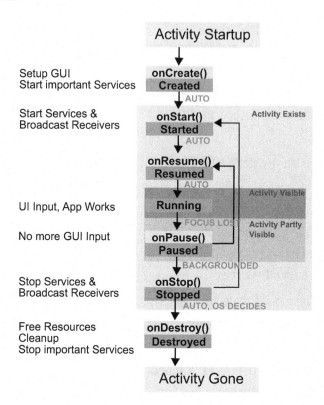

Figure 3-1. *Activity State Transitions*

Preserving State in Activities

We almost overly stressed the need for you to take precautions your app restarts in a well-behaving manner when it forcibly got stopped by the Android OS. Here we give you an advice how that can be done.

Looking at the lifecycle of an activity – see section "Activities Lifecycle" – we can see that an activity about to be killed by the Android OS calls the method onStop(). But there are two more callbacks we haven't talked about yet. They have the names onSaveInstanceState() and onRestoreInstanceState(), and they get called whenever Android decides that an activity's data needs to be saved or restored. This is not the same as onStart() and onStop(), because it is sometimes not necessary to preserve the state. For example, if an activity will not be destroyed but just suspended, the state is going to be kept anyways, and onSaveInstanceState() and onRestoreInstanceState() will not be invoked.

Android already helps us here: the default implementations of
onSaveInstanceState() and onRestoreInstanceState() already save and restore
UI elements that have an ID. So if that is all what you need, you don't have to do
anything. Of course your activity might be more complex and maybe contains other
fields you need to preserve. In this case you can override both onSaveInstanceState()
and onRestoreInstanceState(). Just make sure you call the superclass's methods.
Otherwise, you must be taking care of all UI elements yourself:

```
override
fun onSaveInstanceState(outState:Bundle?) {
    super.onSaveInstanceState(outState)
    // add your own data to the Bundle here...
    // you can use one of the put* methods here
    // or write your own Parcelable types
}
```

```
override
fun onRestoreInstanceState(savedInstanceState: Bundle?) {
    super.onRestoreInstanceState(savedInstanceState)
    // restore your own data from the Bundle here...
    // use one of the get* methods here
}
```

Note that the saved state goes to the onCreate() callback as well, so it is up to you
whether you want to use the onRestoreInstanceState() or the onCreate() method for
restoring the state.

Under other circumstances the standard mechanism for saving and restoring state
might not suit your needs. For example, what it can't accomplish is to preserve data
when you stop your app. In this case the onSaveInstanceState() is not getting called. If
you need to preserve data in such cases as well, what you can do is inside onDestroy()
saving your app's data in a database and reading the database during the onCreate()
callback. See section "Databases" in Chapter 8.

CHAPTER 4

Services

Services are components running without a user interface apart from notifications in the *status bar* or per *Toast* and with a conceptual affinity toward long-running processes. Services can be started by apps, or they can be bound to by apps, or both.

Services come in two flavors: foreground services and background services. While at first glance it seems to be a contradiction speaking of "foreground" services, since so many people tend to tell you that "services run in the background," foreground services do actually exist, and the distinction between foreground and background services is crucial, because their behavior is different.

Caution   Do not misinterpret services as constructs for running anything that needs to be calculated in the background, that is, not disturbing GUI activities. If you need a process that does not interfere with the GUI, but is otherwise not eligible to run while your app is inactive and also not subject to being used from outside your app, consider using an extra thread instead. See Chapter 11.

To wholly understand services is not an easy task, especially with noticeable differences across various Android versions. While this chapter tries to give you an overview and shows you one or the other detail-level hint, it cannot possibly handle all aspects of service development. It is therefore advisable to also consult the online documentation at https://developer.android.com/guide/components/services.

© Peter Späth 2022
P. Späth, *Pro Android with Kotlin*, https://doi.org/10.1007/978-1-4842-8745-3_4

Foreground Services

The intrinsic functioning of foreground services differs with different Android versions. While foreground services prior to Android 8.0 or API level 26 are just background services with an entry inside the status bar and otherwise no stringent influence on how the Android OS handles them, with Android 8.0 or API level 26, foreground services exhibit a special behavior and receive an improved attention by the Android OS, making them less likely to be killed because of resource shortage. In detail

- **Foreground services before Android 8.0 or API level 26** are services that just present a notification entry in the status bar. The client component that needs to use a service doesn't know whether the service started is a foreground service or not; it just starts the service via startService(intent). See Chapter 13.

- **Foreground services starting with Android 8.0 or API level 26** run with the user being made aware of them. They *must* interfere with the operating system by notifications in the status bar. A client component explicitly starts a foreground service by invoking sta rtForeroundService(intent), and the service itself must readily tell the Android OS within a few seconds that it wishes to run as a foreground service by calling startForeground(notificationId, notification).

  One noticeable lifetime characteristic of a foreground service is less likely being killed by Android because of an available resource shortage. The documentation is however not precise about that. Sometimes you'll read "will not be killed" and sometimes "less likely to be killed." Also, the way Android handles such things is subject to change with new Android versions. As a general rule of thumb, you should be very conservative and expect the worst. In this case, read "less likely to be killed" and take precautions if the service ceases functioning while your app is performing some work.

Background Services

Background services run in the background, that is, they will not show an entry in the status bar. They are however allowed to use *Toasts* to send short notification messages to the user. Background services are more brittle compared with foreground services, since Android expects them to be more loosely connected to user activities and thus more readily decides to kill them when there is a resource shortage.

Starting with Android 8.0 (API level 26), a couple of limitations hold instantiating background services the old way, and a shift toward using the *JobScheduler* methodology is recommended. Apps running on Android 8.0 or later are considered to run services in the background, if none of the following is true:

- The app has a visible activity, currently active or paused.

- The app has a foreground service, that is, a service calling `startForegound()` during its operation.

- Another foreground app is connected to it, either by using one of its services or using it as a content provider.

Once an Android 8.0 (or later) app started its life as a background app or switched to being a background app, it has a window of a couple of minutes before it is considered *idle*. Once *idle*, the background services of an app get stopped. As an exception to this, a background app will go on a *whitelist* and is allowed to execute background services, if it handles tasks visible to the user, for example, handling a *Firebase Cloud Messaging* (FCM) message, receiving a broadcast such as an SMS or MMS message, executing a *PendingIntent* from a notification (an Intent to be executed by a different app with the originating app's permission), or starting a *VpnService*.

Most things that were formerly accomplished by executing background jobs are as of Android 8.0 considered to be eligible to be handled by the *JobScheduler* API – see Chapter 8.

Declaring Services

Services get declared inside the app's `AndroidManifest.xml` file like

```
<?xml version="1.0" encoding="utf-8"?>
<manifest ...>
```

```
<application ...>
    <activity ...>
    </activity>
    <service
        android:name=".MyService"
        android:enabled="true"
        android:exported="true">
    </service>
</application>
</manifest>
```

See Table 4-1 for the flags available.

Table 4-1. *Manifest Flags for Services*

Name	Description
android:description	A resource ID pointing to a description of the service. You should use it, because users can kill services, but if you tell them what your service does, this is less likely to happen.
android:directBootAware	One of `true`, `false`. Default is false. If true, the service can run even if the device is not yet unlocked after a restart. The *Direct Boot* mode was introduced in Android 7.0 or API level 24. Note that a *Direct Boot–aware* service must store its data in the *device-protected storage*.
android:enabled	One of `true`, `false`. Default is true. If false, the service is effectively disabled. You wouldn't normally set it to false for a production service.
android:exported	One of `true`, `false`. Whether or not other applications can use the service. Default is false, if there are no intent filters, or true otherwise. The presence of intent filters implies external usage, thus this distinction.

(*continued*)

Table 4-1. (*continued*)

Name	Description
android:icon	The icon resource ID. Default is the app's icon.
android:isolatedProcess	One of `true`, `false`. Default is false. If true, the service has no means to communicate with the system, only through the service methods. It is actually a good idea to use this flag, but in most cases your service will need to talk to the system, so you have to leave it false unless the service is really self-contained.
android:foregroundServiceType	One of "camera", "connectedDevice", "dataSync", "location", "mediaPlayback", "mediaProjection", "microphone", "phoneCall". Android behaves differently for different foreground service types. You can improve user experience if you explicitly specify the type of foreground service using this attribute.
android:label	A label for the service displayed to the user. Default is the app's label.
android:name	The name of the service's class. If you use a dot as the first character, it automatically gets prepended the name of the package specified in the `manifest` element.
android:permission	The permission name adjoint to this service. Default is the permission attribute in the `application` element. If specified nowhere, the service will not be protected.
android:process	The name of the service's process. If specified, the service will run in its own process. If it starts with a colon ":", the process will be private to the app. If it starts with a lowercase letter, the process spawned will be a global process. Security restrictions might apply.

See also `https://developer.android.com/guide/topics/manifest/service-element`.

The `<service>` element allows for child elements:

- **intent-filter**: Zero, one, or many intent filters. They are described in section "Intent Filters" of Chapter 3.

- **meta-data**: An arbitrary name-value pair in the form `<meta-data android:name="..." android:resource="..." android:value="..." />`. You can have several of them, and they go into an `android.os.Bundle` element available as `PackageItemInfo.metaData`.

Starting with Android 9 (API level 28), foreground services must request an additional permission inside the `AndroidManifest.xml` file:

```
<manifest ...>
    <uses-permission android:name="android.permission.FOREGROUND_SERVICE"/>
    ...
</manifest>
```

For you as a professional developer, understanding what a *process* actually is and how it gets treated by the Android OS is quite important; see the `android:service` flag in the manifest for process control. And it can be tricky, because process internals tend to change with new Android versions and they seem to change on a per-minute basis if you look inside blogs. As a matter of fact, a *process* is a computational unit that gets started by the Android OS to perform computational tasks. Also it gets stopped when Android decides it runs out of system resources. If you decide to stop working with a particular app, it doesn't automatically mean the corresponding process or processes get killed. Whenever you start an app for the first time and you don't explicitly tell the app to use another app's process, surely a new process gets created and started, and with subsequent computational tasks, existing processes get used or new processes get started, depending on their settings and relations to each other.

Without any precaution an own service started by an app will run in the app's process. This means the services possibly live and inevitably die with the app. A service needs to be started to actually live, but when it runs in the app's main process, it will die when the app dies. This automatically means a service's resource needs count to the app's resource needs. In former times when resources were more scarce, this was more important than nowadays with stronger devices, but it is still good to know if a service needs a lot of resources, and if there is some kind of resource shortage, it makes a difference if the whole app needs to be killed to free resources or just that greedy service.

If you however tell the service to use its own process by virtue of the android:service manifest entry, the service's lifecycle can be treated independently by the Android OS. You have to decide: either let it use its own process and accept a possible proliferation of processes for just one app, or let them run in one process and couple the lifecycles more closely.

Letting several computation units run in one process bears another consequence: they do not run concurrently! This is crucial for GUI activities and processes, because we know GUI activities must be fast to not obstruct user interactions, and services are conceptionally bound to longer-running computations. A way out of this dilemma is to use asynchronous tasks or threads. We will be talking more about concurrency in Chapter 11.

If the service needs to address the *device-protected storage*, as in the *Direct Boot* mode triggered by the android:directBootAware flag in the manifest, it needs to access a special context:

```
val directBootContext:Context =
        appContext.createDeviceProtectedStorageContext()
// For example open a file from there:
val inStream:FileInputStream =
        directBootContext.openFileInput(filename)
```

You should not use this context normally, only for special services that need to be active directly after the boot process.

Service Classes

Services must extend the

android.app.Service

class or one of its subclasses, and they must be declared inside the app's AndroidManifest.xml file as described previously.

The interface methods from android.app.Service get described in section "Intent Constituent Parts" in the online text companion.

Note that to stop a service that was explicitly started via startService() or startForeroundService, there are two ways: either the service stops itself by calling stopSelf() or stopSelfResult() or from outside by calling stopService().

Starting Services

A service can be explicitly started from any component that is a subclass of `android.content.Context` or has access to a `Context`. This is the case for activities, other services, broadcast receivers, and content providers.

In order to explicitly start a service, you need an appropriate Intent. We basically have two cases: First, if the service lives in the same app as the client (invoker) of the service, you can write

```
val intent = Intent(this, TheService::class.java)
startService(intent)
```

for a normal service or

```
val intent = Intent(this, TheService::class.java)
if (Build.VERSION.SDK_INT >= Build.VERSION_CODES.O) {
    startForegroundService(intent)
} else {
    startService(intent)
}
```

for a foreground service as defined starting in Android 8.0 or API level 26 (for versions prior to that, we start it the normal way). So we can directly refer to the service class. The `TheService::class.java` notation may look strange at first glance if you are a new Kotlin developer – it is just the Kotlin way of providing Java classes as an argument.

Note   Since Intents allow general-purpose extra attributes by using one of the various `putExtra()` methods, we can also pass data to the service.

Second, if the service we want to start is part of another app and thus is an *external* service, first you have to add an intent filter inside the service declaration, for example

```
<service
    android:name=".MyService"
    android:enabled="true"
    android:exported="true">
    <intent-filter>
```

```
<action android:name="<PCKG_NAME>.START_SERVICE" />
    </intent-filter>
</service>
```

where `<PCKG_NAME>` is the name of the app's package and instead of `START_SERVICE` you can write a different identifier if you like. Now, inside the service client, you can write

```
val intent = Intent("<PCKG_NAME>.START_SERVICE")
intent.setPackage("<PCKG_NAME>")
startService(intent)

// ... do something ...

stopService(intent)
```

to start and stop the external service, where inside the intent constructor you have to write the very same string as in the intent filter declaration of the service. The setPackage() statement is important here (of course you have to substitute the service's package name); otherwise, a security restriction applies, and you get an error message.

Binding to Services

Starting a service is one part of the story – the other part is using it while it is running. This is what the *binding* of services is used for.

To create a service that can be bound to from the same app, write something like

```
/**
 * Class used for binding locally, i.e. in the same App.
 */
class MyBinder(val servc:MyService) : Binder() {
    fun getService():MyService {
        return servc
    }
}

class MyService : Service() {
    // Binder given to clients
    private val binder: IBinder = MyBinder(this)
```

```kotlin
    // Random number generator
    private val generator: Random = Random()

    override
    fun onBind(intent: Intent):IBinder  {
        return binder
    }

    /** method for clients */
    fun getRandomNumber():Int {
        return generator.nextInt(100)
    }
}
```

To bind to this service internally, from the same app, inside the service client, write

```kotlin
val servcConn = object : ServiceConnection {
    override
    fun onServiceDisconnected(compName: ComponentName?) {
        Log.e("LOG","onServiceDisconnected: " + compName)
    }
    override
    fun onServiceConnected(compName: ComponentName?,
                           binder: IBinder?) {
        Log.e("LOG","onServiceConnected: " + compName)
        val servc = (binder as MyBinder).getService()
        Log.i("LOG", "Next random number from service: " +
            servc.getRandomNumber())
    }
    override
    fun onBindingDied(compName:ComponentName) {
        Log.e("LOG","onBindingDied: " + compName)
    }
}
val intent = Intent(this, MyService::class.java)
val flags = BIND_AUTO_CREATE
bindService(intent, servcConn, flags)
```

where the object : ServiceConnection {...} construct is the Kotlin way of implementing an interface by creating an object of an anonymous inner class, as new ServiceConnection(){ ... } in Java. The construct is called *object expression* in Kotlin. The this inside the intent constructor in this case refers to a Context object. You can use it like this inside an activity. If you have the Context in a variable instead, use that variable's name here.

Of course instead of the logging, you should do more meaningful things. Especially inside the onSeviceConnected() method, you can save the binder or service in a variable for further use. Just make sure, having said all these, that you appropriately react to a died binding or a killed service connection. You could, for example, try to bind to the service again or tell the user or both.

The preceding code starts the service automatically once you bind to it, and it doesn't exist yet. This happens by virtue of the

```
val flags = BIND_AUTO_CREATE
[...]
```

statement. If you don't need it because you are sure the service is running, you can omit it. In most cases it is however better to include that flag. The flags you can use for setting binding characteristics are as follows:

- **BIND_AUTO_CREATE**: We just used that. It means the service gets started automatically if it hasn't started yet. You'll sometimes read that explicitly starting a service is unnecessary if you bind to it, but this is only true if you set this flag.

- **BIND_DEBUG_UNBIND**: This leads to saving the callstack of a following unbindService(), just in case subsequent unbind commands are wrong. If this happens, a more verbose diagnostic output will be shown. Since this imposes a memory leak, this feature should be used only for debugging purposes.

- **BIND_NOT_FOREGROUND**: Only if the client runs in a foreground process and the target service runs in a background process. With this flag the binding process will not raise the service to foreground scheduling priority.

- **BIND_ABOVE_CLIENT**: With this flag, we express the service to be more important than the client (i.e., service invoker). In case of a resource shortage, the system will kill the client prior to the service invoked.

- **BIND_ALLOW_OOM_MANAGEMENT**: This flag tells the Android OS that you more willingly accept Android treating the binding as noncritical and killing the service under low-memory circumstances.

- **BIND_WAIVE_PRIORITY**: This flag leads to leaving the scheduling of the service invocation up to the process where the service runs in.

Just add them together in a combination that suits your needs.

Note   Binding is not possible from inside a BroadcastReceiver component, unless the BroadcastReceiver has been registered via `registerReceiver(receiver.intentfilter)`. In the latter case, the lifetime of the receiver is tied to the registering component. You can however from broadcast receivers pass instruction strings inside the Intent you used for starting, that is, not binding, the service.

To bind to an external service, that is, a service belonging to another app, you cannot use the same binding technique as described for internal services. The reason for that is the `IBinder` interface we are using cannot directly access the service class, since the class is not visible across process boundaries. We can however wrap data to be transported between the service and the service client into an `android.os.Handler` object and use this object to send data from the service client to the service. To achieve this, for the service we first need to define a `Handler` for receiving messages, for example:

```
internal class InHandler(val ctx: Context) : Handler() {
    override
    fun handleMessage(msg: Message) {
        val s = msg.data.getString("MyString")
        Toast.makeText(ctx, s, Toast.LENGTH_SHORT).show()
    }
}
[...]
class MyService : Service() {
```

```
    val myMessg:Messenger = Messenger(InHandler(this))
    [...]
}
```

Instead of just creating a Toast message, you can of course do more interesting things when a message arrives. Now in the service's onBind() method, we return the binder object provided by the messenger:

```
override
fun onBind(intent:Intent):IBinder {
    return myMessg.binder
}
```

As for the entries inside the AndroidManifest.xml file, we can write the same as for *starting* remote services; see the preceding section "Starting Services."

In the service client, you'd add a Messenger attribute and a ServiceConnection object, for example:

```
var remoteSrvc:Messenger? = null
private val myConnection = object : ServiceConnection {
    override
    fun onServiceConnected(className: ComponentName,
                           service: IBinder) {
        remoteSrvc = Messenger(service)
    }
    override
    fun onServiceDisconnected(className: ComponentName) {
        remoteSrvc = null
    }
}
```

To actually perform the binding, we can proceed as for internal services. For example, inside an activity's onCreate() method, you could write

```
val intent:Intent = Intent("<PCKG_NAME>.START_SERVICE")
intent.setPackage("<PCKG_NAME>")
bindService(intent, myConnection, Context.BIND_AUTO_CREATE)
```

with the <PCKG_NAME> appropriately substituted by the service package's name.

Now to send a message from the client to the service across the process boundary, you can write

```
val msg = Message.obtain()
val bundle = Bundle()
bundle.putString("MyString", "A message to be sent")
msg.data = bundle
remoteSrvc?.send(msg)
```

Note that for this example you cannot add these lines into the activity's onCreate() method after the bindService() statement, because the remoteSrvc only gets a value after the connection fired up. But you could, for example, add it to the onServiceConnected() method of the ServiceConnection class.

Note   In the preceding code, no precautions were taken to ensure connection sanity. You should add sanity checks for production code. Also, unbind from the service inside the onStop() method.

Data Sent by Services

Up to now we were talking of messages sent from the service client to the service. Sending data the opposite direction from the service to the service client is possible as well – it best can be achieved by using either an extra *messenger* inside the client, a broadcast message, or a ResultReceiver class.

For the first method, provide another *handler* and *messenger* in the service client, and once the client receives an *onServiceConnected()* callback, send a *message* to the service with the second messenger passed by the replyTo parameter:

```
internal class InHandler(val ctx: Context) : Handler() {
    override
    fun handleMessage(msg: Message) {
        // do something with the message from the service
    }
}
```

```kotlin
class MainActivity : AppCompatActivity() {
    private var remoteSrvc:Messenger? = null
    private var backData:Messenger? = null

    private val myConn = object : ServiceConnection {
      override
      fun onServiceConnected(className: ComponentName,
            service: IBinder) {
        remoteSrvc = Messenger(service)
        backData = Messenger(
            InHandler(this@MainActivity))

        // establish backchannel
        val msg0 = Message.obtain()
        msg0.replyTo = backData
        remoteSrvc?.send(msg0)

        // handle forward (client -> service)
        // connectivity...
      }

      override
      fun onServiceDisconnected(clazz: ComponentName) {
        remoteSrvc = null
      }
    }

    override fun onCreate(savedInstanceState: Bundle?) {
        super.onCreate(savedInstanceState)
        setContentView(R.layout.activity_main)

        // bind to the service, use ID from the manifest!
        val intent = Intent("<PCKG>.START_SERVICE")
        intent.setPackage("<PCKG>")
        val flags = Context.BIND_AUTO_CREATE
        bindService(intent, myConn, flags)
    }
}
```

The service can then use this message, extract the replyTo attribute, and use it to send messages to the service client:

```
internal class IncomingHandler(val ctx: Context) :
        Handler() {
    override
    fun handleMessage(msg: Message) {
        val s = msg.data.getString("MyString")
        val repl = msg.replyTo
        Toast.makeText(ctx, s, Toast.LENGTH_SHORT).show()
        Log.e("IncomingHandler", "!!! " + s)
        Log.e("IncomingHandler", "!!! replyTo = " + repl)

        // If not null, we can now use the 'repl' to send
        // messages to the client. Of course we can save
        // it elsewhere and use it later as well
        if(repl != null) {
          val thr = Thread( object : Runnable {
            override fun run() {
                Thread.sleep(3000)
                val msg = Message.obtain()
                val bundle = Bundle()
                bundle.putString("MyString",
                    "A reply message to be sent")
                msg.data = bundle
                repl?.send(msg)
            }
          } )
          thr.start()
        }
    }
}
```

The other two methods, using a broadcast message or a ResultReceiver class, get handled in Chapters 5 and 13.

Service Subclasses

Up to now we were always using the `android.app.Service` as a base class for services we described. There are other classes supplied by Android usable as base classes though, with different semantics. For Android 8.0 (and above), there are not less than 20 service classes or base classes you can use. You can see them all if inside the Android API documentation,

---

Note   At the time of writing this book, you can find it at `https://developer.android.com/reference/android/app/Service.html`.

---

you investigate "Known Direct Subclasses." Outstanding are the following three:

- **android.app.Service**: The one we've been using so far. This is the most basic service class. Unless you use multithreading *inside* the service class or the service is explicitly configured to execute in another process, the service will be running inside the service caller's main thread. If this is the GUI thread, and unless you expect the service invocation to run really fast, it is strongly recommended to send service activities to a background thread.

- **android.app.IntentService**: While a service by design does not naturally handle incoming start requests simultaneously to the main thread, an `IntentService` uses a dedicated worker thread to receive multiple start messages. Still it uses just one thread to work on start requests, so they get executed one after the other. `IntentService` classes take care of correctly stopping services, so you don't need to care about this yourself. You have to provide the service's work to be done for each start request inside an overwritten `onHandleIntent()` method. Since basically you don't need anything else, `IntentService` services are very easy to implement. Note that starting with Android 8.0 or API level 26, restrictions apply to background processes – see section "Background Services" – so under appropriate circumstances, consider using `JobIntentService` classes instead.

- **android.support.v4.app.JobIntentService** uses a `JobScheduler` to enqueue service execution requests. Starting with Android 8.0 or

API level 26, consider using this service base class for background services. To implement such a service, you basically have to create a subclass of `JobIntentService` and override the method `onHandleWork(intent: Intent): Unit` to contain the service's workload.

Services Lifecycle

Having described various service characteristics in the preceding sections, the actual lifecycle of a service from a bird's-eye view is arguably easier than that of an activity. But be careful. Because of services being able to run in the background and also because services are more readily subject to stops forced by the Android OS, they may require special attention in correspondence with service clients.

In your service implementation, you can overwrite any of the lifecycle callbacks

- onCreate()

- onStartCommand()

- onBind()

- onUnbind()

- onRebind()

- onDestroy()

at will, for example, to log service invocation information while developing or debugging. Figure 4-1 shows you an overview of the lifecycle of a service.

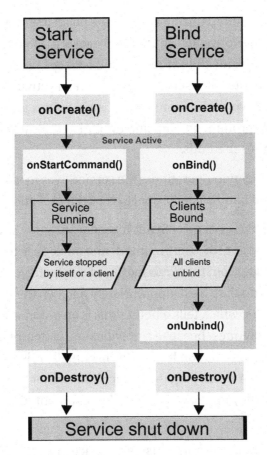

Figure 4-1. *Services Lifecycle*

More Service Characteristics

More observations for services are as follows:

1. Services get declared alongside with activities inside
   AndroidManifest.xml. The question of how they interact with
   each other comes up. Surely, somebody needs to invoke services
   in order to use them, but this can also be done from other services,
   other activities, or even other apps.

2. Do not bind or unbind during an activity's `onResume()` and
    `onPause()` for performance and stability reasons. Do bind and
    unbind instead inside the `onStart()` and `onStop()` methods, if
    you need to interact with services only when an activity is visible.
    If you need service connections also when activities are stopped
    and in the background, do bind and unbind in the `onCreate()`
    and `onRestore()` methods.

3. In remote connection operations (the service lives in another
    app), catch and handle `DeadObjectException` exceptions.

4. If you overwrite a service's `onStartCommand(intent: Intent,`
    `flags: Int, startId: Int)` method, first make sure to also
    call method `super.onStartCommand()` unless you have good
    reasons not to do that. Next, appropriately react on the incoming
    `flags` parameter, which tells whether this is an automatic
    follow-up start request because a previous start attempt failed.
    See the API documentation for details. Eventually this method
    returns an integer describing the service's state after leaving the
    `onStartCommand()` method – see the API documentation for
    details.

5. Calling `stopService()` from outside a service or `stopSelf()` from
    inside a service does not guarantee that the service gets stopped
    immediately. Expect the service to hang around for a little while
    until Android really stops it.

6. If a service is not designed to react on binding requests, if
    you overwrite the `onBind()` method of the service, it should
    return `null`.

7. While not forbidden explicitly, for a service that is designed
    for communicating with service clients via binding, consider
    disallowing the service to be started by `startService()`. In this
    case you *must* provide the `Context.BIND_AUTO_CREATE` flag in the
    `bindService()` method call.

CHAPTER 5

Broadcasts

Android broadcasts are messages following the publish-subscribe pattern. They are sent across the Android OS, with the internals hidden by the Android OS, so both publishers and subscribers only see a lean asynchronous interface for sending and receiving messages. Broadcasts can be published by the Android OS itself, by standard apps, and by any other app installed on the system. Likewise, any app can be configured or programmed to receive broadcast messages it is interested in. As with activities, broadcasts can be explicitly or implicitly routed – whichever is used is the responsibility of the broadcast sender.

Broadcast receivers are declared either in the `AndroidManifest.xml` file or programmatically. Starting with Android 8.0 or API level 26, the developers of Android have abandoned the usual symmetry between XML and programmatic declaration of broadcast receivers for implicit Intents. The reason is the general idea of imposing restrictions on processes running in background mode – such processes, especially related to broadcasts, resulted in a high load on the Android OS, making devices slow down considerably and leading to a bad user experience. For that reason the declaration of broadcast receivers inside `AndroidManifest.xml` is now limited to a smaller set of use cases. See the following section "Implicit Broadcasts."

Note We want to write modern apps runnable also on Android 8.0 and later. For that reason take this broadcast limits for implicit Intents serious and make your app live with those limitations.

Explicit Broadcasts

An explicit broadcast is a broadcast published in such a way that there is exactly one receiver addressed by it. This usually makes sense only if both broadcast publishers and subscribers are part of the same app or, less frequently, part of the same app collection if there is a strong functional dependency among them.

51

© Peter Späth 2022
P. Späth, *Pro Android with Kotlin*, https://doi.org/10.1007/978-1-4842-8745-3_5

Also, there is a difference between local and remote broadcasts: Local broadcast receivers *must* reside in the same app, they run fast, and these receivers cannot be declared inside AndroidManifest.xml. Instead, a programmatic registration method must be used for local broadcast receivers. Also, you must use

```
// send local broadcast
LocalBroadcastManager.getInstance(Context).
    sendBroadcast(...)
```

to send local broadcast messages. Remote broadcast receivers on the other hand *can* reside in the same app, they are slower, and it is possible to use AndroidManifest.xml to declare them. To send remote broadcasts, you write

```
// send remote broadcast (this App or other Apps)
sendBroadcast(...)
```

Note   Local broadcasts should be favored over remote broadcasts for performance reasons. The apparent disadvantage that you cannot use AndroidManifest.xml to declare local receivers does not weigh too much, since starting with Android 8.0 or API level 26, the use cases of declaring broadcast receivers inside the manifest files are limited anyways.

Explicit Local Broadcasts

To send a local broadcast message to a local broadcast receiver inside the same app, you write

```
val intent = Intent(this, MyReceiver::class.java)
intent.action = "de.pspaeth.simplebroadcast.DO_STH"
intent.putExtra("myExtra", "myExtraVal")
Log.e("LOG", "Sending broadcast")
LocalBroadcastManager.getInstance(this).
    sendBroadcast(intent)
Log.e("LOG", "Broadcast sent")
```

where MyReceiver is the receiver class:

```kotlin
class MyReceiver : BroadcastReceiver() {
  override
  fun onReceive(context: Context?, intent: Intent?) {
    Toast.makeText(context, "Intent Detected.",
                   Toast.LENGTH_LONG).show()
    Log.e("LOG", "Received broadcast")
    Thread.sleep(3000)
    // or real work of course...
    Log.e("LOG", "Broadcast done")
  }
}
```

For local broadcasts the receiver *must* be declared inside the code. To avoid a resource leakage, we create and register the receiver inside onCreate() and unregister it inside onDestroy():

```kotlin
class MainActivity : AppCompatActivity() {
    private var bcReceiver:BroadcastReceiver? = null

    override fun onCreate(savedInstanceState: Bundle?) {
        super.onCreate(savedInstanceState)
        // ...

        bcReceiver = MyReceiver()
        val ifi:IntentFilter =
            IntentFilter("de.pspaeth.myapp.DO_STH")
        LocalBroadcastManager.getInstance(this).
            registerReceiver(bcReceiver, ifi)
    }

    override fun onDestroy() {
        super.onDestroy()
        // ...

        LocalBroadcastManager.getInstance(this).
            unregisterReceiver(bcReceiver)
    }
}
```

Explicit Remote Broadcasts

We already pointed out that we can send broadcast messages of the *remote* type to other apps or to the same app where the receivers live. The difference is how the data is sent – for remote messages the data goes through an IPC channel. Now to send such remote broadcast messages to the same app, you write

```
val intent = Intent(this, MyReceiver::class.java)
intent.action = "de.pspaeth.myapp.DO_STH"
intent.putExtra("myExtra", "myExtraVal")
sendBroadcast(intent)
```

On the receiving side, for remote messages the receiver *must* be declared inside the manifest file:

```
<application ...>
  ...
  <receiver android:name=".MyReceiver">
    <intent-filter>
      <action android:name=
            "de.pspaeth.myapp.DO_STH">
      </action>
    </intent-filter>
  </receiver>
</application>
```

Looking at the differences between local and remote broadcasts, it is helpful to keep the following in mind:

- **Local explicit broadcasts**

  Sender uses explicit receiver class, receiver must be declared programmatically, and both sender and receiver use the LocalBroadcastManager to send messages and to register the receiver.

- **Remote explicit broadcasts**

  Sender uses explicit receiver class, and receiver must be declared in AndroidManifest.xml.

For the class that is responsible to handle received broadcasts, there is no difference compared to that of explicit local broadcasts:

```
class MyReceiver : BroadcastReceiver() {
  override
  fun onReceive(context: Context?, intent: Intent?) {
    // handle incoming broadcasts...
  }
}
```

Explicit Broadcasts Sent to Other Apps

The senders and receivers of explicit broadcasts can live in different apps. In order for this to work, we can no longer use the intent constructor we used earlier:

```
val intent = Intent(this, MyReceiver::class.java)
intent.action = "de.pspaeth.myapp.DO_STH"
// add other coords...
sendBroadcast(intent)
```

This is because the receiving class, here MyReceiver, is not part of the class path. There is however another construct we can use instead

```
val intent = Intent()
intent.component = ComponentName("de.pspaeth.xyz",
        "de.pspaeth.xyz.MyReceiver")
intent.action = "de.pspaeth.simplebroadcast.DO_STH"
// add other coords...
sendBroadcast(intent)
```

where the first argument to ComponentName is the package string of the receiving package and the second argument is the class name there.

Caution   Unless you are broadcasting to apps that have been built by yourself as well, this way of sending explicit broadcasts is of limited use only. The developer of the other app may easily decide to change class names, so then your communication to the other app using broadcasts will be broken.

Implicit Broadcasts

Implicit broadcasts are broadcasts with an undefined number of possible receivers. For explicit broadcasts we learned that we have to build the corresponding Intents by using the constructor, which point to the recipient component: `val intent = Intent(this, TheReceiverClass::class.java)`. Contrary to that, for an implicit broadcast, we no longer specify the recipient, but instead give hints on which components might be interested to receive it. For example, in

```
val intent = Intent()
intent.action = "de.pspaeth.myapp.DO_STH"
sendBroadcast(intent)
```

we actually express the following: "Send a broadcast message to all receivers that are interested in action 'de.pspaeth.myapp.DO_STH." The Android OS determines which components are eligible to receive such broadcast message then – this might result in zero, one, or many actual recipients.

There are three decisions you must take before you start programming implicit broadcasts:

1. **Do we want to listen to system broadcasts?**

    A quite large number of predefined broadcast message types exist for Android. Inside the Android SDK, which you installed alongside with Android Studio, more precisely at `SDK_INST_DIR/platforms/VERSION/data/broadcast_actions.txt`, you find a list of system broadcast actions. In case we want to listen to such messages, we just need to program appropriate broadcast receivers as described in the following in sections "Receiving Implicit Broadcasts" and "Listening to System Broadcasts." In the online text companion in section "System Broadcasts," you'll find a comprehensive list of the system broadcasts.

2. **How do we classify broadcast message types?**

    Broadcast senders and broadcast receivers join based on intent filter matches, just as activities do, as described in section "Intent Filters" of Chapter 3. The classification is threefold for broadcasts as well: first, you have an obligatory "action" specifier, second a "category," and third a "data-and-type" specifier, which you can all use to define filters. We describe this matching procedure in the following.

3. **Are we heading for local or remote broadcasts?**

   If all the broadcasting happens completely inside your app, you should use local broadcasting for sending and receiving messages. For implicit broadcasts this will probably not be the case too often, but for large complex apps, this is totally acceptable. If system broadcasts are involved, or broadcasts from other apps, you *must* use remote broadcasts. The latter is the default case in most examples, so you will see this pattern quite often.

Intent Filter Matching

Broadcast receivers express they're accepting broadcasts by means of declaring *action*, *category*, and *data specifiers*.

We first talk about *actions*. Prima facie those are just strings without any syntax restriction. Looking more thoroughly at them, you see that we first have a more or less stringently defined set of predefined action names. We listed them all in section "Intent Filters" of Chapter 3. Also, you can define your own actions. A convention is to use your package name plus a dot and then an action specifier. You are not forced to follow this convention, but it is strongly recommended to do it that way, so your apps do not mess up with other apps. Without specifying any other filter criteria, a sender specifying that particular action you specified in the filter will reach all matching receivers:

- For an intent filter to match, the *action* specified on the receiver side must match the *action* specified on the sender side. For implicit broadcasts, zero, one, or many receivers might be addressed by one broadcast.

- A receiver may specify more than one filter. If one of the filters contains the specified *action*, this particular filter will match the broadcast.

Examples are shown in Table 5-1.

Table 5-1. *Action Matches*

Receiver	Sender	Match
One-filter action = "com.xyz.ACTION1"	action = "com.xyz. ACTION1"	YES
One-filter action = "com.xyz.ACTION1"	action = "com.xyz. ACTION2"	NO
Two-filter action = "com.xyz.ACTION1"action = "com.xyz. ACTION2"	action = "com.xyz. ACTION1"	YES
Two-filter action = "com.xyz.ACTION1"action = "com.xyz. ACTION2"	action = "com.xyz. ACTION3"	NO

Apart from *actions*, a *category* specifier may be used to restrict an intent filter. We have a couple of predefined categories listed in section "Intent Filters" of chapter 3, but again you can define your own categories. And as with *actions*, for your own *categories*, you should follow the naming convention to prepend your app's package name to your category name. Once during the intent matching process a match in the *action* is found, all the categories that were declared by the sender must be present as well in the receiver's intent filter for the match to further prevail.

- Once an *action* inside an intent filter matches a broadcast and the filter also contains a list of categories specified by the sender, only such filter will match the broadcast.

Examples are shown in Table 5-2 (one filter only – if there are several filters, the matching happens on an "or" basis).

Table 5-2. *Category Matches*

Recv. Act.	Recv. Categ.	Sender	Match
com.xyz.ACT1	com.xyz.cate1	action = "com.xyz.ACT1"	YES
com.xyz.ACT1	-	action = "com.xyz.ACT1" categ = "com.xyz.cate1"	NO
com.xyz.ACT1	com.xyz.cate1	action = "com.xyz.ACT1" categ = "com.xyz.cate1"	YES
com.xyz.ACT1	com.xyz.cate1	action = "com.xyz.ACT1" categ = "com.xyz.cate1" categ = "com.xyz.cate2"	NO
com.xyz.ACT1	com.xyz.cate1com.xyz.cate2	action = "com.xyz.ACT1" categ = "com.xyz.cate1" categ = "com.xyz.cate2"	YES
com.xyz.ACT1	com.xyz.cate1com.xyz.cate2	action = "com.xyz.ACT1" categ = "com.xyz.cate1"	YES
com.xyz.ACT1	any	action = "com.xyz.ACT2" categ = any	NO

Lastly, a *data-and-type* specifier allows for filtering data types. Such a specifier is one of

- **type**: The MIME type, for example, "text/html" or "text/plain"
- **data**: A data URI, for example, "`http://xyz.com/type1`"
- **data** and **type**: Both of them

where the `data` element allows for wildcard matching. The details are shown in section "Receiving Implicit Broadcasts."

- Presumed *action* and *category* match, and a *type* filter element matches if the sender's specified MIME type is contained in the receiver's list of allowed MIME types.

- Presumed *action* and *category* match, and a *data* filter element matches if the sender's specified data URI matches any of the receiver's list of allowed data URIs (wildcard matching might apply).

- Presumed *action* and *category* match, and a *data-and-type* filter element matches if both the MIME type and the data URI match, that is, are contained within the receiver's specified list.

Examples are shown in Table 5-3 (one filter only – if there are several filters, the matching happens on an "or" basis).

Table 5-3. *Data Matches*

Recv. Type	Recv. URI (.* = any string)	Sender	Match
text/html	-	type = "text/html"	YES
text/html|text/plain	-	type = "text/html"	YES
text/html|text/plain	-	type = "image/jpeg"	NO
-	http://a.b.c/xyz	data = "http://a.b.c/xyz"	YES
-	http://a.b.c/xyz	data = "http://a.b.c/qrs"	NO
-	http://a.b.c/xyz/.*	data = "http://a.b.c/xyz/3"	YES
-	http://.*/xyz	data = "http://a.b.c/xyz"	YES
-	http://.*/xyz	data = "http://a.b.c/qrs"	NO
text/html	http://a.b.c/xyz/.*	type = "text/html" data = "http://a.b.c/xyz/1"	YES
text/html	http://a.b.c/xyz/.*	type = "image/jpeg" data = "http://a.b.c/xyz/1"	NO

Active or On-Hold Listening

The question is in which state an app must be in order to be able to receive implicit broadcasts. If we want a broadcast receiver to be just registered in the system and fired up only on demand when a matching broadcast arrives, the listener must be specified in the manifest file of the app. However, for implicit broadcasts this cannot be freely done, only for predefined system broadcasts as listed in section "Listening to System Broadcasts."

Note   This restriction on implicit intent filters has been introduced in Android 8.0 or API level 26. Before that, any implicit filters could be specified inside the manifest file.

If however you start your broadcast listeners programmatically from inside an app and this app is running, you can define as many implicit broadcast listeners as you wish, and there is no restriction on whether the broadcasts come from the system, your app, or other apps. Likewise, there is no restriction on usable *action* or *category* names.

Since listening for booting completed events is included in the list for allowed listeners inside the manifest file, you are free to start apps there as activities or services, and inside those apps you can register any implicit listener. That means you can legally work around the restrictions imposed starting with Android 8.0. Just be aware that such apps may be killed by the Android OS if resource shortages occur, so you have to take appropriate precautions.

Sending Implicit Broadcasts

To prepare sending an implicit broadcast, you specify an action, categories, data, and extra data as follows:

```
val intent = Intent()
intent.action = "de.pspaeth.myapp.DO_STH"
intent.addCategory("de.pspaeth.myapp.CATEG1")
intent.addCategory("de.pspaeth.myapp.CATEG2")
// ... more categories
intent.type = "text/html"
intent.data = Uri.parse("content://myContent")
intent.putExtra("EXTRA_KEY", "extraVal")
intent.flags = ...
```

Only the action is mandatory; all the others are optional. Now to send the broadcast, you'd write

```
sendBroadcast(intent)
```

for a remote broadcast or

```
LocalBroadcastManager.getInstance(this).
     sendBroadcast(intent)
```

for a local broadcast. The "this" must be a Context or a subclass thereof – it will work exactly like shown here if the code is from inside an activity or a service class.

For remote messages there is also a variant sending a broadcast to applicable receivers one at a time:

```
...
sendOrderedBroadcast(...)
...
```

This makes the receivers get the message sequentially, and each receiver may cancel forwarding the message to the next receiver in the line by using BroadcastReceiver. abortBroadcast().

Receiving Implicit Broadcasts

To receive an implicit broadcast, for a limited set of broadcast types (see section "Listening to System Broadcasts"), you can specify a BroadcastListener inside AndroidManifest.xml as follows:

```
<application ...>
  ...
  <receiver android:name=".MyReceiver">
    <intent-filter>
      <action android:name=
          "com.xyz.myapp.DO_STH" />
      <category android:name=
          "android.intent.category.DEFAULT"/>
      <category android:name=
          "com.xyz.myapp.MY_CATEG"/>
      <data android:scheme="http"
          android:port="80"
          android:host="com.xyz"
          android:path="items/7"
          android:mimeType="text/html" />
```

```
        </intent-filter>
      </receiver>
</application>
```

The <data> element shown here is just an example – all possibilities are shown in Chapter 3, section "Intent Filters."

In contrast to that, adding a programmatic listener for implicit broadcasts to your code is unrestricted:

```
class MainActivity : AppCompatActivity() {
  private var bcReceiver:BroadcastReceiver? = null

  override fun onCreate(savedInstanceState: Bundle?) {
    super.onCreate(savedInstanceState)
    // ...
    bcReceiver = MyReceiver()
    val ifi:IntentFilter =
        IntentFilter("de.pspaeth.myapp.DO_STH")
    registerReceiver(bcReceiver, ifi)
  }

  override fun onDestroy() {
    super.onDestroy()
    // ...
    unregisterReceiver(bcReceiver)
  }
}
```

The MyReceiver shown here is an implementation of class android.content.BroadcastReceiver.

Listening to System Broadcasts

In order to listen to system broadcasts – see the list in the online text companion's section "System Broadcasts" – you can just use a programmatic registration as shown earlier. For most of them, you cannot use the manifest registration way, for background execution limits imposed since Android 8.0 or API level 26. However, for a number of them, you can also use the manifest file to specify listeners:

- **ACTION_LOCKED_BOOT_COMPLETED, ACTION_BOOT_ COMPLETED**:

  Apps may need those to schedule jobs, alarms, and so on.

- **ACTION_USER_INITIALIZE, "android.intent.action.USER_ ADDED", "android.intent.action.USER_REMOVED"**:

  Protected by privileged permissions, so use cases are limited.

- **"android.intent.action.TIME_SET", ACTION_TIMEZONE_ CHANGED, ACTION_NEXT_ALARM_CLOCK_CHANGED**:

  Needed by clock apps.

- **ACTION_LOCALE_CHANGED**:

  The locale changed, and apps might need to update their data when this happens.

- **ACTION_USB_ACCESSORY_ATTACHED, ACTION_USB_ ACCESSORY_DETACHED, ACTION_USB_DEVICE_ATTACHED, ACTION_USB_DEVICE_DETACHED**:

  USB-related events.

- **ACTION_CONNECTION_STATE_CHANGED, ACTION_ACL_ CONNECTED, ACTION_ACL_DISCONNECTED**:

  Bluetooth events.

- **ACTION_CARRIER_CONFIG_CHANGED, TelephonyIntents. ACTION_SUBSCRIPTION_CHANGED, "TelephonyIntents. SECRET_CODE_ACTION"**:

  OEM telephony apps may need to receive these broadcasts.

- **LOGIN_ACCOUNTS_CHANGED_ACTION**:

  Needed by some apps to set up scheduled operations for new and changed accounts.

- **ACTION_PACKAGE_DATA_CLEARED**:

  Data cleared by the OS "Settings" app. A running app likely is interested in that.

- **ACTION_PACKAGE_FULLY_REMOVED:**

  Related apps may need to be informed if some apps get
  uninstalled and their data removed.

- **ACTION_NEW_OUTGOING_CALL:**

  Intercepting outgoing calls.

- **ACTION_DEVICE_OWNER_CHANGED:**

  Some apps may need to receive it, so that they know that the
  device's security status has changed.

- **ACTION_EVENT_REMINDER:**

  Sent by the calendar provider to post an event reminder to the
  calendar app.

- **ACTION_MEDIA_MOUNTED, ACTION_MEDIA_CHECKING,
  ACTION_MEDIA_UNMOUNTED, ACTION_MEDIA_EJECT,
  ACTION_MEDIA_UNMOUNTABLE, ACTION_MEDIA_REMOVED,
  ACTION_MEDIA_BAD_REMOVAL:**

  Apps may need to know about the user's physical interactions
  with the device.

- **SMS_RECEIVED_ACTION, WAP_PUSH_RECEIVED_ACTION:**

  Needed by SMS recipient apps.

Adding Security to Broadcasts

Security in broadcasting messages is handled by the *permission* system, which gets
described in more detail in Chapter 7.

In the following sections, we distinguish between explicit and implicit broadcasts.

Securing Explicit Broadcasts

For non-local broadcasting, that is, not using the `LocalBroadcastManager`, permissions
can be specified on both sides, the receiver *and* the sender. For the latter, the broadcast
sending methods have overloaded versions including a permission specifier:

```
...
val intent = Intent(this, MyReceiver::class.java)
...
sendBroadcast(intent, "com.xyz.theapp.PERMISSION1")
...
```

This expresses sending a broadcast to a receiver that is protected by "com.xyz. theapp.PERMISSION1". Of course you should write your own package names here and use appropriate permission names.

In contrast, sending a broadcast without permission specification

```
...
val intent = Intent(this, MyReceiver::class.java)
...
sendBroadcast(intent)
...
```

may address receivers with and without permission protection. That means specifying permissions on the sender side is not supposed to tell the receiver that the sender is protected in any way.

For adding a permission to the receiver side, we first need to declare using it inside AndroidManifest.xml on an app level:

```
<manifest ...>
    <uses-permission android:name=
        "com.xyz.theapp.PERMISSION1"/>
    ...
    <application ...
```

Next, we explicitly add it to the receiver element inside the same manifest file

```
<receiver android:name=".MyReceiver"
        android:permission="com.xyz.theapp.PERMISSION1">
    <intent-filter>
        <action android:name=
                    "com.xyz.theapp.DO_STH" />
    </intent-filter>
</receiver>
```

where MyReceiver is an implementation of `android.content.BroadcastReceiver`. Then, since this is a custom permission, you have to declare itself in the manifest file:

```
<manifest ...>
    <permission android:name=
        "com.xyz.theapp.PERMISSION1"/>
    ...
```

The `<permission>` allows for a couple of more attributes (see section "Manifest Top-Level Entries" in the online text companion), namely, the protection level. The details for and implications of that get explained thoroughly in Chapter 7.

For non-custom permissions, you don't need to use the `<permission>` element.

Caution   Specifying a permission on the sender side without having a matching permission on the receiver side silently fails when you try to send a broadcast. There are also no logging entries, so be careful with sender-side permissions.

If you use local broadcasts with the `LocalBroadcastManager`, you cannot specify permissions on neither the sender nor the receiver side.

Securing Implicit Broadcasts

Same as for non-local explicit broadcasts, permissions in implicit broadcasts can be specified on both broadcast sender and receiver sides. On the sender side, you would write

```
val intent = Intent()
intent.action = "de.pspaeth.myapp.DO_STH"
// ... more intent coordinates
sendBroadcast(intent, "com.xyz.theapp.PERMISSION1")
```

which expresses sending a broadcast to all matching receivers that are additionally protected by "com.xyz.theapp.PERMISSION1". Of course you should write your own package names here and use appropriate permission names. As with the usual sender-receiver matching procedure for implicit broadcasts, adding a permission kind of serves as an additional matching criterion, so if there are several receiver candidates, looking at the intent filters, for actually receiving this broadcast, only those that additionally provide this permission flag will be picked out.

One more thing that needs to be taken care of for implicit broadcasts is specifying the permission usage in `AndroidManifest.xml`. So for this sender to be able to use the permission, add

```
<uses-permission
        android:name="com.xyz.theapp.PERMISSION1"/>
```

to the manifest file.

Same as for explicit broadcasts, sending a broadcast without permission specification

```
...
sendBroadcast(intent)
...
```

may address receivers with and without permission protection. That means specifying permissions on the sender side is not supposed to tell the receiver that the sender is protected in any way.

In order for a receiver to be able to get hold of such a broadcast, the permission must be added to the code like

```
private var bcReceiver: BroadcastReceiver? = null

override fun onCreate(savedInstanceState: Bundle?) {
  super.onCreate(savedInstanceState)
  ...
  bcReceiver = object : BroadcastReceiver() {
    override fun onReceive(context: Context?,
         intent: Intent?) {
      // do s.th. when receiving...
    }
  }
  val ifi: IntentFilter =
         IntentFilter("de.pspaeth.myapp.DO_STH")
  registerReceiver(bcReceiver, ifi,
       "com.xyz.theapp.PERMISSION1", null)
}
```

```
override fun onDestroy() {
  super.onDestroy()
  unregisterReceiver(bcReceiver)
}
```

In addition you must both define the permission and declare using it in the receiver's manifest file:

```
...
<uses-permission android:name=
      "com.xyz.theapp.PERMISSION1" />
<permission android:name=
      "com.xyz.theapp.PERMISSION1" />
...
```

Again, for non-custom permissions, you don't need to use the <permission> element. For more about permissions, see Chapter 7.

Note   As an additional means to improve security, in applicable cases you can use Intent.setPackage() to restrict possible receivers.

Sending Broadcasts from the Command Line

For devices you can connect to via the *Android Debug Bridge* (ADB) – see Chapter 19, section "The SDK Platform Tools" – you can use a shell command on your development PC to send a broadcast message. An example would be

```
./adb shell am broadcast -a de.pspaeth.myapp.DO_STH \
      de.pspaeth.simplebroadcast MyReceiver
```

sending an action "de.pspaeth.myapp.DO_STH" to the dedicated receiver "MyReceiver" of the package "de.pspaeth.simplebroadcast" (this thus is an explicit broadcast message).

To get a complete synopsis for that way of sending broadcasts, you can use the shell as follows:

```
./adb shell
am
```

This command will show you all the possibilities to create broadcast messages and do other things using that "am" command.

Random Notes on Broadcasts

- You can register and unregister programmatically managed receivers also in callback methods `onPause()` and `onResume()`. Obviously, registering and unregistering will then happen more often compared with using the `onCreate()`/`onDestroy()` pair.

- A currently executing `onReceive()` method will upgrade the process priority to "foreground" level, preventing the Android OS from killing the receiving process – it would then happen only under extreme resource shortage conditions.

- If you have long-running processes inside `onReceive()`, you might think of running them on a background thread, finishing `onReceive()` early. However, since the process priority will be reverted to the normal level after finishing `onReceive()`, your background process is more likely to be killed, breaking your app. You can prevent this by using `Context.goAsync()` and then starting an `AsyncTask` (inside, at the end you must call `finish()` on the `PendingResult` object you got from `goAsync()` to eventually free resources), or you can use a `JobScheduler`.

- Custom permissions (we used such in the "Securing Implicit Broadcasts" section) get registered when the app gets installed. Because of that the app defining the custom permissions must be installed prior to the apps using them.

- Be cautious with sending sensitive information through implicit broadcasts. Potentially malicious apps may try to receive them as well. At the least you can secure the broadcast by specifying permissions on the sender side.

- For clarity and to not mess up with other apps, always use namespaces for broadcast action and permission names.

- Avoid starting activities from broadcasts – this contradicts Android usability principles.

CHAPTER 6

Content Providers

The Content Provider Framework

The *content provider* framework allows for

1. Using (structured) data provided by other apps

2. Providing (structured) data for use by other apps

3. Supporting copying data from one app to another

4. Providing data to the *search framework*

5. Providing data to special data-related UI widgets

6. Doing all that by virtue of a well-defined standardized interface

The data communicated can have a strictly defined structure, for example, the rows from a database with defined column names and types, but it can also be files or byte arrays without any semantics associated.

If the requirements of your app concerning data storage do not fit in any of the preceding cases, you don't need to implement content provider components – use the normal data storage options instead.

Note It is not strictly forbidden for an app to provide data to its own components or use its own data provider for accessing content; however, looking at content providers, you usually think of inter-app data exchange. But if you need it, you always can consider intra-app data exchange patterns as a straightforward special case of inter-app communication.

© Peter Späth 2022
P. Späth, *Pro Android with Kotlin*, https://doi.org/10.1007/978-1-4842-8745-3_6

If we want to create content-aware apps, both looking at providing and consuming content, the main questions are as follows:

- How do apps provide content?

- How do apps access content provided by other apps?

- How do apps handle content provided by other apps?

- How do we secure the provided data?

And we will be looking at exactly these topics in the following sections. An outline is shown in Figure 6-1.

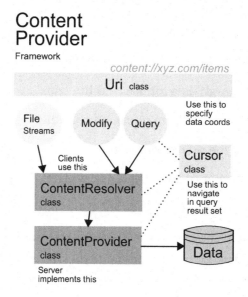

Figure 6-1. *Content Provider Framework*

Providing Content

Content can be provided by your app, but of course also by system apps. Think, for example, of pictures taken by the camera or contacts from your contacts list. The content provider framework is a little easier to grasp if we first look at the content providing side. In later sections we will also be looking at consumers and other topics.

First of all we need to know where the data lives. However, the content provider framework makes no assumptions on where the data actually comes from – it can reside in files, databases, in-memory storages, or any other place you might think of. This improves the maintenance of your app. For example, in an early project stage, data may come from files, but later you switch to a database or cloud storage, and the possible consumers don't have to care about those changes, because they don't have to change the way of addressing your content. The content provider framework thus provides an abstraction layer for your data.

The single interface you need to implement for providing content is the abstract class

```
android.content.ContentProvider
```

In the following subsections, we will be looking at the implementation of this class from a use case perspective.

Initializing the Provider

Inside your instantiable subclass of the ContentProvider class, you *have* to implement the method

```
onCreate()
```

This method gets called by the Android OS when the content provider is being instantiated. Here you can initialize the content provider, but you should avoid putting time-consuming initialization processes at this place, since instantiation does not necessarily mean the content provider will be actually used at all.

If you don't have anything interesting to do here, just implement it as an empty method.

To find out more about the environment your content provider is running in when instantiated, you can overwrite its attachInfo() method – there you will be told about the context the content provider is running in and also get a ProviderInfo object. Just don't forget to also call super.attachInfo() from inside.

Querying Data

For querying database-like data sets, there is one method you *must* implement and two more you *can* implement:

```
abstract fun query(          // ----- Variant A -----
    uri:Uri,
    projection:Array<String>,
```

```
    selection:String,
    selectionArgs:Array<String>,
    sortOrder:String) : Cursor

                        // ----- Variant B -----
// You don't have to implement this. The default
// implementation calls variant A, but disregards the
// 'cancellationSignal' argument.
fun query(
    uri:Uri,
    projection:Array<String>,
    selection:String,
    selectionArgs:Array<String>,
    String sortOrder:String,
    cancellationSignal:CancellationSignal) : Cursor

                        // ----- Variant C -----
// You don't have to implement this. The default
// implementation converts the bundle argument to
// appropriate arguments for calling variant B.
// The bundle keys used are:
//      ContentResolver.QUERY_ARG_SQL_SELECTION
//      ContentResolver.QUERY_ARG_SQL_SELECTION_ARGS
//      ContentResolver.QUERY_ARG_SQL_SORT_ORDER -or-
//          ContentResolver.QUERY_ARG_SORT_COLUMNS
//          (this being a String array)
fun query(
    uri:Uri,
    projection:Array<String>,
    queryArgs:Bundle,
    cancellationSignal:CancellationSignal) : Cursor
```

These methods are not intended to present file data like images and sound. To return links or identifiers to file data is acceptable, though.

In the following paragraphs, we describe all the parameters by name and variant:

- **uri**: This is an important parameter specifying the type coordinates of the query in the data space. Content consumers will tell what *kind* of data they are interested in by appropriately specifying this parameter. Since URIs are so important, we describe them in an own subsection; see the following section "Designing Content URIs." This parameter has the same meaning for all variants A, B, and C.

- **projection**: This will tell the implementation which columns the requester is interested in. Looking at the SQL database type of storing data, this lists the column names that should be included in the result. There is however no strict requirement for a one-to-one mapping – a requester might ask for a selection parameter "X", and the values for "X" might be calculated any way you might possibly think of. If null, return all fields. This parameter has the same meaning for all variants A, B, and C.

- **selection**: Only for variants A and B, this specifies a selection for the data to be returned. The content provider framework makes no assumptions how this selection parameter must look like – it is completely up to the implementation, and content requesters must yield to what the implementation defines. In many cases you will however have something like a SQL selection string like "name = Jean AND age < 45" here. If null, return all data sets.

- **selectionArgs**: The selection parameter may contain placeholders like "?". If so, the values to be inserted for the placeholders are specified in this array. Again the framework makes no strict assumptions here, but in most cases the "?" serves as a placeholder like in "name = ? AND age < ?", as for SQL. This may be null if there are no selection placeholders.

- **sortOrder**: Only for variants A and B, this specifies a sort order for the data to be returned. The content provider framework does not prescribe a syntax here, but for SQL-like access, this will usually be something like "name DESC, age ASC".

- **queryArgs**: For variant C, all three – selection, selection arguments, and sort order – may or may not be specified using an `android.os.Bundle` object. By convention, for SQL-like queries, the bundle keys are

  - ContentResolver.QUERY_ARG_SQL_SELECTION

  - ContentResolver.QUERY_ARG_SQL_SELECTION_ARGS

  - ContentResolver.QUERY_ARG_SQL_SORT_ORDER

- **cancellationSignal**: For variants B and C, if this is not `null`, you can use it to cancel the current operation. The Android OS will then appropriately inform the requesters.

All the query methods are supposed to return an `android.database.Cursor` object. This allows to iterate over the data sets, with the convention that each data set contains an "_id"-keyed technical ID. See the following sections "A Cursor Class Basing on AbstractCursor and Co." and "A Cursor Class Basing on the Cursor Interface" to see how to design appropriate cursor objects.

Modifying Content

Content providers do not just allow to read content; they also allow to alter content. For this aim the following methods exist:

```
abstract fun insert(
    Uri uri:Uri,
    values:ContentValues) : Uri

// You don't have to overwrite this, the default
// implementation correctly iterates over the input
// array and calls insert(...) on each element.
fun bulkInsert(
    uri:Uri,
    values:Array<ContentValues>) : Int

abstract fun update(
    uri:Uri,
    values:ContentValues,
```

```
    selection:String,
    selectionArgs:Array<String>) : Int
abstract fun delete(
    uri:Uri,
    selection:String,
    selectionArgs:Array<String>) : Int
```

We describe the parameters and their meanings in the following paragraphs:

- **uri**: Specifies the type coordinates of the data in the data space. Content consumers will tell what *kind* of data they are targeting at by appropriately specifying this parameter. See the following section "Designing Content URIs" for a detailed description. Note that for deleting or updating single data sets, it is generally assumed that the URI contains the (technical) ID of the data at the end of the URI path, for example, `content://com.android.contacts/contact/42`.

- **values**: These are the values to be inserted or updated. You use the various `get*()` methods of this class to access the values.

- **selection**: This specifies a selection for the data to be updated or deleted. The content provider framework makes no assumptions how this selection parameter must look like – it is completely up to the implementation, and content requesters must yield to what the implementation defines. In many cases you will however have something like a SQL selection string like "name = Jean AND age < 45" here. If `null`, all items of the data set will be addressed.

- **selectionArgs**: The selection parameter may contain placeholders like "?". If so, the values to be inserted for the placeholders are specified in this array. Again the framework makes no strict assumptions here, but in most cases the "?" serves as a placeholder like in "name = ? AND age < ?", as for SQL. This may be `null` if there are no selection placeholders.

The `insert()` method is supposed to return the URI specifying the inserted data. This return value may be `null`, so there is no strict requirement to return something here. If it returns something, this should contain the technical ID. All the `Int`-returning methods are supposed to return the number of affected data sets.

If you don't want the content provider to be able to alter any data, you can just provide empty implementations to all the insert, update, and delete methods and let them return 0 or `null`.

Finishing the ContentProvider Class

In order to finish the implementation of your `ContentProvider` class, you must – apart from the query, insert, update, and delete methods – implement one more method:

```
abstract getType(uri:Uri) : String
```

This maps any usable URI to the appropriate MIME type. For a possible implementation, you can, for example, use URIs as follows

```
ContentResolver.CURSOR_DIR_BASE_TYPE +
    "/vnd.<name>.<type>"
ContentResolver.CURSOR_ITEM_BASE_TYPE +
    "/vnd.<name>.<type>"
```

for URIs referring to *possibly* many items or *at most* one item, respectively. For "<name>" use a globally unique name, maybe the reverse company domain or the package name or a prominent part of it. For "<type>" use an identifier defining the table name or the data domain.

Registering the Content Provider

Once you finish the `ContentProvider` implementation, you must register it inside the `AndroidManifest.xml` file as follows:

```
<provider android:authorities="list"
        android:directBootAware=["true" | "false"]
        android:enabled=["true" | "false"]
        android:exported=["true" | "false"]
        android:grantUriPermissions=["true" | "false"]
        android:icon="drawable resource"
        android:initOrder="integer"
        android:label="string resource"
        android:multiprocess=["true" | "false"]
        android:name="string"
```

```
    android:permission="string"
    android:process="string"
    android:readPermission="string"
    android:syncable=["true" | "false"]
    android:writePermission="string" >
```

    . . .

</provider>

The attributes are described in Table 6-1.

Table 6-1. *The <provider> Element*

Attribute (Prepend "android:" to Each)	Description
authorities	A semicolon ";"–separated list of authorities. In many cases this will be just one, and you usually use the app (package) name or the full class name of the ContentProvider implementation. There is no default; you must have at least one.
directBootAware	Whether the content provider can run before the user unlocks the device. Default is false.
enabled	Whether the content provider is enabled. Default is true.
exported	Whether other apps can access contents here. Depending on the architecture of your app, access might be restricted to components from the same app, but usually you want other apps to access the content and thus set this to true. Starting with API level 17, default is false. Prior to that the flag doesn't exist, and apps behave like this is set to true.
grantUriPermissions	Whether permission to other apps accessing content from this provider by URI can be temporarily granted or not. *Temporarily granted* means a permission denial as defined by <permission>, <readPermission>, or writePermission gets overridden temporarily if the content-accessing client is invoked by an Intent with intent.addFlags(Intent.FLAG_ GRANT__URI_PERMISSION). If you set this attribute to false, a more fine-grained temporary permission can still be granted by setting one or more <grant-uri-permission> sub-elements. Default is false.

(continued)

Table 6-1. (*continued*)

Attribute (Prepend "android:" to Each)	Description
icon	The resource ID of an icon to use for the provider. Default is to use the parent component's icon.
initOrder	Here you can impose some order for content providers of the same app to be instantiated. Higher numbers get instantiated first. Use this with care, since startup order dependencies might indicate a bad application design.
label	A string resource ID for a label to use. Default is the app's `label`.
multiprocess	If set to `true`, an app running in more than one process possibly will have multiple instances of the content provider running. Otherwise, at most one instance of the content provider will exist. Default is false.
name	The fully qualified class name of the `ContentProvider` implementation.
permission	A convenient way of setting both `readPermission` and `writePermission` – see in the following. Specifying one of the latter has precedence.
process	Specify a process name if you want the content provider to run in another process than the app itself. If it starts with a ":", the process will be private to the app; if it starts with a lowercase letter, a global process will be used (permission to do so required). Default is to run in the app's process.
readPermission	A permission a client must have in order to have read access to content of the content provider. You can have a client without that permission still being able to access the content by virtue of the `grantUriPermissions` attribute.
syncable	Whether data of the content provider should be synchronized with a server.
readPermission	A permission a client must have in order to have write access to content of the content provider. You can have a client without that permission still being able to access the content by virtue of the `grantUriPermissions` attribute.

If you use `grantUriPermissions` to temporarily give URI permissions to components from other apps called by an implicit Intent, you have to carefully tailor such an Intent: (1) add flag `Intent.FLAG_GRANT_READ_URI_PERMISSION`, (2) and add the URI you want to allow access for inside the Intent's `data` field. An example would be

```
intent.action =
        "com.example.app.VIEW" // SET INTENT ACTION
intent.flags =
        Intent.FLAG_ACTIVITY_NEW_TASK
intent.addFlags(Intent.FLAG_GRANT_READ_URI_PERMISSION)
        // GRANT TEMPORARY READ PERMISSION
intent.data = Uri.parse("content://<AUTHORITY>/<PATH>")
        // USE YOUR OWN!
startActivity(intent)
```

Inside the intent filter of the called component, you then must specify a `<data>` element, and it must contain an appropriate URI *and* a MIME type. The reason a MIME type must be specified, although we haven't explicitly stated one, is that the Android OS uses the content provider's `getType(Uri)` method to automatically add the MIME type while the Intent gets resolved, for example:

```
<intent-filter>
    <action android:name=
            "de.pspaeth.crcons.VIEW"/>
    <category android:name=
            "android.intent.category.DEFAULT"/>
    <data android:mimeType="*/*"
            android:scheme="content"
            android:host="*"
            android:pathPattern=".*"/>
</intent-filter>
```

The called component is then granted to access this URI in the specified way. After it finishes its work, it is supposed to call `revokeUriPermission(String, Uri, Int)` to revoke the temporary permission it has been given to:

```
revokePermission(getPackageName(), uri,
    Intent.FLAG_GRANT_READ_URI_PERMISSION
    or Intent.FLAG_GRANT_WRITE_URI_PERMISSION)
```

Inside the `<provider>` element, there are a couple of child elements you can add:

- **meta-data**

```
<meta-data android:name="string"
       android:resource="resource specification"
       android:value="string" />
```

Where either "resource" or "value" must be specified. If you use "resource", a resource ID like "@string/someString" would assign the resource ID itself to the meta-entry, while using "value" and "@string/someString" would assign the *contents* of the resource to the meta-entry.

- **grant-uri-permission**

```
<grant-uri-permission android:path="string"
               android:pathPattern="string"
               android:pathPrefix="string" />
```

Grant a specific URI permission (use zero to many of this child). Only if the parent's attribute "grantUriPermissions" is set to `false`, this child allows the access to specific URIs. Use exactly one of the following attributes: "path" is for the complete URI, "pathPrefix" is for URIs starting with a certain value, and "pathPattern" allows for wildcards – "X*" is for zero to many repetitions of any character "X", and ".*" is for zero to many repetitions of any character.

- **path-permission**

```
<path-permission android:path="string"
            android:pathPrefix="string"
            android:pathPattern="string"
            android:permission="string"
            android:readPermission="string"
            android:writePermission="string" />
```

To define a subset of data a content provider can serve, you can use this element to specify a path and a required permission. The "path" attribute specifies a complete path, the "pathPrefix" attribute allows matching the initial part of a path, and "pathPattern" is a complete path, but with wildcards: "*" matches zero to many occurrences of a certain character, and ".*" matches zero to many occurrences of any character. The "permission" attribute specifies a read and write permission, and the attributes "readPermission" and "writePermission" draw a distinction between read and write permissions. If any of the latter two is specified, it takes precedence over the "permission" attribute.

Designing Content URIs

URIs describe the domain of the data a content requester is interested in. Thinking of SQL, this would be the table name. URIs can do more, however. The official syntax of a URI is

```
scheme:[//[user[:password]@]host[:port]]
    [/path][?query][#fragment]
```

You can see that the "user," "password," and "port" parts are optional, and in fact you usually wouldn't specify them in an Android environment. It is not forbidden, though, and makes sense under certain circumstances. The "host" part however is interpreted in the most general way as something that provides something, and this is exactly the way it is interpreted here, with "something" being the data. To make that notion somewhat clearer, the "host" part is for Android commonly referred to as *authority*. For example, in the *Contacts* system app, the authority would be "com.android.contacts" (don't use strings; use class constant fields instead – see in the following in the "Contract" section). The "scheme" is by convention normally "content." So a general contacts URI starts with

```
content://com.android.contacts
```

The "path" part of the URI specifies the data domain, or table if you think of SQL. The user profile data inside the contacts, for example, gets addressed by

```
content://com.android.contacts/profile
```

In this example the path has just one element, but in can be more complex like "pathpart1/pathpart2/pathpart3".

A URI may also have a "query" part specifying a selection. Looking at the query methods from class android.content.ContentProvider, we already have a possibility to specify a selection on an API basis, but it is totally acceptable, although not mandatory, to also allow query parameters inside the URI. If you need to put several elements into the query parameter, you can follow the usual convention to use "&" as a separator, for example, "name=John&age=37".

The "fragment" specifies a secondary resource and is not used often for content providers. But you can use it, if it helps you.

Since a URI is such a generic construct and guessing correct URIs for accessing content provided by some app is almost impossible, a content provider app usually provides a contract class that helps in building correct URIs for the task at hand – see the following section "Building a Content Interface Contract."

Building a Content Interface Contract

The URIs a client has to use to access data represent the interface to the contents. It is therefore a good idea to have a central place a client can look at to find out which URIs to use. The Android documentation suggests using a content contract class for that purpose. The outline of such a class will look like

```
class MyContentContract {
    companion object {
        // The authority and the base URI
        @JvmField
        val AUTHORITY = "com.xyz.whatitis"
        @JvmField
        val CONTENT_URI = Uri.parse("content://" +
                        AUTHORITY)

        // Selection for ID bases query
        @JvmField
        val SELECTION_ID_BASED = BaseColumns._ID +
                        " = ? "

    }
    // For various tables (or item types) it is
    // recommended to use inner classes to specify
    // them. This is just an example
    class Items {
        companion object {
```

```kotlin
    // The name of the item.
    @JvmField
    val NAME = "item_name"

    // The content URI for items
    @JvmField
    val CONTENT_URI = Uri.withAppendedPath(
        MyContentContract.CONTENT_URI, "items")
    // The MIME type of a directory of items
    @JvmField
    val CONTENT_TYPE =
        ContentResolver.CURSOR_DIR_BASE_TYPE +
        "/vnd." + MyContentContract.AUTHORITY +
        ".items"
    // The mime type of a single item.
    @JvmField
    val CONTENT_ITEM_TYPE =
        ContentResolver.CURSOR_ITEM_BASE_TYPE +
        "/vnd." + MyContentContract.AUTHORITY +
        ".items"

    // You could add database column names or
    // projection specifications here, or sort
    // order specifications, and more
    // ...
  }
 }
}
```

Of course part of your interface design must be using meaningful names for the classes, field names, and field values.

Note   The interface described in the contract class does *not* have to correspond to actual database tables – it is completely feasible and beneficial to conceptually decouple the interface from the actual implementation and also provide table joins or other item types here derived in any way you might think of.

Here are a couple of notes about this construct:

- If you can make sure clients will ever be using only Kotlin
  as a platform, this can be written much shorter without any
  boilerplate code:

```kotlin
object MyContentContract2 {
  val AUTHORITY = "com.xyz.whatitis"
  val CONTENT_URI = Uri.parse("content://"
                     + AUTHORITY)
  val SELECTION_ID_BASED =
      BaseColumns._ID + " = ? "
  object Items {
    val NAME = "item_name"
    val CONTENT_URI =
        Uri.withAppendedPath(
        MyContentContract.CONTENT_URI, "items")
    val CONTENT_TYPE =
        ContentResolver.CURSOR_DIR_BASE_TYPE +
        "/vnd." + MyContentContract.AUTHORITY +
        ".items"
    val CONTENT_ITEM_TYPE =
        ContentResolver.CURSOR_ITEM_BASE_TYPE +
        "/vnd." + MyContentContract.AUTHORITY +
        ".items"
  }
}
```

  However, if we want Java clients to use the interface as well,
  we have to use all that `companion object` and `@JvmObject`
  declarations and modifiers.

- Using companion objects and `JvmObject` annotations allows for
  writing `TheClass.THE_FIELD` as for static fields in Java.

- You might consider providing an equivalent Java construct to your
  clients, so they don't have to learn the Kotlin syntax if they use
  only Java.

- The Uri.parse() and Uri.withAppendedPath() method calls are just two examples of using the Uri class. The class contains a couple of more methods that help manage constructing correct URIs.

- You can also provide helper methods inside the contract class. If you do so, make sure the interface class does not depend on other classes, and add a modifier JvmStatic to the fun function declaration to make it callable from Java.

You would then provide this contract class, or classes if you want to document the interface using both Kotlin and Java, publicly to any possible clients that are supposed to use your content provider app.

A Cursor Class Basing on AbstractCursor and Co.

All of the query*() methods from ContentProvider return an android.database.Cursor object. From the package you can see that this is a database-centric class, and this is actually a small design flaw of Android, since the content interface better had been access methodology agnostic.

Apart from that the Cursor interface is a random-access interface for clients wishing to scan through result sets. You can use the base implementation android.database.AbstractCursor for your cursor class – it already implements a couple of the interface methods. To do so write class MyCursor : AbstractCursor { ... } or val myCursor = object : AbstractCursor { ... } and implement all abstract methods and overwrite some of the other methods for the class to do meaningful things:

- **override fun getCount(): Int**

  The number of data sets available.

- **override fun getColumnNames(): Array<String>**

  The ordered array of column names.

- **override fun getInt(column: Int): Int**

  Get a long value (the column index is zero based).

- **override fun getLong(column: Int): Long**

  Get a long value (the column index is zero based).

- **override fun getShort(column: Int): Short**

  Get a short value (the column index is zero based).

- **override fun getFloat(column: Int): Float**

  Get a float value (the column index is zero based).

- **override fun getDouble(column: Int): Double**

  Get a double value (the column index is zero based).

- **override fun getString(column: Int): String**

  Get a string value (the column index is zero based).

- **override fun isNull(column: Int): Boolean**

  Tells whether the value is `null` (the column index is zero based).

- **override fun getType(column: Int): Int**

  You don't have to overwrite this, but if you don't it will always
  return `Cursor.FIELD_TYPE_STRING`, assuming that `getString()`
  will always return something meaningful. For more fine-grained
  control, let it return one of `FIELD_TYPE_NULL`, `FIELD_TYPE_`
  `INTEGER`, `FIELD_TYPE_FLOAT`, `FIELD_TYPE_STRING`, and `FIELD_`
  `TYPE_BLOB`. The column index is zero based.

- **override fun getBlob(column: Int): ByteArray**

  Overwrite this, if you want to support blobs. Otherwise, an
  `UnsupportedOperationException` will be thrown.

- **override fun onMove(oldPosition: Int, newPosition: Int): Boolean**

  Although not marked `abstract`, you `must` overwrite this. Your
  implementation must move the cursor to the corresponding position
  in the result set. Possible values range from `-1` (before the first pos,
  not a valid position) to `count` (after the last pos, not a valid position).
  Let it return `true` if the move was successful. If you don't overwrite it,
  nothing will happen, and the function returns always `true`.

The `AbstractCursor` also provides a method `fillWindow(position: Int, window: CursorWindow?): Unit`, which you can use to fill an `android.database.CursorWindow` object based on the result set from the query. See the online API documentation of `CursorWindow` to proceed with this approach.

Besides `AbstractCursor`, the `Cursor` interface has a couple of more (abstract) implementations you can use. We briefly summarize them in Table 6-2.

Table 6-2. *More Cursor Implementations*

Name Inside android.database	Description
AbstractWindowedCursor	Inherits from `AbstractCursor` and owns a `CursorWindow` object holding the data. Subclasses are responsible for filling the cursor window with data during their `onMove(Int, Int)` operation, allocating a new cursor window if necessary. Easier to implement compared with `AbstractCursor`, but you have to add a lot of functionality to `onMove()`.
CrossProcessCursor	A cursor implementation that allows using it from remote processes. It is just an extension of the `android.database.Cursor` interface, containing three more methods: `fillWindow(Int, CursorWindow)`, `getWindow(): CursorWindow`, and `onMove(Int, Int): Boolean`. It does not provide its own implementation; you have to overwrite all the methods defined in `Cursor`.
CrossProcessCursorWrapper	A cursor implementation that allows using it from remote processes. Implements `CrossProcessCursor` and holds a `Cursor` delegate, which can also be a `CrossProcessCursor`.
CursorWrapper	Holds a `Cursor` delegate all method calls are forwarded to.
MatrixCursor	A full implementation of `Cursor`, with in-memory storage of data as an object array. You have to use `addRow(...)` to add data. The inner class `MatrixCursor.RowBuilder` can be used to build rows to be used by `MatrixCursor.addRow(Array<Object>)`.
MergeCursor	Use this to transparently merge, or concatenate, cursor objects.
sqlite.SQLiteCursor	An implementation of `Cursor` with the data backed by a SQLite database. Use one of the constructors to connect the cursor with a SQLite database object.

A Cursor Class Basing on the Cursor Interface

A more low-level approach of implementing a cursor is not relying on `AbstractCursor` but instead implementing all the interface methods yourself.

You can then use subclassing as in `class MyCursor : Cursor { ... }` or use an anonymous object as in `val myCursor = object : Cursor { ... }`. In section "Cursor Interface" in the online text companion, we list and describe all the interface methods.

Dispatching URIs Inside the Provider Code

In order to simplify dispatching incoming URIs, the class `android.content.UriMatcher` comes handy. If you have query-related URIs like

```
people              #list all people from a directory
people/37           #inquire a person with ID 37
people/37/phone     #get phone info of person with ID 37
```

and want to use an easy switch statement, you can write inside your class or object

```
val PEOPLE_DIR_AUTHORITY = "directory"
val PEOPLE = 1
val PEOPLE_ID = 2
val PEOPLE_PHONES = 3
val uriMatcher = UriMatcher(UriMatcher.NO_MATCH)
init {
    uriMatcher.addURI(PEOPLE_DIR_AUTHORITY,
        "people", PEOPLE)
    uriMatcher.addURI(PEOPLE_DIR_AUTHORITY,
        "people/#", PEOPLE_ID)
    uriMatcher.addURI(PEOPLE_DIR_AUTHORITY,
        "people/#/phone", PEOPLE_PHONES)
}
```

where "#" stands for any number and "*" matches any string.

In your `ContentProvider` implementation, you can then use the following construct to dispatch incoming string URLs:

```
when(uriMatcher.match(url)) {
    PEOPLE ->
      // incoming path = people, do s.th. with that...
    PEOPLE_ID ->
      // incoming path = people/#, do s.th. with that...
    PEOPLE_PHONES ->
      // incoming path = people/#/phone, ...
    else ->
      // do something else
}
```

Providing Content Files

Content providers can not only give access to database-like content; they may also expose methods for the retrieval of file-like data, like image or sound files. For this aim the following methods are provided:

- **override fun getStreamTypes(uri:Uri, mimeTypeFilter:String) : Array<String>**

  If your content provider offers files, overwrite this method to allow clients to determine supported MIME types given a URI. The mimeTypeFilter is supposed not to be null, and you can use it to filter the output. It supports wildcards, so if a client wants to retrieve all values, it will write "*/*" here, and your provider code needs to correctly handle this. The output must also contain all those types that may be the result of suitable type conversions performed by the provider. May return null to indicate an empty result set. Examples are "image/png" or "audio/mpeg".

- **override fun openFile(uri:Uri, mode:String): ParcelFileDescriptor**

  Override this to handle requests to open a file blob. The parameter "mode" must be one of (there is no default)

  - "r" for read-only access

  - "w" for write-only access (first erasing if data is already present)

  - "wa" like "w", but possibly appends data

- — "rw" for reading and appending writing

- — "rwt" like "rw", but truncates existing data

To learn what to do with the returned `ParcelFileDescriptor`, see in the following.

- **override fun openFile(uri:Uri, mode:String, signal:CancellationSignal): ParcelFileDescriptor**

Same as `openFile(Uri, String)`, but additionally the client may signal a cancellation while reading the file is in progress – the provider can save the `signal` object and catch the client's cancellation request by periodically calling `throwIfCancelled()` on the `signal` object.

- **override fun openAssetFile(uri:Uri, mode:String): AssetFileDescriptor**

This is like `openFile(Uri, String)`, but can be implemented by providers that need to be able to return subsections of files, often assets inside of their APK. For implementing this you probably want to use the `android.content.res.AssetManager` class. You have it in the `asset` field of a context, so, for example, in an activity you can directly use `asset` to address the `AssetManager`.

- **override fun openAssetFile(uri:Uri, mode:String, signal:CancellationSignal): AssetFileDescriptor**

Same as `openAssetFile(Uri, String)`, but allows for cancellation from the client side. The provider can save the `signal` object and catch the client's cancellation request by periodically calling `throwIfCancelled()` on the `signal` object.

- **override fun : openTypedAssetFile(uri:Uri, mimeTypeFilter:String, opts:Bundle): AssetFileDescriptor**

Implement this if you want clients to be able to read (not write!) asset data by MIME type. The default implementation compares the "mimeTypeFilter" with whatever it gets from `getType(Uri)`, and if they match, it simply forwards to `openAssetFile(...)`.

- **override fun : openTypedAssetFile(uri:Uri, mimeTypeFilter:String, opts:Bundle, signal:CancellationSignal): AssetFileDescriptor**

  Same as openTypedAssetFile(Uri, String, Bundle), but allows for cancellation from the client side. The provider can save the signal object and catch the client's cancellation request by periodically calling throwIfCancelled() on the signal object.

- **override fun <T : Any?> openPipeHelper(uri: Uri?, mimeType: String?, opts: Bundle?, args: T, func: PipeDataWriter<T>?): ParcelFileDescriptor**

  A helper function for implementing openTypedAssetFile(Uri, String, Bundle). It creates a data pipe and a background thread allowing you to stream generated data back to the client. This function returns a new ParcelFileDescriptor. After work is done, the caller must close it.

- **override fun openFileHelper(uri:Uri, mode:String): ParcelFileDescriptor**

  This is a convenience method for subclasses. The default implementation opens a file whose path is given by the result of a query() using the URI provided. For the file path, the "_data" member gets extracted from the query result, and the result set count must be 1.

Those methods that return a ParcelFileDescriptor object can invoke appropriate constructors as in

```
val fd = ... // get the ParcelFileDescriptor
val inpStream =
    ParcelFileDescriptor.AutoCloseInputStream(fd)
val outpStream =
    ParcelFileDescriptor.AutoCloseOutputStream(fd)
```

to build input and output streams for the files. You must use the close() method on the stream once its work is done – the "Auto" means the ParcelFileDescriptor gets closed for you automatically when you close the streams.

Similarly, those methods that return an `AssetFileDescriptor` object can invoke appropriate constructors as in

```
val fd = ... // get the AssetFileDescriptor
val inpStream =
  AssetFileDescriptor.AutoCloseInputStream(fd)
val outpStream =
  AssetFileDescriptor.AutoCloseOutputStream(fd)
```

to build input and output streams for the files. Here again, you must use the `close()` method on the stream once its work is done – only the `AssetFileDescriptor` gets closed for you automatically when you close the streams.

Informing Listeners of Data Changes

A client addressing a content provider via its `ContentResolver` field (e.g., `Activity.contentResolver`) can register for being notified of content changes by calling

```
val uri = ... // a content uri
contentResolver.registerContentObserver(uri, true,
    object : ContentObserver(null) {
      override fun onChange(selfChange: Boolean) {
        // do s.th.
      }
      override fun onChange(selfChange: Boolean,
          uri: Uri?) {
        // do s.th.
      }
    }
)
```

The second argument to `registerContentObserver()` specifies whether sub-URIs (the URI plus any more path elements) will lead to a notification as well. The constructor argument to `ContentObserver` can also be a `Handler` object for receiving onChange messages in a different thread.

In order for this to work, on the content provider side, you may need to take care the event gets correctly emitted. For example, inside any data modification method, you should add

```
context.contentResolver.notifyChange(uri, null)
```

Also, to make change listening bulletproof, you might want to inform any `Cursor` objects returned by the `query()` methods. For this aim a `cursor` has a `registerContentObserver()` method that you can use to collect cursor-based content observers. The content provider may then send messages to those content observers as well.

Extending a Content Provider

We have seen that a content provider allows for accessing database-like content and files. If you don't like the way this is done too much or have your own ideas about what a content provider should be able to do, you can implement the `call()` method as in

```
override call(method:String, arg:String, extras:Bundle)
      : Bundle {
    super.call(method, arg, extras)
    // do your own stuff...
}
```

This way you can design your own content access framework. Of course you should inform possible clients of ways how to use the interface, for example, inside the contract class.

Caution   No security checks apply to calling this method. You have to implement appropriate security checks yourself, for example, by using `checkSelfPermission()` on the context.

Client Access Consistency by URI Canonicalization

Quite often query results contain IDs or list index numbers or other information that depends on some short-term database context. For example, a query may return item IDs like 23, 67, and 56, and if you need to get the details for an item, you query again using another URI containing this ID, for example, `content://com.xyz/people/23`. The problem with such URIs is that a client usually wouldn't save them for later retrievals – the ID might have changed, so the URI is thus not very reliable.

To overcome this problem, a content provider may implement a *URI canonicalization*. To do so, your content provider class has to implement the following two methods:

- **canonicalize(url:Uri): Uri**

    Let this method return a canonicalized URI, for example, by adding some domain-specific query parameters like in

    ```
    content://com.xyz/people/23  ->
    content://com.xyz/people?
         firstName=John&
         lastName=Bird&
         Birthday=20010534&
         SSN=123-99-1624
    ```

- **uncanonicalize(url:Uri): Uri**

    Does the exact opposite of `canonicalize()`. Let it return `null` if the item got lost and the uncanonicalization cannot be performed.

Consuming Content

In order to consume content, content provider clients use an `android.content.ContentResolver` object. Any `Context` object, including activities, services, and more, provides one: `getContentResolver()` or, with Kotlin in short, `contentResolver`.

Using the Content Resolver

To access database-like content, you use one of the following `ContentResolver` methods:

- **insert(url: Uri, values: ContentValues): Int**

  Insert a record.

- **delete(url: Uri, where: String, selectionArgs: Array<String>): Int**

  Delete records.

- **update(uri: Uri, values: ContentValues, where: String, selectionArgs: Array<String>): Int**

  Update records.

- **query(uri: Uri, projection: Array<String>, queryArgs: Bundle, cancellationSignal: CancellationSignal): Cursor**

  Query.

- **query(uri: Uri, projection: Array<String>, selection: String, selectionArgs: Array<String>, sortOrder: String, cancellationSignal: CancellationSignal): Cursor**

  Query.

- **query(uri: Uri, projection: Array<String>, selection: String, selectionArgs: Array<String>, sortOrder: String): Cursor**

  Query.

Their signatures and meanings closely relate to the corresponding `ContentProvider` methods – see the preceding section "Providing Content." Also have a look at the online API reference.

To instead access file content, you can use one of the following methods:

- **openAssetFileDescriptor(uri: Uri, mode: String, cancellationSignal: CancellationSignal): AssetFileDescriptor**

  Open inner (asset) file.

- **openAssetFileDescriptor(uri: Uri, mode: String): AssetFileDescriptor**

  Open inner (asset) file, no cancellation signal.

97

- **openTypedAssetFileDescriptor(uri: Uri, mimeType: String, opts: Bundle, cancellationSignal: CancellationSignal): AssetFileDescriptor**

  Open typed inner (asset) file.

- **openTypedAssetFileDescriptor(uri: Uri, mimeType: String, opts: Bundle): AssetFileDescriptor**

  Open typed inner (asset) file, no cancellation signal.

- **openFileDescriptor(uri: Uri, mode: String, cancellationSignal: CancellationSignal): ParcelFileDescriptor**

  Open file.

- **openFileDescriptor(uri: Uri, mode: String): ParcelFileDescriptor**

  Open file, no cancellation signal.

- **openInputStream(uri: Uri): InputStream**

  Open an input stream.

- **openOutputStream(uri: Uri, mode: String): OutputStream**

  Open an output stream.

- **openOutputStream(uri: Uri): OutputStream**

  Open an output stream, "w" mode.

The open*Descriptor() methods again closely relate to the corresponding ContentProvider methods from section "Providing Content." The two others, openInputStream() and openOutputStream(), are convenience methods to more readily access file (stream) data.

To register content observers for asynchronously being signaled when content changes – see the preceding section "Informing Listeners of Data Changes" – use one of the methods.

- registerContentObserver(uri: Uri, notifyForDescendants: Boolean, observer: ContentObserver)

- unregisterContentObserver(observer: ContentObserver)

To use a content provider that exhibits an extension by virtue of an implementation of its `call()` method, you use the corresponding

- call(uri: Uri, method: String, arg: String, extras: Bundle): Bundle

method of the content resolver.

Accessing System Content Providers

The Android OS including preinstalled apps provides several content provider components. Inside the online API documentation, the content provider contract classes can be found at "android.provider/Classes". The following sections summarize what they are and how they can be accessed.

BlockedNumberContract

Exposes a table containing blocked numbers. Only the system, the default phone app, the default SMS app, and carrier apps can access this table – except for `canCurrentUserBlockNumbers()` that can be called by any app. To use it, you, for example, write

```
val values = ContentValues()
values.put(BlockedNumbers.COLUMN_ORIGINAL_NUMBER,
      "1234567890")
Uri uri = contentResolver.insert(
      BlockedNumbers.CONTENT_URI, values)
```

CalendarContract

A rather complex content provider with many tables. As an example, we access the calendars list and add an event:

```
val havePermissions =
    ContextCompat.checkSelfPermission(this,
            Manifest.permission.WRITE_CALENDAR)
    == PackageManager.PERMISSION_GRANTED
    && ContextCompat.checkSelfPermission(this,
            Manifest.permission.READ_CALENDAR)
    == PackageManager.PERMISSION_GRANTED
```

99

```kotlin
if(!havePermissions) {
    // Acquire permissions...
}else{
    data class CalEntry(val name: String, val id: String)
    val calendars = HashMap<String, CalEntry>()
    val uri = CalendarContract.Calendars.CONTENT_URI
    val cursor = contentResolver.query(
            uri, null, null, null, null)
    cursor.moveToFirst()
    while (!cursor.isAfterLast) {
        val calName = cursor.getString(
            cursor.getColumnIndex(
                CalendarContract.Calendars.NAME))
        val calId = cursor.getString(
            cursor.getColumnIndex(
                CalendarContract.Calendars._ID))
        calendars[calName] = CalEntry(calName, calId)
        cursor.moveToNext()
    }
    Log.e("LOG", calendars.toString())

    val calId = "4" // You should instead fetch an
                    // appropriate entry from the map!
    val year = 2018
    val month = Calendar.AUGUST
    val dayInt = 27
    val hour = 8
    val minute = 30

    val beginTime = Calendar.getInstance()
    beginTime.set(year, month, dayInt, hour, minute)
    val event = ContentValues()
    event.put(CalendarContract.Events.CALENDAR_ID,
            calId)
    event.put(CalendarContract.Events.TITLE,
            "MyEvent")
```

```
event.put(CalendarContract.Events.DESCRIPTION,
        "This is test event")
event.put(CalendarContract.Events.EVENT_LOCATION,
        "School")
event.put(CalendarContract.Events.DTSTART,
        beginTime.getTimeInMillis())
event.put(CalendarContract.Events.DTEND,
        beginTime.getTimeInMillis())
event.put(CalendarContract.Events.ALL_DAY,
        0)
event.put(CalendarContract.Events.RRULE,
        "FREQ=YEARLY")
event.put(CalendarContract.Events.EVENT_TIMEZONE,
        "Germany")
val retUri = contentResolver.insert(
        CalendarContract.Events.CONTENT_URI, event)
Log.e("LOG", retUri.toString())
}
```

We didn't implement the permission inquiry – permissions are described in detail in Chapter 7.

CallLog

This is a table listing placed and received calls. We show an example to list the table:

```
val havePermissions =
    ContextCompat.checkSelfPermission(this,
        Manifest.permission.READ_CALL_LOG)
            == PackageManager.PERMISSION_GRANTED
    && ContextCompat.checkSelfPermission(this,
        Manifest.permission.WRITE_CALL_LOG)
            == PackageManager.PERMISSION_GRANTED
if(!havePermissions) {
    // Acquire permissions...
}else {
    val uri = CallLog.Calls.CONTENT_URI
```

```
val cursor = contentResolver.query(
    uri, null, null, null, null)
cursor.moveToFirst()
while (!cursor.isAfterLast) {
    Log.e("LOG", "New entry:")
    for(name in cursor.columnNames) {
        val v = cursor.getString(
            cursor.getColumnIndex(name))
        Log.e("LOG"," > " + name + " = " + v)
    }
    cursor.moveToNext()
}
}
```

We didn't implement the permission inquiry – permissions are described in detail in Chapter 7.

The table columns are listed in Table 6-3.

Table 6-3. *CallLog Table Columns*

Name	Description
date	The date of the call, in milliseconds since the epoch.
transcription	Transcription of the call or voicemail entry.
photo_id	The cached photo ID of an associated photo.
subscription_ component_name	The component name of the account used to place or receive the call.
type	The type of the call. One of (constant names in `CallLog.Calls`) INCOMING_TYPE, OUTGOING_TYPE, MISSED_TYPE, VOICEMAIL_TYPE, REJECTED_TYPE, BLOCKED_TYPE, ANSWERED_EXTERNALLY_TYPE
geocoded_location	A geocoded location for the number associated with this call.

(*continued*)

Table 6-3. (*continued*)

Name	Description
presentation	The number presenting rules set by the network. One of (constant names in `CallLog.Calls`) PRESENTATION_ALLOWED, PRESENTATION_RESTRICTED, PRESENTATION_UNKNOWN, PRESENTATION_PAYPHONE.
duration	The duration of the call in seconds.
subscription_id	The identifier for the account used to place or receive the call.
is_read	Whether this item has been read or otherwise consumed by the user (0 = false, 1 = true).
number	The phone number as the user entered it.
features	Bit mask describing features of the call, built of (constant names in `CallLog. Calls`) **FEATURES_HD_CALL**: Call was HD. **FEATURES_PULLED_EXTERNALLY**: Call was pulled externally. **FEATURES_VIDEO**: Call had video. **FEATURES_WIFI**: Call was WIFI call.
voicemail_uri	URI of the voicemail entry, if applicable.
normalized_ number	The cached normalized (E164) version of the phone number, if it exists.
via_number	For an incoming call, the secondary line number the call was received via. When a SIM card has multiple phone numbers associated with it, the via number indicates which of the numbers associated with the SIM was called.
matched_number	The cached phone number of the contact that matches this entry, if it exists.
last_modified	The date the row is last inserted, updated, or marked as deleted. In milliseconds since the epoch. Read-only.
new	Whether or not the call has been acknowledged (0 = false, 1 = true).
numberlabel	The cached number label, for a custom number type, associated with the phone number, if it exists.
lookup_uri	The cached URI to look up the contact associated with the phone number, if it exists.

(*continued*)

Table 6-3. (*continued*)

Name	Description
photo_uri	The cached photo URI of the picture associated with the phone number, if it exists.
data_usage	The data usage of the call in bytes.
phone_account_ address	Undocumented.
formatted_number	The cached phone number, formatted with rules based on the country the user was in when the call was made or received.
add_for_all_users	Undocumented.
numbertype	The cached number type associated with the phone number, if applicable. One of (constant names in `CallLog.Calls`) INCOMING_TYPE OUTGOING_TYPE MISSED_TYPE VOICEMAIL_TYPE REJECTED_TYPE BLOCKED_TYPE ANSWERED_EXTERNALLY_TYPE
countryiso	The ISO 3166-1 two-letter country code of the country where the user received or made the call.
name	The cached name associated with the phone number, if it exists.
post_dial_digits	The post-dial portion of a dialed number.
transcription_state	Undocumented.
_id	The (technical) ID of the table entry.

ContactsContract

This is a complex contract describing the phone contacts. Contact information is stored in a three-tier data model:

- **ContactsContract.Data**

  Any kind of personal data.

- **ContactsContract.RawContacts**

  A set of data describing a person.

- **ContactsContract.Contacts**

  An aggregated view on a person, possibly related to several rows inside the "RawContacts" table. Due to its aggregating nature, it is writable only in parts.

There are more contract-related tables described as inner classes of ContactsContract. Instead of explaining all possible use cases for the contacts content provider, to get you started, we just present code to list the contents of the three main tables listed previously, show what a single new contact writes there, and otherwise refer to the online documentation of the ContactsContract class. To list the contents of the three tables, use

```kotlin
fun showTable(tbl:Uri) {
    Log.e("LOG", "################################")
    Log.e("LOG", tbl.toString())
    val cursor = contentResolver.query(
            tbl, null, null, null, null)
    cursor.moveToFirst()
    while (!cursor.isAfterLast) {
        Log.e("LOG", "New entry:")
        for(name in cursor.columnNames) {
            val v = cursor.getString(
                    cursor.getColumnIndex(name))
            Log.e("LOG","  > " + name + " = " + v)
        }
        cursor.moveToNext()
    }
}
...
showTable(ContactsContract.Contacts.CONTENT_URI)
showTable(ContactsContract.RawContacts.CONTENT_URI)
showTable(ContactsContract.Data.CONTENT_URI)
```

If you create a new contact using Android's pre-installed Contacts app, inside the Contacts view table, you will find the following new entry (only important columns):

```
_id = 1
display_name_alt = Mayer, Hugo
sort_key_alt = Mayer, Hugo
has_phone_number = 1
contact_last_updated_timestamp = 1518451432615
display_name = Hugo Mayer
sort_key = Hugo Mayer
times_contacted = 0
name_raw_contact_id = 1
```

And as an associated entry inside table RawContacts, you will find among others

```
_id = 1
account_type = com.google
contact_id = 1
display_name_alt = Mayer, Hugo
sort_key_alt = Mayer, Hugo
account_name = pmspaeth1111@gmail.com
display_name = Hugo Mayer
sort_key = Hugo Mayer
times_contacted = 0
account_type_and_data_set = com.google
```

Obviously you find many of these entries also inside the Contacts view listed before. Associated are zero to many entries inside the Data table (only the most important shown):

```
Entry:
  _id = 3
  mimetype = vnd.android.cursor.item/phone_v2
  raw_contact_id = 1
  contact_id = 1
  data1 = (012) 345-6789
```

```
Entry:
  _id = 4
  mimetype = vnd.android.cursor.item/phone_v2
  raw_contact_id = 1
  contact_id = 1
  data1 = (098) 765-4321

Entry:
  _id = 5
  mimetype = vnd.android.cursor.item/email_v2
  raw_contact_id = 1
  contact_id = 1
  data1 = null

Entry:
  _id = 6
  mimetype = vnd.android.cursor.item/name
  raw_contact_id = 1
  contact_id = 1
  data3 = Mayer
  data2 = Hugo
  data1 = Hugo Mayer

Entry:
  _id = 7
  mimetype = vnd.android.cursor.item/nickname
  raw_contact_id = 1
  contact_id = 1
  data1 = null

Entry:
  _id = 8
  mimetype = vnd.android.cursor.item/note
  raw_contact_id = 1
  contact_id = 1
  data1 = null
```

You can see that the rows inside the `Data` table correspond to edit fields inside the GUI – you see two phone numbers, a first and second name, no nickname, and no email address.

DocumentsContract

This is not a content contract in the same sense as the other contracts we see here – it corresponds to `android.provider.DocumentsProvider,` which is a subclass of `android.content.ContentProvider`. We will be dealing with documents providers in the following in section "Documents Provider."

FontsContract

This is a contract that deals with downloadable fonts and does not correspond to content providers.

MediaStore

The media store handles metadata for all media-related files on both internal and external storage devices. This includes audio files, images, and videos. Apart from that it handles files in a usage-agnostic manner – that means media and non-media files that by whatever means relate to media files. The root class `android.provider.MediaStore` itself does not contain content provider–specific assets, but the following inner classes do:

- **MediaStore.Audio**

  Audio files. Contains more inner classes for music albums, artists, the audio files themselves, genres, and playlists

- **MediaStore.Images**

  Images

- **MediaStore.Videos**

  Videos

- **MediaStore.Files**

  Files in general

You can investigate any of the media store tables by scanning through the online API documentation. For your own experiments, you can start with the tables as a whole by watching out for constants EXTERNAL_CONTENT_URI and INTERNAL_CONTENT_URI, or method getContentUri(), and then sending those through the same code we already used previously:

```
showTable(MediaStore.Audio.Media.getContentUri(
      "internal"))  // <- other option: "external"

fun showTable(tbl:Uri) {
  Log.e("LOG", "####################################")
  Log.e("LOG", tbl.toString())
  val cursor = contentResolver.query(
        tbl, null, null, null, null)
  cursor.moveToFirst()
  while (!cursor.isAfterLast) {
    Log.e("LOG", "New entry:")
    for(name in cursor.columnNames) {
      val v = cursor.getString(
            cursor.getColumnIndex(name))
      Log.e("LOG"," > " + name + " = " + v)
    }
    cursor.moveToNext()
  }
}
```

Settings

This is a content provider that deals with various global and system-level settings. The following are the main URIs as constants from the contract class:

- **Settings.Global.CONTENT_URI**

  Global settings. All entries are triples of

  - "_id"
  - android.provider.Settings.NameValueTable.NAME
  - android.provider.Settings.NameValueTable.VALUE

- **Settings.System.CONTENT_URI**

  Global system-level settings. All entries are triples of

  - " _id"

  - android.provider.Settings.NameValueTable.NAME

  - android.provider.Settings.NameValueTable.VALUE

- **Settings.Secure.CONTENT_URI**

  Secured system settings – apps are not allowed to alter them. All
  entries are triples of

  - " _id"

  - android.provider.Settings.NameValueTable.NAME

  - android.provider.Settings.NameValueTable.VALUE

To investigate these tables, have a look at the online API documentation of android.
provider.Settings. It shows and describes all possible settings entries. To list the
complete settings, you can use the same function as earlier for the ContactsContract
contract class:

```
showTable(Settings.Global.CONTENT_URI)
showTable(Settings.System.CONTENT_URI)
showTable(Settings.Secure.CONTENT_URI)
...
fun showTable(tbl:Uri) {
  Log.e("LOG", "##################################")
  Log.e("LOG", tbl.toString())
  val cursor = contentResolver.query(
        tbl, null, null, null, null)
  cursor.moveToFirst()
  while (!cursor.isAfterLast) {
    Log.e("LOG", "New entry:")
    for(name in cursor.columnNames) {
      val v = cursor.getString(
            cursor.getColumnIndex(name))
      Log.e("LOG"," > " + name + " = " + v)
    }
```

```
    cursor.moveToNext()
  }
}
```

Your app doesn't need a special permission to read the settings. However, writing is only possible for the Global and System tables, and you also need a special construct to acquire permission:

```
if(!Settings.System.canWrite(this)) {
    val intent = Intent(
            Settings.ACTION_MANAGE_WRITE_SETTINGS)
    intent.data = Uri.parse(
            "package:" + getPackageName())
    startActivity(intent)
}
```

Usually you acquire permissions by calling

```
ActivityCompat.requestPermissions(this,
        arrayOf(Manifest.permission.WRITE\_SETTINGS), 42)
```

For settings permissions this request however gets denied immediately by current Android versions. So you cannot use that and need to call the Intent as shown earlier instead.

To access a certain entry, you can again use constants and methods from the contract class:

```
val uri = Settings.System.getUriFor(
        Settings.System.HAPTIC_FEEDBACK_ENABLED)
Log.e("LOG", uri.toString())

val feedbackEnabled = Settings.System.getInt(
            contentResolver,
            Settings.System.HAPTIC_FEEDBACK_ENABLED)
Log.e("LOG", Integer.toString(feedbackEnabled))

Settings.System.putInt(contentResolver,
        Settings.System.HAPTIC_FEEDBACK_ENABLED, 0)
```

Caution   While it is possible to acquire an individual URI for a certain setting, you should not use the `ContentResolver.update()`, `ContentResolver.insert()`, or `ContentResolver.delete()` method to alter values. Instead use the methods provided by the contract class.

SyncStateContract

This contract is used by the Browser app, the Contacts app, and the Calendar app to help synchronize user data with external servers.

UserDictionary

This refers to a content provider that allows for administering and using predictive input based on a word dictionary. As of API level 23, the user dictionary can only be used from IMEs, that is, Input Method Editors, or the Spelling Checker Framework. You should for modern apps not try to use it from some other place. This contract thus plays only an informational role.

VoicemailContract

This contract allows for accessing information referring to voicemail providers. It primarily consists of two tables described by inner classes:

- **VoicemailContract.Status**

  A voicemail source app uses this contract to tell the system about its state.

- **VoicemailContract.Voicemails**

  Contains the actual voicemails.

You can list the contents of these tables – for example, for the Voicemails table, write

```
val uri = VoicemailContract.Voicemails.CONTENT_URI.
    buildUpon().
    appendQueryParameter(
        VoicemailContract.PARAM_KEY_SOURCE_PACKAGE,
```

```
        packageName)
      .build()
showTable(uri)

fun showTable(tbl:Uri) {
  Log.e("LOG", "#################################")
  Log.e("LOG", tbl.toString())
  val cursor = contentResolver.query(
        tbl, null, null, null, null)
  cursor.moveToFirst()
  while (!cursor.isAfterLast) {
    Log.e("LOG", "New entry:")
    for(name in cursor.columnNames) {
      val v = cursor.getString(
            cursor.getColumnIndex(name))
      Log.e("LOG"," > " + name + " = " + v)
    }
    cursor.moveToNext()
  }
}
```

Adding the VoicemailContract.PARAM_KEY_SOURCE_PACKAGE URI parameter is important; otherwise, you'll get a security exception.

Batch-Accessing Content Data

The *android.content.ContentProvider* class allows your implementation to use

```
applyBatch(
      operations: ArrayList<ContentProviderOperation>):
      Array<ContentProviderResult>
```

The default implementation iterates through the list and performs each operation in turn, but you can also override the method to use your own logic. The ContentProviderOperation objects provided in the parameter describe the operation to perform – it can be one of update, delete, and insert. For your convenience, the class provides a builder, which you can use, for example, as follows:

```
val oper:ContentProviderOperation =
        ContentProviderOperation.newInsert(uri)
                .withValue("key1", "val1")
                .withValue("key2", 42)
        .build()
```

Securing Content

From the moment you declare a content provider inside AndroidManifest.xml and export it by setting its "exported" attribute to "true", other apps are allowed to access the complete contents exposed by the provider.

This might not be what you want for sensitive information. As a remedy, in order to impose restrictions on the content or part of the content, you add permission-related attributes to the <provider> element or its sub-elements.

You basically have the following options:

1. **Securing all content by one criterion**

   To do so, use the "permission" attribute of <provider> as in

   <provider ...
           android:permission="PERMISSION-NAME"
           ... >
       ...
   </provider>

   where PERMISSION-NAME is a system permission or a permission you defined in the <permission> element of the app. If you do it that way, the complete content of the provider is accessible only to such clients that successfully acquired exactly this permission. More precisely, any read or write access requires clients to have this permission. If you need to distinguish between *read* permission and *write* permission, you can instead use the "readPermission" and "writePermission" attributes. If you use a mixture, the more specific attributes win. This means

- permission = A → writePermission = A, readPermission = A

- permission = A, readPermission = B → writePermission = A, readPermission = B

- permission = A, writePermission = B → writePermission = B, readPermission = A

- permission = A, writePermission = B, readPermission = C → writePermission = B, readPermission = C

2. **Securing specific URI paths**

   By using the `<path-permission>` sub-element of `<provider>`, you can impose restrictions on specific URI paths:

   ```
   <path-permission android:path="string"
               android:pathPrefix="string"
               android:pathPattern="string"
               android:permission="string"
               android:readPermission="string"
               android:writePermission="string" />
   ```

   In the "*permission" attributes, you specify the permission name and permission scope, just as described previously in item "Securing all content by one criterion." For the path specification, you use exactly one of the three possible attributes: "path" is for an exact path match, "pathPrefix" is for matching the start of a path, and "pathPattern" allows for wildcards: "X*" is for zero to many occurrences of any character "X", and ".*" is for zero to many occurrences of any character. Since you can use several `<path-permission>` elements, you can build a very fine-grained permission structure in your content provider.

3. **Permission exemptions**

By using the "grantUriPermission" attribute of the `<provider>` element, you can temporarily grant permissions to components called by the Intent from the app that owns the content provider. If you set "grantUriPermission" to "true" and the Intent for calling the other component gets constructed using the help of

```
intent.addFlags(
    Intent.FLAG_GRANT_READ_URI_PERMISSION)
/*or*/
intent.addFlags(
    Intent.FLAG_GRANT_WRITE_URI_PERMISSION)
/*or*/
intent.addFlags(
    Intent.FLAG_GRANT_WRITE_URI_PERMISSION and
    Intent.FLAG_GRANT_READ_URI_PERMISSION)
```

the called component will have full access to all content of the provider. You can instead set "grantUriPermission" to "false" and add sub-elements

```
<grant-uri-permission android:path="string"
                android:pathPattern="string"
                android:pathPrefix="string" />
```

which then control the exemptions in a more fine-grained way. For both to make sense, you obviously must have restrictions by "*permission" attributes in effect; otherwise, there is nothing you can have exemptions for. The rules for the `<grant-uri-permission>` element's attributes are as explained previously: "path" is for an exact path match, "pathPrefix" is for matching the start of a path, and "pathPattern" allows for wildcards: "X*" is for zero to many occurrences of any character "X", and ".*" is for zero to many occurrences of any character.

Providing Content for the Search Framework

The Android *search framework* provides a feature to users to search any data that is available to them by whatever means and using whatever data source. We will be talking about the search framework in Chapter 8, section "Search Framework." For now it is important to know that for

- Recent query suggestions

- Custom suggestions

content providers play a role. For both of them, you provide special content provider subclasses and add them to `AndroidManifest.xml` as any other content provider.

Documents Provider

The documents provider is part of the *Storage Access Framework (SAF)*. It allows for a document-centric view of data access, and it also exhibits a hierarchical super-structure of document directories.

Note   The Storage Access Framework (SAF) was included in API level 19. This is as of mid-2022 the case for more than 99% of active Android devices.

The main idea of a documents provider is that your app provides access to documents, wherever the corresponding data is stored, and otherwise doesn't care about how the documents and the document structure get presented to the user or other apps. The documents provider data model consists of one to many trees starting at root nodes, with sub-nodes either being documents or directories spanning subtrees, again with other directories and documents. It thus resembles the structure of data in a file system.

To start with a documents provider, you create a class implementing `android.provider.DocumentsProvider`, which itself is a specialized subclass of `android.content.ContentProvider`. As a bare minimum, you have to implement the following methods:

- **override fun onCreate(): Boolean**

  Use this to initialize the documents provider. Since this runs on the app's main thread, you must not perform lengthy operations here. But you can prepare the data access to the provider. Return true if the provider was successfully loaded and false otherwise.

- **override fun queryRoots(projection: Array<out String>?): Cursor**

  This is supposed to query the roots of the provider's data structure. In many cases the data will fit into one tree, and you thus need to provide just one root, but you can have as many roots as making sense for your requirements. The `projection` argument may present a list of columns to be included in the result set. The names are the same as the `COLUMN_` constants inside `DocumentsContract.Root`. It may be `null`, which means return all columns. The method must return cursors with at maximum the following fields (shown are the constant names from `DocumentsContract.Root`):

  - **COLUMN_AVAILABLE_BYTES**: (long) Available bytes under the root. Optional and may be `null` to indicate "unknown."

  - **COLUMN_CAPACITY_BYTES**: (long) The capacity of the tree at that root, in bytes. Think of a file system capacity. Optional and may be `null` to indicate "unknown."

  - **COLUMN_DOCUMENT_ID**: The ID (string) of the directory corresponding to that root. Required.

  - **COLUMN_FLAGS**: Flags that apply to a root (Int). A combination of (constants in `DocumentsContract.Root`) FLAG_LOCAL_ONLY (local to the device, no network access)

FLAG_SUPPORTS_CREATE (at least one document under the root supports creating content)

FLAG_SUPPORTS_RECENTS (root can be queried to show recently changed documents)

FLAG_SUPPORTS_SEARCH (the tree allows for searching documents)

- **COLUMN_ICON**: (Int) Icon resource ID for a root. Required.

- **COLUMN_MIME_TYPES**: (string) Supported MIME types. If more than one, use a newline "\n" as a separator. Optional and may be `null` to indicate support for all MIME types.

- **COLUMN_ROOT_ID**: (string) A unique ID of the root. Required.

- **COLUMN_SUMMARY**: (string) Summary for this root, might be shown to a user. Optional and may be `null` to indicate "unknown."

- **COLUMN_TITLE**: (string) Title for the root, might be shown to a user. Required.

If this set of roots changes, you must call `ContentResolver.notifyChange` with `DocumentsContract.buildRootsUri` to notify the system.

- **override fun queryChildDocuments(parentDocumentId: String?, projection: Array<out String>?, sortOrder: String?): Cursor**

Return the immediate child documents and sub-directories contained in the requested directory. Apps targeting API level 26 or higher should instead implement `fun queryChildDocuments(par entDocumentId: String?, projection: Array<out String>?, queryArgs: Bundle?): Cursor` and in this method use

```
override fun queryChildDocuments(
    parentDocumentId: String?,
    projection: Array<out String>?,
```

```
        sortOrder: String?): Cursor {
    val bndl = Bundle()
    bndl.putString(
        ContentResolver.QUERY_ARG_SQL_SORT_ORDER,
        sortOrder)
    return queryChildDocuments(
        parentDocumentId, projection, bndl)
}
```

- **override fun queryChildDocuments(parentDocumentId: String?, projection: Array<out String>?, queryArgs: Bundle?): Cursor**

  Return the immediate child documents and sub-directories contained in the requested directory. The bundle argument contains query parameters at keys

```
ContentResolver.QUERY_ARG_SQL_SELECTION
ContentResolver.QUERY_ARG_SQL_SELECTION_ARGS
ContentResolver.QUERY_ARG_SQL_SORT_ORDER -or-
    ContentResolver.QUERY_ARG_SORT_COLUMNS
    (this being a String array)
```

  The `parentDocumentId` is the ID of the directory we want to have listed, and inside `projection` you can specify the columns that should be returned – use a list of constants `COLUMN_` from `DocumentsContract.Document`. Or write `null` to return all columns. The resulting `Cursor` at a maximum returns the following fields (keys are constants from `DocumentsContract.Document`):

  - **COLUMN_DISPLAY_NAME**: (string) The display name of a document, used as the primary title displayed to a user. Required

  - **COLUMN_DOCUMENT_ID**: (string) The unique ID of a document. Required

  - **COLUMN_FLAGS**: Flags for the document. A combination of (constant names from `DocumentsContract.Document`)

FLAG_SUPPORTS_WRITE (writing supported)

FLAG_SUPPORTS_DELETE (deleting supported)

FLAG_SUPPORTS_THUMBNAIL (representation as thumbnail supported)

FLAG_DIR_PREFERS_GRID (for directories, if they should be shown as a grid)

FLAG_DIR_PREFERS_LAST_MODIFIED (for directories, sorting by "last modified" preferred)

FLAG_VIRTUAL_DOCUMENT (a virtual document without MIME type)

FLAG_SUPPORTS_COPY (copying supported)

FLAG_SUPPORTS_MOVE (moving – inside the tree – supported)

FLAG_SUPPORTS_REMOVE (removing from the hierarchical structure (not deleting!) supported)

- **COLUMN_ICON**: (Int) A specific icon resource ID for a document. May be null to use the system default

- **COLUMN_LAST_MODIFIED**: (long) The timestamp when a document was last modified, in milliseconds since January 1, 1970, 00:00:00.0 UTC. Required, but may be null if undefined.

- **COLUMN_MIME_TYPE**: (string) The MIME type of a document. Required

- **COLUMN_SIZE**: (long) Size of a document, in bytes, or null if unknown. Required

- **COLUMN_SUMMARY**: (string) The summary of a document, may be shown to a user. Optional and may be null

For network-related operations, you might return data partly and set DocumentsContract.EXTRA_LOADING on the Cursor to indicate that you are still fetching additional data. Then, when the network data is available, you can send a change notification to trigger a requery and return the complete contents. To support change notifications, you must fire `Cursor.setNotificationUri()` with a relevant URI, maybe from `DocumentsContract.buildChildDocumentsUri()`. Then you can call `ContentResolver.notifyChange()` with that URI to send change notifications.

- **fun openDocument(documentId: String?, mode: String?, signal: CancellationSignal?): ParcelFileDescriptor**

  Open and return the requested document. This should return a reliable `ParcelFileDescriptor` to detect when the remote caller has finished reading or writing the document. If you block while downloading content, you should periodically check `CancellationSignal.isCanceled()` to abort abandoned open requests. The parameters are as follows: `documentId` is for the document to return. The `mode` specifies the "open" mode, such as "r", "w", or "rw". Mode "r" should always be supported. The provider should throw `UnsupportedOperationException` if the passed mode is not supported. You may return a pipe or socket pair if the mode is exclusively "r" or "w", but complex modes like "rw" imply a normal file on disk that supports seeking. The `signal` may be used from the caller if the request should be canceled. May be `null`.

- **override fun queryDocument(documentId: String?, projection: Array<out String>?): Cursor**

  Return metadata for a single requested document. Parameters are as follows: `documentId` is the ID of the document to return and `projection` a list of columns to put into the cursor. Use the constants from `DocumentsContract.Document`; for a list see earlier inside the description of method `queryChildDocuments()`. If you use `null` here, all columns are to be returned.

Inside the file `AndroidManifest.xml`, you register the documents provider almost like any other provider:

```
<provider
    android:name="com.example.YourDocumentProvider"
```

```
      android:authorities="com.example.documents"
      android:exported="true"
      android:grantUriPermissions="true"
      android:permission=
            "android.permission.MANAGE_DOCUMENTS">
  <intent-filter>
    <action android:name=
          "android.content.action.DOCUMENTS_PROVIDER"/>
  </intent-filter>
</provider>
```

Inside the preceding queries, we have seen that the Cursor object returns flags to indicate that recent documents and searching inside the tree be supported. In order for this to work, you must implement one or two more methods in your DocumentsProvider implementation:

- **override fun queryRecentDocuments(rootId: String, projection: Array<String>): Cursor**

  Supposed to return recently modified documents under the requested root. The returned documents should be sorted by COLUMN_LAST_MODIFIED in descending order, and at most 64 entries should be shown. Recent documents do not support change notifications.

- **querySearchDocuments(rootId: String, query: String, projection: Array<String>): Cursor**

  Supposed to return documents that match the given query under the requested root. The returned documents should be sorted by relevance in descending order. For slow queries you can return data in part and set EXTRA_LOADING on the cursor to indicate that you are fetching additional data. Then, when the data is available, you can send a change notification to trigger a requery and return the complete contents. To support change notifications, you must use setNotificationUri(ContentResolver, Uri) with a relevant

URI, maybe from buildSearchDocumentsUri(String, String, String). Then you can call the method notifyChange(Uri, android.database.ContentObserver, boolean) with that URI to send change notifications.

Once your documents provider is configured and running, a client component can then use an ACTION_OPEN_DOCUMENT or ACTION_CREATE_DOCUMENT Intent to open or create a document. The Android system picker will be taking care of presenting the appropriate documents to the user – you don't have to provide an own GUI for your documents provider.

An example of such a client access would be

```
// An integer you can use to identify that call when the
// called Intent returns
val READ_REQUEST_CODE = 42

// ACTION_OPEN_DOCUMENT used in this example is the
// intent to choose a document like for example a file
// file via the system's file browser.
val intent = Intent(Intent.ACTION_OPEN_DOCUMENT)

// Filter to only show results that can be "opened", such
// as a file (as opposed to a list of informational items)
intent.addCategory(Intent.CATEGORY_OPENABLE)

// You can use a filter to for example show only images.
// To search for all documents instead, you can use "*/*"
// here.
intent.type = "image/*"

// The actual Intent call - the system will provide the
// GUI
startActivityForResult(intent, READ_REQUEST_CODE)
```

Once an item is selected from inside the system picker, to catch the intent return, you'd write something like

```
override fun onActivityResult(requestCode:Int,
        resultCode:Int,
        resultData:Intent) {
```

```
// The ACTION_OPEN_DOCUMENT intent was sent with the
// request code READ_REQUEST_CODE. If the request
// code seen here doesn't match, it's the
// response to some other intent, and the code below
// shouldn't run at all.

if (requestCode == READ_REQUEST_CODE
        && resultCode == Activity.RESULT_OK) {
    // The document selected shows up in
    // intent.getData()
    val uri = resultData.data
    Log.i("LOG", "Uri: " + uri.toString())
    showImage(uri) // Do s.th. with it
    }
}
```

Instead of opening a file as shown in the example, you can do other things with the URI you received in the Intent's return. You could, for example, also issue a query to fetch metadata as shown in the preceding query methods. Since the DocumentsProvider inherits from ContentProvider, you can use the methods described there – see the preceding section "Providing Content Files," to open a stream for the document's bytes.

CHAPTER 7

Permissions

Securing sensitive data is an important task during the development of an app. With more and more apps on handheld devices being used for sensitive everyday tasks like banking and communicating, security has been gaining more and more importance over time, and it will continue to do so in the future. You as a developer must yield to this evolvement and take every precaution possible to handle your app users' data responsibly.

Fully handling each and every possible security aspect is a challenging task and would fill a whole book on its own. Fortunately, there is a vast amount of online resources you can consult to get updated with Android OS security matters. Just be cautious to filter out inappropriate information. A good place to start is the security-related topics of the Android OS's online resources – by mid-2022 two relevant page URLs for that read are `https://developer.android.com/design-for-safety#security` and `https://developer.android.com/guide/topics/permissions/overview`. If these links are broken when you read the book, enter "Android best practices security" and "Android best practices permissions" in your favorite search engine, and you'll readily get to these resources.

Having said that, we still want to deal with the *permission* system inside the Android OS to some depth, because this is the place you as a developer will definitely have to feel at home once your app addresses sensitive data. Permissions add security to using system data and features, by using predefined permissions or defining them yourself. In `AndroidManifest.xml` you add custom permissions and declare permissions that your app wants to use. Dependent on the permission type, you must add dialogs in your code to inform the user about which permissions are needed, and you request confirmation for accessing secured resources or features.

127

© Peter Späth 2022
P. Späth, *Pro Android with Kotlin*, https://doi.org/10.1007/978-1-4842-8745-3_7

Permission Types

Permissions come in several flavors according to the desired protection level:

- **Normal**: This level corresponds to low-level security sensitive information. The system will automatically grant such permissions for installed apps without explicitly asking the user, but the permission is listed in the package description before the app gets installed. And it can be queried by explicit demand using the system settings app.

- **Dangerous**: This level corresponds to high-level security sensitive information. The user will be asked whether they want to allow using that permission during runtime. Once allowed for an app, the allowance will be saved, and the user possibly won't be asked again until the app gets reinstalled or the permission gets explicitly revoked by using the system settings app.

- **Signature**: This level corresponds to extremely high-level security sensitive information. Only apps signed with the same certificate as the app defining the permission can acquire it. The system will check whether the signatures match and then automatically grant the permission. This level makes sense only for a collection of apps developed by the same developer.

- **Special**: Only for a couple of use cases, the system grants access to certain system resources only by off-bands acquisition methods. Such special permissions are defined by the platform.

- **Privileged** or **System**: Only for system image apps. You normally should not and should not have to use them.

Permissions are gathered in permission groups. The idea behind that is that once the user has accepted a permission request from permission A of group G1, another permission inquiry for another permission B of the same group G1 is not needed. From a user experience perspective, permission groups show only an effect if we are talking of *Dangerous*-type permissions – permission groups for *Normal* permissions have no impact.

Note   The mapping of permissions to permission groups may change with future versions of Android – your app thus should not rely on such a mapping. From a development perspective, you should just ignore permission groups, unless you define your own permissions and permission groups.

Defining Permissions

The Android OS includes a number of permissions defined by various built-in apps or the OS itself. In addition, you as a developer can define your own permissions to secure apps or parts of your apps. You define such permissions inside AndroidManifest.xml:

```
<permission android:description="string resource"
        android:icon="drawable resource"
        android:label="string resource"
        android:name="string"
        android:permissionGroup="string"
        android:protectionLevel=["normal" | "dangerous" |
                "signature" | "signatureOrSystem"] />
```

The meaning of the attributes gets described in section "Manifest Top-Level Entries" of the online text companion. At a bare minimum, you must provide the "name" and the "protectionLevel" attribute, but it certainly is a good idea to also add label and/or icon and a description to help your users understand what the permission does.

In case you need to group your permissions, you can use one of two methods:

1. Use the <permission-group> element and add "permissionGroup" attributes to <permission> – see section "Manifest Top-Level Entries" in the online text companion.

2. Use the <permission-tree> element and name your permissions accordingly – see "Manifest Top-Level Entries" again inside the online text companion.

If you then acquire a permission of a group, the sibling permissions from the same group will be implicitly included in the grant.

Caution   To adhere to security guidelines and to have your app design clear and stable, keep the number of permissions you define yourself at the absolute bare minimum.

Using Permissions

To use permissions, inside your `AndroidManifest.xml` file add one or more

```
<uses-permission-sdk-23 android:name="string"
      android:maxSdkVersion="integer" />
```

The "name" attribute specifies the permission name and "maxSdkVersion" the maximum API level this permission requirement will take into account. The reason this special `<uses-permission-sdk-23>` element was introduced is a major change in permission semantics for Android 6.0.

The question is: How would we know which permissions exactly we need for our app? The answer has three parts:

- Android Studio tells you about a permission your app needs. If you, for example, write

  ```
  val uri = CallLog.Calls.CONTENT_URI
  val cursor = contentResolver.query(
          uri, null, null, null, null)
  ```

  Android Studio tells you a certain permission is required – see Figure 7-1.

- During development and testing, your app crashes, and in the logs you see an entry like

  ```
  Caused by: java.lang.SecurityException: Permission
  Denial: opening provider
  com.android.providers.contacts.CallLogProvider
  from
  ProcessRecord{faeda9c 4127:de.pspaeth.cp1/u0a96}
  ```

```
(pid=4127, uid=10096) requires
android.permission.READ_CALL_LOG or
android.permission.WRITE_CALL_LOG
```

- The list of system permissions tells you that you need a certain permission for a certain task. See Table 7-1 (not exhaustive).

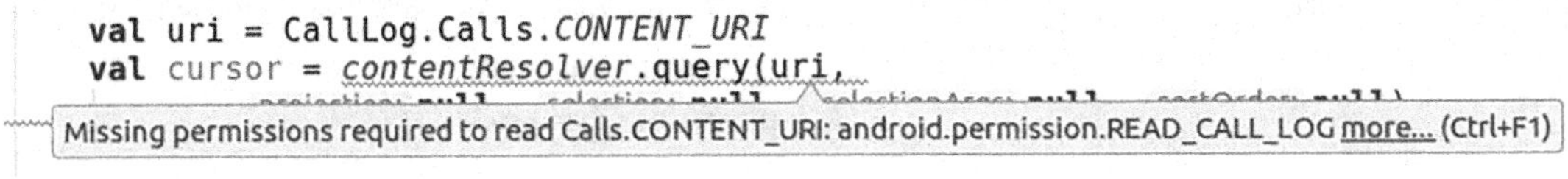

```
val uri = CallLog.Calls.CONTENT_URI
val cursor = contentResolver.query(uri,
```

Missing permissions required to read Calls.CONTENT_URI: android.permission.READ_CALL_LOG more... (Ctrl+F1)

Figure 7-1. *Android Studio Tells About a Permission Requirement*

In order to enforce an activity or the whole app being protected by a custom permission, you declare the permission inside the "permission" attribute as in

```
...
<activity android:name=
        "com.example.myapp.ExampleActivity"
    android:permission=
        "com.eample.myapp.ABC_PERMISSION"/>
...
```

or likewise inside the <application> element.

Table 7-1. *System Permissions*

Permission	Group	Description
READ_CALENDAR	CALENDAR	Allows for reading the calendar. Manifest entry: android.permission.- READ_CALENDAR
WRITE_CALENDAR	CALENDAR	Allows for writing the calendar. Manifest entry: android.permission.- READ_CALENDAR
CAMERA	CAMERA	Allows for accessing the camera. Manifest entry: android.permission.- CAMERA
READ_CONTACTS	CONTACTS	Read from the contacts table. Manifest entry: android.permission.- READ_CONTACTS
WRITE_CONTACTS	CONTACTS	Write into the contacts table. Manifest entry: android.permission.- WRITE_CONTACTS
GET_ACCOUNTS	CONTACTS	Allows for listing accounts from the *Accounts Service*. Manifest entry: android.permission.- GET_ACCOUNTS
ACCESS_FINE_LOCATION	LOCATION	Allows an app to access fine-grained location. Manifest entry: android.permission.- ACCESS_FINE_LOCATION
ACCESS_COARSE_LOCATION	LOCATION	Allows an app to access approximate location. Manifest entry: android.permission.- ACCESS_COARSE_LOCATION

(continued)

Table 7-1. (*continued*)

Permission	Group	Description
RECORD_AUDIO	MICROPHONE	Allows for recording audio. Manifest entry: android.permission.-RECORD_AUDIO
READ_PHONE_STATE	PHONE	Allows read access to phone state (phone number of the device, current cellular network information, the status of any ongoing calls, and a list of any PhoneAccounts registered on the device). Manifest entry: android.permission.-READ_PHONE_STATE
READ_PHONE_NUMBERS	PHONE	Read access to the device's phone number(s). Manifest entry: android.permission.-READ_PHONE_NUMBERS
CALL_PHONE	PHONE	Allows an application to initiate a phone call without going through the dialer user interface. Manifest entry: android.permission.-CALL_PONE
ANSWER_PHONE_CALLS	PHONE	Allows for answering an incoming phone call. Manifest entry: android.permission.-ANSWER_PHONE_CALLS
READ_CALL_LOG	PHONE	Reading from the call log table. Manifest entry: android.permission.-READ_CALL_LOG

(*continued*)

Table 7-1. (*continued*)

Permission	Group	Description
WRITE_CALL_LOG	PHONE	Writing to the call log table. Manifest entry: android.permission.-WRITE_CALL_LOG
ADD_VOICEMAIL	PHONE	Allows for adding a voicemail. Manifest entry: com.android.voicemail.-permission.ADD_VOICEMAIL
USE_SIP	PHONE	Allows for using the SIP service. Manifest entry: android.permission.-USE_SIP
PROCESS_OUTGOING_CALLS	PHONE	Allows an application to see the number being dialed during an outgoing call with the option to redirect the call to a different number or abort the call. Manifest entry: android.permission.-PROCESS_OUTGOING_CALLS
BODY_SENSORS	SENSORS	Allows an application to access data from sensors that the user uses to measure what is happening inside their body. Manifest entry: android.permission.-BODY_SENSORS
SEND_SMS	SMS	Allows sending an SMS. Manifest entry: android.permission.-SEND_SMS
RECEIVE_SMS	SMS	Allows receiving an SMS. Manifest entry: android.permission.-RECEIVE_SMS
READ_SMS	SMS	Allows reading an SMS. Manifest entry: android.permission.-READ_SMS

(*continued*)

Table 7-1. (*continued*)

Permission	Group	Description
RECEIVE_WAP_PUSH	SMS	Allows receiving a WAP Push message. Manifest entry: android.permission.-RECEIVE_WAP_PUSH
RECEIVE_MMS	SMS	Allows receiving an MMS. Manifest entry: android.permission.-RECEIVE_MMS
READ_EXTERNAL_STORAGE	STORAGE	Allows for reading from the external storage. Only required if the API level is below 19. Manifest entry: android.permission.-READ_EXTERNAL_STORAGE
WRITE_EXTERNAL_STORAGE	STORAGE	Allows for writing to the external storage. Only required if the API level is below 19. Manifest entry: android.permission.-WRITE_EXTERNAL_STORAGE

Acquiring Permissions

Permission inquiry for "Dangerous" permissions happens during the runtime of an app. This makes the permission system quite flexible – users of your app might never use certain parts of it, and thus not asking for unneeded permission avoids unnecessary annoyance.

The downside of this runtime approach is that more programming work is needed – the permission inquiry must be included in your code. To do so, at any suitable place before the permission is needed, you add

```
val activity = this
val perm = Manifest.permission.CAMERA
val cameraPermReturnId = 7239 // any suitable constant
```

```
val permissionCheck = ContextCompat.checkSelfPermission(
    activity, perm)
if (permissionCheck !=
        PackageManager.PERMISSION_GRANTED) {
    // Should we show an explanation?
    if (ActivityCompat.
        shouldShowRequestPermissionRationale(
            activity, perm)) {
        // Show an explanation to the user
        // *asynchronously* -- don't block
        // this thread waiting for the user's
        // response! After the user sees the
        // explanation, try again to request
        // the permission.
        val dialog = AlertDialog.Builder(activity) ...
            .create()
        dialog.show()
    } else {
        // No explanation needed, we can request
        // the permission.
        ActivityCompat.requestPermissions(activity,
            arrayOf(perm), cameraPermReturnId)
        // cameraPermReturnId is an app-defined
        // int constant. The callback method gets
        // the result of the request.
    }
}
```

What this code does is as follows:

- First, we check whether the permission has already been granted or not. If the permission was granted before, the user wouldn't be asked again unless the app got reinstalled or the permission got revoked explicitly.

- The `ActivityCompat.shouldShowRequestPermissionRationale()` checks whether a rationale should be shown to the user. The idea behind that is if the user denied the permission inquiry request a couple of times, they maybe did that because the need for the permission was not well understood. In this case the app gets a chance to tell the user more about the permission need. How often `shouldShowRequestPermissionRationale()` returns true is up to the Android OS. The example here shows a dialog. You can of course do whatever you want here for informing the user.

- The `ActivityCompat.requestPermissions(...)` finally performs the permission inquiry. This happens asynchronously, so the call returns immediately.

Once the call to `ActivityCompat.requestPermissions(...)` happens, the user gets asked by the Android OS, outside your app, whether they want to grant the permission. The result of that will show up in an asynchronous callback method as follows:

```
override
fun onRequestPermissionsResult(
        requestCode: Int, permissions: Array<String>,
        grantResults: IntArray) {
    when (requestCode) {
      cameraPermReturnId -> {
        // If request is canceled, the result
        // arrays are empty. Here we know it just
        // can be one entry
        if ((grantResults.isNotEmpty()
              && grantResults[0] ==
                PackageManager.PERMISSION_GRANTED)) {
          // permission was granted
          // act accordingly...
        } else {
          // permission denied
          // act accordingly...
        }
        return
```

```
      }
      // Add other 'when' lines to check for other
      // permissions this App might request.
      else -> {
        // Ignore all other requests.
        // Or whatever makes sense to you.
      }
    }
  }
}
```

This methods needs to be implemented inside an `android.content.Activity` class. In other contexts this is not possible.

System-Managed Permission Requests

In case you don't like the tight coupling of the permission inquiry process to the activity – remember you have to implement the onRequestPermissionsResult() method inside the activity class – there is an alternative using a callback registration mechanism.

In order to use it, you must first add two additional dependencies to your `build. gradle` file:

```
implementation "androidx.activity:" +
    "activity-ktx:1.4.0"
implementation "androidx.fragment:" +
    "fragment-ktx:1.4.1"
```

Then, inside the initialization part of the activity, you write

```
import androidx.activity.result.contract.
    ActivityResultContracts
...

class MainActivity : AppCompatActivity() {

    private lateinit var requestPermissionLauncher:
        ActivityResultLauncher<String>
    ....
```

```
override fun onCreate(savedInstanceState: Bundle?) {
    super.onCreate(savedInstanceState)

    ...
    requestPermissionLauncher =
        registerForActivityResult(
            ActivityResultContracts.RequestPermission()
        ) { isGranted: Boolean ->
            if (isGranted) {
                // Permission is granted. Continue the
                // workflow in your app.
                ...
            } else {
                // The features requires a permission
                // that the user has denied. Explain to
                // the user that the feature is
                // unavailable.
                ...
            }
        }
}
```

Note   This registration must be performed *before* the activity enters the ACTIVE state. To do it inside create() certainly isn't a bad idea.

To actually check for and possibly acquire the permission, you add something like the following to your code:

```
if(checkSelfPermission(Manifest.permission.CAMERA) !=
        PackageManager.PERMISSION_GRANTED) {
    if(shouldShowRequestPermissionRationale(
            Manifest.permission.CAMERA)) {
        // Explain to the user why your app requires
        // this permission. The view should show
```

```
             // a button linked to
             //   requestPermissionLauncher.launch(
             //      Manifest.permission.CAMERA
             //   )
             ...
         } else {
             // Ask the system for the permission.
             requestPermissionLauncher.launch(
                 Manifest.permission.CAMERA
             )
         }
     } else {
         // Use the API that requires the permission.
         ....
     }
}
```

The only connection to the `Activity` class is the `requestPermissionLauncher` variable, so it is easy to factor out the permission-related code to a separate class.

Acquiring Special Permissions

Using `ActivityCompat.requestPermissions()` under circumstances is not enough to acquire special permissions like SYSTEM_ALERT_WINDOW or WRITE_SETTINGS. For those two permissions and possibly others, you need to follow a different approach.

The permission WRITE_SETTINGS must be acquired using a special Intent as follows:

```
val backFromSettingPerm = 6183   // any suitable constant
if (Build.VERSION.SDK_INT >= Build.VERSION_CODES.M) {
    val activity = this
    if (!Settings.System.canWrite(activity)) {
        // This is just a suggestion: present a special
        // dialog to the user telling about the special
        // permission. Important is the Activity start
        AlertDialog dialog =
          new AlertDialog.Builder(activity)
            .setTitle(...)
```

```
        .setMessage(...)
        .setPositiveButton("OK", { dialog, id ->
            val intent = Intent(
              Settings.ACTION_MANAGE_WRITE_SETTINGS)
            intent.data = Uri.parse("package:" +
              getPackageName())
            activity.startActivityForResult(intent,
              backFromSettingPerm)
        }).setNegativeButton("Cancel",
            { dialog, id ->
              // ...
        })
        .create();
      dialog.show();
      systemWillAsk = true;
    }
} else {
    // do as with any other permissions...
}
```

Once done with that Intent, the callback method onActivityResult() can be used to continue with the GUI flow:

```
override
protected fun onActivityResult(requestCode:Int,
      resultCode:Int, data:Intent) {
  if ((requestCode and 0xFFFF) == backFromSettingPerm) {
      if (resultCode == Activity.RESULT_OK) {
         // act accordingly...
      }
  }
}
```

For the SYSTEM_ALERT_WINDOW permission, you possibly have to follow the same approach, but use ACTION_MANAGE_OVERLAY_PERMISSION instead for creating the Intent.

> **Note**   For this special SYSTEM_ALERT_WINDOW permission, the Google Play
> Store will automatically grant the permission if the app gets installed from the
> Google Play Store. For local development and testing, you have to use the Intent
> as described. Also note that for Android 11, the policy for this setting was updated;
> see https://developer.android.com/about/versions/11/privacy/
> permissions.

Feature Requirements and Permissions

In Chapter 2 we have seen that by virtue of the <uses-feature> element inside
AndroidManifest.xml, you can specify which features your app will use. This
information is important for the Google Play Store to find out on which devices your
app can run after being published. However, there is another important aspect to take
into account if you specify this requirement: which permissions will be implied by such
requirement, and how will they be handled depending on the API level in use?

Feature constants and API levels do not necessarily strictly relate to each other – for
example, the android.hardware.bluetooth feature was added in API level 8, but the
corresponding Bluetooth API was added in API level 5. Because of this, some apps were
able to use the API before they had the ability to declare that they required the API using
the <uses-feature> declaration. To remedy this discrepancy, Google Play assumes that
certain hardware-related permissions indicate that the underlying hardware features
are required by default. For instance, applications that use Bluetooth must request
the BLUETOOTH permission in a <uses-permission> element, and for apps targeting
older API levels, Google Play assumes that the permission declaration implies that
the underlying android.hardware.bluetooth feature is required by the application.
Table 7-2 lists the permissions that imply such feature requirements.

Note that the <uses-feature> declarations take precedence over features implied by
the permissions in Table 7-2. For any of these permissions, you can disable filtering based
on the implied feature by explicitly declaring the implied feature, in a <uses-feature>
element, with an android:required="false" attribute. For example, to disable any
filtering based on the CAMERA permission, you would add this to the manifest file:

```
<uses-feature android:name="android.hardware.camera"
              android:required="false" />
```

Table 7-2. *Permissions That Imply Feature Requirements*

Category	Permission...	...Implies Feature
Bluetooth	BLUETOOTH	android.hardware.bluetooth
	BLUETOOTH_ADMIN	android.hardware.bluetooth
Camera	CAMERA	android.hardware.camera and android. hardware.camera.autofocus
Location	ACCESS_MOCK_LOCATION	android.hardware.location
	ACCESS_LOCATION_EXTRA_ COMMANDS	android.hardware.location
	INSTALL_LOCATION_PROVIDER	android.hardware.location
	ACCESS_COARSE_LOCATION	android.hardware.location android.hardware. location.network (API level < 21)
	ACCESS_FINE_LOCATION	android.hardware.location android.hardware. location.gps (API level < 21)
Microphone	RECORD_AUDIO	android.hardware.microphone
Telephony	CALL_PHONE	android.hardware.telephony
	CALL_PRIVILEGED	android.hardware.telephony
	MODIFY_PHONE_STATE	android.hardware.telephony
	PROCESS_OUTGOING_CALLS	android.hardware.telephony
	READ_SMS	android.hardware.telephony
	RECEIVE_SMS	android.hardware.telephony
	RECEIVE_MMS	android.hardware.telephony
	RECEIVE_WAP_PUSH	android.hardware.telephony
	SEND_SMS	android.hardware.telephony
	WRITE_APN_SETTINGS	android.hardware.telephony
	WRITE_SMS	android.hardware.telephony
Wi-Fi	ACCESS_WIFI_STATE	android.hardware.wifi
	CHANGE_WIFI_STATE	android.hardware.wifi
	CHANGE_WIFI_MULTICAST_STATE	android.hardware.wifi

Permission Handling Using a Terminal

To see the permissions you have registered on your device, you can scan through the apps list in the system settings app or, more easily, use the ADB shell to get various permission-related information in a terminal.

For that aim, connect the hardware device via USB to your laptop or PC, open a terminal, cd to the platform-tools folder in your SDK installation, find your device in

```
./adb devices
```

and then enter

```
./adb shell -s <DEVICE-NAME>
```

If there is only one device, you can omit that -s switch.

Once inside the shell, you can use a couple of commands to get permission information. First, you can list all packages installed via

```
cmd package list package
```

To show *all* Dangerous permissions or to see the permission state for a certain package or to grant or revoke one or more permissions, you can use

```
cmd package list permissions -d -g
dumpsys package <PACKAGE-NAME>
pm [grant|revoke] <PERMISSION-NAME> ...
```

Note   Current versions of dumpsys will show both requested *and* granted permissions – do not get confused by old blog entries about that matter.

CHAPTER 8

APIs

The subject of this chapter is APIs that are the cornerstones of your app. This includes

- *Databases*
- *Scheduling*
- *Notifications*
- *Contacts*
- *Search framework*
- *Location and maps*
- *Preferences*

Databases

Android provides two realms for dealing with databases: either you use the *SQLite* library included in the Android OS, or you use the *Room* architecture component. The latter is recommended, since it adds an abstraction layer between the database and the client, simplifying the mapping between Kotlin objects and database storage objects. You can find exhaustive information about SQLite in the online docs and lots of examples on the Web – in this book we talk about Room, since the separation of concerns introduced by the abstraction helps you write better code, and since Room also helps avoid boilerplate code, you can shorten your database code significantly.

© Peter Späth 2022
P. Späth, *Pro Android with Kotlin*, https://doi.org/10.1007/978-1-4842-8745-3_8

Configuring Your Environment for Room

Since Room is a support architecture component, using it must be configured inside your Android Studio build script. To do so, open the *module's* `build.gradle` file (not the one from the project!), and on the top level (not inside any of the curly braces), write

```
apply plugin: 'kotlin-kapt'
```

This is the Kotlin compiler plugin to support annotation processing. Inside the "dependencies" section, add

```
def room_version = "2.4.2"
implementation "androidx.room:" +
    "room-runtime:$room_version"
kapt "androidx.room:" +
    "room-compiler:$room_version"
```

Room Architecture

Room is designed with easiness in mind – you basically deal with three kinds of objects:

- **Database**

  A holder for the database. Talking in SQL language idioms, it contains several tables. Technology agnostic, a database contains several entity containers.

- **Entity**

  Represents a table in the SQL world. Technology agnostic, this is a usage-centric aggregate of fields. An example would be an *Employee* inside a company or a *Contact* holding information about how to communicate with people or partners.

- **DAO or Data Access Object**

  Contains the access logic to retrieve data from the database. It thus serves as an interface between the program logic and the database model. You often have one DAO per entity class, but possibly more DAOs for various combinations. You could, for example, have an EmployeeDao and a ContactDao for the two Employee and Contact entities, but also a PersonDao that combines the employee and their contact information.

The Database

To declare a database, you write as follows:

```
import androidx.room.*

@Database(entities =
    arrayOf(Employee::class, Contact::class),
    version = 1)
abstract class MyDatabase : RoomDatabase() {
    abstract fun employeeDao(): EmployeeDao
    abstract fun contactDao(): ContactDao
    abstract fun personDao(): PersonDao
}
```

Inside the @Database annotation, you declare all entity classes used, and as abstract functions you provide factory methods for the DAO classes. You don't have to implement this abstract database class – the Room library will automatically provide an implementation for you based on the signatures and the annotations! The version number will help you upgrade different data model versions – more about that in the following.

Entities

Next, we implement the entity classes, which is extremely easy to do in Kotlin:

```
@Entity
data class Employee(
    @PrimaryKey(autoGenerate = true) var uid:Int = 0,
    var firstName:String,
    var lastName:String)
```

```
@Entity
data class Contact(
    @PrimaryKey(autoGenerate = true) var uid:Int = 0,
    var emailAddr:String)
```

You can see that we need a primary key of type Int for each entity. The `autoGenerate` `= true` takes care of automatically making it unique.

The column names from the database table defined by these entity classes match the variable names. If you want to change that, you can add another annotation @ `ColumnInfo`:

```
@Entity
data class Employee(
    @PrimaryKey(autoGenerate = true) var uid:Int = 0,
    @ColumnInfo(name = "first_name") var firstName:String,
    @ColumnInfo(name = "last_name") var lastName:String)
```

This would lead to using "first_name" and "last_name" as table column names.

Also, the table name is taken from the entity class names "Employee" and "Contact" for these examples. You can also change that: just add a parameter "tableName" to the `@Entity` annotation as in

```
@Entity(tableName = "empl")
data class Employee(
    @PrimaryKey(autoGenerate = true) var uid:Int = 0,
    @ColumnInfo(name = "first_name") var firstName:String,
    @ColumnInfo(name = "last_name") var lastName:String)
```

While it is generally a good idea to have a single integer-valued primary key, you can also use a combined key. For that aim there is an additional annotation parameter in `@Entity` you can use:

```
@Entity(tableName = "empl",
        primaryKeys = tableOf("first_name","last_name"))
data class Employee(
    @ColumnInfo(name = "first_name") var firstName:String,
    @ColumnInfo(name = "last_name") var lastName:String)
```

Entities can also have fields that are not going to be persisted. From a design perspective, this is maybe not a good idea, but if you need such a field, you can add it and use the annotation @Ignore as in

```
@Entity(tableName = "empl")
data class Employee(
    @PrimaryKey(autoGenerate = true) var uid:Int = 0,
    var firstName:String = "",
    var lastName:String = "",
    @Ignore var salary:Int)
```

As a restriction imposed by the way Room is implemented, in case you add such an "@Ignore" annotation, *all* fields must have default values assigned, even if unused.

Relationships

Room by design doesn't allow direct relationships between entities. You cannot, for example, add a list of Contact entities as a class member of an Employee entity. However, it is possible to declare foreign key relationships, which helps in maintaining data consistency.

Note   See also `https://developer.android.com/training/data-storage/room/relationships`.

To do so, add a foreignKeys annotation attribute as in the following code snippet:

```
@Entity(
    foreignKeys = arrayOf(
        ForeignKey(entity = Employee::class,
            parentColumns = arrayOf( "uid" ),
            childColumns = arrayOf( "employeeId" ),
            onDelete = ForeignKey.CASCADE,
            onUpdate = ForeignKey.CASCADE,
            deferred = true)),
    indices = arrayOf(
        Index("employeeId"))
```

```
)
@Entity
data class Contact(
        @PrimaryKey(autoGenerate = true) var uid:Int = 0,
        var employeeId:Int,
        var emailAddr:String)
```

Here are a few notes about that construct:

- In Java you would write @Entity(foreignKeys = @ForeignKey(...). Kotlin doesn't allow annotations inside annotations. In this case using the constructor serves as a substitute, which boils down to omitting the "@" for inner annotations.

- In Java annotation attribute value arrays are written like name = { ..., ... }. This cannot be used in Kotlin, because the curly braces do not serve as array initializers. Instead, the arrayOf(...) library method gets used.

- The childColumns attribute points to the reference key in *this* entity, that is, Contact.employeeId in this case.

- The parentColumns attribute points to the referred-to foreign key entity, in this case the Employee.uid.

- The onDelete attribute tells what to do if the parent gets deleted. A value ForeignKey.CASCADE means to also automatically remove all children, that is, the associated Contact entities. All possible values are as follows:

  - **CASCADE**: Transport all actions to the root of the child-parent relation tree.

  - **NO_ACTION**: Don't do anything. This is the default, and it leads to an exception if the relationship breaks due to update or delete actions.

  - **RESTRICT**: Similar to NO_ACTION, but the check will be made immediately when a delete or an update happens.

  - **SET_NULL**: All child key columns get set to null if a parent delete or update happens.

- **SET_DEFAULT**: All child key columns get set to their default if a
  parent delete or update happens.

- The onUpdate attribute tells what to do if the parent gets updated. A
  value ForeignKey.CASCADE means to also automatically update all
  children, that is, the associated Contact entities. The possible values
  are the same as for onDelete earlier.

- The deferred = true setting will postpone the consistency check
  until the database transaction is committed. This might, for example,
  be important if both parent and child get created inside the same
  transaction.

- Foreign keys must be part of a corresponding index. Here the
  Contact.employeeId gets the index. Find more about indexes in the
  following.

Nested Objects

Although it is not possible to define inter-object relations other than manually by foreign
keys, you can on the object side define a nesting of hierarchical objects. For example,
from the Employee entity

```
@Entity
data class Employee(
    @PrimaryKey(autoGenerate = true) var uid:Int = 0,
    var firstName:String,
    var lastName:String)
```

you can factor out the first and last names and instead write

```
data class Name(var firstName:String, var lastName:String)
```

```
@Entity
data class Employee(
    @PrimaryKey(autoGenerate = true) var uid:Int = 0,
    @Embedded var name:Name)
```

Note that this does not have any impact on the database side of the data model. The associated table will still have the columns "uid", "firstName", and "lastName". Since the database identity of such an embedded object is tied to the names of its fields, in case of several embedded objects of the same embedded type, you must disambiguate the names by using a `prefix` attribute as in

```
data class Name(var firstName:String, var lastName:String)

@Entity
data class Employee(
    @PrimaryKey(autoGenerate = true) var uid:Int = 0,
    @Embedded var name:Name,
    @Embedded(prefix="spouse_") var spouseName:Name)
```

which makes the table have columns "uid", "firstName", "lastName", "spouse_firstName", and "spouse_lastName".

If you like, inside the embeddable class, you can use Room annotations, for example, the `@ColumnInfo` annotation to specify custom column names:

```
data class Name(
  @ColumnInfo(name = "first_name") var firstName:String,
  @ColumnInfo(name = "last_name") var lastName:String)

@Entity
data class Employee(
    @PrimaryKey(autoGenerate = true) var uid:Int = 0,
    @Embedded var name:Name)
```

Using Indexes

To improve database query performance, you can declare one or more indexes to be used on certain fields or field combinations. You don't have to do that for the unique key; this is done automatically for you. But for any other index you want to define, write something like

```
@Entity(indices = arrayOf(
    Index("employeeId"),
    Index(value = arrayOf("country","city"))
```

```
    )
)
data class Contact(
        @PrimaryKey(autoGenerate = true) var uid:Int = 0,
        var employeeId:Int,
        var emailAddr:String,
        var country:String,
        var city:String)
```

This adds an index that allows for fast queries using the foreign key field "employeeId" and another one for fast queries given both country and city.

If you add unique = true as an attribute to the @Index annotation, Room will make sure the table cannot have two entries with the same value for that particular index. As an example we add a SSN (social security number) field to Employee and define a unique index for it:

```
@Entity(indices = arrayOf(
    Index(value = arrayOf("ssn"), unique = true)
    )
)
data class Employee(
    @PrimaryKey(autoGenerate = true) var uid:Int = 0,
    var ssn:String,
    @Embedded var name:Name)
```

If you now try to add two employees with the same SSN to the database, Room will throw an exception.

Data Access: DAOs

Data Access Objects or DAOs provide the logic to access the database. We have already seen that inside the database declaration, we have to list all DAOs in factory methods like

```
@Database(entities =
    arrayOf(Employee::class, Contact::class),
    version = 1)
abstract class MyDatabase : RoomDatabase() {
```

```
    abstract fun employeeDao(): EmployeeDao
    abstract fun contactDao(): ContactDao
    abstract fun personDao(): PersonDao
}
```

In this example we declare three DAOs for use by Room. For the actual implementation, we don't need full-fledged DAO classes. It is enough to declare interfaces or abstract classes; Room will do the rest for us.

The DAO classes, for example, for the entity

```
@Entity
data class Employee(
    @PrimaryKey(autoGenerate = true) var uid:Int = 0,
    @ColumnInfo(name = "first_name") var firstName:String,
    @ColumnInfo(name = "last_name") var lastName:String)
```

might look like

```
@Dao
interface EmployeeDao {
    @Query("SELECT * FROM employee")
    fun getAll(): List<Employee>

    @Query("SELECT * FROM employee" +
        " WHERE uid IN (:uIds)")
    fun loadAllByIds(uIds: IntArray): List<Employee>

    @Query("SELECT * FROM employee" +
        " WHERE last_name LIKE :name")
    fun findByLastName(name: String): List<Employee>

    @Query("SELECT * FROM employee" +
        " WHERE last_name LIKE :lname AND " +
        "        first_name LIKE :fname LIMIT 1")
    fun findByName(lname: String, fname: String): Employee

    @Query("SELECT * FROM employee" +
        " WHERE uid = :uid")
    fun findById(uid: Int): Employee
```

```
@Insert
fun insert(vararg employees: Employee): LongArray

@Update
fun update(vararg employees: Employee)

@Delete
fun delete(vararg employees: Employee)
}
```

You see that we used an interface here, which is possible because the complete access logic is defined by method signatures and annotations. Also, for insert, update, and delete, the method signature is all that Room needs – it will send the right commands to the database just by looking at the signatures.

For the various query methods, we use @Query annotations to provide the correct database commands. You can see that Room is smart enough to see whether we want to return a list of objects or a single object. Also we can pass method arguments into the pseudo-SQL by using ":name" identifiers.

The @Insert annotation allows for adding an attribute onConflict = "<strategy>" where you can specify what to do if a conflict occurs because a unique or primary key constraint is violated. Possible values for the <strategy> are given inside constants:

- OnConflictStrategy.ABORT to abort the transaction

- OnConflictStrategy.FAIL to fail the transaction

- OnConflictStrategy.IGNORE to ignore the conflict

- OnConflictStrategy.REPLACE to just replace the entity and otherwise continue the transaction

- OnConflictStrategy.ROLLBACK to roll back the transaction

The other DAOs from the example entities used previously will look very similar – the PersonDao maybe will do outer joins to combine the Employee and Contact entities:

```
@Dao
interface ContactDao {
    @Insert
    fun insert(vararg contacts: Contact)

    @Query("SELECT * FROM Contact WHERE uid = :uId")
```

```
    fun findById(uId: Int): List<Contact>

    @Query("SELECT * FROM Contact WHERE" +
            " employeeId = :employeeId")
    fun loadByEmployeeId(employeeId: Int): List<Contact>
}

data class Person(@Embedded var name:Name?,
                  var emailAddr: String?)
@Dao
interface PersonDao {
    @Query("SELECT * FROM empl" +
            " LEFT OUTER JOIN Contact ON" +
            "      empl.uid = Contact.employeeId" +
            " WHERE empl.uid = :uId")
    fun findById(uId: Int): List<Person>
}
```

Observable Queries

In addition to performing a query with returning entities or lists or arrays of entities as they are in the moment when the query happens, it is also possible to retrieve the query result *plus* the possibility to register an observer, which gets invoked when the underlying data changes.

The construct to achieve this for a method inside a DAO class looks as follows:

```
@Query("SELECT * FROM employee")
    fun getAllSync(): LiveData<List<Employee>>
```

So you basically wrap a LiveData class around the result, and this is what you can do with all your queries.

However, this is only possible if you add the corresponding architecture component. For this aim add

```
implementation "androidx.lifecycle:" +
    "lifecycle-livedata-ktx:2.4.1"
```

to your module's build.gradle file.

This LiveData object now allows for adding an observer as follows:

```
val ld: LiveData<List<Employee>> =
        employeeDao.getAllSync()
ld.observeForever { l ->
    l?.forEach { empl ->
      Log.e("LOG", empl.toString())
      // do s.th. else with the employee
    }
}
```

This is particularly useful if inside the observer callback you update GUI components.

Your production code should do a better job in doing correct housekeeping – if we use the observeForever() method, the LiveData object should have the observer unregistered by calling ld.removeObserver(...) at an appropriate place in your code.

For a better solution for correct housekeeping, the LiveData object also allows for adding an observer tied to a lifecycle object. This is done by

```
val ld: LiveData<List<Employee>> =
        employeeDao.getAllSync()
val lcOwn : LifecycleOwner = ...
ld.observe(lcOwn, { l ->
    l?.forEach { empl ->
      Log.e("LOG", empl.toString())
      // do s.th. else with the employee
    }
} )
```

An AppCompatActivity, for example, is a possible LifecycleOwner, so if you can get hold of the activity reference, you just write

```
val lcOwn : LifecycleOwner = activity
```

For more details about lifecycle objects, please have a look at the online API documentation for androidx.compose.runtime.LiveData.

A similar but maybe more comprehensive approach to add observables to your database code is using *RxJava/RxKotlin*, which is the Java/Kotlin platform implementation of *ReactiveX*. We do not give an introduction into *ReactiveX* programming here, but to include it into queries, using it boils down to wrapping the results into RxJava objects. Not as a complete example, but as an impression on how to do that, you, for example, write

```
@Query("SELECT * FROM employee" +
    " WHERE uid = :uid")
fun findByIdRx(uid: Int): Flowable<Employee> {
    [...] // Wrap query results into a Flowable
}
```

which returns a `Flowable`, allowing *observers* to *react* on retrieved database rows in an asynchronous manner.

For this to work, you have to include RxJava support into the build file:

```
// RxJava support for Room
implementation "androidx.room:room-rxjava3:2.4.2"
```

For more details about RxKotlin, please consult the online resources about ReactiveX in general or RxKotlin for the Kotlin language binding of ReactiveX.

With Android Room now integrating with Kotlin coroutines, you also have a genuine technique to couple database access with non-preemptive concurrency. Just add suspend to the Dao methods to convert them into suspending functions, or add the Flow<> type qualifier for returned lists:

```
@Dao
interface ContactDao {
    @Insert
    suspend fun insert(vararg contacts: Contact)

    @Query("SELECT * FROM Contact WHERE uid = :uId")
    suspend fun findById(uId: Int): List<Contact>

    @Query("SELECT * FROM Contact WHERE" +
      " employeeName like = '%' || :name || '%'")
    fun loadByEmployeeNameLike(name: String):
    Flow<List<Contact>>
}
```

Database Clients

To actually include Room into the app, we need to know how we can get hold of databases and DAOs. To achieve this, we first acquire a reference to a database via

```
fun fetchDb() =
    Room.databaseBuilder(
        this, MyDatabase::class.java,
        "MyDatabase.db")
    .build()
val db = fetchDb()
```

which creates a file-backed database. The string argument is the name of the file holding the data. To instead open a memory-based database, say for testing purposes or because you favor speed over data loss when the application stops, use

```
fun fetchDb() =
    Room.inMemoryDatabaseBuilder(
        this, MyDatabase::class.java)
    .build()
val db = fetchDb()
```

The builder allows for certain configuration activities in a fluent builder style. Interesting configuration options are shown in Table 8-1. You just chain them before the final .build() call. One option you might use often during early development phases is relaxing the foreground operation restriction by

```
fun fetchDb() =
    Room.databaseBuilder(
        this, MyDatabase::class.java,
        "MyDatabase.db")
    .allowMainThreadQueries()
    .build()
val db = fetchDb()
```

Table 8-1. *Room Builder Options*

Option	Description
addCallback(RoomDatabase. Callback)	Adds a `RoomDatabase.Callback` to this database. You can use it, for example, to have some code executed when the database gets created or opened.
allowMainThreadQueries()	Use this to disable the no-main-thread restriction in Room. If you don't use this and try to perform database operations in the main thread, Room will throw an exception. There is a good reason for Room to work this way – GUI-related threads should not be blocked because of lengthy DB operations. So for your code, you should not call this method – it makes sense only for experiments to avoid dealing with asynchronicity.
addMigrations(vararg Migration)	Adds migration plans. Migration gets handled in more detail in the following in section "Migrating Databases."
fallbackToDestructiveMigration()	If a matching migration plan is missing – that is, for a necessary upgrade from the data version *inside* the database to the version specified in the `@Database` annotation, no registered migration plan can be found – Room normally throws an exception. If you instead want the current database to be purged and then the database be built up from scratch for the new version, use this method.
fallbackToDestructiveMigration(vararg Int)	Same as `fallbackToDestructiveMigration()` earlier, but restricts to certain starting versions. For all other versions, an exception will be thrown if the migration plan is missing.

Then, once you have a database object, just call any of the DAO factory methods we defined inside the database class in an abstract manner – Room automatically provides implementations. So, for example, write

```
val db = ...
val employeeDao = db.employeeDao()
// use the DAO...
```

Transactions

Room allows for transactions in EXCLUSIVE mode. This means that if transaction A is in progress, no other processes or threads are allowed to access a database in another transaction B until transaction A is finished. More precisely, transaction B will have to wait until A is finished.

To run a set of database operations inside a transaction in Kotlin, you can write

```
val db = ...
db.runInTransaction { ->
    // do DB work...
}
```

The transaction is marked "successful" if the code inside the closure does not throw any exception. Otherwise, the transaction will be rolled back.

Migrating Databases

In order to migrate databases from one version of your app to another version, you add migration plans while accessing the database as in

```
val migs = arrayOf(
  object : Migration(1,2) {
    override fun migrate(db: SupportSQLiteDatabase) {
      // code for the 1->2 migration...
      // this is already running inside a transaction,
      // don't add your own transaction code here!
    }
  }, object : Migration(2,3) {
    override fun migrate(db: SupportSQLiteDatabase) {
      // code for the 2->3 migration...
      // this is already running inside a transaction,
      // don't add your own transaction code here!
    }
  } // more migrations ...
)
```

```
private fun fetchDb() =
    Room.databaseBuilder(
            this, MyDatabase::class.java,
            "MyDatabase.db")
        .addMigrations(*migs)
        .build()
```

It obviously makes no sense to use DAO classes here, because then you'd have to manage several DAO variants, one for each version. That is why inside the `migrate()` methods, you need to access the DB on a lower level, for example, by executing SQL statements without bindings to Kotlin objects. As an example, say you have an `Employee` table and by upgrading from versions 1 to 2 need to add a column "salary" and by upgrading from versions 2 to 3 another column "childCount". Inside the `migs` array from the preceding code, you then write

```
//...
object : Migration(1,2) {
  override fun migrate(db: SupportSQLiteDatabase) {
    db.execSQL("ALTER TABLE components "+
            "ADD COLUMN salary INTEGER DEFAULT 0;")
  }
}
//...
object : Migration(2,3) {
  override fun migrate(db: SupportSQLiteDatabase) {
    db.execSQL("ALTER TABLE components "+
            "ADD COLUMN childCount INTEGER DEFAULT 0;")
  }
}
//...
object : Migration(1,3) {
  override fun migrate(db: SupportSQLiteDatabase) {
    db.execSQL("ALTER TABLE components "+
        "ADD COLUMN salary INTEGER DEFAULT 0;")
    db.execSQL("ALTER TABLE components "+
        "ADD COLUMN childCount INTEGER DEFAULT 0;")
```

```
    }
  }
  //...
```

If you provide small-step migrations as well as large-step migrations, the latter will have precedence. This means if you have migration plans 1 →2, 2 →3, and 1 →3 and the system demands a migration 1 →3, the plan 1 →3 will run, not the chain 1 →2 →3.

Scheduling

With user experience in mind, running tasks in an asynchronous manner is an important matter. It is vital that no lengthy operations disturb the front-end flow, leaving the impression that your app is doing its job fluently.

It is not too easy to write stable apps that have important parts run in the background, though. The reasons for that are manyfold: The device maybe gets powered off on demand or because of low battery, or the user might have started a more important app with higher priority, expecting to temporarily run background jobs in a low-priority mode. Also, the Android OS might decide to interrupt or postpone background jobs for other reasons like resource shortage or because a timeout condition applies. And with the advent of Android 8, it has become even more important to think about clever ways of performing background tasks, since this version imposes important restrictions on background execution of program parts.

For running jobs in an asynchronous manner, several techniques exist, all of them with downsides and advantages:

- **Java threads**

  Java or Kotlin threads – remember both are targeting the same Java Virtual Machine – are a very low-level technique of running things in the background. In Kotlin you can use a construct as easy as

  ```
  Thread{-> do s.th.}.start()
  ```

  to process program parts in a background thread. This being a very basic approach, you can expect a high performance of your background execution tasks. However, you are completely running outside of any Android OS component lifecycle, so you do not really have a good control of what happens to long-running background threads while the lifecycle status of Android processes changes.

- **Java concurrency classes**

  Java and Kotlin allow the use of concurrency-related classes from the `java.util.concurrency` package. This is a higher-level approach of running things in the background with improved background task management capabilities, but it still has the downside of running outside any Android component lifecycle control.

- **Kotlin coroutines**

  Kotlin coroutines introduce a totally new software design pattern for handling concurrency. Functions can be transformed to *suspending functions*, subject to temporarily giving away program flow to other suspending functions.

- **AlarmManager**

  This was originally designed for running tasks at very specific times, and you can use it if you need to send notifications to the user at specific instances in time. It has been there since API level 1. Only starting at API level 19 (Android 4.4) the system allows for postponing alarms under certain conditions. The downside is you don't have control over more general device conditions – when the device is up, it will fire alarm events at its own discretion, no matter what else happens on your device.

- **SyncAdapter**

  This methodology was added in Android API level 5. It is particularly useful for synchronization tasks. For more general background execution tasks, you should instead use a *JobScheduler* as described in the following. Use a SyncAdapter only if you need one of the additional functionalities it provides.

- **JobScheduler**

     This is an integrated library for scheduling jobs on the Android
     OS. It runs on any device starting at API level 21, which is about
     98% of the Android devices in use.

The more low-level approaches get handled in Chapter 11. The rest of this section is about the *JobScheduler* and the *AlarmManager*.

JobScheduler

A JobScheduler is the dedicated method to schedule and run background tasks in any Android device starting at API level 21.

Note   Also, the documentation of Android 8 strongly recommends using JobSchedulers to overcome the background task execution restrictions imposed since Android 8.

To start using a JobScheduler, we first implement the job itself. To do so, implement the class `android.app.job.JobService`, as, for example, in

```
class MyJob : JobService() {
    var jobThread:Thread? = null

    override
    fun onStartJob(params: JobParameters) : Boolean {
        Log.i("LOG", "MyJob: onStartJob() : " +
                params.jobId)

        jobThread?.interrupt()
        jobThread = Thread {
            Log.i("LOG", "started job thread")
            // do job work...
            jobFinished(params, false)
            jobThread = null
            Log.i("LOG", "finished job thread")
        }
```

```
        jobThread.start()
        return true
    }

    override
    fun onStopJob(params:JobParameters) : Boolean {
        Log.i("LOG", "MyJob: onStopJob()")
        jobThread?.interrupt()
        jobThread = null
        return true

    }
}
```

The most important part of the implementation is the onStartJob() method – here you'll enter the work the job is actually supposed to do. Note that we pushed the actual work into a thread. This is important, because the onStartJob() runs in the app's main thread, thus blocking maybe important other work if it stays too long inside. Starting a thread instead finishes immediately. Also we return true signaling that the job continues doing its work in a background thread. Once the job finishes, it must call jobFinished(); otherwise, the system wouldn't know that the job finished doing its work.

The overridden onStopJob() method is *not* part of the normal job lifecycle – it instead gets called when the system decides to finish the job prematurely. We let it return true to tell the system that it is allowed to reschedule the job, in case it was configured accordingly.

To finish the job implementation, we must still configure the service class inside AndroidManifest.xml. To do so, add

```
<service android:name=".MyJob"
         android:label="MyJob Service"
         android:permission=
             "android.permission.BIND_JOB_SERVICE" />
```

The permission configured here is *not* a "Dangerous" permission, so you don't have to implement a process to acquire this permission. However, you must add this permission here; otherwise, the job gets ignored.

To actually schedule a job governed by the JobScheduler, you first need to obtain a JobScheduler object as a system service. Then you can build a JobInfo object, and in the end you register it with the JobScheduler:

```
val jsched = getSystemService(JobScheduler::class.java)
val JOB_ID : Int = 7766

val service = ComponentName(this, MyJob::class.java)
val builder = JobInfo.Builder(JOB_ID, service)
    .setMinimumLatency((1 * 1000).toLong())
        // wait at least 1 sec
    .setOverrideDeadline((3 * 1000).toLong())
        // maximum delay 3 secs

jsched.schedule(builder.build())
```

This example schedules the job to be started the earliest after 1 second and the latest after 3 seconds. By construction it gets the ID 7766 assigned – this is a value passed to onStartJob() inside the job implementation. The number is just an example – you can use any unique number for the ID.

While building the JobInfo object, you can set various job characteristics, as shown in Table 8-2.

Table 8-2. *JobInfo Builder Options*

Method	Description
setMinimumLatency(minLatencyMillis: Long)	This job should be delayed by the specified amount of time or longer.
setOverrideDeadline(maxExecutionDelayMillis: Long)	The maximum time a job can be delayed.
setPeriodic(intervalMillis: Long)	Make the job repeat and set a recurrence interval. The actual interval can be higher, but will not be lower.
setPeriodic(intervalMillis: Long, flexMillis: Long)	Make the job repeat and set a recurrence interval and a flexibility window. So the real interval will be between *intervalMillis* − 0.5 · *flexMillis* and *intervalMillis* + 0.5 · *flexMillis*. Both numbers get their lowest possible value clamped to getMinPeriodMillis() and MAX(getMinFlexMillis(), 0.05 * intervalMillis), respectively.

(continued)

167

Table 8-2. (*continued*)

Method	Description
setBackoffCriteria(init ialBackoffMillis:Long, backoffPolicy:Int)	A back-off might happen when inside your job implementation you write jobFinished(params, true). Here you specify what happens in such a case. Possible values for "backoffPolicy" are given by the constants in • **JobInfo.BACKOFF_POLICY_LINEAR**: Back-offs happen at intervals *initialBackoffMillis · retry − number*. • **JobInfo.BACKOFF_POLICY_EXPONENTIAL**: Back-offs happen at intervals *initialBackoffMillis* $\cdot$ $2^{retry - number}$.
setExtras(extras: PersistableBundle)	Set optional extras. These extras get passed to onStartJob() inside the job implementation.
setTransientExtras(extras: Bundle)	Only for API level 26 and higher. Set optional unpersisted extras. These extras get passed to onStartJob() inside the job implementation.
setPersisted(isPersisted: Boolean)	Whether the job gets persisted across device reboots. Needs permission "android.Manifest.permission.RECEIVE_BOOT_ COMPLETED".
setRequiredNetworkType(net workType: Int)	Specifies an additional condition that needs to be met for the job to run. Possible argument values are • JobInfo.NETWORK_TYPE_NONE • JobInfo.NETWORK_TYPE_ANY • JobInfo.NETWORK_TYPE_UNMETERED • JobInfo.NETWORK_TYPE_NOT_ROAMING • JobInfo.NETWORK_TYPE_METERED
setRequiresBatteryNotLow(b atteryNotLow: Boolean)	Only for API level 26 and higher. Specifies an additional condition that needs to be met for the job to run, that is, the battery must not be low. False resets to not care.
setRequiresCharging(require sCharging: Boolean)	Specifies an additional condition that needs to be met for the job to run, that is, the device must be plugged in. False resets to not care.

(*continued*)

Table 8-2. (*continued*)

Method	Description
setRequiresDeviceIdle(requiresDeviceIdle: Boolean)	Specifies an additional condition that needs to be met for the job to run, that is, the device must be in idle state. False resets to not care.
setRequiresStorageNotLow(storageNotLow: Boolean)	Only for API level 26 and higher. Specifies an additional condition that needs to be met for the job to run, that is, the device memory must not be low. False resets to not care.
addTriggerContentUri(uri:JobInfo.TriggerContentUri)	Only for API level 24 and higher. Add a content URI that will be monitored for changes. If a change happens, the job gets executed.
setTriggerContentUpdateDelay(durationMs: Long)	Only for API level 24 and higher. Set the minimum delay in milliseconds from when a content change is detected until the job is scheduled.
setTriggerContentMaxDelay(durationMs: Long)	Only for API level 24 and higher. Set the maximum total delay in milliseconds that is allowed from the first time a content change is detected until the job is scheduled.
setClipData(clip:ClipData,grantFlags:Int)	Only for API level 26 and higher. Set a ClipData associated with this job. Possible values for the `grantFlags` are FLAG_GRANT_READ_URI_PERMISSION, FLAG_GRANT_WRITE_URI_PERMISSION, and FLAG_GRANT_PREFIX_URI_PERMISSION (all constants inside class `Intent`).

AlarmManager

If you need actions to happen at specific times, regardless of whether associated components are running or not, the AlarmManager is the system service that you can use for such tasks.

As for matters concerning the AlarmManager, your device is in one of the following states:

- **Device awake**: The device is running. Usually this means also the screen is on, but there is no guarantee that if the screen is off, the device is no longer awake. However, quite often if the screen gets switched off, the device shortly after that leaves the awake state. The details depend on the hardware and the device's software configuration. The AlarmManager can do its work if the device is awake, but being awake is not necessary for the AlarmManager to fire events – see the other states in the following.

- **Device locked**: The device is locked, and the user needs to unlock it before it can be handled again. A locked device *might* lead to the device going asleep; however, locking per se is a security measure and has no primary impact on the AlarmManager's functioning.

- **Device asleep**: The screen is switched off, and the device runs in a low-power-consumption mode. Events triggered by the AlarmManager will be able to wake up the device, which then fires them, but this needs to be explicitly specified.

- **Device switched off**: The AlarmManager stops working and resumes working only the next time the device is switched on. Alarm events get lost when the device is switched off – there is nothing like a retry functionality here.

Alarm events are one of the following:

- A *PendingIntent* gets fired. Since PendingIntents may target either Services, activities, or broadcasts, an alarm event may start an activity or a service or send a broadcast.

- A *handler* gets invoked. This is a direct version of sending alarm events to the same component that is issuing the alarms.

In order to schedule alarms, you first need to get the AlarmManager as a system service as follows:

```
val alrm = getSystemService(AlarmManager::class.java)
```

You can then issue alarms by various methods as shown in Table 8-3. If for API levels 24 and higher you choose to have a listener receive alarm events, the details about how to use the associated handlers get presented in section "Multithreading" of Chapter 11. If instead aiming at Intents, all corresponding methods have a `type:Int` parameter with the following possible values:

- **AlarmManager.RTC_WAKEUP**

  Time parameter is wall clock time in UTC (milliseconds since January 1, 1970, 00:00:00). The device will be woken up if necessary.

- **AlarmManager.RTC**

  Time parameter is wall clock time in UTC (milliseconds since January 1, 1970, 00:00:00). If the device is asleep, the event will be discarded, and no alarm will be triggered.

- **AlarmManager.ELAPSED_REALTIME_WAKEUP**

  Time parameter is the time in milliseconds since last boot, including sleep time. The device will be woken up if necessary.

- **AlarmManager.ELAPSED_REALTIME**

  Time parameter is the time in milliseconds since last boot, including sleep time. If the device is asleep, the event will be discarded, and no alarm will be triggered.

Table 8-3. *Issuing Alarms*

Method	Description
set(type: Int, triggerAtMillis: Long, operation: PendingIntent): Unit	Schedule an alarm. An Intent gets invoked, triggered according to the type and the time parameter provided. Starting with API level 19, alarm event delivery might be inexact to optimize system resource usage. Use one of the "setExact" methods if you need exact delivery.
set(type: Int, triggerAtMillis: Long, tag: String, listener: AlarmManager. OnAlarmListener, targetHandler: Handler): Unit	Requires API level 24 or higher. Direct callback version of set(Int, Long, PendingIntent). The Handler parameter can be null to invoke the listener on the app's main looper. Otherwise, the call of the listener will be performed from inside the handler provided.
setAlarmClock(info: AlarmManager. AlarmClockInfo, operation: PendingIntent): Unit	Requires API level 21 or higher. Schedule an alarm represented by an alarm clock. The alarm clock info object allows for adding an Intent, which is able to describe the trigger. The system may choose to display information about this alarm to the user. Other than that, this method is like setExact(Int, Long, PendingIntent), but implies the RTC_WAKEUP trigger type.

(continued)

Table 8-3. (*continued*)

Method	Description
setAndAllowWhileIdle(type: Int, triggerAtMillis: Long, operation: PendingIntent): Unit	Requires API level 23 or higher. Like `set(Int, Long, PendingIntent)`, but this alarm will be allowed to execute even when the system is in low-power idle modes.
setExact(type: Int, triggerAtMillis: Long, operation: PendingIntent): Unit	Requires API level 19 or higher. Schedule an alarm to be delivered precisely at the stated time.
setExact(type: Int, triggerAtMillis: Long, tag: String, listener: AlarmManager. OnAlarmListener, targetHandler: Handler): Unit	Requires API level 24 or higher. Direct callback version of `setExact(Int, Long, PendingIntent)`. The Handler parameter can be `null` to invoke the listener on the app's main looper. Otherwise, the call of the listener will be performed from inside the handler provided.
setExactAndAllowWhileIdle(type: Int, triggerAtMillis: Long, operation: PendingIntent): Unit	Requires API level 23 or higher. Like `setExact(Int, Long, PendingIntent)`, but this alarm will be allowed to execute even when the system is in low-power idle modes.
setInexactRepeating(type: Int, triggerAtMillis: Long, intervalMillis: Long, operation: PendingIntent): Unit	Schedule a repeating alarm that has inexact trigger time requirements, for example, an alarm that repeats every hour, but not necessarily at the top of every hour.
setRepeating(type: Int, triggerAtMillis: Long, intervalMillis: Long, operation: PendingIntent): Unit	Schedule a repeating alarm. Starting at API level 19, this is the same as `setInexactRepeating()`.
setWindow(type: Int, windowStartMillis: Long, windowLengthMillis: Long, operation: PendingIntent): Unit	Schedule an alarm to be delivered within a given window of time.
setWindow(int type: Int, windowStartMillis: Long, windowLengthMillis: Long, tag: String, listener: AlarmManager.OnAlarmListener, targetHandler: Handler) : Unit	Requires API level 24 or higher. Direct callback version of setWindow(int, long, long, PendingIntent). The Handler parameter can be `null` to invoke the listener on the app's main looper. Otherwise, the call of the listener will be performed from inside the handler provided.

The AlarmManager also has a couple of auxiliary methods. A listing is provided in Table 8-4.

Table 8-4. *Auxiliary AlarmManager Methods*

Method	Description
cancel(operation: PendingIntent) : Unit	Removes any alarms with a matching Intent.
cancel(listener: AlarmManager. OnAlarmListener): Unit	Removes any alarm scheduled to be delivered to the given `AlarmManager.OnAlarmListener`.
getNextAlarmClock() : AlarmManager. AlarmClockInfo	Gets information about the next alarm clock currently scheduled.
setTime(long millis): Unit	Sets the system wall clock time, UTC (milliseconds since January 1, 1970, 00:00:00).
setTimeZone(String timeZone): Unit	Sets the system's persistent default time zone.

Notifications

A notification is a message an app can present to the user outside its normal GUI flow. Notifications show up at a special region of the screen, most prominently inside the status bar and notification drawer on top of a screen, in special dialogs, on the lock screen, on a paired Android Wear device, or on an app icon badge. See Figures 8-1 and 8-2 for a smartphone example. There, you can see the notification icon and the notification content after the user expands the notification drawer.

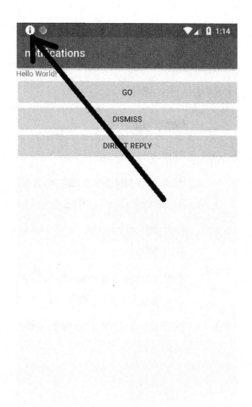

Figure 8-1. *Smartphone Notification*

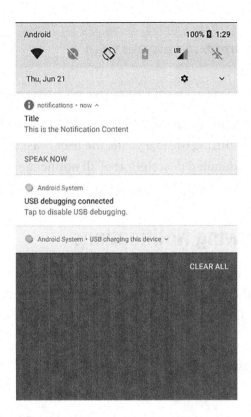

Figure 8-2. *Notification Content*

Notifications also allow for actions, like calling custom activities when tapped, or they can contain special action buttons or even edit fields a user can fill out. Likewise, although notifications were primarily built to show only short text snippets, with current Android versions, it is possible to present larger texts there as well.

The online API documentation suggests using the NontificationCompat API from the support library. Using this compatibility layer allows older versions to present similar or no-op variants on features that were made available only later, simplifying the development. Although using this compatibility layer removes the burden from the developer to present many branches inside the code to take care of different Android API levels, caution must be taken to not make an app unusable, which depends too much on latest notification API features.

To make sure the compatibility API is available for your project inside Android Studio, check whether the build.gradle of your module contains the following inside the "dependencies" section:

```
dependencies {
    implementation "androidx.core:core:1.6.0"
    ...
}
```

The following sections present an outline of the notification API – with this API having grown considerably during the last years, the user is asked to consult the online documentation for a more detailed description of all notification features: `https://developer.android.com/guide/topics/ui/notifiers/notifications`.

Creating and Showing Notifications

To create and show a notification, you prepare action Intents for a tap-on and additional action buttons, use a notification builder to construct the notification, register a notification channel, and finally make the framework show the notification. An example for that would be

```
val NOTIFICATION_CHANNEL_ID = "1"
val NOTIFICATION_ID = 1

// Make sure this Activity exists
val intent = Intent(this, AlertDetails::class.java)
intent.flags = Intent.FLAG_ACTIVITY_NEW_TASK
        //or Intent.FLAG_ACTIVITY_CLEAR_TASK
val tapIntent = PendingIntent.getActivity(this, 0,
        intent, 0)

// Make sure this broadcast receiver  exists and can
// be called by explicit Intent like this
val actionIntent = Intent(this, MyReceiver::class.java)
actionIntent.action = "com.xyz.MAIN"
actionIntent.putExtra(EXTRA_NOTIFICATION_ID, 0)
val actionPendingIntent =
    PendingIntent.getBroadcast(this, 0, actionIntent, 0)

val builder = NotificationCompat.Builder(this,
        NOTIFICATION_CHANNEL_ID)
    .setSmallIcon( ... an icon resource id... )
```

```
        .setContentTitle("Title")
        .setContentText("Content Content Content Content ...")
        .setPriority(NotificationCompat.PRIORITY_DEFAULT)
        // add the default tap action
        .setContentIntent(tapIntent)
        .setAutoCancel(true)
        // add a custom action button
        .addAction( ... an icon resource id ...,
            "Go",
            actionPendingIntent)

buildChannel(NOTIFICATION_CHANNEL_ID)

val notificationManager =
        NotificationManagerCompat.from(this)
notificationManager.notify(
        NOTIFICATION_ID, builder.build())
```

The function buildChannel() is needed for Android API levels 26 (Android 8.0) and higher – it reads

```
fun buildChannel(channelId:String) {
    if (Build.VERSION.SDK_INT >= Build.VERSION_CODES.O) {
        // Create the NotificationChannel, but only
        // on API 26+ only after that it is needed
        val channel = if (Build.VERSION.SDK_INT >=
                Build.VERSION_CODES.O) {
            NotificationChannel(channelId,
                    "Channel Name",
                    NotificationManager.IMPORTANCE_DEFAULT)
        } else {
            throw RuntimeException("Internal error")
        }
        channel.description = "Description"
        // Register the channel with the system
        val notificationManager =
            if (Build.VERSION.SDK_INT >=
```

```
            Build.VERSION_CODES.M) {
        getSystemService(
                NotificationManager::class.java)
      } else {
        throw RuntimeException("Internal error")
      }
    notificationManager.
          createNotificationChannel(channel)
  }
}
```

An explanation for the other code follows here:

- The notification itself needs a unique ID; we save that inside
  NOTIFICATION_ID.

- The action button, here for sending a broadcast, is for the example
  only – having no action button is allowed.

- The setAutoCancel(true) will lead to automatically dismissing the
  notification once the user taps the notification. This works only if
  setContentIntent() is used as well.

- Creating the notification channel is necessary only for API level 26
  (Android 8.0) or higher. The superfluous checks inside the outer
  "if" are necessary to make Android Studio not complain about
  compatibility issues.

- For all the strings, you should use resource IDs where feasible;
  otherwise, use texts that better suit your needs.

Adding Direct Reply

Starting with API level 24 or Android 7.0, the possibility for the user entering text as a
reply to a notification message has been added. A major use case for this is of course a
notification message from a messaging system like a chat client or email. See Figure 8-3
for an example.

Figure 8-3. *Reply Notification*

Since API levels below 24 are not able to provide that, your app should not rely on this functionality. Usually this is easy to achieve – for API levels 23 and lower, the activity called by tapping a notification can of course contain a facility to reply if needed.

A method that issues a notification with reply functionality might look as follows:

```
fun directReply(view:View) {
    // Key for the string that's delivered in the
    // action's intent.
    val KEY_TEXT_REPLY = "key_text_reply"
    val remoteInput = RemoteInput.Builder(KEY_TEXT_REPLY)
            .setLabel("Reply label")
            .build()

    // Make sure this broadcast receiver exists
    val CONVERSATION_ID = 1
    val messageReplyIntent =
```

```
            Intent(this, MyReceiver2::class.java)
    messageReplyIntent.action = "com.xyz2.MAIN"
    messageReplyIntent.putExtra("conversationId",
        CONVERSATION_ID)

    // Build a PendingIntent for the reply
    // action to trigger.
    val replyPendingIntent = PendingIntent.
        getBroadcast(applicationContext,
            CONVERSATION_ID,
            messageReplyIntent,
            PendingIntent.FLAG_UPDATE_CURRENT)

    // Create the reply action and add the remote input.
    val action = NotificationCompat.Action.Builder(
        ... a resource id for an icon ...,
        "Reply", replyPendingIntent)
        .addRemoteInput(remoteInput)
        .build()

    val builder = NotificationCompat.Builder(this,
        NOTIFICATION_CHANNEL_ID)
      .setSmallIcon(... a resource id for an icon ...)
      .setContentTitle("Title")
      .setContentText("Content Content Content ...")
      .setPriority(NotificationCompat.PRIORITY_DEFAULT)
      // add a reply action button
      .addAction(action)

    buildChannel(NOTIFICATION_CHANNEL_ID)

    val notificationManager =
        NotificationManagerCompat.from(this)
    notificationManager.notify(
        NOTIFICATION_ID, builder.build())
  }
```

Here are a few notes about this code:

- The `KEY_TEXT_REPLY` is used to identify the reply text in the intent receiver.

- The `CONVERSATION_ID` is used to identify the conversation chain – here the notification and the intent that receives the reply must know they refer to each other.

- As usual make sure that in production code you use string resources and appropriate texts.

When the notification shows up, it will contain a "Reply" button, and when the user presses it, the system will inquire some reply text, which is then going to be sent to the intent receiver ("messageReplyIntent" in the example).

The intent receiver for the reply text might then have a receive callback, which looks like

```
override fun onReceive(context: Context,
        intent: Intent) {
  Log.e("LOG", intent.toString())
  val KEY_TEXT_REPLY = "key_text_reply"

  val remoteInput = RemoteInput.
        getResultsFromIntent(intent)
  val txt = remoteInput?.
        getCharSequence(KEY_TEXT_REPLY)?:"undefined"
  val conversationId =
        intent.getIntExtra("conversationId",0)
  Log.e("LOG","reply text = " + txt)

  // Do s.th. with the reply...

  // Build a new notification, which informs the user
  // that the system handled their interaction with
  // the previous notification.
  val NOTIFICATION_CHANNEL_ID = "1"
  val repliedNotification =
        NotificationCompat.Builder(context,
            NOTIFICATION_CHANNEL_ID)
```

```
        .setSmallIcon(android.R.drawable.ic_media_play)
        .setContentText("Replied")
        .build()

    buildChannel(NOTIFICATION_CHANNEL_ID)

    // Issue the new notification.
    val notificationManager =
        NotificationManagerCompat.from(context)
    notificationManager.notify(conversationId,
        repliedNotification)
}
```

This method

- Fetches the reply text by using RemoteInput.
  getResultsFromIntent() using the same key as used for the
  reply input

- Fetches the conversation ID we added as an extra value to the Intent

- Does whatever is appropriate to handle the reply

- Issues a reply to the reply by setting another notification

Notification Progress Bar

To add a progress bar to the notification, add to the builder

```
.setProgress(PROGRESS_MAX, PROGRESS_CURRENT, false)
```

with PROGRESS_MAX the maximum integer value and PROGRESS_CURRENT 0 at the beginning. Or, if you want an indeterminate progress bar, you instead use

```
.setProgress(0, 0, true)
```

In a background thread that does the work you, then update a determinate progress bar by periodically executing

```
builder.setProgress(PROGRESS_MAX, currentProgress, false)
notificationManager.notify(
    NOTIFICATION_ID, builder.build())
```

with new `currentProgress` values.

To finish a determinate or an indeterminate progress bar, you can write

```
builder.setContentText("Download complete")
        .setProgress(0,0,false)
notificationManager.notify(
        NOTIFICATION_ID, builder.build())
```

Expandable Notifications

Notifications cannot only contain short messages. Using the expandable features, it is also possible to show larger amounts of information to the user.

For details on how to do that, please consult the online documentation: enter, for example, "Android create expandable notification" in your favorite search engine to find the corresponding pages.

Rectifying Activity Navigation

To improve the user experience, an activity that was started from inside a notification can have its expected task behavior added. For example, if pressing the back button, the activity down in the stack gets called. For this to work, you must define an activity hierarchy inside `AndroidManifest.xml`, for example, as follows:

```
<activity
    android:name=".MainActivity"
    ... >
</activity>
<!-- MainActivity is the parent for ResultActivity -->
<activity
    android:name=".ResultActivity"
    android:parentActivityName=".MainActivity" />

    ...
</activity>
```

You can then use a `TaskStackBuilder` to inflate a task stack for the Intent called:

```
// Create an Intent for the Activity you want to start
val resultIntent =
        Intent(this, ResultActivity::class.java)
// Create the TaskStackBuilder
val stackBuilder = TaskStackBuilder.create(this)
stackBuilder.
        addNextIntentWithParentStack(resultIntent)
// Get the PendingIntent containing the back stack
val resultPendingIntent =
        stackBuilder.getPendingIntent(
                0, PendingIntent.FLAG_UPDATE_CURRENT)
// -> this can go to .setContentIntent() inside
//    the builder
```

For more details about activities and task management, please see section "Activities and Tasks" of Chapter 3.

Grouping Notifications

Beginning with API level 24 (Android 7.0), notifications can be grouped to improve the representation of several notifications that by one or the other way are related. To create such a group, all you have to do is add

```
.setGroup(GROUP_KEY)
```

to the builder chain, with the `GROUP_KEY` being a string of your choice. If you need a custom sorting – the default is to sort by incoming date – you can use the method `setSortKey()` from the builder. Sorting then happens lexicographically given that key. A grouping inside the notification drawer might look like that shown in Figure 8-4.

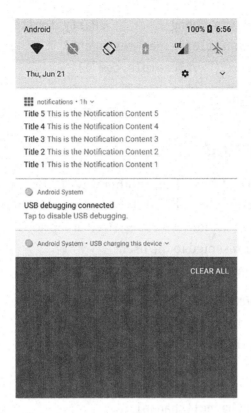

Figure 8-4. *Notification Group*

For API levels below 24 where some kind of Android-managed auto-summary for groups is not available, you can add a notification summary. To do so, just create a notification like any other notification, but additionally call `.setGroupSummary(true)` inside the builder chain. Make sure all the notifications from the group *and* the summary use the same `setGroup(GROUP_KEY)`.

Caution   It seems like due to a bug at least in API level 27 you *must* add a summary notification for the grouping to be enabled at all. So the advice is, no matter what API level you are targeting, to add a notification summary anyways.

For the summary you maybe want to tailor the display style for displaying an appropriate number of summary items. For this aim you can use a construct like

```
.setStyle(NotificationCompat.InboxStyle()
      .addLine("MasterOfTheUniverse    Go play PacMan")
```

```
         .addLine("Silvia Cheng          Party tonite")
         .setBigContentTitle("2 new messages")
         .setSummaryText("xyz@example.com"))
```

inside the builder chain.

Notification Channels

Starting with Android 8.0 or API level 26, another way of grouping notifications by
notification channels has been introduced. The idea behind that is to give the device user
more control over how notifications get categorized and prioritized by the system and
the way notifications get presented to the user.

To create a notification channel, you write

```
if (Build.VERSION.SDK_INT >= Build.VERSION_CODES.O) {
    // Create the NotificationChannel, but only
    // on API 26+ only after that it is needed
    val channel = if (Build.VERSION.SDK_INT >=
             Build.VERSION_CODES.O) {
        NotificationChannel(channelId,
             "Channel Name",
             NotificationManager.IMPORTANCE_DEFAULT)
    } else {
        throw RuntimeException("Internal error")
    }
    channel.description = "Description"
    // Register the channel with the system
    val notificationManager =
      if (Build.VERSION.SDK_INT >=
             Build.VERSION_CODES.M) {
        getSystemService(
             NotificationManager::class.java)
      } else {
        throw RuntimeException("Internal error")
```

```
    }
    notificationManager.
        createNotificationChannel(channel)
}
```

which we have already seen in the preceding sections. Speaking of Kotlin language styling, this looks a little clumsy – the superfluous if constructs have been introduced to avoid Android Studio complaining about compatibility issues. Adapt the channel ID, the channel name, and the importance in the channel constructor according to your needs, just as the description text.

By the way, the createNotificationChannel() in the last line is idempotent – if a channel with the same characteristics already exists, nothing will happen.

The possible importance levels in the NotificationChannel constructor are IMPORTANCE_HIGH for sound and heads-up notification, IMPORTANCE_DEFAULT for sound, IMPORTANCE_LOW for no sound, and IMPORTANCE__MIN for neither sound nor status bar presence.

Having said that it is up to the user how notification channels get handled, inside your code you can still read the settings a user made by using one of the get*() methods of the NotificationChannel object you can get from the manager via getNotificationChannel() or getNotificationChannels(). Please consult the online API documentation for details.

There is also a notification channel settings UI you can call by

```
val intent = Intent(
    Settings.ACTION_CHANNEL_NOTIFICATION_SETTINGS)
intent.putExtra(Settings.EXTRA_APP_PACKAGE,
    getPackageName())
intent.putExtra(Settings.EXTRA_CHANNEL_ID,
    myNotificationChannel.getId())
startActivity(intent)
```

You can further organize notification channels by gathering them in groups, for example, to separate work-related and private-type channels. To create a group, you write

```
val groupId = "my_group"
// The user-visible name of the group.
```

```
val groupName = "Group Name"
val notificationMngr =
    getSystemService(Context.NOTIFICATION_SERVICE)
    as NotificationManager
notificationMngr.createNotificationChannelGroup(
    NotificationChannelGroup(groupId, groupName))
```

You can then add the group to each notification channel by using its setGroup() method.

Notification Badges

Starting with Android 8.0 or API level 26, once a notification arrives in the system, a *notification badge* will show up in the app's icon – see Figure 8-5.

Figure 8-5. *A Notification Badge*

You can control this badge by one of the NotificationChannel methods listed in Table 8-5.

Table 8-5. *Notification Badges*

Method	Description
setShowBadge(Boolean)	Whether or not to show the badge.
setNumber(Int)	Long-tapping an app icon with a badge will show the number of notifications that arrived. You can tailor this number according to your needs by using this method.
setBadgeIconType(Int)	Long-tapping an app icon with a badge will show an icon associated with the notification. You can tailor the icon's size by using this method. Possible values are given as constants in class NotificationCompat: BADGE_ICON_NONE, BADGE_ICON_SMALL, and BADGE_ICON_LARGE.

Contacts

Managing and using contacts is one of the tasks a handheld device must really be good at. After all, handheld devices and especially smartphones get often used to communicate with other people, and contacts are abstracted entities representing people, groups, companies, or other "things" you use as address points for communication needs.

Contacts thus being so important, the built-in contacts framework has become quite complex during the history of Android. Fortunately, the complexity can be reduced somewhat if we restrict ourselves to looking solely at the back-end part and omit user interface peculiarities, which are described in other chapters of this book. What is left for the description of the contacts framework is

- Looking at the internals, especially the database model used

- Finding out how to read contacts data

- Finding out how to write contacts data

- Calling system activities to handle single contacts

- Synchronizing contacts

- Using quick contact badges

Contacts Framework Internals

The basic class to communicate with the contacts framework is the `android.content.ContentResolver` class. This makes a lot of sense, since contact data very well fits into what content providers deal with. You thus very often use content provider operations to handle contact data. See Chapter 6.

The data model consists of three main tables, the *Contacts*, *Raw Contacts*, and *Data* tables. In addition, a couple of auxiliary tables for administrative tasks exist. You usually don't have to deal with any kind of direct table access, but in case you are interested, have a look at the online contacts framework documentation and the documentation for the `ContactsContract` class, which extensively describes the content provider contract for the contacts.

If you want to look at the contacts tables directly, using ADB for a virtual or rooted device, you can create a shell access to your device by cd SDK_INST/platform-tools ; ./adb root ; ./adb shell in a terminal – see section "The SDK Platform Tools" of Chapter 19 – and from there investigate the tables as follows:

```
cd /data
find . -name 'contacts*.db'
# <- this is to locate the contacts DB
cd <folder-for-contacts-db>
sqlite3 <name-of-contacts-db-file>
```

For example, enter .header on to switch on table header output, .tables to list all table names, and select * from raw_contacts; to list the *Raw Contacts* table.

Reading Contacts

For reading a number of contacts, maybe based on some criterion, you best use a ViewModel as a view data holder, wrap model elements with LiveData to make sure model changes reflect in redisplaying the screen, apply coroutines to load data asynchronously, and adopt the Jetpack Compose library for an elegant front-end design.

Note   In former times you'd have used loaders, but those are deprecated, and using the combination of ViewModel, LiveData, coroutines, and Jetpack Compose makes sure you are on track with the most recent and most elegant Android development technologies.

For all this to work, add the following dependencies to build.gradle:

```
def compose_version = '1.1.1'

implementation 'androidx.core:core-ktx:1.7.0'
implementation "androidx.compose.ui:" +
    "ui:$compose_version"
implementation "androidx.compose.foundation:" +
    "foundation:$compose_version"
implementation "androidx.compose.material:" +
    "material:$compose_version"
```

```
implementation "androidx.compose.ui:" +
    "ui-tooling-preview:$compose_version"
implementation 'androidx.lifecycle:' +
    'lifecycle-runtime-ktx:2.3.1'
implementation 'androidx.lifecycle:' +
    'lifecycle-extensions:2.2.0'
implementation "androidx.lifecycle:" +
    "lifecycle-livedata-ktx:2.4.1"
implementation "androidx.compose.runtime:" +
    "runtime-livedata:$compose_version"
implementation 'androidx.activity:' +
    'activity-compose:1.3.1'
// We need this for permission inquiry
// using JetPack compose:
implementation "com.google.accompanist:" +
    "accompanist-permissions:0.23.1"
```

For reading the data from the contacts-related content databases, we declare a per-contact data class and a data source class for reading the data:

```
package book.andrkotlpro.mycontacts1.db

import android.content.ContentResolver
import android.content.ContentUris
import android.net.Uri
import android.provider.ContactsContract

data class MyContact(val id:String, val lookupKey,
                val display:String, val email:String)

class MyContactsDataSource(
        private val contentResolver: ContentResolver) {
    fun fetchContactsPrimary(): List<MyContact> {
        val result: MutableList<MyContact> =
            mutableListOf()

        val CONTENT_URI =
            ContactsContract.Contacts.CONTENT_URI
```

```
    val PROJECTION = arrayOf(
        ContactsContract.Contacts._ID,
        ContactsContract.Contacts.LOOKUP_KEY,
        ContactsContract.Contacts.DISPLAY_NAME_PRIMARY)

    val SORT_ORDER = ContactsContract.Contacts.
        DISPLAY_NAME_PRIMARY

    val cursor = contentResolver.query(
        CONTENT_URI,
        PROJECTION,
        null,
        null,
        SORT_ORDER
    )
    cursor?.let {
        cursor.moveToFirst()
        while (!cursor.isAfterLast) {
            result.add(
                MyContact(
                    cursor.getString(0),
                    cursor.getString(1),
                    cursor.getString(2),
                    ""
                )
            )
            cursor.moveToNext()
        }
        cursor.close()
    }
    return result.toList()
}

fun fetchContactsData(): List<MyContact> {
    val result: MutableList<MyContact> =
        mutableListOf()
```

```kotlin
val CONTENT_URI =
    ContactsContract.Data.CONTENT_URI

val PROJECTION = arrayOf(
    ContactsContract.Data._ID,
    ContactsContract.Data.LOOKUP_KEY,
    ContactsContract.Data.DISPLAY_NAME_PRIMARY,
    ContactsContract.CommonDataKinds.Email.ADDRESS)

val SELECTION =
    ContactsContract.Data.MIMETYPE + " = '" +
    ContactsContract.CommonDataKinds.Email.
        CONTENT_ITEM_TYPE +
    "'"

val SORT_ORDER = ContactsContract.Data.
    DISPLAY_NAME_PRIMARY

val cursor = contentResolver.query(
    CONTENT_URI,
    PROJECTION,
    SELECTION,
    null,
    SORT_ORDER
)
cursor?.let {
    cursor.moveToFirst()
    while (!cursor.isAfterLast) {
        result.add(
            MyContact(
                cursor.getString(0),
                cursor.getString(1),
                cursor.getString(2),
                cursor.getString(3)
            )
        )
        cursor.moveToNext()
```

```
            }
            cursor.close()
        }
        return result.toList()
    }
}
```

The MyContactsDataSource class provides two functions fetchContactsPrimary() and fetchContactsData() for reading data from the primary contacts table and from the contacts Data table, respectively. Only the latter contains the email address, so the first one is here only for illustration purposes, and we won't use it in the rest of the code.

Inside the SELECTION string, you can add search criteria, if you like. A "?" serves as a placeholder then, and you can populate it in the penultimate parameter of the query() call, like in

```
val SELECTION =
    ContactsContract.CommonDataKinds.Email.ADDRESS +
    " LIKE ? " + "AND " +
    ContactsContract.Data.MIMETYPE + " = '" +
    ContactsContract.
        CommonDataKinds.Email.CONTENT_ITEM_TYPE +
    "'"
val selectionArgs = arrayOf("%" + search + "%")
...
val cursor = contentResolver.query(
        CONTENT_URI,
        PROJECTION,
        SELECTION,
        selectionArgs,
        SORT_ORDER
)
```

There are also special URIs you can use, for example, for finding contacts by email address, you could use the content URI ContactsContract.CommonDataKinds.Email. CONTENT_URI. As another option, the URI given by ContactsContract.Contacts. CONTENT_FILTER_URI allows for adding search criteria inside the URI instead of specifying them as a parameter for the query() call:

```
...
val PROJECTION : Array<String>? = null
val SELECTION : String? = null
val selectionArgs : Array<String>? = null

val contentUri = Uri.withAppendedPath(
        ContactsContract.Contacts.CONTENT_FILTER_URI,
        Uri.encode(search))
Log.e("LOG", contentUri.toString())
...
```

Note that in this case it is not allowed to pass an empty string "" as a search criterion.

A class `MyContactsRepository` wraps the query into a `suspend` function, which is the coroutine idiom for "allow for asynchronous invocation." For more information about coroutines, see `https://kotlinlang.org/docs/coroutines-overview.html`:

```
package book.andrkotlpro.mycontacts1.db

import kotlinx.coroutines.CoroutineDispatcher
import kotlinx.coroutines.withContext

class MyContactsRepository(
        private val source: MyContactsDataSource,
        private val myDispatcher: CoroutineDispatcher) {
    suspend fun fetchContacts(): List<MyContact> {
        return withContext(myDispatcher) {
            source.fetchContactsData()
        }
    }
}
```

For the ViewModel we define the classes `ContactsViewModel` and `ContactsViewModelFactory`, the former wrapping the query result list into a LiveData object (for data binding between the model and the UI layer) and the latter serving as a factory for creating the ViewModel instance:

```
package book.andrkotlpro.mycontacts1

import android.app.Application
```

```kotlin
import androidx.lifecycle.*
import book.andrkotlpro.mycontacts1.db.*
import kotlinx.coroutines.Dispatchers

class ContactsViewModel (
    context: Application,
    private val myContactsRepository: MyContactsRepository
) : AndroidViewModel(context) {

    var myContacts: LiveData<List<MyContact>> = liveData {
        emit(myContactsRepository.fetchContacts())
    }
}

class ContactsViewModelFactory(
        private val application: Application)
        : ViewModelProvider.AndroidViewModelFactory(
                application) {
    override fun <T : ViewModel?>
    create(modelClass: Class<T>): T {
        return if (modelClass.isAssignableFrom(
                ContactsViewModel::class.java)) {
            val source = MyContactsDataSource(
                application.contentResolver)
            ContactsViewModel(application,
                MyContactsRepository(source,
                    Dispatchers.IO)) as T
        } else
            throw IllegalArgumentException(
                "Unknown ViewModel class")
    }
}
```

Inside ContactsViewModelFactory we use a Dispatchers.IO parameter for the MyContactsRepository instantiation, which enables suspend function execution in a thread pool especially tailored for IO background processing.

The manifest file `AndroidManifest.xml` contains the permissions necessary to access the contacts database tables:

```xml
<?xml version="1.0" encoding="utf-8"?>
<manifest xmlns:android=
        "http://schemas.android.com/apk/res/android"
    xmlns:tools="http://schemas.android.com/tools"
    package="book.andrkotlpro.mycontacts1">

    <uses-permission android:name=
        "android.permission.READ_CONTACTS" />
    <uses-permission android:name=
        "android.permission.WRITE_CONTACTS" />
    <application ...>
        ...
    </application>
</manifest>
```

The activity class looks very different from what you are used to, in case this is your first Jetpack Compose project. The most noticeable difference is that a layout XML file no longer is in use. Instead a builder-like syntax gets applied for front-end view structures, as in

```
Column() {
    Text(textToShow)
    Button(onClick = { ... }) {
        Text("Request permission")
    }
}
```

The full code of the activity class reads

```
package book.andrkotlpro.mycontacts1

import android.os.Bundle
import android.util.Log
import androidx.activity.ComponentActivity
import androidx.activity.compose.setContent
import androidx.compose.foundation.
```

```
    ExperimentalFoundationApi
import androidx.compose.foundation.layout.Column
import androidx.compose.foundation.layout.fillMaxSize
import androidx.compose.foundation.layout.padding
import androidx.compose.foundation.lazy.LazyColumn
import androidx.compose.foundation.lazy.items
import androidx.compose.material.*
import androidx.compose.runtime.*
import androidx.compose.ui.Modifier
import androidx.compose.ui.unit.dp
import androidx.compose.runtime.livedata.observeAsState
import androidx.lifecycle.ViewModelProvider
import book.andrkotlpro.mycontacts1.ui.theme.
    MyContacts1Theme
import com.google.accompanist.permissions.*

class MainActivity : ComponentActivity() {
    // The @OptIn is needed, because the library with
    // classes at com.google.accompanist.permissions are
    // experimental
    @OptIn(ExperimentalPermissionsApi::class)
    override fun onCreate(savedInstanceState: Bundle?) {
        super.onCreate(savedInstanceState)

        // These two lines are all we need to access
        // the model data.
        val myViewModelFactory =
            ContactsViewModelFactory(application)
        val contactsViewModel = ViewModelProvider(
            this, myViewModelFactory).get(
                ContactsViewModel::class.java)

        setContent { // the UI builder starts here
            // Wrap in a theme. Note that the theme
            // classes are generated by the Studio's
            // 'new project' wizard
            MyContacts1Theme {
```

```
            // A surface container using the
            //'background' color from the theme
            Surface(
                modifier = Modifier.fillMaxSize(),
                color = MaterialTheme.colors.background
            ) {
                // Inquire permission state
                val contactsPermissionState =
                    rememberMultiplePermissionsState (
                      listOf(
                      android.Manifest.permission.
                          WRITE_CONTACTS,
                      android.Manifest.permission.
                          READ_CONTACTS
                ) )
                with(contactsPermissionState) {
                    if(allPermissionsGranted) {
                        ContactsContentLazy(
                            contactsViewModel)
                    }else{
                        InquirePermission(this)
                    }
                }
            }
        }
    }
}

// The @Composable is an important JetPack compose feature
// It allows to extract UI builder fragments. This
// composable requests permissions.
@OptIn(ExperimentalPermissionsApi::class)
@Composable
fun InquirePermission(
        contactsPermissionState: MultiplePermissionsState) {
```

```
    val textToShow =
    if(contactsPermissionState.shouldShowRationale) {
        "Contacts access is important for this app." +
        " Please grant the permission."
    }else{
        "Contacts permission required for this feature" +
        " to be available. Please grant the permission"
    }
    Column() {
        Text(textToShow)
        Button(onClick = { contactsPermissionState.
                launchMultiplePermissionRequest() }) {
            Text("Request permission")
        }
    }
}

// The contacts list
@Composable
fun ContactsContentLazy(viewModel: ContactsViewModel) {
    // Just in case you need it...
    //val composableScope = rememberCoroutineScope()
    //val ctx = LocalContext.current

    // An important line. The 'observeAsState' makes
    // sure the UI gets recomposed if the underlying
    // data change. It _will_ do so, because by virtue
    // of Coroutines the data get fetched asynchronously
    val list by viewModel.myContacts.
        observeAsState(mutableListOf())

    // The LazyColumn renders only visible items. It
    // also makes the list view scrollable
    LazyColumn(modifier = Modifier.padding(16.dp)) {
        //items(list, {itm -> itm.id}) { itm ->
        items(list) { itm ->
            Log.e("LOG", "-------------------------")
```

```
            Log.e("LOG", itm.id)
            Log.e("LOG", itm.lookupKey)
            Log.e("LOG", itm.display)
            Log.e("LOG", itm.email)
            Text(
                text = itm.id + "\n  " + itm.display +
                    "\n  " + itm.email,
                modifier = Modifier.padding(bottom = 8.dp),
                style = MaterialTheme.typography.h5
            )
        }
    }
}
```

Writing Contacts

Inserting or updating contacts best happens in batch mode. You start with a list of item type ContentProviderOperation and fill it with operations as follows:

```
import android.content.Context
import android.content.ContentProviderOperation
import android.content.ContentResolver
import android.provider.ContactsContract
import android.content.ContentValues.TAG
import android.util.Log
import android.widget.Toast

class ContactsWriter(val ctx:Context, val contentResolver:
        ContentResolver) {
    val opList = mutableListOf<ContentProviderOperation>()

    fun addContact(accountType:String, accountName:String,
                firstName:String, lastName:String,
                emailAddr:String, phone:String) {
        val firstOperationIndex = opList.size
```

Inside this method we first create a new contact. The "Contacts" table will be filled automatically; a direct access is not possible anyways. The device's user account and account type are needed; otherwise, the operations silently will fail!

```
// Creates a new raw contact.
var op = ContentProviderOperation.newInsert(
        ContactsContract.RawContacts.CONTENT_URI)
    .withValue(
        ContactsContract.RawContacts.ACCOUNT_TYPE,
        accountType)
    .withValue(
        ContactsContract.RawContacts.ACCOUNT_NAME,
        accountName)
opList.add(op.build())
```

Next, still inside the method, we create a display name for the new row. This is a row inside table "StructuredName":

```
// Creates the display name for the new row
op = ContentProviderOperation.newInsert(
        ContactsContract.Data.CONTENT_URI)
    // withValueBackReference will make sure the
    // foreign key relations will be set
    // correctly
    .withValueBackReference(
        ContactsContract.Data.RAW_CONTACT_ID,
        firstOperationIndex)
    // The data row's MIME type is StructuredName
    .withValue(ContactsContract.Data.MIMETYPE,
        ContactsContract.CommonDataKinds.
            StructuredName.CONTENT_ITEM_TYPE)
    // The row's display name is the name in the UI.
    .withValue(ContactsContract.CommonDataKinds.
        StructuredName.DISPLAY_NAME,
        firstName + " " + lastName)
opList.add(op.build())
```

Likewise, we add the phone number and the email address:

```
// The specified phone number
op = ContentProviderOperation.newInsert(
     ContactsContract.Data.CONTENT_URI)
  // Fix foreign key relation
  .withValueBackReference(
    ContactsContract.Data.RAW_CONTACT_ID,
        firstOperationIndex)
  // Sets the data row's MIME type to Phone
  .withValue(ContactsContract.Data.MIMETYPE,
          ContactsContract.CommonDataKinds.
              Phone.CONTENT_ITEM_TYPE)
  // Phone number and type
  .withValue(ContactsContract.CommonDataKinds.
        Phone.NUMBER, phone)
  .withValue(ContactsContract.CommonDataKinds.
        Phone.TYPE,
           android.provider.ContactsContract.
           CommonDataKinds.Phone.TYPE_HOME)
opList.add(op.build())

// Inserts the email
op = ContentProviderOperation.newInsert(
     ContactsContract.Data.CONTENT_URI)
  // Fix the foreign key relation
  .withValueBackReference(
       ContactsContract.Data.RAW_CONTACT_ID,
     firstOperationIndex)
  // Sets the data row's MIME type to Email
  .withValue(ContactsContract.Data.MIMETYPE,
          ContactsContract.CommonDataKinds.
             Email.CONTENT_ITEM_TYPE)
  // Email address and type
  .withValue(ContactsContract.CommonDataKinds.
        Email.ADDRESS, emailAddr)
```

```
        .withValue(ContactsContract.CommonDataKinds.
            Email.TYPE,
        android.provider.ContactsContract.
            CommonDataKinds.Email.TYPE_HOME)
```

Finally, before closing the method, we add a yield point. This has no functional influence, but introduces a break so the system can do other work to improve usability. The following snippet also contains the rest of the class:

```
    // Add a yield point.
    op.withYieldAllowed(true)

    opList.add(op.build())
  }

  fun reset() {
      opList.clear()
  }

  fun doAll() {
      try {
          contentResolver.applyBatch(
              ContactsContract.AUTHORITY,
              opList as ArrayList)
      } catch (e: Exception) {
          // Display a warning
          val duration = Toast.LENGTH_SHORT
          val toast = Toast.makeText(ctx,
              "Something went wrong", duration)
          toast.show()

          // Log exception
          Log.e("LOG", "Exception encountered "+
              "while inserting contact: " + e, e)
      }
  }
}
```

This uses a fixed phone type and a fixed email type, but I guess you get the point. Also make sure in production code you use resource strings instead of hard-coded strings as shown here. To use the class, all you have to do from inside an activity is

```
val cwr = ContactsWriter(this, contentResolver)
cwr.addContact("com.google","user@gmail.com",
    "Peter","Kappa",
    "post@kappa.com","0123456789")
cwr.addContact("com.google","user@gmail.com",
    "Hilda","Kappa",
    "post2@kappa.com","0123456789")
cwr.doAll()
```

In order to update a contacts entry, we introduce another function inside the ContactsWriter class:

```
fun updateContact(id:String, firstName:String?,
    lastName:String?, emailAddr:String?, phone:String?) {
  var op : ContentProviderOperation.Builder? = null
  if(firstName != null && lastName != null) {
    op = ContentProviderOperation.newUpdate(
            ContactsContract.Data.CONTENT_URI)
      .withSelection(ContactsContract.Data.CONTACT_ID +
          " = ? AND " + ContactsContract.Data.MIMETYPE +
          " = ?",
          arrayOf(id, ContactsContract.CommonDataKinds.
                    StructuredName.CONTENT_ITEM_TYPE))
      .withValue(ContactsContract.Contacts.DISPLAY_NAME,
          firstName + " " + lastName)
    opList.add(op.build())
  }
  if(emailAddr != null) {
    op = ContentProviderOperation.newUpdate(
            ContactsContract.Data.CONTENT_URI)
      .withSelection(ContactsContract.Data.CONTACT_ID +
          " = ? AND " + ContactsContract.Data.MIMETYPE +
          " = ?",
```

```
                arrayOf(id, ContactsContract.CommonDataKinds.
                        Email.CONTENT_ITEM_TYPE))
        .withValue(ContactsContract.CommonDataKinds.Email.
                ADDRESS, emailAddr)
      opList.add(op.build())
  }
  if(phone != null) {
    op = ContentProviderOperation.newUpdate(
            ContactsContract.Data.CONTENT_URI)
      .withSelection(ContactsContract.Data.CONTACT_ID +
          " = ? AND " + ContactsContract.Data.MIMETYPE +
          " = ?",
          arrayOf(id, ContactsContract.CommonDataKinds.
                  Phone.CONTENT_ITEM_TYPE))
      .withValue(ContactsContract.CommonDataKinds.Phone.
              NUMBER, phone)
    opList.add(op.build())
  }
}
```

As an input you need the ID key from the *Raw Contacts* table; any function argument not null gets updated. For example, you can write inside the activity

```
val rawId = ...
val cwr = ContactsWriter(this, contentResolver)
cwr.updateContact(rawId, null, null,
                "postXXX@kappa.com", null)
cwr.doAll()
```

As a last function, we add the possibility to delete a contact, again based on the ID:

```
fun delete(id:String) {
    var op = ContentProviderOperation.newDelete(
        ContactsContract.RawContacts.CONTENT_URI)
    .withSelection(ContactsContract.RawContacts.
```

```
        CONTACT_ID + " = ?",
        arrayOf(id))
    opList.add(op.build())
}
```

Using it is similar to an update:

```
val rawId = ...
val cwr = ContactsWriter(this, contentResolver)
cwr.delete(rawId)
cwr.doAll()
```

Using Contacts System Activities

To read or update a single contact, you can avoid having to write your own user interface. Just use the system activity to access a contact. An appropriate intent call for creating a single contact looks like

```
val intent = Intent(Intents.Insert.ACTION)
intent.setType(ContactsContract.RawContacts.CONTENT_TYPE)
intent.putExtra(Intents.Insert.EMAIL, emailAddress)
    .putExtra(Intents.Insert.EMAIL_TYPE,
        CommonDataKinds.Email.TYPE_WORK)
    .putExtra(Intents.Insert.PHONE, phoneNumber)
    .putExtra(Intents.Insert.PHONE_TYPE,
        Phone.TYPE_WORK)
startActivity(intent)
```

This will open the contacts screen for creating a new contact and prefill the given fields.

To instead edit an existing contact, once you have the look-up key and the raw contact ID – see the preceding section "Reading Contacts" – write as follows:

```
val uri = Contacts.getLookupUri(id, lookupKey)
val intent = Intent(Intent.ACTION_EDIT)
// the following must be done in _one_ call, do not
// chain .setData() and .setType(), because they
// overwrite each other!
```

```
intent.setDataAndType(uri, Contacts.CONTENT_ITEM_TYPE)
intent.putExtra("finishActivityOnSaveCompleted", true)

// now put any data to update, for example
intent.putExtra(Intents.Insert.EMAIL, newEmail)
...
startActivity(intent)
```

Using Quick Contact Badges

Quick contact badges allow you to use a GUI widget that your user can tap to see a contact's details and take any suitable action from there like sending an email, issuing a call, or whatever makes sense. This details screen gets presented by the system, you don't have to implement it in your app. See Figure 8-6.

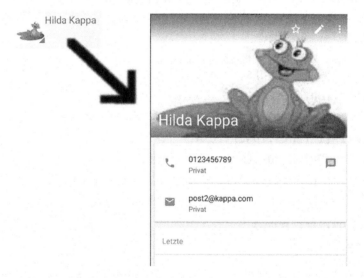

Figure 8-6. *A Quick Contact Badge*

In order to generate such a quick contact badge using the traditional XML description way, inside your layout file you must add

```
<QuickContactBadge
        android:id="@+id/quickBadge"
        android:layout_width="60dp"
        android:layout_height="60dp"
        android:scaleType="centerCrop"/>
```

We talk about using Jetpack Compose instead for including quick contact badges in the following.

Inside your code you must connect the badge to the following information you get from the contacts provider: the raw contact ID, the look-up key, and a thumbnail URI. The corresponding code might look like

```
val id = row[ContactsContract.Contacts.
    _ID]

val lookup = row[ContactsContract.Contacts.
    LOOKUP_KEY]

val photo = row[ContactsContract.Contacts.
    PHOTO_THUMBNAIL_URI]
```

where the row, for example, is a map you get from a contacts content provider query. In this case a query inside the *Raw Contacts* table is enough; you don't need to also query the *Data* table.

From here we configure the badge as follows, for example, after you load the contact information by user interface activities:

```
val contactUri = ContactsContract.Contacts.getLookupUri(
    id.toLong(), lookup)
quickBadge.assignContactUri(contactUri)
val thumbnail =
    loadContactPhotoThumbnail(photo.toString())
quickBadge.setImageBitmap(thumbnail)
```

where the loadContactPhotoThumbnail() function loads the thumbnail image data:

```
private fun loadContactPhotoThumbnail(photoData: String):
    Bitmap? {
  var afd: AssetFileDescriptor? = null
  try {
    val thumbUri = Uri.parse(photoData)
    afd = contentResolver.
        openAssetFileDescriptor(thumbUri, "r")
    afd?.apply {
        fileDescriptor?.apply {
```

```
            return BitmapFactory.decodeFileDescriptor(
                this, null, null)
        }
    }
} catch (e: FileNotFoundException) {
    // Handle file not found errors ...
} finally {
    afd?.close()
}
return null
}
```

If we want to use Jetpack Compose as a front-end development technology, we immediately realize that there is no "QuickContactBadge" composable element available. This is not a real problem, though, because with `AndroidView` there is a compatibility bridge between Jetpack Compose and traditional AndroidViews. All you have to do is to add

```
AndroidView(
    modifier = Modifier.width(60.dp).height(60.dp),
    factory = { context ->
        // This instantiates a non-Compose View:
        QuickContactBadge(context).apply {
            val contactUri = ContactsContract.
                Contacts.getLookupUri(
                    itm.id.toLong(),
                    itm.lookupKey)
            assignContactUri(contactUri)
            val thumbnail =
                loadContactPhotoThumbnail(
                    itm.photoThumbnailUri)
            setImageBitmap(thumbnail)
        }
    },
    update = { view ->
        // View's been inflated or state has been
```

```
        // updated. Add logic here if necessary.
        // Because the QuickContactBadge does not
        // represent a state, we don't need to add
        // anything here.
    }
)
```

to your composable's structure. The `itm` is a data holder (data class) for the ID, the lookup-key, and the photo thumbnail URI. Remember that for Jetpack Compose, no entry in whatever layout XML file is needed.

Search Framework

The *search framework* allows you to seamlessly add search functionality to your app and register your app as a searchable items provider in the Android OS.

Talking of the user interface, you have two options:

- Open the search dialog provided by the OS.

- Add a search widget to your UI via `SearchView`.

More precisely, in order to include search facilities inside your app, you have to

1. Provide a searchable configuration as an XML file.

2. Provide a dialog or search widget.

3. Provide an activity that (A) is able to receive a search query, (B) performs the search inside your app's data, (C) and displays the search result.

The rest of this section walks through these requirements.

The Searchable Configuration

The searchable configuration is a file named `searchable.xml` and resides inside the folder `/res/xml` of your project. The most basic contents of this file read

```
<?xml version="1.0" encoding="utf-8"?>
<searchable xmlns:android=
```

```
      "http://schemas.android.com/apk/res/android"
   android:label="@string/app_label"
   android:hint="@string/search_hint" >
</searchable>
```

The "@string/..." entries point to localized string resources. The "@string/app_label" points to a label and should equal the name of the "label" attribute of the <application> element. The other one, "@string/search_hint", is the string to be shown inside search fields if nothing has been entered yet. It is recommended and should show something like "Search <content>" with <content> being specific to the data being searched for. There are a lot more possible attributes and some optional child elements – we will mention some in the following sections. For the complete list, please see the online documentation under the "Searchable Configuration" document.

The Searchable Activity

For the activity that handles search-related issues inside your app, start with its declaration inside AndroidManifest.xml. The activity needs to have a special signature there, as in

```
<activity android:name=".SearchableActivity" >
  <intent-filter>
    <action android:name=
        "android.intent.action.SEARCH" />
  </intent-filter>
  <meta-data android:name="android.app.searchable"
          android:resource="@xml/searchable"/>

  ...
</activity>
```

The name of the activity is up to you. All the other tags and attributes must be as shown here.

Next, we let this activity receive the search request. This is done inside its onCreate() callback as in

```
override fun onCreate(savedInstanceState: Bundle?) {
  super.onCreate(savedInstanceState)
  setContentView(R.layout.activity_searchable)
```

```
  // This is the standard way a system search dialog
  // or the search widget communicates the query
  // string:
  if (Intent.ACTION_SEARCH == intent.action) {
    val query =
        intent.getStringExtra(SearchManager.QUERY)
    doMySearch(query)
  }

  // More initialization if necessary...
}
```

The doMySearch() function is supposed to perform the search and present the result or whatever inside the SearchableActivity. The way this is done is totally up to the application – it could be a database search or a search using a content provider or any other way you might think of.

The Search Dialog

In order for any activity to open the system's search dialog and have it pass the query entered there to the SearchableActivity, inside AndroidManifest.xml you write

```
<activity android:name=".SearchableActivity" >
  <!-- same as above -->
</activity>
<activity android:name=".MainActivity"
          android:label="Main">
  <!-- ... -->

  <!-- Enable the search dialog and let it send -->
  <!-- the queries to SearchableActivity -->
  <meta-data android:name=
      "android.app.default_searchable"
          android:value=
      ".SearchableActivity" />

  ...
</activity>
```

This example allows for the MainActivity to open the system's search dialog – in fact you can use any suitable activity from inside your app for that purpose.

To open the search dialog inside your searchable activity, write

```
onSearchRequested()
```

Note   Usually, directly executing an obvious callback function starting with "on…" has a bad smell. You sometimes do that for half-legal shortcuts. The reason we have to do it here is that your device might have a dedicated search button. In this case onSearchRequested() gets called from the system, and it is a real callback method. Because such a button is optional, it is however necessary always to provide a search initiator from inside your app.

A dialog-based search flow gets depicted in Figure 8-7.

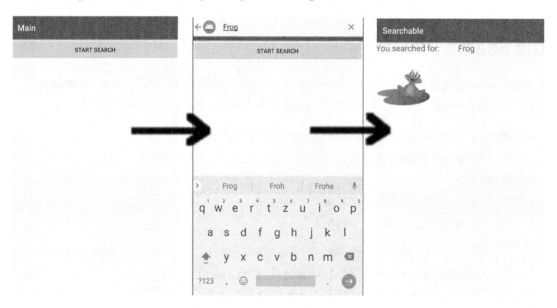

Figure 8-7. *A Dialog-Based Search Flow*

The Search Widget

Instead of opening the system's search dialog, you can also place a `<SearchView>` widget inside your UI. While in principle you can place it wherever you like, it is recommended to put it in the action bar. For this aim, provided you have set up an action bar and defined a menu there, inside the menu XML definition, write

```xml
<menu xmlns:android=
    "http://schemas.android.com/apk/res/android"
     xmlns:app=
    "http://schemas.android.com/apk/res-auto">

  <!-- Usually you have Settings in any menu -->
  <item android:id="@+id/action_settings"
        android:title="Settings"
        app:showAsAction="never"/>

  <item android:id="@+id/action_search"
        android:title="Search"
        app:showAsAction="ifRoom|collapseActionView"
        app:actionViewClass=
            "android.support.v7.widget.SearchView"
      android:icon=
            "@android:drawable/ic_menu_search"/>

  <!-- more items ... ->
</menu>
```

What then needs to be done inside your app in order to connect the widget with the search framework is

```kotlin
// Set the searchable configuration
val searchManager = getSystemService(SEARCH_SERVICE)
      as SearchManager
val searchView = menu.findItem(R.id.action_search).
      actionView as SearchView
searchView.setSearchableInfo(
```

```
        searchManager.getSearchableInfo(componentName))
// Do not iconify the widget; expand it by default:
searchView.setIconifiedByDefault(false)
```

This is it! The flow looks like that shown in Figure 8-8 (you'd press the search icon in the action bar).

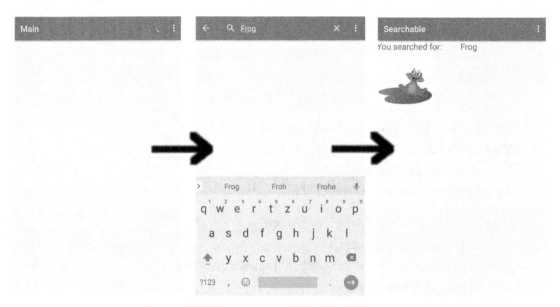

Figure 8-8. *A Widget-Based Search Flow*

If you want to do the same using Jetpack Compose as a front-end technology, you must use AndroidView, because there is no built-in composable for the search widget:

```
@Composable
fun MySearchWidget() {
    var searchTxt by remember { mutableStateOf("") }
    AndroidView(
        modifier = Modifier
            .fillMaxWidth()
            .height(60.dp),
        factory = { context ->
            // This instantiates a non-Compose
            // View:
            val searchManager =
```

```
        getSystemService(SEARCH_SERVICE)
            as SearchManager
    SearchView(context).apply {
        setSearchableInfo(
            searchManager.
                getSearchableInfo(
                    componentName))
        isIconifiedByDefault = false
        setQuery(searchTxt, false)
    }
},
update = { view ->
    // View's been inflated or state has
    // been updated. Add logic here if
    // necessary.
    view.setQuery(searchTxt, false)
}
)
}
```

Search Suggestions

There are two ways you can help the user input search query strings: First, you can let
the system memorize queries for the next times the searches get used. Second, you can
let your app provide fully customizable suggestions.

Recent Query Suggestions

For the recent query suggestions, you implement a content provider subclass of
SearchRecentSuggestionsProvider and add it to AndroidManifest.xml like any other
content provider. A basic but nevertheless already fully implemented content provider
looks like

```
class RecentsProvider :
        SearchRecentSuggestionsProvider {
    val AUTHORITY = "com.example.RecentsProvider"
```

```
    val MODE = DATABASE_MODE_QUERIES

    init {
        setupSuggestions(AUTHORITY, MODE)
    }
}
```

Register it inside /res/xml/searchable.xml as follows:

```
<?xml version="1.0" encoding="utf-8"?>
<searchable xmlns:android=
        "http://schemas.android.com/apk/res/android"
    android:label="@string/app_label"
    android:hint="@string/search_hint"
    android:searchSuggestAuthority=
        "com.example.RecentsProvider"
    android:searchSuggestSelection=
        " ?">
</searchable>
```

New are the last two attributes. The "android:searchSuggestAuthority" here draws a connection to the provider.

The content provider must still be registered inside AndroidManifest.xml. This, for example, reads

```
<provider
    android:name=".RecentsProvider"
    android:authorities="com.example.RecentsProvider"
    android:enabled="true"
    android:exported="true"> .
</provider>
```

This reads previous queries from an automatically generated database. What is left to do is to add the search queries. For this aim, inside the SearchableActivity class, write

```
override fun onCreate(savedInstanceState: Bundle?) {
  super.onCreate(savedInstanceState)
  setContentView(R.layout.activity_searchable)
```

```
// This is the standard way a system search dialog
// or the search widget communicates the query
// string:
if (Intent.ACTION_SEARCH == intent.action) {
  val query =
      intent.getStringExtra(SearchManager.QUERY)

  // Add it to the recents suggestion database
  val suggestions = SearchRecentSuggestions(this,
      RecentsProvider.AUTHORITY, RecentsProvider.MODE)
  suggestions.saveRecentQuery(q, null)

  doMySearch(query)
}

// More initialization if necessary...
}
```

The second parameter for the saveRecentQuery() method could be a second line for annotation purposes. For this to work, you (A) have to use val MODE = DATABASE_MODE_QUERIES or DATABASE_MODE_2LINES in the RecentsProvider and (B) find a way to retrieve annotation texts inside the SearchableActivity class.

Custom Suggestions

Custom suggestions are more powerful compared with recent query suggestions. They can be fully app or domain specific, and you can provide intelligent suggestions to the user, tailored for the current user action. Compared with recent query suggestions, you instead implement and register a ContentProvider obeying certain rules:

- The Android OS will fire ContentProvider.query(uri, projection, selection, selectionArgs, sortOrder) calls with URIs like

```
content://your.authority/
    optional.suggest.path/
    SUGGEST_URI_PATH_QUERY/
    <query>
```

where "your.authority" is the content provider authority, "/optional.suggest.path" might be added by the search configuration for disambiguation, and SUGGEST_URI_PATH_QUERY is the value of the constant SearchManager.SUGGEST_URI_PATH_QUERY. The "<query>" contains the string to be searched for. Both the selection and selectionArgs parameters will be filled only if appropriately configured in the search configuration.

- The resulting Cursor must return the following fields (shown are constant names):

  - **BaseColumns._ID**

    A (technical) unique ID you must provide

  - **SearchManager.SUGGEST_COLUMN_TEXT_1**

    The search suggestion

  - **SearchManager.SUGGEST_COLUMN_TEXT_2**

    (optional) A second, less important string representing an annotation text

  - **SearchManager.SUGGEST_COLUMN_ICON_1**

    (optional) A drawable resource ID, content, or file URI string for an icon to be shown on the left

  - **SearchManager.SUGGEST_COLUMN_ICON_2**

    (optional) A drawable resource ID, content, or file URI string for an icon to be shown on the right

  - **SearchManager.SUGGEST_COLUMN_INTENT_ACTION**

    (optional) An intent action string that is used to call an Intent when the suggestion gets clicked

  - **SearchManager.SUGGEST_COLUMN_INTENT_DATA**

    An intent data member to be sent with the Intent

  - **SearchManager.SUGGEST_COLUMN_INTENT_DATA_ID**

    A string to be appended to the intent data member

- **SearchManager.SUGGEST_COLUMN_INTENT_EXTRA_DATA**

  Extra data to be sent with the Intent

- **SearchManager.SUGGEST_COLUMN_QUERY**

  The original query string

- **SearchManager.SUGGEST_COLUMN_SHORTCUT_ID**

  Used when providing suggestions for the *Quick Search Box* –
  indicates whether a search suggestion should be stored as a
  shortcut and whether it should be validated

- **SearchManager.SUGGEST_COLUMN_SPINNER_WHILE_
  REFRESHING**

  Used when providing suggestions for the *Quick Search Box* – a
  spinner should be shown instead of the icon from SUGGEST_
  COLUMN_ICON_2 while the shortcut of this suggestion is being
  refreshed in the Quick Search Box

Let us try to build a valid example for custom suggestions. We start with a working
example of a recent query suggestion provider as described previously. It doesn't matter
whether you use the dialog or the widget method. Now the difference is the content
provider and the search configuration.

As a search configuration defined by file /res/xml/searchable.xml, enter

```xml
<?xml version="1.0" encoding="utf-8"?>
<searchable xmlns:android=
      "http://schemas.android.com/apk/res/android"
   android:label=
      "@string/app_label"
   android:hint=
      "@string/search_hint"
   android:searchSuggestAuthority=
      "com.example.CustomProvider"
   android:searchSuggestIntentAction=
      "android.intent.action.VIEW">
</searchable>
```

And we define a new content provider

```kotlin
class CustomProvider : ContentProvider() {
  override fun query(uri: Uri,
          projection: Array<String>?,
          selection: String?,
          selectionArgs: Array<String>?,
          sortOrder: String?): Cursor? {
      Log.e("LOG", "query(): " + uri +
              " - projection=" +
                  Arrays.toString(projection) +
              " - selection=" + selection +
              " - selectionArgs=" +
                  Arrays.toString(selectionArgs) +
              " - sortOrder=" + sortOrder)
      return null
  }

  override fun delete(uri: Uri, selection: String?,
        selectionArgs: Array<String>?): Int {
      throw UnsupportedOperationException(
          "Not yet implemented")
  }

  override fun getType(uri: Uri): String? {
      throw UnsupportedOperationException(
          "Not yet implemented")
  }

  override fun insert(uri: Uri, values: ContentValues?):
        Uri? {
      throw UnsupportedOperationException(
          "Not yet implemented")
  }

  override fun onCreate(): Boolean {
      return false
  }
```

```
override fun update(uri: Uri, values: ContentValues?,
    selection: String?,
    selectionArgs: Array<String>?): Int {
  throw UnsupportedOperationException(
      "Not yet implemented")
  }
}
```

and register it inside AndroidManifest.xml:

```
<provider
    android:name=".CustomProvider"
    android:authorities="com.example.CustomProvider"
    android:enabled="true"
    android:exported="true">
</provider>
```

What happens so far when the user starts a search is as follows:

- Whenever the user enters or removes a character, the system will go to the search configuration and see by looking at the "searchSuggestAuthority" attribute that it needs to address a content provider with this authority assigned to it.

- By looking into AndroidManifest.xml, it sees that this authority is connected to the provider class CustomProvider.

- It invokes a query() on this provider and expects a Cursor return the custom suggestions.

- If the user taps a suggestion, by virtue of the "searchSuggestIntentAction" attribute set to "android.intent.action. VIEW", the SearchableActivity's onCreate() will see the incoming Intent with the "VIEW" action.

Up to now we let the query() method return null, which is equivalent to *no* suggestions, but we added a logging statement, so we can see what arrives at the query() method. For example, when the user enters "sp", the arguments so far will read

```
query(): content://com.example.CustomProvider/
    search_suggest_query/sp?limit=50
```

```
projection=null
selection=null
selectionArgs=null
sortOrder=null
```

The arguments sent to the query() method by the search framework can be tailored extensively by various search configuration attributes. At this place however, we refer to the online documentation and continue with extracting the information from the first uri parameter. How to build Cursor objects is described in Chapter 6. For this example, we use a MatrixCursor, and instead of returning null, we could, for example, return

```
override fun query(uri: Uri,
                   projection: Array<String>?,
                   selection: String?,
                   selectionArgs: Array<String>?,
                   sortOrder: String?): Cursor? {
    Log.e("LOG", "query(): " + uri +
            " - projection=" +
                Arrays.toString(projection) +
            " - selection=" + selection +
            " - selectionArgs=" +
                Arrays.toString(selectionArgs) +
            " - sortOrder=" + sortOrder)

    val lps = uri.lastPathSegment // the query
    val qr = uri.encodedQuery     // e.g. "limit=50"

    val curs = MatrixCursor(arrayOf(
            BaseColumns._ID,
            SearchManager.SUGGEST_COLUMN_TEXT_1,
            SearchManager.SUGGEST_COLUMN_INTENT_DATA
    ))
    curs.addRow(arrayOf(1, lps + "-Suggestion 1",
        lps + "-Suggestion 1"))
    curs.addRow(arrayOf(2, lps + "-Suggestion 2",
        lps + "-Suggestion 2"))
```

```
    return curs
}
```

from inside the `SearchableActivity`. This example provides only silly suggestions – you can write something more clever to the `MatrixCursor`.

As a last modification, you can make your search suggestions available to the system's *Quick Search Box*. All you have to do for that is add `android:includeInGlobalSearch = "true"` to your search configuration. The user must allow this inside the settings for this connection to take effect.

Location and Maps

Handheld devices may track their geographic position, and they may interact with map services to graphically interfere with a user's location needs. Geographical position is not only about latitude and longitude numbers but also about finding out street addresses and points of interest. While it is certainly an important ethical question how far apps can go to track their users' personal life, the possibilities for interesting apps and games are potentially endless. In this section we talk about the technical possibilities. Just be cautious with your user's data and be transparent with what you are doing with them.

The Android OS itself contains a location framework with classes at package `android.location`. However, the official position of Google is to favor the `Google Play Services location API` for it is more elaborate and simpler to use. We follow this suggestion and talk about the services location API in the following paragraphs. Location is about finding out (A) the geographical position of a device as a latitude-longitude pair and (B) street names, house numbers, and other points of interest given the geographical position.

In order to make the services location API available to your app, inside your app module's `build.gradle` file, add as dependencies

```
implementation
   'com.google.android.gms:play-services-location:11.8.0'
implementation
   'com.google.android.gms:play-services-maps:11.8.0'
```

(There are just two lines; remove the newlines after "implementation.")

Last Known Location

The easiest way to get the device's position is to get the *last known location.* To do so, in your app request permissions

```
<uses-permission android:name=
    "android.permission.ACCESS_COARSE_LOCATION"/>
<uses-permission android:name=
    "android.permission.ACCESS_FINE_LOCATION"/>
```

The GPS resolution with less than ten yards needs the *FINE* location permission, while the more coarse network-based resolution with approximately 100 yards needs the *COARSE* location permission. Adding both to the manifest file gives us the most options, but depending on your needs, you could go along with just the coarse one.

Then, inside your component, for example, inside onCreate(), you construct a FusedLocationProviderClient as in

```
var fusedLocationClient: FusedLocationProviderClient? =
    null

override fun onCreate(savedInstanceState: Bundle?) {
  super.onCreate(savedInstanceState)

  ...

  fusedLocationClient = LocationServices.
        getFusedLocationProviderClient(this)
}
```

Wherever needed in your app, you can use it to get the last known location:

```
if (checkPermission(
      Manifest.permission.ACCESS_COARSE_LOCATION,
      Manifest.permission.ACCESS_FINE_LOCATION)) {
  fusedLocationClient?.lastLocation?.
        addOnSuccessListener(this,
      {location : Location? ->
          // Got last known location. In some rare
          // situations this can be null.
```

```
            if(location == null) {
                // TODO, handle it
            } else location.apply {
                // Handle location object
                Log.e("LOG", location.toString())
            }
        })
    }
```

where checkPermission() checks and possibly acquires the needed permissions as described in Chapter 7. This could be, for example

```
val PERMISSION_ID = 42
private fun checkPermission(vararg perm:String) :
      Boolean {
  val havePermissions = perm.toList().all {
      ContextCompat.checkSelfPermission(this,it) ==
          PackageManager.PERMISSION_GRANTED
  }
  if (!havePermissions) {
    if(perm.toList().any {
      ActivityCompat.
      shouldShowRequestPermissionRationale(this, it)}
    ) {
        val dialog = AlertDialog.Builder(this)
            .setTitle("Permission")
            .setMessage("Permission needed!")
            .setPositiveButton("OK",{
                id, v ->
                ActivityCompat.requestPermissions(
                    this, perm, PERMISSION_ID)
            })
            .setNegativeButton("No",{
                id, v ->
            })
            .create()
```

```
        dialog.show()
    } else {
      ActivityCompat.requestPermissions(this, perm,
          PERMISSION_ID)
    }
    return false
  }
  return true
}
```

For simplicity I used strings for button labels and messages – for production code make sure you use resources! The function checkPermission() if necessary tries to acquire permission from a system activity. Whether or not the user grants permissions, upon return from this activity, your app may accordingly react to the result inside

```
override
fun onRequestPermissionsResult(requestCode: Int,
        permissions: Array<String>,
        grantResults: IntArray) {
    when (requestCode) {
      PERMISSION_ID -> {
        ...
      }
      ...
    }
}
```

Caution   The concept of a "last known location" is somewhat blurry. In an emulated device, for example, it is not sufficient to set the location by the provided device control for changing the "last known location." Only after an app like Google Maps uses location update mechanisms the code as described here also returns the correct value. The mechanisms described in the following sections are more complex, but also more reliable.

Tracking Position Updates

If your app needs to track updates on changing locations, you follow a different approach. First, the permissions needed are the same as stated previously in section "Last Known Location," so no change there. The difference is requesting periodic updates from the *Fused Location Provider*. For that we need to define a location settings object. Confusingly, the corresponding class is called `LocationRequest` (it better had been called "LocationRequestSettings" or something). To create one, write

```
val reqSetting = LocationRequest.create().apply {
    fastestInterval = 10000
    interval = 10000
    priority = LocationRequest.PRIORITY_HIGH_ACCURACY
    smallestDisplacement = 1.0f
}
```

The `.apply` construct lets us configure the object faster – for example, the `fastestInterval = 10000` internally gets translated to `reqSetting.setFastestInterval(10000)`. The meanings of the individual settings are as follows:

- **fastestInterval**

  The fastest possible total update interval in milliseconds for the location provider.

- **interval**

  The requested interval in milliseconds. This setting is only approximative.

- **priority**

  The requested accuracy. This setting influences the battery usage. Possible values are (constants from `LocationRequest`)

  – **PRIORITY_NO_POWER**: Fetch only passive updates if other requestors actively request updates.

  – **PRIORITY_LOW_POWER**: Only updates on "city" levels.

- – **PRIORITY_BALANCED_POWER_ACCURACY**: Only updates on "city street block" levels.

- – **PRIORITY_HIGH_ACCURACY**: Use highest possible accuracy available.

  This value will be internally adapted according to available permissions.

- **smallestDisplacement**

  The smallest displacement in meters necessary for an update message to be fired.

With the location request settings at hand, we check whether the system is able to fulfill our request. This happens in the following code snippet:

```
val REQUEST_CHECK_STATE = 12300 // any suitable ID
val builder = LocationSettingsRequest.Builder()
        .addLocationRequest(reqSetting)
val client = LocationServices.getSettingsClient(this)
client.checkLocationSettings(builder.build()).
        addOnCompleteListener { task ->
    try {
        val state: LocationSettingsStates = task.result.
            locationSettingsStates
        Log.e("LOG", "LocationSettings: \n" +
          " BLE present: ${state.isBlePresent} \n" +
          " BLE usable: ${state.isBleUsable} \n" +
          " GPS present:  ${state.isGpsPresent} \n" +
          " GPS usable: ${state.isGpsUsable} \n" +
          " Location present: " +
              "${state.isLocationPresent} \n" +
          " Location usable: " +
              "${state.isLocationUsable} \n" +
          " Network Location present: " +
              "${state.isNetworkLocationPresent} \n" +
```

```
        "  Network Location usable: " +
            "${state.isNetworkLocationUsable} \n"
      )
  } catch (e: RuntimeExecutionException) {
     if (e.cause is ResolvableApiException)
       (e.cause as ResolvableApiException).
         startResolutionForResult(
             this@MainActivity,
             REQUEST_CHECK_STATE)
  }
}
```

This asynchronously performs a check, and in case high accuracy is requested and the device's setting wouldn't allow updates based on GPS data, the corresponding system settings dialog gets called. The latter happens somewhat awkwardly inside the exception catch. The result of the corresponding system intent call ends up in

```
override fun onActivityResult(requestCode: Int,
      resultCode: Int, data: Intent) {
  if (requestCode and 0xFFFF == REQUEST_CHECK_STATE) {
     Log.e("LOG", "Back from REQUEST_CHECK_STATE")
     ...
  }
}
```

With all set up correctly and enough permissions, we now can register for location updates via

```
val locationUpdates = object : LocationCallback() {
    override fun onLocationResult(lr: LocationResult) {
        Log.e("LOG", lr.toString())
        Log.e("LOG", "Newest Location: " + lr.locations.last())
        // do something with the new location...
    }
}
fusedLocationClient?.requestLocationUpdates(reqSetting,
    locationUpdates,
    null /* Looper */)
```

In order to stop location updates, you move the `locationUpdates` to a class field and react to stop requests via

```
fun stopPeriodic(view:View) {
  fusedLocationClient?.
        removeLocationUpdates(locationUpdates)
}
```

Geocoding

The Geocoder class allows to determine the geo-coordinates (`longitude, latitude`) for a given address or, the other way round, possible addresses for given geo-coordinates. These processes are known as forward and reverse geocoding. The `Geocoder` class internally uses an online Google service, but the details are hidden inside the implementation – you as a developer use the `Geocoder` class without the need to understand where the data comes from.

This section is about *reverse* geocoding – we use a `Location` object with longitude and latitude to find nearby street names. To start, we first have to decide what we do with a potentially long-running operation – to do the look-up, a network operation is necessary, and the online service needs to look up a huge database. An `IntentService` will do the job for us, and among the methods that can return us the value, we choose a `ResultReceiver` passed by intent extras. First, we define a kind of contract between the service and the service clients in a class holding some constants:

```
class GeocoderConstants {
  companion object Constants {
      val SUCCESS_RESULT = 0
      val FAILURE_RESULT = 1
      val PACKAGE_NAME = "<put your package name here>"
      val RECEIVER = "$PACKAGE_NAME.RECEIVER"
      val RESULT_DATA_KEY =
          "$PACKAGE_NAME.RESULT_DATA_KEY"
      val LOCATION_DATA_EXTRA =
          "$PACKAGE_NAME.LOCATION_DATA_EXTRA"
  }
}
```

Now the full service class reads

```kotlin
class FetchAddressService :
      IntentService("FetchAddressService") {

  override
  fun onHandleIntent(intent: Intent?) {
      val geocoder = Geocoder(this, Locale.getDefault())
      var errorMessage = ""

      // Get the location passed to this service through
      // an extra.
      val location = intent?.getParcelableExtra(
              GeocoderConstants.LOCATION_DATA_EXTRA)
          as Location

      // Get the Intent result receiver
      val receiver = intent.getParcelableExtra(
          GeocoderConstants.RECEIVER) as ResultReceiver

      var addresses: List<Address>? = null
      try {
          addresses = geocoder.getFromLocation(
                  location.getLatitude(),
                  location.getLongitude(),
                  1) // Get just a single address!
      } catch (e: IOException) {
          // Catch network or other I/O problems.
          errorMessage = "service_not_available"
          Log.e("LOG", errorMessage, e)
      } catch (e: IllegalArgumentException) {
          // Catch invalid latitude or longitude values.
          errorMessage = "invalid_lat_long_used"
          Log.e("LOG", errorMessage + ". " +
                  "Latitude = " + location.getLatitude() +
                  ", Longitude = " +
                  location.getLongitude(), e)
      }
```

```kotlin
        if (addresses == null || addresses.size == 0) {
            // No address was found.
            if (errorMessage.isEmpty()) {
                errorMessage = "no_address_found"
                Log.e("LOG", errorMessage)
            }
            deliverResultToReceiver(
                receiver,
                GeocoderConstants.FAILURE_RESULT,
                errorMessage)
        } else {
            val address = addresses[0]
            val addressFragments =
                (0..address.maxAddressLineIndex).
                map { i -> address.getAddressLine(i) }
            val addressStr = addressFragments.joinToString(
                separator =
                    System.getProperty("line.separator"))
            Log.i("LOG", "address_found")
            deliverResultToReceiver(
                receiver,
                GeocoderConstants.SUCCESS_RESULT,
                addressStr)
        }
    }

    private fun deliverResultToReceiver(
            receiver:ResultReceiver,
            resultCode: Int,
            message: String) {
        val bundle = Bundle()
        bundle.putString(GeocoderConstants.RESULT_DATA_KEY,
            message)
        receiver.send(resultCode, bundle)
    }
}
```

Again, for production code you should use resource strings instead of literals as shown in this example. The service must be registered inside AndroidManifest.xml:

```
<service android:name=".FetchAddressService"
         android:exported="false"/>
```

For using this service, we first build a ResultReceiver class, check the permissions, and, for example, use the *last known location* to call the service:

```
class AddressResultReceiver(handler: Handler?) :
    ResultReceiver(handler) {
  override
  fun onReceiveResult(resultCode: Int,
                      resultData: Bundle) {
    val addressOutput =
        resultData.getString(
            GeocoderConstants.RESULT_DATA_KEY)
    Log.e("LOG", "address result = " +
        addressOutput.toString())
    ...
  }
}
val resultReceiver = AddressResultReceiver(null)
fun startFetchAddress(view:View) {
  if (checkPermission(
        Manifest.permission.ACCESS_COARSE_LOCATION,
        Manifest.permission.ACCESS_FINE_LOCATION))
  {
      fusedLocationClient?.lastLocation?.
          addOnSuccessListener(this, {
              location: Location? ->
            if (location == null) {
              // TODO
            } else location.apply {
              Log.e("LOG", toString())
              val intent = Intent(
                  this@MainActivity,
```

235

```
                        FetchAddressService::class.java)
                intent.putExtra(
                  GeocoderConstants.RECEIVER,
                  resultReceiver)
                intent.putExtra(
                  GeocoderConstants.LOCATION_DATA_EXTRA,
                  this)
                startService(intent)
            }
        })
    }
}
```

You can see we use an explicit Intent. That is why we don't need an intent filter inside the service declaration in `AndroidManifest.xml`.

Using ADB to Fetch Location Information

For development and debugging purposes, you can use ADB to fetch the location information of a device connected to your PC or laptop:

```
./adb shell dumpsys location
```

For more information on CLI commands, see Chapter 19.

Maps

Adding a map to your location-related app greatly improves the usability for your users. To add a Google Maps API, the easiest is to use the wizard provided by Android Studio. Do as follows:

1. Add a map activity: Right-click your module. Then in the menu, choose New ➤ Activity ➤ Gallery…, and from the gallery choose a Google Maps activity. Press Next and inside the screen that follows, enter activity parameters according to your needs. However, choosing an appropriate activity name basically is all you need – the defaults make sense in most cases.

2. You need an API key in order to use Google Maps. For this purpose, inside the file /res/values/google_maps_api.xml, locate the link inside the comments; it might look like https:// console.developers.google.com/flows/enableapi?.... Open this link in a browser and follow the instructions there. Finally, enter the key generated online as the text of the <string name = "google_maps_key" ... > element in that file.

What we have now is an activity class prepared for us, a fragment layout file that we can include in our app, and a registered API key that allows us to fetch map data from the Google server.

To include the fragment as defined by /res/layout/activity_maps.xml, you write

```
<include
    android:layout_width="fill_parent"
    android:layout_height="250dp"
    layout="@layout/activity_maps" />
```

inside your layout, with sizes adapted according to your needs.

Inside the code we first add a snippet to fetch a map from the server. You do this inside your onCreate() callback as follows:

```
override fun onCreate(savedInstanceState: Bundle?) {
    ...
    val mapFragment = supportFragmentManager
            .findFragmentById(R.id.map)
        as SupportMapFragment
    mapFragment.getMapAsync(this)
}
```

where R.id.map points to the map's ID inside /res/layout/activity_maps.xml.

Next, we add a callback that gets called when the map is loaded and ready to receive commands. To do so, we extend the activity that handles the map to also implement the interface com.google.android.gms.maps.OnMapReadyCallback

```
class MainActivity : AppCompatActivity(),
    OnMapReadyCallback { ... }
```

and add the callback implementation, for example:

```
/**
 * Use this to save and manipulate the map once
 * available.
 */
override fun onMapReady(map: GoogleMap) {
    // Add a marker in Austin, TX and move the camera
    val austin = LatLng(30.284935, -97.735464)
    map.addMarker(MarkerOptions().position(austin).
        title("Marker in Austin"))
    map.moveCamera(CameraUpdateFactory.
        newLatLng(austin))
}
```

In case Google Play Services is not installed on the device, the user automatically gets prompted to install it. The map object can of course be saved as a class object field, and you can do lots of interesting things with it, including adding markers, lines, zoom, movement, and more. The possibilities get described in the online API documentation for `com.google.android.gms.maps.GoogleMap`.

Preferences

Preferences allow the user to change the way the app performs certain parts of its functionalities. Contrary to the input given by the user during the app's functional workflows, preferences are less likely to be changed, so the access to preferences gets usually provided by a single "Preferences" entry in the app's menu.

There was a major overhaul in Android's Preferences API. It is now part of Jetpack, and you can find its documentation at `https://developer.android.com/guide/topics/ui/settings/`, `https://developer.android.com/jetpack/androidx/releases/preference/`, and `https://developer.android.com/reference/androidx/preference/package-summary`.

In order to be able to use Jetpack for preferences, we have to correctly add the dependencies to the build file:

```
// Project build.gradle **********************************
buildscript {
    ext.kotlin_version = '1.6.21'
    repositories {
        google()
        mavenCentral()
    }
    dependencies {
        classpath 'com.android.tools.build:gradle:7.2.1'
        classpath "org.jetbrains.kotlin:" +
            "kotlin-gradle-plugin:$kotlin_version"
    }
}

allprojects {
    repositories {
        google()
        mavenCentral()
    }
}

// Module build.gradle **********************************
plugins {
    id 'com.android.application'
    id 'kotlin-android'
    id 'kotlin-kapt'
}
android {
    compileSdkVersion 32
    defaultConfig {
        applicationId "com.example.myapp"
        minSdkVersion 23
        targetSdkVersion 32
        versionCode 1
        versionName "1.0"
```

```
            testInstrumentationRunner 'androidx.test.runner.' +
                'AndroidJUnitRunner'
        }
        buildFeatures {
            // Enables Jetpack Compose for this module
            compose true
        }
        compileOptions {
            sourceCompatibility JavaVersion.VERSION_1_8
            targetCompatibility JavaVersion.VERSION_1_8
        }
        kotlinOptions {
            jvmTarget = "1.8"
        }
        composeOptions {
            //kotlinCompilerExtensionVersion '1.1.1'
            kotlinCompilerExtensionVersion '1.2.0-beta03'
        }
        buildTypes {
            release {
                minifyEnabled false
                proguardFiles getDefaultProguardFile(
                    'proguard-android.txt'), 'proguard-rules.pro'
            }
        }
    }

dependencies {
    implementation "org.jetbrains.kotlin:" +
        "kotlin-stdlib-jdk7:$kotlin_version"
    implementation 'androidx.appcompat:appcompat:1.4.2'
    implementation 'androidx.activity:activity-ktx:1.4.0'
    implementation 'androidx.fragment:fragment-ktx:1.4.1'
    implementation 'com.google.android.material:' +
        'material:1.6.1'
```

```
implementation 'androidx.constraintlayout:' +
    'constraintlayout:2.1.4'
implementation "androidx.datastore:" +
    "datastore-preferences:1.0.0"
implementation "androidx.preference:" +
    "preference-ktx:1.2.0"
testImplementation 'junit:junit:4.13.2'
androidTestImplementation 'androidx.test.ext:' +
    'junit:1.1.3'
androidTestImplementation 'androidx.test.espresso:' +
    'espresso-core:3.4.0'

def lifecycle_version = "2.4.1"

implementation "androidx.lifecycle:" +
    "lifecycle-viewmodel-ktx:$lifecycle_version"
implementation "androidx.lifecycle:" +
    "lifecycle-viewmodel-compose:$lifecycle_version"
implementation "androidx.lifecycle:" +
    "lifecycle-livedata-ktx:$lifecycle_version"
implementation "androidx.lifecycle:" +
    "lifecycle-runtime-ktx:$lifecycle_version"
implementation "androidx.lifecycle:" +
    "lifecycle-viewmodel-savedstate:$lifecycle_version"
implementation "androidx.lifecycle:" +
    "lifecycle-common-java8:$lifecycle_version"

implementation 'androidx.compose.ui:ui:1.1.1'
implementation 'androidx.compose.foundation:' +
    'foundation:1.1.1'
implementation 'androidx.activity:' +
    'activity-compose:1.4.0'
implementation 'androidx.compose.material:' +
    'material:1.1.1'
implementation 'androidx.compose.material:' +
    'material-icons-core:1.1.1'
```

```
    implementation 'androidx.compose.material:' +
        'material-icons-extended:1.1.1'
    implementation 'androidx.compose.animation:' +
        'animation:1.1.1'
    implementation 'androidx.compose.ui:' +
        'ui-tooling:1.1.1'
    implementation 'androidx.lifecycle:' +
        'lifecycle-viewmodel-compose:2.4.1'
    implementation 'androidx.compose.runtime:' +
        'runtime-livedata:1.1.1'
    implementation 'androidx.compose.runtime:' +
        'runtime-rxjava2:1.1.1'
    implementation 'androidx.navigation:' +
        'navigation-compose:2.4.0'
    implementation 'androidx.constraintlayout:' +
        'constraintlayout-compose:1.0.0'
    androidTestImplementation 'androidx.compose.ui:' +
        'ui-test-junit4:1.1.1'
}
```

To start with an example preferences workflow, let your activity class read

```
package com.example.myapp

import android.content.Context
import android.os.Bundle
import androidx.core.app.ActivityCompat
import androidx.core.content.ContextCompat
import androidx.appcompat.app.AppCompatActivity
import androidx.activity.compose.setContent
import androidx.activity.viewModels
import androidx.compose.material.*
import androidx.compose.runtime.*
import androidx.datastore.preferences.preferencesDataStore
import androidx.lifecycle.*
import androidx.navigation.compose.NavHost
import androidx.navigation.compose.composable
```

```
import androidx.navigation.compose.rememberNavController

import com.example.myapp.ui.*
import com.example.myapp.vm.SettingsViewModel

// Add a preferences DataStore to the Context. The
// documentation suggests to do it that way, so we have
// a central single access location.
val Context.settingsDataStore by
    preferencesDataStore(name = "settings")

class MainActivity : AppCompatActivity() {
    ...

    override fun onCreate(savedInstanceState: Bundle?) {
        super.onCreate(savedInstanceState)
        ...

        // view models ------------------------------------
        ...
        // Obtain a ViewModel for the settings. Because we
        // need a context object inside the ViewModel, we
        // must use a ViewModelProvider as shown here
        val settingsViewModel: SettingsViewModel by
        viewModels {
            ViewModelProvider.AndroidViewModelFactory.
            getInstance(application)
        }
        // ------------------------------------------------

        setContent {
            // We are now inside JetPack Compose...
            // First a navigation controller. We use
            // rememberNavController(), so Compose
            // knows about the navigation controller
            // and appropriately handles navigation
            // state changes.
            val navController = rememberNavController()
            ...
```

```
Scaffold(
  topBar = {
    // Indicates whether or not the dropdown
    // menu is shown. Because of remember() the
    // value prevails for recomposition, and
    // because of mutableStateOf() Compose can
    // dynamically react on state changes:
    val displayMenu = remember {
        mutableStateOf(false) }
    TopAppBar(
      title = { Text(...) },
      actions = {
        // Icon button for dropdown menu
        IconButton(onClick = {
            displayMenu.value =
                  !displayMenu.value }) {
          Icon(Icons.Default.MoreVert, "")
        }
        DropdownMenu(
          expanded = displayMenu.value,
          onDismissRequest = {
              displayMenu.value = false }
        ) {
          // A dropdown menu item to navigate
          // to the settings screen:
          DropdownMenuItem(onClick = {
            displayMenu.value = false
            nav.navigate("settings")
          }) {
            Text(text = "Settings")
          }
          ...
        }
      }
    )
  },
```

```
        content = {
            // The content area. We let the navigation
            // controller decide what to show here.
            NavHost(navController = navController,
                    startDestination = "home") {
                composable("home"){
                    // The contents of the "home" screen
                    ...
                }
                ...
                composable("settings"){
                    // The settings screen
                    SettingsScreen(settingsViewModel).make()
                }
            }
        }
    )
    }
}
    ...
}
```

Don't forget to register the activity in the manifest file. In case the rest of your app does not yet use Compose, you still can use the preceding code. Just use a dedicated settings activity, and place the SettingsScreen(...).make() directly inside content = { }.

The SettingsViewModel serves as a holder for preferences, and this is also the place where storing in and retrieving from the preferences database happens:

```
package com.example.myapp.vm

import android.app.Application
import androidx.compose.runtime.getValue
import androidx.compose.runtime.mutableStateOf
import androidx.compose.runtime.setValue
import androidx.compose.runtime.snapshotFlow
import androidx.lifecycle.AndroidViewModel
```

```
import androidx.lifecycle.viewModelScope
import kotlinx.coroutines.flow.*
import kotlinx.coroutines.launch

import com.example.myapp.vm.prefs.Prefs

class SettingsViewModel(application: Application):
    AndroidViewModel(application) {
  private val dataStore = Prefs(application)

  var user by mutableStateOf("")
  var flag by mutableStateOf(false)
  var count by mutableStateOf(0)
  init {
      viewModelScope.launch {
          user = dataStore.loadString("app_user","")
              .first()
          launch { snapshotFlow { user }.onEach {
              dataStore.save("app_user", it) }.collect() }
          flag = dataStore.loadBoolean("app_flag",false)
              .first()
          launch { snapshotFlow { flag }.onEach {
              dataStore.save("app_flag", it) }.collect() }
          count = dataStore.loadInt("app_count","")
              .first()
          launch { snapshotFlow { count }.onEach {
              dataStore.save("app_count", it) }.collect() }

      }
  }
}
```

The launch { snapshotFlow { ... registers an asynchronous handler and makes sure that any value change automatically leads to saving the new value in the preferences DataStore.

The Prefs class is a generic facade for interfering with the DataStore implementation:

```
package com.example.myapp.prefs

import android.content.Context
import androidx.datastore.preferences.core.
    booleanPreferencesKey
import androidx.datastore.preferences.core.
    intPreferencesKey
import androidx.datastore.preferences.core.
    stringPreferencesKey
import androidx.datastore.preferences.core.edit
import kotlinx.coroutines.flow.Flow
import kotlinx.coroutines.flow.first
import kotlinx.coroutines.flow.map
import kotlinx.coroutines.runBlocking

import com.example.myapp.settingsDataStore

class Prefs(val context: Context) {
    suspend fun <T> save(key:String, v: T) {
        context.settingsDataStore.edit { preferences ->
            when(v) {
                is String -> preferences[
                    stringPreferencesKey(key)] =
                        v as String
                is Boolean -> preferences[
                    booleanPreferencesKey(key)] =
                        v as Boolean
                is Int -> preferences[
                    intPreferencesKey(key)] =
                        v as Int
                else -> throw
                  IllegalArgumentException(
                      v!!::class.java.toString())
            }
        }
    }
```

```
    fun loadBoolean(key:String, defVal:Boolean = false)
        : Flow<Boolean> {
    return context.settingsDataStore.data
        .map { preferences ->
            preferences[
                booleanPreferencesKey(key)] ?: defVal
        }
}

    fun loadString(key:String, defVal:String = "")
        : Flow<String> {
    return context.settingsDataStore.data
        .map { preferences ->
            preferences[
                stringPreferencesKey(key)] ?: defVal
        }
}

    fun loadInt(key:String, defVal:Int = 0)
        : Flow<Int> {
    return context.settingsDataStore.data
        .map { preferences ->
            preferences[
                intPreferencesKey(key)] ?: defVal
        }
}

    // Non-coroutines getters
    fun getString(key:String, defVal:String = "") =
        runBlocking { loadString(key, defVal).first() }
    fun getInt(key:String, defVal:Int = 0) =
        runBlocking { loadInt(key, defVal).first() }
    fun getBoolean(key:String, defVal:Boolean = false) =
        runBlocking { loadBoolean(key, defVal).first() }
}
```

The SettingsScreen contains the complete UI for showing and adjusting the preferences:

```
package com.example.myapp.ui

import androidx.compose.foundation.clickable
import androidx.compose.foundation.layout.*
import androidx.compose.foundation.rememberScrollState
import androidx.compose.foundation.verticalScroll
import androidx.compose.material.*
import androidx.compose.material.icons.Icons
import androidx.compose.material.icons.twotone.Help
import androidx.compose.runtime.*
import androidx.compose.ui.Modifier
import androidx.compose.ui.graphics.Color
import androidx.compose.ui.platform.LocalContext
import androidx.compose.ui.res.stringResource
import androidx.compose.ui.text.font.FontWeight
import androidx.compose.ui.unit.dp
import androidx.compose.ui.unit.sp
import androidx.constraintlayout.compose.ConstraintLayout

import com.example.myapp.vm.SettingsViewModel

class SettingsScreen(private val vm: SettingsViewModel) {

    @Composable
    fun make() {
        val ctx = LocalContext.current
        val DROPDOWN_TITLES: Array<String> =
            arrayOf("Item 1", "Item 2")

        var selectMenu by
            remember { mutableStateOf(false) }
        Box(modifier = Modifier.verticalScroll(
            rememberScrollState())) {
            Column {
                // ----------------------------------------
```

```
SectionHeader("Header 1")
// ----------------------------------------
Label("Some String")
TextFieldAndDescription(
    text = vm.someString,
    onValueChange = {
      vm.someString = it },
    description = "Description")
...
Label("Some String")
Box {
    ButtonForDropDown(
        DROPDOWN_TITLES[vm.selector],
        { selectMenu = !selectMenu },
        description = "Description"
    )
    DropdownMenu(expanded = selectMenu,
        onDismissRequest = {
            selectMenu = false }) {
        DROPDOWN_TITLES.forEachIndexed {
            i, s ->
            DropdownMenuItem(onClick = {
                vm.selector = i
                selectMenu = false
            }) {
                Text(s)
            }
        }
    }
}
// ----------------------------------------
SectionHeader( ... )
// ----------------------------------------
...
    }
```

```
    }
}

/////////////////////////////////////////////////////
/////////////////////////////////////////////////////

@Composable
private fun Label(text:String) {
    Spacer(modifier = Modifier.height(5.dp))
    Text(text = text)
}

@Composable
private fun SectionHeader(text:String) {
    Spacer(modifier = Modifier.height(25.dp))
    Text(text = text, fontSize = 20.sp,
        fontWeight = FontWeight.Bold)
}

@Composable
private fun
ButtonForDropDown(text:String, onClick:()->Unit,
    description:String="") {
    ConstraintLayout(modifier =
        Modifier.fillMaxWidth()) {
        var helpShown by
            remember { mutableStateOf(false) }
        val icon = createRef()
        Button( colors = ButtonDefaults.
            buttonColors(
                backgroundColor =
                    Color(200,200,255)),
            modifier = Modifier.fillMaxWidth(),
            onClick = onClick
        ) {
            Text(text = text)
        }
```

```
            Icon(Icons.TwoTone.Help,
                contentDescription = "",
                modifier = Modifier
                  .constrainAs(icon) {
                    top.linkTo(parent.top, margin = 5.dp)
                    end.linkTo(parent.end, margin = 5.dp)
                  }
                  .height(35.dp)
                  .width(35.dp)
                  .clickable { helpShown = true })
            HelpDialog(text = description,
                shown = helpShown,
                onDismiss = { helpShown = false })
        }
    }
}
```

The UI uses a couple of custom Compose components. You can put them alongside the UI class, or even inside it, but since they are of the general-purpose kind of components, you can also place them inside a utilities package:

```
@Composable
fun TextFieldAndDescription(text:String,
    onValueChange: (String) -> Unit = {},
    description: String) {
  ConstraintLayout(modifier = Modifier.fillMaxWidth()) {
    MyBasicTextField(value = text,
        onValueChange = onValueChange)
    var helpShown by remember { mutableStateOf(false) }
    val icon = createRef()
    Icon(Icons.TwoTone.Help, contentDescription = "",
        modifier = Modifier
            .constrainAs(icon) {
                top.linkTo(parent.top, margin = -6.dp)
                end.linkTo(parent.end, margin = 5.dp)
            }
```

```
                .height(33.dp)
                .width(33.dp)
                .clickable { helpShown = true })
        HelpDialog(text = description, shown = helpShown,
            onDismiss = { helpShown = false })
    }
}

@Composable
fun HelpDialog(text:String, shown:Boolean,
      onDismiss:()->Unit) {
    if(shown) {
        AlertDialog(
            onDismissRequest = onDismiss,
            confirmButton = {},
            dismissButton = {},
            text = {
                Text(text = text, fontSize = 17.sp)
            },
            modifier = Modifier
                .fillMaxWidth()
                .fillMaxHeight()
                .padding(10.dp),
            shape = RoundedCornerShape(5.dp),
            backgroundColor = Color.White,
            properties = DialogProperties(
                dismissOnBackPress = true,
                dismissOnClickOutside = true
            )
        )
    }
}

@Composable
fun MyBasicTextField(
    value: String,
```

```
    singleline: Boolean = true,
    onValueChange: (String) -> Unit = {},
    placeholder: String = "",
    keyboardOptions: KeyboardOptions =
        KeyboardOptions.Default,
    keyboardActions: KeyboardActions =
        KeyboardActions.Default,
    onFocusLost: ()->Unit  = {},
    modifier: Modifier = Modifier
){
    BasicTextField(value = value,
        onValueChange = onValueChange,
        singleLine = singleline,
        textStyle = TextStyle.Default.merge(
            TextStyle(fontSize = 18.sp)),
        modifier = modifier
            .padding(horizontal = 5.dp)
            .fillMaxWidth()
            .onFocusChanged { fs->
                if(!fs.isFocused) onFocusLost() },
        decorationBox = { innerTextField ->
            Box(modifier = Modifier
                    .fillMaxWidth()
                    .offset(x = 2.dp),
                contentAlignment = Alignment.CenterStart,
            ) {
                if (value.isEmpty()) {
                    Text(placeholder, fontSize = 18.sp,
                        color = Color.Gray)
                }
                innerTextField()
            }
        },
        keyboardOptions = keyboardOptions,
        keyboardActions = keyboardActions)
}
```

In order to read preferences from inside your app, write

```
val someString = Prefs(context).readString("app_key",
                                            "default")
```

where context could be the activity itself, or LocalContext.current if you are inside a @Composable. The "app_key" corresponds to one of the values used as keys inside SettingsViewModel.

CHAPTER 9

User Interface

The user interface is certainly the most important part of any end user app. For corporate usage apps without user interfaces are of course possible, but even then in most cases, you will have some kind of rudimentary UI, if for no other reason then maybe just to avoid the Android OS to kill your app too readily during resource housekeeping tasks.

In this chapter we will not cover the basics of UI development for Android – instead, it is expected you've read some introductory-level book or worked through the official tutorials or any number of the other tutorials you will find on the Web. What we do here is to cover a couple of important UI-related issues, which help you create more stable apps or apps with special outstanding requirements.

Background Tasks

Android relies on a single-threaded execution model. This means when an app starts, it by default starts only a single thread, called the main thread, in which all actions run unless you explicitly use background threads for certain tasks. Talking of user experience, this automatically means you have to take special precautions if you have long-running tasks that would interrupt a fluent UI workflow. It is just not acceptable for modern apps that the UI freezes after the user presses a button, just because this action leads to a process running for a few seconds or longer. It is therefore vital to put long-running tasks into the background.

One way to accomplish putting things into the background is using `IntentService` objects as described in section "Service Subclasses" of Chapter 4. Depending on circumstances it might however blow up your app design to put all background work into services, and having too many services run on a device will not help keep resource usage low. For low-level tasks, it is therefore better to use a more low-level approach. You have several options here, which we describe in the following sections.

257

© Peter Späth 2022
P. Späth, *Pro Android with Kotlin*, https://doi.org/10.1007/978-1-4842-8745-3_9

Java Concurrency

On a very low level, you can use Java threads and classes from the `java.util.`
`concurrent` package to handle background jobs. Beginning with Java 7, those classes
have become quite powerful, but it needs some time to fully understand all options and
implications.

You will quite often read that directly handling threads from inside the Android OS is
not a good idea because threads are expensive in terms of system resources. While this
was certainly true for older devices and old Android versions, nowadays this is just no
longer the case. A simple test on a Motorola Moto G4 starting 1000 threads and waiting
until all were running took approximately 0.0006 seconds per thread. So if you are used
to Java threads and less than a millisecond for the thread to start is good for you, there is
no performance reason for not using Java threads. However, you must take into account
that threads run outside any Android component lifecycle, so you have to handle
lifecycle issues manually if you use threads.

In Kotlin threads are defined and started easily:

```
val t = Thread{ ->
  // do background work...
}.also { it.start() }
```

Note   To just access the UI from inside a thread is not allowed in Android. You
must do that as follows:

```
val t = Thread{ ->
  // do background work...
  runOnUiThread {
    // use the UI...
  }
}.also { it.start() }
```

The AsyncTask Class

An AsyncTask object is a medium-level helper class to run some code in the background. You override its doInBackground() method to do some background work, and if you need to communicate with the UI, you also implement onProgressUpdate() to do the communication and fire publishProgress() from inside the background work to trigger it.

   AsyncTasks are deprecated starting with Android 11. We mention it here because of its widespread use.

> **Note**   Android Studio will as a warning complain about a possible memory leak if you create AsyncTask objects like val at = object : AsyncTask< Int, Int, Int >() { ... }. This is because internally a static reference to the background code will be held. The warning can be suppressed by annotating the method with @SuppressLint("StaticFieldLeak").

> **Caution**   A number of N AsyncTask jobs will not lead to a parallel execution of all N of them – instead they all run sequentially in *one* background thread.

Handlers

A Handler is an object maintaining a message queue for asynchronous processing of messages or Runnable objects. You can use a Handler for asynchronous processes as follows:

```
var handlerThread : HandlerThread? = null
// or: lateinit var handlerThread : HandlerThread
...
fun doSomething() {
  handlerThread = handlerThread ?:
        HandlerThread("MyHandlerThread").apply {
    start()
  }
  val handler = Handler(handlerThread?.looper)
```

```
handler.post {
  // do s.th. in background
  }
}
```

If you create one HandlerThread as in this code snippet, everything that is posted gets run in the background, but there executed sequentially. This means a handler. post{} ; handler.post{} will run the posts in series. You can however create more HandlerThread objects to handle the posts in parallel. For a true parallelism, you'd have to use one HandlerThread for each execution.

Note   Handlers had been introduced in Android a long time before the new java. util.concurrent package came up in Java 7. Nowadays for your own code, you might decide to favor the generic Java classes over Handlers without missing anything. Handlers however quite often show up in Android's libraries.

Loaders

Loaders also do their work in the background – they are primarily used for loading data from an external source.

Loaders are deprecated starting with API level 28. You should now use ViewModels and LiveData for background loading purposes – see in the following. We mention loaders here for completeness and because of their widespread use.

Coroutines

Coroutines are Kotlin's answer to non-preemptive background processing. If you are used to Java's preemptive concurrency and to Android's AsyncTasks, handlers, and loaders, understanding how coroutines work takes some time.

We don't give a thorough introduction into coroutines at this place, since it somewhat imposes a major paradigm change and fully incorporating coroutines into your code is a complex task and requires extensively using the libraries provided by Jetpack, which is out of scope for this edition of the book. It is however in the pipeline of anticipated updates for a third edition to come up. For now please visit https:// developer.android.com/kotlin/coroutines and https://kotlinlang.org/docs/ coroutines-overview.html.

Just as an appetizer, consider inside a `ViewModel` (you use a ViewModel as a data holder for UI-related classes) you want to send some IO-related task to the background. With coroutines you can write as follows:

```
class MyViewModel(): ViewModel() {
    fun doSomething() {
        // Create a coroutine to move the execution off
        // the UI thread
        viewModelScope.launch(Dispatchers.IO) {
            // do some background work...
        }
    }
}
```

Here the `viewModelScope` (from the base class) is a contextual object especially suited for background processing in ViewModels, and `Dispatchers.IO` expresses the need for IO-related background process housekeeping. You can see that configuring executors or handlers or whatever is needed for controlling the concurrency is left to the framework and thus not part of our code, which is what *non-preemptive* actually means.

Loading Data in ViewModels

Asynchronously loading external data in ViewModels best happens based on a combination of coroutines and LiveData. While far away from a complete fits-all example, consider a ViewModel for preferences:

```
import android.content.Context
import androidx.datastore.preferences.preferencesDataStore
import androidx.lifecycle.*
import android.app.Application
import androidx.compose.runtime.getValue
import androidx.compose.runtime.mutableStateOf
import androidx.compose.runtime.setValue
import androidx.compose.runtime.snapshotFlow
import kotlinx.coroutines.flow.*
import kotlinx.coroutines.launch
import androidx.datastore.preferences.core.edit
```

```
import androidx.datastore.preferences.core.
    stringPreferencesKey
import kotlinx.coroutines.runBlocking

// A central "singleton" DataStore. You maybe put this
// alongside (not inside) the main Activity.
val Context.settingsDataStore by
    preferencesDataStore(name = "settings")

// A wrapper for using the settings datastore
class Prefs(val context: Context) {
    suspend fun <T> save(key:String, v: T) {
        context.settingsDataStore.edit { preferences ->
            when(v) {
                is String -> preferences[
                    stringPreferencesKey(key)] =
                        v as String
                else -> throw IllegalArgumentException(
                    v!!::class.java.toString())
            }
        }
    }

    fun loadString(key:String, defVal:String = "")
            : Flow<String> {
        return context.settingsDataStore.data
            .map { preferences ->
                preferences[stringPreferencesKey(key)]
                    ?: defVal
            }
    }

    // Non-coroutines getter. For use outside of Coroutines
    fun getString(key:String, defVal:String = "") =
        runBlocking { loadString(key, defVal).first() }
}
```

```
// A ViewModel. You use this in client code to read
// (and write) preferences.
class SettingsViewModel(application: Application):
     AndroidViewModel(application) {
   private val dataStore = Prefs(application)

   // Because of mutableStateOf(""), this is an observed
   // variable
   var someString by mutableStateOf("")

   init {
       viewModelScope.launch {
           // async loading from the datastore
           someString = dataStore.loadString(
               "some_string","").first()
           // automatically save changes to the datastore
           launch { snapshotFlow { someString }.onEach {
               dataStore.save("some_string", it) }.
                   collect() }
       }
   }
}
```

The suspend inside suspend fun <T> save() (class Prefs) makes sure that saving preferences, for example, in a preferences screen, happens asynchronously. The counterpart for loading preferences, loadString(...), returns a Flow<String>, which is the coroutines' way of saying something that eventually evaluates to a string, available in coroutines for asynchronously getting values. For the other constructs, see the inline comments.

Supporting Multiple Devices

Device compatibility is an important issue for apps. Whenever you create an app, it is of course your goal to address as many device configurations as possible and to make sure users who install your app on a certain device can actually use it. Compatibility boils down to

- Finding a way your app can run with different screen capabilities, including pixel width, pixel height, pixel density, color space, and screen shape

- Finding a way your app can run with different API versions

- Finding a way your app can run with different hardware features, including sensors and keyboards

- Finding a way you can filter your app's visibility inside the Google Play Store

- Possibly providing different APKs for one app, depending on device features

In this chapter we talk about UI-related issues for compatibility, that is, we focus on screen and user input capabilities.

Screen Sizes

To allow your app looking nice on different screen sizes, you have the following measures at hand:

- **Use flexible layouts.**

  Avoid specifying absolute positions and absolute width. Instead, use layouts that allow specifications like "on the right of" or "use half of the available space" or similar.

- **Use alternative layouts.**

  Using alternative layouts is a very powerful means for supplying different screen sizes. The layout XML files can be put into different directories with names containing size filters. For example, you could put one layout into the file `res/layout/main_activity.xml` and another one into `res/layout-sw480dp/main_activity.xml` expressing a "smallest width" of 480 dp (large phone screens 5" or higher). The naming schema gets extensively described online in the "Providing Resources" and "Providing Alternative Resources" documents, respectively, from inside the Android developer documentation. The Android OS then automatically picks the best matching layout at runtime on the user's device.

- **Use stretchable images.**

  You can provide *nine-patch* bitmaps for UI elements. Inside such images you provide a one-pixel-wide border telling which parts of an image can be repeated to stretch an image and optionally which parts can be used for inner contents. Such nine-patch images are PNG files with the suffix `.9.png`. Android Studio allows for converting conventional PNGs into nine-patch PNGs – use the context menu for that purpose.

Pixel Densities

Devices have different pixel densities. To make your app as device independent as possible, wherever you need pixel sizes, use *density-independent pixel* sizes instead of *pixel sizes*. Density-independent pixel sizes use "dp" as a unit, while pixels use "px".

Besides that, you can also provide different layout files based on different densities – the separation is similar to the separation for different screen sizes described previously.

Declare Restricted Screen Support

In some situations you want to restrict your app by saying that some screen characteristics just cannot be used. Obviously you want to avoid such situations, but in case it is inevitable, you can inside `AndroidManifest.xml`

- Tell the app certain activities can run in multi-window modes available in API level 24 (Android 7.0) or later. For that aim use attribute `android:resizeableActivity` and set it to "true" or "false."

- Tell certain activities should be letter-boxed (margins added accordingly) above certain aspect ratios. For that aim use attribute `android:maxAspectRatio` and specify the aspect ratio as a value. For Android 7.1 and lower, duplicate this setting inside the `<application>` element as in `<meta-data android:name = "android.max_aspect" android:value = "s.th." />`.

- Tell certain activities should not be stretched above a certain limit by using the largestWidthLimitDp attribute inside a <supports-screens> element.

- Use more <supports-screens> and <compatible-screens> elements and attributes as described in Chapter 2.

Detect Device Capabilities

From inside your app, you can check for certain features like in

```
if(packageManager.
    hasSystemFeature(PackageManager.FEATURE_...)) {
  // ...
}
```

where "FEATURE_..." is one of the various constants from inside PackageManager.

An additional source of feature information is the Configuration. In Kotlin from inside an activity, you can obtain the configuration object via

```
val conf = resources.configuration
```

and from there obtain information about the color mode in use, available keyboards, the screen orientation, and touchscreen capabilities. To get the screen's size, you can write

```
val size = Point()
windowManager.defaultDisplay.getSize(size)
// or (getSystemService(Context.WINDOW_SERVICE)
//    as WindowManager).defaultDisplay.getSize(size)
val (width,height) = Pair(size.x, size.y)
```

and to get the resolution

```
val metrics = DisplayMetrics()
windowManager.defaultDisplay.getMetrics(metrics)
val density = metrics.density
```

Programmatic UI Design

Usually UI design happens by declaring UI objects (`View` objects) and containers (`ViewGroup` objects) inside one or more XML layout files. While this is the suggested way of designing a UI and most people probably tell you, you shouldn't do anything else, there are reasons to take away the layout design from XML and do a programmatic layout instead:

- You need more dynamics on a layout. For example, your app adds, removes, or moves layout elements by user actions. Or you want to create a game with game elements represented by `View` objects, which are dynamically moving, appearing, and disappearing.

- Your layout is defined on a server. Especially in a corporate environment, defining the layout on a server makes sense – whenever the layout of an app changes, you don't need a new version to be installed on all devices. Instead, only a central layout engine needs to be updated.

- You define a layout builder that allows to specify layouts in Kotlin in a way more expressive and concise compared with XML. Think of, for example

```
LinearLayout(orientation="vertical") {
  TextView(id="tv1",
        width="match_parent", height="wrap_content")
  Button(id="btn1", text="Go",
        onClick = { btn1Clicked() })
}
```

which is valid Kotlin syntax.

- You need special constructs that are not defined in XML. While the standard way is to define in XML as much as possible and do the rest in the code, you might want to prefer a single-technology solution, and in this case you have to do all from inside the code.

> **Note**   Using Jetpack Compose is an extremely good way of programmatically building layouts. See in the following and the documentation in order to find out how to do that.

Note that if you abandon descriptive layouting via XML files and use programmatic layouting instead, you manually have to take care of different screen sizes, screen densities, and other hardware characteristics. While this is always possible, it under circumstances could be a complicated and error-prone procedure. Certain characteristics like UI element sizes can be much more easily expressed in XML than in the code.

Adding Views Manually

In order to start with a programmatic UI design, it is the easiest if you define a single container inside XML and use this in your code. I say deliberately simple, because layouts have their own idea how and when to place their children, so you might end up in a nightmare of timing, layout, and clipping issues if your code has another idea how and when to place views. A good candidate is a FrameLayout, and you can write

```
<?xml version="1.0" encoding="utf-8"?>
<FrameLayout
  xmlns:android =
        "http://schemas.android.com/apk/res/android"
  android:id="@+id/fl"
  android:layout_width="match_parent"
  android:layout_height="match_parent">
</FrameLayout>
```

as a layout XML, say /res/layout/activity_main.xml, and

```
class MainActivity : AppCompatActivity() {
  var tv:TextView? = null
  override fun onCreate(savedInstanceState: Bundle?) {
      super.onCreate(savedInstanceState)
      setContentView(R.layout.activity_main)
```

```
    // For example add a text at a certain position
    tv = TextView(this).apply {
        text = "Dynamic"
        x = 37.0f
        y = 100.0f
    }
    fl.addView(tv)
  }
}
```

as a sample activity. To, for example, add a button that shifts the text from the preceding example around, you can write

```
val WRAP = ViewGroup.LayoutParams(
            ViewGroup.LayoutParams.WRAP_CONTENT,
            ViewGroup.LayoutParams.WRAP_CONTENT)
fl.addView(
    Button(this).apply {
        text = "Go"
        setOnClickListener { v ->
          v?.run {
            x += 30.0f *
                (-0.5f + Math.random().toFloat())
            y += 30.0f *
                (-0.5f + Math.random().toFloat())
          }
        }
    }, WRAP
)
```

If you don't need total control and want a layout object to do its child positioning and sizing job the way it is designed, adding children to other layout types, like a LinearLayout, is of course also possible from inside the code. Just use the addView() method without explicitly setting the position via setX() or setY(). Under circumstances you must use layoutObject.invalidate() to trigger a re-layouting afterward. The latter has to be done from inside the UI thread or else inside a runOnUiThread{ ... }.

Using Jetpack Compose Builders

Android Jetpack is a very ambitious project inside Android's technology universe. It serves as an umbrella for libraries simplifying a developer's work and improving code quality with respect to best practices and embracing Kotlin as a source for writing elegant code.

The reason we didn't talk about Jetpack earlier in this book is the mere size of the Jetpack library collection – Jetpack could very well be the subject of another book. Besides, Jetpack's approach for a front-end design somewhat contradicts the basic idea for screen transitions being described by switching from one activity to another. Well, to be honest the pre-Jetpack methodology already contained something similar called *fragments*, which simplified the redrawing of screen parts inside one activity. Jetpack's UI technology, called *Jetpack Compose*, just follows this trail to a genuine single-activity approach. In addition, Jetpack heavily concentrates on functions instead of classes, somewhat leaving the realm of object-oriented design. This has advantages and disadvantages – with Jetpack it is possible to more readily obtain a working front end, but the code is not that easy to understand, because functions are not that easily recognizable as belonging to a class describing a unique concern.

Nevertheless, in this section we investigate a Jetpack Compose–based front-end design example, without describing all functionalities Jetpack has to offer. You are asked to study the online documentation at `https://developer.android.com/jetpack/`, to learn more about the other libraries included within Jetpack.

We start with the two build files necessary to declare the dependencies:

```
// ---------- Project build.gradle ----------
buildscript {
    ext.kotlin_version = '1.6.21'
    repositories {
        google()
        mavenCentral()
    }
    dependencies {
        classpath 'com.android.tools.build:gradle:7.2.1'
        classpath "org.jetbrains.kotlin:" +
            "kotlin-gradle-plugin:$kotlin_version"
    }
```

```
}

allprojects {
    repositories {
        google()
        mavenCentral()
    }
}
// ---------- Module build.gradle ----------
plugins {
    id 'com.android.application'
    id 'kotlin-android'
    id 'kotlin-kapt'
}
android {
    compileSdkVersion 32
    defaultConfig {
        applicationId "com.example.myapp"
        minSdkVersion 23
        targetSdkVersion 32
        versionCode 1
        versionName "1.0"
        testInstrumentationRunner ""+
            'androidx.test.runner.AndroidJUnitRunner'
    }
    buildFeatures {
        // Enables Jetpack Compose for this module
        compose true
    }
    compileOptions {
        sourceCompatibility JavaVersion.VERSION_1_8
        targetCompatibility JavaVersion.VERSION_1_8
    }
    kotlinOptions {
        jvmTarget = "1.8"
```

```
    }
    composeOptions {
        //kotlinCompilerExtensionVersion '1.1.1'
        kotlinCompilerExtensionVersion '1.2.0-beta03'
    }
    buildTypes {
        release {
            minifyEnabled false
            proguardFiles getDefaultProguardFile(
                'proguard-android.txt'), 'proguard-rules.pro'
        }
    }
}

dependencies {
    implementation "org.jetbrains.kotlin:" +
        "kotlin-stdlib-jdk7:$kotlin_version"
    implementation 'androidx.appcompat:appcompat:1.4.2'
    implementation 'androidx.activity:activity-ktx:1.4.0'
    implementation 'androidx.fragment:fragment-ktx:1.4.1'
    implementation 'com.google.android.material:' +
        'material:1.6.1'
    implementation 'androidx.constraintlayout:' +
        'constraintlayout:2.1.4'
    implementation 'com.jakewharton.timber:timber:5.0.1'
    implementation "androidx.datastore:" +
        "datastore-preferences:1.0.0"
    implementation "androidx.preference:" +
        "preference-ktx:1.2.0"
    testImplementation 'junit:junit:4.13.2'
    androidTestImplementation 'androidx.test.ext:' +
        'junit:1.1.3'
    androidTestImplementation 'androidx.test.espresso:' +
        'espresso-core:3.4.0'

    def lifecycle_version = "2.4.1"
```

```
implementation "androidx.lifecycle:" +
    "lifecycle-viewmodel-ktx:$lifecycle_version"
implementation "androidx.lifecycle:" +
    "lifecycle-viewmodel-compose:$lifecycle_version"
implementation "androidx.lifecycle:" +
    "lifecycle-livedata-ktx:$lifecycle_version"
implementation "androidx.lifecycle:" +
    "lifecycle-runtime-ktx:$lifecycle_version"
implementation "androidx.lifecycle:" +
    "lifecycle-viewmodel-savedstate:$lifecycle_version"
implementation "androidx.lifecycle:" +
    "lifecycle-common-java8:$lifecycle_version"
implementation 'androidx.compose.ui:ui:1.1.1'
implementation 'androidx.compose.foundation:' +
    'foundation:1.1.1'
implementation 'androidx.activity:' +
    'activity-compose:1.4.0'
implementation 'androidx.compose.material:' +
    'material:1.1.1'
implementation 'androidx.compose.material:' +
    'material-icons-core:1.1.1'
implementation 'androidx.compose.material:' +
    'material-icons-extended:1.1.1'
implementation 'androidx.compose.animation:' +
    'animation:1.1.1'
implementation 'androidx.compose.ui:ui-tooling:1.1.1'
implementation 'androidx.lifecycle:' +
    'lifecycle-viewmodel-compose:2.4.1'
implementation 'androidx.compose.runtime:' +
    'runtime-livedata:1.1.1'
implementation 'androidx.compose.runtime:' +
    'runtime-rxjava2:1.1.1'
implementation "androidx.navigation:" +
    "navigation-compose:2.4.0"
androidTestImplementation 'androidx.compose.ui:' +
```

```
        'ui-test-junit4:1.1.1'
    implementation "androidx.constraintlayout:" +
        "constraintlayout-compose:1.0.0"
}
```

We start with the main activity, which serves as a container for UI units, in Jetpack Compose called *composables*. A navigation controller, also provided by Jetpack Compose, switches between different screens, so a single activity is all we need even for a more complex app:

```
import android.content.Context
import android.content.pm.PackageManager
import android.os.Bundle
import androidx.core.app.ActivityCompat
import androidx.core.content.ContextCompat
import androidx.appcompat.app.AppCompatActivity
import androidx.activity.compose.setContent
import androidx.activity.viewModels
import androidx.compose.material.*
import androidx.compose.runtime.*
import androidx.lifecycle.*
import androidx.navigation.compose.NavHost
import androidx.navigation.compose.composable
import androidx.navigation.compose.rememberNavController

class MainActivity : AppCompatActivity() {
    override fun onCreate(savedInstanceState: Bundle?) {
        super.onCreate(savedInstanceState)

        // view models -----------------------------------
        val homeViewModel: HomeViewModel by viewModels()
        ...
        // -----------------------------------------------

        setContent {
          val navController = rememberNavController()
          val topBar by remember { mutableStateOf(
              MyTopBar(navController, this)) }
```

```
        val startDestination = "home"

        Scaffold(
          topBar = { topBar.make() },
          content = {
            NavHost(navController = navController,
                  startDestination = startDestination) {
              composable("home"){
                  HomeScreen(homeViewModel,
                      navController).make()
              }
              composable("otherScreen"){
                  ...
              }
              ...
            }
          }
        )
      }
    }
}
```

The "remember" and "mutableStateOf" constructs for navController and topBar
are important, because they make sure a variable's state survives recomposition because
of UI state changes and they take care of UI updates that happen, for example, if the
value of a text field changes (see the following listings).

Class MyTopBar is responsible for the top action bar's content:

```
import android.app.Activity
import android.content.Context
import android.content.DialogInterface
import androidx.compose.material.*
import androidx.compose.material.icons.Icons
import androidx.compose.material.icons.filled.MoreVert
import androidx.compose.runtime.*
import androidx.compose.ui.platform.LocalContext
import androidx.navigation.NavHostController
```

```kotlin
class MyTopBar(private val nav:NavHostController,
      private val activity:Activity) {
   // A boolean variable to store the display menu state
   private lateinit var displayMenu:MutableState<Boolean>

   @Composable
   fun make() {
      displayMenu = remember { mutableStateOf(false) }

      // fetching local context
      val context = LocalContext.current

      TopAppBar(
         title = { Text("My App") },
         actions = {
            // Icon button for dropdown menu
            IconButton(onClick = { displayMenu.value =
                  !displayMenu.value }) {
               Icon(Icons.Default.MoreVert, "")
            }

            DropdownMenu(
               expanded = displayMenu.value,
               onDismissRequest = {
                  displayMenu.value = false }
            ) {

               DropdownMenuItem(onClick = {
                  displayMenu.value = false
                  nav.navigate("settings")
               }) {
                  Text(text = "Settings")
               }

               ... more items
            }
         }
      )
```

```
        }
}
```

Because of the `mutableStateOf()` while defining `displayMenu`, the dropdown menu automatically reacts and updates its UI as soon as the value of `displayMenu` changes.

A starting point for the HomeScreen could read as follows:

```
import androidx.compose.material.Button
import androidx.compose.material.Text
import androidx.compose.material.TextField
import androidx.compose.runtime.*
import androidx.navigation.NavHostController

class HomeScreen(
    private val vm: HomeViewModel,
    private val navController: NavHostController
) {

    @Composable
    fun make() {
        Column {
            Text(text = vm.text1)
            TextField(value = vm.text2,
                onValueChange = {
                vm.text2 = it } )
        }
    }
}
```

And a simple ViewModel for now contains just the two string variables `text1` and `text2`:

```
import androidx.compose.runtime.*
import androidx.lifecycle.ViewModel

class HomeViewModel : ViewModel() {
    var text1 by mutableStateOf("Hello")
    var text2 by mutableStateOf("")
}
```

In an elaborated app, the ViewModel would also be the place where you initialize and persist values using some kind of external storage, like a Room database.

Adapters and List Controls

The need to display a list with a variable number of items happens quite often, especially in a corporate environment. While `AdapterView` and `Adapter` objects with various subclasses have been around for a while, we concentrate on the relatively new and high-performing *recycler views*. You will see that with Kotlin's conciseness, implementing a recycler view happens in a very elegant and comprehensive manner.

The basic idea is as follows: you have an array or a list or another collection of data items, maybe from a database, and you want to send them to a single UI element that does all the presentation, including rendering all visible items and providing a scroll facility if necessary. Each item's presentation either should depend on an *item* XML layout file or could be generated dynamically from inside the code. The mapping from each data item's member to the corresponding view element from inside the item's UI representation is to be handled by an *adapter* object.

With recycler views this all happens in a straightforward manner, but first we have to include a support library, because the recycler views are not part of the framework. To do so, inside your *module*'s `build.gradle`, add

```
implementation
        'com.android.support:recyclerview-v7:26.1.0'
```

inside the `dependencies{ ... }` section (one line – remove the newline after "implementation").

To tell the app we want to use a recycler view, inside your activity's layout file, add

```
<android.support.v7.widget.RecyclerView
    android:id="@+id/recycler_view"
    android:scrollbars="vertical"
    ... />
```

and specify its layouting options as for any other `View`.

For the layouting of an item from the list, create another layout file inside `res/layout`, say `item.xml`, with sample content:

```xml
<?xml version="1.0" encoding="utf-8"?>
<RelativeLayout xmlns:android="http://schemas.android.com/apk/res/android"
                android:layout_width="fill_parent"
                android:layout_height="?android:attr/
                listPreferredItemHeight"
                android:padding="8dip" >

    <ImageView
        android:id="@+id/icon"
        android:layout_width="wrap_content"
        android:layout_height="fill_parent"
        android:layout_alignParentBottom="true"
        android:layout_alignParentTop="true"
        android:layout_marginRight="8dip"
        android:contentDescription="TODO"
        android:src="@android:drawable/star_big_on" />

    <TextView
        android:id="@+id/secondLine"
        android:layout_width="fill_parent"
        android:layout_height="26dip"
        android:layout_alignParentBottom="true"
        android:layout_alignParentRight="true"
        android:layout_toRightOf="@id/icon"
        android:singleLine="true"
        android:text="Description"
        android:textSize="12sp" />

    <TextView
        android:id="@+id/firstLine"
        android:layout_width="fill_parent"
        android:layout_height="wrap_content"
        android:layout_above="@id/secondLine"
        android:layout_alignParentRight="true"
        android:layout_alignParentTop="true"
        android:layout_alignWithParentIfMissing="true"
        android:layout_toRightOf="@id/icon"
```

```
        android:gravity="center_vertical"
        android:text="Example application"
        android:textSize="16sp" />
</RelativeLayout>
```

As stated previously, you could also omit this step and define an item's layout solely from inside the code! Next, we provide an adapter. In Kotlin this could be as easy as

```kotlin
class MyAdapter(val myDataset:Array<String>) :
    RecyclerView.Adapter
            <MyAdapter.Companion.ViewHolder>() {
  companion object {
    class ViewHolder(val v:RelativeLayout) :
        RecyclerView.ViewHolder(v)
  }

  override
  fun onCreateViewHolder(parent:ViewGroup,
        viewType:Int) : ViewHolder {
    val v = LayoutInflater.from(parent.context)
            .inflate(R.layout.item, parent, false)
        as RelativeLayout
    return ViewHolder(v)
  }

  override
  fun onBindViewHolder(holder:ViewHolder,
                    position:Int) {
    // replace the contents of the view with
    // the element at this position
    holder.v.findViewById<TextView>(
        R.id.firstLine).text =
        myDataset[position]
  }

  override
  fun getItemCount() : Int = myDataset.size
}
```

Here are a couple of notes on that listing:

- The class inside "companion object" is the Kotlin way of declaring a static inner class. This one designates a reference to each data item as a UI element. More precisely, the recycler view will internally hold only so many view holders as are necessary to represent the *visible* items.

- Only when really needed the function onCreateViewHolder() to create a view holder gets called – more precisely, more or less only as often as is necessary to render the items visible to the user.

- The function onBindViewHolder() connects one of the visible view holders with a certain data item. Here we must replace the contents of a view holder's view.

Inside the activity all that is needed to define the recycler view is

```
with(recycler_view) {
    // use this setting to improve performance if you know
    // that changes in content do not change the layout
    // size of the RecyclerView
    setHasFixedSize(true)
    // use for example a linear layout manager
    layoutManager = LinearLayoutManager(this@MainActivity)
    // specify the adapter, use some sample data
    val dataset = (1..21).map { "Itm" + it }.toTypedArray()
    adapter = MyAdapter(dataset)
}
```

This will look like that shown in Figure 9-1. Useful extensions to the program are the following:

- Add on-click listeners to all items.

- Make items selectable.

- Make items or item parts editable.

- Automatically react to changes in the underlying data.

- Tailor graphical transition effects.

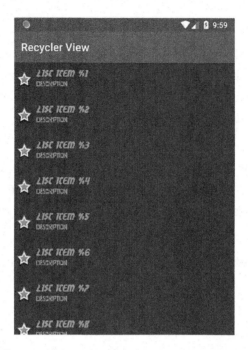

Figure 9-1. *Recycler View*

For all that I refer to the online documentation of recycler views. The code presented here however should give you a good starting point.

Styles and Themes

The predefined styles an Android app uses by default already give a good starting point for professionally looking apps. If however you want to apply your company's style guidelines or otherwise create a visually outstanding app, creating your own styles is worth the effort. Or even better, create your own theme, which is a collection of styles to be applied to groups of UI elements.

Styles and themes get created inside `res/values/` as XML files. To make a new theme, you use or create a file `themes.xml` and write something like

```xml
<?xml version="1.0" encoding="utf-8"?>
<resources>
  <style name="MyTheme" parent="Theme.AppCompat">
      <item name="colorPrimary">
            @color/colorPrimary</item>
```

```
<item name="colorPrimaryDark">
    @color/colorPrimaryDark</item>
<item name="colorAccent">
    @color/colorAccent</item>
<item name="android:textColor">
    #FF0000</item>
<item name="android:textSize">
    22sp</item>
  </style>
</resources>
```

Here are a couple of notes on that:

- The "parent" attribute is important. It expresses that we want to create a theme overriding parts of the "Theme.AppCompat" theme from the compatibility library.

- Because of the naming schema "Theme" + DOT + "AppCompat", we can infer that the theme "Theme.AppCompat" inherits from theme "Theme". This dot-induced inheritance could have more elements.

- Instead of the parent "Theme.AppCompat", we could use one of its sub-themes. You can see a list of them if inside Android Studio, you click the "AppCompat" part and then press Ctrl+B. Android Studio will open a file with the list of all sub-themes, for example, "Theme. AppCompat.CompactMenu", "Theme.AppCompat.Light", and more.

- In the example we see two methods to overwrite styles: Those with "android:" at the beginning refer to style settings as defined for UI elements the same way as if we wanted to set styles from inside a layout file. You find all of them in the online API documentation for all the views. Better however, you use those without "android:" at the beginning, for those refer to abstract style identifiers that actually make up a theme. You get a list of possible item names if inside the online documentation you search for "R.styleable.Theme".

- The styling system has become complex over the years – if you are brave and have some time, you can inside Android Studio navigate through all files by repeatedly pressing Ctrl+B on the parents.

- The "@color/..." refer to entries inside "res/values/colors.xml" files – you should adopt that method and define new colors in your app module's "res/values/colors.xml" file.

- The values of `<item>` elements can refer to styles via "@style/...", for example, the item `<item name="buttonStyle">@style/Widget. AppCompat.Button</item>`. You can overwrite such items as well – just define your own styles in `styles.xml` and refer to them.

In order to use that new theme for your whole app at once, you write in the manifest file `AndroidManifest.xml`

```
<manifest ... >
  <application android:theme="@style/MyTheme" ... >
  </application>
</manifest>
```

Note   You don't have to use a complete theme to overwrite styles – instead, you can overwrite or create single styles you can then apply to single widgets. Using a theme however greatly improves the design consistency of your app.

You can assign styles to different API levels. For that aim, for example, create a folder `res/values-v21/` or any level number that suits you. Styles from inside there then get applied *additionally* if the current API level is *greater than or equal to* that number.

Fonts in XML

Android starting at API level 26 (Android 8.0) and also prior versions if using the support library 26 allow you to add your own fonts in TTF or OTF format.

Note   To use this support library, inside your module's `build.gradle` file, add `implementation 'com.android.support:appcompat-v7:26.1.0'` inside the "dependencies" section.

To add font files, create a font resource directory: select New ➤ Android resource directory, then enter "font" as a directory name and "font" as a resource type, and press OK. Copy your font files to that new resource directory, but first convert all file names to only contain characters from "a to z and 0 to 9_" before the suffix.

To apply the new font, use the `android:fontFamily` attribute as, for example, in

```
<TextView ...
  android:fontFamily="@font/<FONT_NAME>"
/>
```

where <FONT_NAME> is the file name of the font without suffix.

To add fonts with different font styles, say you have a `myfont_regular.ttf`, a `myfont_bold.ttf`, a `myfont_italic.ttf`, and a `myfont_bold_italic.ttf` inside the font resource folder, add a file `myfont.xml` by choosing New ➤ Font resource file. Inside write

```
<?xml version="1.0" encoding="utf-8"?>
<font-family
    xmlns:android=
        "http://schemas.android.com/apk/res/android"
    xmlns:app=
        "http://schemas.android.com/apk/res-auto">
  <font
            android:fontStyle="normal"
            app:fontStyle="normal"
            android:fontWeight="400"
            app:fontWeight="400"
            android:font="@font/myfont_regular"
            app:font="@font/myfont_regular"/>
  <font
            android:fontStyle="normal"
            app:fontStyle="normal"
            android:fontWeight="700"
            app:fontWeight="700"
            android:font="@font/myfont_bold"
            app:font="@font/myfont_bold"/>
  <font
            android:fontStyle="italic"
```

285

```
            app:fontStyle="italic"
            android:fontWeight="400"
            app:fontWeight="400"
            android:font="@font/myfont_italic"
            app:font="@font/myfont_italic"/>
    <font
            android:fontStyle="italic"
            app:fontStyle="italic"
            android:fontWeight="700"
            app:fontWeight="700"
            android:font="@font/myfont_bold_italic"
            app:font="@font/myfont_bold_italic"/>
</font-family>
```

and ignore Android Studio's version warning – for compatibility all attributes use a standard and additionally a compatibility namespace.

Then you can use the name of this XML file, without the suffix, for UI views inside the "android:fontFamily" attribute:

```
<TextView ...
    android:fontFamily="@font/myfont"
    android:textStyle="normal"
/>
```

As "textStyle" you could now also use "italic" or "bold" or "bold|italic".

2D Animation

Animation makes your apps look more fancy, and while too much animation might look kinky, the right amount of it helps your users understand what your app does.

The Android OS provides several animation techniques you can use, and we describe them in the following sections.

Auto-animating Layouts

A very easy way to add animation is using the built-in automatic animation for layouts. All you have to do is add android:animateLayoutChanges="true" to the layout declaration, for example

```
<LinearLayout
  ...
  android:animateLayoutChanges="true"
  ...
/>
```

Animated Bitmaps

You can add animation to bitmaps by providing a number of different versions of a bitmap and letting Android switch between them. First, add all the images to res/ drawable, for example, img1.png, img2.png, ..., img9.png. Then create a file inside the same folder named, for example, anim.xml and inside write

```
<?xml version="1.0" encoding="utf-8"?>
<animation-list
      xmlns:android=
        "http://schemas.android.com/apk/res/android"
      android:oneshot="false">
  <item android:drawable="@drawable/img1"
      android:duration="250" />
  <item android:drawable="@drawable/img2"
      android:duration="250" />
  ...
  <item android:drawable="@drawable/img9"
      android:duration="250" />
</animation-list>
```

where the duration for each bitmap slide is given in milliseconds. To make it non-repeating, set android:oneshot="true". Add the image, for example, as an ImageView to your layout as follows:

```
<ImageView
```

```
android:id="@+id/img"
android:adjustViewBounds="true"
android:scaleType="centerCrop"
android:layout_width="match_parent"
android:layout_height="wrap_content"
android:background="@drawable/anim1" />
```

This prepares the animation, but it needs to be started from inside the program, for example, as follows:

```
img.setBackgroundResource(R.drawable.anim1)
img.setOnClickListener{
    val anim = img.background as AnimationDrawable
    anim.start()
}
```

Here the animation starts when the user clicks the image.

Property Animation

The property animation framework allows you to animate everything you might think of. Using the class android.animation.ValueAnimator, you can specify

- Duration and repeating mode

- Type of the interpolated value

- Time interpolation during the animation

- A listener for value updates

Most of the time, you will however use the android.animation.ObjectAnimator class, because it already targets objects and their properties, so you don't have to implement listeners. This class has various static factory methods to create instances of ObjectAnimator, where as arguments you specify the object to animate, the name of the property of this object to use, and the values to use during the animation. On the object you can then set a certain interpolator (default is the AccelerateDecelerateInterpolator that starts and ends slowly and in between accelerates and decelerates) and add a value update listener (set in onAnimationUpdate()) in case, for example, a target object of type View needs to be informed that it must update itself (by calling invalidate()).

As an example we define a TextView object inside a FrameLayout and move it from x=0 to x=500 in an accelerating manner. The layout file contains

```
<FrameLayout
     android:id="@+id/fl"
     android:layout_width="match_parent"
     android:layout_height="400dp">
     <TextView
          android:id="@+id/tv"
          android:layout_width="wrap_content"
          android:layout_height="wrap_content"
          android:text="XXX"/>
</FrameLayout>
```

And inside the code, for example, after a button is clicked, is

```
val anim = ObjectAnimator.ofFloat(tv, "x", 0.0f, 500.0f)
    .apply {
       duration = 1000 // default is 300ms
       interpolator = AccelerateInterpolator()
    }
anim.start()
```

Note   This only works if the object in question, here a TextView, has a setter method for the property specified, here an "x". More precisely, the object needs a setX(Float), which however is the case for all View objects.

Caution   Your mileage varies largely depending on the layout your UI object is placed in – after all the layout object might have its own idea how to position objects, thwarting the animation. A FrameLayout is quite handsome here, but you have to do all layouting inside the code.

Using the `android.animation.AnimatorSet` you can also choreograph a set of several animations. The online API documentation will tell you more about how to use it.

View Property Animator

With certain constraints imposed, a couple of `View`-related properties can also be animated using an `android.view.ViewPropertyAnimator`. It seems to be less invasive compared with general property animation, but only a small number of properties can be animated, and only the drawing gets affected by the animation – the position for on-click listeners, for example, gets orphaned if views move away.

Other than that you can use it to (A) translate views, (B) scale views, (C) rotate views, and (D) fade in or fade out views. For details please see the online documentation.

As an extension to the built-in *view property* animation, you might want to have a look at *fling animation* as well. This type of animation applies a frictional force on moving objects, letting the animation appear more natural. To find information about fling animation, search for "Android fling animation" inside your favorite search engine.

Spring Physics

Adding spring physics to your animations improves the user experience by making moves more realistic. To add spring physics, you need to include the corresponding support library: in your module's `build.gradle` file, add "implementation 'com.android. support:support-dynamic-animation:27.1.0'" inside the "dependencies" element.

For details I refer to the online API documentation of class `android.support. animation.SpringAnimation`. The most important settings are the following:

- Inside the constructor, set the property. Available are alpha, translation, rotation, scroll value, and scale.

- Add listeners: use `addUpdateListener()` and/or `addEndListener()`.

- Use `setStartVelocity()` to start the animation with an initial speed (default is 0.0f).

- Use `getSpring().setDampingRatio()` or in Kotlin just `.spring. dampingRatio = ...` to set the damping factor.

- Use `getSpring().setStiffness()` or in Kotlin just `.spring. stiffness = ...` to set the spring stiffness.

Use `start()` or `animateToFinalPosition()` to start the animation. This must happen inside the GUI thread or inside `runOnUiThread { ... }`.

An example for a spring animation would be, for example, after a button press

```
val springAnim = SpringAnimation(tv, DynamicAnimation.TRANSLATION_X,
500.0f).apply {
    setStartVelocity(1.0f)
    spring.stiffness =
        SpringForce.STIFFNESS_LOW
    spring.dampingRatio =
        SpringForce.DAMPING_RATIO_LOW_BOUNCY
}
springAnim.start()
```

Transitions

The transition framework allows for applying animated transitions between different layouts. You basically create `android.transition.Scene` objects from a starting and an end layout and then let the `TransitionManager` act, for example:

```
val sceneRoot:ViewGroup = ...

// Obtain the view hierarchy to add as a child of
// the scene root when this scene is entered
val startViewHierarchy:ViewGroup = ...

// Same for the end scene
val endViewHierarchy:ViewGroup = ...

// Create the scenes
val startScene = Scene(sceneRoot, startViewHierarchy)
val endScene = Scene(sceneRoot, endViewHierarchy)

val fadeTransition = Fade()
TransitionManager.go(endScene, fadeTransition)
```

The sceneRoot could, for instance, be a FrameLayout with the transition supposed to happen inside. You'd then at the beginning add the starting layout (startViewHierarchy) inside. The preceding code will establish a transition to the end layout (endViewHierarchy), all happening *inside* the sceneRoot.

Such transitions can be specified from inside the code, but also as by special XML files. For details please see the online documentation.

Caution   Certain restrictions apply – not all View types will correctly take part of such layout transitions. It is however possible to exclude elements from the transition by using the removeTarget() method.

Start an Activity Using Transitions

While one activity gets replaced by another activity, it is possible to (A) specify an exit transition for the first, (B) specify an enter transition for the second, and (C) allow for a smooth transition of common view elements. Such transitions can be specified either by special XML files or from inside the code. We briefly describe the latter. For the XML way and also for more details, please consult the online documentation.

Such activity switch transitions are available for API levels 21 (Android 5.0) and up. To make sure your code works with versions prior to that, inside the following code snippet, we write a check:

```
if (Build.VERSION.SDK_INT >=
        Build.VERSION_CODES.LOLLIPOP) ...
```

To set an *exit* and an *enter* transition, use the following snippet inside both activities:

```
override fun onCreate(savedInstanceState: Bundle?) {
    super.onCreate(savedInstanceState)

    if (Build.VERSION.SDK_INT >=
            Build.VERSION_CODES.LOLLIPOP) {
        with(window) {
            requestFeature(
                Window.FEATURE_CONTENT_TRANSITIONS)
            exitTransition = Explode()
```

```
                    // if inside the CALLED transition,
                    // instead use:
                    // enterTransition = Explode()

                    // use this in the CALLED transition to
                    // primordially start the enter transition:
                    // allowEnterTransitionOverlap = true
                }
        } else {
            // Go without transition - this can be empty
        }

        ...
    }
```

where instead of Explode() you can also choose Slide(), Fade(), or AutoTransition(). *Fade* and *Slide* do the obvious thing; the AutoTransition fades out elements that are not common (see in the following what that means), moves and resizes common elements, and then fades in new elements.

Note   The requestFeature() must happen at the beginning of onCreate().

The transition gets only activated when you start a new activity via

```
if (Build.VERSION.SDK_INT >=
        Build.VERSION_CODES.LOLLIPOP) {
    startActivity(intent,
        ActivityOptions.
        makeSceneTransitionAnimation(this).toBundle())
}else{
    startActivity(intent)
}
```

When the *called* activity exists, you could use Activity.finishAfterTransition() instead of the usual finish() to have the reverse transition more nicely handled. Again you have to put that inside an if (Build.VERSION.SDK_INT >= Build.VERSION_CODES. LOLLIPOP) check.

To improve user experience, you can identify elements that are common to both activities and let the transition framework handle them in a special way. To do so you do two things:

- Give the common UI elements a special *transition name*:

```
if (Build.VERSION.SDK_INT >=
        Build.VERSION_CODES.LOLLIPOP) {
    img.transitionName = "imgTrans"
        // for a certain "img" UI element
}
```

This name must be unique, and the setting should happen inside `onCreate()` in both the calling and the called activity.

- Replace the preceding `ActivityOptions.makeSceneTransitionAnimation(this)` by

```
ActivityOptions.
    makeSceneTransitionAnimation(
        this@MainActivity,
        UPair.create(img,"imgTrans"),
        ...more pairs...
    )
```

where the `UPair` is an import alias to avoid name clashes: `import android.util.Pair as UPair`.

You can then, for example, use the `AutoTransition()` transition to get such common UI elements handled in a special way during the animation.

Animation in Jetpack Compose

Jetpack Compose has its own, very concise and elegant animation methodology. The online documentation of Jetpack Compose tells you more about it and also gives examples.

Fast Graphics OpenGL ES

For Android apps you can use the industry-standard OpenGL ES to render high-performance graphics in 2D and 3D. The user interface development differs significantly from the standard Android OS way, and you have to expect to spend some time learning how to use OpenGL ES. In the end however, you might end up with an outstanding graphics, which pays off for the effort.

Note   It doesn't make sense to use OpenGL ES if the Android OS user interface provides the same functionality and performance is not an issue.

OpenGL ES comes in different versions: 1.x, 2.0, and 3.x. While there is a huge difference in terms of methodology between 1.x and the later versions, the difference between 2.0 and 3.x is not so big. But setting 3.x as a strict requirement, you may miss a considerable part of all possible users, so the recommendation is

- Develop for OpenGL ES 2.0 and only in case you really need it add 3.x features. If using 3.x you best supply fallbacks for devices that do not speak 3.x.

In the following sections, we will be talking about version 2.0.

Note   OpenGL ES for Android is supported by both the framework and also the *Native Development Kit* (NDK). In the book we will be putting more weight on the framework classes.

OpenGL ES is extremely versatile, and usage patterns are potentially endless. To cover all what OpenGL ES provides goes beyond the scope of the book, but I will present the following scenarios to get you started:

- Configure the activity to use OpenGL ES.

- Provide a custom GLSurfaceView class to hold the OpenGL scene.

- Provide two graphics primitives: a triangle that uses a vertex buffer and a shader program and a quad that uses a vertex buffer, an index buffer, and a shader program.

- Provide a renderer to paint the graphics.

- Briefly outline how to introduce view projection.

- Briefly outline how to add motion.

- Briefly outline how to add light.

- Briefly outline how to react to user input.

Showing an OpenGL Surface in Your Activity

You can make a custom OpenGL view element be the only UI element to show in an activity via

```
class MyActivity : AppCompatActivity() {
  var glView:GLSurfaceView? = null

  override fun onCreate(savedInstanceState: Bundle?) {
      super.onCreate(savedInstanceState)

      // Create a GLSurfaceView instance and set it
      // as the ContentView for this Activity.
      glView = MyGLSurfaceView(this)
      setContentView(glView)
  }
}
```

where MyGLSurfaceView is the custom GLSurfaceView we will define in the following.

Or you could use a normal XML layout file and add the custom GL view there by, for example, writing

```
<com.example.opengl.glapp.MyGLSurfaceView
    android:layout_width="400dp"
    android:layout_height="400dp"/>
```

where you have to specify the full class path of the custom GL view class.

Creating a Custom OpenGL View Element

A custom OpenGL view element could be as easy as subclassing android.opengl.
GLSurfaceView and specifying a renderer for the graphics data, a rendering mode, and
maybe listeners for user interactions. We however want to go a step further and include
an OpenGL ES version check, so you can decide whether the inclusion of OpenGL ES 3.x
constructs is possible. The code reads

```
import android.app.ActivityManager
import android.content.Context
import android.opengl.GLSurfaceView
import android.util.Log
import javax.microedition.khronos.egl.EGL10

class MyGLSurfaceView(context: Context) :
      GLSurfaceView(context) {
  val renderer: MyGLRenderer
  var supports3x = false
  var minVers = 0

  init {
      fetchVersion()

      // Create an OpenGL ES 2.0 context
      setEGLContextClientVersion(2)

      // We set the 2.x context factory to use for
      // the view
      setEGLContextFactory()

      // We set the renderer for drawing the graphics
      renderer = MyGLRenderer()
      setRenderer(renderer)

      // This setting prevents the GLSurfaceView frame
      // from being redrawn until you call
      // requestRender()
      renderMode = GLSurfaceView.RENDERMODE_WHEN_DIRTY
  }
```

```
private fun fetchVersion() {
    val activityManager =
        context.getSystemService(
            Context.ACTIVITY_SERVICE)
        as ActivityManager
    val configurationInfo =
        activityManager.deviceConfigurationInfo
    val vers = configurationInfo.glEsVersion
        // e.g. "2.0"
    supports3x = vers.split(".")[0] == "3"
    minVers = vers.split(".")[1].toInt()
    Log.i("LOG", "Supports OpenGL 3.x = " +
        supports3x)
    Log.i("LOG", "OpenGL minor version = " +
        minVers)
}

private fun setEGLContextFactory() {
    val EGL_CONTEXT_CLIENT_VERSION = 0x3098
        // from egl.h c-source
    class ContextFactory :
        GLSurfaceView.EGLContextFactory {
      override fun createContext(egl: EGL10,
          display: javax.microedition.khronos.
                  egl.EGLDisplay?,
          eglConfig: javax.microedition.khronos.
                  egl.EGLConfig?)
      :javax.microedition.khronos.egl.EGLContext? {
          val attrib_list =
              intArrayOf(EGL_CONTEXT_CLIENT_VERSION,
                      2, EGL10.EGL_NONE)
          val ectx = egl.eglCreateContext(display,
              eglConfig,
              EGL10.EGL_NO_CONTEXT,
              attrib_list)
        return ectx
```

```
        }

        override fun destroyContext(egl: EGL10,
                display: javax.microedition.khronos.
                        egl.EGLDisplay?,
                context: javax.microedition.khronos.
                        egl.EGLContext?) {
            egl.eglDestroyContext(display, context)
        }
    }
    setEGLContextFactory(ContextFactory())
  }
}
```

You can then use .supports3x to see whether OpenGL ES 3.x is supported and .minVers for the minor version number in case you need it. The renderer used by this class gets defined in the following. Also note that by virtue of RENDERMODE_WHEN_DIRTY a redrawing only happens on demand. If you need fully dynamic changes, comment that line out.

A Triangle with a Vertex Buffer

A class responsible for drawing graphics primitives, in this case a simple triangle, reads

```
class Triangle {
  val vertexShaderCode = """
      attribute vec4 vPosition;
      void main() {
        gl_Position = vPosition;
      }
      """.trimIndent()

  val fragmentShaderCode = """
      precision mediump float;
      uniform vec4 vColor;
      void main() {
        gl_FragColor = vColor;
```

```kotlin
        }
        """.trimIndent()

    var program:Int? = 0

    val vertexBuffer: FloatBuffer

    var color = floatArrayOf(0.6f, 0.77f, 0.22f, 1.0f)

    var positionHandle: Int? = 0
    var colorHandle: Int? = 0

    val vertexCount =
        triangleCoords.size / COORDS_PER_VERTEX
    val vertexStride = COORDS_PER_VERTEX * 4
        // 4 bytes per vertex

    companion object {
        // number of coordinates per vertex
        internal val COORDS_PER_VERTEX = 3
        internal var triangleCoords =
            floatArrayOf( // in counterclockwise order:
              0.0f, 0.6f, 0.0f,    // top
              -0.5f, -0.3f, 0.0f, // bottom left
              0.5f, -0.3f, 0.0f    // bottom right
        )
    }
}
```

Inside the class's init block, the shaders get loaded and initialized, and a vertex buffer gets prepared:

```kotlin
init {
    val vertexShader = MyGLRenderer.loadShader(
        GLES20.GL_VERTEX_SHADER,
        vertexShaderCode)
    val fragmentShader = MyGLRenderer.loadShader(
        GLES20.GL_FRAGMENT_SHADER,
        fragmentShaderCode)
```

```
// create empty OpenGL ES Program
program = GLES20.glCreateProgram()

// add the vertex shader to program
GLES20.glAttachShader(program!!, vertexShader)

// add the fragment shader to program
GLES20.glAttachShader(program!!, fragmentShader)

// creates OpenGL ES program executables
GLES20.glLinkProgram(program!!)

// initialize vertex byte buffer for shape
// coordinates
val bb = ByteBuffer.allocateDirect(
        // (4 bytes per float)
        triangleCoords.size * 4)
// use the device hardware's native byte order
bb.order(ByteOrder.nativeOrder())

// create a floating point buffer from bb
vertexBuffer = bb.asFloatBuffer()
// add the coordinates to the buffer
vertexBuffer.put(triangleCoords)
// set the buffer to start at 0
vertexBuffer.position(0)
}
```

The draw() method performs the rendering work. Note that, as usual in OpenGL rendering, this method must run really fast. Here we just move around references:

```
fun draw() {
    // Add program to OpenGL ES environment
    GLES20.glUseProgram(program!!)

    // get handle to vertex shader's vPosition member
    positionHandle = GLES20.glGetAttribLocation(
        program!!, "vPosition")

    // Enable a handle to the triangle vertices
```

```
GLES20.glEnableVertexAttribArray(
        positionHandle!!)

// Prepare the triangle coordinate data
GLES20.glVertexAttribPointer(positionHandle!!,
        COORDS_PER_VERTEX,
        GLES20.GL_FLOAT, false,
        vertexStride, vertexBuffer)

// get handle to fragment shader's vColor member
colorHandle = GLES20.glGetUniformLocation(
        program!!, "vColor")

// Set color for drawing the triangle
GLES20.glUniform4fv(colorHandle!!, 1, color, 0)

// Draw the triangle
GLES20.glDrawArrays(GLES20.GL_TRIANGLES, 0,
        vertexCount)

// Disable vertex array
GLES20.glDisableVertexAttribArray(
        positionHandle!!)
    }
}
```

To see how this triangle class gets used from inside the renderer, please look in the following.

A Quad with a Vertex Buffer and an Index Buffer

In OpenGL polygons with more than three vertices best get described by gluing together as many triangles as necessary. So for a quad, we need two triangles. Obviously some vertices then show up several times: if we have a quad A-B-C-D, we need to declare the triangles A-B-C and A-C-D, so the vertices A and C get used twice each.

Uploading vertices to the graphics hardware several times is not a good solution, and that is why there are *index lists*: we upload vertices A, B, C, and D and in addition a list

0, 1, 3, and 2, pointing *into* the vertices list and describing the two triangles as a triangle strip (first is 0-1-3; second is 1-3-2). The corresponding code for a quad reads

```
class Quad {

    val vertexBuffer: FloatBuffer
    val drawListBuffer: ShortBuffer

    val vertexShaderCode = """
        attribute vec4 vPosition;
        void main() {
          gl_Position = vPosition;
        }
    """.trimIndent()

    val fragmentShaderCode = """
        precision mediump float;
        uniform vec4 vColor;
        void main() {
          gl_FragColor = vColor;
        }
    """.trimIndent()

    // The shader program
    var program:Int? = 0

    var color = floatArrayOf(0.94f, 0.67f, 0.22f, 1.0f)

    val vbo = IntArray(1) // one vertex buffer
    val ibo = IntArray(1) // one index buffer

    var positionHandle: Int? = 0
    var colorHandle: Int? = 0

    companion object {
        val BYTES_PER_FLOAT = 4
        val BYTES_PER_SHORT = 2
        val COORDS_PER_VERTEX = 3
        val VERTEX_STRIDE = COORDS_PER_VERTEX *
```

```
            BYTES_PER_FLOAT
    var quadCoords = floatArrayOf(
            -0.5f, 0.2f, 0.0f, // top left
            -0.5f, -0.5f, 0.0f, // bottom left
            0.2f, -0.5f, 0.0f, // bottom right
            0.2f, 0.2f, 0.0f) // top right
    val drawOrder = shortArrayOf(0, 1, 3, 2)
            // order to draw vertices
}
```

As with the preceding triangle, we initialize the shaders and the buffers in the init block:

```
init {
    val vertexShader = MyGLRenderer.loadShader(
            GLES20.GL_VERTEX_SHADER,
            vertexShaderCode)
    val fragmentShader = MyGLRenderer.loadShader(
            GLES20.GL_FRAGMENT_SHADER,
            fragmentShaderCode)

    program = GLES20.glCreateProgram().apply {
        // add the vertex shader to program
        GLES20.glAttachShader(this, vertexShader)

        // add the fragment shader to program
        GLES20.glAttachShader(this, fragmentShader)

        // creates OpenGL ES program executables
        GLES20.glLinkProgram(this)
    }

    // initialize vertex byte buffer for shape coords
    vertexBuffer = ByteBuffer.allocateDirect(
            quadCoords.size * BYTES_PER_FLOAT).apply{
        order(ByteOrder.nativeOrder())
    }.asFloatBuffer().apply {
        put(quadCoords)
```

```
        position(0)
    }

    // initialize byte buffer for the draw list
    drawListBuffer = ByteBuffer.allocateDirect(
            drawOrder.size * BYTES_PER_SHORT).apply {
        order(ByteOrder.nativeOrder())
    }.asShortBuffer().apply {
        put(drawOrder)
        position(0)
    }

    GLES20.glGenBuffers(1, vbo, 0);
    GLES20.glGenBuffers(1, ibo, 0);
    if (vbo[0] > 0 && ibo[0] > 0) {
        GLES20.glBindBuffer(GLES20.GL_ARRAY_BUFFER,
            vbo[0])
        GLES20.glBufferData(GLES20.GL_ARRAY_BUFFER,
            vertexBuffer.capacity() * BYTES_PER_FLOAT,
            vertexBuffer, GLES20.GL_STATIC_DRAW)

        GLES20.glBindBuffer(
            GLES20.GL_ELEMENT_ARRAY_BUFFER, ibo[0])
        GLES20.glBufferData(
            GLES20.GL_ELEMENT_ARRAY_BUFFER,
            drawListBuffer.capacity() *
                BYTES_PER_SHORT,
            drawListBuffer, GLES20.GL_STATIC_DRAW)

        GLES20.glBindBuffer(
            GLES20.GL_ARRAY_BUFFER, 0);
        GLES20.glBindBuffer(
            GLES20.GL_ELEMENT_ARRAY_BUFFER, 0)
    } else {
        //TODO: some error handling
    }
}
```

The draw() method performs the rendering, as is the case for the triangle class we described previously:

```
fun draw() {
    // Add program to OpenGL ES environment
    GLES20.glUseProgram(program!!)

    // Get handle to fragment shader's vColor member
    colorHandle = GLES20.glGetUniformLocation(
            program!!, "vColor")
    // Set color for drawing the quad
    GLES20.glUniform4fv(colorHandle!!, 1, color, 0)

    // Get handle to vertex shader's vPosition member
    positionHandle = GLES20.glGetAttribLocation(
            program!!, "vPosition")

    // Enable a handle to the vertices
    GLES20.glEnableVertexAttribArray(
            positionHandle!!)

    // Prepare the coordinate data
    GLES20.glVertexAttribPointer(positionHandle!!,
            COORDS_PER_VERTEX,
            GLES20.GL_FLOAT, false,
            VERTEX_STRIDE, vertexBuffer)

    // Draw the quad
    GLES20.glBindBuffer(
            GLES20.GL_ARRAY_BUFFER, vbo[0]);

    // Bind Attributes
    GLES20.glBindBuffer(
            GLES20.GL_ELEMENT_ARRAY_BUFFER, ibo[0])
    GLES20.glDrawElements(GLES20.GL_TRIANGLE_STRIP,
            drawListBuffer.capacity(),
            GLES20.GL_UNSIGNED_SHORT, 0)

    GLES20.glBindBuffer(
```

```
        GLES20.GL_ARRAY_BUFFER, 0)
    GLES20.glBindBuffer(
        GLES20.GL_ELEMENT_ARRAY_BUFFER, 0)

    // Disable vertex array
    GLES20.glDisableVertexAttribArray(
        positionHandle!!)
  }
}
```

In the constructor, the shader program, the vertex buffer, and the index buffer get uploaded to the graphics hardware. Inside the draw() method, which potentially gets called often, only pointers to the uploaded buffers get used. The usage of this Quad class is described in the following section.

Creating and Using a Renderer

A renderer is responsible for drawing the graphics objects. Since we are using a subclass of android.opengl.GLSurfaceView, the renderer must be a subclass of GLSurfaceView. Renderer. Since the classes Triangle and Quad have their own shaders, all the renderer needs to do is instantiate a quad and a triangle and use their draw() methods, besides some boilerplate code:

```
class MyGLRenderer : GLSurfaceView.Renderer {
  companion object {
    fun loadShader(type: Int, shaderCode: String)
        : Int {
      // create a vertex shader type
      //     (GLES20.GL_VERTEX_SHADER)
      // or a fragment shader type
      //     (GLES20.GL_FRAGMENT_SHADER)
      val shader = GLES20.glCreateShader(type)

      // add the source code to the shader and
      // compile it
      GLES20.glShaderSource(shader, shaderCode)
      GLES20.glCompileShader(shader)
```

```
        return shader
    }
}

var triangle:Triangle? = null
var quad:Quad? = null

// Called once to set up the view's OpenGL ES
// environment.
override
fun onSurfaceCreated(gl: GL10?, config:
        javax.microedition.khronos.egl.EGLConfig?) {
    // enable face culling feature
    GLES20.glEnable(GL10.GL_CULL_FACE)
    // specify which faces to not draw
    GLES20.glCullFace(GL10.GL_BACK)
    // Set the background frame color
    GLES20.glClearColor(0.0f, 0.0f, 0.0f, 1.0f)
}

// Called for each redraw of the view.
// If renderMode =
//      GLSurfaceView.RENDERMODE_WHEN_DIRTY
// (see MyGLSurfaceView)
// this will not be called every frame
override
fun onDrawFrame(unused: GL10) {
    // Redraw background color
    GLES20.glClear(GLES20.GL_COLOR_BUFFER_BIT)

    triangle = triangle ?: Triangle()
    triangle?.draw()

    quad = quad ?: Quad()
    quad?.draw()
}

override
```

```
   fun onSurfaceChanged(unused: GL10, width: Int,
        height: Int) {
     GLES20.glViewport(0, 0, width, height)
   }
 }
```

Projection

Once we start using the third dimension, we need to talk about projection. Projection describes how the three dimensions of the vertices get mapped to two-dimensional screen coordinates. The Triangle and Quad graphics primitives we built so far both use their own shader program. While this gives us the maximum flexibility, to avoid a proliferation of shader programs, it is better to extract the shader program and use just one from inside the renderer. Also, the projection calculation then needs to be done only at one place.

In addition, we let the renderer prepare N times 2 buffer objects and one pair of vertex and index buffers per object and provide corresponding handles to each graphics primitive constructor. The new Square class then looks like

```
class Square(val program: Int?,
             val vertBuf:Int, val idxBuf:Int) {
  val vertexBuffer: FloatBuffer
  val drawListBuffer: ShortBuffer

  var color = floatArrayOf(0.94f, 0.67f, 0.22f, 1.0f)

  companion object {
      val BYTES_PER_FLOAT = 4
      val BYTES_PER_SHORT = 2
      val COORDS_PER_VERTEX = 3
      val VERTEX_STRIDE = COORDS_PER_VERTEX *
          BYTES_PER_FLOAT
      var coords = floatArrayOf(
              -0.5f, 0.2f, 0.0f, // top left
              -0.5f, -0.5f, 0.0f, // bottom left
              0.2f, -0.5f, 0.0f, // bottom right
```

```
                0.2f, 0.2f, 0.0f) // top right
        val drawOrder = shortArrayOf(0, 1, 3, 2)
            // order to draw vertices
    }
```

The class no longer contains shader code, so what is left for the init block is preparing the buffers to use:

```
init {
    // initialize vertex byte buffer for shape
    // coordinates
    vertexBuffer = ByteBuffer.allocateDirect(
            coords.size * BYTES_PER_FLOAT).apply{
        order(ByteOrder.nativeOrder())
    }.asFloatBuffer().apply {
        put(coords)
        position(0)
    }

    // initialize byte buffer for the draw list
    drawListBuffer = ByteBuffer.allocateDirect(
            drawOrder.size * BYTES_PER_SHORT).apply {
        order(ByteOrder.nativeOrder())
    }.asShortBuffer().apply {
        put(drawOrder)
        position(0)
    }

    if (vertBuf > 0 && idxBuf > 0) {
        GLES20.glBindBuffer(GLES20.GL_ARRAY_BUFFER,
                vertBuf)
        GLES20.glBufferData(GLES20.GL_ARRAY_BUFFER,
                vertexBuffer.capacity() *
                    BYTES_PER_FLOAT,
                vertexBuffer, GLES20.GL_STATIC_DRAW)

        GLES20.glBindBuffer(
                GLES20.GL_ELEMENT_ARRAY_BUFFER, idxBuf)
```

```
    GLES20.glBufferData(
        GLES20.GL_ELEMENT_ARRAY_BUFFER,
        drawListBuffer.capacity() *
            BYTES_PER_SHORT,
        drawListBuffer, GLES20.GL_STATIC_DRAW)

    GLES20.glBindBuffer(
        GLES20.GL_ARRAY_BUFFER, 0)
    GLES20.glBindBuffer(
        GLES20.GL_ELEMENT_ARRAY_BUFFER, 0)
} else {
    //TODO: error handling
}
}
```

The draw() method does not substantially differ from before – this time we use the shader program provided in the constructor. Again this method runs fast, since it only shifts around references:

```
fun draw() {
    // Add program to OpenGL ES environment
    GLES20.glUseProgram(program!!)

    // get handle to fragment shader's vColor member
    val colorHandle = GLES20.glGetUniformLocation(
        program!!, "vColor")
    // Set color for drawing the square
    GLES20.glUniform4fv(colorHandle!!, 1, color, 0)

    // get handle to vertex shader's vPosition member
    val positionHandle = GLES20.glGetAttribLocation(
        program!!, "vPosition")

    // Enable a handle to the vertices
    GLES20.glEnableVertexAttribArray(
        positionHandle!!)

    // Prepare the coordinate data
    GLES20.glVertexAttribPointer(positionHandle!!,
```

```
                    COORDS_PER_VERTEX,
                    GLES20.GL_FLOAT, false,
                    VERTEX_STRIDE, vertexBuffer)

        // Draw the square
        GLES20.glBindBuffer(GLES20.GL_ARRAY_BUFFER,
                vertBuf)
        GLES20.glBindBuffer(
                GLES20.GL_ELEMENT_ARRAY_BUFFER, idxBuf)
        GLES20.glDrawElements(GLES20.GL_TRIANGLE_STRIP,
                drawListBuffer.capacity(),
                GLES20.GL_UNSIGNED_SHORT, 0)

        GLES20.glBindBuffer(
                GLES20.GL_ARRAY_BUFFER, 0)
        GLES20.glBindBuffer(
                GLES20.GL_ELEMENT_ARRAY_BUFFER, 0)

        // Disable vertex array
        GLES20.glDisableVertexAttribArray(
                positionHandle!!)
    }
}
```

Here, inside the constructor, we fetch handles to the program, a vertex buffer name
(an integer), and an index buffer name (another integer) and furthermore prepare and
upload the vertex and index buffers to the graphics hardware. To let a new `Triangle`
class use the same method is left as an exercise to you.

The new renderer class now contains the shader program and prepares handles for
the buffers. But we go one step further and also add projection matrices:

```
class MyGLRenderer : GLSurfaceView.Renderer {
  companion object {
      fun loadShader(type: Int, shaderCode: String)
            : Int {
        // create a vertex shader type
        //      (GLES20.GL_VERTEX_SHADER)
        // or a fragment shader type
```

```kotlin
        //        (GLES20.GL_FRAGMENT_SHADER)
        val shader = GLES20.glCreateShader(type)

        // add the source code to the shader and
        // compile it
        GLES20.glShaderSource(shader, shaderCode)
        GLES20.glCompileShader(shader)

        return shader
    }
}

val vertexShaderCode = """
    attribute vec4 vPosition;
    uniform mat4 uMVPMatrix;
    void main() {
      gl_Position = uMVPMatrix * vPosition;
    }
    """.trimIndent()

val fragmentShaderCode = """
    precision mediump float;
    uniform vec4 vColor;
    void main() {
      gl_FragColor = vColor;
    }
    """.trimIndent()

var triangle:Triangle? = null
var square:Square? = null
var program:Int? = 0

val vbo = IntArray(2) // vertex buffers
val ibo = IntArray(2) // index buffers

val vMatrix:FloatArray = FloatArray(16)
val projMatrix:FloatArray = FloatArray(16)
val mvpMatrix:FloatArray = FloatArray(16)
```

The method onSurfaceCreated() just gets called once by the system when the OpenGL rendering is ready to go. We use it to set some rendering flags and to initialize the shaders:

```kotlin
// Called once to set up the view's
// OpenGL ES environment.
override fun onSurfaceCreated(gl: GL10?, config:
        javax.microedition.khronos.egl.EGLConfig?) {
  // enable face culling feature
  GLES20.glEnable(GL10.GL_CULL_FACE)
  // specify which faces to not draw
  GLES20.glCullFace(GL10.GL_BACK)

  // Set the background frame color
  GLES20.glClearColor(0.0f, 0.0f, 0.0f, 1.0f)

  val vertexShader = loadShader(
          GLES20.GL_VERTEX_SHADER,
          vertexShaderCode)
  val fragmentShader = loadShader(
          GLES20.GL_FRAGMENT_SHADER,
          fragmentShaderCode)

  // create empty OpenGL ES Program
  program = GLES20.glCreateProgram()

  // add the vertex shader to program
  GLES20.glAttachShader(program!!, vertexShader)

  // add the fragment shader to program
  GLES20.glAttachShader(program!!, fragmentShader)

  // creates OpenGL ES program executables
  GLES20.glLinkProgram(program!!)

  GLES20.glGenBuffers(2, vbo, 0) // just buffer names
  GLES20.glGenBuffers(2, ibo, 0)

  // Create a camera view and an orthogonal projection
  // matrix
```

```
Matrix.setLookAtM(vMatrix, 0, 0f, 0f, 3.0f, 0f, 0f,
        0f, 0f, 1.0f, 0.0f)
Matrix.orthoM(projMatrix,0,-1.0f,1.0f, -1.0f, 1.0f,
        100.0f, -100.0f)
}
```

The callback method onDrawFrame() gets called for each redraw of the view. If renderMode = GLSurfaceView.RENDERMODE_WHEN_DIRTY – see class MyGLSurfaceView – this will however not be called every frame, only if changes are detected. The following snippet also closes the class:

```
override fun onDrawFrame(unused: GL10) {
    // Redraw background color
    GLES20.glClear(GLES20.GL_COLOR_BUFFER_BIT)

    GLES20.glUseProgram(program!!)
    val muMVPMatrixHandle = GLES20.glGetUniformLocation(
            program!!, "uMVPMatrix");
    Matrix.multiplyMM(mvpMatrix, 0,
            projMatrix, 0, vMatrix, 0)

    // Apply the combined projection and camera view
    // transformations
    GLES20.glUniformMatrix4fv(muMVPMatrixHandle, 1,
            false, mvpMatrix, 0);

    triangle = triangle ?:
            Triangle(program,vbo[0],ibo[0])
    triangle?.draw()

    square = square ?:
            Square(program,vbo[1],ibo[1])
    square?.draw()
}

override
fun onSurfaceChanged(unused: GL10, width: Int,
        height: Int) {
    GLES20.glViewport(0, 0, width, height)
```

315

```
    }
  }
```

You can see the projection matrices get calculated inside the Kotlin code, but uploaded as shader *uniform* variables and used from inside the vertex shader.

Applying projection to three-dimensional objects makes of course more sense. As a very general assumption for such 3D objects, we expect

- Vertex coordinates in four-dimensional homogeneous coordinates
- RGBA colors assigned to vertices
- Face normals assigned to vertices

Using four coordinate values instead of the usual three (x, y, z) helps for perspective projection. Colors assigned to vertices can be used from inside the shader code to apply a coloring scheme. But they can also be ignored or used for non-coloring purposes – this is totally up to the shader code. The normals help for a realistic lighting.

The renderer gets just new shader code:

```
val vertexShaderCode = """
    attribute vec4 vPosition;
    attribute vec4 vNorm;
    attribute vec4 vColor;

    varying vec4 fColor;
    varying vec4 fNorm;

    uniform mat4 uMVPMatrix;

    void main() {
      gl_Position = uMVPMatrix * vPosition;
      fColor = vColor;
      fNorm = vNorm;
    }
    """.trimIndent()

val fragmentShaderCode = """
    precision mediump float;
    varying vec4 fColor;
```

```
varying vec4 fNorm;

void main() {
  gl_FragColor = fColor;
}
""".trimIndent()
```

As a sample 3D object, I present a cube with an interpolated coloring according to the vertex colors and with the normals ignored for now:

```
class Cube(val program: Int?, val vertBuf:Int,
      val idxBuf:Int) {
  val vertexBuffer: FloatBuffer
  val drawListBuffer: ShortBuffer
```

The companion object holds all the coordinates and indices we need for the cube:

```
companion object {
    val BYTES_PER_FLOAT = 4
    val BYTES_PER_SHORT = 2
    val COORDS_PER_VERTEX = 4
    val NORMS_PER_VERTEX = 4
    val COLORS_PER_VERTEX = 4
    val VERTEX_STRIDE = (COORDS_PER_VERTEX +
          NORMS_PER_VERTEX +
          COLORS_PER_VERTEX) * BYTES_PER_FLOAT
    var coords = floatArrayOf(
          // positions  + normals + colors
          // --- front
          -0.2f, -0.2f, 0.2f, 1.0f,
                0.0f, 0.0f, 1.0f, 0.0f,
                    1.0f, 0.0f, 0.0f, 1.0f,
          0.2f, -0.2f, 0.2f, 1.0f,
                0.0f, 0.0f, 1.0f, 0.0f,
                    1.0f, 0.0f, 0.0f, 1.0f,
          0.2f, 0.2f, 0.2f, 1.0f,
                0.0f, 0.0f, 1.0f, 0.0f,
                    1.0f, 0.0f, 0.0f, 1.0f,
```

```
       -0.2f, 0.2f, 0.2f, 1.0f,
          0.0f, 0.0f, 1.0f, 0.0f,
                1.0f, 0.0f, 0.0f, 1.0f,
       // --- back
       -0.2f, -0.2f, -0.2f, 1.0f,
          0.0f, 0.0f, -1.0f, 0.0f,
                0.0f, 1.0f, 0.0f, 1.0f,
       0.2f, -0.2f, -0.2f, 1.0f,
          0.0f, 0.0f, -1.0f, 0.0f,
                0.0f, 1.0f, 0.0f, 1.0f,
       0.2f, 0.2f, -0.2f, 1.0f,
          0.0f, 0.0f, -1.0f, 0.0f,
                0.0f, 1.0f, 0.0f, 1.0f,
       -0.2f, 0.2f, -0.2f, 1.0f,
          0.0f, 0.0f, -1.0f, 0.0f,
                0.0f, 1.0f, 0.0f, 1.0f,
       // --- bottom
       -0.2f, -0.2f, 0.2f, 1.0f,
          0.0f, -1.0f, 0.0f, 0.0f,
                0.0f, 0.0f, 1.0f, 1.0f,
       0.2f, -0.2f, 0.2f, 1.0f,
          0.0f, -1.0f, 0.0f, 0.0f,
                0.0f, 0.0f, 1.0f, 1.0f,
       0.2f, -0.2f, -0.2f, 1.0f,
          0.0f, -1.0f, 0.0f, 0.0f,
                0.0f, 0.0f, 1.0f, 1.0f,
       -0.2f, -0.2f, -0.2f, 1.0f,
          0.0f, -1.0f, 0.0f, 0.0f,
                0.0f, 0.0f, 1.0f, 1.0f,
       // --- top
       -0.2f, 0.2f, 0.2f, 1.0f,
          0.0f, 1.0f, 0.0f, 0.0f,
                1.0f, 0.0f, 1.0f, 1.0f,
       0.2f, 0.2f, 0.2f, 1.0f,
          0.0f, 1.0f, 0.0f, 0.0f,
```

```
            1.0f, 0.0f, 1.0f, 1.0f,
    0.2f, 0.2f, -0.2f, 1.0f,
        0.0f, 1.0f, 0.0f, 0.0f,
            1.0f, 0.0f, 1.0f, 1.0f,
    -0.2f, 0.2f, -0.2f, 1.0f,
        0.0f, 1.0f, 0.0f, 0.0f,
            1.0f, 0.0f, 1.0f, 1.0f,
    // --- right
    0.2f, -0.2f, 0.2f, 1.0f,
        1.0f, 0.0f, 0.0f, 0.0f,
            0.0f, 1.0f, 1.0f, 1.0f,
    0.2f, 0.2f, 0.2f, 1.0f,
        1.0f, 0.0f, 0.0f, 0.0f,
            0.0f, 1.0f, 1.0f, 1.0f,
    0.2f, 0.2f, -0.2f, 1.0f,
        1.0f, 0.0f, 0.0f, 0.0f,
            0.0f, 1.0f, 1.0f, 1.0f,
    0.2f, -0.2f, -0.2f, 1.0f,
        1.0f, 0.0f, 0.0f, 0.0f,
            0.0f, 1.0f, 1.0f, 1.0f,
    // --- left
    -0.2f, -0.2f, 0.2f, 1.0f,
        -1.0f, 0.0f, 0.0f, 0.0f,
            1.0f, 1.0f, 0.0f, 1.0f,
    -0.2f, 0.2f, 0.2f, 1.0f,
        -1.0f, 0.0f, 0.0f, 0.0f,
            1.0f, 1.0f, 0.0f, 1.0f,
    -0.2f, 0.2f, -0.2f, 1.0f,
        -1.0f, 0.0f, 0.0f, 0.0f,
            1.0f, 1.0f, 0.0f, 1.0f,
    -0.2f, -0.2f, -0.2f, 1.0f,
        -1.0f, 0.0f, 0.0f, 0.0f,
            1.0f, 1.0f, 0.0f, 1.0f
)
val drawOrder = shortArrayOf( // vertices order
```

```
        0, 1, 2,      0, 2, 3,      // front
        4, 6, 5,      4, 7, 6,      // back
        8, 10, 9,     8, 11, 10,    // bottom
        12, 13, 14,   12, 14, 15,   // top
        16, 18, 17,   16, 19, 18,   // right
        20, 21, 22,   20, 22, 23    // left
    )
}
```

As in the listings before, we use the init block to prepare and initialize the buffers we need for the shaders:

```
init {
    // initialize vertex byte buffer for shape
    // coordinates, normals and colors
    vertexBuffer = ByteBuffer.allocateDirect(
            coords.size * BYTES_PER_FLOAT).apply{
        order(ByteOrder.nativeOrder())
    }.asFloatBuffer().apply {
        put(coords)
        position(0)
    }

    // initialize byte buffer for the draw list
    drawListBuffer = ByteBuffer.allocateDirect(
            drawOrder.size * BYTES_PER_SHORT).apply {
        order(ByteOrder.nativeOrder())
    }.asShortBuffer().apply {
        put(drawOrder)
        position(0)
    }

    if (vertBuf > 0 && idxBuf > 0) {
        GLES20.glBindBuffer(
                GLES20.GL_ARRAY_BUFFER, vertBuf)
        GLES20.glBufferData(GLES20.GL_ARRAY_BUFFER,
                vertexBuffer.capacity() *
```

```
                    BYTES_PER_FLOAT,
            vertexBuffer, GLES20.GL_STATIC_DRAW)

    GLES20.glBindBuffer(
            GLES20.GL_ELEMENT_ARRAY_BUFFER, idxBuf)
    GLES20.glBufferData(
            GLES20.GL_ELEMENT_ARRAY_BUFFER,
            drawListBuffer.capacity() *
                    BYTES_PER_SHORT,
            drawListBuffer, GLES20.GL_STATIC_DRAW)

    GLES20.glBindBuffer(
            GLES20.GL_ARRAY_BUFFER, 0)
    GLES20.glBindBuffer(
            GLES20.GL_ELEMENT_ARRAY_BUFFER, 0)
    } else {
        // TODO: error handling
    }
}
```

The draw() method for rendering the graphics this time reads

```
fun draw() {
    // Add program to OpenGL ES environment
    GLES20.glUseProgram(program!!)

    // get handle to vertex shader's vPosition member
    val positionHandle =
        GLES20.glGetAttribLocation(program,
                                    "vPosition")
    // Enable a handle to the vertices
    GLES20.glEnableVertexAttribArray(positionHandle)
    // Prepare the coordinate data
    GLES20.glVertexAttribPointer(
            positionHandle, COORDS_PER_VERTEX,
            GLES20.GL_FLOAT, false,
            VERTEX_STRIDE, vertexBuffer)
```

```
// !!!!!!!!!!!!!!!!!!!!!!!!!!!!!!!!!!!!!!!!!!!!!!!!
// Buffer offsets are a little bit strange in the
// Java binding - for the normals and colors we
// create new views and then reset the vertex
// array
// !!!!!!!!!!!!!!!!!!!!!!!!!!!!!!!!!!!!!!!!!!!!!!!!

// get handle to vertex shader's vPosition member
vertexBuffer.position(COORDS_PER_VERTEX)
val normBuffer = vertexBuffer.slice()
    // create a new view
vertexBuffer.rewind()
    // ... and rewind the original buffer
val normHandle = GLES20.glGetAttribLocation(
    program, "vNorm")
if(normHandle >= 0) {
  // Enable a handle to the vertices
  GLES20.glEnableVertexAttribArray(normHandle)
  // Prepare the coordinate data
  GLES20.glVertexAttribPointer(normHandle,
    COORDS_PER_VERTEX,
    GLES20.GL_FLOAT, false,
    VERTEX_STRIDE, normBuffer)
}

// get handle to vertex shader's vColor member
vertexBuffer.position(COORDS_PER_VERTEX +
                    NORMS_PER_VERTEX)
val colorBuffer = vertexBuffer.slice()
    // create a new view
vertexBuffer.rewind()
    // ... and rewind the original buffer
val colorHandle = GLES20.glGetAttribLocation(
    program, "vColor")
if(colorHandle >= 0) {
  // Enable a handle to the vertices
```

```
    GLES20.glEnableVertexAttribArray(colorHandle)
    // Prepare the coordinate data
    GLES20.glVertexAttribPointer(colorHandle,
        COLORS_PER_VERTEX,
        GLES20.GL_FLOAT, false,
        VERTEX_STRIDE, colorBuffer)
}

// Draw the cube
GLES20.glBindBuffer(GLES20.GL_ARRAY_BUFFER,
    vertBuf)
GLES20.glBindBuffer(
    GLES20.GL_ELEMENT_ARRAY_BUFFER, idxBuf)
GLES20.glDrawElements(GLES20.GL_TRIANGLES,
        drawListBuffer.capacity(),
        GLES20.GL_UNSIGNED_SHORT, 0)

GLES20.glBindBuffer(GLES20.GL_ARRAY_BUFFER,
        0)
GLES20.glBindBuffer(GLES20.GL_ELEMENT_ARRAY_BUFFER,
        0)

// Disable attribute arrays
GLES20.glDisableVertexAttribArray(positionHandle)
if(normHandle >= 0)
    GLES20.glDisableVertexAttribArray(normHandle)
if(colorHandle >= 0)
    GLES20.glDisableVertexAttribArray(colorHandle)
    }
}
```

Motion

Up to now our objects were kind of static, and by virtue of renderMode =
GLSurfaceView.RENDERMODE_WHEN_DIRTY in class MyGLSurfaceView, redrawing happens
only on demand. If instead you use GLSurfaceView.RENDERMODE_CONTINUOUSLY, the
redrawing happens every frame.

Note that you still can and should use vertex and index buffers for feeding the shaders – you can easily introduce motion by adjusting the matrices inside Kotlin or by directly editing the shader code, for example, after adding more *uniform* variables.

Light

Lighting can be added inside the *fragment shader* code. This time we will have to use the normal vectors, because they determine how light gets reflected on the surface elements. If we introduce light, we need to tell where its position is. For this aim inside the renderer's companion object, add

```
val lightPos = floatArrayOf(0.0f, 0.0f, 4.0f, 0.0f)
```

With the shader code now getting more complex, we should have to find out how to get hold of the error messages. To achieve this you can add inside the renderer's loadShader() function

```
val statusShader = IntArray(1)
GLES20.glGetShaderiv(shader, GLES20.GL_COMPILE_STATUS,
        IntBuffer.wrap(statusShader))
if (statusShader[0] == GLES20.GL_FALSE) {
  val s = GLES20.glGetShaderInfoLog(shader)
  Log.e("LOG", "Shader compilation: " + s)
}
```

Similarly, after the program linking, add the following snippet:

```
val statusShader = IntArray(1)
GLES20.glGetShaderiv(program!!, GLES20.GL_LINK_STATUS,
        IntBuffer.wrap(statusShader))
if (statusShader[0] == GLES20.GL_FALSE) {
  val s = GLES20.glGetShaderInfoLog(program!!)
  Log.e("LOG", "Shader linking: " + s)
}
```

The new vertex shader transports a transformed normal vector according to rotation and scaling, *not* including translation (that is why the fourth component of the normal vectors reads 0.0), and also a transformed position vector, this time including translation:

```
val vertexShaderCode = """
    attribute vec4 vPosition;
    attribute vec4 vNorm;
    attribute vec4 vColor;

    varying vec4 fColor;
    varying vec3 N;
    varying vec3 v;

    uniform mat4 uVMatrix;
    uniform mat4 uMVPMatrix;

    void main() {
      gl_Position = uMVPMatrix * vPosition;
      fColor = vColor;
      v = vec3(uVMatrix * vPosition);
      N = normalize(vec3(uVMatrix * vNorm));
    }
    """.trimIndent()
```

Note that we also transport the vertex colors, although we are not going to use them any longer. You could however merge the color information, so we don't remove it. The following code ignores the vertex colors.

The new fragment shader takes the interpolated positions and normals from the vertex shader, adds a *uniform* variable for the light's position, and in our case uses the *Phong* shading model to apply light:

```
val fragmentShaderCode = """
  precision mediump float;
  varying vec4 fColor;
  varying vec3 N;
  varying vec3 v;
  uniform vec4 lightPos;

  void main() {
    vec3 L = normalize(lightPos.xyz - v);
    vec3 E = normalize(-v); // eye coordinates!
    vec3 R = normalize(-reflect(L,N));
```

```
//calculate Ambient Term:
vec4 Iamb = vec4(0.0, 0.1, 0.1, 1.0);

//calculate Diffuse Term:
vec4 Idiff = vec4(0.0, 0.0, 1.0, 1.0) *
    max(dot(N,L), 0.0);
Idiff = clamp(Idiff, 0.0, 1.0);

// calculate Specular Term:
vec4 Ispec = vec4(1.0, 1.0, 0.5, 1.0) *
    pow(max(dot(R,E),0.0),
      /*shininess=*/5.0);
Ispec = clamp(Ispec, 0.0, 1.0);

// write Total Color:
gl_FragColor = Iamb + Idiff + Ispec;
//gl_FragColor = fColor; // use vertex color instead
}
""".trimIndent()
```

Don't forget to add a handle for the light's position inside the renderer's onDrawFrame() function:

```
// The light position
val lightPosHandle = GLES20.glGetUniformLocation(
    program!!, "lightPos");
GLES20.glUniform4f(lightPosHandle,
    lightPos[0],lightPos[1],lightPos[2],lightPos[3])
```

The vectors used in the Phong shading algorithm get depicted in Figure 9-2. You find the same vector names used in the shader code.

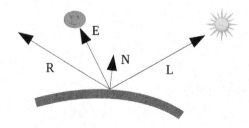

Figure 9-2. *Phong Shading Vectors*

You can of course add more dynamics to the lighting by using uniforms for the color components – for simplicity I hard-coded them inside the fragment shaders (all those vec4(...) constructors). A lighted cube looks as shown in Figure 9-3.

Figure 9-3. *A Lighted Cube*

Textures

Images in OpenGL get handled by *textures* – those are bitmap data uploaded to the graphics hardware and usually spanned over surfaces defined by textures. To allow for textures, the companion object from the renderer we introduced in the preceding sections gets another function to load texturable images from the Android resource folder:

```kotlin
companion object {
    ...
    fun loadTexture(context: Context, resourceId: Int):
        Int {
      val textureHandle = IntArray(1)

      GLES20.glGenTextures(1, textureHandle, 0)

      if (textureHandle[0] != 0) {
          val options = BitmapFactory.Options().apply {
              inScaled = false    // No pre-scaling
          }

          // Read in the resource
          val bitmap = BitmapFactory.decodeResource(
              context.getResources(),
              resourceId, options)
```

```
        // Bind to the texture in OpenGL
        GLES20.glBindTexture(GLES20.GL_TEXTURE_2D,
            textureHandle[0])

        // Set filtering
        GLES20.glTexParameteri(GLES20.GL_TEXTURE_2D,
            GLES20.GL_TEXTURE_MIN_FILTER,
            GLES20.GL_NEAREST)
        GLES20.glTexParameteri(GLES20.GL_TEXTURE_2D,
            GLES20.GL_TEXTURE_MAG_FILTER,
            GLES20.GL_NEAREST)

        // Load the bitmap into the bound texture.
        GLUtils.texImage2D(GLES20.GL_TEXTURE_2D, 0,
            bitmap, 0)

        // The bitmap is no longer needed.
        bitmap.recycle()
    }else{
        // TODO: handle error
    }
    return textureHandle[0]
}
```

In addition to that, the renderer gets a new code for both the vertex and the fragment shader:

```
val vertexShaderCode = """
    attribute vec4 vPosition;
    attribute vec2 vTexture;
    attribute vec4 vColor;

    varying vec2 textureCoords;
    varying vec4 fColor;

    uniform mat4 uMVPMatrix;

    void main() {
      gl_Position = uMVPMatrix * vPosition;
```

```
    textureCoords = vTexture;
    fColor = vColor;
  }
  """.trimIndent()

val fragmentShaderCode = """
    precision mediump float;
    uniform sampler2D texture;   // The input texture.
    varying vec2 textureCoords;
    varying vec4 fColor;

    void main() {
      gl_FragColor = texture2D(texture, textureCoords);
      // use vertex color instead:
      // gl_FragColor = fColor;
    }
    """.trimIndent()
```

The attribute vTexture corresponds to a new data section in the vertex definition of an object, and the uniform sampler2D texture; describes the connection to a texture object defined in Kotlin code.

As a sample object, we define a plane that very much resembles one of the faces from the Cube class we defined previously, apart from additionally feeding the texture:

```
class Plane(val program: Int?, val vertBuf:Int,
      val idxBuf:Int, val context: Context) {

  val vertexBuffer: FloatBuffer
  val drawListBuffer: ShortBuffer

  // Used to pass in the texture.
  var textureUniformHandle: Int = 0
  // A handle to our texture data
  var textureDataHandle: Int = 0
```

The companion object is used to define the coordinates and some constants:

```
companion object {
    val BYTES_PER_FLOAT = 4
```

```kotlin
        val BYTES_PER_SHORT = 2
        val COORDS_PER_VERTEX = 4
        val TEXTURE_PER_VERTEX = 2
        val NORMS_PER_VERTEX = 4
        val COLORS_PER_VERTEX = 4
        val VERTEX_STRIDE = (COORDS_PER_VERTEX +
                TEXTURE_PER_VERTEX +
                NORMS_PER_VERTEX +
                COLORS_PER_VERTEX) * BYTES_PER_FLOAT
    var coords = floatArrayOf(
            // positions, normals, texture, colors
            -0.2f, -0.2f, 0.2f, 1.0f,
                0.0f, 0.0f, 1.0f, 0.0f,
                    0.0f, 1.0f,
                        1.0f, 0.0f, 0.0f, 1.0f,
            0.2f, -0.2f, 0.2f, 1.0f,
                0.0f, 0.0f, 1.0f, 0.0f,
                    1.0f, 1.0f,
                        1.0f, 0.0f, 0.0f, 1.0f,
            0.2f, 0.2f, 0.2f, 1.0f,
                0.0f, 0.0f, 1.0f, 0.0f,
                    1.0f, 0.0f,
                        1.0f, 0.0f, 0.0f, 1.0f,
            -0.2f, 0.2f, 0.2f, 1.0f,
                0.0f, 0.0f, 1.0f, 0.0f,
                    0.0f, 0.0f,
                        1.0f, 0.0f, 0.0f, 1.0f
    )
    val drawOrder = shortArrayOf( // vertices order
            0, 1, 2,    0, 2, 3
    )
}
```

Inside the init block, the buffers get defined and initialized, and we also load a texture image:

```
init {
    // initialize vertex byte buffer for shape
    // coordinates
    vertexBuffer = ByteBuffer.allocateDirect(
            coords.size * BYTES_PER_FLOAT).apply{
        order(ByteOrder.nativeOrder())
    }.asFloatBuffer().apply {
        put(coords)
        position(0)
    }

    // initialize byte buffer for the draw list
    drawListBuffer = ByteBuffer.allocateDirect(
            drawOrder.size * BYTES_PER_SHORT).apply {
        order(ByteOrder.nativeOrder())
    }.asShortBuffer().apply {
        put(drawOrder)
        position(0)
    }

    if (vertBuf > 0 && idxBuf > 0) {
        GLES20.glBindBuffer(GLES20.GL_ARRAY_BUFFER,
            vertBuf)
        GLES20.glBufferData(GLES20.GL_ARRAY_BUFFER,
            vertexBuffer.capacity() * BYTES_PER_FLOAT,
            vertexBuffer, GLES20.GL_STATIC_DRAW)

        GLES20.glBindBuffer(
            GLES20.GL_ELEMENT_ARRAY_BUFFER, idxBuf)
        GLES20.glBufferData(
            GLES20.GL_ELEMENT_ARRAY_BUFFER,
            drawListBuffer.capacity() *
                BYTES_PER_SHORT,
            drawListBuffer, GLES20.GL_STATIC_DRAW)

        GLES20.glBindBuffer(GLES20.GL_ARRAY_BUFFER, 0)
        GLES20.glBindBuffer(
```

```
                GLES20.GL_ELEMENT_ARRAY_BUFFER, 0)
    } else {
        // TODO: handle error
    }

    // Load the texture
    textureDataHandle =
        MyGLRenderer.loadTexture(context,
        R.drawable.myImage)
}
```

The draw() callback gets used to draw the buffers including the texture. Inside the following snippet, we also close the class:

```
fun draw() {
    // Add program to OpenGL ES environment
    GLES20.glUseProgram(program!!)

    // get handle to vertex shader's vPosition member
    val positionHandle =
        GLES20.glGetAttribLocation(program,
        "vPosition")
    // Enable a handle to the vertices
    GLES20.glEnableVertexAttribArray(positionHandle)
    // Prepare the coordinate data
    GLES20.glVertexAttribPointer(positionHandle,
        COORDS_PER_VERTEX,
        GLES20.GL_FLOAT, false,
        VERTEX_STRIDE, vertexBuffer)

    // !!!!!!!!!!!!!!!!!!!!!!!!!!!!!!!!!!!!!!!!!!!!!!!!!
    // Buffer offsets are a little bit strange in the
    // Java binding - For the other arrays we create
    // a new view and then reset the vertex array
    // !!!!!!!!!!!!!!!!!!!!!!!!!!!!!!!!!!!!!!!!!!!!!!!!!

    // get handle to vertex shader's vNorm member
    vertexBuffer.position(COORDS_PER_VERTEX)
```

```
val normBuffer = vertexBuffer.slice()
    // create a new view
vertexBuffer.rewind()
    // ... and rewind the original buffer
val normHandle =
    GLES20.glGetAttribLocation(program, "vNorm")
if(normHandle >= 0) {
    // Enable a handle to the vertices
    GLES20.glEnableVertexAttribArray(normHandle)
    // Prepare the coordinate data
    GLES20.glVertexAttribPointer(normHandle,
        COORDS_PER_VERTEX,
        GLES20.GL_FLOAT, false,
        VERTEX_STRIDE, normBuffer)
}

// get handle to vertex shader's textureCoords
vertexBuffer.position(COORDS_PER_VERTEX +
    NORMS_PER_VERTEX)
val textureBuffer = vertexBuffer.slice()
    // create a new view
vertexBuffer.rewind()
    // ... and rewind the original buffer
val textureHandle =
    GLES20.glGetAttribLocation(program,
    "vTexture")
if(textureHandle >= 0) {
    // Enable a handle to the texture coords
    GLES20.glEnableVertexAttribArray(
        textureHandle)
    // Prepare the coordinate data
    GLES20.glVertexAttribPointer(textureHandle,
        COORDS_PER_VERTEX,
        GLES20.GL_FLOAT, false,
        VERTEX_STRIDE, textureBuffer)
}
```

```
// get handle to vertex shader's vColor member
vertexBuffer.position(COORDS_PER_VERTEX +
    NORMS_PER_VERTEX + TEXTURE_PER_VERTEX)
val colorBuffer = vertexBuffer.slice()
    // create a new view
vertexBuffer.rewind()
    // ... and rewind the original buffer
val colorHandle =
    GLES20.glGetAttribLocation(program, "vColor")
if(colorHandle >= 0) {
    // Enable a handle to the vertices
    GLES20.glEnableVertexAttribArray(colorHandle)
    // Prepare the coordinate data
    GLES20.glVertexAttribPointer(colorHandle,
        COLORS_PER_VERTEX,
        GLES20.GL_FLOAT, false,
        VERTEX_STRIDE, colorBuffer)
}

textureUniformHandle =
    GLES20.glGetUniformLocation(program,
    "texture")
if(textureHandle >= 0) {
    // Set the active texture unit to
    // texture unit 0.
    GLES20.glActiveTexture(GLES20.GL_TEXTURE0)
    // Tell the texture uniform sampler to use
    // this texture in the shader by binding to
    // texture unit 0.
    GLES20.glUniform1i(textureUniformHandle, 0)
}

// Draw the plane
GLES20.glBindBuffer(GLES20.GL_ARRAY_BUFFER,
    vertBuf)
GLES20.glBindBuffer(
```

```
        GLES20.GL_ELEMENT_ARRAY_BUFFER, idxBuf)
    GLES20.glDrawElements(GLES20.GL_TRIANGLES,
            drawListBuffer.capacity(),
            GLES20.GL_UNSIGNED_SHORT, 0)

    GLES20.glBindBuffer(GLES20.GL_ARRAY_BUFFER, 0)
    GLES20.glBindBuffer(
        GLES20.GL_ELEMENT_ARRAY_BUFFER, 0)

    // Disable vertex array
    GLES20.glDisableVertexAttribArray(
        positionHandle)
    if(normHandle >= 0)
        GLES20.glDisableVertexAttribArray(
        normHandle)
    if(textureHandle >= 0)
        GLES20.glDisableVertexAttribArray(
        textureHandle)
    if(colorHandle >= 0)
        GLES20.glDisableVertexAttribArray(
        colorHandle)
    }
}
```

User Input

To respond to user touch events, all you have to do is overwrite the function
onTouchEvent(e: MotionEvent) : Boolean { ... }. The MotionEvent you receive
is able to tell many things:

- **Touch events:** Touchdown and touch-up

- **Move events**: Moving while touched

- **Pointer events**: Second, third,… finger touching

Besides that, a couple more events are registered – see the online documentation of
MotionEvent.

If we want to listen to touch and move events, the minimum implementation for such a listener reads

```
override
fun onTouchEvent(event: MotionEvent): Boolean {
    var handled = true
    when(event.actionMasked) {
        MotionEvent.ACTION_DOWN -> {
            Log.e("LOG","Action: ACTION_DOWN " +
                    event.toString())
        }
        MotionEvent.ACTION_UP -> {
            Log.e("LOG","Action: ACTION_UP " +
                    event.toString())
        }
        MotionEvent.ACTION_MOVE -> {
            Log.e("LOG","Action: MOVE " +
                    event.toString())
        }
        else -> handled = false
    }
    return handled || super.onTouchEvent(event)
}
```

You can see that we return true when our listener handles events. Especially if we receive an ACTION_DOWN event, returning true is important; otherwise, both move and up actions will be ignored.

Note   We check the actionMasked accessor of the event object, not the action accessor as is suggested often. The reason for this is that the action accessor might contain additional bits if a multi-touch event happens. The masked variant is just more reliable.

Fast Graphics with Vulkan

The *Vulkan* API is an alternative way for addressing high-performance 3D graphics needs on Android devices. Compared with OpenGL, Vulkan somewhat better fits video game programming methodologies, and with its development starting in 2016, it is arguably the more modern framework (OpenGL exists since 1992).

In this book we don't further talk about Vulkan, but `https://developer.android.com/ndk/guides/graphics/getting-started` and `www.khronos.org/vulkan/` give you a good starting point if you want to learn more about it.

UI Design with Movable Items

If your app needs movable UI elements, you best use the `FrameLayout` class or a subclass of it. We want to take care of UI element positions ourselves and don't want a layout class to interfere with that. The `FrameLayout` class does not position its elements dynamically, so using it is a good choice for that kind of positioning.

If you want your view movable, you create a subclass and overwrite its `onTouchEvent()` method. For example, say you have an `ImageView` and want to have it movable. For that aim create a subclass as follows:

```
class MyImageView : ImageView {
  constructor(context: Context)
      : super(context)
  constructor(context: Context, attrs: AttributeSet)
      : super(context, attrs)

  var dx : Float = 0.0f
  var dy : Float = 0.0f

  override
  fun onTouchEvent(event: MotionEvent): Boolean {
      var handled = true
      when(event.actionMasked) {
          MotionEvent.ACTION_DOWN -> {
              //Log.e("LOG","Action: ACTION_DOWN " +
              //        event.toString())
              dx = x - event.rawX
```

```
            dy = y - event.rawY
        }
        MotionEvent.ACTION_UP -> {
            //Log.e("LOG","Action: ACTION_UP " +
            //           event.toString())
        }
        MotionEvent.ACTION_MOVE -> {
            //Log.e("LOG","Action: MOVE " +
            //           event.toString())
            x = event.rawX + dx
            y = event.rawY + dy
        }
        else -> handled = false
    }
    return handled || super.onTouchEvent(event)
  }
}
```

If instead you want to have moving handled by a single point inside your code, you can do one of the following:

- Create a base class for movable views and let all UI elements inherit from it.

- Add the touch event listener to the layout container. You then however have to provide some logic to find the touched UI element by checking pixel coordinate bounds.

Menus and Action Bars

Menus and action bars are important user interface elements if you want to present your user a list of selectable choices. In the following sections, we present different kinds of menus and explain when and how to use them.

Options Menu

The options menu shows up inside the app bar. Android Studio will help you start developing an app with an app bar. If you want to do that yourself, inside your layout, add

```
<android.support.design.widget.AppBarLayout
    android:layout_width="match_parent"
    android:layout_height="wrap_content"
    android:theme="@style/AppTheme.AppBarOverlay">

    <android.support.v7.widget.Toolbar
        android:id="@+id/toolbar"
        android:layout_width="match_parent"
        android:layout_height="?attr/actionBarSize"
        android:background="?attr/colorPrimary"
        app:popupTheme="@style/AppTheme.PopupOverlay"/>
</android.support.design.widget.AppBarLayout>
```

Inside the activity's onCreate(...) method, we need to tell the Android OS that we are using an app bar. To do so, register the app bar via

```
setSupportActionBar(toolbar)
```

Also, in the activity overwrite onCreateOptionsMenu(...) to create the menu and onOptionsItemSelected(...) to listen to menu click events:

```
override
fun onOptionsItemSelected(item: MenuItem): Boolean {
  when (item.getItemId()) {
    menu_item1 -> {
        Toast.makeText(this,"Item 1",
            Toast.LENGTH_LONG).show()
        return true
    }
    menu_item2 -> {
        Toast.makeText(this,"Item 2",
            Toast.LENGTH_LONG).show()
        return true
```

```
        }
        else -> return
                super.onOptionsItemSelected(item)
    }
}

override
fun onCreateOptionsMenu(menu: Menu): Boolean {
  val inflater = menuInflater
  inflater.inflate(R.menu.my_menu, menu)
  return true
}
```

What is left is the definition of the menu itself: inside res/menu add an XML file my_
menu.xml and inside write

```xml
<?xml version="1.0" encoding="utf-8"?>
<menu xmlns:android=
        "http://schemas.android.com/apk/res/android">
  <item android:id="@+id/menu_item1"
      android:title="@string/title_item1"/>
  <item android:id="@+id/menu_item2"
      android:title="@string/title_item2"/>
</menu>
```

where the <item> element accepts more attributes – see the online
documentation (search for "Android menu resource"). Particularly interesting is the
android:showAsAction attribute – setting it to "ifRoom" allows for prominently placing
the menu item inside the action bar as a separate action element.

Context Menu

A context menu shows up after a long tap on a registered view. To do this registration,
inside the activity call registerForContextMenu() and provide the view as an argument:

```
override fun onCreate(savedInstanceState: Bundle?) {
    ...
    registerForContextMenu(myViewId)
}
```

This can be done several times if you want the context menu to show up for several views.

Once a context menu is registered, you define it by overwriting onCreateContextMenu(...) inside the activity and furthermore overwriting onContextItemSelected to listen to menu select events. An example would be

```
override
fun onCreateContextMenu(menu: ContextMenu, v: View,
                        menuInfo: ContextMenuInfo?) {
    super.onCreateContextMenu(menu, v, menuInfo)
    val inflater = menuInflater
    inflater.inflate(R.menu.context_menu, menu)
}

override
fun onContextItemSelected(item: MenuItem): Boolean {
    when (item.itemId) {
        ctxmenu_item1 -> {
            Toast.makeText(this,"CTX Item 1",
                Toast.LENGTH_LONG).show()
        }
        ctxmenu_item2 -> {
            Toast.makeText(this,"CTX Item 2",
                Toast.LENGTH_LONG).show()
        }
        else -> return
                super.onContextItemSelected(item)
    }
    return true
}
```

The XML definition goes to a standard menu XML file, for the example res/context_menu.xml:

```
<?xml version="1.0" encoding="utf-8"?>
<menu xmlns:android=
    "http://schemas.android.com/apk/res/android">
```

```
<item android:id="@+id/ctxmenu_item1"
      android:title="@string/ctxtitle_item1"/>
<item android:id="@+id/ctxmenu_item2"
      android:title="@string/ctxtitle_item2"/>
</menu>
```

It is also possible to open a context menu programmatically by `openContextMenu(` `someView` `)` inside an activity.

Contextual Action Mode

The *contextual action mode* behaves like a context-relative app bar. While a standard app bar is static to the app, a contextual action mode is view specific. What you have to do for this kind of context menu is as follows:

- Implement the `ActionMode.Callback` interface.

  - Inside `onCreateActionMode(...)` create the menu, similar to `onCreateContextMenu()` earlier for the standard context menu.

  - Inside `onPrepareActionMode(...)` return `false`, unless you need special preparation steps.

  - Implement `onActionItemClicked(...)` to listen to touch events.

- Create a menu XML resource file, as for the standard context menu.

- Inside your code, open the contextual action mode by calling `startActionMode(` `theActionModeCallback` `)`.

Popup Menus

While context-related menus are mostly for settings that are not subject to be changed often, menus that belong to a front-end workflow best are implemented as popup menus. Popups usually show up as a result of the user interacting with a certain view, so popup menus are assigned to UI elements.

Showing the popup menu of a view after some user action can be as easy as calling a function:

```
fun showPopup(v: View) {
   PopupMenu(this, v).run {
      setOnMenuItemClickListener { menuItem ->
         Toast.makeText(this@TheActivity,
               menuItem.toString(),
               Toast.LENGTH_LONG).show()
         true
      }
      menuInflater.inflate(popup, menu)
      show()
   }
}
```

As usual, you also need to define the menu inside the res/menu resources – for the example, a file popup.xml (as seen by the first argument to inflate(...)).

Progress Bars

Showing progress bars is a good means to improve user experience for tasks that are running a couple of seconds. To implement progress bars, add a ProgressBar view to your layout. It doesn't matter whether you do that inside the XML layout file or from inside the Kotlin program. In XML you write

```
<ProgressBar
    android:id="@+id/progressBar"
    android:layout_width="wrap_content"
    android:layout_height="wrap_content"
    />
```

for an indeterminate bar (if you can't tell the progress as a percentage value) or

```
<ProgressBar
    android:id="@+id/progressBar"
    style="@android:style/Widget.ProgressBar.Horizontal"
    android:layout_width="wrap_content"
    android:layout_height="wrap_content"
    android:progress="0"
    />
```

for a determinate progress bar (you know the percentage while updating the progress bar).

Inside the code you toggle the visibility of an indeterminate progress bar by using

```
progressBar.visibility = View.INVISIBLE
// or .. = View.VISIBLE
```

To set the progress value for a determinate progress bar, see the following example:

```
with(progressBar) {
    if (Build.VERSION.SDK_INT >= Build.VERSION_CODES.O)
        min = 0
    max = 100
}
var value = 0
Thread {
    while(value < 100) {
        value += 1
        Thread.sleep(200)
        runOnUiThread {
            progressBar.progress = value
        }
    }
    progressBar.visibility = View.INVISIBLE
}.start()
```

Here we use a background thread to simulate the longer-running task – in a real-world app, something more sensible will be happening in the background. And maybe you use an AsyncTask instead of a thread.

Working with Fragments

A *fragment* is a reusable modular part of an activity. If you develop a nontrivial app without fragments, you will have a number of activities calling each other. The problem with that is that on devices with larger screens, this is maybe not the optimal solution if the activities stay in close relation to each other. Consider, for example, a list of some items in one activity and a details view of a selected item in another activity. On a small device, it is perfectly acceptable to start the details activity once the user clicks an item in the list activity. On a larger screen however, it might improve user experience if both views, the list and the details, show up side by side.

That is where fragments come handy. Instead of switching between activities, you create several fragments that are part of the *same* activity. Then, depending on the device, you choose either the one-pane view or the two-pane view.

Developing for fragments is easy if you perform a transition from an app that consists only of activities. Fragments have a lifecycle just as activities do, and the lifecycle callbacks are very similar if not the same as for activities. This is where the story gets a little bit complicated, though, because the lifecycle of the container activity and the lifecycles of the contained fragments are connected to each other and fragments also exhibit a dedicated callstack behavior. The online documentation for fragments gives you a detailed reference for all fragment-related issues. Here in this section, we however limit the survey to basic aspects of creating and using fragments.

Creating Fragments

To create fragments you have two options: either you specify `Fragment` elements inside a layout file, or you add fragments programmatically from inside Kotlin code.

To use the XML way of adding fragments to your app, inside a layout file, you identify appropriate places where to add fragments and write

```
<fragment android:name=
    "com.example.android.fragments.TheFragment"
    android:id="@+id/fragment_id1"
    android:layout_weight="..."
    android:layout_width="..."
    android:layout_height="..." />
```

where layouting parameters are to be chosen according to your app's layouting needs. For different devices, more precisely different screen sizes, you can provide several distinct layout files that contain varying numbers of fragments at varying places.

For the fragment class, designated by the "name" attribute in the XML file, start with a bare minimum like

```
import android.support.v4.app.Fragment
...
class MyFragment : Fragment() {
  override
  fun onCreateView(inflater: LayoutInflater?,
       container: ViewGroup?,
       savedInstanceState: Bundle?): View? {
     return inflater!!.inflate(
         my_fragment, container, false)
  }
}
```

and add a layout file my_fragment.xml to the res/layout resource folder.

To add fragments from inside your Kotlin code, you identify a layout container or ViewGroup where to place a fragment and then use a fragment manager to perform that insertion:

```
with(supportFragmentManager.beginTransaction()) {
    val fragment = MyFragment()
    add(fragm_container.id, fragment, "fragmTag")
    val fragmentId = fragment.id // can use that later...
    commit()
}
```

which can happen, for example, inside the activity's onCreate() callback or more dynamically at any other suitable place. The fragm_container is, for example, a <FrameLayout> element inside the layout XML.

Note   A fragment gets its ID from the fragment manager during adding it inside a transaction. You cannot use it before that, and you cannot provide your own ID if you add fragments in Kotlin code.

Handling Fragments from Activities

Handling fragments from inside activities includes

- Adding fragments, as shown previously in the "Creating Fragments" section

- Getting references to fragments, given an ID or a tag

- Handling the back stack

- Registering listeners for lifecycle events

For all these needs, you use getSupportFragmentManager(), which gives you the fragment manager, which is capable of doing all that, or in Kotlin simply just use the accessor

```
supportFragmentManager
```

to fetch a reference.

Note   There is also a fragmentManager without the "support" in the name. That one points to the framework's fragment manager as opposed to the support library fragment manager. Using the support fragment manager however improves the compatibility with older API levels.

Communicating with Fragments

Activities can communicate with their fragments by using the fragment manager and finding fragments given their ID or tag:

```
val fragm = supportFragmentManager.
       findFragmentByTag("fragmTag")
// or val fragm = supportFragmentManager.
//           findFragmentById(fragmId)
```

But fragments also can talk to their activity. This might indicate a poor application design, for fragments should be self-contained entities. If you still need it, you can use getActivity() inside the fragment class or in Kotlin simply

```
activity
```

to access it. And from there a fragment can even fetch references to other fragments.

App Widgets

App widgets are their own class of applications that show informational messages and/ or controllers in other apps, especially the home screen. App widgets get implemented as special broadcast receivers and as such are subject to being killed by the Android OS once the callback methods have done their work and a couple of seconds have passed by after that. If you need to have longer process run, consider starting *services* from inside the app widgets.

To start creating an app widget, write inside `AndroidManifest.xml`, more precisely as a child element of `<application>`

```
<receiver android:name=".ExampleAppWidgetProvider" >
    <intent-filter>
        <action android:name="android.appwidget.action.APPWIDGET_
        UPDATE" />
    </intent-filter>
    <meta-data android:name="android.appwidget.provider"
               android:resource="@xml/example_appwidget_info" />
</receiver>
```

Next, create metadata inside the resources: create a new file `example_appwidget_ info.xml` inside `res/xml` and write inside

```
<appwidget-provider xmlns:android=
        "http://schemas.android.com/apk/res/android"
    android:minWidth="40dp"
    android:minHeight="40dp"
    android:updatePeriodMillis="86400000"
    android:resizeMode="horizontal|vertical"
    android:widgetCategory="home_screen">
</appwidget-provider>
```

What is left is creating the broadcast listener class – for this aim it is easiest to inherit from class `android.appwidget.AppWidgetProvider` and, for example, write

```
class ExampleAppWidgetProvider : AppWidgetProvider() {
  override
  fun onUpdate(context: Context,
```

```
        appWidgetManager: AppWidgetManager,
        appWidgetIds:IntArray) {
    // Perform this loop procedure for each App
    // Widget that belongs to this provider
    for(appWidgetId in appWidgetIds) {
        // This is just an example, you can do other
        // stuff here...
        // Create an Intent to launch MainActivity
        val intent = Intent(context,
                MainActivity::class.java)
        val pendingIntent = PendingIntent.
                getActivity(context, 0, intent, 0)

        // Attach listener to the button
        val views =
                RemoteViews(context.getPackageName(),
                R.layout.appwidget_provider_layout)
        views.setOnClickPendingIntent(
                R.id.button, pendingIntent)

        // Tell the AppWidgetManager to perform an
        // update on the app widget
        appWidgetManager.updateAppWidget(
                appWidgetId, views)
    }
  }
}
```

An *app widget provider* can serve several app widgets; that is why we have to go through a loop inside the setup. Since this needs a layout file ciappwidget_provider_layout.xml, we create this one inside res/layout and, for example, write

```
<?xml version="1.0" encoding="utf-8"?>
<RelativeLayout
    xmlns:android=
            "http://schemas.android.com/apk/res/android"
    android:layout_width="match_parent"
```

349

```
    android:layout_height="match_parent"
    android:orientation="horizontal">

    <Button
        android:id="@+id/button"
        android:layout_width="match_parent"
        android:layout_height="wrap_content"
        android:text="Go"/>
</RelativeLayout>
```

Note   Not all layout containers and views are allowed inside the layout file
for an app widget – you can use one of `FrameLayout`, `LinearLayout`,
`RelativeLayout`, `GridLayout`, `AnalogClock`, `Button`, `Chronometer`,
`ImageButton`, `ImageView`, `ProgressBar`, `TextView`, `ViewFlipper`,
`ListView`, `GridView`, `StackView`, and `AdapterViewFlipper`.

The user must still decide to activate an app widget by long-tapping the app icon
and then placing it on the home screen. Because not all users know this, the
functionality of an app should not depend on whether it gets set as an app widget
on the home screen or not.

App widgets can have a configuration activity attached to them. This special activity
gets called once the user tries to place the app widget on the home screen. The user then
may, for example, be asked for some settings concerning appearance or functioning. To
install such an activity, you write inside `AndroidManifest.xml`

```
<activity android:name=".ExampleAppWidgetConfigure">
  <intent-filter>
    <action android:name=
        "android.appwidget.action.APPWIDGET_CONFIGURE"/>
  </intent-filter>
</activity>
```

The intent filter shown here is important – it tells the system about this special nature of the activity.

The app widget configuration activity must then be added to the XML configuration file example_appwidget_info.xml: add

```
android:configure=
      "full.class.name.ExampleAppWidgetConfigure"
```

as an additional attribute, using the fully qualified name of the configuration class.

The configuration activity itself is asked to return the app widget ID as follows:

```
class ExampleAppWidgetConfigure : AppCompatActivity() {
  var awi:Int = 0

  override fun onCreate(savedInstanceState: Bundle?) {
      super.onCreate(savedInstanceState)
      setContentView(R.layout.activity_conf)

      awi = intent.extras.getInt(
          AppWidgetManager.EXTRA_APPWIDGET_ID)
      Toast.makeText(this,"" + awi, Toast.LENGTH_LONG).
          show()
      // do more configuration stuff...
  }

  fun goBack(view: View) {
      // just an example...
      val data = Intent()
      data.putExtra(AppWidgetManager.EXTRA_APPWIDGET_ID,
          awi)
      setResult(RESULT_OK, data)
      finish()
  }
}
```

Note   The app widget's `onUpdate()` method does not get called *the first time* the configuration activity exits – it is the responsibility of the configuration activity to accordingly call `updateAppWidget()` on the app widget manager if needed.

Drag-and-Drop

Android supports drag-and-drop for any kind of UI element and layout. The idea is as follows:

- The app defines a gesture that defines the start of a drag operation. You are totally free to define this gesture – usual candidates are touch or touch and move operations, but you can also start drag operations programmatically.

- If the drag-and-drop designates some kind of data transfer, you may assign a data snippet of type `android.content.ClipData` to the drag operation.

- Views that take part of this drag-and-drop operation – this includes *any* drag source and *all* possible drop targets – get a customized `View.OnDragListener` object assigned.

- While the dragging is in progress, the dragged target gets visually represented by a moving *shadow* object. You are free to define it – it could be a star, a box, or any kind of graphics resembling the drag source. You only have to tell the system how to paint it – the positioning during the drag operation gets automatically handled by the Android OS. Because the drag source stays in place during the drag operation, the layout remains static all the time, and the dragging does not thwart layout operations by the layout manager.

- When the drag shadow enters the area of a possible drop target, the listener gets informed about that, and you can react by, for example, changing the visual appearance of the drop candidate.

- Because all drag sources and possible drop targets get informed about the various dragging states, you are free to visually express that by using different view appearances.

- Once a drop happens, the listener gets informed, and you can freely react on such drop events.

It is also possible to not use a dedicated drag-and-drop listener but instead overwrite some specific methods of the views taking part in drag-and-drop operations. The downside of that is you have to use the customized views inside the layout description, which makes it somewhat less readable. Also from an architectural point of view, the views then know too much of what is happening *to* them, which is an external concern and as such better gets handled from outside objects. We therefore follow the listener approach and in the following sections describe what exactly to do for this methodology.

Defining Drag Data

If your drag-and-drop operation defines some kind of data transfer from one object represented by a view to another, you define a ClipData object, for example, as follows:

```
val item = ClipData.Item(myView.tag.toString())
val dragData = ClipData(myView.tag.toString(),
      arrayOf(MIMETYPE_TEXT_PLAIN), item)
```

The first argument to the constructor is a user-readable label for the clip data, the second describes the type of the contents by assigning appropriate MIME types, and the item argument represents the data to be transported, here the string given by the tag attribute of the view. Other item types are Intents and URIs, to be specified in the constructor of ClipData.Item.

Defining a Drag Shadow

The drag shadow is the visible element painted underneath your finger while the dragging is in progress. You define the shadow in an object like in

```
class DragShadow(val resources: Resources, val resId:Int,
      view: ImageView) : View.DragShadowBuilder(view) {
   val rect = Rect()
```

```kotlin
// Defines a callback that sends the drag shadow
// dimensions and touch point back to the
// system.
override
fun onProvideShadowMetrics(size: Point, touch: Point) {
    val width = view.width
    val height = view.height

    rect.set(0, 0, width, height)

    // Back to the system through the size parameter.
    size.set(width, height)

    // The touch point's position in the middle
    touch.set(width / 2, height / 2)
}

// Defines a callback that draws the drag shadow in a
// Canvas
override
fun onDrawShadow(canvas: Canvas) {
    canvas.drawBitmap(
            BitmapFactory.decodeResource(
                    resources, resId),
            null, rect, null)
}
}
```

This example draws a bitmap resource, but you can do anything you like here.

Starting a Drag

To start a drag you invoke startDragAndDrop() for API levels 24 and higher, or startDrag() else, on the view object, which serves as a drag source. An example would be

```kotlin
theView.setOnTouchListener { view, event ->
    if(event.action == MotionEvent.ACTION_DOWN) {
```

```
        val shadow = DragShadow(resources,
                R.the_dragging_image, theView)

        val item = ClipData.Item(frog.tag.toString())
        val dragData = ClipData(frog.tag.toString(),
                arrayOf(MIMETYPE_TEXT_PLAIN), item)

        if (Build.VERSION.SDK_INT >=
                Build.VERSION_CODES.N) {
          theView.startDragAndDrop(dragData, shadow,
                null, 0)
        } else {
          theView.startDrag(dragData, shadow,
                null, 0)
        }
      }
    }
    true
}
```

If the drag operation is *not* associated with a data type, you can just as well let dragData be null. In this case you don't have to build a ClipData object.

Listening to Drag Events

The complete set of events occurring during a drag-and-drop operation is governed by a drag-and-drop listener. An example would be

```
class MyDragListener : View.OnDragListener {
  override
  fun onDrag(v: View, event: DragEvent): Boolean {
      var res = true
      when(event.action) {
          DragEvent.ACTION_DRAG_STARTED -> {
              when(v.tag) {
                  "DragSource" -> { res = false
                          /*not a drop receiver*/ }
                  "OneTarget" -> {
```

```kotlin
                    // could visibly change
                    // possible drop receivers
                }
            }
        }
        DragEvent.ACTION_DRAG_ENDED -> {
            when(v.tag) {
                "OneTarget" -> {
                    // could visibly change
                    // possible drop receivers
                }
            }
        }
        DragEvent.ACTION_DROP -> {
            when(v.tag) {
                "OneTarget" -> {
                    // visually revert drop
                    // receiver ...
                }
            }
            Toast.makeText(v.context, "dropped!",
                Toast.LENGTH_LONG).show()
        }
        DragEvent.ACTION_DRAG_ENTERED -> {
            when(v.tag) {
                "OneTarget" -> {
                    // could visibly change
                    // possible drop receivers
                }
            }
        }
        DragEvent.ACTION_DRAG_EXITED -> {
            when(v.tag) {
                "OneTarget" -> {
                    // visually revert drop
```

```
            // receiver ...
         }
      }
   }
}
      return res
   }
}
```

You can see that we are listening to drag start and end events and also to the shadow entering or exiting a possible drop area and to drop events. As pointed out, how you react to all these events is totally up to you.

Note   In the example we use a `tag` attribute assigned to a view to identify the view as part of a drag-and-drop operation. In fact you can also use the ID or any other way you might think of.

What is left is inside, for example, the activity's `onCreate()` callback you register the listener to all views that participate in a drag-and-drop operation:

```
override fun onCreate(savedInstanceState: Bundle?) {
   super.onCreate(savedInstanceState)
   setContentView(R.layout.activity_main)

   theView.setOnTouchListener ...

   val dragListener = MyDragListener()
   theView.setOnDragListener(dragListener)
   otherView.setOnDragListener(dragListener)
   ...
}
```

Multitouch

Multitouch events in Android OS are surprisingly easy to handle. All you need is overwrite the onTouchEvent() method of a View or a ViewGroup element. Inside the onTouchEvent() you fetch the masked action and act upon it:

```
frog.setOnTouchListener { view, event ->
    true
}
```

Note   In older versions of Android, you usually dispatch on the action as in event.action. With multitouch gestures it is better to act on the maskedAction – see in the following.

Inside the listener, you get the masked action by event.actionMasked and pass it to a when(){ .. } statement.

The magic now lies in this listener being invoked for all fingers (here called *pointers*) consecutively. To find out how many fingers currently are registered, you use event.pointerCount, and if you want to know which finger the event belongs to, you use val index = event.actionIndex. A starting point is thus

```
theView.setOnTouchListener { view,event ->
  fun actionToString(action:Int) : String = mapOf(
    MotionEvent.ACTION_DOWN to "Down",
    MotionEvent.ACTION_MOVE to "Move",
    MotionEvent.ACTION_POINTER_DOWN to "Pointer Down",
    MotionEvent.ACTION_UP to "Up",
    MotionEvent.ACTION_POINTER_UP to "Pointer Up",
    MotionEvent.ACTION_OUTSIDE to "Outside",
    MotionEvent.ACTION_CANCEL to "Cancel").
           getOrDefault(action,"")

  val action = event.actionMasked
  val index = event.actionIndex
  var xPos = -1
  var yPos = -1
```

```
Log.d("LOG", "The action is " +
        actionToString(action))

if (event.pointerCount > 1) {
  Log.d("LOG", "Multitouch event")
  // The coordinates of the current screen contact,
  // relative to the responding View or Activity.
  xPos = event.getX(index).toInt()
  yPos = event.getY(index).toInt()
} else {
  // Single touch event
  Log.d("LOG", "Single touch event")
  xPos = event.getX(index).toInt()
  yPos = event.getY(index).toInt()
}

// do more things...


  true
}
```

Picture-in-Picture Mode

Starting with Android 8.0 or API level 26, there exists a picture-in-picture mode where an activity gets shrunk and pinned to an edge of the screen. This is especially useful if the activity plays a video and you want the video to keep playing while another activity shows up.

To enable the picture-in-picture mode, inside AndroidManifest.xml add the following attributes to <activity>:

```
android:resizeableActivity="true"
android:supportsPictureInPicture="true"
android:configChanges=
    "screenSize|smallestScreenSize|
    screenLayout|orientation"
```

Then, wherever feasible in your app, you start the picture-in-picture mode by

```
enterPictureInPictureMode()
```

You might want to change and later revert the layout if the picture-in-picture mode gets entered or exited. To do so, overwrite the onPictureInPictureModeChanged(isInPictureInPictureMode : Boolean, newConfig : Configuration) and react accordingly.

Text-to-Speech

The text-to-speech framework allows for text to be converted to audio, either directly sent to the audio hardware or sent to a file. Using the corresponding TextToSpeech class is easy, but you should make sure all necessary resources are loaded. For this aim an Intent with action TextToSpeech.Engine.ACTION_CHECK_TTS_DATA should be fired. It is expected to return TextToSpeech.Engine.CHECK_VOICE_DATA_PASS; if it does not, call another Intent with action TextToSpeech.Engine.ACTION_INSTALL_TTS_DATA to let the user install text-to-speech data.

An example activity doing all that reads

```kotlin
class MainActivity : AppCompatActivity() {
  companion object {
      val MY_DATA_CHECK_CODE = 42
  }

  var tts: TextToSpeech? = null

  override
  fun onCreate(savedInstanceState: Bundle?) {
      super.onCreate(savedInstanceState)
      setContentView(R.layout.activity_main)

      val checkIntent = Intent()
      checkIntent.action = TextToSpeech.Engine.
          ACTION_CHECK_TTS_DATA
      startActivityForResult(checkIntent,
          MY_DATA_CHECK_CODE)
  }
```

```kotlin
fun go(view: View) {
    tts?.run {
        language = Locale.US
        val myText1 = "Did you sleep well?"
        val myText2 = "It's time to wake up."
        speak(myText1, TextToSpeech.QUEUE_FLUSH, null)
        speak(myText2, TextToSpeech.QUEUE_ADD, null)
    }
}

override
fun onActivityResult(requestCode: Int,
        resultCode: Int, data: Intent) {
  if (requestCode == MY_DATA_CHECK_CODE) {
    if (resultCode ==
          TextToSpeech.Engine.CHECK_VOICE_DATA_PASS) {
      // success, create the TTS instance
      tts = TextToSpeech(this, { status ->
        // do s.th. if you like
      })
    } else {
      // data are missing, install it
      val installIntent = Intent()
      installIntent.action =
          TextToSpeech.Engine.ACTION_INSTALL_TTS_DATA
      startActivity(installIntent)
    }
  }
}
}
```

This example also contains a go() method, which, for example, could be triggered by a button press. It will produce some speech and send it immediately to the loudspeakers.

If instead you want to write the audio to a file, use the tts.synthesizeToFile() method. More details will be given to you in the online documentation of TextToSpeech.

CHAPTER 10

Firebase

Firebase is the name of Google's cloud and (offshore) development platform. In this chapter we talk about cloud data storage and cloud-based messaging.

Note Firebase is more than just messaging and data storage – please consult the online documentation (e.g., `https://firebase.google.com/products-build`) and information you find in the Firebase console, and the information Android Studio gives you, to see what else can be done.

Firebase Cloud Storage

You can save files to and read them from Google Cloud Storage using the Cloud Storage API. You need a Google account with Firebase activated and a Firebase project set up via `https://console.firebase.google.com`.

Note The notion "file" is meant in a very broad sense – this could just be a series of bytes from your device's memory, a byte stream, or an actual file from the device's storage.

A verbatim copy of the app setup and storage configuration documentation in this book would not have much value. Instead, just follow the detailed instructions given at `https://firebase.google.com/docs/storage`, especially `https://firebase.google.com/docs/storage/android/start` therein.

363

© Peter Späth 2022
P. Späth, *Pro Android with Kotlin*, https://doi.org/10.1007/978-1-4842-8745-3_10

Firebase Cloud Messaging

Firebase Cloud Messaging (FCM) is a cloud-based message broker you can use to send and receive messages to and from various devices, including other operating systems like Apple iOS. The idea is as follows: you register an app in the Firebase console and henceforth can receive and send messages in connected devices, including other installations of your app on other devices.

Note   Firebase Cloud Messaging (FCM) is a successor of *Google Cloud Messaging* (GCM).

To start FCM from inside Android Studio, from your open project, go to Tools ➤ Firebase. Select Cloud Messaging and then Set up Firebase Cloud Messaging. If you follow the instructions there, you will end up using two services:

- A subclass of `FirebaseInstanceIdService` where you will receive a message token. The class basically looks like

```
class MyFirebaseInstanceIdService :
    FirebaseInstanceIdService() {
  override
  fun onTokenRefresh() {
    // Get updated InstanceID token.
    val refreshedToken =
        FirebaseInstanceId.getInstance().token
    Log.d(TAG, "Refreshed token: " +
        refreshedToken!!)

    // If you want to send messages to this
    // application instance or manage this apps
    // subscriptions on the server side, send the
    // Instance ID token to your app server.
    sendRegistrationToServer(refreshedToken)
  }
}
```

and it has a corresponding entry inside `AndroidManifest.xml`:

```
<service
  android:name=".MyFirebaseInstanceIdService"
  android:enabled="true"
  android:exported="true">
    <intent-filter>
      <action android:name=
          "com.google.firebase.INSTANCE_ID_EVENT"/>
    </intent-filter>
</service>
```

The token you receive here when you first start an app that is connected to Firebase is important – you need it to use the Firebase-based communication channel. And it is subject to infrequent automated renewal, so you need to find a way to reliably store the token whenever you receive it in this service. And do yourself a favor: unless you implemented a way to store the token, be sure to save the token you receive in the logs, because to recover a lost token results in annoying administrative work.

- Another service for receiving FCM-based messages. It could read

```
class MyFirebaseMessagingService :
      FirebaseMessagingService() {
  override
  fun onMessageReceived(remoteMessage:
      RemoteMessage) {
    // ...
    // Check if message contains a data payload.
    if (remoteMessage.data.size > 0) {
      Log.d(TAG, "Message data payload: " +
          remoteMessage.data)

      // Implement a logic:
      // For long-running tasks (10 seconds or more)
      // use Firebase Job Dispatcher.
      scheduleJob()
      // ...or else handle message within 10 seconds
      // handleNow()
    }
```

```
        // Message contains a notification payload?
        remoteMessage.notification?.run {
          Log.d(TAG, "Message Notification Body: " +
                body)
        }
      }

      private fun handleNow() {
          Log.e("LOG","handleNow()")
      }

      private fun scheduleJob() {
          Log.e("LOG","scheduleJob()")
      }
    }
```

and this too has a corresponding entry in AndroidManifest.xml:

```
<service
    android:name=".MyFirebaseMessagingService"
    android:enabled="true"
    android:exported="true">
  <intent-filter>
    <action android:name=
        "com.google.firebase.MESSAGING_EVENT"/>
  </intent-filter>
</service>
```

In order for this all to work, you need to have Firebase active in your Google account. There are several options. For a high-traffic messaging service, you need to buy a plan. The free variant (as of March 2018) however will give you more than enough power for development and testing.

If all is set up correctly, you can use the web-based Firebase console to test sending messages to your running app and see the messages arriving there in the logs.

For sending messages the suggested solution is to set up a trusted environment in the form of an application server. This is beyond the scope of the book, but the online Firebase documentation gives you various hints to get started with that matter.

CHAPTER 11

Development

This chapter is about issues closer to development matters, compared with the previous chapters. The topics we will be talking about here are less tightly coupled to specific Android OS APIs – it is more our concern here to find out how technical requirements can best be accomplished using Kotlin methodologies.

The chapter gets amended by a section for transcribing Kotlin code to JavaScript code, which can serve `WebView` widgets.

Writing Reusable Libraries in Kotlin

Most tutorials you will find on the Web are about activities, services, broadcast receivers, and content providers. These components are reusable in the sense that you can more or less easily extract them from a project and copy them to another project. The encapsulation in the Android OS has reached a quite elaborate stage, which makes this reusing possible. On a lower level, however, in quite some cases, the libraries or APIs that are provided inside Android maybe do not suit all your needs, so you might be tempted to develop such libraries yourself and then *copy* the sources from project to project wherever feasible.

Surely, such a copying on the source code level does not fit well into modern methodologies for reusable libraries. Just think about maintenance and versioning issues, which introduce a lot of boilerplate efforts. The best is you design such reusable libraries as dedicated development artifacts that then can be easily reused from different projects.

In the following sections, we develop a rudimentary *Regular Expression* library, serving as a conceptual basis for your own library projects.

© Peter Späth 2022   367
P. Späth, *Pro Android with Kotlin*, https://doi.org/10.1007/978-1-4842-8745-3_11

Starting a Library Module

Library projects come as projects containing one or more modules. With Android Studio open, create a new project. Then, inside the new project, go to *New* ➤ *New Module* and choose *Android Library*.

Note   An Android library is more than just a collection of classes. It may also contain resources and configuration files. For our purposes we just look at the classes – from a development perspective, these additional possibilities don't hurt, and you just can ignore them. For your projects using the Android library type however gives you many more possibilities for future extensions, compared with using just JAR files.

Creating the Library

Inside the library module, create a new Kotlin class, and inside write

```
package com.example.regularexpressionlib

infix operator fun String.div(re:String) :
      Array<MatchResult> =
  Regex(re).findAll(this).toList().toTypedArray()

infix operator fun String.rem(re:String) :
      MatchResult? =
  Regex(re).findAll(this).toList().firstOrNull()

operator fun MatchResult.get(i:Int) =
  this.groupValues[i]

fun String.onMatch(re:String, func: (String)-> Unit)
      : Boolean =
  this.matches(Regex(re)).also { if(it) func(this) }
```

What these four operators and functions do is not less than allowing us to write `searchString / regExpString` to search for regular expression matches and searchString % regExpString to search for the first match. Besides, we can use searchString.onMatch() to have some block execute only if there is a match.

This listing is different from all the listings we have seen so far in this book. First of all you can see that we don't have any class here. This is possible, because Kotlin knows the concept of a file artifact – behind the scenes it generates a hidden class based on the package name. Any client of the library that imports it via import com.example. regularexpressionlib.* can act as if it performed a static import of all these functions in Java.

The infix operator fun String.div(re:String) defines a division operator for strings. Such a division is not possible in the standard, so there is no clash with Kotlin built-in operators. It uses the Regex class from the Kotlin libraries to find all occurrences of a regular expression in a search string and converts it to an array, so we can later use the [ ] operator to access the results by index. The infix operator fun String.rem(re:String) does almost the same, but it defines the % operator for strings, performs a regular expression search, and takes only the first result or returns null if no result exists.

The operator fun MatchResult.get(i:Int) = ... is an extension of the MatchResult returned by the preceding operators. It allows for accessing the groups of a match by index. Say you searched for "(el)" inside "Hello Nelo", you could write ("Hello Nelo" / "(e.)") [0][1] to get the first group of the first match, in this case the "el" from "Hello".

Testing the Library

We need a way to test the library while developing it. Unfortunately, Android Studio version 3.0 does not allow for something like a main() function it could start. The only thing we can do is to create a *unit test*, and for our case such a unit test could read

```
import org.junit.Assert.*
import org.junit.Test
...

class RegularExpressionTest {
  @Test
  fun proof_of_concept() {
      assertEquals(1, ("Hello Nelo" / ".*el.*").size)
      assertEquals(2, ("Hello Nelo" / ".*?el.*?").size)
```

```
    var s1:String = ""
    ("Hello Nelo" / "e[lX]").forEach {
        s1 += it.groupValues
    }
    assertEquals("[el][el]", s1)

    var s2: String = ""
    ("Hello Nelo" / ".*el.*").firstOrNull()?.run {
        s2 += this[0]
    }
    assertEquals("Hello Nelo", s2)

    assertEquals("el",
        ("Hello Nelo" % ".*(el).*")?.let{ it[1] } )

    assertEquals("el",
        ("Hello Nelo" / ".*(el).*")[0][1])

    var match1: Boolean = false
    "Hello".onMatch(".*el.*") {
        match1 = true
    }
    assertTrue(match1)
  }
}
```

You can then run this test like any other unit test using Android Studio's context menu. Note that at early stages of the development, you can add `println()` statements to the test in order to print some information on the test console while the test runs.

Using the Library

Once you invoke *Build ➤ Rebuild Project*, you can find the Android library inside the

```
build/outputs/aar
```

folder of the module. To use it from clients, create a new module in the client project via *New ➤ New Module,* choose "Import .JAR/.AAR Package," and navigate to the .aar file generated by the library project.

Caution   This procedure copies the .aar file. If you have a new version of the library, you can either remove the library project inside the client project (!) and import it again or copy the .aar file manually from the library project to the client project.

To use the library in the client, you just add `import com.example.regularexpressionlib.*` to the header, and henceforth you can apply the new matching constructs as shown in the preceding test.

Publishing the Library

So far we have used the library locally, which means you have the library project somewhere on your development machine and use it from other projects on the same machine. You can also publish libraries, meaning to make them either available for other developers inside a corporate environment if you have a corporate repository at hand or truly public for libraries you want to provide to the community.

Unfortunately, the process of publishing libraries is rather complex and involves altering the build files at several places and using third-party plugins and repository websites. This makes the process of publishing libraries a complex and brittle task, and giving you a detailed description of one possible publishing process might easily be outdated when you read this book. I therefore ask you to do your own research – entering "publishing Android libraries" in your favorite search engine will readily point you to online resources that will help you. If you find several processes that might suit your needs, a general rule of thumb is to use one that (A) has a large support community and (B) is as easy as possible.

Also, make sure for corporate projects you have the allowance to use public repositories if you want to use one of them. If you cannot use public repositories, to install a corporate repository is not an overly complex task. To, for example, establish a corporate Maven repository, you can use the software suite "Artifactory."

Advanced Listeners Using Kotlin

Whatever kind of app you are creating for Android, at one or the other place or more probably quite often, you will have to provide listeners for API function calls. While in Java you have to create classes or anonymous inner classes that implement the listener interface, in Kotlin you can do that more elegantly.

If you have a SAM (or *single abstract method*) class or interface, the story goes very easy. For example, if you want to add an on-click listener to a button, which means you have to provide an implementation of interface View.OnClickListener, doing it the Java way looks like

```
btn.setOnClickListener(object : View.OnClickListener {
    override fun onClick(v: View?) {
        // do s.th.
    }
})
```

However, since this interface just has only one method, you can write more shortly

```
btn.setOnClickListener {
  // do s.th.
}
```

and let the compiler find out how the interface method is to implement.

If a listener is not a SAM, that is, it has more than one method, this short notation is not possible any longer. If, for example, you have an EditText view and want to add a text changed listener, you basically have to write

```
val et = ... // the EditText view
et.addTextChangedListener( object : TextWatcher {
    override fun afterTextChanged(s: Editable?) {
        // ...
    }
    override fun beforeTextChanged(s: CharSequence?,
          start: Int, count: Int, after: Int) {
        // ...
    }
    override fun onTextChanged(s: CharSequence?,
```

```
        start: Int, before: Int, count: Int) {
    // ...
  }
})
```

even if you are only interested in the onTextChanged() callback method. What you could
do however is extend the EditText class in a utility file and there add the possibility to
provide a simplified text changed listener. To do so, start with such a file, for example,
utility.kt, inside package com.example or of course any package of your app.
Inside add

```
fun EditText.addTextChangedListener(l:
      (CharSequence?, Int, Int, Int) -> Unit) {
  this.addTextChangedListener(object : TextWatcher {
    override fun afterTextChanged(s: Editable?) {
    }
    override fun beforeTextChanged(s: CharSequence?,
         start: Int, count: Int, after: Int) {
    }
    override fun onTextChanged(s: CharSequence?,
         start: Int, before: Int, count: Int) {
      l(s, start, before, count)
    }
  })
}
```

which adds the desired method to that class dynamically.

You can now import com.example.utility.* anywhere needed and then write

```
val et = ... // the EditText view
et.addTextChangedListener({ s: CharSequence?,
      start: Int, before: Int, count: Int ->
  // do s.th.
})
```

which looks considerably more concise compared with the original construct.

Multithreading

We already talked about multithreading to some extent inside section "Background Tasks" of Chapter 9. In this section we just point out what Kotlin on a language level can do to simplify multithreading.

Kotlin contains a couple of utility functions inside its standard library. They help start threads and timers more easily compared with using the Java API – see Table 11-1.

Table 11-1. *Kotlin Concurrency*

Name	Parameters	Return	Description
fixedRateTimer	name: String? daemon: Boolean initialDelay: Long period: Long action: TimerTask.() -> Unit	Timer	Creates and starts a timer object for fixed-rate scheduling. The period and initialDelay parameters are in milliseconds.
fixedRateTimer	name: String? daemon: Boolean startAt: Date period: Long action: TimerTask.() -> Unit	Timer	Creates and starts a timer object for fixed-rate scheduling. The period parameter is in milliseconds.
timer	name: String? daemon: Boolean initialDelay: Long period: Long action: TimerTask.() -> Unit	Timer	Creates and starts a timer object for fixed-rate scheduling. The period parameter is the time in milliseconds between the end of the previous and the start of the next task.
timer	name: String? daemon: Boolean startAt: Date period: Long action: TimerTask.() -> Unit	Timer	Creates and starts a timer object for fixed-rate scheduling. The period parameter is the time in milliseconds between the end of the previous and the start of the next task.
thread	start: Boolean isDaemon: Boolean contextClassLoader: ClassLoader? name: String? priority: Int block: () -> Unit	Thread	Creates and possibly starts a thread, executing its `block`. Threads with higher priority are executed in preference to threads with lower priority.

For the timer functions, the "action" parameter is a closure with `this` being the corresponding `TimerTask` object. Using it you may, for example, cancel the timer from inside its execution block. Threads or timers that have `daemon` or `isDaemon` set to `true` will not prevent the JVM from shutting down when all non-daemonized threads have exited.

By virtue of its general functional abilities, Kotlin anyway does a good job in helping us with concurrency – many of the classes inside `java.util.concurrent` that deal with parallel execution take a `Runnable` or `Callable` as an argument, and in Kotlin you can always replace such SAM (single abstract method) constructs via direct `{ ... }` lambda constructs, for example:

```
val es = Executors.newFixedThreadPool(10)
// ...
val future = es.submit({
      Thread.sleep(2000L)
      println("executor over")
      10
  } as ()->Int)
val res:Int = future.get()
```

So you don't have to write

```
ExecutorService es = Executors.newFixedThreadPool(10);
// ...
Callable<Integer> c = new Callable<>() {
    public Integer call() {
      try {
        Thread.sleep(2000L);
      } catch(InterruptedException e { }
      System.out.println("executor over");
      return 10;
    };
Future<Integer> f = es.submit(c);
int res = f.get();
```

as in Java. Note the cast to `()->Int` is necessary in the Kotlin code, even with Android Studio complaining that it be superfluous. The reason for that is if we didn't do it, the other method with a `Runnable` as argument would get called instead and the executor would be unable to return a value.

Compatibility Libraries

There is an important and at the beginning not-so-easy-to-understand distinction between the *Framework API* and the *compatibility libraries*. If you start developing Android apps, you quite often see classes of the same name showing up in different packages. Or even worse, you see classes of different names from different packages seemingly doing the same thing.

Note   The Jetpack library collection simplifies compatibility. If you use Jetpack compatibility classes from the `androidx.*` namespace, you can forget about compatibility libraries as described in the following. Android Studio helps for migrating older projects. `https://developer.android.com/jetpack/androidx/` tells you more about it.

Let us take a look at a prominent example: to create activities you can either subclass `android.app.Activity` or subclass `android.support.v7.app.AppCompatActivity`. Looking at examples and tutorials you find on the Web, there seems to be no noticeable difference in usage. In fact `AppCompatActivity` inherits from `Activity`, so wherever an `Activity` is required, you can substitute `AppCompatActivity` for it, and it will compile. So is there a difference in function? It depends. If you look at the documentation or at the code, you can see that the `AppCompatActivity` allows for adding an `android.support.v7.app.ActionBar`, while `android.app.Activity` does not. Instead, `android.app.Activity` allows for adding an `android.app.ActionBar`. And this time `android.support.v7.app.ActionBar` does *not* inherit from `android.app.ActionBar`, so you cannot add `android.support.v7.app.ActionBar` to an `android.app.Activity`.

This basically says that if you favor `android.support.v7.app.ActionBar` over `android.app.ActionBar`, you must use the `AppCompatActivity` for an activity. Why would one use `android.support.v7.app.ActionBar` instead of `android.app.ActionBar`? The answer is easy: the latter is quite old – it is available since API level 11. Newer versions of `android.app.ActionBar` cannot break the API to maintain compatibility with older devices. But `android.support.v7.app.ActionBar` can have new functions added – it is much newer and exists since API level 24.

The magic now works as follows: if you use a device that speaks API level 24 or higher, you can use `android.support.v7.app.AppCompatActivity` and add an `android.support.v7.app.ActionBar`. You could also use `android.app.Activity`, but then you cannot add an `android.support.v7.app.ActionBar` and instead have to use an `android.app.ActionBar`. So for new devices, it makes sense to use `android.support.v7.app.AppCompatActivity` for your activities if the support library action bar better suits your needs compared with the framework action bar.

How about older devices? You still can use `android.support.v7.app.AppCompatActivity` because it is provided as a library added to the app. So you also can use the modern `android.support.v7.app.ActionBar` as an action bar and have more functionalities compared with the old `android.app.ActionBar` genuinely provided by the device. And this is actually how the trick goes: *using support libraries even older devices can take advantage of new functionalities added later*! The implementation of the support class internally checks for the device version and provides sensible fallback functionalities to resemble modern devices as much as possible.

The caveat is that you as a developer have to live in two worlds at the same time: you have to explicitly or implicitly use framework classes if there is no other choice, and you have to think about using support library classes if available and if you want to ensure the maximum compatibility with older devices. It is therefore vital to check, before using a class, if there is also a matching support library class. You might not be happy with this two-world methodology used in Android, and it also means more thinking work to build an app, but that is how Android handles backward compatibility.

You will readily find detailed information about the support libraries if you enter "Android support library" in your favorite search engine.

Support libraries get bundled with your app, so they must be declared as dependencies in the build file. If you start a new project in Android Studio, it by default writes inside the module's `build.gradle` file

```
dependencies {
  ...
  implementation 'com.android.support:appcompat-v7:26.1.0'
  implementation 'com.android.support.constraint:constraint-layout:1.0.2'
  ...
}
```

So you see the support library version v7 is available by default, so you can use it right from the start.

Kotlin Best Practices

Development is not only about solving IT-related problems or implementing requirements; you also want to write "good" software. What "good" exactly means in this context is a little blurry, though. A lot of aspects play a role here: quick development, high execution performance, short programs, readable programs, high program stability, and so on. All of them have their merits, and exaggerating any of them will thwart the other aspects.

In fact, you should have all of them in mind. Experience tells however to put some stress on the following aspects:

- Make programs comprehensive (or expressive). A super-elegant solution that nobody else understands maybe makes you happy, but bear in mind that later maybe other people need to understand your software.

- Keep programs simple. Overly complex solutions are subject to instabilities. Of course you will not wake up one morning and say, "OK, today I will write a simple program to solve requirement XYZ." Writing simple programs that reliably solve problems is a matter of experience, and it comes with years of practice. But you can always try to constantly get better in writing simple programs. A good starting point is always asking yourself "Shouldn't there be a simpler solution to this?" for any part of your software, and looking at the API documentations and the programming language reference in quite some cases, you *will* find easier solutions doing the same as what you currently have.

- Don't repeat yourself. This principle, commonly referred to as "DRY" programming, cannot be overemphasized. Whenever you find yourself using Ctrl+C and Ctrl+V to copy some program passages, think of instead using one function or one lambda expression providing just one place where things are done.

- Do expectable and anticipatable things. You can overwrite class methods and operators in Kotlin, and you can dynamically add functions to existing classes, even to such basic classes like `String`. In any case make sure such extensions work as expected looking at their names, for if they didn't, the program would be hard to understand.

Kotlin helps with all of these aspects and quite often does a better job than the venerable Java. In the following sections, we point out a couple of Kotlin concepts you can use to make your program short, simple, and expressive. Note that the sum of these concepts is far away from being a complete documentation of Kotlin. So for more details, please see the online documentation or a Kotlin book.

Functional Programming

While functional programming as a development paradigm entered Java with version 8, Kotlin supports a functional programming style from the beginning. In functional programming you prefer non-mutable values over variables, avoid state machines, and allow functions as parameters to functions. Also, the lambda calculus allows for passing functions without names. Kotlin provides us with all that.

In Java you have the `final` modifier to express a variable isn't going to be changed after first initialization. While most Java developers use `final` modifiers for constants as in

```
public class Constants {
  public final static int CALCULATION_PRECISION = 10;
  public final static int MAX_ITERATIONS = 1000;
  ...
}
```

I barely ever saw developers using it inside the coding, which is a pity, since it improves both readability and stability. The temptation to omit it for saving a few keystrokes is just too big. In Kotlin the story is different – you say `val` to express a data object remains constant during its lifetime and `var` if you need a real variable:

```
fun getMaxFactorial():Int = 13
fun fact(n:Int):Int {
    val maxFactorial = getMaxFactorial()
    if(n > maxFactorial)
        throw RuntimeException("Too big")
    var x = 1
    for( i in 1..(n) ) {
        x *= i
    }
```

```
    return x
}
val x = fact(12)
System.out.println("12! = ${x}")
```

In this short snippet, you see the maxFactorial as a val, and by that you say "this is not subject to change." The x however is a var, and it gets changed after initialization.

We can even avoid the var x in the snippet for the factorial calculation and replace it with a functional construct. This is another functional imperative: prefer expressions over a statement or a chain of statements. To do so, we use a recursion and write

```
fun fact(n:Int):Int = if(n>getMaxFactorial())
  throw RuntimeException("Too big") else
  if(n > 1) n * fact(n-1) else 1
val x = fact(10)
System.out.println("10! = ${x}")
```

This little factorial calculator is just a short example – with collections the story gets more interesting. The Kotlin standard library includes a lot of functional constructs you can use to write elegant code. Just to give you a glimpse of all the possibilities, we rewrite the factorial calculator once again and use a fold function from the collections package:

```
fun fact(n:Int) = (1..n).fold(1, { acc,i -> acc * i })
System.out.println("10! = ${fact(10)}")
```

For simplicity I removed the range check; if you like you can add that if... check from earlier to the lambda expression inside {...}. You see that we even don't have a val left – internally the i and acc get handled as vals though. This can even be shortened one step further. Since all we use is the "times" functionality of type Int, we can directly refer to it and write

```
fun fact(n:Int) = (1..n).fold(1, Int::times)
System.out.println("10! = ${fact(10)}")
```

With the other functional constructs from the collections package, you can perform more interesting transformations with sets, lists, and maps. But functional programming is also about passing around functions as objects in your code. In Kotlin you can assign functions to vals or vars as in

```
val factEngine:  (acc:Int,i:Int) -> Int =
      { acc,i -> acc * i }
fun fact(n:Int) = (1..n).fold(1, factEngine)
System.out.println("10! = ${fact(10)}")
```

or even shorter since Kotlin under circumstances can infer the type:

```
val factEngine = { acc:Int, i:Int -> acc * i }
fun fact(n:Int) = (1..n).fold(1, factEngine)
System.out.println("10! = ${fact(10)}")
```

In this book we are using functional constructs wherever feasible to improve comprehensiveness and conciseness.

Top-Level Functions and Data

While in the Java world it is considered a bad style to have too many globally available functions and data, for example, by definitions with static scope inside some utility class, in Kotlin this experiences a renaissance and also looks somewhat more natural. That is because you can declare functions and variables/values in a file outside any class. Still to use them, you have to import such elements like in import com.example.global.* where a file with arbitrary name inside package com/example.global contains no classes but only fun, var, and val elements.

For example, write a file "common.kt" in com/example/app/util and inside add

```
package com.example.app.util

val PI_SQUARED = Math.PI * Math.PI

fun logObj(o:Any?) =
      o?.let { "(" + o::class.toString() + ") " +
            o.toString() } ?: "<null>"
```

and more utility functions and constants. To use them, write

```
import com.example.app.util.*
...
val ps = PI_SQUARED
logObj(ps)
```

You should however be cautious using that feature – overly using it easily leads to a structural mess. And avoid putting mutable variables in such a scope altogether! You can and should however put utility functions and global constants in such a global file.

Class Extensions

Unlike in the Java language, Kotlin allows you to dynamically add methods to classes. To do so write

```
fun TheClass.newFun(...){ ... }
```

The same works for operators, which allows you to create extensions like "Some Text" % "magic" (it is left to your fantasy what this does) to such common classes like String. You'd implement this particular extension like

```
infix operator fun String.rem(s:String){ ... }
```

Just make sure you don't unintentionally overwrite existing class methods and operators – this makes your program unreadable because it does unexpected things. Note that most standard operators like Double.times() cannot be overwritten anyways since they are marked *final* internally.

A list of operators you can define via operator fun TheClass.<OPERATOR> is shown in Table 11-2.

Table 11-2. *Kotlin Operators*

Symbol	Translates to	Infix	Default Function
+a	a.unaryPlus()		Usually does nothing
-a	a.unaryMinus()		Negates a number
!a	a.not()		Negates a Boolean expression
a++	a.inc()		Increments a number
a- -	a.dec()		Decrements a number
a + b	a.plus(b)	x	Addition

(continued)

Table 11-2. (*continued*)

Symbol	Translates to	Infix	Default Function
a – b	a.minus(b)	x	Subtraction
a * b	a.times(b)	x	Multiplication
a / b	a.div(b)	x	Division
a % b	a.rem(b)	x	Remainder after division
a .. b	a.rangeTo(b)	x	Defines a range
a in b	b.contains(a)	x	Containment check
a !in b	!b.contains(a)	x	Non-containment check
a[i]	a.get(i)		Indexed access
a[i,j,...]	a.get(i,j,...)		Indexed access, normally not used
a[i] = b	a.set(i,b)		Indexed setting access
a[i,j,...] = b	a.set(i,j,...,b)		Indexed setting access, normally not used
a()	a.invoke()		Invocation
a(b)	a.invoke(b)		Invocation
a(b,c,...)	a.invoke(b,c,...)		Invocation
a += b	a.plusAssign(b)	x	Adds to a. Must not return a value – instead, you must modify this
a -= b	a.minusAssign(b)	x	Subtracts from a. Must not return a value – instead, you must modify this
a *= b	a.timesAssign()	x	Multiplies by a. Must not return a value – instead, you must modify this
a /= b	a.divAssign(b)	x	Divides a by b and then assigns. Must not return a value – instead, you must modify this
a %= b	a.remAssign(b)	x	Takes the remainder of the division by b and then assigns. Must not return a value – instead, you must modify this

(*continued*)

Table 11-2. (*continued*)

Symbol	Translates to	Infix	Default Function
a == b	a?.equals(b) ?: (b === null)	x	Checks equality
a != b	!(a?.equals(b) ?: (b === null))	x	Checks inequality
a > b	a.compareTo(b) > 0	x	Comparison
a < b	a.compareTo(b) < 0	x	Comparison
a >= b	a.compareTo(b) >= 0	x	Comparison
a <= b	a.compareTo(b) <= 0	x	Comparison

To define an extension, for any operator from the table of type "Infix", you write

```
infix operator fun TheClass.<OPERATOR>( ... ){ ... }
```

where the function arguments are the second and any subsequent operands and this inside the function body refers to the first operand. For operators not of type "Infix", just omit the "infix".

Defining operators for your own classes certainly is a good idea. To amend standard Java or Kotlin library classes by operators might improve the readability of your code as well.

Named Arguments

Using named arguments as in

```
fun person(fName:String = "", lName:String = "",
        age:Int=0) {
    val p = Person().apply { ... }
    return p
}
```

you can make more expressive calls like

```
val p = person(age = 27, lName = "Smith")
```

Using parameter names you don't have to care about argument order, and in many cases you can avoid overloading constructors for various parameter combinations.

Scoping Functions

The scoping functions allow you to structure your code in a way different from using classes and methods. Consider, for example, the code

```
val person = Person()
person.lastName = "Smith"
person.firstName = "John"
person.birthDay = "2011-01-23"
val company = Company("ACME")
```

While this is valid code, the repetition of "person." is annoying. Besides, the first four lines are about constructing a person, while the last line has nothing to do with a person. It would be nice if this could be visually expressed and the repetition could also be avoided. There is a construct in Kotlin, and it reads

```
val person = Person().apply {
  lastName = "Smith"
  firstName = "John"
  birthDay = "2011-01-23"
}
val company = Company("ACME")
```

This looks more expressive compared with the original code. It clearly says: Construct a person and do something with it; then do something else. There are five such constructs, and despite being similar, they differ in meaning and usage: **also**, **apply**, **let**, **run**, and **with**. Table 11-3 describes them.

Table 11-3. *Scoping Functions*

Syntax	What Is "this"	What Is "it"	Returns	Use
a.also { ... }	this of outer context	a	a	Use for some crosscutting concern, for example, to add logging.
a.apply { ... }	a	-	a	Use for post-construction object forming.
a.let { ... }	this of outer context	a	Last expression	Use for transformations.
a.run { ... }	a	-	Last expression	Do some computation using an object, with only side effects. For clarity better don't use what it returns.
with(a) { ... }	a	-	Last expression	Group operations on an object. For clarity better don't use what it returns.

Using scoping functions greatly improves the expressiveness of your code – I use them often in this book.

Nullability

Kotlin addresses the problem of nullability on a language level, to avoid annoying NullPointerException throws. For any variable or constant, the assignment of null values is not allowed by default – you have to explicitly declare nullability by adding a "?" at the end as in

```
var name:String? = null
```

The compiler then knows that name from the example can be null and takes various precautions to avoid NullPointerExceptions. You, for example, cannot write name. toUpperCase(), but you have to use name?.toUpperCase() instead, which does the capitalization only if name is not null and otherwise returns null itself.

Using the scoping functions we described previously, there is a very elegant method to avoid constructs like if(x != null) { ... }. You can instead write

```
x?.run {
    ...
}
```

which does the same but is more expressive: by virtue of the "?." the execution of run{} happens only if x is not null.

The elvis operator "?:" is also quite useful, for it handles cases where you want to calculate an expression only if the receiver variable is null, as in

```
var x:String? = ...
...
var y:String = x ?: "default"
```

which is the same as String y = (x != null) ? x : "default"); in Java.

Data Classes

Data classes are classes whose responsibility is to carry structured data. Actually doing something with the data inside the data class usually is not necessary or at least not important.

The declaration of data classes in Kotlin is very easy; all you have to do is write

```
data class Person(
        val fName:String,
        val lName:String,
        val age:Int)
```

or, if you want to use default values for some arguments

```
data class Person(
        val fName:String="",
        val lName:String,
        val age:Int=0)
```

This simple declaration already defines a constructor, an appropriate `equals()` method for comparison, a default `toString()` implementation, and the ability to be part of a destructuring – see in the following. To create an object, you just have to write

```
val pers = Person("John","Smith",37)
```

or more expressive

```
val pers = Person(fName="John", lName="Smith", age=37)
```

in which case you can also omit parameters if they have defaults declared.

This, and the fact that you can declare classes and functions also inside functions, makes it very easy to define ad hoc complex function return types, as in

```
fun someFun() {
    ...
    data class Person(
        val fName:String,
        val lName:String,
        val age:Int)
    fun innerFun():Person = ...
    ...
    val p1:Person = innerFun()
    val fName1 = p1.fName
    ...
```

Destructuring

A *destructuring declaration* allows you to multi-assign values or variables. Say you have a data class `Person` as defined in the previous section. You can then write

```
val p:Person = ...
val (fName,lName,age) = p
```

which gives you three different values. The order for data classes is defined by the order of the class's member declaration. Generally, any object that has `component1()`, `component2()`, ... accessors can take part in a destructuring, so you can use destructuring for your own classes as well. This is, for example, by default given for map entries, so you can write

```
val m = mapOf( 1 to "John", 2 to "Greg", ... )
for( (k,v) in m) { ... }
```

because the "to" is an infix operator that creates a Pair class, which in turn has fun
component1() and fun component2() defined.

As an additional feature to a destructuring declaration, you can use "_" wildcards for
unused parts, as in

```
val p:Person = ...
val (fName,lName,_) = p
```

Multiline String Literals

Multiline string literals in Java always are a little clumsy to define:

```
String s = "First line\n" +
    "Second line";
```

In Kotlin you can define multiline string literals as in

```
val s = """
    First line
    Second Line"""
```

and you can even get rid of the preceding indent spaces by adding .trimIndent() as in

```
val s = """
    First line
    Second Line""".trimIndent()
```

which removes the leading newline and the common spaces at the beginning of
each line.

Inner Functions and Classes

In Kotlin functions and classes can also be declared inside other functions, which further
helps in structuring your code:

```
fun someFun() {
  ...
  class InnerClass { ... }
  fun innerFun() = ...
  ...
}
```

The scope of such inner constructs is of course limited to the function in which they are declared.

String Interpolation

In Kotlin you can pass values into strings as in

```
val i = 7
val s = "And the value of 'i' is ${i}"
```

This is borrowed from the Groovy language, and you can use it for all types, since all types have a `toString()` member. The only requirement is that the contents of `${}` evaluate to an expression, so you even can write

```
val i1 = 7
val i2 = 8
val s = "The sum is: ${i1+i2}"
```

or more complex constructs using method calls and lambda functions:

```
val s = "8 + 1 is: ${ { i: Int -> i + 1 }(8) }"
```

Qualified "this"

If "this" is not what you want but you instead want to refer to `this` from an outer context, in Kotlin you use the "@" qualifier as in

```
class A {
    val b = 7
    init {
        val p = arrayOf(8,9).apply {
            this[0] += this@A.b
```

```
        }
        ...
    }
}
```

Delegation

Kotlin allows for easily following the *delegation* pattern. In

```
interface Printer {
    fun print()
}

class PrinterImpl(val x: Int) : Printer {
    override fun print() { print(x) }
}

class Derived(b: Printer) : Printer by b
```

the class Derived is of type Printer and delegates all its method calls to the b object. So you can write

```
val pi = PrinterImpl(7)
Derived(pi).print()
```

You are free to overwrite method calls at will, so you can adapt the delegate to use new functionalities:

```
class Derived(val b: Printer) : Printer by b {
    override fun print() {
        print("Printing:")
        b.print()
    }
}
```

Renamed Imports

In some cases imported classes may use long names, and you use them very often, so you'd wish they had shorter names, for example, if you often use `SimpleDateFormat` classes in your code and don't want to write the full class name all the time. To help us with that and shorten this a little, you can introduce import aliases and write

```
import java.text.SimpleDateFormat as SDF
```

Henceforth, you can use `SDF` as a substitute for `SimpleDateFormat`, as in

```
val dateStr = SDF("yyyy-MM-dd").format(Date())
```

Don't overuse this feature though, since your fellow developers may need to memorize too many new names, which makes your code hard to read.

Kotlin on JavaScript

If you hear Android and Kotlin together, the obvious thing you will think about is that Kotlin serves as a substitute for Java and addresses the Android Runtime and Android APIs. But there is another possibility, which is not that obvious but nevertheless opens interesting possibilities. If you look at Kotlin alone, you can see that it can create bytecode to be run on a Java Virtual Machine or on a somewhat Java-like Dalvik Virtual Machine in the case of Android. *Or* it can produce JavaScript to be used in a browser. The question is: Can we use that in Android as well? The answer is yes, and in the following sections, I will show you how this can be done.

Creating a JavaScript Module

We start with a JavaScript module containing Kotlin files, which are compiled to JavaScript files. There is nothing like a "JavaScript" module wizard available when you start a new module, but we can easily start with a standard smartphone app module and convert it to serve our needs.

In an Android Studio project, select New ➤ New Module and then choose Phone & Tablet Module. Give it a decent name, say "kotlinjsSample" for now. Once the module is generated, remove the following folders and files, because we don't need them:

```
src/test
src/androidTest
src/main/java
src/main/res
src/main/AndroidManifest.xml
```

Note   If you want to do that removal from inside Android Studio, you have to switch the view type from "Android" to "Project" first.

Instead, add two folders:

```
src/main/kotlinjs
src/main/web
```

Now replace the contents of the module's build.gradle file to read

```
buildscript {
    ext.kotlin_version = '1.2.31'
    repositories {
        mavenCentral()
    }
    dependencies {
        classpath "org.jetbrains.kotlin:" +
                "kotlin-gradle-plugin:$kotlin_version"
    }
}

apply plugin: 'kotlin2js'

sourceSets {
    main.kotlin.srcDirs += 'src/main/kotlinjs'
}

task prepareForExport(type: Jar) {
    baseName = project.name + '-all'
    from {
        configurations.compile.collect {
```

```
                it.isDirectory() ? it : zipTree(it) } +
                'src/main/web'
    }
    with jar
}

repositories {
    mavenCentral()
}

dependencies {
    implementation "org.jetbrains.kotlin:" +
            "kotlin-stdlib-js:$kotlin_version"
}
```

This build file enables the Kotlin ➤ JavaScript compiler and introduces a new export task.

You can now open the "Gradle" view on the right side of Android Studio's window, and there under "others" you will find the task "prepareForExport". To run it, double-click it. After that inside build/libs, you will find a new file kotlinjsSample-all.jar. It is this file that represents the JavaScript module for use by other apps or modules.

Create a first file Main.kt inside src/main/kotlinjs and let it read

```
import kotlin.browser.document

fun main(args: Array<String>) {
    val message = "Hello JavaScript!"
    document.getElementById("cont")!!.innerHTML = message
}
```

In the end we will be targeting a website, so we need a first HTML page as well. Make it the standard landing page index.html, create it inside src/main/web, and enter

```
<!DOCTYPE html>
<html lang="en">
<head>
  <meta charset="UTF-8">
  <title>Kotlin-JavaScript</title>
</head>
```

```
<body>
  <span id="cont"></span>
  <script type="text/javascript"
       src="kotlin.js"></script>
  <script type="text/javascript"
       src="kotlinjsSample.js"></script>
</body>
</html>
```

Execute the task "prepareForExport" once again to let the module output artifact reflect the changes we just made.

Using the JavaScript Module

To use the JavaScript module we constructed in the last section, we add a couple of lines in the app's build.gradle file:

```
task syncKotlinJs(type: Copy) {
  from zipTree('../kotlinjsSample/build/libs/' +
               'kotlinjsSample-all.jar')
  into 'src/main/assets/kotlinjs'
}
preBuild.dependsOn(syncKotlinJs)
```

This will import the JavaScript module's output file and extract it inside the assets folder of the app. This extra build task gets executed automatically for you during a normal build by virtue of the "dependsOn()" declaration.

Now inside your layout file, place a WebView element, like in

```
<WebView
    android:id="@+id/wv"
    android:layout_width="match_parent"
    android:layout_height="match_parent">
</WebView>
```

To fill that view with a web page, inside your main activity's onCreate() callback, write

```
wv.webChromeClient = WebChromeClient()
wv.settings.javaScriptEnabled = true
wv.loadUrl("file:///android_asset/kotlinjs/index.html")
```

This will enable JavaScript support for the WebView widget and load the main HTML page from the JavaScript module.

As an extension you maybe want to connect the JavaScript inside the web page to the Kotlin code from the app (not the JavaScript module). This is not overly complicated. You just have to add

```
class JsObject {
    @JavascriptInterface
    override fun toString(): String {
      return "Hi from injectedObject"
    }
}
wv.addJavascriptInterface(JsObject(), "injectedObject")
```

and henceforth can use "injectedObject" from the JavaScript module as follows:

```
val message = "Hello JavaScript! injected=" +
      window["injectedObject"]
```

Using these techniques you could design your complete app using HTML, CSS, Kotlin transcribing to JavaScript, and a couple of accessor objects to address Android APIs.

CHAPTER 12

Building

In this chapter we talk about the building process of your apps. While building an app given source files can be done using both a terminal and buttons and menu entries from inside the Android Studio IDE, this is not an introduction to Android Studio nor a reference – for these please refer to the help included or books and online resources.

What we will do in this chapter is look at build-related concepts and methods for adapting the build process to your needs.

Build-Related Files

Once you create a new project inside Android Studio, you will see the following build-related files:

- **build.gradle**

  This is the top-level project-related build file. It contains the declaration of repositories and dependencies common to all modules the project contains. There is normally no need for you to edit this file for simple apps.

- **gradle.properties**

  Technical settings related to Gradle builds. There is normally no need for you to edit this file.

- **gradlew** and **gradlew.bat**

  Wrapper scripts so you can run builds using a terminal instead of the Android Studio IDE.

- **local.properties**

  Generated technical properties related to your Android Studio installation. You should not edit this file.

© Peter Späth 2022
P. Späth, *Pro Android with Kotlin*, https://doi.org/10.1007/978-1-4842-8745-3_12

- **settings.gradle**

  Tells which modules are part of the project. Android Studio will handle this file if you add new modules.

- **app/build.gradle**

  Module-related build file. This is important – here dependencies and the build process for the module get configured. Android Studio will create a first module named "app" including the corresponding build file for you, but this "app" as a name is just a convention. Additional modules will have different names you choose at will, and they all have their own build files. It is even possible to rename "app" to a different name that better suits your needs, if you like.

Module Configuration

Each module of a project contains its own build file `build.gradle`. If you let Android Studio create a new project or module for you, it also creates an initial build file. Such a basic build file for a module with Kotlin support looks like

```
plugins {
    id 'com.android.application'
    id 'org.jetbrains.kotlin.android'
    id 'com.google.gms.google-services'
}

android {
    compileSdk 32

    defaultConfig {
        applicationId "book.andrkotlpro.example1"
        minSdk 23
        targetSdk 32
        versionCode 1
        versionName "1.0"
```

```
        testInstrumentationRunner -
          "androidx.test.runner.AndroidJUnitRunner"
        vectorDrawables {
            useSupportLibrary true
        }
    }

    buildTypes {
        release {
            minifyEnabled false
            proguardFiles getDefaultProguardFile(
              'proguard-android-optimize.txt'),
                'proguard-rules.pro'
        }
    }
    compileOptions {
        sourceCompatibility JavaVersion.VERSION_1_8
        targetCompatibility JavaVersion.VERSION_1_8
    }
    kotlinOptions {
        jvmTarget = '1.8'
    }
    buildFeatures {
        compose true
    }
    composeOptions {
        kotlinCompilerExtensionVersion compose_version
    }
    packagingOptions {
        resources {
            excludes += '/META-INF/{AL2.0,LGPL2.1}'
        }
    }
}
```

```
dependencies {
    implementation 'androidx.core:core-ktx:1.7.0'
    implementation -
      "androidx.compose.ui:ui:$compose_version"
    implementation -
      "androidx.compose.material:material:$compose_version"
    implementation "androidx.compose.ui:" +
      "ui-tooling-preview:$compose_version"
    implementation -
      'androidx.lifecycle:lifecycle-runtime-ktx:2.3.1'
    implementation -
      'androidx.activity:activity-compose:1.3.1'
    implementation -
      'com.google.firebase:firebase-messaging:20.1.0'
    testImplementation 'junit:junit:4.13.2'
    androidTestImplementation -
      'androidx.test.ext:junit:1.1.3'
    androidTestImplementation -
      'androidx.test.espresso:espresso-core:3.4.0'
    androidTestImplementation -
      "androidx.compose.ui:ui-test-junit4:$compose_version"
    debugImplementation -
      "androidx.compose.ui:ui-tooling:$compose_version"
    debugImplementation -
      "androidx.compose.ui:ui-test-manifest:$compose_version"
}
```

(Disregard the ¬ and the following line breaks.) Note that "" strings in Gradle allow to contain ${} placeholders, while ' ' strings do not. Other than that they are interchangeable.

Its elements are as follows:

- The **plugins { }** lines load and apply Gradle plugins necessary for Android and Kotlin development.

- The **android { }** element specifies settings for the Android plugin.

- The **dependencies { }** element describes dependencies of the module. The implementation keyword means the dependency is needed both for compiling the module and running it. The latter implies that the dependency gets included in the APK file. Identifiers like "xyzImplementation" refer to a build type or source set "xyz" – you can see that for the unit tests located at src/test, the JUnit libraries get added, while for src/androidTest both the test runner and Espresso get used. If you refer to build types or product flavors (more about build types and product flavors in the following), you can substitute the build type name or product flavor name for "xyz". If you want to refer to a variant, which is a combination of a build type and a product flavor, you additionally must declare it inside a configurations { } element, for example:

```
configurations {
  // flavor = "free", type = "debug"
  freeDebugCompile {}
}
```

- For **defaultConfig { }** and **buildTypes { }**, see the following sections.

Other keywords inside the dependencies {...} section include

- **implementation**

  We talked about that one. It expresses the dependency is needed both for compiling and running the app.

- **api**

  Same as implementation, but in addition lets the dependency leak through to clients of the app.

- **compile**

  This is an old alias for api. Don't use it.

- **compileOnly**

  The dependency is needed for compilation, but will not be included in the app. This frequently happens for source-only libraries like source code preprocessors and alike.

401

- **runtimeOnly**

  The dependency is not needed for compilation, but will be included inside the app.

Note that variable compose_version is defined in the *project's* build.gradle file:

```
buildscript {
    ext {
        compose_version = '1.1.0-beta01'
    }
    dependencies {
        classpath 'com.google.gms:google-services:4.3.3'
    }
}
// Top-level build file where you can add configuration
// options common to all sub-projects/modules.
plugins {
    id 'com.android.application' version '7.2.1'
      apply false
    id 'com.android.library' version '7.2.1'
      apply false
    id 'org.jetbrains.kotlin.android' version '1.5.31'
      apply false
}

task clean(type: Delete) {
    delete rootProject.buildDir
}
```

(Remove the line breaks in front of the "apply false". In this file you also find other very general settings applicable to all project modules.)

Module Common Configuration

The element defaultConfig { ... } inside a module's build.gradle file specifies configuration settings for a build, independent of the variant chosen (see the next section). The possible setting can be looked up in the Android Gradle DSL reference, but a common setup reads like

```
defaultConfig {

  // Uniquely identifies the package for publishing.
  applicationId 'com.example.myapp'

  // The minimum API level required to run the app.
  minSdk 23

  // The API level used to test the app.
  targetSdk 32

  // The version number of your app.
  versionCode 42

  // A user-friendly version name for your app.
  versionName "42.0"
}
```

Module Build Variants

Build variants correspond to different .apk files, which are generated by the build process. The number of build variants is given by

```
Number of Build Variants =
    (Number of Build Types) x (Number of Product Flavors)
```

Inside Android Studio, you choose the build variant via Build ➤ Select Build Variant in the menu. In the following sections, we describe what build types and product flavors are.

Build Types

Build types correspond to different stages of the app development – if you start a project, Android Studio will set up two build types for you: *development* and *release*. If you open the module's build.gradle file, you can see inside android { ... }

```
buildTypes {
  release {
    minifyEnabled false
```

```
      proguardFiles ¬
        getDefaultProguardFile('proguard-android.txt'), ¬
        'proguard-rules.pro'
    }
  }
```

(Disregard the ¬ including the following newlines.) Even though you don't see a "debug" type there, it exists. The fact that it doesn't appear just means the "debug" type uses its default settings. If you need to change the defaults, just add a "debug" section here as in

```
buildTypes {
    release {
        ...
    }
    debug {
        ...
    }
}
```

You are not restricted to use one of the predefined build types. Define additional build types as in

```
buildTypes {
    release {
        ...
    }
    debug {
        ...
    }
    integration {
        initWith debug
        manifestPlaceholders = ¬
            [hostName:"internal.mycompany.com"]
        applicationIdSuffix ".integration"
    }
}
```

This defines a new build type "integration" that inherits from "debug" by virtue of "initWith" and otherwise adds a custom app file suffix and provides a placeholder to be used in the manifest file. The settings you can specify there are rather numerous – you can find them if you enter "Android Gradle plugin DSL reference" in your favorite search engine.

Another identifier we haven't talked about yet is the `proguardFiles` identifier. That one is used for filtering and/or obfuscating files that are to be included in the app before distributing it. If you use it for filtering, please first weigh the benefit against the effort – with modern devices saving a few megabytes doesn't play a big role nowadays. And if you want to use it for obfuscation, note that this might cause trouble if reflection gets used either by your code or from the libraries referred to. And obfuscation does not really prevent hijackers from using your code after decompilation – it just makes it a little harder. So carefully consider the advantages of using Proguard. If you think it will suit your needs, details about how to use it can be found in the online documentation.

Product Flavors

Product flavors allow distinctions between things like different *feature sets* or different *device requirements*, but you can draw the distinction wherever best suits you.

By default Android Studio doesn't prepare different product flavors for a new project or module – if you need them, you must add a `productFlavors { ... }` section inside the `android { ... }` element of file `build.gradle`. An example would be

```
buildTypes {...}
flavorDimensions "monetary"
productFlavors {
    free {
        dimension "monetary"
        applicationIdSuffix ".free"
        versionNameSuffix "-free"
    }
    paid {
        dimension "monetary"
        applicationIdSuffix ".paid"
        versionNameSuffix "-paid"
    }
}
```

where the possible setting can be looked up in the Android Gradle DSL reference. This will lead to APKs of the form

```
app-free-debug.apk
app-paid-debug.apk
app-free-release.apk
app-paid-release.apk
```

The dimensionality can even be extended. If you add more elements to the flavorDimensions line, for example, flavorDimensions "monetary", "apilevel", you can add more flavors

```
flavorDimensions "monetary", "apilevel"
productFlavors {
    free {
        dimension "monetary" ... }
    paid {
        dimension "monetary" ... }
    sinceapi21 {
        dimension "apilevel"
        versionNameSuffix "-api21" ... }
    sinceapi24 {
        dimension "apilevel"
        versionNameSuffix "-api24" ... }
}
```

which in the end will give us the following set of APK files:

```
app-free-api21-debug.apk
app-paid-api21-debug.apk
app-free-api21-release.apk
app-paid-api21-release.apk
app-free-api24-debug.apk
app-paid-api24-debug.apk
app-free-api24-release.apk
app-paid-api24-release.apk
```

To filter out certain variants of the possible variants, add a `variantFilter` element into the build file and write

```
variantFilter { variant ->
  def names = variant.flavors*.name  // this is an array
  // To filter out variants, make a check here and then
  // do a "setIgnore(true)" if you don't need a variant.
  // This is just an example:
  if (names.contains("sinceapi24") &&
        names.contains("free")) {
    setIgnore(true)
  }
}
```

Source Sets

If you create a project in Android Studio and switch to the "Project" view, you can see that there is a "main" folder inside the "src" folder. This corresponds to the "main" source set, which is the single source set configured and used by default. See Figure 12-1.

Figure 12-1. *The "main" Source Set*

You can however have more sets, and they correspond to the build types, the product flavors, and the build variants. As soon as you add more source sets, a build will lead to merging the current build variant, the build type it includes, the product flavor it includes, and finally the "main" source set. To see which source sets will be included in a build, open the Gradle view on the right side of the window and run the "sourceSets" task. This will produce a long listing, and you can see entries like

```
main
Java sources: [app/src/main/java]

debug
Java sources: [app/src/debug/java]

free
Java sources: [app/src/free/java]
```

```
freeSinceapi21
Java sources: [app/src/freeSinceapi21/java]

freeSinceapi21Debug
Java sources: [app/src/freeSinceapi21Debug/java]

freeSinceapi21Release
Java sources: [app/src/freeSinceapi21Release/java]

paid
Java sources: [app/src/paid/java]

paidSinceapi21
Java sources: [app/src/paidSinceapi21/java]

release
Java sources: [app/src/release/java]

sinceapi21
Java sources: [app/src/sinceapi21/java]
```

This will tell you that if you choose a build variant freeSinceapi21Debug, the build process will look into folders

```
app/src/freeSinceapi21Debug/java
app/src/freeSinceapi21/java
app/src/free/java
app/src/sinceapi21/java
app/src/debug/java
app/src/main/java
```

for classes and likewise into the corresponding folders for resources, assets, and the AndroidManifest.xml file. While the Java or Kotlin classes must not repeat in such a build chain, the manifest files and resource and assets files will be merged by the build process.

Inside the "dependencies { ... }" section of file build.gradle, you can dispatch dependencies according to build variants. Just add a camel-cased version of the source set in front of any of the settings there. For example, if for the "freeSinceapi21" variant you want to include a compile dependency ":mylib", write

```
freeSinceapi21Compile ':mylib'
```

Running a Build from the Console

You don't have to use Android Studio to build apps. While it is a good idea to bootstrap an app project using Android Studio, after this you can build the app using a terminal. This is what the Gradle wrapper scripts `gradlew` and `gradlew.bat` are for – the first one is for Linux, and the second one is for Windows. In the following paragraphs, we will have a look at some command line commands for Linux; if you have a Windows development machine, just use the BAT script instead.

In the preceding sections, we have seen that the basic building blocks of each build consist of one or more tasks that get executed during the build. So we first want to know which tasks actually exist. For this aim, to list all tasks available, enter

```
./gradlew tasks
```

This will give you an extensive list and some description of each task. In the following we will have a look at some of these tasks.

To build the app APK file for build type "debug" or "release," enter one of

```
./gradlew assembleDebug
./gradlew assembleRelease
```

which creates an APK file inside `<PROJECT>/<MODULE>/build/outputs`. Of course you can also specify any custom build type you defined inside `build.gradle`.

To build the debug type APK and then install it on a connected device or emulator, enter

```
./gradlew installDebug
```

where for the "Debug" part in the argument, you can substitute any build variant using the variant's camel-cased name. This installs the app on connected devices. It does not automatically run it though – you have to do that manually! To install *and* run an app, please see Chapter 19.

In case you want to find out which dependencies any of your app's modules has, to see the dependency tree, enter

```
./gradlew dependencies :app:dependencies
```

or with "app" substituted by the module name in question. This provides a rather lengthy listing, so you maybe want to pipe it into a file

```
./gradlew dependencies :app:dependencies > deps.txt
```

and then investigate the result in an editor.

Signing

Each app's APK file needs to be signed before it can be run on a device. For the "debug" build type, a suitable signing configuration will be chosen for you automatically, so for the debugging development stage, you don't need to care about signing.

A release APK however needs a proper signing configuration. If you use Android Studio's menu Build ➤ Generate Signed APK, Android Studio will help you create and/ or use an appropriate key. But you can also specify the signing configuration inside the module's build.gradle file. To do so, add a signingConfigs { ... } section as in

```
android {
    ...
    defaultConfig {...}
    signingConfigs {
        release {
            storeFile file("myrelease.keystore")
            storePassword "passwd"
            keyAlias "MyReleaseKey"
            keyPassword "passwd"
        }
    }
    buildTypes {
        release {
            ...
            signingConfig signingConfigs.release
        }
    }
}
```

and also from inside the release build type refer to a signing config as shown at "signingConfig ..." inside the listing. The keystore you need to provide for that is a standard Java keystore – please see Java's online documentation to learn how to build one. Or you let Android Studio help you create a keystore using the dialog that pops up when you chose Build ➤ Generate Signed APK in the menu.

CHAPTER 13

Communication

Communication is about sending data through component or app or device boundaries. A standardized way of components of one or more apps communicating with each other is using *broadcasts*, which we talked about in Chapter 5.

Another possibility for inter-app communication on one device is using ResultReceiver objects, which are passed by Intents. Despite their name they can not only be used to send data back to an invoker when an invoked component has done its work, but also anytime while it is alive. We used them at a couple of places in this book, but in this chapter, we will revise using them to have all communication means together.

ResultReceiver Classes

A ResultReceiver object can be passed from any one component to another component by assigning it to an Intent, so you can use it to send data between components of any kind, provided they live on the same device.

We first subclass a ResultReceiver, which will later receive messages from an invoked component, and write

```
class MyResultReceiver : ResultReceiver(null) {
  companion object {
    val INTENT_KEY = "my.result.receiver"
    val DATA_KEY = "data.key"
  }
  override fun onReceiveResult(resultCode: Int,
      resultData: Bundle?) {
    super.onReceiveResult(resultCode, resultData)
```

© Peter Späth 2022
P. Späth, *Pro Android with Kotlin*, https://doi.org/10.1007/978-1-4842-8745-3_13

```
      val d = resultData?.get(DATA_KEY) as String
      Log.e("LOG", "Received: " + d)
    }
  }
```

Of course you can write more meaningful things inside its onReceiveResult() function. To pass an instance of MyResultReceiver over to an invoked component, we can now write

```
Intent(this, CalledActivity::class.java).apply {
    putExtra(MyResultReceiver.INTENT_KEY,
           MyResultReceiver())
}.run{ startActivity(this) }
```

or any other means to invoke another component.

Inside the invoked component, you can now at any suitable place send data to the invoking component via something like

```
var myReceiver:ResultReceiver? = null

override fun onCreate(savedInstanceState: Bundle?) {
  super.onCreate(savedInstanceState)
  setContentView(R.layout.activity_called)
  ...
  myReceiver = intent.
        getParcelableExtra<ResultReceiver>(
        MyResultReceiver.INTENT_KEY)
}

fun go(v: View) {
  val bndl = Bundle().apply {
      putString(MyResultReceiver.DATA_KEY,
        "Hello from called component")
  }
  myReceiver?.send(42, bndl) ?:
        throw IllegalStateException("myReceiver is null")
}
```

Inside a production environment, you additionally need to take care of checking whether the recipient is still alive – I left this check out for brevity. Also note that on the sending side, a reference to the `ResultReceiver` implementation is actually not needed – if you communicate through app boundaries, you can just write

```
...
val INTENT_KEY = "my.result.receiver"
val DATA_KEY = "data.key"
...
val myReceiver = intent.
    getParcelableExtra<ResultReceiver>(
    INTENT_KEY)
...
val bndl = Bundle().apply {
  putString(DATA_KEY,
    "Hello from called component")
}
myReceiver?.send(42, bndl)
```

Communication with Back Ends

Using a cloud-based provider like Firebase for connecting your app to other apps on other devices, as described in Chapter 10, certainly exhibits different merits. You have a reliable message broker with message backup facilities, analytics, and more.

But using the cloud has its disadvantages as well. Your data, be it encrypted or not, will leave your house even for corporate apps, and you cannot be 100% sure the provider will not change the API at some point in the future, forcing you to change your app. So, if you need more control, you can abandon the cloud and use direct networking instead.

For directly using network protocols to communicate with devices or application servers, you basically have two options:

- **Use javax.net.ssl.HttpsURLConnection.**

  This provides for a low-level connectivity, but with already TLS, streaming capabilities, timeouts, and connection pooling included. As you can see from the class name, it is part of the standard Java API, so you will find lots of information about it on the Web. We nevertheless give a description in the following section.

- **Use the Volley API included with Android.**

  This is a higher-level wrapper around basic networking functions. Using Volley considerably simplifies network-based development, so it is generally the first candidate for using networking in Android.

In both cases you need to add appropriate permissions inside `AndroidManifest.xml`:

```
<uses-permission android:name=
    "android.permission.INTERNET" />
<uses-permission android:name=
    "android.permission.ACCESS_NETWORK_STATE" />
```

Communication with HttpsURLConnection

Before using a network communication API, we need to make sure networking operations happen in the background – modern Android versions even won't allow you to perform networking in the UI thread. But even without that restriction, it is highly recommended to always perform networking in a background task. We talked about background operation in section "Background Tasks" of Chapter 9. A first method you want to look at is running network operations inside a suspending function (part of the coroutines technology), but you are free to choose other means as well. The following sections assume the snippets presented there are running in the background.

Using class `HttpsURLConnection`-based communication boils down to

```kotlin
fun convertStreamToString(istr: InputStream): String {
  val s = Scanner(istr).useDelimiter("\\A")
  return if (s.hasNext()) s.next() else ""
}

// This is a convention for emulated devices
// addressing the host (development PC)
val HOST_IP = "10.0.2.2"

val url = "https://${HOST_IP}:6699/test/person"
var stream: InputStream? = null
var connection: HttpsURLConnection? = null
var result: String? = null
try {
```

```
  connection = (URL(uri.toString()).openConnection()
        as HttpsURLConnection).apply {

    // ! ONLY FOR TESTING !  No SSL hostname verification
    class TrustAllHostNameVerifier : HostnameVerifier {
      override
      fun verify(hostname: String, session: SSLSession):
          Boolean = true
    }
    hostnameVerifier = TrustAllHostNameVerifier()

    // Timeout for reading InputStream set to 3000ms
    readTimeout = 3000
    // Timeout for connect() set to 3000ms.
    connectTimeout = 3000
    // For this use case, set HTTP method to GET.
    requestMethod = "GET"
    // Already true by default, just telling. Needs to
    // be true since this request is carrying an input
    // (response) body.
    doInput = true
    // Open communication link
    connect()
    responseCode.takeIf {
          it != HttpsURLConnection.HTTP_OK }?.run {
      throw IOException("HTTP error code: $this")
    }
    // Retrieve the response body
    stream = inputStream?.also {
      result = it.let { convertStreamToString(it) }
    }
  }
} finally {
  stream?.close()
  connection?.disconnect()
}
```

```
Log.e("LOG", result)
```

This example tries to access a GET URL https://10.0.2.2:6699/test/person
targeting your development PC and prints the result in the logs.

Note, if your server happens to hold a self-signed certificate for SSL, you must at an
initialization place, say inside the onCreate() callback, add

```
val trustAllCerts =
        arrayOf<TrustManager>(object : X509TrustManager {
    override
    fun getAcceptedIssuers():
      Array<java.security.cert.X509Certificate>? = null
    override
    fun checkClientTrusted(
      certs: Array<java.security.cert.X509Certificate>,
      authType: String) {
    }
    override
    fun checkServerTrusted(
        certs: Array<java.security.cert.X509Certificate>,
        authType: String) {
    }
})
SSLContext.getInstance("SSL").apply {
  init(null, trustAllCerts, java.security.SecureRandom())
}.apply {
  HttpsURLConnection.setDefaultSSLSocketFactory(
        socketFactory)
}
```

Otherwise, the preceding code will complain and fail. Of course you shouldn't do
this in production code and instead add a check for the validity of the certificate.

Networking with Volley

Volley is a networking library that simplifies networking for Android. First of all Volley sends its work to the background by itself; you don't have to take care about that. Other goodies provided by Volley are

- Scheduling mechanisms

- Parallel working of several requests

- Handling of JSON requests and responses

- Caching

- Diagnosis tools

To start developing with Volley, add the dependency to your module's `build.gradle` file:

```
dependencies {
  ...
  implementation 'com.android.volley:volley:1.2.1'
}
```

The next thing to do is set up a `RequestQueue` that Volley uses to handle requests in the background. The easiest way to do that is

```
val queue = Volley.newRequestQueue(this)
```

inside an activity. But you can also customize the creation of a `RequestQueue` and instead write

```
val CACHE_CAPACITY = 1024 * 1024 // 1MB
val cache = DiskBasedCache(cacheDir, CACHE_CAPACITY)
// ... or a different implementation
val network = BasicNetwork(HurlStack())
// ... or a different implementation

val requestQueue = RequestQueue(cache, network).apply {
  start()
}
```

The question is: Under which scope is the request queue best defined? We could create and run the request queue in an activity's scope, which means that that queue needs to be recreated each time the activity gets recreated itself. This is a valid option, but the documentation suggests you use the application scope instead to reduce the recreation of caches. The recommended way is to use the `Singleton` pattern, which results in

```
class RequestQueueSingleton
    constructor (context: Context) {
  companion object {
    @Volatile
    private var INSTANCE: RequestQueueSingleton? = null
    fun getInstance(context: Context) =
        INSTANCE ?: synchronized(this) {
            INSTANCE ?: RequestQueueSingleton(context)
        }
  }
  val requestQueue: RequestQueue by lazy {
    val alwaysTrusting = object : HurlStack() {
      override
      fun createConnection(url: URL): HttpURLConnection {
        fun getHostnameVerifier():HostnameVerifier {
          return object : HostnameVerifier {
            override
            fun verify(hostname:String,
                    session:SSLSession):Boolean = true
          }
        }
        return (super.createConnection(url) as
              HttpsURLConnection).apply {
          hostnameVerifier = getHostnameVerifier()
        }
      }
    }
    // Using the Application context is important.
    // This is for testing:
```

```
Volley.newRequestQueue(context.applicationContext,
        alwaysTrusting)
// ... for production use:
// Volley.newRequestQueue(context.applicationContext)
  }
}
```

where for development and testing purposes, an accept-all SSL hostname verifier was added.

So, instead of writing `val queue = Volley.newRequestQueue(this)` or `val requestQueue = RequestQueue(...)` as shown earlier, you then use

```
val queue = RequestQueueSingleton(this).requestQueue
```

Now for sending a string request, you have to write

```
// This is a convention for emulated devices
// addressing the host (development PC)
val HOST_IP = "10.0.2.2"

val stringRequest =
    StringRequest(Request.Method.GET,
        "https://${HOST_IP}:6699/test/person",
        Response.Listener<String> { response ->
          val shortened =
              response.substring(0,
                  Math.min(response.length, 500))
          tv.text = "Response is: ${shortened}"
        },
        Response.ErrorListener { err ->
          Log.e("LOG", err.toString())
          tv.text = "That didn't work!"
        })
queue.add(stringRequest)
```

where `tv` points to a `TextView` UI element. For that to work, you need to have a server responding to `https://localhost:6699/test/person`. Note that the response listener automatically runs in the UI thread, so you don't have to take care of that yourself.

To cancel single requests, use `cancel()` on the request object anywhere. You can also cancel a group of requests: add a tag to each request in question as in `val stringRequest = ... .apply {tag = "TheTag"}` and then write `queue?.cancelAll( "TheTag" )`. Volley makes sure the response listener never gets called once a request is canceled.

To request a JSON object or JSON array, you have to substitute

```
val request =
    JsonArrayRequest(Request.Method.GET, ...)
```

or

```
val request =
    JsonObjectRequest(Request.Method.GET, ...)
```

for the `StringRequest` we used previously. For example, for a JSON request and the POST method, you can write

```
val reqObj:JSONObject =
    JSONObject("""{"a":7, "b":"Hello"}""")
val json1 = JsonObjectRequest(Request.Method.POST,
    "https://${HOST_IP}:6699/test/json",
    reqObj,
    Response.Listener<JSONObject> { response ->
        Log.e("LOG", "Response: ${response}")
    },
    Response.ErrorListener{ err ->
        Log.e("LOG", "Error: ${err}")
    })
```

Volley can do more for you. You can use other HTTP methods like "PUT" and also write custom requests handling and returning other data types. Please see Volley's online documentation or its API documentation for more details.

Setting Up a Test Server

This is not really an Android topic and not even anything that necessarily has to do with Kotlin, but to test the communication, you need to have some kind of web server running. To have things easy, I usually configure a very simple yet powerful server

based on Groovy and Spark – not Apache Spark but instead Java Spark from http://
sparkjava.com/.

To use it, for example, in Eclipse, first install the Groovy plugin. Then create a Maven
project and add as dependencies

```
<dependency>
    <groupId>com.sparkjava</groupId>
    <artifactId>spark-core</artifactId>
    <version>2.9.4</version>
</dependency>
<dependency>
    <groupId>org.slf4j</groupId>
    <artifactId>slf4j-simple</artifactId>
    <version>1.7.25</version>
    <scope>test</scope>
</dependency>
```

After that create a Java keystore file and write a Groovy script

```
import static spark.Spark.*

def keystoreFilePath = "keystore.jks"
def keystorePassword = "passw7%d"
def truststoreFilePath = null
def truststorePassword = null

secure(keystoreFilePath, keystorePassword,
        truststoreFilePath, truststorePassword)
port(6699)

get("/test/person", { req, res -> "Hello World" })

post("/test/json", { req, res ->
    println(req.body())
    '{ "msg":"Hello World", "val":7 }'
})
```

and start it.

> **Caution**   In order for inside Eclipse to avoid Servlet API version clashes, remove the dependency on the Servlet API in the Groovy settings dialog you get at Properties after right-clicking Groovy Libraries in the project.

To create a keystore file, for example, under Linux, you could use the Bash script

```
#!/bin/bash
export JAVA_HOME=/opt/jdk
$JAVA_HOME/bin/keytool -genkey -keyalg RSA \
  -alias selfsigned -keystore keystore.jks \
  -storepass passw7%d -validity 360 -keysize 2048
```

with the Java path adapted.

Android and NFC

NFC is for short-range wireless connectivity for the transport of small data packages between NFC-capable devices. The range is limited to a few centimeters between the communication partners. Typical use cases are

- Connecting and then reading from or writing to NFC tags

- Connecting and then communicating with other NFC-capable devices (peer-to-peer mode)

- Emulating an NFC card: connecting and then communicating with NFC card readers and writers

To start developing an app that speaks NFC, you need to acquire the permission to do so inside `AndroidManifest.xml`:

```
<uses-permission android:name="android.permission.NFC" />
```

To also limit visibility in the Google Play Store, add

```
<uses-feature android:name="android.hardware.nfc"
    android:required="true" />
```

to the same file.

Talking to NFC Tags

Once a device with NFC enabled discovers an NFC tag in the vicinity, it tries to dispatch the tag according to a certain algorithm: If the system determines an NDEF data and finds an intent filter that is able to handle NDEF, the corresponding component gets called. If the tag does not exhibit NDEF data but otherwise identifies itself by providing information about technology and/or payload, this set of data gets mapped to a "tech" record, and the system tries to find a component that is able to handle that. If both fail, the discovery information is limited to the bare fact that an NFC tag was discovered. In this case the system tries to find a component that can handle NFC tags without NDEF and without "tech"-type data.

Based on the information found on the NFC tag, Android also creates a URI and a MIME type you can use for intent filters. The procedure for that gets described in more detail on page "NFC Basics" of the Android online developer documentation – for example, enter "Android develop NFC basics" in your favorite search engine to find it.

For writing appropriate intent filters, please see section "Intent Filters" of Chapter 3, with the addition that for "tech"-style discovery, you need to add a certain `<meta-data>` element inside `<activity>` as in

```
<meta-data android:name="android.nfc.action.TECH_DISCOVERED"
    android:resource="@xml/nfc_tech_filter" />
```

which points to a file `nfc_tech_filter.xml` inside `res/xml`, containing

```
<resources xmlns:xliff=
        "urn:oasis:names:tc:xliff:document:1.2">
    <tech-list>
        <tech>android.nfc.tech.IsoDep</tech>
        <tech>android.nfc.tech.NfcA</tech>
        <tech>android.nfc.tech.NfcB</tech>
        <tech>android.nfc.tech.NfcF</tech>
        <tech>android.nfc.tech.NfcV</tech>
        <tech>android.nfc.tech.Ndef</tech>
        <tech>android.nfc.tech.NdefFormatable</tech>
        <tech>android.nfc.tech.MifareClassic</tech>
        <tech>android.nfc.tech.MifareUltralight</tech>
    </tech-list>
</resources>
```

or any subset of it.

The actions you need to add to the intent filter to contribute to the NFC dispatching process are as follows:

- For NDEF discovery style, use

```
<intent-filter>
  <action android:name=
       "android.nfc.action.NDEF_DISCOVERED"/>
  ...more filter specs...
</intent-filter>
```

- For tech discovery style, use

```
<intent-filter>
  <action android:name=
       "android.nfc.action.TECH_DISCOVERED"/>
</intent-filter>
<meta-data android:name=
     "android.nfc.action.TECH_DISCOVERED"
     android:resource="@xml/nfc_tech_filter" />
```

- For failback discovery style, use

```
<intent-filter>
  <action android:name=
       "android.nfc.action.TAG_DISCOVERED"/>
  ...more filter specs...
</intent-filter>
```

Once the NFC-related Intent gets dispatched, a matching activity can extract NFC information from the Intent. To do so, fetch intent extra data via one or a combination of the following:

- **NfcAdapter.EXTRA_TAG**: Required, gives back an `android.nfc.Tag` object.

- **NfcAdapter.EXTRA_NDEF_MESSAGES**: Optional, NDEF messages from the tag. You can retrieve them via

```
val rawMessages : Parcelable[] =
    intent.getParcelableArrayExtra(
    NfcAdapter.EXTRA_NDEF_MESSAGES)
```

- **NfcAdapter.EXTRA_ID**: Optional, the low-level ID of the tag.

If you want to write to NFC tags, the procedure for that gets described on page "NFC Basics" of the Android online developer documentation.

Peer-to-Peer NFC Data Exchange

Android allows for the NFC communication between two Android devices via its *Beam* technology. The procedure goes as follows: Let the activity of an NFC-capable device extend CreateNdefMessageCallback and implement the method createNdefMessage(event : NfcEvent) : NdefMessage. Inside this method, create and return an NdefMessage like in

```
val text = "A NFC message at " +
        System.currentTimeMillis().toString()
val msg = NdefMessage( arrayOf(
      NdefRecord.createMime(
          "application/vnd.com.example.android.beam",
          text.toByteArray() ) )
) )

/*
 * When a device receives an NFC message with an Android
 * Application Record (AAR) added, the application
 * specified in the AAR is guaranteed to run. The AAR
 * thus overrides the tag dispatch system.
 */
//val msg = NdefMessage( arrayOf(
//      NdefRecord.createMime(
//          "application/vnd.com.example.android.beam",
//          text.toByteArray() ),
```

```
//        NdefRecord.createApplicationRecord(
//            "com.example.android.beam")
//) )
return msg
```

An NFC data–receiving app could then, for example, in its `onResume()` callback, detect whether it got initiated by an NFC discovery action:

```
override
fun onResume() {
    super.onResume()
    // Check to see that the Activity started due to an
    // Android Beam event
    if (NfcAdapter.ACTION_NDEF_DISCOVERED ==
            intent.action) {
        processIntent(intent)
    }
}
```

NFC Card Emulation

Letting an Android device act as if it was a smartcard with NFC chip requires involved setting and programming tasks. This especially makes sense if you think about security – some Android devices may contain a *secure element* that performs the communication with the card reader on a hardware basis. Some other device may apply *host-based card emulation* to let the device CPU perform the communication. An exhaustive description of all the details for NFC card emulation is out of scope for this book, but you can find information on the Web and if you open the page "Host-based Card Emulation" from the online developer guides of Android.

That said we describe the basic artifacts to start with a *host-based card emulation*. The example is based on the HCE example provided by the developer guides of Android, but converted to Kotlin and boiled down to important NFC-related aspects only (the example runs under an Apache license – see `www.apache.org/licenses/LICENSE-2.0`). The code reads

```
/**
 * This is a sample APDU Service which demonstrates how
```

```
 * to interface with the card emulation support added
 * in Android 4.4, KitKat.
 *
 * This sample replies to any requests sent with the
 * string "Hello World". In real-world situations, you
 * would need to modify this code to implement your
 * desired communication protocol.
 *
 * This sample will be invoked for any terminals
 * selecting AIDs of 0xF11111111, 0xF22222222, or
 * 0xF33333333. See src/main/res/xml/aid_list.xml for
 * more details.
 *
 * Note: This is a low-level interface. Unlike the
 * NdefMessage many developers are familiar with for
 * implementing Android Beam in apps, card emulation
 * only provides a byte-array based communication
 * channel. It is left to developers to implement
 * higher level protocol support as needed.
 */
class CardService : HostApduService() {
```

The onDeactivated() callback gets called if the connection to the NFC card is lost, in order to let the application know the cause for the disconnection (either a lost link or another AID being selected by the reader):

```
/**
 * Called if the connection to the NFC card is lost.
 * @param reason Either DEACTIVATION_LINK_LOSS or
 *      DEACTIVATION_DESELECTED
 */
override fun onDeactivated(reason: Int) {}
```

The processCommandApdu() will be called when a command APDU has been received. A response APDU can be provided directly by returning a byte array in this method. In general response APDUs must be sent as quickly as possible, given the fact that the user is likely holding their device over an NFC reader when this method is called. If there are multiple services that have registered for the same AIDs in their metadata entry, you will only get called if the user has explicitly selected your service, either as a default or just for the next tap. This method is running in the main thread of your application. If you cannot return a response APDU immediately, return null and use the sendResponseApdu() method later:

```
/**
 * This method will be called when a command APDU has
 * been received from a remote device.
 *
 * @param commandApdu The APDU that received from the
 *     remote device
 * @param extras A bundle containing extra data. May
 *     be null.
 * @return a byte-array containing the response APDU,
 *     or null if no response APDU can be sent
 *     at this point.
 */
override
fun processCommandApdu(commandApdu: ByteArray,
        extras: Bundle): ByteArray {
    Log.i(TAG, "Received APDU: " +
            byteArrayToHexString(commandApdu))
    // If the APDU matches the SELECT AID command for
    // this service, send the loyalty card account
    // number, followed by a SELECT_OK status trailer
    // (0x9000).
    if (Arrays.equals(SELECT_APDU, commandApdu)) {
        val account = AccountStorage.getAccount(this)
        val accountBytes = account!!.toByteArray()
        Log.i(TAG, "Sending account number: $account")
        return concatArrays(accountBytes, SELECT_OK_SW)
    } else {
        return UNKNOWN_CMD_SW
    }
}
```

The companion object contains a couple of constants and utility functions:

```
companion object {
    private val TAG = "CardService"
    // AID for our loyalty card service.
    private val SAMPLE_LOYALTY_CARD_AID = "F222222222"
    // ISO-DEP command HEADER for selecting an AID.
    // Format: [Class | Instruction | Parameter 1 |
    //          Parameter 2]
    private val SELECT_APDU_HEADER = "00A40400"
    // "OK" status word sent in response to SELECT AID
    // command (0x9000)
    private val SELECT_OK_SW =
        hexStringToByteArray("9000")
    // "UNKNOWN" status word sent in response to
    // invalid APDU command (0x0000)
    private val UNKNOWN_CMD_SW =
        hexStringToByteArray("0000")
    private val SELECT_APDU =
        buildSelectApdu(SAMPLE_LOYALTY_CARD_AID)

    /**
     * Build APDU for SELECT AID command. This command
     * indicates which service a reader is
     * interested in communicating with. See
     * ISO 7816-4.
     *
     * @param aid Application ID (AID) to select
     * @return APDU for SELECT AID command
     */
    fun buildSelectApdu(aid: String): ByteArray {
        // Format: [CLASS | INSTRUCTION |
        //          PARAMETER 1 | PARAMETER 2 |
        //          LENGTH | DATA]
        return hexStringToByteArray(
            SELECT_APDU_HEADER +
```

```
                String.format("%02X",
                        aid.length / 2) +
            aid)
    }

    /**
     * Utility method to convert a byte array to a
     * hexadecimal string.
     */
    fun byteArrayToHexString(bytes: ByteArray):
        String {
        val hexArray = charArrayOf('0', '1', '2', '3',
            '4', '5', '6', '7', '8', '9', 'A', 'B',
            'C', 'D', 'E', 'F')
        val hexChars = CharArray(bytes.size * 2)
        var v: Int
        for (j in bytes.indices) {
            v = bytes[j].toInt() and 0xFF
            // Cast bytes[j] to int, treating as
            // unsigned value
            hexChars[j * 2] = hexArray[v.ushr(4)]
            // Select hex character from upper nibble
            hexChars[j * 2 + 1] = hexArray[v and 0x0F]
            // Select hex character from lower nibble
        }
        return String(hexChars)
    }

    /**
     * Utility method to convert a hexadecimal string
     * to a byte string.
     *
     * Behavior with input strings containing
     * non-hexadecimal characters is undefined.
     */
    fun hexStringToByteArray(s: String): ByteArray {
```

```kotlin
    val len = s.length
    if (len % 2 == 1) {
        // TODO, throw exception
    }
    val data = ByteArray(len / 2)
    var i = 0
    while (i < len) {
        // Convert each character into a integer
        //   (base-16), then bit-shift into place
        data[i / 2] =
            ((Character.digit(s[i], 16) shl 4) +
            Character.digit(s[i + 1], 16)).
            toByte()
        i += 2
    }
    return data
}

/**
 * Utility method to concatenate two byte arrays.
 */
fun concatArrays(first: ByteArray,
        vararg rest: ByteArray): ByteArray {
    var totalLength = first.size
    for (array in rest) {
        totalLength += array.size
    }
    val result =
            Arrays.copyOf(first, totalLength)
    var offset = first.size
    for (array in rest) {
        System.arraycopy(array, 0,
                result, offset, array.size)
        offset += array.size
    }
    return result
```

```
        }
    }
}
```

The corresponding service declaration inside `AndroidManifest.xml` reads

```xml
<service android:name=".CardService"
        android:exported="true"
        android:permission=
                "android.permission.BIND_NFC_SERVICE">
    <!-- Intent filter indicating that we support
        card emulation. -->
    <intent-filter>
        <action android:name=
                "android.nfc.cardemulation.action.
                HOST_APDU_SERVICE"/>
        <category android:name=
                "android.intent.category.DEFAULT"/>
    </intent-filter>
    <!-- Required XML configuration file, listing the
        AIDs that we are emulating cards
        for. This defines what protocols our card
        emulation service supports. -->
    <meta-data android:name=
            "android.nfc.cardemulation.host_apdu_service"
            android:resource="@xml/aid_list"/>
</service>
```

And we need a file `aid_list.xml` inside `res/xml`:

```xml
<?xml version="1.0" encoding="utf-8"?>
<!-- This file defines which AIDs this application
    should emulate cards for.

    Vendor-specific AIDs should always start with an "F",
    according to the ISO 7816 spec. We recommended
    vendor-specific AIDs be at least 6 characters long,
    to provide sufficient uniqueness. Note, however, that
```

longer AIDs may impose a burden on non-Android NFC
terminals. AIDs may not exceed 32 characters
(16 bytes).

Additionally, AIDs must always contain an even number
of characters, in hexadecimal format.

In order to avoid prompting the user to select which
service they want to use when the device is scanned,
this app must be selected as the default handler for
an AID group by the user, or the terminal must
select *all* AIDs defined in the category
simultaneously ("exact match").
-->

```
<host-apdu-service
    xmlns:android=
        "http://schemas.android.com/apk/res/android"
    android:description="@string/service_name"
    android:requireDeviceUnlock="false">
<!--
If category="payment" is used for any aid-groups, you
must also add an android:apduServiceBanner attribute
above, like so:

android:apduServiceBanner="@drawable/settings_banner"

 apduServiceBanner should be 260x96 dp. In pixels,
 that works out to...
    - drawable-xxhdpi: 780x288 px
    - drawable-xhdpi:  520x192 px
    - drawable-hdpi:   390x144 px
    - drawable-mdpi:   260x96  px
```

The apduServiceBanner is displayed in the "Tap & Pay"
menu in the system Settings app, and is only displayed
for apps which implement the "payment" AID category.

Since this sample is implementing a non-standard card

type (a loyalty card, specifically), we do not need
to define a banner.

Important: category="payment" should only be used for
    industry-standard payment cards. If you are
    implementing a closed-loop payment system (e.g.
    stored value cards for a specific merchant or
    transit system), use category="other". This is
    because only one "payment" card may be active at
    a time, whereas all "other" cards are active
    simultaneously (subject to AID dispatch).
-->

```
<aid-group android:description=
    "@string/card_title" android:category="other">
    <aid-filter android:name="F222222222"/>
</aid-group>
</host-apdu-service>
```

The service class also depends on object AccountStorage, which, for example, reads

```
/**
 * Utility class for persisting account numbers to disk.
 *
 * The default SharedPreferences instance is used as
 * the backing storage. Values are cached in memory for
 * performance.
 */
object AccountStorage {
  private val PREF_ACCOUNT_NUMBER = "account_number"
  private val DEFAULT_ACCOUNT_NUMBER = "00000000"
  private val TAG = "AccountStorage"
  private var sAccount: String? = null
  private val sAccountLock = Any()

  fun setAccount(c: Context, s: String) {
      synchronized(sAccountLock) {
          Log.i(TAG, "Setting account number: $s")
```

```
        val prefs = PreferenceManager.
            getDefaultSharedPreferences(c)
        prefs.edit().
            putString(PREF_ACCOUNT_NUMBER, s).
            commit()
        sAccount = s
    }
}

fun getAccount(c: Context): String? {
    synchronized(sAccountLock) {
        if (sAccount == null) {
            val prefs = PreferenceManager.
                getDefaultSharedPreferences(c)
            val account = prefs.getString(
                PREF_ACCOUNT_NUMBER,
                DEFAULT_ACCOUNT_NUMBER)
            sAccount = account
        }
        return sAccount
    }
  }
}
```

Android and Bluetooth

Android allows for adding your own Bluetooth functionality. An exhaustive description of all that can be done to serve Bluetooth needs is beyond the scope of this book, but to learn

- How to scan for available local Bluetooth devices (in case you have more than one)

- How to scan for paired remote Bluetooth devices

- How to scan for services a remote device provides

- How to establish communication channels

- How to transfer data between local and remote devices

- About working with profiles

- About Bluetooth servers on your Android device

please see the online documentation for Bluetooth in Android at `https://developer.android.com/guide/topics/connectivity/bluetooth`.

What we will do here is describe the implementation of a RfComm channel to transfer serial data between your smartphone and an external Bluetooth service. With this use case, you already have a powerful means for Bluetooth communication at hand – you can, for example, use it to control robots or smarthome gadgets.

A Bluetooth RfComm Server

It is surprisingly hard to find valuable information about setting up Bluetooth servers on the Web. However, for development it is necessary to implement a Bluetooth server, so you can test the Android app. And such a test server might also serve as a basis for real-world scenarios you might think of.

A good candidate for a Bluetooth server technology is *BlueCove*, which is an open source project. Parts of it are licensed under an Apache license V2.0 and other parts under GPL, so while it is easy to incorporate in your own projects, you need to check if for commercial projects the license is applicable for your needs. In the following paragraphs, I will describe how to set up a RfComm Bluetooth server on Linux using *BlueCove* and *Groovy*. For Windows you'll have to adapt the startup script and use DLL libraries instead.

Start with downloading and installing Groovy. Any modern version should do. Next, download *BlueCove*. The version I tested is 2.1.0, but you might try newer versions as well. You need the files `bluecove-2.1.0.jar`, `bluecove-emu-2.1.0.jar`, and `bluecove-gpl-2.1.0.jar`. Temporarily extract the JARs as zip files somewhere, and create a folder structure:

```
libbluecove.jnilib
startRfComm.sh
libbluecove.so
libbluecove_x64.so
libs/
    bluecove-2.1.0.jar
```

```
    bluecove-emu-2.1.0.jar
    bluecove-gpl-2.1.0.jar
scripts/
    rfcomm.groovy
```

Note   Depending on the Linux distribution you use, you might have to add an additional symlink as follows:

cd /usr/lib/x86_64-linux-gnu/

ln -s libbluetooth.so.3 libbluetooth.so

You must do this as root.

In addition, still as root, make

mkdir /var/run/sdb

chmod 777 /var/run/sdp

Also, to remedy compatibility issues, you must adapt the Bluetooth server process:

cd /etc/systemd/system/bluetooth.target.wants/

Change inside bluetooth.service

ExecStart=/usr/lib/bluetooth/bluetoothd→

ExecStart=/usr/lib/bluetooth/bluetoothd –C

and then

systemctl daemon-reload and systemctl restart bluetooth

The file startRfComm.sh is the startup script. Create it and inside write

```
#!/bin/bash

export JAVA_HOME=/opt/jdk8
export GROOVY_HOME=/opt/groovy

$GROOVY_HOME/bin/groovy \
  -cp libs/bluecove-2.1.0.jar:libs/bluecove-emu-2.1.0.jar:libs/bluecove-
  gpl-2.1.0.jar \
```

```
   -Dbluecove.debug=true \
   -Djava.library.path=. \
   scripts/rfcomm.groovy
```

fixing paths accordingly.

The server code lives inside scripts/rfcomm.groovy. Create it and let it read

```groovy
import javax.bluetooth.*
import javax.obex.*
import javax.microedition.io.*
import groovy.transform.Canonical

// Run server as root!

// setup the server to listen for connection
// retrieve the local Bluetooth device object
LocalDevice local = LocalDevice.getLocalDevice()
local.setDiscoverable(DiscoveryAgent.GIAC)

UUID uuid = new UUID(80087355)
String url = "btspp://localhost:" + uuid.toString() +
      ";name=RemoteBluetooth"
println("URI: " + url)
StreamConnectionNotifier notifier = Connector.open(url)
// waiting for connection
while(true) {
  println("waiting for connection...")
  StreamConnection connection = notifier.acceptAndOpen()
  InputStream inputStream = connection.openInputStream()
  println("waiting for input")
  while (true) {
    int command = inputStream.read()
    if(command == -1) break
    println("Command: " + command)
  }
}
```

The server must be started as root. Once you invoke sudo ./startRfComm.sh on a system with a Bluetooth adapter installed, the output with timestamps removed should look like

```
Java 1.4+ detected: 1.8.0_60; Java HotSpot(TM) 64-Bit Server VM; Oracle
Corporation
...
localDeviceID 0
...
BlueCove version 2.1.0 on bluez
URI: btspp://localhost:04c6093b00001000800000805f9b34fb;name=Remot
eBluetooth
open using BlueCove javax.microedition.io.Connector
...
connecting btspp://localhost:04c6093b00001000800000805f9b34fb;name=Remot
eBluetooth
...
created SDPSession 139982379587968
...
BlueZ major verion 4 detected
...
function sdp_extract_pdu of bluez major version 4 is called
...
waiting for connection...
```

An Android RfComm Client

With the RfComm Bluetooth server process from the preceding section running, we now develop the client for the Android platform. It is supposed to

- Provide an activity to select the remote Bluetooth device to connect to.

- Provide another activity to initiate a connection and send a message to the Bluetooth RfComm server.

Start with a new project and don't forget to add Kotlin support. Change file
AndroidManifest.xml to read

```xml
<?xml version="1.0" encoding="utf-8"?>
<manifest xmlns:android=
        "http://schemas.android.com/apk/res/android"
    package="de.pspaeth.bluetooth">

  <uses-permission android:name=
        "android.permission.BLUETOOTH_ADMIN"/>
  <uses-permission android:name=
        "android.permission.BLUETOOTH"/>

  <application
        android:allowBackup="true"
        android:icon="@mipmap/ic_launcher"
        android:label="@string/app_name"
        android:roundIcon="@mipmap/ic_launcher_round"
        android:supportsRtl="true"
        android:theme="@style/AppTheme">
      <activity android:name=".MainActivity">
          <intent-filter>
              <action android:name=
                    "android.intent.action.MAIN"/>
              <category android:name=
                    "android.intent.category.LAUNCHER"/>
          </intent-filter>
      </activity>
      <activity
          android:name=".DeviceListActivity"
          android:configChanges=
                "orientation|keyboardHidden"
          android:label="Select Device"
          android:theme=
                "@android:style/Theme.Holo.Dialog"/>
  </application>
</manifest>
```

Next, create three layout files inside res/layout. The first, activity_main.xml, contains a status line and two buttons:

```xml
<?xml version="1.0" encoding="utf-8"?>
<LinearLayout
  xmlns:android=
        "http://schemas.android.com/apk/res/android"
  xmlns:app="http://schemas.android.com/apk/res-auto"
  xmlns:tools="http://schemas.android.com/tools"
  android:layout_width="match_parent"
  android:layout_height="match_parent"
  tools:context=".MainActivity"
  android:orientation="vertical">

  <LinearLayout
      android:layout_width="match_parent"
      android:layout_height="wrap_content"
      android:orientation="horizontal">
    <TextView
        android:layout_width="wrap_content"
        android:layout_height="wrap_content"
        android:text="State: " />
    <TextView
        android:id="@+id/state"
        android:layout_width="wrap_content"
        android:layout_height="wrap_content"/>
  </LinearLayout>

  <Button
      android:layout_width="match_parent"
      android:layout_height="wrap_content"
      android:text="Scan Devices"
      android:onClick="scanDevices"/>
  <Button
      android:layout_width="match_parent"
      android:layout_height="wrap_content"
      android:text="RfComm"
```

```
            android:onClick="rfComm"/>
    </LinearLayout>
```

Note   For simplicity I added texts as literals – in a production environment, you
should of course use string resources.

The next layout file, device_list.xml, is for the remote device selector activity:

```xml
<?xml version="1.0" encoding="utf-8"?>
<LinearLayout xmlns:android=
        "http://schemas.android.com/apk/res/android"
    android:layout_width="match_parent"
    android:layout_height="match_parent"
    android:orientation="vertical">

    <TextView
        android:id="@+id/title_paired_devices"
        android:layout_width="match_parent"
        android:layout_height="wrap_content"
        android:background="#666"
        android:paddingLeft="5dp"
        android:text="Paired Devices"
        android:textColor="#fff"
        android:visibility="gone"
        />

    <ListView
        android:id="@+id/paired_devices"
        android:layout_width="match_parent"
        android:layout_height="wrap_content"
        android:layout_weight="1"
        android:stackFromBottom="true"
        />

    <TextView
        android:id="@+id/title_new_devices"
```

```
    android:layout_width="match_parent"
    android:layout_height="wrap_content"
    android:background="#666"
    android:paddingLeft="5dp"
    android:text="Other Devices"
    android:textColor="#fff"
    android:visibility="gone"
    />

<ListView
    android:id="@+id/new_devices"
    android:layout_width="match_parent"
    android:layout_height="wrap_content"
    android:layout_weight="2"
    android:stackFromBottom="true"
    />

<Button
    android:id="@+id/button_scan"
    android:layout_width="match_parent"
    android:layout_height="wrap_content"
    android:text="Scan"
    />
</LinearLayout>
```

The last, device_name.xml, is for layouting list items from the device lister activity:

```
<?xml version="1.0" encoding="utf-8"?>
<TextView xmlns:android=
        "http://schemas.android.com/apk/res/android"
    android:layout_width="match_parent"
    android:layout_height="wrap_content"
    android:padding="5dp"
    android:textSize="18sp" />
```

The DeviceListActvity class is an adapted version of the device lister activity of the Bluetooth chat example from the Android developer documentation:

```
/**
 * This Activity appears as a dialog. It lists any
 * paired devices and devices detected in the area after
 * discovery. When a device is chosen by the user, the
 * MAC address of the device is sent back to the parent
 * Activity in the result Intent.
 */
class DeviceListActivity : Activity() {
  companion object {
      private val TAG = "DeviceListActivity"
      var EXTRA_DEVICE_ADDRESS = "device_address"
  }

  private var mBtAdapter: BluetoothAdapter? = null
  private var mNewDevicesArrayAdapter:
      ArrayAdapter<String>? = null
```

The OnItemClickListener is an example for the implementation of a *single method interface* in Kotlin:

```
  private val mDeviceClickListener =
      AdapterView.OnItemClickListener {
              av, v, arg2, arg3 ->
      // Cancel discovery because it's costly and we're
      // about to connect
      mBtAdapter!!.cancelDiscovery()

      // Get the device MAC address, which is the last
      // 17 chars in the View
      val info = (v as TextView).text.toString()
      val address = info.substring(info.length - 17)

      // Create the result Intent and include the MAC
      // address
      val intent = Intent()
```

```
    intent.putExtra(EXTRA_DEVICE_ADDRESS, address)

    // Set result and finish this Activity
    setResult(Activity.RESULT_OK, intent)
    finish()
}
```

The BroadcastReceiver listens for discovered devices and changes the title when discovery is finished:

```kotlin
/**
 * Listening for discovered devices.
 */
private val mReceiver = object : BroadcastReceiver() {
    override
    fun onReceive(context: Context, intent: Intent) {
        val action = intent.action

        // When discovery finds a device
        if (BluetoothDevice.ACTION_FOUND == action) {
            // Get the BluetoothDevice object from
            // the Intent
            val device = intent.
                getParcelableExtra<BluetoothDevice>(
                BluetoothDevice.EXTRA_DEVICE)
            // If it's already paired, skip it,
            // because it's been listed already
            if (device.bondState !=
                BluetoothDevice.BOND_BONDED) {
                mNewDevicesArrayAdapter!!.add(
                    device.name + "\n" +
                    device.address)
            }
            // When discovery is finished, change the
            // Activity title
        } else if (BluetoothAdapter.
            ACTION_DISCOVERY_FINISHED == action) {
```

```
            setProgressBarIndeterminateVisibility(
                false)
            setTitle("Select Device")
            if (mNewDevicesArrayAdapter!!.count
                == 0) {
                val noDevices = "No device"
                mNewDevicesArrayAdapter!!.add(
                    noDevices)
            }
        }
    }
}
```

As usual, the onCreate() callback method sets up the user interface:

```
override fun onCreate(savedInstanceState: Bundle?) {
    super.onCreate(savedInstanceState)

    // Setup the window
    requestWindowFeature(Window.
        FEATURE_INDETERMINATE_PROGRESS)
    setContentView(R.layout.activity_device_list)

    // Set result CANCELED in case the user backs out
    setResult(Activity.RESULT_CANCELED)

    // Initialize the button to perform device
    // discovery
    button_scan.setOnClickListener { v ->
        doDiscovery()
        v.visibility = View.GONE
    }

    // Initialize array adapters. One for already
    // paired devices and one for newly discovered
    // devices
    val pairedDevicesArrayAdapter =
        ArrayAdapter<String>(this,
```

```
              R.layout.device_name)
mNewDevicesArrayAdapter =
      ArrayAdapter(this,
              R.layout.device_name)

// Find and set up the ListView for paired devices
val pairedListView = paired_devices as ListView
pairedListView.adapter = pairedDevicesArrayAdapter
pairedListView.onItemClickListener =
      mDeviceClickListener

// Find and set up the ListView for newly
// discovered devices
val newDevicesListView = new_devices as ListView
newDevicesListView.adapter =
      mNewDevicesArrayAdapter
newDevicesListView.onItemClickListener =
      mDeviceClickListener

// Register for broadcasts when a device is
// discovered
var filter =
      IntentFilter(BluetoothDevice.ACTION_FOUND)
this.registerReceiver(mReceiver, filter)

// Register for broadcasts when discovery has
// finished
filter = IntentFilter(BluetoothAdapter.
      ACTION_DISCOVERY_FINISHED)
this.registerReceiver(mReceiver, filter)

// Get the local Bluetooth adapter
mBtAdapter = BluetoothAdapter.getDefaultAdapter()

// Get a set of currently paired devices
val pairedDevices = mBtAdapter!!.bondedDevices

// If there are paired devices, add each one to
// the ArrayAdapter
```

```
        if (pairedDevices.size > 0) {
            title_paired_devices.visibility = View.VISIBLE
            for (device in pairedDevices) {
                pairedDevicesArrayAdapter.add(
                    device.name + "\n" + device.address)
            }
        } else {
            val noDevices = "No devices"
            pairedDevicesArrayAdapter.add(noDevices)
        }
    }
```

And the onDestroy() callback method gets used to clean up stuff. Finally, the doDiscovery() method performs the actual discovery work:

```
override fun onDestroy() {
    super.onDestroy()

    // Make sure we're not doing discovery anymore
    if (mBtAdapter != null) {
        mBtAdapter!!.cancelDiscovery()
    }

    // Unregister broadcast listeners
    this.unregisterReceiver(mReceiver)
}

/**
 * Start device discover with the BluetoothAdapter
 */
private fun doDiscovery() {
    Log.d(TAG, "doDiscovery()")

    // Indicate scanning in the title
    setProgressBarIndeterminateVisibility(true)
    setTitle("Scanning")

    // Turn on sub-title for new devices
    title_new_devices.visibility = View.VISIBLE
```

```
    // If we're already discovering, stop it
    if (mBtAdapter!!.isDiscovering) {
        mBtAdapter!!.cancelDiscovery()
    }

    // Request discover from BluetoothAdapter
    mBtAdapter!!.startDiscovery()
  }
}
```

The MainActivity class is responsible for checking and acquiring permissions and constructs a BluetoothCommandService, which we will describe later:

```
class MainActivity : AppCompatActivity() {
  companion object {
      val REQUEST_ENABLE_BT = 42
      val REQUEST_QUERY_DEVICES = 142
  }
  var mBluetoothAdapter: BluetoothAdapter? = null
  var mCommandService:BluetoothCommandService? = null
```

The onCreate() callback inside the activity gets used to set up the user interface and register the Bluetooth adapter:

```
override fun onCreate(savedInstanceState: Bundle?) {
    super.onCreate(savedInstanceState)
    setContentView(R.layout.activity_main)

    val permission1 = ContextCompat.
        checkSelfPermission(
        this, Manifest.permission.BLUETOOTH)
    val permission2 = ContextCompat.
        checkSelfPermission(
        this, Manifest.permission.BLUETOOTH_ADMIN)
    if (permission1 !=
        PackageManager.PERMISSION_GRANTED ||
        permission2 !=
        PackageManager.PERMISSION_GRANTED)
```

```
    {
        ActivityCompat.requestPermissions(this,
            arrayOf(
              Manifest.permission.BLUETOOTH,
              Manifest.permission.BLUETOOTH_ADMIN),
            642)
    }

    mBluetoothAdapter =
          BluetoothAdapter.getDefaultAdapter()

    if (mBluetoothAdapter == null) {
        Toast.makeText(this,
            "Bluetooth is not supported",
            Toast.LENGTH_LONG).show()
        finish()
    }

    if (!mBluetoothAdapter!!.isEnabled()) {
        val enableIntent = Intent(
            BluetoothAdapter.ACTION_REQUEST_ENABLE)
        startActivityForResult(
            enableIntent, REQUEST_ENABLE_BT)
    }
}
```

The scanDevices() method is used for calling the system's Bluetooth device scanner:

```
/**
 * Launch the DeviceListActivity to see devices and
 * do scan
 */
fun scanDevices(v:View) {
    val serverIntent = Intent(
          this, DeviceListActivity::class.java)
    startActivityForResult(serverIntent,
        REQUEST_QUERY_DEVICES)
}
```

And methods `rfComm` and `sendMessage()` handle the sending of Bluetooth messages:

```kotlin
fun rfComm(v: View) {
    sendMessage("The message")
}

/**
 * Sends a message.
 *
 * @param message A string of text to send.
 */
private fun sendMessage(message: String) {
    if (mCommandService?.mState !==
            BluetoothCommandService.Companion.
            State.CONNECTED)
    {
        Toast.makeText(this, "Not connected",
                Toast.LENGTH_SHORT).show()
        return
    }

    // Check that there's actually something to send
    if (message.length > 0) {
        val send = message.toByteArray()
        mCommandService?.write(send)
    }
}
```

The actual connection to a device gets done from inside method `connectDevice()`:

```kotlin
private
fun connectDevice(data: Intent, secure: Boolean) {
    val macAddress = data.extras!!
            .getString(
            DeviceListActivity.EXTRA_DEVICE_ADDRESS)
    mBluetoothAdapter?.
```

```
            getRemoteDevice(macAddress)?.run {
        val device = this
        mCommandService =
                BluetoothCommandService(
                this@MainActivity, macAddress).apply {
            addStateChangeListener { statex ->
                runOnUiThread {
                    state.text = statex.toString()
                }
            }
            connect(device)
        }
    }
}

private fun fetchUuids(device: BluetoothDevice) {
    device.fetchUuidsWithSdp()
}
```

The callback method onActivityResult() handles the return from the system's device chooser – here we just perform a connection to the device chosen:

```
override
fun onActivityResult(requestCode: Int,
        resultCode: Int, data: Intent) {
    when (requestCode) {
        REQUEST_QUERY_DEVICES -> {
            if (resultCode == Activity.RESULT_OK) {
                connectDevice(data, false)
            }
        }
    }
}
```

Class BluetoothCommandService is, despite its name, not an Android service. It handles the communication with the Bluetooth server and reads

```kotlin
class BluetoothCommandService(context: Context,
        val macAddress:String) {
   companion object {
       // Unique UUID for this application
       private val MY_UUID_INSECURE = UUID.fromString(
             "04c6093b-0000-1000-8000-00805f9b34fb")

       // Constants that indicate the current connection
       // state
       enum class State {
           NONE,       // we're doing nothing
           LISTEN,     // listening for incoming conns
           CONNECTING, // initiating an outgoing conn
           CONNECTED   // connected to a remote device
       }
   }

   private val mAdapter: BluetoothAdapter
   private var createSocket: CreateSocketThread? = null
   private var readWrite: SocketReadWrite? = null
   var mState: State = State.NONE

   private var stateChangeListeners =
         mutableListOf<(State)->Unit>()
   fun addStateChangeListener(l:(State)->Unit) {
       stateChangeListeners.add(l)
   }

   init {
       mAdapter = BluetoothAdapter.getDefaultAdapter()
       changeState(State.NONE)
   }
```

Its public methods are for connecting, disconnecting, and writing data:

```kotlin
/**
```

```
 * Initiate a connection to a remote device.
 *
 * @param device The BluetoothDevice to connect
 */
fun connect(device: BluetoothDevice) {
    stopThreads()

    // Start the thread to connect with the given
    // device
    createSocket = CreateSocketThread(device).apply {
        start()
    }
}

/**
 * Stop all threads
 */
fun stop() {
    stopThreads()
    changeState(State.NONE)
}

/**
 * Write to the ConnectedThread in an unsynchronized
 * manner
 *
 * @param out The bytes to write
 * @see ConnectedThread.write
 */
fun write(out: ByteArray) {
    if (mState != State.CONNECTED) return
    readWrite?.run { write(out) }
}
```

Its private methods handle the connection threads:

```
//////////////////////////////////////////////////////
//////////////////////////////////////////////////////
```

```kotlin
/**
 * Start the ConnectedThread to begin managing a
 * Bluetooth connection
 *
 * @param socket The BluetoothSocket on which the
 *        connection was made
 * @param device The BluetoothDevice that has been
 *        connected
 */
private fun connected(socket: BluetoothSocket,
        device: BluetoothDevice) {
    stopThreads()

    // Start the thread to perform transmissions
    readWrite = SocketReadWrite(socket).apply {
        start()
    }
}

private fun stopThreads() {
    createSocket?.run {
        cancel()
        createSocket = null
    }
    readWrite?.run {
        cancel()
        readWrite = null
    }
}

/**
 * Indicate that the connection attempt failed.
 */
private fun connectionFailed() {
    changeState(State.NONE)
}
```

```
/**
 * Indicate that the connection was lost.
 */
private fun connectionLost() {
    changeState(State.NONE)
}
```

The connection socket handling thread itself is a dedicated Thread implementation:

```
/**
 * This thread runs while attempting to make an
 * outgoing connection with a device. It runs straight
 * through; the connection either succeeds or fails.
 */
private inner
class CreateSocketThread(
        private val mmDevice: BluetoothDevice) :
        Thread() {
    private val mmSocket: BluetoothSocket?

    init {
        // Get a BluetoothSocket for a connection
        // with the given BluetoothDevice
        mmSocket = mmDevice.
            createInsecureRfcommSocketToServiceRecord(
            MY_UUID_INSECURE)
        changeState(Companion.State.CONNECTING)
    }

    override fun run() {
        name = "CreateSocketThread"

        // Always cancel discovery because it will
        // slow down a connection
        mAdapter.cancelDiscovery()

        // Make a connection to the BluetoothSocket
        try {
```

```
            // This is a blocking call and will only
            // return on a successful connection or an
            // exception
            mmSocket!!.connect()
        } catch (e: IOException) {
            Log.e("LOG","Connection failed", e)
            Log.e("LOG", "Maybe device does not " +
                " expose service " +
                MY_UUID_INSECURE)
            // Close the socket
            mmSocket!!.close()

            connectionFailed()
            return
        }

        // Reset the thread because we're done
        createSocket = null

        // Start the connected thread
        connected(mmSocket, mmDevice)
    }

    fun cancel() {
        mmSocket!!.close()
    }
}
```

For reading and writing data from and to the connection socket, we use
another thread:

```
/**
 * This thread runs during a connection with a
 * remote device. It handles all incoming and outgoing
 * transmissions.
 */
private inner
class SocketReadWrite(val mmSocket: BluetoothSocket) :
```

```kotlin
        Thread() {
    private val mmInStream: InputStream?
    private val mmOutStream: OutputStream?

    init {
        mmInStream = mmSocket.inputStream
        mmOutStream = mmSocket.outputStream
        changeState(Companion.State.CONNECTED)
    }

    override fun run() {
        val buffer = ByteArray(1024)
        var bytex: Int

        // Keep listening to the InputStream while
        // connected
        while (mState ==
            Companion.State.CONNECTED) {
            try {
                // Read from the InputStream
                bytex = mmInStream!!.read(buffer)
            } catch (e: IOException) {
                connectionLost()
                break
            }
        }
    }

    /**
     * Write to the connected OutStream.
     *
     * @param buffer The bytes to write
     */
    fun write(buffer: ByteArray) {
        mmOutStream!!.write(buffer)
    }
```

```
    fun cancel() {
        mmSocket.close()
    }
}
```

Finally, we provide a method to tell interested parties when a socket connection state changes. Here this also emits a logging statement – for production code you'd remove this or provide this information to the user some other way:

```
private fun changeState(newState:State) {
    Log.e("LOG",
            "changing state: ${mState} -> ${newState}")
    mState = newState
    stateChangeListeners.forEach { it(newState) }
}
}
```

Note   The UUID from the companion object must match the UUID you see in the server startup logs.

What this class does is as follows:

- Once its connect(...) method gets called, it starts a connection attempt.

- If the connection succeeds, another thread for initializing input and output streams using the connection object gets started. Note: The input stream is not used in this example – it is here for informational purposes.

- By virtue of its mState member, clients can check for the connection state.

- If connected, the method write(...) can be called to send data through the connection channel.

To test the connection, press the "RFCOMM" button on the UI. The server application should then log

```
Command: 84
Command: 104
Command: 101
Command: 32
Command: 109
Command: 101
Command: 115
Command: 115
Command: 97
Command: 103
Command: 101
```

which is the numerical representation of the message "The message".

CHAPTER 14

Hardware

Android can do more than presenting a GUI on a smartphone. Android is also about wearables, talking to appropriately equipped TV sets, and infotainment in cars. And smartphones have cameras, NFC and Bluetooth adapters, and sensors for position, movement, orientation, and fingerprints. And, yes, smartphones can do phone calls as well. This chapter describes how the Android OS can run on devices other than smartphones and how to interact with the device's hardware.

Programming with Wearables

Google Wear is about small devices you wear on your body. While as of now this is practically restricted to smartwatches you can buy and then wrap around your wrist, future devices will maybe be part of your glasses, your clothes, or what else you might think of. Also, talking of Google Wear, you usually think of a smartphone you need to carry with you and connect to a Google Wear device via some pairing mechanism, but modern devices also may run in a standalone fashion. This means to function they don't need paired smartphones any longer and themselves can connect to the Internet, a cellular network, or a local network via Wi-Fi, Bluetooth, or a cellular adapter.

If you happen to use a paired smartphone for a Google Wear app, this no longer is restricted to Android running there, so you can pair a Google Wear device with both an Android smartphone and an Apple iOS phone. The Wear OS works with paired phones running Android version 4.4 or higher and iOS 9.3 or higher.

Google's design guidelines for smartphone apps, more precisely the demand for an easy and expressive user interface, are even more important for Wear apps. Due to the limited space and input capabilities, it is absolutely vital for Wear-related development to reduce UI elements and front-end workflows to a bare minimum. Otherwise, you risk your app's usability and acceptance degrading significantly.

© Peter Späth 2022
P. Späth, *Pro Android with Kotlin*, https://doi.org/10.1007/978-1-4842-8745-3_14

Common use cases for Google Wear apps are as follows:

- Designing own watch faces (time and date display)

- Adding face complications (custom face elements)

- Displaying notifications

- Messaging

- Voice interaction

- Google Assistant

- Playing music

- Making and receiving calls

- Alarms

- Apps with simple user interfaces

- Companion apps to smartphone and tablet apps

- Sensor apps

- Location-based services

- Pay apps

In the following sections, we will be looking at development matters for Google Wear apps.

Wearables Development

While to develop Wear apps you can mostly use the same tools and techniques you use for smartphone or tablet app development, you have to take care of the limited space on smartwatches and the different way users interact with watches compared with other devices.

Nevertheless, the prominent place to start Wear development is Android Studio, and in this section we describe what to do to set up your IDE to start Wear development and how to get devices connected to Android Studio.

For developing Wear apps, we first have to point out that there are two operation modes:

- **Pairing a wearable device with a smartphone**

  Due to technical restrictions, it is not possible to pair a virtual smartwatch with a virtual smartphone. So you have to use a real phone to pair a virtual smartwatch.

- **Standalone mode**

  The Wear app runs on its own, without needing pairing to a smartphone. It is highly recommended for modern apps to be able to do sensible things also in standalone mode.

In either case create a new Android Studio project and in the "Target Android Devices" check only the Wear checkbox. In the subsequent screen, select one of the following:

- **Add No Activity**

  Proceed without adding an activity. You will have to do that later manually.

- **Blank Wear Activity**

  Add as layout

  ```
  <android.support.wear.widget.BoxInsetLayout ...>
    <FrameLayout ...>
    </FrameLayout>
  </android.support.wear.widget.BoxInsetLayout>
  ```

  and an activity class

  ```
  class MainActivity : WearableActivity() {
    override
    fun onCreate(savedInstanceState: Bundle?) {
      super.onCreate(savedInstanceState)
      setContentView(R.layout.activity_main)
      setAmbientEnabled() // Enables Always-on
    }
  }
  ```

- **Watch Face**

  Does not create an activity. Instead, it builds a service class needed to define a watch face.

This choice corresponds to the development paradigm to choose. You will create one of the following:

- A smartphone-like app that needs explicitly to be started on the watch in order to run.

- A watch face. This is more or less a graphics design issue – a face is the visual appearance of time and date on the watch's surface.

- A face complication. This is a feature added to a face.

We will be talking about the different development paths in the following sections.

Next, open Tools ➤ AVD Manager and create a new virtual Wear device. You can now start your app on a virtual Wear device. Unless you chose "Add No Activity," the emulator should already show a starting UI on the face.

To pair the virtual watch with your smartphone, connect the smartphone to your development PC with a USB cable, make it a development device (tap seven times the build number at the bottom of the system settings), and then install the "Wear OS by Google" app on the smartphone. On your development PC, set up the communication via

```
./adb -d forward tcp:5601 tcp:5601
```

Start the app, and from the menu choose "Connect to Emulator."

If you want to develop using a real smartwatch and need debugging capabilities, the online resource https://developer.android.com/training/wearables/get-started/debugging shows more information about how to set up a smartwatch debugging process.

Wearables App User Interface

Before you start creating a user interface for your Wear app, consider using one of the built-in mechanisms, namely, a notification or a face complication as described in the following sections. If however you think it is necessary your Wear app presents its own layout, do not just copy a smartphone app layout and use it for Wear. Instead, to build a genuine Wear user interface, use the special UI elements provided by the Wear support library. To use it, make sure the module's build.gradle file contains

```
dependencies {
    ...
    implementation "androidx.wear:wear:1.2.0"

    // Add support for wearable specific inputs
    implementation "androidx.wear:wear-input:1.1.0"
    implementation "androidx.wear:wear-input-testing:1.1.0"

    // Use to implement wear ongoing activities
    implementation "androidx.wear:wear-ongoing:1.0.0"

    // Use to implement support for interactions from the
    // Wearables to Phones
    implementation "androidx.wear:" +
        "wear-phone-interactions:1.1.0-alpha03"
    // Use to implement support for interactions between
    // the Wearables and Phones
    implementation "androidx.wear:" +
        "wear-remote-interactions:1.0.0"
}
```

These libraries contain various classes helping to build a UI with elements especially tailored for Wear development. The page at https://developer.android.com/ jetpack/androidx/releases/wear of the online API documentation contains detailed information about how to use those classes.

Wearables Faces

If you want to create a Wear face showing time and date in a certain custom design, start with the project creation wizard as described previously, using the "Watch Face" option.

The wizard service class generated provides a pretty elaborate example for a watch face you can use as a starting point for your own faces.

Adding Face Complications

Face complications are placeholders for data snippets in a face. The complication data providers are strictly separated from the complication renderers, so in your face you do not say you want to show certain complications. Instead, you specify places where to show complications, and you also specify possibly complication data types, but you let the user decide which complications to show where exactly.

In this section we talk about how to enhance your face to show complication data. For this aim I present a minimally invasive way to update your face implementation, so it will be easier for you to realize your own ideas. Having a running face as described previously is a requirement for this section.

We start with the entries in `AndroidManifest.xml`. What we need here is the following:

- We need a way to tell Android that we are going to have a configuration activity for complication UI elements. This happens by adding

  ```
  <meta-data
      android:name=
          "com.google.android.wearable. ¬
          watchface.wearableConfigurationAction"
      android:value=
          "com.example.xyz88.CONFIG_COMPLICATION"/>
  ```

  inside the `service` element (remove the line breaks indicated by ¬). This shows Android that there exists a complication administration activity. We map it to the new activity we describe next.

- We add the information about a permission inquiry activity and a configuration activity as follows:

  ```
  <activity android:name=
          "android.support.wearable. ¬
          complications. ¬
          ComplicationHelperActivity"/>
  <activity
      android:name=
  ```

```
        ".ComplicationConfigActivity"
        android:label="@string/app_name">
    <intent-filter>
      <action android:name=
          "com.example.xyz88. ¬
          CONFIG_COMPLICATION"/>
      <category android:name=
          "com.google.android. ¬
          wearable.watchface.category. ¬
          WEARABLE_CONFIGURATION"/>
      <category android:name=
          "android.intent.category. ¬
          DEFAULT"/>
    </intent-filter>
</activity>
```

Next, we add inside the face class at any suitable place:

```
lateinit var compl : MyComplications

private fun initializeComplications() {
  compl = MyComplications()
  compl.init(this@MyWatchFace, this)
}

override
fun onComplicationDataUpdate(
      complicationId: Int,
      complicationData: ComplicationData)
{
  compl.onComplicationDataUpdate(
      complicationId,complicationData)
}

private fun drawComplications(
      canvas: Canvas, drawWhen: Long) {
  compl.drawComplications(canvas, drawWhen)
}
```

```
// Fires PendingIntent associated with
// complication (if it has one).
private fun onComplicationTap(
        complicationId:Int) {
  Log.d("LOG", "onComplicationTap()")
  compl.onComplicationTap(complicationId)
}
```

In the same file, add to `ci.onCreate(...)`

```
initializeComplications()
```

and at the end of onSurfaceChanged(...)

```
compl.updateComplicationBounds(width, height)
```

Inside the onTapCommand(...) function, replace the corresponding where block branch as follows:

```
WatchFaceService.TAP_TYPE_TAP -> {
  // The user has completed the tap gesture.
  // Toast.makeText(applicationContext, R.string.message, Toast.
    LENGTH_SHORT)
  //         .show()
  compl.getTappedComplicationId(x, y)?.run {
    onComplicationTap(this)
  }
}
```

This figures out if the user tapped one of the shown complications and, if this is the case, forwards the event to one of the new functions we defined. Finally, inside onDraw(...) write

```
...
drawBackground(canvas)
drawComplications(canvas, now)
drawWatchFace(canvas)
...
```

To handle the complications, create a new class MyComplications and let it read

```
class MyComplications {
```

We first in the companion object define a couple of constants and utility methods:

```
companion object {
    fun getComplicationId(
            pos: ComplicationConfigActivity.
                ComplicationLocation): Int {
        // Add supported locations here
        return when(pos) {
            ComplicationConfigActivity.
                ComplicationLocation.LEFT ->
                LEFT_COMPLICATION_ID
            ComplicationConfigActivity.
                ComplicationLocation.RIGHT ->
                RIGHT_COMPLICATION_ID
            else -> -1
        }
    }

    fun getSupportedComplicationTypes(
            complicationLocation:
                ComplicationConfigActivity.
                ComplicationLocation): IntArray? {
        return when(complicationLocation) {
            ComplicationConfigActivity.
                ComplicationLocation.LEFT ->
                COMPLICATION_SUPPORTED_TYPES[0]
            ComplicationConfigActivity.
                ComplicationLocation.RIGHT ->
                COMPLICATION_SUPPORTED_TYPES[1]
            else -> IntArray(0)
        }
    }

    private val LEFT_COMPLICATION_ID = 0
```

```kotlin
        private val RIGHT_COMPLICATION_ID = 1
        val COMPLICATION_IDS = intArrayOf(
            LEFT_COMPLICATION_ID, RIGHT_COMPLICATION_ID)
        private val complicationDrawables =
            SparseArray<ComplicationDrawable>()
        private val complicationDat =
            SparseArray<ComplicationData>()

        // Left and right dial supported types.
        private val COMPLICATION_SUPPORTED_TYPES =
          arrayOf(
            intArrayOf(ComplicationData.TYPE_RANGED_VALUE,
                    ComplicationData.TYPE_ICON,
                    ComplicationData.TYPE_SHORT_TEXT,
                    ComplicationData.TYPE_SMALL_IMAGE),
            intArrayOf(ComplicationData.TYPE_RANGED_VALUE,
                    ComplicationData.TYPE_ICON,
                    ComplicationData.TYPE_SHORT_TEXT,
                    ComplicationData.TYPE_SMALL_IMAGE)

        )
    }

    private lateinit var ctx:CanvasWatchFaceService
    private lateinit var engine:MyWatchFace.Engine
```

Inside an init() method, we register the complications to draw. Method onComplicationDataUpdate() is used to handle complication data updates, and updateComplicationBounds() reacts to complication size changes:

```kotlin
    fun init(ctx:CanvasWatchFaceService,
        engine: MyWatchFace.Engine) {
        this.ctx = ctx
        this.engine = engine

        // A ComplicationDrawable for each location
        val leftComplicationDrawable =
            ctx.getDrawable(custom_complication_styles)
            as ComplicationDrawable
```

```
    leftComplicationDrawable.setContext(
        ctx.applicationContext)
    val rightComplicationDrawable =
        ctx.getDrawable(custom_complication_styles)
        as ComplicationDrawable
    rightComplicationDrawable.setContext(
        ctx.applicationContext)

    complicationDrawables[LEFT_COMPLICATION_ID] =
        leftComplicationDrawable
    complicationDrawables[RIGHT_COMPLICATION_ID] =
        rightComplicationDrawable

    engine.setActiveComplications(*COMPLICATION_IDS)
}

fun onComplicationDataUpdate(
        complicationId: Int,
        complicationData: ComplicationData) {
    Log.d("LOG", "onComplicationDataUpdate() id: " +
        complicationId);
    complicationDat[complicationId] = complicationData
    complicationDrawables[complicationId].
        setComplicationData(complicationData)
    engine.invalidate()
}

fun updateComplicationBounds(width: Int,
    height: Int) {
    // For most Wear devices width and height
    // are the same
    val sizeOfComplication = width / 4
    val midpointOfScreen = width / 2

    val horizontalOffset =
        (midpointOfScreen - sizeOfComplication) / 2
    val verticalOffset =
        midpointOfScreen - sizeOfComplication / 2
```

```
complicationDrawables.get(LEFT_COMPLICATION_ID).
    bounds =
      // Left, Top, Right, Bottom
      Rect(
        horizontalOffset,
        verticalOffset,
        horizontalOffset + sizeOfComplication,
        verticalOffset + sizeOfComplication)
complicationDrawables.get(RIGHT_COMPLICATION_ID).
    bounds =
      // Left, Top, Right, Bottom
      Rect(
        midpointOfScreen + horizontalOffset,
        verticalOffset,
        midpointOfScreen + horizontalOffset +
              sizeOfComplication,
        verticalOffset + sizeOfComplication)
}
```

Method `drawComplications()` actually draws the complications. For this aim we scan through the complications we registered inside the `init` block:

```
fun drawComplications(canvas: Canvas, drawWhen: Long) {
    COMPLICATION_IDS.forEach {
        complicationDrawables[it].
              draw(canvas, drawWhen)
    }
}
```

We need a possibility to find out whether one of our complications has been tapped. The method `getTappedComplicationId()` is responsible for that. Finally, a method `onComplicationTap()` reacts to such events:

```
// Determines if tap happened inside a complication
// area, or else returns null.
fun getTappedComplicationId(x:Int, y:Int):Int? {
    val currentTimeMillis = System.currentTimeMillis()
```

```
    for(complicationId in
         MyComplications.COMPLICATION_IDS) {
       val res =
            complicationDat[complicationId]?.run {
          var res2 = -1
          if(isActive(currentTimeMillis)
             && (getType() !=
               ComplicationData.TYPE_NOT_CONFIGURED)
             && (getType() !=
               ComplicationData.TYPE_EMPTY))
          {
              val complicationDrawable =
                complicationDrawables[complicationId]
              val complicationBoundingRect =
                complicationDrawable.bounds
              if (complicationBoundingRect.width()
                    > 0) {
                 if (complicationBoundingRect.
                       contains(x, y)) {
                    res2 = complicationId
                 }
              } else {
                 Log.e("LOG",
                 "Unrecognized complication id.")
              }
          }
          res2
       } ?: -1
       if(res != -1) return res
    }
    return null
}

// The user tapped on a complication
fun onComplicationTap(complicationId:Int) {
    Log.d("LOG", "onComplicationTap()")
```

```kotlin
        val complicationData =
            complicationDat[complicationId]
        if (complicationData != null) {
            if (complicationData.getTapAction()
                    != null) {
                try {
                    complicationData.getTapAction().send()
                } catch (e: Exception ) {
                    Log.e("LOG",
                      "onComplicationTap() tap error: " +
                      e);
                }
            } else if (complicationData.getType() ==
                    ComplicationData.TYPE_NO_PERMISSION) {
                // Launch permission request.
                val componentName = ComponentName(
                        ctx.applicationContext,
                        MyComplications::class.java)
                val permissionRequestIntent =
                  ComplicationHelperActivity.
                  createPermissionRequestHelperIntent(
                        ctx.applicationContext,
                        componentName)
                ctx.startActivity(permissionRequestIntent)
            }
        } else {
            Log.d("LOG",
                "No PendingIntent for complication " +
                complicationId + ".")
        }
    }
}
```

What is left to do is writing the configuration activity. For that purpose create a new Kotlin class ComplicationConfigActivity and let it read

```
class ComplicationConfigActivity :
        ActivityCompat(), View.OnClickListener {
    companion object {
        val TAG = "LOG"
        val COMPLICATION_CONFIG_REQUEST_CODE = 1001
    }

    var mLeftComplicationId: Int = 0
    var mRightComplicationId: Int = 0
    var mSelectedComplicationId: Int = 0

    // Used to identify a specific service that renders
    // the watch face.
    var mWatchFaceComponentName: ComponentName? = null

    // Required to retrieve complication data from watch
    // face for preview.
    var mProviderInfoRetriever:
        ProviderInfoRetriever? = null

    var mLeftComplicationBackground: ImageView? = null
    var mRightComplicationBackground: ImageView? = null

    var mLeftComplication: ImageButton? = null
    var mRightComplication: ImageButton? = null

    var mDefaultAddComplicationDrawable: Drawable? = null

    enum class ComplicationLocation {
        LEFT,
        RIGHT
    }
```

As usual, we use the onCreate() and onDestroy() callbacks to set up and clean up our user interface, respectively. Also, method retrieveInitialComplicationsData() gets used by onCreate() to initialize the complications:

```
override
fun onCreate(savedInstanceState: Bundle?) {
    super.onCreate(savedInstanceState)
```

```
setContentView(R.layout.activity_config)

mDefaultAddComplicationDrawable =
    getDrawable(R.drawable.add_complication)

mSelectedComplicationId = -1

mLeftComplicationId =
    MyComplications.getComplicationId(
    ComplicationLocation.LEFT)
mRightComplicationId =
    MyComplications.getComplicationId(
    ComplicationLocation.RIGHT)

mWatchFaceComponentName =
    ComponentName(applicationContext,
    MyWatchFace::class.java!!)

// Sets up left complication preview.
mLeftComplicationBackground =
    left_complication_background
mLeftComplication = left_complication
mLeftComplication!!.setOnClickListener(this)

// Sets default as "Add Complication" icon.
mLeftComplication!!.setImageDrawable(
    mDefaultAddComplicationDrawable)
mLeftComplicationBackground!!.setVisibility(
    View.INVISIBLE)

// Sets up right complication preview.
mRightComplicationBackground =
    right_complication_background
mRightComplication = right_complication
mRightComplication!!.setOnClickListener(this)

// Sets default as "Add Complication" icon.
mRightComplication!!.setImageDrawable(
    mDefaultAddComplicationDrawable)
mRightComplicationBackground!!.setVisibility(
```

```
        View.INVISIBLE)

    mProviderInfoRetriever =
        ProviderInfoRetriever(applicationContext,
        Executors.newCachedThreadPool())
    mProviderInfoRetriever!!.init()

    retrieveInitialComplicationsData()
}

override fun onDestroy() {
    super.onDestroy()
    mProviderInfoRetriever!!.release()
}

fun retrieveInitialComplicationsData() {
    val complicationIds =
        MyComplications.COMPLICATION_IDS
    mProviderInfoRetriever!!.retrieveProviderInfo(
        object : ProviderInfoRetriever.
            OnProviderInfoReceivedCallback() {
            override fun onProviderInfoReceived(
                watchFaceComplicationId:
                    Int,
                complicationProviderInfo:
                    ComplicationProviderInfo?)
            {
                Log.d(TAG,
                    "onProviderInfoReceived: " +
                    complicationProviderInfo)
                updateComplicationViews(
                    watchFaceComplicationId,
                    complicationProviderInfo)
            }
        },
        mWatchFaceComponentName,
        *complicationIds)
}
```

Methods onClick() and launchComplicationHelperActivity() are used to handle on-complication taps:

```
override
fun onClick(view: View) {
    if (view.equals(mLeftComplication)) {
        Log.d(TAG, "Left Complication click()")
        launchComplicationHelperActivity(
            ComplicationLocation.LEFT)
    } else if (view.equals(mRightComplication)) {
        Log.d(TAG, "Right Complication click()")
        launchComplicationHelperActivity(
            ComplicationLocation.RIGHT)
    }
}

fun launchComplicationHelperActivity(
    complicationLocation: ComplicationLocation) {

    mSelectedComplicationId =
            MyComplications.getComplicationId(
            complicationLocation)

    if (mSelectedComplicationId >= 0) {
        val supportedTypes = MyComplications.
            getSupportedComplicationTypes(
            complicationLocation)!!

        startActivityForResult(
                ComplicationHelperActivity.
                createProviderChooserHelperIntent(
                    applicationContext,
                    mWatchFaceComponentName,
                    mSelectedComplicationId,
                    *supportedTypes),
                ComplicationConfigActivity.
                COMPLICATION_CONFIG_REQUEST_CODE)
    } else {
```

```
        Log.d(TAG,
            "Complication not supported by watch face.")
    }
}
```

To handle updates we get signaled by the Android OS, we provide methods
updateComplicationViews() and onActivityResult():

```
fun updateComplicationViews(
        watchFaceComplicationId:
          Int,
        complicationProviderInfo:
          ComplicationProviderInfo?)
{
    Log.d(TAG, "updateComplicationViews(): id: "+
        watchFaceComplicationId)
    Log.d(TAG, "\tinfo: " + complicationProviderInfo)

    if (watchFaceComplicationId ==
        mLeftComplicationId) {
        if (complicationProviderInfo != null) {
            mLeftComplication!!.setImageIcon(
                complicationProviderInfo.providerIcon)
            mLeftComplicationBackground!!.
                setVisibility(View.VISIBLE)
        } else {
            mLeftComplication!!.setImageDrawable(
                mDefaultAddComplicationDrawable)
            mLeftComplicationBackground!!.
                setVisibility(View.INVISIBLE)
        }

    } else if (watchFaceComplicationId ==
          mRightComplicationId) {
        if (complicationProviderInfo != null) {
            mRightComplication!!.
                setImageIcon(
```

```
                complicationProviderInfo.providerIcon)
            mRightComplicationBackground!!.
                setVisibility(View.VISIBLE)

        } else {
            mRightComplication!!.setImageDrawable(
                mDefaultAddComplicationDrawable)
            mRightComplicationBackground!!.
                setVisibility(View.INVISIBLE)
        }
    }
}

override
fun onActivityResult(requestCode: Int,
        resultCode: Int, data: Intent) {
    if (requestCode ==
            COMPLICATION_CONFIG_REQUEST_CODE
        && resultCode == Activity.RESULT_OK) {

        // Retrieves information for selected
        //  Complication provider.
        val complicationProviderInfo =
            data.getParcelableExtra<
                ComplicationProviderInfo>(
                ProviderChooserIntent.
                EXTRA_PROVIDER_INFO)
        Log.d(TAG, "Provider: " +
            complicationProviderInfo)

        if (mSelectedComplicationId >= 0) {
            updateComplicationViews(
                mSelectedComplicationId,
                complicationProviderInfo)
        }
    }
}
```

Note that we added a couple of logging statements you maybe want to remove for production code. A corresponding layout may read

```xml
<?xml version="1.0" encoding="utf-8"?>
<RelativeLayout
  xmlns:android=
      "http://schemas.android.com/apk/res/android"
  android:layout_width="match_parent"
  android:layout_height="match_parent">

  <View
      android:id="@+id/watch_face_background"
      android:layout_width="180dp"
      android:layout_height="180dp"
      android:layout_centerHorizontal="true"
      android:layout_centerVertical="true"
      android:background=
        "@drawable/settings_face_preview_background"/>

  <View
      android:id="@+id/watch_face_highlight"
      android:layout_width="180dp"
      android:layout_height="180dp"
      android:layout_centerHorizontal="true"
      android:layout_centerVertical="true"
      android:background=
        "@drawable/settings_face_preview_highlight"/>

  <View
      android:id="@+id/watch_face_arms_and_ticks"
      android:layout_width="180dp"
      android:layout_height="180dp"
      android:layout_centerHorizontal="true"
      android:layout_centerVertical="true"
      android:background=
        "@drawable/settings_face_preview_arms_n_ticks"/>
```

```
<ImageView
    android:id="@+id/left_complication_background"
    android:layout_width="wrap_content"
    android:layout_height="wrap_content"
    android:src="@drawable/added_complication"
    style="?android:borderlessButtonStyle"
    android:background="@android:color/transparent"
    android:layout_centerVertical="true"
    android:layout_alignStart=
        "@+id/watch_face_background"/>

<ImageButton
    android:id="@+id/left_complication"
    android:layout_width="wrap_content"
    android:layout_height="wrap_content"
    style="?android:borderlessButtonStyle"
    android:background="@android:color/transparent"
    android:layout_alignTop=
        "@+id/left_complication_background"
    android:layout_alignStart=
        "@+id/watch_face_background"/>

<ImageView
    android:id="@+id/right_complication_background"
    android:layout_width="wrap_content"
    android:layout_height="wrap_content"
    android:src="@drawable/added_complication"
    style="?android:borderlessButtonStyle"
    android:background="@android:color/transparent"
    android:layout_alignTop=
        "@+id/left_complication_background"
    android:layout_alignStart=
        "@+id/right_complication"/>

<ImageButton
    android:id="@+id/right_complication"
    android:layout_width="wrap_content"
```

```
    android:layout_height="wrap_content"
    style="?android:borderlessButtonStyle"
    android:background="@android:color/transparent"
    android:layout_alignTop=
        "@+id/right_complication_background"
    android:layout_alignEnd=
        "@+id/watch_face_background"/>
</RelativeLayout>
```

With all these additions, the face provides for two possible complications to be added on user demand. More complication positions are possible. Just rewrite the appropriate parts of the code.

Note   Entering the code as shown here, Android Studio will complain for missing resources, especially drawables. For the code presented here to run, you must provide for missing resources. Usually from looking at the names or by just trying, you can find out what they get used for.

Providing Complication Data

A Google Wear device by default includes several complication data providers, so the user can choose among them to fill the complication placeholders in a face.

If you want to create your own complication data provider, prepare a new service as declared inside AndroidManifest.xml:

```
<service
    android:name=".CustomComplicationProviderService"
    android:icon="@drawable/ic_watch_white"
    android:label="Service label"
    android:permission="com.google.android.wearable. ¬
        permission.BIND_COMPLICATION_PROVIDER">

    <intent-filter>
      <action android:name="android.support.wearable. ¬
        complications. ¬
```

```
        ACTION_COMPLICATION_UPDATE_REQUEST"/>
  </intent-filter>

  <meta-data
        android:name="android.support.wearable. ¬
            complications.SUPPORTED_TYPES"
        android:value=
            "SHORT_TEXT,LONG_TEXT,RANGED_VALUE"/>

        <!--
        UPDATE_PERIOD_SECONDS specifies how
        often you want the system to check for updates
        to the data. A zero value means you will
        instead manually trigger updates.

        If not zero, set the interval in the order
        of minutes. The actual update may however
        differ - the system might have its own idea.
        -->
        <meta-data
            android:name="android.support.wearable. ¬
                complications.UPDATE_PERIOD_SECONDS"
            android:value="0"/>

  </service>
```

Start with a service class CustomComplicationProviderService as follows:

```
class CustomComplicationProviderService :
    ComplicationProviderService() {
  // This method is for any one-time per complication set-up.
  override
  fun onComplicationActivated(
        complicationId: Int, dataType: Int,
        complicationManager: ComplicationManager?) {
    Log.d(TAG,
        "onComplicationActivated(): $complicationId")
  }
```

```kotlin
// The complication needs updated data from your
// provider. Could happen because of one of:
//    1. An active watch face complication is changed
//       to use this provider
//    2. A complication using this provider becomes
//       active
//    3. The UPDATE_PERIOD_SECONDS (manifest) has
//       elapsed
//    4. Manually: an update via
//       ProviderUpdateRequester.requestUpdate()
override fun onComplicationUpdate(
        complicationId: Int, dataType: Int,
        complicationManager: ComplicationManager) {
    Log.d(TAG,
      "onComplicationUpdate() $complicationId")

    // ... add code for data generation ...

    var complicationData: ComplicationData? = null
    when (dataType) {
        ComplicationData.TYPE_SHORT_TEXT ->
          complicationData = ComplicationData.
              Builder(ComplicationData.TYPE_SHORT_TEXT)
                . ... create datum ...
                .build()
        ComplicationData.TYPE_LONG_TEXT ->
          complicationData = ComplicationData.
              Builder(ComplicationData.TYPE_LONG_TEXT)
                ...
        ComplicationData.TYPE_RANGED_VALUE ->
          complicationData = ComplicationData.
              Builder(ComplicationData.
                    TYPE_RANGED_VALUE)

                ...
        else ->
          Log.w("LOG",
```

```
            "Unexpected complication type $dataType")
    }

    if (complicationData != null) {
        complicationManager.updateComplicationData(
            complicationId, complicationData)
    } else {
        // Even if no data is sent, we inform the
        // ComplicationManager
        complicationManager.noUpdateRequired(
            complicationId)
    }
  }

  override
  fun onComplicationDeactivated(complicationId: Int) {
      Log.d("LOG",
        "onComplicationDeactivated(): $complicationId")
  }
}
```

To manually fire requests for the system to inquire new complication data, you use the ProviderUpdateRequester class as follows:

```
val compName =
  ComponentName(applicationContext,
      MyService::class.java)

val providerUpdateRequester =
  ProviderUpdateRequester(
      applicationContext, componentName)

providerUpdateRequester.requestUpdate(
    complicationId)
// To instead all complications, instead use
// providerUpdateRequester.requestUpdateAll()
```

Notifications on Wearables

Notifications on wearables can run in a bridged mode and in a standalone mode. In bridged mode, notifications get automatically synchronized with a paired smartphone; in standalone mode, the Wear device shows notifications independently.

To start creating your own notifications, begin with a Wear project using "Blank Wear Activity" in the project setup wizard. We change the layout file to add a button for creating a notification:

```xml
<?xml version="1.0" encoding="utf-8"?>
<android.support.wear.widget.BoxInsetLayout
  xmlns:android=
      "http://schemas.android.com/apk/res/android"
  xmlns:app="http://schemas.android.com/apk/res-auto"
  xmlns:tools="http://schemas.android.com/tools"
  android:layout_width="match_parent"
  android:layout_height="match_parent"
  android:background="@color/dark_grey"
  android:padding="@dimen/box_inset_layout_padding"
  tools:context=".MainActivity"
  tools:deviceIds="wear">

  <LinearLayout
      android:layout_width="match_parent"
      android:layout_height="match_parent"
      android:padding=
          "@dimen/inner_frame_layout_padding"
      app:boxedEdges="all"
      android:orientation="vertical">

    <TextView
        android:id="@+id/text"
        android:layout_width="wrap_content"
        android:layout_height="wrap_content"
        android:text="@string/hello_world"/>
```

```
<Button
    android:layout_width="wrap_content"
    android:layout_height="wrap_content"
    android:text="Go"
    android:onClick="go"/>

    </LinearLayout>
</android.support.wear.widget.BoxInsetLayout>
```

The activity gets a function to react to the button press. Inside, we create and send a notification:

```
class MainActivity : WearableActivity() {
  override fun onCreate(savedInstanceState: Bundle?) {
      super.onCreate(savedInstanceState)
      setContentView(activity_main)
      setAmbientEnabled() // Enables Always-on
  }

  fun go(v: View) {
      val notificationId = 1

      // The channel ID of the notification.
      val id = "my_channel_01"
      if (Build.VERSION.SDK_INT >=
          Build.VERSION_CODES.O) {
        // Create the NotificationChannel
        val name = "My channel"
        val description = "Channel description"
        val importance =
            NotificationManager.IMPORTANCE_DEFAULT
        val mChannel = NotificationChannel(
            id, name, importance)
        mChannel.description = description
        // Register the channel with the system
        val notificationManager = getSystemService(
            Context.NOTIFICATION_SERVICE)
          as NotificationManager
```

```
        notificationManager.
            createNotificationChannel(mChannel)
    }

    // Notification channel ID is ignored for Android
    // 7.1.1 (API level 25) and lower.
    val notificationBuilder =
        NotificationCompat.Builder(this, id)
        .setSmallIcon(android.R.drawable.ic_media_play)
        .setContentTitle("Title")
        .setContentText("Content Text")

    // Get NotificationManager service
    val notificationManager =
        NotificationManagerCompat.from(this)

    // Issue the notification
    notificationManager.notify(
        notificationId, notificationBuilder.build())
    }
}
```

If you start this app, it shows a simple UI with a text and a button. Pressing the button leads to shortly displaying the notification icon, which is a "play" rectangle in our example. Using the back button and swiping up, the notification shows up with title and contents. Also, the face your user uses might have a notification preview added. See Figure 14-1.

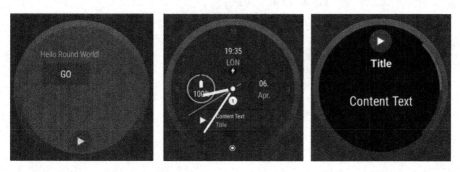

Figure 14-1. *A Notification on Wear*

You can also add a `PendingIntent` to your code and register it with `setContentIntent(...)` inside the builder to allow for sending an Intent once the user clicks an appearing notification. Also, inside the builder you can add additional action icons by using `addAction(...)` or `addActions(...)`.

Wearable-specific features can be added to a notification by constructing a `NotificationCompat.WearableExtender` object and calling `extent(...)` on the builder, passing this extender object. Note by adding actions to the `WearableExtender` object instead of the builder, you can make sure the actions only show up on a wearable.

For adding voice features to Wear notifications, using predefined text responses, and special features to be used in the bridged mode, please see the online documentation of wearable notifications at `https://developer.android.com/training/wearables/notifications/index.html`.

Controlling App Visibility on Wearables

Wear OS devices since Android 5.1 allow for running Wear apps in foreground even when the power-saving or *ambient* mode was engaged. You have two options for handling the ambient mode:

- Use the `AmbientModeSupport` class.

- Use the `WearableActivity` class.

For using the `AmbientModeSupport` class, implement a subclass of `Activity`, implement the `AmbientCallbackProvider` interface, and declare and save an `AmbientController` as in

```
class MainActivity : FragmentActivity(),
      AmbientModeSupport.AmbientCallbackProvider {
   override
   fun getAmbientCallback():
         AmbientModeSupport.AmbientCallback
   {
      ...
   }

   lateinit
   var mAmbientController:
```

```
        AmbientModeSupport.AmbientController

    override
    fun onCreate(savedInstanceState:Bundle?) {
        super.onCreate(savedInstanceState)
        ...
        mAmbientController =
            AmbientModeSupport.attach(this)
    }
}
```

Inside the getAmbientCallback() function, create and return a subclass of AmbientModeSupport.AmbientCallback. This callback is then responsible for the switch between standard and ambient modes. What ambient mode actually does is up to you as a developer, but you should engage power-saving measure as dimmed and black-and-white graphics, augmented update intervals, and so on.

The second possibility to allow for an ambient mode is to let your activity inherit from class WearableActivity, call setAmbientEnabled() in its onCreate(...) callback, and overwrite onEnterAmbient() and onExitAmbient(). If you also overwrite onUpdateAmbient(), you can put your screen updating logic there and let the system decide which update frequency to use in ambient mode.

Authentication in Wear

With Wear apps being able to run in standalone mode, authentication becomes more important. Describing the appropriate procedures for this matter is out of scope for this book, but the page at https://developer.android.com/training/wearables/overlays/auth-wear gives you detailed information about authentication in Wear.

Voice Capabilities in Wear

Adding voice capabilities to Wear devices makes a lot of sense, since other methods for user input are limited due to the small device dimensions. You have two options: connect your app to one or more of the system-provided voice actions, or define your own actions.

Caution   The Wear emulator cannot handle voice commands – you have to use real devices to test them.

Connecting system voice events to activities your app provides is easy – all you have to do is to add an intent filter to your activity as follows:

```
<intent-filter>
    <action android:name=
        "android.intent.action.SEND" />
    <category android:name=
        "com.google.android.voicesearch.SELF_NOTE" />
</intent-filter>
```

Possible voice keys are listed in Table 14-1.

Table 14-1. *System Voice Commands*

Command	Manifest Key	Extras
"OK, Google, get me a taxi" "OK, Google, call me a car"	com.google.android.gms.actions. RESERVE_TAXI_RESERVATION	-
"OK, Google, take a note" "OK, Google, note to self"	android.intent.action. SEND Category:com.android.voicesearch. SELF_NOTE	android.content.Intent.EXTRA_ TEXT – a string with note body
"OK, Google, set an alarm for 8 AM" "OK, Google, wake me up at 6 tomorrow"	android.intent.action.SET_ALARM	android.provider.AlarmClock. EXTRA_HOUR – an integer with the hour of the alarm. android. provider.AlarmClock.EXTRA_ MINUTES – an integer with the minute of the alarm

(continued)

Table 14-1. (*continued*)

Command	Manifest Key	Extras
"OK, Google, set a timer for 10 minutes"	android.intent.action.SET_TIMER	android.provider.AlarmClock. EXTRA_LENGTH – an integer in the range of 1–86400 (number of seconds in 24 hours) representing the length of the timer
"OK, Google, start stopwatch"	com.google.android.wearable.action. STOPWATCH	-
"OK, Google, start cycling" "OK, Google, start my bike ride" "OK, Google, stop cycling"	vnd.google.fitness.TRACK Mime Type:vnd.google.fitness.activity/biking	actionStatus – a string with the value ActiveActionStatus when starting and CompletedActionStatus when stopping
"OK, Google, track my run" "OK, Google, start running" "OK, Google, stop running"	vnd.google.fitness.TRACK MimeType:vnd.google.fitness.activity/ running	actionStatus – a string with the value ActiveActionStatus when starting and CompletedActionStatus when stopping
"OK, Google, start a workout" "OK, Google, track my workout" "OK, Google, stop workout"	vnd.google.fitness.TRACK MimeType:vnd.google.fitness.activity/ other	actionStatus – a string with the value ActiveActionStatus when starting and CompletedActionStatus when stopping
"OK, Google, what's my heart rate?" "OK, Google, what's my BPM?"	vnd.google.fitness.VIEW Mime Type:vnd.google.fitness.data_type/ com.google.heart_rate.bpm	-
"OK, Google, how many steps have I taken?" "OK, Google, what's my step count?"	vnd.google.fitness.VIEW Mime Type:vnd.google.fitness.data_type/ com.google.step_count.cumulative	-

Extra data can be extracted from incoming Intents as usual via one of the various `Intent.get*Extra(...)` methods.

You may also provide app-defined voice actions, *which can start custom activities.* To do so, inside `AndroidManifest.xml` define each `<action>` element in question as follows:

```
<activity android:name="MyActivity" android:label="MyRunningApp">
    <intent-filter>
        <action android:name="android.intent.action.MAIN" />
        <category android:name="android.intent.category.LAUNCHER" />
    </intent-filter>
</activity>
```

which by virtue of the "label" attribute will allow you to speak "Start MyRunningApp" to start the activity.

You can also let speech recognition fill edit fields. For this purpose, write

```
val SPEECH_REQUEST_CODE = 42
val intent = Intent(
        RecognizerIntent.ACTION_RECOGNIZE_SPEECH).apply {
  putExtra(RecognizerIntent.EXTRA_LANGUAGE_MODEL,
        RecognizerIntent.LANGUAGE_MODEL_FREE_FORM)
}.run {
  startActivityForResult(this, SPEECH_REQUEST_CODE)
}
```

and fetch the result in the overwritten `onActivityResult(...)` callback:

```
fun onActivityResult(requestCode:Int, resultCode:Int,
        data:Intent) {
  if (requestCode and 0xFFFF == SPEECH_REQUEST_CODE
        && resultCode == RESULT_OK) {
    val results = data.getStringArrayListExtra(
            RecognizerIntent.EXTRA_RESULTS)
    String spokenText = results[0]
    // ... do something with spoken text
  }
```

```
    super.onActivityResult(
        requestCode, resultCode, data)
}
```

Speakers on Wearables

If you want to use the speakers connected to a Wear device to play some audio, you first
check whether the Wear app can connect to speakers:

```
fun hasSpeakers(): Boolean {
    val packageManager = context.getPackageManager()
    val audioManager =
            context.getSystemService(
            Context.AUDIO_SERVICE) as AudioManager

    if (Build.VERSION.SDK_INT >= Build.VERSION_CODES.M) {
        // Check FEATURE_AUDIO_OUTPUT to guard against
        // false positives.
        if (!packageManager.hasSystemFeature(
                PackageManager.FEATURE_AUDIO_OUTPUT)) {
            return false
        }

        val devices =
                audioManager.getDevices(
                AudioManager.GET_DEVICES_OUTPUTS)
        for (device in devices) {
            if (device.type ==
                    AudioDeviceInfo.TYPE_BUILTIN_SPEAKER) {
                return true
            }
        }
    }
    return false
}
```

You can then play sound the same way as for any other app on any other device. This gets described in detail in the following in section "Playing Media."

Location in Wear

To use location detection in a Wear device, you must first check if location data is available:

```
fun hasGps():Boolean {
  return packageManager.hasSystemFeature(
      PackageManager.FEATURE_LOCATION_GPS);
}
```

If the wearable has no own location sensor, you must instead constantly check whether the wearable is connected. You do so by handling callbacks as in

```
var wearableConnected = false
fun onCreate(savedInstanceState: Bundle?) {
    ...
    Wearable.getNodeClient(this@MainActivity).
        connectedNodes.addOnSuccessListener {
        wearableConnected = it.any {
            it.isNearby
        }
    }.addOnCompleteListener {
    }.addOnFailureListener {
      ...
    }
}
```

Starting from there you can handle location detection using the *Fused Location Provider* as described in section "Location and Maps" of Chapter 8.

Data Communication in Wear

Data communication in the Wear OS happens in one of two ways:

- **Direct network communication**: This is for Wear devices able to connect to a network by themselves, wishing to talk to non-paired devices.

- **Using the wearable data layer API**: This is for communication to paired handheld devices.

For a direct network communication, use class `android.net.ConnectivityManager` for both checking for capabilities like bandwidth and requesting new capabilities like increased bandwidth. Please see the class's online API documentation for details. To actually perform network communication, use the classes and interfaces from package `android.net`.

The rest of this section is for describing the *wearable data layer API* for communication to paired handhelds.

To access the wearable data layer API, retrieve a `DataClient` or a `MessageClient` via

```
val dataClient = Wearable.getDataClient(this)
val msgClient = Wearable.getMessageClient(this)
```

from inside an activity. You can do this often, for both calls are inexpensive. A message client is best used for data with a small payload; for larger payloads, use a data client instead. Also, a data client is a reliable means of synchronizing data between Wear devices and handhelds, while a message client uses a fire-and-forget mode. A message client thus does not know whether sent data actually arrives or not.

For sending data items using a data client, create a `PutDataMapRequest` object, call `getDataMap()` on it, and use one of the various `put...()` methods to add data. Finally, call `asPutDataRequest()` and use its result to call `DataClient.putDataItem(...)`. The latter starts the synchronization with other devices and returns a `com.google.android.gms.tasks.Task` object to which you can add listeners to watch the communication.

On the receiver side, you can observe data synchronization by extending your activity with `DataClient.OnDataChangedListener` and implementing the fun `onDataChanged( dataEvents: DataEventBuffer )` function.

For larger binary data sets like images, you can use an `Asset` as a data type to be sent over the data client, as in

```
fun createAssetFromBitmap(bitmap: Bitmap): Asset {
  val byteStream = ByteArrayOutputStream()
  bitmap.compress(Bitmap.CompressFormat.PNG, 100,
```

```
            byteStream)
     return Asset.createFromBytes(byteStream.
           toByteArray())
  }
  val bitmap = BitmapFactory.decodeResource(
         getResources(), android.R.drawable.ic_media_play)
  val asset = createAssetFromBitmap(bitmap)
  val dataMap = PutDataMapRequest.create("/image")
  dataMap.getDataMap().putAsset("profileImage", asset)
  val request = dataMap.asPutDataRequest()
  val putTask: Task<DataItem> =
         Wearable.getDataClient(this).putDataItem(request)
```

To instead use a message client, we first need to find suitable message receivers. You do so by first assigning capabilities to suitable handheld apps. This can be accomplished by adding a file wear.xml to res/values and letting it read

```
<resources>
  <string-array name="android_wear_capabilities">
      <item>my_capability1</item>
      <item>my_capability2</item>
      ...
  </string-array>
</resources>
```

To find a handheld (or network node) with suitable capabilities and then send messages to it, you write

```
val capabilityInfo = Tasks.await(
    Wearable.getCapabilityClient(this).getCapability(
        "my_capability1",
        CapabilityClient.FILTER_REACHABLE))
capabilityInfo.nodes.find {
  it.isNearby
}?.run {
  msgClient.sendMessage(
        this.id,"/msg/path","Hello".toByteArray())
}
```

Instead of this you could also add a `CapabilityClient.`
`OnCapabilityChangedListener` listener directly to the client like in

```
Wearable.getCapabilityClient(this).addListener({
  it.nodes.find {
    it.isNearby
  }?.run {
    msgClient.sendMessage(
        this.id,"/msg/path","Hello".toByteArray())
  }
}, "my_capability1")
```

To receive such a message, anywhere in an app installed on a handheld, register a
message event listener via

```
Wearable.getMessageClient(this).addListener {
    messageEvent ->
  // do s.th. with the message event
}
```

Programming with Android TV

App development targeting an Android TV device does not substantially differ from
development on smartphones. However, due to the user expectation coming from
decades of TV consumption, conventions are more strict compared with smartphones.
Fortunately, the project builder wizard of Android Studio helps you get started. And in
this section too, we will be talking about important aspects of Android TV development.

Android TV Use Cases

The typical use cases for an Android TV app are

- Playback of video and music data streams and files

- A catalog to help users find content

- A game that can be played on Android TV (without touchscreen)

- Presenting channels with content

Starting an Android TV Studio Project

If you start a new Android TV project in Android Studio, the prominent points of interest are as follows:

- Inside the manifest file, add the items

```
<uses-feature
    android:name="android.hardware.touchscreen"
    android:required="false"/>
<uses-feature
    android:name="android.software.leanback"
    android:required="true"/>
```

  This will make sure the app *could* also work on a smartphone with a touchscreen and that the leanback user interface needed by Android TV gets included.

- Still inside the manifest file, you will see the start activity to have an intent filter like

```
<intent-filter>
  <action android:name=
    "android.intent.action.MAIN"/>
  <category android:name=
    "android.intent.category.LEANBACK_LAUNCHER"/>
</intent-filter>
```

  The category shown here is important; otherwise, Android TV will not properly recognize the app. The activity also needs to have an "android:banner" attribute, which points to a banner prominently shown on the Android TV user interface.

- Inside the module's `build.gradle` file, the leanback support library gets added inside the dependencies section:

```
implementation 'com.android.support:leanback-v17:27.1.1'
```

For development you can either use a virtual or a real device. Virtual devices get installed via the AVD Manager in the Tools menu. For real devices, tap seven times the build number in Settings ➤ Device ➤ About. Back in Settings, go to Preferences and enable debugging in the Developer Options.

Android TV Hardware Features

To find out whether an app is running on an Android TV, you can use the `UiModeManager` as follows:

```
val isRunnigOnTv =
    (getSystemService(Context.UI_MODE_SERVICE)
            as UiModeManager).currentModeType ==
    Configuration.UI_MODE_TYPE_TELEVISION
```

Also, available features vary from device to device. If your app needs certain hardware features, you can check the availability as follows:

```
getPackageManager().
        hasSystemFeature(PackageManager.FEATURE_*)
```

For all possible features, see the API documentation of the `PackageManager`.

User input on Android TV devices normally happens via a D-pad controller. To build stable apps, you should react to changes on the availability of the D-pad controller: inside the `AndroidManifest.xml` file, add `android:configChanges = "keyboard|keyboardHidden|navigation"` as an activity attribute. The app then gets informed about configuration changes via the overwritten callback function `fun onConfigurationChanged( newConfig : Configuration )`.

UI Development for Android TV

For Android TV development, using the *leanback theme* is suggested. For this aim replace the "theme" attribute in the `<application>` element of the `AndroidManifest.xml` file with

```
android:theme="@style/Theme.Leanback"
```

This implies not using an action bar, which makes sense since Android TV does not support action bars. Also, the activity must not extend `AppCompatActivity`, but instead must extend `android.support.v4.app.FragmentActivity`.

Another specialty of Android TV apps is that an occasional overscan might happen: depending on pixel size and aspect ratio, Android TV might clip away parts of the screen. In order to avoid your layout being destroyed, adding a margin of 48 dp × 27 dp to the main container is suggested, as in

```
<RelativeLayout xmlns:android=
        "http://schemas.android.com/apk/res/android"
    android:layout_width="match_parent"
    android:layout_height="match_parent"
    android:layout_marginTop="27dp"
    android:layout_marginBottom="27dp"
    android:layout_marginLeft="48dp"
    android:layout_marginRight="48dp">

    <!-- Screen elements ... -->

</RelativeLayout>
```

Besides, for Android TV a development for 1920 × 1080 pixels is suggested. With other hardware pixel sizes, Android will then automatically downscale layout elements if necessary.

Since users cannot navigate through tappable UI elements and instead use a D-pad for navigation, an alternative way to switch between UI elements is needed for Android TV. This can easily be accomplished by adding "nextFocusUp", "nextFocusDown", "nextFocusLeft", and "nextFocusRight" attributes to UI elements. The arguments are then ID specifications of navigate-to elements as in `"@+id/xyzElement"`.

For TV playback components, the *leanback* library provides a couple of classes and concepts, which come in handy:

- For a media browser, let your fragment extend `android.support.v17.leanback.app.BrowseSupportFragment`. The project builder wizard instead creates a deprecated `BrowseFragment,` but you can walk through the API documentation of `BrowseSupportFragment` to learn the new methodology.

- The actual media items to be presented inside the media browser are governed by a card view. The corresponding class to overwrite is `android.support.v17.leanback.widget.Presenter`.

- To show details of a selected media item, extend class `android.support.v17.leanback.app.DetailsSupportFragment`. The wizard creates the deprecated `DetailFragment` instead, but their usage is similar, and you can have a look at the API documentation for more details.

- For a UI element showing video playback, use one of `android.support.v17.leanback.app.PlaybackFragment` and `android.support.v17.leanback.app.VideoFragment`.

- Use class `android.media.session.MediaSession` to configure a *Now Playing* card.

- Direct rendering of a video stream onto a UI element is supported by class `android.media.tv.TvInputService`. Calling `onTune(...)` will start rendering the direct video stream.

- If your app needs a guide using several steps, for example, to present a purchasing workflow to the user, you can use class `android.support.v17.leanback.app.GuidedStepSupportFragment`.

- To present an app to the first-time user in a non-interactive way, use class `android.support.v17.leanback.app.OnboardingSupportFragment`.

Recommendation Channels for Content Search

Recommendations shown to users come in two forms: as a recommendation row before Android 8.0 and as recommendation channels starting with Android 8.0 or API level 26. To not miss users, your app should serve both in a switch:

```
if (android.os.Build.VERSION.SDK_INT >=
        Build.VERSION_CODES.O) {
  // Recommendation channels API ...
} else {
  // Recommendations row API ...
}
```

For Android 8.0 and later, the Android TV home screen shows a global *Play Next* row at the top of the channel list and a number of channels each belonging to a certain app. A channel other than the *Play Next* row cannot belong to more than one app. Each app can define a *default channel*, which automatically shows up in the channel view – for all other channels an app might define, the user must approve first before the channel gets shown on the home screen.

An app needs to have the following permissions in order to be able to manage channels:

```
<uses-permission android:name=
    "com.android.providers.tv.permission.READ_EPG_DATA"
    />
<uses-permission android:name=
    "com.android.providers.tv.permission.WRITE_EPG_DATA"
    />
```

So add them to file `AndroidManifest.xml`.

In addition inside your module's `build.gradle` file, add to the `dependencies` section (one line)

```
implementation
        'com.android.support:support-tv-provider:27.1.1'
```

To create a channel, add a channel logo, and possibly make it the default channel, write

```
val builder = Channel.Builder()

// Intent to execute when the App link gets tapped.
val appLink = Intent(...).toUri(Intent.URI_INTENT_SCHEME)

// You must use type `TYPE_PREVIEW`
builder.setType(TvContractCompat.Channels.TYPE_PREVIEW)
        .setDisplayName("Channel Name")
        .setAppLinkIntentUri(Uri.parse(appLink))
val channel = builder.build()
val channelUri = contentResolver.insert(
        TvContractCompat.Channels.CONTENT_URI,
        channel.toContentValues())
```

```
val channelId = ContentUris.parseId(channelUri)
// Choose one or the other
ChannelLogoUtils.storeChannelLogo(this, channelId,
      /*Uri*/ logoUri)
ChannelLogoUtils.storeChannelLogo(this, channelId,
      /*Bitmap*/ logoBitmap)

// optional, make it the default channel
if (Build.VERSION.SDK_INT >= Build.VERSION_CODES.O)
    TvContractCompat.requestChannelBrowsable(this,
          channelId)
```

To update or delete a channel, you use the channel ID gathered from the channel creation step and then write

```
// to update:
contentResolver.update(
      TvContractCompat.buildChannelUri(channelId),
      channel.toContentValues(), null, null)

// to delete:
contentResolver.delete(
      TvContractCompat.buildChannelUri(channelId),
      null, null)
```

To add a program, use

```
val pbuilder = PreviewProgram.Builder()

// Intent to launch when a program gets selected
val progLink = Intent().toUri(Intent.URI_INTENT_SCHEME)

pbuilder.setChannelId(channelId)
    .setType(TvContractCompat.PreviewPrograms.TYPE_CLIP)
    .setTitle("Title")
    .setDescription("Program description")
    .setPosterArtUri(largePosterArtUri)
    .setIntentUri(Uri.parse(progLink))
    .setInternalProviderId(appProgramId)
```

```
val previewProgram = pbuilder.build()
val programUri = contentResolver.insert(
      TvContractCompat.PreviewPrograms.CONTENT_URI,
            previewProgram.toContentValues())
val programId = ContentUris.parseId(programUri)
```

To instead add a program to the *Play Next*, you somewhat similarly use a WatchNextProgram.Builder and write

```
val wnbuilder = WatchNextProgram.Builder()
val watchNextType = TvContractCompat.
      WatchNextPrograms.WATCH_NEXT_TYPE_CONTINUE
wnbuilder.setType(
        TvContractCompat.WatchNextPrograms.TYPE_CLIP)
    .setWatchNextType(watchNextType)
    .setLastEngagementTimeUtcMillis(time)
    .setTitle("Title")
    .setDescription("Program description")
    .setPosterArtUri(largePosterArtUri)
    .setIntentUri(Uri.parse(progLink))
    .setInternalProviderId(appProgramId)
val watchNextProgram = wnbuilder.build()
val watchNextProgramUri = contentResolver
    .insert(
          TvContractCompat.WatchNextPrograms.CONTENT_URI,
          watchNextProgram.toContentValues())
val watchnextProgramId =
      ContentUris.parseId(watchNextProgramUri)
```

where for the watchNextType you can use one of the following constants from TvContractCompat.WatchNextPrograms:

- **WATCH_NEXT_TYPE_CONTINUE**: The user stopped while watching content and can resume here.

- **WATCH_NEXT_TYPE_NEXT**: The next program in a series is available.

- **WATCH_NEXT_TYPE_NEW**: The next program in a series is newly available.

- **WATCH_NEXT_TYPE_WATCHLIST**: Inserted by the system or the app when the user saves a program.

To update or delete a program, use the program ID you memorized from the program generation:

```
// to update:
contentResolver.update(
    TvContractCompat.
        buildPreviewProgramUri(programId),
    watchNextProgram.toContentValues(), null, null)
```

```
// to delete:
contentResolver.delete(
    TvContractCompat.
        buildPreviewProgramUri(programId),
    null, null)
```

A Recommendation Row for Content Search

For Android up to version 7.1 or API level 25, recommendations were handled by a special recommendation row. You must not use a recommendation row for any later version.

In order for an app to participate in the recommendation row for the pre-8.0 Android versions, we first create a new recommendation service as follows:

```
class UpdateRecommendationsService :
    IntentService("RecommendationService") {
  companion object {
      private val TAG = "UpdateRecommendationsService"
      private val MAX_RECOMMENDATIONS = 3
  }
  override fun onHandleIntent(intent: Intent?) {
      Log.d("LOG", "Updating recommendation cards")

      val recommendations:List<Movie> =
```

```kotlin
            ArrayList<Movie>()
        // TODO: fill recommendation movie list...

        var count = 0
        val notificationManager =
            getSystemService(Context.NOTIFICATION_SERVICE)
            as NotificationManager
        val notificationId = 42
        for (movie in recommendations) {
            Log.d("LOG", "Recommendation - " +
                    movie.title!!)
            val builder = RecommendationBuilder(
                context = applicationContext,
                smallIcon = R.drawable.video_by_icon,
                id = count+1,
                priority = MAX_RECOMMENDATIONS - count,
                title = movie.title ?: "",
                description = "Description",
                image = getBitmapFromURL(
                        movie.cardImageUrl ?:""),
                intent = buildPendingIntent(movie))
            val notification = builder.build()
            notificationManager.notify(
                    notificationId, notification)
            if (++count >= MAX_RECOMMENDATIONS) {
              break
            }
        }
    }

    private fun getBitmapFromURL(src: String): Bitmap {
        val url = URL(src)
        return (url.openConnection() as HttpURLConnection).
        apply {
            doInput = true
        }.let {
```

```
        it.connect()
        BitmapFactory.decodeStream(it.inputStream)
    }
}

private fun buildPendingIntent(movie: Movie):
    PendingIntent {
    val detailsIntent =
        Intent(this, DetailsActivity::class.java)
    detailsIntent.putExtra("Movie", movie)

    val stackBuilder = TaskStackBuilder.create(this)
    stackBuilder.addParentStack(
        DetailsActivity::class.java)
    stackBuilder.addNextIntent(detailsIntent)
    // Ensure a unique PendingIntents, otherwise all
    // recommendations end up with the same
    // PendingIntent
    detailsIntent.action = movie.id.toString()

    return stackBuilder.getPendingIntent(
        0, PendingIntent.FLAG_UPDATE_CURRENT)
}
}
```

The corresponding entry in `AndroidManifest.xml` reads

```
<service
    android:name=".UpdateRecommendationsService"
    android:enabled="true" />
```

The `RecommendationBuilder` mentioned in the code refers to a wrapper class around a notification builder:

```
class RecommendationBuilder(
    val id:Int = 0,
    val context:Context,
    val title:String,
    val description:String,
```

```kotlin
    var priority:Int = 0,
    val image: Bitmap,
    val smallIcon: Int = 0,
    val intent: PendingIntent,
    val extras:Bundle? = null
) {
    fun build(): Notification {
        val notification:Notification =
            NotificationCompat.BigPictureStyle(
                NotificationCompat.Builder(context)
                    .setContentTitle(title)
                    .setContentText(description)
                    .setPriority(priority)
                    .setLocalOnly(true)
                    .setOngoing(true)
                    .setColor(...)
                    .setCategory(
                        Notification.CATEGORY_RECOMMENDATION)
                    .setLargeIcon(image)
                    .setSmallIcon(smallIcon)
                    .setContentIntent(intent)
                    .setExtras(extras))
                .build()
        return notification
    }
}
```

We need it, because creating and passing a notification is the way to tell the system about a recommendation.

What is left is a component that starts at system bootup and then regularly sends the recommendation. An example would use a broadcast receiver and an alarm for the periodic updates:

```kotlin
class RecommendationBootup : BroadcastReceiver() {
    companion object {
        private val TAG = "BootupActivity"
```

```kotlin
        private val INITIAL_DELAY: Long = 5000
    }

    override
    fun onReceive(context: Context, intent: Intent) {
        Log.d(TAG, "BootupActivity initiated")
        if (intent.action!!.endsWith(
                Intent.ACTION_BOOT_COMPLETED)) {
            scheduleRecommendationUpdate(context)
        }
    }

    private
    fun scheduleRecommendationUpdate(context: Context) {
        Log.d(TAG, "Scheduling recommendations update")

        val alarmManager =
                context.getSystemService(
                Context.ALARM_SERVICE) as AlarmManager
        val recommendationIntent = Intent(context,
                UpdateRecommendationsService::class.java)
        val alarmIntent =
                PendingIntent.getService(
                context, 0, recommendationIntent, 0)

        alarmManager.setInexactRepeating(
                AlarmManager.ELAPSED_REALTIME_WAKEUP,
                INITIAL_DELAY,
                AlarmManager.INTERVAL_HALF_HOUR,
                alarmIntent)
    }
}
```

with a corresponding entry inside AndroidManifest.xml:

```xml
<receiver android:name=".RecommendationBootup"
        android:enabled="true"
        android:exported="false">
```

```
<intent-filter>
  <action android:name=
      "android.intent.action.BOOT_COMPLETED"/>
</intent-filter>
</receiver>
```

For this to work, you need as permission

```
<uses-permission android:name=
    "android.permission.RECEIVE_BOOT_COMPLETED"/>
```

Android TV Content Search

Your Android TV app may contribute to the Android search framework. We described it in section "Search Framework" of Chapter 8 – in this section we point out peculiarities for using search in a TV app.

The search item fields important for TV search *suggestions* are shown in Table 14-2, where in the left column constant names from the SearchManager class are shown. You can use them in your database as shown, or at least you must provide a mapping mechanism inside the app.

Table 14-2. *TV Search Fields*

Field	Description
SUGGEST_COLUMN_TEXT_1	Required: The name of your content
SUGGEST_COLUMN_TEXT_2	A text description of your content
SUGGEST_COLUMN_RESULT_CARD_IMAGE	An image/poster/cover for your content
SUGGEST_COLUMN_CONTENT_TYPE	Required: The MIME type of your media
SUGGEST_COLUMN_VIDEO_WIDTH	The width of your media
SUGGEST_COLUMN_VIDEO_HEIGHT	The height of your media
SUGGEST_COLUMN_PRODUCTION_YEAR	Required: The production year
SUGGEST_COLUMN_DURATION	Required: The duration in milliseconds

As for any other search provider, create a content provider for the search suggestions inside your app.

As soon as the user submits the search dialog to actually *perform* a search query, the search framework fires an Intent with action SEARCH, so you can write an activity with an appropriate intent filter as follows:

```
<activity
    android:name=".DetailsActivity"
    android:exported="true">

    <!-- Receives the search request. -->
    <intent-filter>
        <action android:name=
            "android.intent.action.SEARCH" />
    </intent-filter>

    <!-- Points to searchable meta data. -->
    <meta-data android:name="android.app.searchable"
        android:resource="@xml/searchable" />
</activity>
```

Android TV Games

While game development seems very appealing first due to the large display, it is important to have a couple of things in mind:

- TVs are always in landscape mode, so make sure your app is good at using landscape mode.

- For a multiplayer game, it is normally not possible to hide things from users, for example, in a card game. You could connect TV apps to companion apps running on smartphones to remedy this.

- Your TV game should support gamepads, and it should prominently tell the users how to use them. Inside the AndroidManifest.xml file, you better declare <uses-feature android:name = "android. hardware.gamepad" android:required = "false"/> – if instead you write required = "true", you make your app uninstallable for users who don't own gamepads.

Android TV Channels

The handling of live content, that is, the presentation of continuous, channel-based content, is governed by the *TV Input Framework* and various classes in the `com.android.tv`, `com.android.providers.tv`, and `android.media.tv` packages. It primarily addresses OEM manufacturers to serve as an aid to connect the TV system of Android to live-stream data. For details please have a look at the API documentation of these packages, and/or enter "Android building TV channels" in your favorite search engine.

Programming with Android Auto and Automotive OS

Android support for cars comes in two flavors:

- **Android Auto** for car-related apps running on a smartphone

- **Android Automotive OS** for devices built in your vehicle

On Android Auto and/or Automotive OS, you can run media apps, messaging apps, navigation apps, point-of-interest apps, and video playback apps.

In this book we do not further dig into car-related Android programming. However, `https://developer.android.com/training/cars` gives you a good starting point for automotive projects. Also, in the *New Project* wizard of Android Studio, you can easily set up a project for an Android Automotive media or messaging app. And there is also an emulated Android Automotive OS device available.

Playing and Recording Sound

Playing sound in Android means one of two things or both together:

- **Short sound snippets**: You typically play them as a feedback to user interface actions, like pressing a button or entering something in an edit field. Another use case is games, where certain events could be mapped to short audio fragments. Especially for UI reactivity, make sure you don't annoy users and provide for a possibility to readily mute audio output.

- **Music playback**: You want to play music pieces with a duration longer than a few seconds.

For short audio snippets, you use a SoundPool and for music pieces a MediaPlayer. We talk about them and also audio recording in the following sections.

Short Sound Snippets

For short sound snippets, you use a SoundPool and preload the sounds during initialization. You cannot immediately use the sound snippets after you load them using one of the SoundPool.load(...) methods. Instead, you have to wait until all sounds are loaded. The suggested way is not to wait for some time as you frequently can read in some blogs – instead, listen to sound loaded events and count finished snippets. You can let a custom class do that, for example:

```
class SoundLoadManager(val ctx:Context) {
  var scheduled = 0
  var loaded = 0
  val sndPool:SoundPool
  val soundPoolMap = mutableMapOf<Int,Int>()
  init {
      sndPool =
          if (Build.VERSION.SDK_INT >=
              Build.VERSION_CODES.LOLLIPOP) {
            SoundPool.Builder()
              .setMaxStreams(4)
              .setAudioAttributes(
                AudioAttributes.Builder()
                .setUsage(
                  AudioAttributes.USAGE_MEDIA)
                .setContentType(
                  AudioAttributes.CONTENT_TYPE_MUSIC)
                .build()
              ).build()
          } else {
              SoundPool(4,
                  AudioManager.STREAM_MUSIC,
```

```
                100)
        }
    sndPool.setOnLoadCompleteListener({
        sndPool, sampleId, status ->
        if(status != 0) {
            Log.e("LOG",
                    "Sound could not be loaded")
        } else {
            Log.i("LOG", "Loaded sample " +
                    sampleId + ", status = " +
                    status)
        }
        loaded++
    })
}

fun load(resourceId:Int) {
    scheduled++
    soundPoolMap[resourceId] =
        sndPool.load(ctx, resourceId, 1)
}

fun allLoaded() = scheduled == loaded

fun play(rsrcId: Int, loop: Boolean):Int {
    return soundPoolMap[rsrcId]?.run {
        val audioManager = ctx.getSystemService(
                Context.AUDIO_SERVICE) as AudioManager
        val curVolume = audioManager.
                getStreamVolume(
                AudioManager.STREAM_MUSIC)
        val maxVolume = audioManager.
                getStreamMaxVolume(
                AudioManager.STREAM_MUSIC)
        val leftVolume = 1f * curVolume / maxVolume
        val rightVolume = 1f * curVolume / maxVolume
```

```
        val priority = 1
        val noLoop = if(loop) -1 else 0
        val normalPlaybackRate = 1f
        sndPool.play(this, leftVolume, rightVolume,
                priority, noLoop, normalPlaybackRate)
    } ?: -1
  }
}
```

What this class does is as follows:

- Loads and saves an instance of SoundPool. The constructor is deprecated; that is why we use different ways of initializing it, dependent of the Android API level. The parameters shown here may be adapted according to your needs. Please see the API documentation of SoundPool, SoundPool.Builder, and AudioAttributes.Builder.

- Provides for a load() method with a resource ID as argument – this could, for example, be a WAV file inside the res/raw folder.

- Provides for a allLoaded() method you can use to check whether all sounds have been loaded.

- Provides for a play() method you can use to play a loaded sound. Will do nothing if the sound is not loaded yet. Will return the stream ID if the sound gets actually played, or else -1.

To use the class, create a field with an instance. Upon initialization, for example, in an activity's onCreate(...) method, load the sounds and invoke play() to start playing:

```
...
lateinit var soundLoadManager:SoundLoadManager
...
override
fun onCreate(savedInstanceState: Bundle?) {
    super.onCreate(savedInstanceState)
    setContentView(R.layout.activity_main)

    ...
```

```
    soundLoadManager = SoundLoadManager(this)
    with(soundLoadManager) {
      load(R.raw.click)
      // more ...
    }
}

fun go(v: View) {
    Log.e("LOG", "All sounds loaded = " +
        soundLoadManager.allLoaded())
    val strmId = soundLoadManager.play(
        R.raw.click, false)
    Log.e("LOG", "Stream ID = " + strmId.toString())
}
```

The SoundPool class also allows for stopping and resuming sounds. You can appropriately extend the SoundLoadManager class to take that into account if you need it.

Playing Media

The class MediaPlayer is all you need to register and play a music clip of arbitrary length and arbitrary origin. It is a state machine and as such not particularly easy to handle, but we first talk about permissions we might need to operate a media player:

- If your app needs to play media originating from the Internet, you must allow Internet access by adding

    ```
    <uses-permission android:name=
        "android.permission.INTERNET" />
    ```

    to file AndroidManifest.xml.

- If you want to prevent your playback from being interrupted by the device going asleep, you need to acquire wake locks. We will be talking more about that in the following, but in order for this to be possible at all, you need to add the permission

    ```
    <uses-permission android:name=
        "android.permission.WAKE_LOCK" />
    ```

to `AndroidManifest.xml`.

To see what to do further to acquire permissions inside your code, please go to Chapter 7.

With necessary permissions set up, we can now treat the handling of the `MediaPlayer` class. As already mentioned, an instance of it creates a state machine, and the transitions from state to state correspond to various playback states. In more detail, the object can be in one of the following states:

- **Idle**

  Once constructed by the default constructor, or after a `reset()`, the player is in *idle* state.

- **Initialized**

  Once the data source gets set via `setDataSource(...)`, the player is in *initialized* state. Unless you first use a `reset()`, calling `setDataSource(...)` again results in an error.

- **Prepared**

  The preparation transition prepares some resources and data streams to be used for the playback. Because it might take some time, especially for stream resources originating from data sources on the Internet, there are two possibilities to engage that transition: the `prepare()` method executes that step and blocks the program flow until it finishes, while the `prepareAsync()` sends the preparation to the background. In the latter case, you have to register a listener via `setOnPreparedListener(...)` to find out when the preparation step actually finished. You must do the preparation before you can start after initialization, and you must do it again after a `stop()` before you can start the playback again.

- **Started**

  After a successful preparation, the playback can be started by calling `start()`.

- **Paused**

  After a start(), you can temporarily suspend the playback by calling
  pause. Calling start again resumes the playback at the current
  playback position.

- **Stopped**

  You can stop the playback, either while it is running or while it is
  paused, by invoking stop(). Once stopped, it is not allowed to start
  again, unless the preparation step got repeated first.

- **Completed**

  Once the playback is completed and no looping is active, the
  completed state gets entered. You can either stop from here or
  start again.

Note that the various static create(...) factory methods gather several transitions.
For details please see the API documentation.

To give you an example, a basic player UI for playing a music file from inside the
assets folder, utilizing a synchronous preparation and with a start/pause button and a
stop button, looks like

```
var mPlayer: MediaPlayer? = null
fun btnText(playing:Boolean) {
    startBtn.text = if(playing) "Pause" else "Play"
}
fun goStart(v:View) {
    mPlayer = mPlayer?.run {
        btnText(!isPlaying)
        if(isPlaying)
            pause()
        else
            start()
        this
    } ?: MediaPlayer().apply {
        setOnCompletionListener {
            btnText(false)
            release()
```

```
            mPlayer = null
        }
        val fd: AssetFileDescriptor =
                assets.openFd("tune1.mp3")
        setDataSource(fd.fileDescriptor)
        prepare() // synchronous
        start()
        btnText(true)
    }
}

fun goStop(v:View) {
    mPlayer?.run {
        stop()
        prepare()
        btnText(false)
    }
}
```

The code is mostly self-explanatory. The goStart() and goStop() methods get called once the buttons get pressed, and btnText(...) is used to indicate state changes. The

```
mPlayer = mPlayer?.run {
    (A)
    this
} ?: MediaPlayer().apply {
    (B)
}
```

construct used here might look strange first, but all it does is this: If the mPlayer object is not null, do (A) and finally perform a void assignment to itself. Otherwise, construct it and then apply (B) to it.

For that example to work, you must have buttons with IDs startBtn and stopBtn in your layout, connect them via android:onclick="goStop" and android:onclick="goStart", and have a file "tune1.mp3" inside your assets/ folder. The example switches the button text between "Play" and "Pause" labels – you could of course instead use ImageButton views here and change icons once pressed.

To use any other data source, including online streams from the Internet, apply one of the various setDataSource(...) alternatives, or use one of the static create(...) methods. To monitor the various state transitions, add appropriate listeners via setOn... Listener(...). It is further suggested to immediately call release() on a MediaPlayer object once you are done with it, to free no longer used system resources.

The playback of some music can also be handled in the background, for example, using a service instead of an activity. In such a case, if you want to avoid the device interrupting a playback because it decides to go into a sleep mode, you acquire wake locks as follows

```
mPlayer.setWakeMode(applicationContext,
        PowerManager.PARTIAL_WAKE_LOCK)
```

to avoid the CPU going to sleep and

```
val wifiLock = (applicationContext.getSystemService(Context.WIFI_SERVICE)
as WifiManager)
    .createWifiLock(WifiManager.WIFI_MODE_FULL, "myWifilock")
.run {
  acquire()
  this
}
... later:
wifiLock.release()
```

to avoid the network connection being interrupted.

Recording Audio

For recording audio, you use the class MediaRecorder. Using it is rather straightforward:

```
val mRecorder = MediaRecorder().apply {
    setAudioSource(MediaRecorder.AudioSource.MIC)
    setOutputFormat(MediaRecorder.OutputFormat.THREE_GPP)
    setOutputFile(mFileName)
    setAudioEncoder(MediaRecorder.AudioEncoder.AMR_NB)
}
mRecorder.prepare()
```

```
mRecorder.start()

... later:
mRecorder.stop()
```

For other options regarding input, media format, and output, please see the API documentation of class `MediaRecorder`.

Using the Camera

An application showing things to the user always has been a predominant usage area of computers. First it was text, later pictures, and even later movies. Only during the last decades the opposite, letting the user show things, has more and more gained considerable attention. With handhelds being equipped with cameras of increasing quality, the need for apps that are able to handle camera data has come up. Android helps a lot here. An app can tell the Android OS to take a picture or record a movie and save it somewhere, or it can take complete control over the camera hardware and continuously monitor camera data and change zoom, exposure, and focus on demand.

We will be talking about all that in the following sections. In case you need features or settings we are not going to describe here, the API documentation serves as a starting point for extended research on that matter.

Taking a Picture

A high-level approach to communicate with the camera hardware is the IT counterpart of the order "Take a picture and save it somewhere I tell you." To accomplish that, assuming the handheld actually has a camera and you have the permission to use it, you call a certain Intent telling the path name where to save the image. Upon intent result retrieval, you have access to the image data, both directly to a low-resolution thumbnail and to the full image data at the place requested.

We start with telling Android that our app needs a camera. This happens via an `<uses-feature>` element inside file `AndroidManifest.xml`:

```
<uses-feature android:name="android.hardware.camera"
              android:required="true" />
```

Inside your app you will then do a runtime check

```
if (!packageManager.hasSystemFeature(
        PackageManager.FEATURE_CAMERA)) {
    ...
}
```

and act accordingly.

To declare the permission necessary, you write inside the manifest file AndroidManifrest.xml in the <manifest> element

```
<uses-permission android:name=
        "android.permission.CAMERA" />
```

To check that permission and in case acquire it, see Chapter 7. In case you want to save the picture to a publicly available store, so other apps can see it, you additionally need the permission "android.permission.WRITE_EXTERNAL_STORAGE", declared and acquired the same way. To instead save the picture data to a space private to the app, you declare a slightly different permission need

```
<uses-permission android:name=
        "android.permission.WRITE_EXTERNAL_STORAGE"
        android:maxSdkVersion="18"/>
```

because that declaration is necessary only up to Android 4.4 or API level 18.

We need to do some extra work to access the image data storage. Apart from the permission we just described, we also need access to the storage on a content provider security level. This means, inside the <application> element of AndroidManifest.xml, you add

```
<provider
        android:name=
            "android.support.v4.content.FileProvider"
        android:authorities=
            "com.example.autho.fileprovider"
        android:exported="false"
        android:grantUriPermissions="true">
    <meta-data
        android:name=
            "android.support.FILE_PROVIDER_PATHS"
        android:resource="@xml/file_paths">
```

```
</meta-data>
</provider>
```

and inside a file res/xml/file_paths.xml write

```
<?xml version="1.0" encoding="utf-8"?>
<paths xmlns:android=
       "http://schemas.android.com/apk/res/android">
  <external-path name="my_images" path=
     "Android/data/com.example.pckg.name/files/Pictures"
  />
</paths>
```

The value inside the path attribute depends on whether we save the pictures in the publicly available storage or in the app's private data space:

- Use "Android/data/com.example.package.name/files/Pictures" if you want to save the image to the app's private data space.

- Use "Pictures" if you want to save the image to the public data space.

Note   If you use the app's private data space, all pictures will be deleted if the app gets uninstalled.

In order to start the system's camera, first create an empty file where the picture taken is written. Then create and fire an Intent as follows:

```
val REQUEST_TAKE_PHOTO = 42
var photoFile:File? = null
fun dispatchTakePictureIntent() {
  fun createImageFile():File {
    val timeStamp =
           SimpleDateFormat("yyyyMMdd_HHmmss_SSS",
           Locale.US).format(Date())
    val imageFileName = "JPEG_" + timeStamp + "_"

    val storageDir =
           Environment.getExternalStoragePublicDirectory(
           Environment.DIRECTORY_PICTURES)
```

```
    // To instead take the App's private space:
    // val storageDir =
    // getExternalFilesDir(
    // Environment.DIRECTORY_PICTURES)
    val image = File.createTempFile(
         imageFileName,
         ".jpg",
         storageDir)
    return image
  }

  val takePictureIntent =
       Intent(MediaStore.ACTION_IMAGE_CAPTURE)
  val canHandleIntent = takePictureIntent.
       resolveActivity(packageManager) != null
  if (canHandleIntent) {
    photoFile = createImageFile()
    Log.e("LOG","Photo output File: ${photoFile}")
    val photoURI = FileProvider.getUriForFile(this,
         "com.example.autho.fileprovider",
         photoFile!!)
    Log.e("LOG","Photo output URI: ${photoURI}")
    takePictureIntent.putExtra(
         MediaStore.EXTRA_OUTPUT, photoURI)
    startActivityForResult(takePictureIntent,
         REQUEST_TAKE_PHOTO)
  }
 }
dispatchTakePictureIntent()
```

Note that the second parameter in `FileProvider.getUriForFile()` designates the authority and as such must also show up in file `AndroidManifest.xml` inside the `<provider>` element, as shown previously.

After the photo has been taken, the app's `onActivityResult()` can be used to fetch the image data:

```
override
```

```kotlin
fun onActivityResult(requestCode: Int, resultCode: Int,
        data: Intent) {
  if ((requestCode and 0xFFFF) == REQUEST_TAKE_PHOTO
        && resultCode == Activity.RESULT_OK) {
    val bmOptions = BitmapFactory.Options()
    BitmapFactory.decodeFile(
          photoFile?.getAbsolutePath(), bmOptions)?.run {
      imgView.setImageBitmap(this)
    }
  }
}
```

where `imgView` points to an `ImageView` element inside the UI layout.

Caution   Other than suggested by the API documentation, the returned Intent does not reliably contain a thumbnail image in its `data` field – some devices do that and some do not.

Since we use the `photoFile` field to transport the image file's name, we must take care of it surviving activity restarts. To make sure it gets persisted, write

```kotlin
override
fun onSaveInstanceState(outState: Bundle?) {
  super.onSaveInstanceState(outState)
  photoFile?.run{
    outState?.putString("imgFile", absolutePath)
  }
}
```

and inside `onCreate(...)` add

```kotlin
savedInstanceState?.run {
  photoFile = getString("imgFile")?.let {File(it)}
}
```

Only in case you used the publicly available space to store the picture, you can advertise the image to the system's media scanner. Do so by writing

```
val mediaScanIntent =
        Intent(Intent.ACTION_MEDIA_SCANNER_SCAN_FILE)
val contentUri = Uri.fromFile(photoFile)
mediaScanIntent.setData(contentUri)
sendBroadcast(mediaScanIntent)
```

Recording a Video

To record a video using the system's app does not substantially differ from taking a picture as described in the preceding section. The rest of this section assumes you worked through that section before.

First of all we need a different entry inside file res/xml/file_paths.xml. Since we now address the videos section, write

```
<?xml version="1.0" encoding="utf-8"?>
<paths xmlns:android=
            "http://schemas.android.com/apk/res/android">
  <external-path name="my_videos"
    path="Android/data/de.pspaeth.camera/files/Movies" />
</paths>
```

for saving videos into the app's private data space or

```
<?xml version="1.0" encoding="utf-8"?>
<paths xmlns:android=
            "http://schemas.android.com/apk/res/android">
    <external-path name="my_videos"
                    path="Movies" />
</paths>
```

to instead use the public data space available to all apps.

Then, in order to signal the Android OS to start recording a video and save the data to a file of our choice, write

```
var videoFile:File? = null
val REQUEST_VIDEO_CAPTURE = 43
```

```kotlin
fun dispatchRecordVideoIntent() {
  fun createVideoFile(): File {
    val timeStamp =
          SimpleDateFormat("yyyyMMdd_HHmmss_SSS",
          Locale.US).format(Date())
    val imageFileName = "MP4_" + timeStamp + "_"
    val storageDir =
          Environment.getExternalStoragePublicDirectory(
          Environment.DIRECTORY_MOVIES)
    // To instead tke the App's private space:
    // val storageDir = getExternalFilesDir(
    // Environment.DIRECTORY_MOVIES)
    val image = File.createTempFile(
          imageFileName,
          ".mp4",
          storageDir)
    return image
  }

  val takeVideoIntent =
        Intent(MediaStore.ACTION_VIDEO_CAPTURE)
  if (takeVideoIntent.resolveActivity(packageManager)
        != null) {
    videoFile = createVideoFile()
    val videoURI = FileProvider.getUriForFile(this,
          "com.example.autho.fileprovider",
          videoFile!!)
    Log.e("LOG","Video output URI: ${videoURI}")
    takeVideoIntent.putExtra(MediaStore.EXTRA_OUTPUT,
          videoURI)
    startActivityForResult(
          takeVideoIntent, REQUEST_VIDEO_CAPTURE)
  }
}
dispatchRecordVideoIntent()
```

To eventually fetch the video data after the recording completes, add to
`onActivityResult(...)`

```
if((requestCode == REQUEST_VIDEO_CAPTURE and 0xFFFF) &&
      resultCode == Activity.RESULT_OK) {
   videoView.setVideoPath(videoFile!!.absolutePath)
   videoView.start()
}
```

where `videoView` points to a `VideoView` inside your layout file.

Also here, since we need to make sure the `videoFile` member survives an activity restart, add it to `onSaveInstanceState(...)` and `onCreate()` as shown before for the `photoFile` field.

Writing Your Own Camera App

Using Intents to signal the Android OS to take a picture for us or record a video might be fine for many use cases. But as soon as we need to have more control over the camera or the GUI, you need to write your own camera access code using the camera API. In this section I will show you an app that can both show you a preview and let you take a still image.

We start with three utility classes. The first class is an extension of a `TextureView`. We use a `TextureView` since it allows for a more rapid connection between the camera hardware and the screen, and we extend it so it gets adapted better to the fixed ratio output of the camera. The listing reads

```
/**
 * A custom TextureView which is able to automatically
 * crop its size according to an aspect ratio set
 */
class AutoFitTextureView : TextureView {
  constructor(context: Context) : super(context)
  constructor(context: Context, attrs: AttributeSet?) :
```

```kotlin
        super(context, attrs)
constructor(context: Context, attrs: AttributeSet?,
        attributeSetId: Int) :
        super(context, attrs, attributeSetId)

var mRatioWidth = 0
var mRatioHeight = 0

/**
 * Sets the aspect ratio for this view. The size of
 * the view will be measured based on the ratio
 * calculated from the parameters. Note that the
 * actual sizes of parameters don't matter, that
 * is, calling setAspectRatio(2, 3) and
 * setAspectRatio(4, 6) make the same result.
 *
 * @param width  Relative horizontal size
 * @param height Relative vertical size
 */
fun setAspectRatio(width:Int, height:Int) {
    if (width < 0 || height < 0) {
        throw IllegalArgumentException(
                "Size cannot be negative.");
    }
    mRatioWidth = width;
    mRatioHeight = height;
    requestLayout()
}

override
fun onMeasure(widthMeasureSpec:Int,
        heightMeasureSpec:Int) {
    super.onMeasure(
            widthMeasureSpec, heightMeasureSpec)
    val width = MeasureSpec.getSize(widthMeasureSpec)
    val height = MeasureSpec.getSize(heightMeasureSpec)
    if (0 == mRatioWidth || 0 == mRatioHeight) {
```

```
            setMeasuredDimension(width, height)
        } else {
            val ratio = 1.0 * mRatioWidth / mRatioHeight
            if (width < height * ratio) {
                setMeasuredDimension(
                        width, (width / ratio).toInt())
            } else {
                setMeasuredDimension(
                        (height * ratio).toInt(), height)
            }
        }
    }
  }
}
```

The next utility class queries the system for a backface camera and once found stores its characteristics. It reads

```
/**
 * Find a backface camera
 */
class BackfaceCamera(context:Context) {
  var cameraId: String? = null
  var characteristics: CameraCharacteristics? = null

  init {
      val manager = context.getSystemService(
            Context.CAMERA_SERVICE) as CameraManager
      try {
          manager.cameraIdList.find {
              manager.getCameraCharacteristics(it).
              get(CameraCharacteristics.LENS_FACING) ==
                  CameraCharacteristics.LENS_FACING_BACK
          }.run {
              cameraId = this
              characteristics = manager.
                      getCameraCharacteristics(this)
          }
```

```
        } catch (e: CameraAccessException) {
            Log.e("LOG", "Cannot access camera", e)
        }
    }
}
```

The third utility class performs a couple of calculations, which help us appropriately map camera output dimensions to the texture view size. It reads

```
/**
 * Calculates and holds preview dimensions
 */
class PreviewDimension {

  companion object {
      val LOG_KEY = "PreviewDimension"

      // Max preview width guaranteed by Camera2 API
      val MAX_PREVIEW_WIDTH = 1920

      // Max preview height guaranteed by Camera2 API
      val MAX_PREVIEW_HEIGHT = 1080

      val ORIENTATIONS = SparseIntArray().apply {
          append(Surface.ROTATION_0, 90);
          append(Surface.ROTATION_90, 0);
          append(Surface.ROTATION_180, 270);
          append(Surface.ROTATION_270, 180);
      }
```

As a companion function, we need a method that, given sizes supported by a camera, chooses the smallest one that is at least as large as the respective texture view size and that is at most as large as the respective max size and whose aspect ratio matches with the specified value. If such a size doesn't exist, it chooses the largest one that is at most as large as the respective max size and whose aspect ratio matches with the specified value:

```
      /**
       * Calculate the optimal size.
       *
```

```
 * @param choices          The list of sizes
 *      that the camera supports for the intended
 *      output class
 * @param textureViewWidth  The width of the
 *      texture view relative to sensor coordinate
 * @param textureViewHeight The height of the
 *      texture view relative to sensor coordinate
 * @param maxWidth          The maximum width
 *      that can be chosen
 * @param maxHeight         The maximum height
 *      that can be chosen
 * @param aspectRatio       The aspect ratio
 * @return The optimal size, or an arbitrary one
 *      if none were big enough
 */
fun chooseOptimalSize(choices: Array<Size>?,
    textureViewWidth: Int,
    textureViewHeight: Int,
    maxWidth: Int, maxHeight: Int,
    aspectRatio: Size): Size {

  // Collect the supported resolutions that are
  // at least as big as the preview Surface
  val bigEnough = ArrayList<Size>()
  // Collect the supported resolutions that are
  // smaller than the preview Surface
  val notBigEnough = ArrayList<Size>()
  val w = aspectRatio.width
  val h = aspectRatio.height
  choices?.forEach { option ->
    if (option.width <= maxWidth &&
        option.height <= maxHeight &&
        option.height ==
            option.width * h / w) {
      if (option.width >= textureViewWidth
        && option.height >=
```

```
                    textureViewHeight) {
                bigEnough.add(option)
            } else {
                notBigEnough.add(option)
            }
        }
    }

    // Pick the smallest of those big enough. If
    // there is no one big enough, pick the
    // largest of those not big enough.
    if (bigEnough.size > 0) {
        return Collections.min(bigEnough,
            CompareSizesByArea())
    } else if (notBigEnough.size > 0) {
        return Collections.max(notBigEnough,
            CompareSizesByArea())
    } else {
        Log.e(LOG_KEY,
            "Couldn't find any suitable size")
        return Size(textureViewWidth,
            textureViewHeight)
    }
}

/**
  * Compares two sizes based on their areas.
  */
class CompareSizesByArea : Comparator<Size> {
    override
    fun compare(lhs: Size, rhs: Size): Int {
        // We cast here to ensure the
        // multiplications won't overflow
        return Long.signum(lhs.width.toLong() *
            lhs.height -
            rhs.width.toLong() * rhs.height)
```

```
            }
        }
    }

    internal var rotatedPreviewWidth: Int = 0
    internal var rotatedPreviewHeight: Int = 0
    internal var maxPreviewWidth: Int = 0
    internal var maxPreviewHeight: Int = 0
    internal var sensorOrientation: Int = 0
    internal var previewSize: Size? = null
```

We need a method that calculates the preview dimension, including the sensor orientation. Method calcPreviewDimension() does exactly that:

```
fun calcPreviewDimension(width: Int, height: Int,
        activity: Activity, bc: BackfaceCamera) {
    // Find out if we need to swap dimension to get
    // the preview size relative to sensor coordinate.
    val displayRotation =
        activity.windowManager.defaultDisplay.rotation

    sensorOrientation = bc.characteristics!!.
        get(CameraCharacteristics.SENSOR_ORIENTATION)
    var swappedDimensions = false
    when (displayRotation) {
        Surface.ROTATION_0, Surface.ROTATION_180 ->
            if (sensorOrientation == 90 ||
                sensorOrientation == 270) {
            swappedDimensions = true
        }
        Surface.ROTATION_90, Surface.ROTATION_270 ->
            if (sensorOrientation == 0 ||
                sensorOrientation == 180) {
            swappedDimensions = true
        }
        else -> Log.e("LOG",
            "Display rotation is invalid: " +
```

```
            displayRotation)
    }

    val displaySize = Point()
    activity.windowManager.defaultDisplay.
        getSize(displaySize)
    rotatedPreviewWidth = width
    rotatedPreviewHeight = height
    maxPreviewWidth = displaySize.x
    maxPreviewHeight = displaySize.y

    if (swappedDimensions) {
        rotatedPreviewWidth = height
        rotatedPreviewHeight = width
        maxPreviewWidth = displaySize.y
        maxPreviewHeight = displaySize.x
    }

    if (maxPreviewWidth > MAX_PREVIEW_WIDTH) {
        maxPreviewWidth = MAX_PREVIEW_WIDTH
    }

    if (maxPreviewHeight > MAX_PREVIEW_HEIGHT) {
        maxPreviewHeight = MAX_PREVIEW_HEIGHT
    }
}

/**
 * Retrieves the JPEG orientation from the specified
 * screen rotation.
 *
 * @param rotation The screen rotation.
 * @return The JPEG orientation
 *         (one of 0, 90, 270, and 360)
 */
fun getOrientation(rotation: Int): Int {
    // Sensor orientation is 90 for most devices, or
    // 270 for some devices (eg. Nexus 5X). We have
```

```
    // to take that into account and rotate JPEG
    // properly. For devices with orientation of 90,
    // we simply return our mapping from ORIENTATIONS.
    // For devices with orientation of 270, we need
    // to rotate the JPEG 180 degrees.
    return (ORIENTATIONS.get(rotation) +
            sensorOrientation + 270) % 360
}
```

In order to allow for a correct preview image presentation, we use the method getTransformationMatrix():

```
fun getTransformationMatrix(activity: Activity,
      viewWidth: Int, viewHeight: Int): Matrix {
    val matrix = Matrix()
    val rotation = activity.windowManager.
            defaultDisplay.rotation
    val viewRect = RectF(0f, 0f,
            viewWidth.toFloat(), viewHeight.toFloat())
    val bufferRect = RectF(0f, 0f,
            previewSize!!.height.toFloat(),
            previewSize!!.width.toFloat())
    val centerX = viewRect.centerX()
    val centerY = viewRect.centerY()
    if (Surface.ROTATION_90 == rotation
            || Surface.ROTATION_270 == rotation) {
        bufferRect.offset(
                centerX - bufferRect.centerX(),
                centerY - bufferRect.centerY())
        matrix.setRectToRect(viewRect, bufferRect,
                Matrix.ScaleToFit.FILL)
        val scale = Math.max(
          viewHeight.toFloat() / previewSize!!.height,
          viewWidth.toFloat() / previewSize!!.width)
        matrix.postScale(
                scale, scale, centerX, centerY)
```

```
            matrix.postRotate(
                (90 * (rotation - 2)).toFloat(),
                centerX, centerY)
        } else if (Surface.ROTATION_180 == rotation) {
            matrix.postRotate(180f, centerX, centerY)
        }
        return matrix
    }
}
```

As in the preceding sections, we need to make sure we can acquire the necessary permissions. For this aim, add inside `AndroidManifest.xml`

```
<uses-permission android:name=
        "android.permission.CAMERA"/>
```

Next, we write an activity, which checks and possibly acquires the permissions necessary, opens a `Camera` object whose class we will define in the following, adds a still image capture button and a captured still image consumer callback, and takes care of a transformation matrix to have the `TextureView` object show the correctly sized preview picture. It, for example, will look like

```
class MainActivity : ActivityCompat() {
  companion object {
      val LOG_KEY = "main"
      val PERM_REQUEST_CAMERA = 642
  }

  lateinit var previewDim:PreviewDimension
  lateinit var camera:Camera

  override
  fun onCreate(savedInstanceState: Bundle?) {
      super.onCreate(savedInstanceState)
      setContentView(R.layout.activity_main)

      val permission1 =
            ContextCompat.checkSelfPermission(
            this, Manifest.permission.CAMERA)
```

541

```
    if (permission1 !=
            PackageManager.PERMISSION_GRANTED) {
        ActivityCompat.requestPermissions(this,
                arrayOf(Manifest.permission.CAMERA),
                PERM_REQUEST_CAMERA)
    }else{
        start()
    }
}

override fun onDestroy() {
    super.onDestroy()
    camera.close()
}

fun go(v: View) {
    camera.takePicture()
}
```

Method start() is used to correctly handle the camera object and set up the preview canvas. Note that, when the screen is turned off and turned back on, the SurfaceTexture is already available and "onSurfaceTextureAvailable" will not be called. In that case, we can open a camera and start preview from here. Otherwise, we wait until the surface is ready in the SurfaceTextureListener:

```
private fun start() {
  previewDim = PreviewDimension()
  camera = Camera(
        this, previewDim, cameraTexture).apply {
     addPreviewSizeListener { w,h ->
        Log.e(LOG_KEY,
            "Preview size by PreviewSizeListener:
            ${w} ${h}")
        cameraTexture.setAspectRatio(w,h)
     }
     addStillImageConsumer(::dataArrived)
  }
```

```kotlin
    // Correctly handle the screen turned off and
    // turned back on.
    if (cameraTexture.isAvailable()) {
        camera.openCamera(cameraTexture.width,
            cameraTexture.height)
        configureTransform(cameraTexture.width,
            cameraTexture.height)
    } else {
        cameraTexture.surfaceTextureListener = object :
            TextureView.SurfaceTextureListener {
            override
            fun onSurfaceTextureSizeChanged(
                surface: SurfaceTexture?,
                width: Int, height: Int) {
                configureTransform(width, height)
            }
            override
            fun onSurfaceTextureUpdated(
                surface: SurfaceTexture?) {
            }
            override
            fun onSurfaceTextureDestroyed(
                surface: SurfaceTexture?): Boolean {
                return true
            }
            override
            fun onSurfaceTextureAvailable(
                surface: SurfaceTexture?,
                width: Int, height: Int) {
                camera.openCamera(width, height)
                configureTransform(width, height)
            }
        }
    }
}
```

```
private fun dataArrived(it: ByteArray) {
    Log.e(LOG_KEY, "Data arrived: " + it.size)
    // do more with the picture...
}

private fun configureTransform(
        viewWidth: Int, viewHeight: Int) {
    val matrix =
            previewDim.getTransformationMatrix(
            this, viewWidth, viewHeight)
    cameraTexture.setTransform(matrix)
}
```

The onRequestPermissionsResult() callback is used to start the preview after the permission check returns from the corresponding system call:

```
override
fun onRequestPermissionsResult(requestCode: Int,
        permissions: Array<out String>,
        grantResults: IntArray) {
    super.onRequestPermissionsResult(requestCode,
            permissions, grantResults)
    when (requestCode) {
        PERM_REQUEST_CAMERA -> {
            if(grantResults[0] ==
                    PackageManager.PERMISSION_GRANTED) {
                start()
            }
        }
    }
}
```

A corresponding layout file with a "Take picture" button and the custom TextureView UI element reads

```xml
<?xml version="1.0" encoding="utf-8"?>
<LinearLayout
  xmlns:android=
        "http://schemas.android.com/apk/res/android"
  xmlns:app="http://schemas.android.com/apk/res-auto"
  xmlns:tools="http://schemas.android.com/tools"
  android:layout_width="match_parent"
  android:layout_height="match_parent"
  tools:context=".MainActivity"
  android:orientation="vertical">

  <Button
      android:layout_width="match_parent"
      android:layout_height="wrap_content"
      android:text="Go"
      android:onClick="go"/>
  <de.pspaeth.camera2.AutoFitTextureView
      android:id="@+id/cameraTexture"
      android:layout_width="400dp"
      android:layout_height="200dp"
      android:layout_marginTop="8dp"
      />
</LinearLayout>
```

where instead of "de.pspaeth.camera2.AutoFitTextureView" you have to use your own class's fully qualified path.

The Camera class will make sure we put important activities into the background, prepare a space where the still image capture data can be placed, and build a camera session object. It also takes care of a couple of sizing issues:

```
/**
 * A camera with a preview sent to a TextureView
 */
class Camera(val activity: Activity,
      val previewDim:PreviewDimension,
      val textureView:TextureView) {
  companion object {
```

```kotlin
        val LOG_KEY = "camera"
        val STILL_IMAGE_FORMAT = ImageFormat.JPEG
        val STILL_IMAGE_MIN_WIDTH = 480
        val STILL_IMAGE_MIN_HEIGHT = 480
    }

    private val previewSizeListeners =
            mutableListOf<(Int,Int) -> Unit>()
    fun addPreviewSizeListener(
            l: (Int,Int) -> Unit ) {
        previewSizeListeners.add(l)
    }

    private val stillImageConsumers =
            mutableListOf<(ByteArray) -> Unit>()
    fun addStillImageConsumer(
            l: (ByteArray) -> Unit) {
        stillImageConsumers.add(l)
    }

    /**
     * An additional thread and handler for running
     * tasks that shouldn't block the UI.
     */
    private var mBackgroundThread: HandlerThread? = null
    private var mBackgroundHandler: Handler? = null

    private var cameraDevice: CameraDevice? = null
    private val backfaceCamera =
            BackfaceCamera(activity)
            // Holds the backface camera's ID

    /**
     * A [Semaphore] to prevent the app from exiting
     * before closing the camera.
     */
```

```
private val cameraOpenCloseLock = Semaphore(1)

private var imageReader:ImageReader? = null

private var paused = false

private var flashSupported = false

private var activeArraySize: Rect? = null

private var cameraSession:CameraSession? = null

private var stillImageBytes:ByteArray? = null
```

The openCamera() method checks for permissions, connects to the camera data output, and initiates the connection to the camera:

```
fun openCamera(width: Int, height: Int) {
    startBackgroundThread()

    val permission1 =
        ContextCompat.checkSelfPermission(
        activity, Manifest.permission.CAMERA)
    if (permission1 !=
        PackageManager.PERMISSION_GRANTED) {
      Log.e(LOG_KEY,
            "Internal error: "+
            "Camera permission missing")
    }

    setUpCameraOutputs(width, height)
    val manager = activity.getSystemService(
        Context.CAMERA_SERVICE)
        as CameraManager
    try {
        if (!cameraOpenCloseLock.tryAcquire(
            2500, TimeUnit.MILLISECONDS)) {
          throw RuntimeException(
                "Time out waiting.")
        }
```

```kotlin
val mStateCallback = object :
    CameraDevice.StateCallback() {
  override
  fun onOpened(cameraDev: CameraDevice) {
    // This method is called when the
    // camera is opened.  We start camera
    // preview here.
    cameraOpenCloseLock.release()
    cameraDevice = cameraDev
    createCameraSession()
  }

  override
  fun onDisconnected(
      cameraDev: CameraDevice) {
    cameraOpenCloseLock.release()
    cameraDevice?.close()
    cameraDevice = null
  }

  override
  fun onError(cameraDev: CameraDevice,
      error: Int) {
    Log.e(LOG_KEY,
        "Camera on error callback: "
        + error);
    cameraOpenCloseLock.release()
    cameraDevice?.close()
    cameraDevice = null
  }
}

manager.openCamera(
    backfaceCamera.cameraId,
    mStateCallback,
    mBackgroundHandler)
```

```
    } catch (e: CameraAccessException) {
        Log.e(LOG_KEY,"Could not access camera", e)
    } catch (e: InterruptedException) {
        Log.e(LOG_KEY,
                "Interrupted while camera opening.", e)
    }
}

/**
 * Initiate a still image capture.
 */
fun takePicture() {
    cameraSession?.takePicture()
}

fun close() {
    stopBackgroundThread()
    cameraSession?.run {
        close()
    }
    imageReader?.run {
        surface.release()
        close()
        imageReader = null
    }
}
```

The following are a couple of private methods to handle the background threads and the camera session:

```
////////////////////////////////////////////////////
////////////////////////////////////////////////////

/**
 * Starts a background thread and its [Handler].
 */
private fun startBackgroundThread() {
    mBackgroundThread =
```

```
                HandlerThread("CameraBackground")
        mBackgroundThread?.start()
        mBackgroundHandler = Handler(
                mBackgroundThread!!.getLooper())
    }

    /**
     * Stops the background thread and its [Handler].
     */
    private fun stopBackgroundThread() {
        mBackgroundThread?.run {
            quitSafely()
            try {
                join()
                mBackgroundThread = null
                mBackgroundHandler = null
            } catch (e: InterruptedException) {
            }
        }
    }

    private fun createCameraSession() {
        cameraSession = CameraSession(mBackgroundHandler!!,
                cameraOpenCloseLock,
                backfaceCamera.characteristics,
                textureView,
                imageReader!!,
                cameraDevice!!,
                previewDim,
                activity.windowManager.defaultDisplay.
                        rotation,
                activeArraySize!!,
                1.0).apply {
            createCameraSession()
            addStillImageTakenConsumer {
                //Log.e(LOG_KEY, "!!! PICTURE TAKEN!!!")
```

```
        for (cons in stillImageConsumers) {
            mBackgroundHandler?.post(
                Runnable {
                  stillImageBytes?.run{
                    cons(this)
                  }
                })
        }
      }
    }
}
```

The setUpCameraOutputs() method performs the hard work of connecting to the camera data output:

```
/**
 * Sets up member variables related to camera:
 * activeArraySize, imageReader, previewDim,
 * flashSupported
 *
 * @param width  The width of available size for
 *       camera preview
 * @param height The height of available size for
 *       camera preview
 */
private fun setUpCameraOutputs(
      width: Int, height: Int) {
    activeArraySize = backfaceCamera.
        characteristics?.
        get(CameraCharacteristics.
        SENSOR_INFO_ACTIVE_ARRAY_SIZE)

    val map =
        backfaceCamera.characteristics!!.get(
            CameraCharacteristics.
            SCALER_STREAM_CONFIGURATION_MAP)
```

```
    val stillSize = calcStillImageSize(map)
    imageReader =
        ImageReader.newInstance(
            stillSize.width,
            stillSize.height,
        STILL_IMAGE_FORMAT, 3).apply {
      setOnImageAvailableListener(
         ImageReader.OnImageAvailableListener {
         reader ->
             if (paused)
               return@OnImageAvailableListener
             val img = reader.acquireNextImage()
             val buffer = img.planes[0].buffer
             stillImageBytes =
               ByteArray(buffer.remaining())
             buffer.get(stillImageBytes)
             img.close()
         }, mBackgroundHandler)
    }

    previewDim.calcPreviewDimension(width, height,
        activity, backfaceCamera)

    val texOutputSizes =
        map?.getOutputSizes(
        SurfaceTexture::class.java)
    val optimalSize =
        PreviewDimension.chooseOptimalSize(
          texOutputSizes,
          previewDim.rotatedPreviewWidth,
          previewDim.rotatedPreviewHeight,
          previewDim.maxPreviewWidth,
          previewDim.maxPreviewHeight,
          stillSize)
    previewDim.previewSize = optimalSize

    // We fit the aspect ratio of TextureView
```

```
    // to the size of preview we picked.
    val orientation =
        activity.resources.configuration.
        orientation
    if (orientation ==
        Configuration.ORIENTATION_LANDSCAPE) {
      previewSizeListeners.forEach{
          it(optimalSize.width,
            optimalSize.height) }
    } else {
      previewSizeListeners.forEach{
          it(optimalSize.height,
            optimalSize.width) }
    }

    // Check if the flash is supported.
    val available =
        backfaceCamera.characteristics?.
        get(CameraCharacteristics.
            FLASH_INFO_AVAILABLE)
    flashSupported = available ?: false
}
```

One last private method calculates the still image size. This plays a role once the
trigger gets pressed or a trigger press gets simulated:

```
private fun calcStillImageSize(
    map: StreamConfigurationMap): Size {
  // For still image captures, we use the smallest
  // one at least some width x height
  val jpegSizes =
      map.getOutputSizes(ImageFormat.JPEG)
  var stillSize: Size? = null
  for (s in jpegSizes) {
      if (s.height >= STILL_IMAGE_MIN_HEIGHT
          && s.width >= STILL_IMAGE_MIN_WIDTH) {
        if (stillSize == null) {
```

```
                stillSize = s
            } else {
                val f =
                        (s.width * s.height).toFloat()
                val still =
                        (stillSize.width *
                         stillSize.height).toFloat()
                if (f < still) {
                    stillSize = s
                }
            }
        }
    }
    return stillSize ?: Size(100,100)
}
}
```

The last and maybe most complex class we need is `CameraSession`. It is a state machine that handles the various camera states including auto-focus and auto-exposure and serves two data drains: the preview texture and the captured still image storage. Before I explain a couple of constructs used here, I present the listing:

```
/**
 * A camera session class.
 */
class CameraSession(val handler: Handler,
        val cameraOpenCloseLock:Semaphore,
        val cameraCharacteristics:CameraCharacteristics?,
        val textureView: TextureView,
        val imageReader: ImageReader,
        val cameraDevice: CameraDevice,
        val previewDim: PreviewDimension,
        val rotation:Int,
        val activeArraySize: Rect,
        val zoom: Double = 1.0) {
    companion object {
```

```
    val LOG_KEY = "Session"

    enum class State {
        STATE_PREVIEW,
            // Showing camera preview.
        STATE_WAITING_LOCK,
            // Waiting for the focus to be locked.
        STATE_WAITING_PRECAPTURE,
            // Waiting for the exposure to be
            // precapture state.
        STATE_WAITING_NON_PRECAPTURE,
            // Waiting for the exposure state to
            // be something other than precapture
        STATE_PICTURE_TAKEN
            // Picture was taken.
    }
}

var mState:State = State.STATE_PREVIEW
```

The inner class MyCaptureCallback is responsible for handling both cases, the preview and the still image capture. For the preview however, state transitions are limited to *on* and *off*:

```
inner class MyCaptureCallback :
    CameraCaptureSession.CaptureCallback() {
    private fun process(result: CaptureResult) {
      if(captSess == null)
          return
      when (mState) {
        State.STATE_PREVIEW -> {
            // We have nothing to do when the
            // camera preview is working normally.
        }
        State.STATE_WAITING_LOCK -> {
            val afState = result.get(
                CaptureResult.CONTROL_AF_STATE)
```

```
            if (CaptureResult.
                CONTROL_AF_STATE_FOCUSED_LOCKED
                == afState
               || CaptureResult.
                CONTROL_AF_STATE_NOT_FOCUSED_LOCKED
                == afState
                || CaptureResult.
                CONTROL_AF_STATE_PASSIVE_FOCUSED
                == afState) {
                if(cameraHasAutoExposure) {
                    mState =
                        State.STATE_WAITING_PRECAPTURE
                    runPrecaptureSequence()
                } else {
                    mState =
                        State.STATE_PICTURE_TAKEN
                    captureStillPicture()
                }
            }
        }
        State.STATE_WAITING_PRECAPTURE -> {
            val aeState = result.get(
                CaptureResult.CONTROL_AE_STATE)
            if (aeState == null ||
                aeState == CaptureResult.
                CONTROL_AE_STATE_PRECAPTURE
                ||
                aeState == CaptureRequest.
                CONTROL_AE_STATE_FLASH_REQUIRED) {
                mState =
                    State.STATE_WAITING_NON_PRECAPTURE
            }
        }
        State.STATE_WAITING_NON_PRECAPTURE -> {
            val aeState = result.get(
```

```
                    CaptureResult.CONTROL_AE_STATE)
            if (aeState == null ||
                aeState != CaptureResult.
                    CONTROL_AE_STATE_PRECAPTURE) {
                mState = State.STATE_PICTURE_TAKEN
                captureStillPicture()
            }
        }
        else -> {}
      }
    }

    override
    fun onCaptureProgressed(
        session: CameraCaptureSession,
        request: CaptureRequest,
        partialResult: CaptureResult) {
      //...
    }

    override
    fun onCaptureCompleted(
        session: CameraCaptureSession,
        request: CaptureRequest,
        result: TotalCaptureResult) {
      process(result)
    }
}

var captSess: CameraCaptureSession? = null
var cameraHasAutoFocus = false
var cameraHasAutoExposure = false
val captureCallback = MyCaptureCallback()

private val stillImageTakenConsumers =
      mutableListOf<() -> Unit>()
fun addStillImageTakenConsumer(l: () -> Unit) {
```

```
        stillImageTakenConsumers.add(l)
    }
```

An auto-focus action is limited to camera devices supporting it. This is checked at the beginning of createCameraSession(). Likewise, an auto-exposure action is limited to appropriate devices:

```
/**
 * Creates a new [CameraCaptureSession] for camera
 * preview and taking pictures.
 */
fun createCameraSession() {
    //Log.e(LOG_KEY,"Starting preview session")

    cameraHasAutoFocus = cameraCharacteristics?.
            get(CameraCharacteristics.
            CONTROL_AF_AVAILABLE_MODES)?.let {
        it.any{ it ==
            CameraMetadata.CONTROL_AF_MODE_AUTO }
    } ?: false

    cameraHasAutoExposure = cameraCharacteristics?.
            get(CameraCharacteristics.
            CONTROL_AE_AVAILABLE_MODES)?.let {
        it.any{ it == CameraMetadata.
                CONTROL_AE_MODE_ON ||
            it == CameraMetadata.
                CONTROL_AE_MODE_ON_ALWAYS_FLASH ||
            it == CameraMetadata.
                CONTROL_AE_MODE_ON_AUTO_FLASH ||
            it == CameraMetadata.
                CONTROL_AE_MODE_ON_AUTO_FLASH_REDEYE }
    } ?: false

    try {
        val texture = textureView.getSurfaceTexture()
        // We configure the size of default buffer
        // to be the size of camera preview we want.
```

```
texture.setDefaultBufferSize(
        previewDim.previewSize!!.width,
        previewDim!!.previewSize!!.height)
// This is the output Surface we need to start
// preview.
val previewSurface = Surface(texture)
val takePictureSurface = imageReader.surface
```

There are two camera output consumers – the texture for the preview and an image reader for the still image capture. Both are constructor parameters, and both are used for creating the session object – see cameraDevice.createCaptureSession(...):

```
// Here, we create a CameraCaptureSession for
// both camera preview and taking a picture
cameraDevice.
createCaptureSession(Arrays.asList(
        previewSurface, takePictureSurface),
    object : CameraCaptureSession.
            StateCallback() {
        override
        fun onConfigured(cameraCaptureSession:
            CameraCaptureSession) {
            // When the session is ready, we
            // start displaying the preview.
            captSess = cameraCaptureSession
            try {
                val captReq =
                  buildPreviewCaptureRequest()
                captSess?.
                  setRepeatingRequest(captReq,
                        captureCallback,
                        handler)
            } catch (e: Exception) {
                Log.e(LOG_KEY,
                "Cannot access camera "+
                "in onConfigured()", e)
```

```
                        }
                    }
                    override fun onConfigureFailed(
                            cameraCaptureSession:
                            CameraCaptureSession) {
                        Log.e(LOG_KEY,
                            "Camera Configuration Failed")
                    }
                    override fun onActive(
                            sess: CameraCaptureSession) {
                    }
                    override fun onCaptureQueueEmpty(
                            sess: CameraCaptureSession) {
                    }
                    override fun onClosed(
                            sess: CameraCaptureSession) {
                    }
                    override fun onReady(
                            sess: CameraCaptureSession) {
                    }
                    override fun onSurfacePrepared(
                            sess: CameraCaptureSession,
                            surface: Surface) {
                    }
                }, handler
            )
        } catch (e: Exception) {
            Log.e(LOG_KEY, "Camera access failed", e)
        }
    }

    /**
     * Initiate a still image capture.
     */
    fun takePicture() {
        lockFocusOrTakePicture()
```

```
}

fun close() {
    try {
        cameraOpenCloseLock.acquire()
        captSess?.run {
            stopRepeating()
            abortCaptures()
            close()
            captSess = null
        }
        cameraDevice.run {
            close()
        }
    } catch (e: InterruptedException) {
        Log.e(LOG_KEY,
            "Interrupted while trying to lock " +
            "camera closing.", e)
    } catch (e: CameraAccessException) {
        Log.e(LOG_KEY, "Camera access exception " +
            "while closing.", e)
    } finally {
        cameraOpenCloseLock.release()
    }
}
```

The following are the private methods. The various build*CaptureRequest() methods show how to prepare requests that then get sent to the camera hardware:

```
/////////////////////////////////////////////////////
/////////////////////////////////////////////////////

private fun buildPreviewCaptureRequest():
    CaptureRequest {
    val texture = textureView.getSurfaceTexture()
    val surface = Surface(texture)

    // We set up a CaptureRequest.Builder with the
```

```
        // preview output Surface.
        val reqBuilder = cameraDevice.
            createCaptureRequest(
            CameraDevice.TEMPLATE_PREVIEW)
        reqBuilder.addTarget(surface)

        // Zooming
        val cropRect = calcCropRect()
        reqBuilder.set(
            CaptureRequest.SCALER_CROP_REGION,
            cropRect)

        // Flash off
        reqBuilder.set(CaptureRequest.FLASH_MODE,
            CameraMetadata.FLASH_MODE_OFF)

        // Continuous autofocus
        reqBuilder.set(CaptureRequest.CONTROL_AF_MODE,
            CaptureRequest.
            CONTROL_AF_MODE_CONTINUOUS_PICTURE)
        return reqBuilder.build()
    }

    private fun buildTakePictureCaptureRequest() :
        CaptureRequest {
        // This is the CaptureRequest.Builder that we use
        // to take a picture.
        val captureBuilder =
            cameraDevice.createCaptureRequest(
            CameraDevice.TEMPLATE_STILL_CAPTURE)
        captureBuilder.addTarget(imageReader.getSurface())

        // Autofocus mode
        captureBuilder.set(CaptureRequest.CONTROL_AF_MODE,
            CaptureRequest.
            CONTROL_AF_MODE_CONTINUOUS_PICTURE)

        // Flash auto
```

```
    captureBuilder.set(CaptureRequest.CONTROL_AE_MODE,
            CaptureRequest.
            CONTROL_AE_MODE_ON_AUTO_FLASH)
    // captureBuilder.set(CaptureRequest.FLASH_MODE,
    // CameraMetadata.FLASH_MODE_OFF)

    // Zoom
    val cropRect = calcCropRect()
    captureBuilder.set(CaptureRequest.
        SCALER_CROP_REGION, cropRect)

    // Orientation
    captureBuilder.set(CaptureRequest.
        JPEG_ORIENTATION,
        previewDim.getOrientation(rotation))
    return captureBuilder.build()
}

private fun buildPreCaptureRequest() :
    CaptureRequest {
    val surface = imageReader.surface
    val reqBuilder =
        cameraDevice.createCaptureRequest(
        CameraDevice.TEMPLATE_STILL_CAPTURE)
    reqBuilder.addTarget(surface)
    reqBuilder.set(CaptureRequest.
        CONTROL_AE_PRECAPTURE_TRIGGER,
        CaptureRequest.
        CONTROL_AE_PRECAPTURE_TRIGGER_START)
    return reqBuilder.build()
}

private fun buildLockFocusRequest() :
    CaptureRequest {
    val surface = imageReader.surface
    val reqBuilder =
        cameraDevice.createCaptureRequest(
```

```
                CameraDevice.TEMPLATE_STILL_CAPTURE)
        reqBuilder.addTarget(surface)
        reqBuilder.set(CaptureRequest.
            CONTROL_AF_TRIGGER,
            CameraMetadata.CONTROL_AF_TRIGGER_START)
        return reqBuilder.build()
    }

    private fun buildCancelTriggerRequest() :
        CaptureRequest {
        val texture = textureView.getSurfaceTexture()
        val surface = Surface(texture)
        val reqBuilder =
            cameraDevice.createCaptureRequest(
            CameraDevice.TEMPLATE_PREVIEW)
        reqBuilder.addTarget(surface)
        reqBuilder.set(CaptureRequest.CONTROL_AF_TRIGGER,
            CameraMetadata.CONTROL_AF_TRIGGER_CANCEL)
        return reqBuilder.build()
    }
```

Capturing a still picture gets handled by method captureStillPicture(). Note that, as for many of the other camera-related functionalities, appropriate tasks get sent to the background and callbacks handle the background processing results:

```
    private fun captureStillPicture() {
        val captureRequest =
            buildTakePictureCaptureRequest()
        if (captSess != null) {
            try {
                val captureCallback = object :
                    CameraCaptureSession.CaptureCallback() {
                    override fun onCaptureCompleted(
                        session: CameraCaptureSession,
                        request: CaptureRequest,
                        result: TotalCaptureResult) {
                        //Util.showToast(activity,
```

```
                  //"Acquired still image")
                  stillImageTakenConsumers.forEach {
                        it() }
                  unlockFocusAndBackToPreview()
             }
        }
      captSess?.run {
           stopRepeating()
           capture(captureRequest,
                 captureCallback, null)
      }
    } catch (e: Exception) {
        Log.e(LOG_KEY,
              "Cannot capture picture", e)
    }
  }
}

private fun lockFocusOrTakePicture() {
    if(cameraHasAutoFocus) {
        captSess?.run {
          try {
            val captureRequest =
                  buildLockFocusRequest()
          mState = State.STATE_WAITING_LOCK
              capture(captureRequest,
                    captureCallback,
                    handler)
          } catch (e: Exception) {
              Log.e(LOG_KEY,
                  "Cannot lock focus", e)
          }
        }
    } else {
        if(cameraHasAutoExposure) {
            mState = State.STATE_WAITING_PRECAPTURE
```

```
                runPrecaptureSequence()
            } else {
                mState = State.STATE_PICTURE_TAKEN
                captureStillPicture()
            }
        }
    }

    /**
     * Unlock the focus. This method should be called when
     * still image capture sequence is finished.
     */
    private fun unlockFocusAndBackToPreview() {
        captSess?.run {
            try {
                mState = State.STATE_PREVIEW
                val cancelAfTriggerRequest =
                        buildCancelTriggerRequest()
                val previewRequest =
                        buildPreviewCaptureRequest()
                capture(cancelAfTriggerRequest,
                        captureCallback,
                        handler)
                setRepeatingRequest(previewRequest,
                        captureCallback,
                        handler)
            } catch (e: Exception) {
                Log.e(LOG_KEY,
                "Cannot go back to preview mode", e)
            }
        }
    }
```

Running the precapture sequence for capturing a still image gets performed by method runPrecaptureSequence(). This method should be called when we get a response in the captureCallback from method lockFocusThenTakePicture():

```
/**
 * Run the precapture sequence for capturing a still
 * image.
 */
private fun runPrecaptureSequence() {
    try {
      captSess?.run {
         val captureRequest = buildPreCaptureRequest()
         mState = State.STATE_WAITING_PRECAPTURE
         capture(captureRequest, captureCallback,
                 handler)
      }
    } catch (e: Exception) {
        Log.e(LOG_KEY, "Cannot access camera", e)
    }
}

private fun calcCropRect(): Rect {
    with(activeArraySize) {
        val cropW = width() / zoom
        val cropH = height() / zoom
        val top = centerY() - (cropH / 2f).toInt()
        val left = centerX() - (cropW / 2f).toInt()
        val right = centerX() + (cropW / 2f).toInt()
        val bottom = centerY() + (cropH / 2f).toInt()
        return Rect(left, top, right, bottom)
    }
}
}
```

Here are a couple of notes on the CameraSession class:

- The emulators don't exhibit auto-focus capabilities. The code takes care of that.

- The term "precapture" is just another name for *auto-exposure*.

- Using the flash is a `todo` in this class. To enable flashing see the places where the flash gets mentioned inside the code.

- By virtue of a listener chain starting in `CameraSession,` the still image capture data eventually arrives in the `dataArrived(...)` method of `MainActivity`. It is there where you can start writing further processing algorithms like saving, sending, converting, reading, and so on.

Android and NFC

NFC adapters, provided the Android device has one, allow for short-range wireless communication with other NFC-capable devices or NFC tags. We talked about NFC in section "Android and NFC" of Chapter 13.

Android and Bluetooth

Most if not all modern Android devices have Bluetooth built in. Via Bluetooth they can wirelessly communicate with other Bluetooth devices. For details please see section "Android and Bluetooth" of Chapter 13.

Android Sensors

Android devices provide various bits of information about their environment to apps:

- Orientation as determined by a compass or gyroscope

- Motion as given by acceleration forces

- Gravitational forces

- Air temperature and pressure, humidity

- Illumination

- Proximity to, for example, find out the distance to the user's ear

The exact geospatial position of a device is not detected by a sensor. For the detection of positional coordinates using GPS, instead see section "Location and Maps" of Chapter 8.

Retrieving Sensor Capabilities

Beginning with Android 4.0 or API level 14, Android devices are supposed to provide all sensor types as defined by the various `android.hardware.Sensor.TYPE_*` constants. To see a list of all sensors including various information about them, use the following code snippet:

```
val sensorManager = getSystemService(
        Context.SENSOR_SERVICE) as SensorManager
val deviceSensors =
        sensorManager.getSensorList(Sensor.TYPE_ALL)
deviceSensors.forEach { sensor ->
  Log.e("LOG", "+++" + sensor.toString())
}
```

To fetch a certain sensor instead, use for example

```
val magneticFieldSensor = sensorManager.getDefaultSensor(
        Sensor.TYPE_MAGNETIC_FIELD)
```

Once you have a `Sensor` object, you can obtain various information about it. Please see the API documentation of `android.hardware.Sensor` for details. To find out sensor values, see the following section.

Listening to Sensor Events

Android allows for the following two sensor event listeners:

- Changes in a sensor's accuracy

- Changes in a sensor's value

To register for a listener, fetch the sensor manager and the sensor as described in the preceding section and then use inside the activity something like

```
val sensorManager = getSystemService(
```

```
        Context.SENSOR_SERVICE) as SensorManager
    val magneticFieldSensor = sensorManager.getDefaultSensor(
        Sensor.TYPE_MAGNETIC_FIELD)
sensorManager.registerListener(this,
        magneticFieldSensor,
        SensorManager.SENSOR_DELAY_NORMAL)
```

For the temporal resolution, you can also use one of the other delay specifications
`SensorManager.SENSOR_DELAY_*`.

The activity must then overwrite `android.hardware.SensorEventListener` and
implement it:

```
class MainActivity : ActivityCompat(),
        SensorEventListener {
    private lateinit var sensorManager:SensorManager
    private lateinit var magneticFieldSensor:Sensor

    override fun onCreate(savedInstanceState: Bundle?) {
        ...
        sensorManager =
                getSystemService(Context.SENSOR_SERVICE)
                as SensorManager
        magneticFieldSensor =
                sensorManager.getDefaultSensor(
                Sensor.TYPE_MAGNETIC_FIELD)
    }

    override
    fun onAccuracyChanged(sensor: Sensor, accuracy: Int) {
        // Do something here if sensor accuracy changes.
    }

    override
    fun onSensorChanged(event: SensorEvent) {
        Log.e("LOG", Arrays.toString(event.values))
        // Do something with this sensor value.
```

```
    }

    override
    fun onResume() {
        super.onResume()
        sensorManager.registerListener(this,
                magneticFieldSensor,
                SensorManager.SENSOR_DELAY_NORMAL)
    }

    override
    fun onPause() {
        super.onPause()
        sensorManager.unregisterListener(this)
    }
}
```

As seen in this example, it is important to unregister sensor event listeners when no longer needed, since sensors may substantially drain battery power.

Note   Other than what the name suggests, onSensorChanged events might be fired even when there is not really a sensor value change,

---

All possible sensor values you get from SensorEvent.values inside onSensorChanged() are listed in Table 14-3.

Table 14-3. *Sensor Event Values*

Type	Values
TYPE_ ACCELEROMETER	Vector3: Acceleration along the x-y-z axes in m/s^2. Includes gravity.
TYPE_AMBIENT_ TEMPERATURE	Scalar: The ambient air temperature in $°C$.
TYPE_GRAVITY	Vector3: Gravitational force along the x-y-z axes in m/s^2.
TYPE_GYROSCOPE	Vector3: Rate of rotation around each of the x-y-z axes, in rad/s.
TYPE_LIGHT	Scalar: Illuminance in lx.
TYPE_LINEAR_ ACCELERATION	Vector3: Acceleration along the x-y-z axes in m/s^2. Without gravity.
TYPE_MAGNETIC_ FIELD	Vector3: Strength of the geomagnetic field in μT.
TYPE_ORIENTATION	Vector3: Azimuth, Pitch, Roll in degrees.
TYPE_PRESSURE	Scalar: Ambient air pressure in hPa.
TYPE_PROXIMITY	Scalar: Distance from object in cm.
TYPE_RELATIVE_ HUMIDITY	Scalar: Ambient relative humidity in %.
TYPE_ROTATION_ VECTOR	Vector4: Rotation vector as a quaternion.
TYPE_SIGNIFICAT_ MOTION	The event gets fired each time a significant motion is detected. To catch this event, you must register via `SensorManager. requestTriggerSensor(...)`.
TYPE_STEP_COUNTER	Scalar: Accumulated step count since reboot and while the sensor is activated.
TYPE_STEP_ DETECTOR	The event gets fired each time a step is detected.
TYPE_TEMPERATURE	Deprecated. Scalar: The device's temperature in $°C$.

Some sensors have an uncalibrated version, which means they show changes more accurately, but less accurately relate to a fixed point:

- TYPE_ACCELEROMETER_UNCALIBRATED

- TYPE_GYROSCOPE_UNCALIBRATED

- TYPE_MAGNETIC_FIELD_UNCALIBRATED.

Instead of the TYPE_ROTATION_VECTOR sensor, you can also use one of the following:

- TYPE_GAME_ROTATION_VECTOR

- TYPE_GEOMAGNETIC_ROTATION_VECTOR

The first one does not use a gyroscope and is more accurate for detecting changes, but not so accurate to find out where *north* is. The second one uses the magnetic field instead of a gyroscope – it is less accurate but also needs less battery power.

Interacting with Phone Calls

Android allows for a couple of ways to interact with incoming or outgoing phone calls and the dialing process. The most prominent use cases your app might implement for telephony are as follows:

- Monitor state changes of the telephone, like being informed of incoming and outgoing calls.

- Initiate a dialing process to start outgoing calls.

- Provide your own UI for managing a call.

You can find telephony-relevant classes and interfaces inside the packages `android.telecom` and `android.telephony` and sub-packages.

Monitoring Phone State Changes

To monitor phone state changes, add the following permissions to `AndroidManifest.xml`:

```
<uses-permission android:name=
```

```
        "android.permission.READ_PHONE_STATE" />
    <uses-permission android:name=
        "android.permission.PROCESS_OUTGOING_CALLS"/>
```

The READ_PHONE_STATE permission allows to detect the status of ongoing calls. The PROCESS_OUTGOING_CALLS permission lets your app see the number of outgoing calls or even use a different number or cancel calls.

For how to acquire permissions from inside your app, please see Chapter 7.

For listening to phone-related events, you then add a broadcast receiver inside AndroidManifest.xml

```
    <application>
      ...
      <receiver android:name=".CallMonitor">
        <intent-filter>
          <action android:name=
                "android.intent.action.PHONE_STATE" />
        </intent-filter>
        <intent-filter>
          <action android:name=
                "android.intent.action.NEW_OUTGOING_CALL" />
        </intent-filter>
      </receiver>
    </application>
```

and implement it, for example, as follows:

```
package ...

import android.telephony.TelephonyManager as TM
import ...

class CallMonitor : BroadcastReceiver() {
    companion object {
        private var lastState = TM.CALL_STATE_IDLE
        private var callStartTime: Date? = null
        private var isIncoming: Boolean = false
        private var savedNumber: String? = null
    }
```

The onReceive() callback handles incoming broadcasts, this time an incoming or outgoing call:

```
override
fun onReceive(context: Context, intent: Intent) {
    if (intent.action ==
            Intent.ACTION_NEW_OUTGOING_CALL) {
        savedNumber = intent.extras!!.
            getString(Intent.EXTRA_PHONE_NUMBER)
    } else {
        val stateStr = intent.extras!!.
            getString(TM.EXTRA_STATE)
        val number = intent.extras!!.
            getString(TM.EXTRA_INCOMING_NUMBER)
        val state = when(stateStr) {
            TM.EXTRA_STATE_IDLE ->
                TM.CALL_STATE_IDLE
            TM.EXTRA_STATE_OFFHOOK ->
                TM.CALL_STATE_OFFHOOK
            TM.EXTRA_STATE_RINGING ->
                TM.CALL_STATE_RINGING
            else -> 0
        }
        callStateChanged(context, state, number)
    }
}

protected fun onIncomingCallReceived(
        ctx: Context, number: String?, start: Date){
    Log.e("LOG",
            "IncomingCallReceived ${number} ${start}")
}

protected fun onIncomingCallAnswered(
        ctx: Context, number: String?, start: Date) {
    Log.e("LOG",
```

```
                "IncomingCallAnswered ${number} ${start}")
    }

    protected fun onIncomingCallEnded(
            ctx: Context, number: String?,
            start: Date?, end: Date) {
        Log.e("LOG",
                "IncomingCallEnded ${number} ${start}")
    }

    protected fun onOutgoingCallStarted(
            ctx: Context, number: String?, start: Date) {
        Log.e("LOG",
                "OutgoingCallStarted ${number} ${start}")
    }

    protected fun onOutgoingCallEnded(
            ctx: Context, number: String?,
            start: Date?, end: Date) {
        Log.e("LOG",
                "OutgoingCallEnded ${number} ${start}")
    }

    protected fun onMissedCall(
            ctx: Context, number: String?, start: Date?) {
        Log.e("LOG",
                "MissedCall ${number} ${start}")
    }
```

The private method callStateChanged() reacts on the various state changes corresponding to phone calls:

```
/**
 * Incoming call:
 *     IDLE -> RINGING when it rings,
 *     -> OFFHOOK when it's answered,
 *     -> IDLE when its hung up
 * Outgoing call:
```

```
*       IDLE -> OFFHOOK when it dials out,
*       -> IDLE when hung up
*/
private fun callStateChanged(
    context: Context, state: Int, number: String?) {
    if (lastState == state) {
        return // no change in state
    }
    when (state) {
        TM.CALL_STATE_RINGING -> {
            isIncoming = true
            callStartTime = Date()
            savedNumber = number
            onIncomingCallReceived(
                context, number, callStartTime!!)
        }
        TM.CALL_STATE_OFFHOOK ->
            if (lastState != TM.CALL_STATE_RINGING) {
                isIncoming = false
                callStartTime = Date()
                onOutgoingCallStarted(context,
                    savedNumber, callStartTime!!)
            } else {
                isIncoming = true
                callStartTime = Date()
                onIncomingCallAnswered(context,
                    savedNumber, callStartTime!!)
            }
        TM.CALL_STATE_IDLE ->
            if (lastState == TM.CALL_STATE_RINGING) {
                //Ring but no pickup-  a miss
                onMissedCall(context,
                    savedNumber, callStartTime)
            } else if (isIncoming) {
                onIncomingCallEnded(context,
```

```
                       savedNumber, callStartTime,
                       Date())
            } else {
               onOutgoingCallEnded(context,
                       savedNumber, callStartTime,
                       Date())
            }
      }
      lastState = state
   }
 }
```

Using such a listener, you can, for example, gather statistical information about phone usage, create a priority phone number list, or do other interesting things. To connect phone calls with contact information, see section "Contacts" of Chapter 8.

Initiate a Dialing Process

To initiate a dialing process from inside your app, you basically have two options:

- Start a dialing process, and the user sees and can change the called number.

- Start a dialing process, and the user cannot change the called number.

For the first case, showing the user the number and letting them change the number, you don't need any special permission. Just write

```
val num = "+34111222333"
val intent = Intent(Intent.ACTION_DIAL,
      Uri.fromParts("tel", num, null))
startActivity(intent)
```

To start a dialing process with a prescribed number, you need as an additional permission

```
<uses-permission android:name=
      "android.permission.CALL_PHONE" />
```

To acquire it, see Chapter 7. The calling process then can be initiated via

```
val num = "+34111222333"
val intent = Intent(Intent.ACTION_CALL,
      Uri.fromParts("tel", num, null))
startActivity(intent)
```

Create a Phone Call Custom UI

The creation of your own phone call activity including your own UI gets described on the online page "Build a calling app" inside the Android documentation. Please see it for details.

Fingerprint Authentication

Fingerprint authentication in Android is part of the biometric authentication framework. An older API for fingerprint authentication, the Android Fingerprint API, entered Android with Android version 6.0 or API level 23. Before that, you had to use vendor-specific APIs if they existed.

For Android 11 (API level 30) or higher, use the information given at `https://developer.android.com/training/sign-in/biometric-auth` for biometric authentication. For lower API levels down to 23, use the same classes, especially `BiometricPrompt`, since the API has an integrated backward compatibility support.

To use it, in the dependencies section of your `build.gradle` file, add

```
implementation "androidx.biometric:biometric:1.1.0"
```

CHAPTER 15

Testing

A lot is said about testing in information technology. There are three reasons for the attention testing has gained during the last decades:

- Testing is the interface between the developers and the users.

- Testing can be engineered to some extent.

- Testing helps gain money.

The developers tend to grow their own biased view on their software. By no means any kind of offense is intended by saying that. It is just natural that if you spend a lot of time with some subject, you potentially lose the ability to anticipate what is going on in a new user's mind. It is therefore a strong advise to regularly step out of your developer role and ask yourself the question: "Suppose I didn't know anything about the app – if I enter this GUI workflow, does it make sense, is it easy to follow, and is it hard to make unrecoverable mistakes?" Testing helps with that – it forces the developer to enter this end user role and ask themselves exactly that question.

Development is far away from being an industrially engineered science. This is good news and bad news at the same time. If it had strong engineering paths, it would be easier to follow agreed-on development patterns, and other developers would much more readily understand what you are doing. On the other hand, not being that precisely engineerable also opens the realm to more creativity and allows for development to become an art. Good developers know that they are constantly swaying between those limits. Testing nowadays tends to prioritize engineerability. This stems from the fact that you can precisely say what a software is supposed to do, totally ignorant of a single line of code. So parts of the tests just don't care how things were accomplished on the coding level, taking away the plethora of possibilities how development demands were satisfied. This is of course not true for low-level unit tests, but even for those you can see a strong overlap of software artifact contracts and testing methodologies. So for testing the grade of engineerability is somewhat higher compared with mere developing.

© Peter Späth 2022
P. Späth, *Pro Android with Kotlin*, https://doi.org/10.1007/978-1-4842-8745-3_15

However, because testing is just one aspect of the development process as a whole, it is still possible to have an interesting job as a developer and live in both worlds: you can be an artist during developing code and an engineer while writing tests.

On the other side of the development chain, depending on your intention, you might want to have end users spending some money for your app. Testing obviously helps avoid frustration because of bugs you didn't anticipate, allowing for the public to more readily acknowledge your app.

A lot is said about testing for Android, and you can find good information and introductory- or advanced-level videos in the official Android documentation. The rest of this chapter should be seen as an advice and a collection of empirical know-how on the matter of testing. I also do not intend to give an introduction into testing, covering each and every aspect of it, but I hope I can give you a starting point for your own deeper research.

Unit Tests

Unit tests aim at the class level and test low-level functional aspects of your app. By "functional" I mean unit tests usually check deterministic relations between input and output of a method call, maybe but not necessarily including state variables of class instances in a deterministic, straightforward manner.

Standard Unit Tests

In an Android environment, standard unit tests run without dependency on the device hardware nor any Android framework classes and are thus executed on the development machine.

This is typically useful for libraries and not so much GUI-related functionalities. That is why the applicability of this kind of unit tests is somewhat limited for most Android apps.

However, if your app's classes contain method calls and you can anticipate the call result given various sets of inputs, using standard unit tests makes sense. It is easy to add unit tests to your app. In fact, if you start a new project using Android Studio, all is set up for you, and you even get a sample test class. See Figure 15-1.

```
▼ ▐▛ app
    ▶ ▤ manifests
    ▼ ▤ java
        ▼ ▐▙ com.example.myapp
            ▼ ⓒ MainActivity
                ⓜ onCreate(savedInstanceState: Bundle?)
        ▶ ▐▙ com.example.myapp (androidTest)
        ▼ ▐▙ com.example.myapp (test)
            ▶ ⓒ ExampleUnitTest
    ▶ ▐▛ res
▼ ⓒ Gradle Scripts
        ⓒ build.gradle (Project: unittests2)
        ⓒ build.gradle (Module: app)
        ▦ gradle-wrapper.properties (Gradle Version)
        ▦ proguard-rules.pro (ProGuard Rules for app)
        ▦ gradle.properties (Project Properties)
        ⓒ settings.gradle (Project Settings)
        ▦ local.properties (SDK Location)
```

Figure 15-1. *Initial Unit Test Setup*

So you immediately can start writing unit tests using that test class as an example – just add more test classes to the *test* section of the source code.

Note   While not technically necessary, a common convention is to use the same names for the test classes as the classes under test, with a "Test" appended. So the test class for com.example.myapp.TheClass should be called com. example.myapp.TheClassTest.

To run the unit tests inside Android Studio, right-click the *test* section and select "Run Tests in ..." or "Debug Tests in ...".

Unit Tests with a Stubbed Android Framework

By default, the Gradle plugin used for executing unit tests contains a stubbed version of the Android framework, throwing an exception whenever an Android class gets called.

You can change this behavior by adding to the app's build.gradle file:

```
android {
  ...
  testOptions {
```

```
        unitTests.returnDefaultValues = true
    }
}
```

Any call of an Android class's method then does nothing and returns `null` on demand.

Unit Tests with a Simulated Android Framework

If you need to access Android classes from inside your unit tests and expect them to do real things, using the community-supported *Robolectric* framework as a unit test implementation is a valid option. With Robolectric you can simulate button clicks, reading and writing text, and lots of other GUI-related activities. Still all that runs on your development machine, which considerably speeds up testing.

To allow your project to use Robolectric, add to your app's `build.gradle` file:

```
android {
  testOptions {
      unitTests {
          includeAndroidResources = true
      }
  }
}

dependencies {
  ...
  //testImplementation 'junit:junit:4.12'
  testImplementation "org.robolectric:robolectric:4.8.1"
}
```

As an example, a test class that simulates a click on a `Button` and then checks whether the click action has updated a `TextView` reads

```
package com.example.robolectric

import org.junit.runner.RunWith
import org.robolectric.RobolectricTestRunner
import org.robolectric.shadows.ShadowApplication
```

```
import android.content.Intent
import android.widget.Button
import android.widget.TextView
import org.junit.Test
import org.robolectric.Robolectric
import org.junit.Assert.*

@RunWith(RobolectricTestRunner::class)
class MainActivityTest {
  @Test
  fun clickingGo_shouldWriteToTextView() {
      val activity = Robolectric.setupActivity(
          MainActivity::class.java!!)
      activity.findViewById<Button>(R.id.go).
          performClick()
      assertEquals("Clicked",
          activity.findViewById<TextView>(
          R.id.tv).text)
  }
}
```

You start that test like any normal unit test by right-clicking the *test* section and selecting "Run Tests in ..." or "Debug Tests in ...".

For more test options and details, please see the home page of Robolectric at www. robolectric.org.

Unit Tests with Mocking

Mocking means you let the test hook into the call of the Android OS functions and simulate their execution by mimicking their functioning.

If you want to include mocking into unit tests, the Android developer documentation suggests using the *Mockito* test library. I suggest going one step further and using *PowerMock* instead, which sits on top of Mockito but adds more power to it like mocking of static or final classes.

To enable PowerMock, add to your app's build.gradle file:

```
android {
```

```
    ...
    testOptions {
        unitTests.returnDefaultValues = true
    }
}

dependencies {
    ...
    def powermock_version = "2.0.2"

    testImplementation ("org.powermock:
        powermock-module-junit4:${powermock_version}")
    }
    testImplementation ("org.powermock:
        powermock-api-mockito2:${powermock_version}")
    testImplementation 'junit:junit:4.13.2'
}
```

(Remove the line breaks after "powermock:".)

The unitTests.returnDefaultValues = true entry takes care of the stubbed Android implementation for unit tests not to throw exceptions, just in case.

As a nontrivial example, I present an activity that writes an entry to a database. We are going to mock out the actual database implementation, but still want to make sure necessary tables get created and the insert statement gets executed. Create a Jetpack Compose activity using the corresponding wizard from Android Studio.

Now, add the following methods to the activity:

```
fun count() {
    val db = openOrCreateDatabase("MyDb",
        MODE_PRIVATE, null)
    with(db) {
        val resultSet = rawQuery(
            "Select * from MyItems", null)
        val cnt = resultSet.count
        Toast.makeText(this@MainActivity,
            "Count: ${cnt}", Toast.LENGTH_LONG).
            show()
```

```
        }
        db.close()
    }

    fun saveInDb(item:String) {
        val tm = System.currentTimeMillis() / 1000
        val db = openOrCreateDatabase("MyDb",
            MODE_PRIVATE, null)
        with(db) {
            execSQL("CREATE TABLE IF NOT EXISTS " +
                    "MyItems(Item VARCHAR,timestamp INT);")
            execSQL("INSERT INTO MyItems VALUES(?,?);",
                arrayOf(item, tm))
        }
        db.close()
    }
```

For the test itself, create a class MainActivityTest inside the *test* section of the sources. Let it read

```
package book.andrkotlpro.mocktest

import android.database.sqlite.SQLiteDatabase
import androidx.activity.ComponentActivity
import org.junit.Test
import org.junit.runner.RunWith
import org.mockito.ArgumentMatchers
import org.mockito.BDDMockito.*
import org.powermock.api.mockito.PowerMockito
import org.powermock.core.classloader.annotations.
    PrepareForTest
import org.powermock.modules.junit4.PowerMockRunner
import org.powermock.reflect.Whitebox
import java.lang.reflect.Constructor
import java.lang.reflect.Method

@RunWith(PowerMockRunner::class)
```

```kotlin
@PrepareForTest(MainActivity::class)
class MainActivityTest {

    @Test
    fun table_created() {
        val componentActivityConstructors:
                Array<Constructor<*>> =
        PowerMockito.constructors(
            ComponentActivity::class.java.getConstructor()
        )
        PowerMockito.suppress(
            componentActivityConstructors)

        val activity = MainActivity()
        val activitySpy = spy(activity)
        val db = mock(SQLiteDatabase::class.java)

        // given
        given(activitySpy.openOrCreateDatabase(
            anyString(), anyInt(), any())).willReturn(db)

        // when
        Whitebox.invokeMethod<Unit>(
            activitySpy,"saveInDb","hello")

        // then
        verify(db).execSQL(ArgumentMatchers.argThat {arg ->
            arg.toString().matches(
                Regex("(?i)create table.*\\bMyItems\\b.*")
            )
        })

    }

    @Test
    fun item_inserted() {
        val componentActivityConstructors:
                Array<Constructor<*>> =
```

```
PowerMockito.constructors(
    ComponentActivity::class.java.getConstructor()
)
PowerMockito.suppress(
    componentActivityConstructors)

val activity = MainActivity()
val activitySpy = spy(activity)
val db = mock(SQLiteDatabase::class.java)

// given
given(activitySpy.openOrCreateDatabase(
    anyString(), anyInt(), any())).willReturn(db)

// when
Whitebox.invokeMethod<Unit>(
    activitySpy,"saveInDb","hello")

// then
verify(db).execSQL(ArgumentMatchers.argThat {arg ->
    arg.toString().matches(
        Regex("(?i)insert into MyItems\\b.*")
    )
}, ArgumentMatchers.argThat { arg ->
    val arr = arg as Array<Any>
    arr[0] == "hello" &&
            arr[1] is Number
})
    }
}
```

The @RunWith(PowerMockRunner::class) will make sure PowerMock gets used as a unit test runner, and @PrepareForTest(MainActivity::class) prepares the MainActivity class, so it can be mocked even though it is marked "final" (something that Kotlin does by default).

The first function table_created() is supposed to make sure the table gets created if necessary. It acts as follows:

- We first make sure the constructor of `ComponentActivity` is not called. This is necessary, because this class is lifecycle aware and thus observed by the UI framework.

- We instantiate `MainActivity`.

- We wrap the `MainActivity` instance into a *Spy*. This allows us to hook into method calls to mock out the actual implementation.

- We create a mock of `SQLiteDatabase` so we can hook into database operations without actually using a real database.

- The following `//given`, `//when`, and `//then` sections follow the BDD style of development.

- Inside the `//given` section, we mock out the `openOrCreateDatabase()` call of the activity and instead let it return our mock database.

- Inside `//when` we call method `saveInDb()` of the activity class.

- In the `//then` section, we can check whether the call of `saveInDb()` invokes the appropriate database operation to create the necessary table. For this aim we use an `ArgMatcher`, which allows us to check for appropriate method call arguments.

The test function `item_inserted()` does almost the same, but instead checks whether an appropriate *insert* statement gets fired to the database.

You can now run the tests, and they should pass without problems.

Integration Tests

Integration tests sit between unit tests that do fine-grained testing work on the development machine and full-fledged user interface tests running on real or virtual devices. Integration tests run on a device, too, but they do not test the app as a whole but instead selected components in an isolated execution environment.

Integration tests happen inside the "androidTest" section of the source code. You also need to add a couple of packages to the app's `build.gradle` file

```
dependencies {
```

```
...
androidTestImplementation
    'com.android.support:support-annotations:27.1.1'
androidTestImplementation
    'com.android.support.test:runner:1.0.2'
androidTestImplementation
    'com.android.support.test:rules:1.0.2'
}
```

with the line breaks after "androidTestImplementation" removed.

Testing Services

In order to test a service with a binding, write something like

```
@RunWith(AndroidJUnit4::class)
class ServiceTest {

    // A @Rule wraps around the test invocation - here we
    // use the 'ServiceTestRule' which makes sure the
    // service gets started and stopped correctly.
    @Rule @JvmField
    val mServiceRule = ServiceTestRule()

    @Test
    fun testWithBoundService() {
        val serviceIntent = Intent(
            InstrumentationRegistry.getTargetContext(),
            MyService::class.java
        ).apply {
            // If needed, data can be passed to the
            // service via the Intent.
            putExtra("IN_VAL", 42L)
        }

        // Bind the service and grab a reference to the
        // binder.
        val binder: IBinder = mServiceRule.
```

```
            bindService(serviceIntent)

      // Get the reference to the service
      val service: MyService =
            (binder as MyService.MyBinder).getService()

      // Verify that the service is working correctly.
      assertThat(service.add(11,27), `is`(38))
   }
}
```

This tests a simple service called MyService with an add(Int, Int) service method:

```
class MyService : Service() {
  class MyBinder(val servc:MyService) : Binder() {
      fun getService():MyService {
          return servc
      }
  }

  private val binder: IBinder = MyBinder(this)

  override fun onBind(intent: Intent): IBinder = binder

  fun add(a:Int, b:Int) = a + b
}
```

To run the integration test, right-click the androidTest section of the sources and choose "Run Tests in …". This will create and upload an APK file, by virtue of InstrumentationRegistry.getTargetContext() create an integration test context, and then run the test on the device.

Testing Intent Services

Other than the official documentation claims, services based on the IntentService class can be subject to integration tests as well. You just cannot use the @Rule ServiceTestRule for handling the service lifecycle, because intent services have their own idea when to start and stop. But you can handle the lifecycle yourself.

As an example, I present a test for a simple intent service working for 10 seconds and continuously sending back data through a ResultReceiver.

The service itself reads

```
class MyIntentService() :
    IntentService("MyIntentService") {
  class MyResultReceiver(val cb: (Double) -> Unit) :
        ResultReceiver(null) {
    companion object {
        val RESULT_CODE = 42
        val INTENT_KEY = "my.result.receiver"
        val DATA_KEY = "data.key"
    }
    override
    fun onReceiveResult(resultCode: Int,
          resultData: Bundle?) {
        super.onReceiveResult(resultCode, resultData)
        val d = resultData?.get(DATA_KEY) as Double
        cb(d)
    }
  }
  var status = 0.0

  override fun onHandleIntent(intent: Intent) {
      val myReceiver = intent.
            getParcelableExtra<ResultReceiver>(
                  MyResultReceiver.INTENT_KEY)
      for (i in 0..100) {
          Thread.sleep(100)
          val bndl = Bundle().apply {
              putDouble(MyResultReceiver.DATA_KEY,
                  i * 0.01)
          }
          myReceiver.send(MyResultReceiver.RESULT_CODE,
                bndl)
      }
```

```
    }
  }
```

and the test class, again inside the "androidTest" section of the sources

```
  @RunWith(AndroidJUnit4::class)
  class MyIntentServiceTest {

    @Test
    fun testIntentService() {
        var serviceVal = 0.0

        val ctx = InstrumentationRegistry.
            getTargetContext()
        val serviceIntent = Intent(ctx,
            MyIntentService::class.java
        ).apply {
            `package`= ctx.packageName
            putExtra(
                MyIntentService.MyResultReceiver.
                    INTENT_KEY,
                MyIntentService.MyResultReceiver( { d->
                        serviceVal = d
            }))
        }
        ctx.startService(serviceIntent)

        val tm0 = System.currentTimeMillis() / 1000
        var ok = false
        while(System.currentTimeMillis() / 1000 - tm0
            < 20) {
            if(serviceVal == 1.0) {
                ok = true
                break
            }
            Thread.sleep(1000)
        }
```

```
        assertThat(ok, `is`(true))
    }
}
```

This test calls the service, listens to its result for a while, and, when it detects that the service did its work as expected, lets the test pass.

Testing Content Providers

For testing content providers, Android provides for a special class `ProviderTestCase2`, which starts an isolated temporary environment so the testing won't interfere with the user data. A test case, for example, reads

```
@RunWith(AndroidJUnit4::class)
class MyContentProviderTest :
    ProviderTestCase2<MyContentProvider>(
    MyContentProvider::class.java,
    "com.example.database.provider.MyContentProvider") {

    @Before public override    // "public" necessary!
    fun setUp() {
        context = InstrumentationRegistry.
                getTargetContext()
        super.setUp()

        val mockRslv: ContentResolver = mockContentResolver
        mockRslv.delete(MyContentProvider.CONTENT_URI,
                "1=1", arrayOf())
    }

    @Test
    fun test_inserted() {
        val mockCtx: Context = mockContext
        val mockRslv: ContentResolver = mockContentResolver

        // add an entry
        val cv = ContentValues()
        cv.put(MyContentProvider.COLUMN_PRODUCTNAME,
```

```
        "Milk")
    cv.put(MyContentProvider.COLUMN_QUANTITY,
        27)
    val newItem = mockRslv.insert(
        MyContentProvider.CONTENT_URI, cv)

    // query all
    val cursor = mockRslv.query(
        MyContentProvider.CONTENT_URI,
        null, null, null)
    assertThat(cursor.count, `is`(1))

    cursor.moveToFirst()
    val ind = cursor.getColumnIndex(
        MyContentProvider.COLUMN_PRODUCTNAME)
    assertThat(cursor.getString(ind), `is`("Milk"))
  }
 }
```

Column names, the authority, and the URI used are biased by the content provider – important for the test case is that you use the mocked content resolver for talking to the content provider.

Note   Observe the order of the first two lines in setUp() – this is different from what you can read in the Android developer docs by May 2018. The docs are wrong here.

Testing Broadcast Receivers

For testing broadcast receivers, the Android testing framework does not pay particular attention. It is also crucial what the broadcast receiver under test actually does. Provided it performs some kind of side effect, for example, writing something to a database, you can mock out that database operation by using the same testing context we used previously for content providers.

For example, if you look at the following test case from inside the "androidTest" source section

```
import android.support.test.InstrumentationRegistry
import android.support.test.runner.AndroidJUnit4
import org.junit.Test
import org.junit.runner.RunWith
import org.junit.Assert.*
import org.hamcrest.Matchers.*
import android.content.Intent

@RunWith(AndroidJUnit4::class)
class BroadcastTest {
  @Test
  fun testBroadcastReceiver() {
      val context = InstrumentationRegistry.
          getTargetContext()

      val intent = Intent(context,
          MyReceiver::class.java)
      intent.putExtra("data", "Hello World!")
      context.sendBroadcast(intent)

      // Give the receiver some time to do its work
      Thread.sleep(5000)

      // Check the DB for the entry added
      // by the broadcast receiver
      val db = MyDBHandler(context)
      val p = db.findProduct("Milk")
      assertThat(p, isA(Product::class.java))
      assertThat(p!!.productName, `is`("Milk"))
  }
}
```

you can see that we used the context provided by `InstrumentationRegistry.getTargetContext()`. This will make sure the database used by the broadcast receiver and later by the test uses a temporary space for its data.

You start this test like any other integration test by right-clicking it or the package it resides in and then selecting "Run …" or "Run Tests in …".

User Interface Tests

Conducting user interface tests, you can work through user stories and see whether your app as a whole acts as expected. I briefly mention two frameworks:

- **Espresso**

  Use *Espresso* to write tests targeting your app, disregarding any inter-app activities. With Espresso you can do things like as follows: when a certain View (Button, TextView, EditText, etc.) shows up, do something (enter text or perform a click), and then check whether some post-conditions occur.

- **UI Automator**

  Use *UI Automator* to write tests that span several apps. With UI Automator you can inspect layouts to find out the UI structure of activities, simulate actions on activities, and do checks on UI elements.

For details on how to use either of them, please consult the online documentation – for example, enter "Android automating UI tests" in your favorite search engine to find resources.

CHAPTER 16

Troubleshooting

In the previous chapter, we talked about ways to test your app. If tests fail, the logs usually tell you what exactly happens, and if this is not enough, you can extend the logging of your app to see where things go wrong.

But even with the best possible testing concept, it might still happen that your app doesn't exactly behave as it is supposed to. First, it might just sometimes not do the right things from a functional perspective. Second, it might be ill-behaving from a non-functional perspective, which means it eats up memory resources as time goes by or it might perform bad in terms of speed.

In this chapter we talk about techniques to remedy problems that your app might expose. We will talk about logging, debugging, and monitoring and the tools from inside Android Studio or the SDK that help us with respect to them.

Logging

Logging in Android is impressively easy – you just import `android.util.Log`, and inside your code you write statements like `Log.e("LOG", "Message")` to issue logging messages. Android Studio then helps you gather, filter, and analyze the logging.

While for developing using this logging is extremely handy, when it comes to publishing your app, it gets problematic. You don't want to thwart the performance of your app, and the documentation suggests to remove all logging, basically negating all the work you put in the logging. If your users later report problems, you add logging statements for troubleshooting, remove them later again after the fix has been done, and so on.

To rectify this procedure, I suggest instead adding a simple wrapper around the logging from the beginning:

```
class Log {
  companion object {
```

© Peter Späth 2022
P. Späth, *Pro Android with Kotlin*, https://doi.org/10.1007/978-1-4842-8745-3_16

```kotlin
fun v(tag: String, msg: String) {
    android.util.Log.v(tag, msg)
}

fun v(tag: String, msg: String, tr: Throwable) {
    android.util.Log.v(tag, msg, tr)
}

fun d(tag: String, msg: String) {
    android.util.Log.d(tag, msg)
}

fun d(tag: String, msg: String, tr: Throwable) {
    android.util.Log.d(tag, msg, tr)
}

fun i(tag: String, msg: String) {
    android.util.Log.i(tag, msg)
}

fun i(tag: String, msg: String, tr: Throwable) {
    android.util.Log.i(tag, msg, tr)
}

fun w(tag: String, msg: String) {
    android.util.Log.w(tag, msg)
}

fun w(tag: String, msg: String, tr: Throwable) {
    android.util.Log.w(tag, msg, tr)
}

fun w(tag: String, tr: Throwable) {
    android.util.Log.w(tag, tr)
}

fun e(tag: String, msg: String) {
    android.util.Log.e(tag, msg)
}
```

```
    fun e(tag: String, msg: String, tr: Throwable) {
        android.util.Log.e(tag, msg, tr)
    }
  }
}
```

You can then use the same simple logging notation as for the Android standard, but are free later to change the logging implementation without touching the rest of your code. You could, for example, add a simple switch:

```
class Log {
  companion object {
      val ENABLED = true

      fun v(tag: String, msg: String) {
          if(!ENABLED) return
          // <- add this to all the other statements
          android.util.Log.v(tag, msg)
      }
      ...
  }
}
```

Or you could enable logging only for virtual devices. Unfortunately, there is no easy and reliable way to find out if your app is running on a virtual device. All solutions presented in blogs have their pros and cons and are subject to change for new Android versions. What you could do instead is to transport build variables to your app. To do so, add in your app's build.gradle file

```
buildTypes {
    release {
        ...
        buildConfigField "boolean", "LOG", "false"
    }
    debug {
        ...
        buildConfigField "boolean", "LOG", "true"
    }
}
```

All you have to do then in your logging implementation is replace

```
val ENABLED = BuildConfig.LOG
```

which switches on the logging for debugging APKs and otherwise turns it off.

Note   In the previous edition, we also talked about adding logging frameworks like Log4j to your Android projects. Because alternative logging frameworks for Android these days seem not to gain considerable attention and even updates because of major security vulnerabilities seem to be missing, I currently do not suggest using them for Android. Instead, use the built-in logger, or a wrapper around it as described previously.

One final measure you could take to improve performance is to use lambdas for logging activities. For this to work, use logging methods as follows in your custom logger:

```
fun v(tag: String, msg: ()->String) {
    if(!ENABLED) return
    Logger.getLogger(tag).trace(msg.invoke())
}
... similar for the other statements
```

Inside your code you then issue log messages like in

```
Log.v("LOG",
    {-> "Number of items added = " + calculate()})
```

The advantage of this approach is that the logging message will not be calculated if logging is not enabled, adding some performance boost to production versions of your app.

Debugging

There is not much to say about debugging from inside Android Studio – it just works as expected.

You set breakpoints inside your code, and once the program flow reaches a breakpoint, you can step through the rest of the program and observe what the program does and how variables change their values.

Performance Monitoring

Android Studio has a quite powerful performance monitor, which lets you analyze performance matters down to the method level. To use it you must first find a way to run that part of your code that is subject to performance issues inside a loop. You can try to use tests for that, but temporarily adding artificial loops to your code is feasible as well.

Then, with that loop running, inside Android Studio open View ➤ Tool Windows ➤ Profiler. Then add profiling sessions.

The profiler monitor shows up, as seen in Figure 16-1. Apart from CPU profiling, it also contains memory usage profiling.

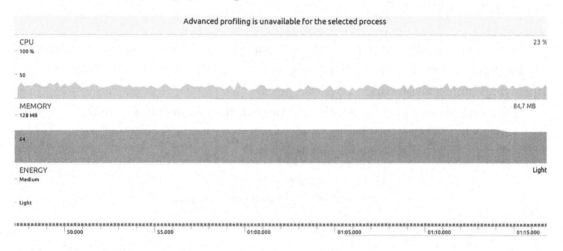

Figure 16-1. *Profiler Lanes*

There, clicking the "CPU" lane narrows the view to the performance monitor diagram you see in Figure 16-2.

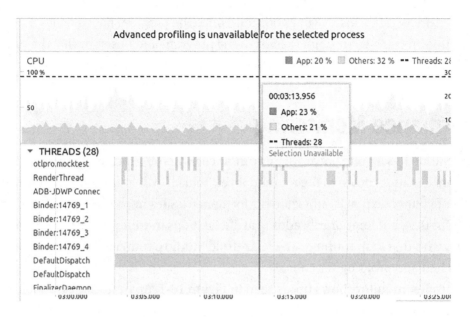

Figure 16-2. *The CPU Profiling Section*

Scrolling through the threads in the lower pane, you can then try to find suspicious threads. For the example I am running here, you can see that the "DefaultDispatch" thread does quite a lot of work.

In the middle pane, you can see the capture control as shown in Figure 16-3.

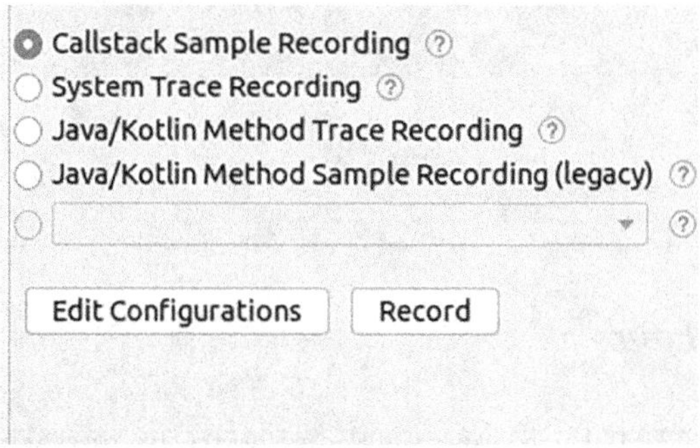

Figure 16-3. *The CPU Profiling Capture Control*

With the capturing mode chosen – "Java/Kotlin Method Trace Recording" usually is a good candidate – you can start a recording by pressing the accordingly named button. After finishing the capturing, the analysis shows you hotspots down to a class method level. From there to find performance bottlenecks usually is easily achievable.

For more information and details about performance monitoring, please see Android Studio's documentation and the onscreen context help.

Memory Usage Monitoring

Apart from profiling the app's performance as shown in the previous section, Android Studio's profiler also allows for finding memory leaks or issues related to poor memory management. Again put the parts of the code subject to problems into a loop and start it. Open the profiler via View ➤ Tool Windows ➤ Profiler. Choose the memory lane, and immediately the profiler shows you a memory usage diagram as shown in Figure 16-4.

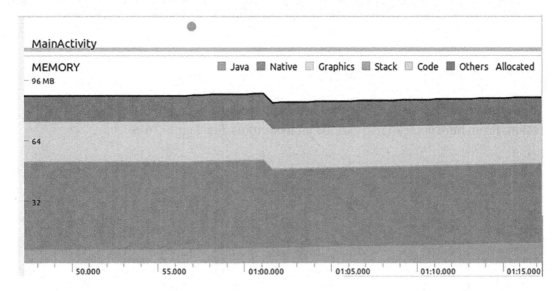

Figure 16-4. *The Memory Monitor*

This running for a while, you can see that the memory usage rises – this is because in the sample app, I added an artificial memory leak. See Figure 16-5.

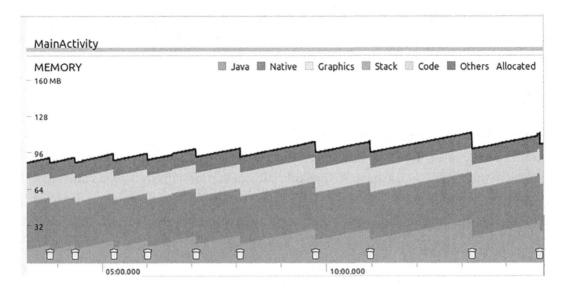

Figure 16-5. *Memory Profiling, Longer Period*

To start an analysis, select "Record Java/Kotlin Allocations" and start a recording session. From here you can use various analysis tools. See Figure 16-6.

Class Name	Allocatio...	Deallocatio...	Total Co...	Shallo... ▾	Shallow S...
app heap	100.984	0	1.369.966	43.214.032	2.726.568
String (java.lang)	50.492	0	985.570	28.588.744	1.211.808
char[]	25.246	0	188.738	7.853.688	1.110.824
Object[] (java.lang)	0	0	1.789	3.425.120	0
Long (java.lang)	12.623	0	97.565	1.561.040	201.968
StringBuilder (java.lang)	12.623	0	87.777	1.404.432	201.968
int[]	0	0	3.120	125.780	0

Figure 16-6. *Memory Profiling, Details*

If you select the "Arrange by Callstack" mode, you can see which method causes a leak. For my example it points to the method

```kotlin
fun go(l:MutableList<String>) {
    Thread {
        while (true) {
            l.add("" + System.currentTimeMillis())
```

```
        Thread.sleep(1)
    }
  }.start()
}
```

where I programmed an artificial memory leak. See Figure 16-7.

Table Visualization					
View app heap ▼ Arrange by callstack ▼ Q⋅		☐ Match Case ☐ Regex ⚠ Selected region does not h			
Callstack Name	Allocations	Deallocatio...	Total Cou...	Shallo... ▼	Shallow S...
🖼 app heap	16.016	0	234.299	7.504.005	432.432
> ≡ <Thread Unknown>	0	0	217.051	7.038.309	0
∨ ≡ <Thread Thread-4>	16.016	0	17.248	465.696	432.432
∨ ⓜ run() (Ljava/lang/Thread;)	16.016	0	17.248	465.696	432.432
∨ ⓜ run() (Lbook/andrkotlpro/mocktest/MainActivity$$ExternalSyntheticLambdi	16.016	0	17.248	465.696	432.432
∨ ⓜ $r8$lambda$7-JVN7jksqP8GIIJHVaxze-GMNU() (Lbook/andrkotlpro/mock	16.016	0	17.248	465.696	432.432
∨ ⚪ go$lambda-0() (Lbook/andrkotlpro/mocktest/MainActivity;)	16.016	0	17.248	465.696	432.432
> ⓜ valueOf() (Ljava/lang/Long;)	2.002	0	2.156	34.496	32.032
> ⓜ stringPlus() (Lkotlin/jvm/internal/Intrinsics;)	14.014	0	15.092	431.200	400.400

Figure 16-7. *Memory Profiling, Pinning Down*

If this is not enough to troubleshoot memory problems, you can in addition acquire a heap dump. To do so, select the "Capture heap dump" recording mode. You can then use the same techniques as described previously or export the heap as an HPROF file and use other tools to analyze the dump.

Note   Such a heap dump allows for determining object reference relationships – something that goes beyond the memory analysis of Android Studio. This gives you the maximum insight into the memory structure, but it takes some time to get acquainted to heap dump analysis tools like Eclipse Memory Analyzer and to find correct answers.

CHAPTER 17

Distributing Apps

If you have finished your app, you need to find a way to distribute it. The primary place to go for that purpose is the *Google Play Store*, but it is also possible to use other distribution channels if you can convince your users to allow for app installations from "other sources." I do not present a list for distribution channels here, nor do I present detailed instructions for using the Google Play Store. There are just too many options depending on which market you are targeting at. Also, this book is not intended to be an introduction into app marketing in general.

For further investigation on that matter, visit
`https://developer.android.com/google/play/dist` or
`https://developer.android.com/distribute/marketing-tools/alternative-distribution` or
`https://support.google.com/googleplay/android-developer/`.

Android App Bundle

With APK as a distribution format having been around for quite some time, Google in 2021 introduced a new packaging format, *Android App Bundle* or AAB. It streamlines distribution to the end user by filtering out unneeded files like localization resources the user would not need.

Android Studio allows for the creation of AAB at Build ➤ Generate Signed Bundle/APK… ➤ Check "Android App Bundle".

Your Own App Store

Once the device allows for installing apps from sources other than the Google Play Store, APK or AAB files can be presented from any server including your own corporate servers. Note that there is a difference for this option depending on the Android version used:

© Peter Späth 2022
P. Späth, *Pro Android with Kotlin*, https://doi.org/10.1007/978-1-4842-8745-3_17

- Up to Android 7 or API level 25, there is a system-wide setting inside the "security" section for allowing the installation from other sources than Google Play.

- Starting with Android 8 or API level 26, the permission to install apps from other sources is handled on a per-app basis, for example, a setting in the browser.

No matter which distribution channel you choose, you must first generate a signed APK or AAB via Build ➤ Generate Signed Bundle/APK... Then, copy it to the server and make sure the file gets assigned the MIME type "application/vnd.android.package-archive" for APK files or one of "application/x-authorware-bin" and "aplication/octet-stream" for AAB files (choose which works best for you).

Note   Although Android Studio automatically uploads debug versions of your app to virtual devices or devices connected per USB, for virtual devices you can also test the signed APK installation procedure. If you have a server running on your local development machine, inside the virtual device, use the IP 10.0.2.2 to connect to the development machine. Better first uninstall versions installed by the development build process.

You can then use the device's browser to download and install APK and AAB files.

The Google Play Store

Despite this not being an introduction into the usage of the Google Play Store, to give you a couple of additional points for the technical aspects of distribution, I list a few random hints here:

- As stated before, you *must* sign you app before it can be distributed to Google Play.

- The online documentation suggests removing all logging statements from inside your app prior to distributing it. As a less destructive alternative, follow the instructions from section "Logging" of Chapter 16 and create a custom logger.

- If your app uses a database, provide for update mechanisms for when the database scheme changes. See class `SQLiteOpenHelper`. If you forget that, updating apps and upgrading the database from version to version can become really cumbersome.

- It is possible to distribute different APKs for different devices. This feature was somewhat neglected inside this book, because nowadays with modern devices, the size an app has no longer plays a vital role and you usually can put all into a single APK file. If you still want to provide multiple APKs, please consult the online documentation – search for "Android multiple APK" or similar inside your favorite search engine.

- If you test your app on a real device, things become a little easier if on your device you use a different Google account compared with the account you use for distributing the app. Google otherwise won't let you install your app using the Play Store. Do this early, because later changing the Google account of a device might be complicated.

- Localize all texts shown to the user! In this book for brevity, localization has not been used, but you definitely should do that for your app. The LINT checker included with Android Studio helps in finding localization deficiencies, and using the custom locale switcher included with the emulators lets you do a check as well.

- Although developing just for a smartphone form factor (screen size, resolution) is somewhat tempting, you should check your design also for other form factors. The various emulators help you with that. You should at least also test your app for a tablet.

The central point for app distribution is the *Google Play Console* at `https://play.google.com/console/`. This is also the place where you would start marketing your app.

CHAPTER 18

Instant Apps

Instant apps allow a device user to use apps without actually installing them. In the Google Play Store, the "Try it" button you sometimes see exactly starts such an instant app.

For more information about instant apps, see `https://developer.android.com/topic/google-play-instant/` or `https://support.google.com/googleplay/android-developer/answer/9900182?hl=en`.

Developing Instant Apps

The development and rollout of instant apps heavily changed during the last couple of years.

A blueprint for developing, building, and rolling out an instant app is as follows:

- Check execution conditions. Allowed are the following permissions: ACCESS_COARSE_LOCATION, ACCESS_FINE_LOCATION, ACCESS_NETWORK_STATE, BILLING (deprecated as of Play Billing Library 1.0), CAMERA, INSTANT_APP_FOREGROUND_SERVICE (Android 8.0 = API level 26 and higher), INTERNET, READ_PHONE_NUMBERS (Android 8.0 = API level 26 and higher), RECORD_AUDIO, VIBRATE, and WAKE_LOCK.

- Declare instant-enabled app modules. Android Studio provides various help facilities here.

- Generate an upload key and keystore (as a tool part of Android Studio).

- Sign your app with your upload key (as a tool part of Android Studio).

- Configure Play App Signing (Google Play Console).

© Peter Späth 2022
P. Späth, *Pro Android with Kotlin*, https://doi.org/10.1007/978-1-4842-8745-3_18

- Upload your app as an AAB to Google Play.

To avoid describing something that is already outdated when you are reading this book, I decided to not further cover this subject in this book. Instead, please visit

```
https://developer.android.com/topic/google-play-instant/getting-started/
instant-enabled-app-bundle
```

which gives you an excellent starting point for developing instant apps.

CHAPTER 19

CLI

In this chapter we briefly summarize the command line tools that you can use for
building, administration, and some maintenance tasks running outside *Android Studio*.

Note

- These tools in part are kind of "semi"-official – you might find them
  at slightly different locations inside the SDK folder, and the online
  documentation is not necessarily up to date.

- The tools shown here are part of the Linux distribution. For other OSs,
  counterparts are provided, and their usage will be similar.

- The list is not exhaustive – it might differ from your installation if you
  have fewer or more SDK packages installed.

The SDK Tools

The following are the platform-independent tools provided inside folder

```
SDK_INST/tools/bin
```

where the SDK installation directory usually resides inside `Android`, which in turn sits
inside your Home folder.

The tools folder includes the management of virtual devices and the SDK itself and
various testing and artifact management tools. Table 19-1 provides a list and describes
these tools.

© Peter Späth 2022
P. Späth, *Pro Android with Kotlin*, https://doi.org/10.1007/978-1-4842-8745-3_19

Table 19-1. *SDK Tools*

Command	Description
apkanalyzer	Use this to analyze APK files you can find, for example, in the PROJECT-DIR/ PROJECT/release folder (PROJECT quite often reads "app"). Invoking the command without argument ./apkanalyzer shows usage information.
archquery	A simple tool to query your OS's architecture: ./archquery outputs, for example, "x86_64"
avdmanager	Use this to manage virtual devices (AVD = Android Virtual Device). You can create, move, and delete devices and list devices, targets, and AVDs. Invoking the command without argument ./avdmanager shows usage information. You can find the data files for virtual devices handled by this command inside ~/.android/avd. The system images used for creating devices are in SDK_INST/system-images.
jobb	Use this to manage OBB (Opaque Binary Blob) files. Those are *APK Expansion Files* that go on an external storage, for example, a SD card, and are accessible only from inside your app. Invoking the command without argument ./jobb shows usage information.
lint	The LINT tool for code inspection. Invoking the command without argument ./lint shows usage information.
monkeyrunner	This is a powerful testing tool for controlling Android apps by use of a Python script on your PC. Invoking ./monkeyrunner shows usage information. Starting it without an argument launches a Jython shell.

(*continued*)

Table 19-1. (*continued*)

Command	Description
screenshot2	Use this to take a screenshot from devices or emulators. Invoking the command without argument `./screenshot2` shows usage information.

sdkmanager	This tool helps you manage packages for the Android SDK. You can install, uninstall, or update SDK packages, and you can use it to list installed and available packages. Invoking
	`./sdkmanager --help`
	shows verbose usage information. For example, to list installed and available packages – this includes build tools, platforms, documentation, sources, system images, and more SDK components – invoke
	`./sdkmanager --list`
	To install new components, the tool needs to download them. A couple of flags exist; see the output of `-help` to find out how to specify proxies or disable the usage of HTTPS.

uiautomatorviewer	Opens the UI Automator GUI. Synopsis: `./uiautomatorviewer` This is broken for current JDKs. Instead, use Record and Playback in the virtual device's extended controls.

In the parent directory

```
SDK_INST/tools
```

you find a couple of more tools. See Table 19-2 for a summary of those.

Table 19-2. *More SDK Tools*

Command	Description
android	DEPRECATED. Invoke it without argument to see a synopsis.
emulator	The emulator management tool. We talked about the emulator in Chapter 1, section "Virtual Devices." Invoke `./emulator -help` to get usage information for this command.
emulator-check	A diagnosis tool for the host system. See the output of `./emulator-check -h` for a synopsis.
mksdcard	Creates a FAT32 image to be used as an emulator image. Invoke it without an argument `./mksdcard` for usage information.
monitor	Starts the graphical device monitor. This is the same device monitor as the one invoked from inside Android Studio at *Tools* ➤ *Android* ➤ *Android Device Monitor*. Note that if you run this command while an instance of Android Studio is running, you might get an error message.
proguard	Inside this directory the Proguard program resides. With Proguard you can shrink APK files by disregarding unneeded files, classes, fields, and methods. Find "Shrink Your Code and Resources" inside the online documentation to learn how Proguard works.

See also `https://developer.android.com/studio/command-line`.

The SDK Build Tools

The following are the build tools provided inside folder

`SDK_INST/build-tools/[VERSION]`

Contained are linkers, compilers, APK file tools, and an AIDL (Android Interface Definition Language) management tool. See Table 19-3.

Table 19-3. *SDK Tools*

Command	Description
aapt	This is the Android asset packaging tool. Invoking the command without argument `./aapt` shows usage information. The tool is able to list the contents of an APK file, and it can extract information from it. Furthermore, it is able to package assets and add and remove elements to and from an APK file. The tool is also responsible for creating the R class, which maps resources to resource IDs usable from inside the code (Android Studio does that automatically for you).
aapt2	This is the successor of the `aapt` tool described previously. Invoking the command without argument `./aapt2` shows some basic usage information. Invoking any of `./aapt2 CMD -h` with CMD one of "compile", "link", "dump", "diff", "optimize", and "version" gives more detailed information. Cross-checking with the help of the `aapt` command gives extra aid.
aarch64-linux-android-ld	A special linker for Android object files, targeting devices with a 64-bit ARM architecture. Invoking the command `./aarch64-linux-android-ld --help` shows verbose usage information. Normally you don't have to invoke that tool directly if you use Android Studio, because it takes care of both compiling and linking for you.
aidl	AIDL is the Android Interface Definition Language handling low-level inter-process communication between *Bound Service* classes of different apps. The `aidl` tool can be used to compile an `*.aidl` interface definition file to the Java language interface files defining the interface. Invoking the command `./aidl` without arguments shows usage information.

(*continued*)

Table 19-3. (*continued*)

Command	Description
apksigner	Manages APK file signing. APK files need to be signed before they can be published. Android Studio helps you with that process – see *Build* ➤ *Generate Signed APK* – but you can also use this tool. Invoke it like `./apksigner -h` for usage information.
arm-linux-androideabi-ld	A special linker for Android object files, targeting devices with 32-bit ARM architecture, and for object files that have been generated by the ABI compiler. Invoking the command `./arm-linux-androideabi-ld --help` shows verbose usage information. Normally you don't have to invoke that tool directly if you use Android Studio, because it takes care of both compiling and linking for you.
bcc_compat	A BCC compiler used for *renderscript* by Android. Invoking the command `./bcc_compat --help` shows usage information.
dexdump	A tool for investigating DEX files, which live inside an APK file and contain the classes. Invoking without arguments `./dexdump` shows usage information.
d8	A tool for managing DEX files. You can, for example, create DEX files or dump their contents. Invoke `./dx --help` to get usage information.
i686-linux-android-ld	A linker for Android object files, targeting devices with an x86 architecture. Invoking the command `./i686-linux-android-ld --help` shows verbose usage information. Normally you don't have to invoke that tool directly if you use Android Studio, because it takes care of both compiling and linking for you.

(*continued*)

Table 19-3. (*continued*)

Command	Description
llvm-rs-cc	The renderscript source compiler (offline mode). Invoke `./llvm-rs-cc --help` to see some usage information.
mipsel-linux-android-ld	A linker for Android object files, targeting devices with an MIPS architecture. Invoking the command `./mipsel-linux-android-ld --help` shows verbose usage information. Normally you don't have to invoke that tool directly if you use Android Studio, because it takes care of both compiling and linking for you.
split-select	Allows for generating the logic for selecting a *Split APK* given a target device configuration. Invoking the command `./split-select --help` shows some usage information.
x86_64-linux-android-ld	A linker for Android object files, targeting devices with an x86 64-bit architecture. Invoking the command `./x86_64-linux-android-ld --help` shows verbose usage information. Normally you don't have to invoke that tool directly if you use Android Studio, because it takes care of both compiling and linking for you.
zipalign	Zip alignment utility. Something developers are not necessarily used to is the fact that an operating system might depend on elements of an archive file aligned a certain way, for example, entries always starting at 32-bit boundaries. This tool can be used to accordingly adapt a zip file. Invoking `./zipalign -h` shows usage information.

See also `https://developer.android.com/studio/command-line`.

The SDK Platform Tools

The following are the platform-dependent tools provided inside folder

`SDK_INST/platform-tools`

See Table 19-4.

Table 19-4. *SDK Platform Tools*

Command	Description
adb	The *Android Debug Bridge*. See under the table for a description of the adb command.
dmtracedump	Creates graphical callstack diagrams from a trace dump. The trace file must have been acquired with the android.os.Debug class. Invoke it without arguments `./dmstracedump` to get information about the command.
e2fsdroid	Mount an image file. CURRENTLY BROKEN.
etc1tool	Use this to convert between the PNG and ETC1 image formats. Invoke `./etc1tool --help` to see usage information.
fastboot	This is the *fastboot* program you can use to modify your device's firmware. Invoke `./fastboot --help` for usage information.
hprof-conv	Use this to convert the HPROF heap file you got from Android OS tools to a standard HPROF format. Invoke it without argument `./hprof-conv` to get usage information.
make_f2fs	Used to make an F2FS file system on some device. Invoke without arguments `./make_f2fs` for usage information.

(continued)

Table 19-3. (*continued*)

Command	Description
mke2fs	Generates a Linux Second Extended file system. Invoke without arguments `./mke2fs` to see options.
sload_f2fs	Used to load files into an F2FS device. Invoke without arguments `./sload_f2fs` to see options.
sqlite3	Starts a SQLITE administration tool. Invoke `./sqlite3 -help` for usage information.

See also `https://developer.android.com/studio/command-line`.

The *Android Debug Bridge* (ADB) invoked by the `adb` command is a versatile tool to connect from your development PC to running emulators and devices connected via USB or Wi-Fi. It consists of a client and transparent server process on the development PC and a daemon running on the device. You can use `adb` to

- Query for accessible devices.

- Install and uninstall apps (APK files).

- Copy files to or from a device.

- Perform backup and restore.

- Connect to the logging output of an app.

- Enable root access on a device.

- Start a shell on a device (to, e.g., see and investigate your app's files).

- Start and stop activities and services.

- Issue broadcasts.

- Start and stop profiling sessions.

- Dump heaps.

- Access the package manager on the device.

- Take screenshots and record videos.

- Restart devices.

For more details find the "Android Debug Bridge" page in the online documentation (`https://developer.android.com/studio/command-line/adb`). Invoke it via

`./adb`

to show the help provided with the command and, for example

`./adb devices`

to list the connected devices and

`./adb -s DEVICE_NAME shell`

to open a shell on a device, with the DEVICE_NAME argument being one of the entries from the first column from the devices list. If there is only one device, in the latter command, you can omit the `-s` flag and the device name.

Note   You must enable debugging on real devices in order for ADB to successfully connect to them.

APPENDIX

Text Companion

To-do: Make available online and add a link to section "Online Text Companion" of the front matter.

Manifest Top-Level Entries

This part of the online text companion describes the `<manifest>` entry as used inside file `AndroidManifest.xml`. See also `https://developer.android.com/guide/topics/manifest/manifest-intro`.

The `<application>` Element

Specifies the application. Because this is the main entry for the application declaration, this gets described in detail in the following section "The Application Declaration."

The `<compatible-screens>` Element

Specifies compatible screens. This is informational only for the app, but it dramatically influences the user base, which can install your app using the Google Play Store. You should not normally use this attribute, but instead provide alternative layouts

© Peter Späth 2022
P. Späth, *Pro Android with Kotlin*, https://doi.org/10.1007/978-1-4842-8745-3

and bitmaps as described in the "Supporting Multiple Devices" section of Chapter 9. Synopsis:

```
<compatible-screens>
  <screen android:screenSize=
        ["small" | "normal" | "large" | "xlarge"]
    android:screenDensity=
        ["ldpi" | "mdpi" | "hdpi" | "xhdpi" | "280" |
         "360" | "420" | "480" | "560" ] />
  <screen ...
</compatible-screens>
```

Both screenSize and screenDensity are required for each <screen> element.

The <instrumentation> Element

Can be used for monitoring interactions. Contains the fully qualified name of a subclass of android.app.Instrumentation. Synopsis:

```
<instrumentation android:functionalTest=["true" | "false"]
            android:handleProfiling=["true" | "false"]
            android:icon="drawable resource"
            android:label="string resource"
            android:name="string"
            android:targetPackage="string"
            android:targetProcesses="string" />
```

The attributes are in detail

- **android:functionalTest**: One of true, false. Whether the instrumentation class is to be run as a functional test. Default is false.

- **android:handleProfiling**: One of true, false. Whether the instrumentation class will handle turning profiling on and off by itself. If false, profiling will run all the time. Default is false.

- **android:icon**: The resource ID of an icon to use for the instrumentation class.

- **android:label**: The resource ID of a label to use for the instrumentation class.

- **android:name**: The fully qualified name of the class extending the base class `android.app.Instrumentation`. If it starts with a dot ".", the package name from the `<manifest>` element gets prepended.

- **android:targetPackage**: Provide the package name of the app you want to be monitored.

- **android:targetProcesses**: Added in API level 26. You can use this to specify the processes to run the instrumentation against. Write a comma-separated list of process names here and use an asterisk "*" as a wildcard for all processes of the app defined by `android:targetPackage`. Default is to monitor only the main process of the app defined by `android:targetPackage`.

The <permission> Element

Specifies a custom, non-system, permission to limit access to components, features, or data, whose careless usage implies a security risk. See Chapter 7. Synopsis:

```
<permission android:description="string resource"
      android:icon="drawable resource"
      android:label="string resource"
      android:name="string"
      android:permissionGroup="string"
      android:protectionLevel=["normal" | "dangerous" |
            "signature" | "signatureOrSystem"] />
```

The attributes of this element are

- **android:description**: The string resource ID of a user-readable description.

- **android:icon**: The drawable resource ID of an icon to use for the permission.

- **android:label**: The resource ID of a label for the permission.

- **android:name**: The name of the permission. To avoid clashes, it is strongly recommended to prepend the package name.

- **android:permissionGroup**: The permission group this permission is supposed to be a part of. Must match with the name of a `<permission-group>` element – see in the following.

- **android:protectionLevel**: A protection level. One of the following:

  – **"normal"**: This is the default. Signifies a lower risk with the permission automatically granted by the system upon installation. The user can investigate such permissions though.

  – **"dangerous"**: A higher risk, and the system will usually require a confirmation before accordingly protected features can be used.

  – **"signature"**: The permission gets only granted if the app requesting the permission is signed with the same certificate as the app declaring the permission.

  – **"signatureOrSystem"**: Same as "signature", but also includes Android system image apps as requestors. You should not use it.

Note that this element *specifies* a permission – it does not impose it. Imposing permissions happens on a component level.

The `<permission-group>` Element

Used for grouping permissions in the UI presented to the user. Contained permissions will have the name of the group added as a `permissionGoup` attribute. Find details in Chapter 7. Synopsis:

```
<permission-group android:description="string resource"
                  android:icon="drawable resource"
                  android:label="string resource"
                  android:name="string" />
```

The attributes are

- **android:description**: A string resource ID for a description of this group

- **android:icon**: A drawable resource ID for an icon

- **android:label**: A string resource ID for a label

- **android:name**: The name of the group, to be added to `<permission>` elements

The <permission-tree> Element

Contains the base name for a permission tree used to gather individual permissions. If, for example, you have permissions like "com.abc.permission.allow1" and "com.abc.permission.allow2", a permission tree with name "com.abc.permission" will automatically gather these two. Find details in Chapter 7. Synopsis:

```
<permission-tree android:icon="drawable resource"
                 android:label="string resource" ]
                 android:name="string" />
```

For the attributes you can use

- **android:icon**: A drawable resource ID for an icon

- **android:label**: A string resource ID for a label.

- **android:name**: The name of the tree, to be matched against the start of names of the `<permission>` elements. Must contain at least three parts separated by dots "."

The <queries> Element

Lists other apps an App wants to interact with. Added in API level 30. Synopsis:

```
<queries>
    ...
</queries>
```

Child elements:

- **<package name="string" />**: The packages name (ID) of the app you want to refer to

- **<intent>...</intent>**: Must contain an intent filter signature (similar to <intent> elements)

- **<provider android:authorities="..." />**: Must contain content provider authorities (similar to <provider> elements)

The <supports-gl-texture> Element

Zero, one, or more elements of this type tell external parties, most prominently the Google Play Store, which OpenGL texture formats the app supports. This is informational to the app; it will not decide anything based on that information. The synopsis is

```
<supports-gl-texture
    android:name="string" />
```

and possible values are

- **GL_OES_compressed_ETC1_RGB8_texture** for Ericsson texture compression (OpenGL ES 2.0)

- **GL_OES_compressed_paletted_texture** for generic paletted texture compression

- **GL_AMD_compressed_3DC_texture** for ATI 3Dc texture compression

- **GL_AMD_compressed_ATC_texture** for ATI texture compression (devices running Adreno GPU)

- **GL_EXT_texture_compression_latc** for luminance alpha texture compression

- **GL_EXT_texture_compression_dxt1** for S3 DXT1 texture compression (Nvidia Tegra2)

- **GL_EXT_texture_compression_s3tc** for S3 texture compression (Nvidia Tegra2)

- **GL_IMG_texture_compression_pvrtc** for PowerVR texture compression (PowerVR SGX530/540 GPU)

The <supports-screens> Element

The possible screen sizes your app supports. Synopsis:

```
<supports-screens android:resizeable=["true"| "false"]
        android:smallScreens=["true" | "false"]
        android:normalScreens=["true" | "false"]
        android:largeScreens=["true" | "false"]
        android:xlargeScreens=["true" | "false"]
        android:anyDensity=["true" | "false"]
        android:requiresSmallestWidthDp="integer"
        android:compatibleWidthLimitDp="integer"
        android:largestWidthLimitDp="integer"/>
```

Here are the attributes explained:

- **android:resizeable**: One of true, false. Whether or not the app is resizable for different screens. The default is true, and because it is deprecated, you should not normally use this attribute.

- **android:smallScreens**: One of true, false. Whether to support small screens (below HVGA). Default is true.

- **android:normalScreens**: One of true, false. Whether to support normal screens (HVGA medium, WQVGA low, WVGA high). Default is true.

- **android:largeScreens**: One of true, false. Whether to support large screens (significantly higher than handset screens). Default is undefined, so you should explicitly set this attribute.

- **android:xlargeScreens**: One of true, false. Whether to support extra-large screens (significantly higher than large screens). Default is undefined, so you should explicitly set this attribute.

- **android:anyDensity**: One of true, false. Tells whether the app can handle different densities by providing different resource sets. Default is true, and you should not change it.

- **android:requiresSmallestWidthDp**: If the smallest screen rectangle your app can handle is P × Q in units of dp, you can set whichever of P and Q is smaller as a value of this attribute. Will not target your app, but Google Play Store filtering (although the availability of this filter is uncertain). You normally don't need this attribute.

- **android:compatibleWidthLimitDp**: If the smaller side of a device's screen is larger than the value here, you let the user decide whether they want to use the *screen compatibility mode*. This is a radio button in the action bar for selecting either to stretch the layout (makes empty areas bigger) or perform a zooming (with possible pixel artifacts). You normally don't need this attribute if you designed the app with different screen sizes covered by different resource sets.

- **android:largestWidthLimitDp**: This is the same as android:compat ibleWidthLimitDp, but the user doesn't have a choice – a zooming-in will happen.

The <uses-configuration> Element

Use this to tell your app needs a certain way for a user inputting data or performing navigation. You should not normally use this attribute and design your app agnostic of the way the user physically interacts with it. Synopsis:

```
<uses-configuration
    android:reqFiveWayNav=["true" | "false"]
    android:reqHardKeyboard=["true" | "false"]
    android:reqKeyboardType=["undefined" | "nokeys" |
                             "qwerty" | "twelvekey"]
    android:reqNavigation=["undefined" | "nonav" |
                           "dpad" | "trackball" | "wheel"]
    android:reqTouchScreen=["undefined" | "notouch" |
                            "stylus" | "finger"] />
```

The attributes are

- **android:reqFiveWayNav**: One of `true`, `false`. Whether or not a five-way navigation must exist. This is a control for navigating up, down, right, and left and a button for invoking the currently selected item. Default is false.

- **android:reqHardKeyboard**: One of `true`, `false`. Whether a hardware keyboard is required. Default is false.

- **android:reqKeyboardType**: The keyboard type. One of the following:

  - **"undefined"**: The default, no special requirement.

  - **"nokeys"**: Keyboard not required.

  - **"qwerty"**: A standard QWERTY keyboard is required.

  - **"twelvekey"**: A phone-like keyboard (0–9, *, #).

- **android:reqNavigation**: A navigation requirement. One of the following:

  - **"undefined"**: The default, no special requirement.

  - **"nonav"**: No navigation required.

  - **"dpad"**: A D-pad is required.

  - **"trackball"**: A trackball is required.

  - **"wheel"**: A wheel is required.

- **android:reqTouchScreen**: A requirement for a touchscreen. One of the following:

  - **"undefined"**: The default, no special requirement.

  - **"notouch"**: No touchscreen required.

  - **"stylus"**: A stylus touchscreen is required.

  - **"finger"**: A finger touchscreen is required.

The <uses-feature> Element

Use this to declare a hardware or software feature your app requires. This has no impact on the app, but serves as a filter criterion in Google Play Store. Synopsis:

```
<uses-feature
    android:name="string"
    android:required=["true" | "false"]
    android:glEsVersion="integer" />
```

For the attributes you can use

- **android:name**: The standardized name of the feature. For a list, see the "Features" section of this online text companion.

- **android:required**: One of `true`, `false`. Whether your app will not work without that feature. Using false here means the feature is nice to have, but your app will work without it. Default is true.

- **android:glEsVersion**: Specify an OpenGL ES version. The higher 16 bits specify the major version code and the lower 16 bits the minor version code. So version 2.0 maps to 0x00020000. The default is to require only version 1.0.

The <uses-permission> Element

Use this to state that your app needs certain permissions to do its work. Up to Android 5.1, permissions get inquired from the user at installation time. Starting with Android 6.0, this happens at runtime. Synopsis:

```
<uses-permission android:name="string"
    android:maxSdkVersion="integer" />
```

The attributes of this element are

- **android:name**: The standardized name of the permission. Contains system and custom permissions (see the preceding `<permission>` element). For a list of system permissions, see the "Permissions" section of this online text companion.

- **android:maxSdkVersion**: Introduced in API level 19. Use this to specify the latest API level a permission explicitly is needed by the app.

The <uses-permission-sdk-23> Element

Same as <uses-permission>, but valid only if the device is running in API level 23 (Android 6.0) or higher. Synopsis:

```
<uses-permission-sdk-23 android:name="string"
        android:maxSdkVersion="integer" />
```

The <uses-sdk> Element

An element specifying the Android API level conformance of your app. This is rather important, because it tells on which Android versions your app will be running and thus defines the possible user base. Synopsis:

```
<uses-sdk android:minSdkVersion="integer"
        android:targetSdkVersion="integer"
        android:maxSdkVersion="integer" />
```

The attributes are

- **android:minSdkVersion**: The minimum API level a device must have in order to run your app. If you make this too low, inside the code you have to take care of too many old Android versions. If you make this too high, you lose too many possible users. See Table A-1 for helping you make a correct decision.

- **android:targetSdkVersion**: You write an API level number into this attribute to express that you developed and tested your app with exactly this number. The Android OS on a device with an API level higher than that will then do its best to make sure your app will run there as well, applying compatibility modes where necessary. It is very reasonable to use this attribute and always write the latest available API level of your test devices or emulated devices you use for development and testing.

- **android:maxSdkVersion**: The maximum API level your app will run in. You usually don't need this attribute, and you should not use it unless you accept losing users.

Note   Despite the name these settings address the *API level*, not actually the SDK version.

Table A-1. *API-Level Cumulated Distribution by 4. Quarter 2021*

Minimum API Level	Android Version	Distribution
16	4.1	> 99%
17	4.2	> 99%
18	4.3	> 99%
19	4.4	> 99%
21	5.0	> 98%
22	5.1	> 97%
23	6.0	> 94%
24	7.0	> 89%
25	7.1	> 85%
26	8.0	> 82%
27	8.1	> 78%
28	9	> 69%
29	10	> 50%
30	11	> 24%

The Application Declaration

An Android app is a container for the components building up the application. It gets described by the `<application>` element as a child element of `<manifest>` inside `AndroidManifest.xml`. The synopsis of the `<application>` element reads

```
<application ...>
    <activity ...>...</activity>
    <activity-alias ...>...</activity-alias>
    <meta-data ...>...</meta-data>
    <service ...>...</service>
    <receiver ...>...</receiver>
    <profileable>...</profileable>
    <provider ...>...</provider>
    <uses-library ...>...</uses-library>
    <uses-native-library ...>...</uses-native-library>
</application>
```

Possible attributes of the `<application>` element are listed in Table A-2; the child elements get described in the following paragraphs.

Table A-2. *Manifest Application Attributes*

Name	Description
android:allowTaskReparenting	One of `true`, `false`. Whether the activities of this app can have their parent activity changed to the value given by the `taskAffinity` attribute. For example, starting a web page from an email with reparenting to the browser means the new web page gets attributed to the browser, so the next time the browser gets activated, this page will be shown. Makes only sense if the `launchMode` attribute of the activities is set to "standard" or "singleTop". Default is false.
android:allowBackup	One of `true`, `false`. If true (the default), allow the app to participate in the backup infrastructure of the Android OS.
android:allowClearUserData	One of `true`, `false`. Not available to non-system image apps. If true (the default for system image apps), the app may reset user data.

(continued)

Table A-2. (*continued*)

Name	Description
android:allowNativeHeapPointerTagging	Whether or not the heap pointer tagging feature is enabled. This is a security feature for some devices using Android 11 or later. For details see `https://source.android.com/devices/tech/debug/tagged-pointers`. Default is true.
android:appCategory	Useful for grouping apps. Set this attribute only for apps that fit well into a category. Possible values: accessibility, audio, game, image, maps, news, productivity, social, video.
android:backupAgent	The fully qualified class name of a backup agent (if starting with a ".", the package name gets prepended) extending `android.app.backup.BackupAgent`.
android:backupInForeground	One of `true`, `false`. If true, an automatic backing up also happens while the app is in a foreground mode. Use with caution, since the app gets shut down from the Android OS during the backing-up operation. Default is false.
android:banner	For Android TV apps, the resource ID of a banner to show in the home screen. There is no default banner.
android:dataExtractionRules	May specify a pointer to an XML resource that describes backup and restore rules. Since API level 31. For details see `https://developer.android.com/guide/topics/data/autobackup`.
android:debuggable	One of `true`, `false`. Whether the app can be debugged. Default is false.
android:description	User-readable longer description of the app, as a resource ID.
android:directBootAware	One of `true`, `false`. Whether the app can run before the user unlocks the device. Default is false.
android:enabled	One of `true`, `false`. If false, the app is disabled. Default is true.

(*continued*)

Table A-2. (*continued*)

Name	Description
android:extractNativeLibs	One of `true`, `false`. If false, do not extract native libraries to the file system while installing the app. The native libraries must then be page aligned and stored uncompressed in the APK file. Default is true.
android:fullBackupContent	Points to an XML file describing what to back up. The syntax for this file is described online in the document "Auto Backup for Apps."
android:fullBackupOnly	For Android starting with API level 23. One of `true`, `false`. If true, the device participates in *Auto Backup* with data synchronized with the Google cloud. Default is false.
android:gwpAsanMode	Helps to find heap memory allocation bugs on some devices running API level 30 or later. See `https://developer.android.com/ndk/guides/gwp-asan` for details. One of "never" (default), "always".
android:hasCode	One of `true`, `false`. Whether the app contains any code. Default is true.
android:hasFragileUserData	If true, the user upon deinstallation will be asked whether to also remove the app's data. Default is false.
android:hardwareAccelerated	One of `true`, `false`. If true, enable graphics hardware acceleration. The memory consumption might be higher. Default is false.
android:icon	The resource ID of an icon to be used for the app, for example, @`mipmap/myapp_icon`.
android:isGame	One of `true`, `false`. Whether the app is a game. Default is false.
android:killAfterRestore	One of `true`, `false`. Whether to kill the app after a full system restore operation. Default is true, and you will not normally change it.
android:largeHeap	One of `true`, `false`. A last-resort setting if your app needs a lot of memory. Default is false.

(*continued*)

Table A-2. (*continued*)

Name	Description
android:label	The resource ID of a label string to be used for the app, for example, `@string/myapp_label`.
android:logo	A resource ID of the app's logo, and a default for the activities included.
android:manageSpaceActivity	The fully qualified name of an activity class (extending `android.app.Activity`), which lets the user administer memory usage of the app. The Android OS might then call it in case of a resource shortage. Default is to not provide such an activity.
android:name	The fully qualified name of a subclass of `android.app.Application`. You may use it for extra investigation of app activities and for special app-related administration purposes. Default is to use the standard class.
android:networkSecurityConfig	Added in API level 24. The resource ID of an XML file containing the network security configuration. The syntax of this file is available online in the "Network Security Configuration" document.
android:permission	The name of a permission the caller needs to be able to call components of this app. If not given here and also not in child elements, no restriction applies.
android:persistent	One of `true`, `false`. Whether the app is supposed to be running at all times. This is left for system-level apps, and you should not use it. Default is false.
android:process	Normally a component starts in the process of the app it is defined in. If you use this attribute, the process given by the value supplied here is used instead for all components of this app, unless you define the `process` attribute on a component basis as well. If the name starts with a ":", a new private process gets created for that aim. If it starts with a lowercase letter, a global process with that name will be used instead.

(*continued*)

Table A-2. (*continued*)

Name	Description
android:restoreAnyVersion	One of `true`, `false`. Whether the backup mechanism is allowed to restore the app even with the backup data coming from newer versions of the app. Default is false.
android:requestLegacyExternalStorage	If true, the older external storage policy should be used instead of the modern scoped storage methodology. See `https://developer.android.com/training/data-storage#scoped-storage` for details.
android:requiredAccountType	Added in API level 18. The name of an account authenticator type necessary for this app to start. This corresponds to an online account. For restricted profiles this effectively disables the app, because they cannot add accounts. Defaults to not requiring an account.
android:resizeableActivity	Added in API level 24. One of `true`, `false`. If set to true, the activities of this App can participate in a multi-window mode, provided the device is capable of doing that. Otherwise, the activities use the whole screen. Default value is true.
android:restrictedAccountType	An addition to the preceding `requiredAccountType` attribute – also add account types here if you want restricted profiles to be able to use the app. Caution: Imposes a security risk if the account is connected with personal user data.
android:supportsRtl	Added in API level 17. One of `true`, `false`. Whether to allow right-to-left layouting. Default is false.
android:taskAffinity	Normally all activities of an app have the same affinity, which means they all go to the same task stack once active. Their affinity is then determined by the root activity's name. If you set an app's `taskAffinity` though, you can express the activities of this app to belong to another task stack, which takes effect once the activity is reparented or launched with the `FLAG_ACTIVITY_NEW_TASK` flag set. If unset and also not set in the child elements, take the package name.

(*continued*)

Table A-2. (*continued*)

Name	Description
android:testOnly	One of `true`, `false`. Set it to true if you want to use this app only for testing purposes. It then cannot be published in the Google Play Store. Default is false.
android:theme	Points to a style resource to be used as the app's style theme. If unset and also not set inside the child elements, take the default system theme.
android:uiOptions	Extra UI options to use. One of "none" for nothing extra (default) and "splitActionBarWhenNarrow" to have an additional action bar at the bottom of the screen when horizontal space gets scarce.
android:usesCleartextTraffic	Added in API level 23. Ignored for API levels 24 and above if a *network security config* is present. One of `true`, `false`. If set to false, platform components might refuse to transport cleartext data over the network, on a best-effort basis. Default is true.
android:vmSafeMode	One of `true`, `false`. Whether the virtual machine should operate in safe mode. Default is false.

Note   For simple apps, the `<application>` element may contain no attributes and just a single `<activity>` element. Of course you want to add attributes for a more professional-looking app, and you will have to add more child elements if your app starts getting more complex.

The `<activity>` Child Element

Describes a user interface component. You can have zero, one, or more of this element in an application. Activities get thoroughly described in Chapter 3.

The `<activity-alias>` Child Element

An alias to an activity from the same application. The alias needs to be declared *after* the target activity. Synopsis:

```
<activity-alias android:enabled=["true" | "false"]
                android:exported=["true" | "false"]
                android:icon="drawable resource"
                android:label="string resource"
                android:name="string"
                android:permission="string"
                android:targetActivity="string" >
    ...
</activity-alias>
```

The attributes are

- **android:enabled**: One of true, false. Whether this alias is enabled. Default is true.

- **android:exported**: One of true, false. Whether this alias is exported, that is, usable from other apps. The default is false, if the element contains no intent filters, and otherwise true.

- **android:icon**: The resource ID of an icon for this alias.

- **android:label**: The string resource ID of a label for this alias.

- **android:name**: The name of this activity alias. Should follow the same naming convention as for activities, but there is actually no restriction for alias names.

- **android:permission**: The name of a permission a client needs to have in order to start the activity declared in attribute targetActivity. Defaults to no restriction.

- **android:targetActivity**: Points to the activity this alias refers to. Enter the activity's name here.

Possible children elements are

- **intent-filter**: See Chapter 3 for a description.

- **meta-data**: An arbitrary name-value pair in the form `<meta-data android:name="..." android:resource="..." android:value="..." />`. You can have several of them, and they go into an `android.os.Bundle` element available as `PackageItemInfo.metaData`.

The `<meta-data>` Child Element

An arbitrary name-value pair in the form `<meta-data android:name = "..." android:resource = "..." android:value = "..." />`. You can have several of them, and they go into an `android.os.Bundle` element available as `PackageItemInfo.metaData`.

The `<profileable>` Child Element

Profiler access capabilities for this app.

The attributes are

- **android:enabled**: One of `true`, `false`

- **Android:shell**: One of `true`, `false`. Whether local debugging tools may access this app

The `<provider>` Child Element

This describes a *content provider*, a component that provides structured data to other components and apps. We handle it in Chapter 6. Here we just summarize the element. You can declare several of them, and one element has the following synopsis:

```
<provider android:authorities="list"
        android:directBootAware=["true" | "false"]
        android:enabled=["true" | "false"]
        android:exported=["true" | "false"]
```

```
android:grantUriPermissions=["true" | "false"]
android:icon="drawable resource"
android:initOrder="integer"
android:label="string resource"
android:multiprocess=["true" | "false"]
android:name="string"
android:permission="string"
android:process="string"
android:readPermission="string"
android:syncable=["true" | "false"]
android:writePermission="string" ›
```
   ...
</provider>

The possible attributes are

- **android:authorities**: A semicolon ";"–separated list of URI
  authorities. Although not strictly prescribed, each authority
  should have a reverse-domain Java-style name like com.example.
  peopleprovider.ThePeople, maybe reflecting the class that extends
  the android.content.ContentProvider subclass. There is no default.
  You must provide at least one.

- **android:directBootAware**: One of true, false. Whether content gets
  provided before the user unlocks the device. Default is false.

- **android:enabled**: One of true, false. Whether this provider is
  enabled. Default is true.

- **android:exported**: One of true, false. Whether this provider is
  exported, that is, usable from other apps. The default is false, if you
  set android:targetSdkVersion to 17 or higher and the device runs in
  API level 17 or higher. Lower API levels run as if it were set to true.

- **android:grantUriPermissions**: One of true, false. For any client
  not listed in a grant-uri-permission sub-element, if you set this
  attribute to true, permissions can still be granted on a temporary
  basis by asking the user. The caller must then set flags like FLAG_
  GRANT_READ_URI_PERMISSION or FLAG_GRANT_WRITE_URI_PERMISSION
  in the calling Intent. Default is false.

- **android:icon**: The resource ID of an icon for this provider.

- **android:initOrder**: If inside a process you need an instantiation order for content providers, you can set an appropriate integer value here. Higher numbers come first.

- **android:label**: The string resource ID of a label for this alias.

- **android:multiprocess**: One of `true`, `false`. By setting this to true and if your app runs in several processes, you can allow several instances of one content provider be instantiated, one per process that needs it. Default is false.

- **android:name**: The class name of this provider. The class must extend the `android.content.ContentProvider` base class. If it starts with a dot ".", the package name gets prepended.

- **android:permission**: The name of a permission a client needs to have in order to use this content provider. A shortcut for using both `readPermission` and `writePermission` with one single value (the latter have precedence though).

- **process**: Normally a component starts in the process of the app it is defined in. If you use this attribute, the process given by the value supplied here is used instead for the content provider. If the name starts with a ":", a new private process gets created for that aim. If it starts with a lowercase letter, a global process with that name will be used instead.

- **android:readPermission**: The name of a permission a client needs to have in order to read from this content provider.

- **android:syncable**: One of `true`, `false`. Whether the data can be synchronized with the data on a server.

- **android:writePermission**: The name of a permission a client needs to have in order to write to this content provider.

Applicable sub-elements of this element are

- **grant-uri-permission**: An element specifying a URI permission or permission pattern. It has the form

```
<grant-uri-permission android:path="string"
    android:pathPattern="string"
    android:pathPrefix="string" />
```

where the path attribute specifies a complete path, the
pathPrefix attribute allows matching the initial part of a path,
and pathPattern is a complete path, but with wildcards: "*"
matches zero to many occurrences of the specified character, and
".*" matches zero to many occurrences of any character.

- **intent-filter**: If you want to allow the content provider to be accessed
  via intent resolution (via PackageManager) – normally you use a
  content resolver for that purpose – you need to specify an intent filter
  using this element.

- **meta-data**: An arbitrary name-value pair in the form <meta-data
  android:name="..." android:resource="..." android:value="..."
  />. You can have several of them, and they go into an android.
  os.Bundle element available as PackageItemInfo.metaData.

- **path-permission**: To define a subset of data a content provider can
  serve, you can use this element to specify a path and a required
  permission. It has the form

```
<path-permission android:path="string"
    android:pathPrefix="string"
    android:pathPattern="string"
    android:permission="string"
    android:readPermission="string"
    android:writePermission="string" />
```

where the path attribute specifies a complete path, the
pathPrefix attribute allows matching the initial part of a path,
and pathPattern is a complete path, but with wildcards: "*"
matches zero to many occurrences of the specified character,
and ".*" matches zero to many occurrences of any character. The
permission attribute specifies a read and write permission, and
the attributes readPermission and writePermission draw a
distinction between read and write permissions. If any of the latter
two is specified, it takes precedence over the permission attribute.

The `<receiver>` Child Element

This element – or these elements, since you can have several of them – specifies *broadcast receivers*. We talked about broadcasts in Chapter 5. Here we just provide a summary. The synopsis of the element is

```
<receiver android:directBootAware=["true" | "false"]
          android:enabled=["true" | "false"]
          android:exported=["true" | "false"]
          android:icon="drawable resource"
          android:label="string resource"
          android:name="string"
          android:permission="string"
          android:process="string" >
    ...
</receiver>
```

It has the following attributes:

- **android:directBootAware**: One of `true`, `false`. Whether broadcasts can be received before the user unlocks the device. Default is false.

- **android:enabled**: One of `true`, `false`. Whether the component is enabled. Default is true.

- **android:exported**: One of `true`, `false`. Whether this receiver is exported, that is, can receive messages from other apps. The default is false, if the element contains no intent filters, and otherwise true.

- **android:icon**: The resource ID of an icon for this receiver.

- **android:label**: The string resource ID for a label.

- **android:name**: The name of this receiver.

- **android:permission**: A permission a broadcast sender must have in order to be able to send messages to this receiver.

- **android:process**: A process name the receiver will run inside when messages arrive. If it begins with a colon ":", the process will be private to the app. If it starts with a lowercase letter, the process will be global and can be shared among apps.

As sub-elements it can contain the same children as an `<activity>` element:

- **intent-filter**: See Chapter 3 for a description.

- **meta-data**: An arbitrary name-value pair in the form `<meta-data android:name="..." android:resource="..." android:value="..." />`. You can have several of them, and they go into an `android.os.Bundle` element available as `PackageItemInfo.metaData`.

The `<service>` Child Element

Describes a service. For details see Chapter 4. You can have zero, one, or more child elements of this type inside the application.

The `<uses-library>` Child Element

If your app needs a shared library to link against, you can specify that here. The synopsis reads

```
<uses-library
    android:name="string"
    android:required=["true" | "false"] />
```

where the `name` attribute is the name of the shared library and by setting `required` to "true" the app won't be installable unless the shared library requirement is met. Setting it to "false" expresses an affinity toward using that library, but your app will work without it too.

The `<uses-native-library>` Child Element

Only for API levels 31 and higher. A vendor-provided shared native library to be linked against. The synopsis reads

```
<uses-native-library
    android:name="string"
    android:required=["true" | "false"] />
```

where the `name` attribute is the name of the shared native library and by setting `required` to "true" the app won't be installable unless the shared native library requirement is met. Setting it to "false" expresses an affinity toward using that library, but your app will work without it too.

Activity-Related Manifest Entries

In this part of the online text companion, we list and describe activity-related declarations inside the manifest file `AndroidManifest.xml`. All attributes of the `<activity>` element inside the manifest file `AndroidManifest.xml` are listed in Table A-3.

Table A-3. *Manifest Flags for Activities*

Name	Description
android:allowEmbedded	One of `true`, `false`. Whether the activity can be embedded inside another activity. Default is false.
android:allowTaskReparenting	One of `true`, `false`. Whether the activity can have its parent activity changed to the value given by the `taskAffinity` attribute. For example, starting a web page from an email with reparenting to the browser means the new web page gets attributed to the browser, so the next time the browser gets activated, this page will be shown. Makes only sense if the `launchMode` attribute is set to "standard" or "singleTop". Default is false.
android:alwaysRetainTaskState	One of `true`, `false`. Only for the root activity of a task. If true, always return to the last state of the task, regardless of how the activity gets started. Otherwise, the Android OS might have decided after some time (say 30 minutes) that the task should be cleared, that is, all activities above the root activity should be removed. Default is false.

(continued)

Table A-3. (*continued*)

Name	Description
android:autoRemoveFromRecents	One of `true`, `false`. If false, leave the activity in the overview screen (recents) of a task until the last activity in the task is completed. The flag overrides the activity caller's flag `FLAG_ACTIVITY_RETAIN_IN_RECENTS`. Default is false.
android:banner	For Android TV apps, the resource ID of a banner to show in the home screen. There is no default banner.
android:clearTaskOnLaunch	One of `true`, `false`. Only for the root activity of a task. If true, returning to a task by relaunching it from the home screen will always return to the task's root activity and remove all activities on top of it. Default is false.
android:colorMode	Set this to "wideColorGamut" if for devices capable of doing it you want to enable more vibrant color. Ignored if the device cannot handle it.
android:configChanges	Use this to list configuration changes the activity wants to handle itself. Normally, an activity gets shut down and restarted if at runtime a configuration value changes, but if inside this list (use "|" as a separator), the `onConfigurationChanged()` method gets called instead. It is recommended to not use this flag. Possible list entries are shown below the table.
android:directBootAware	One of `true`, `false`. Whether the activity can run before the user unlocks the device. Default is false.
android:documentLaunchMode	Specifies how new instances of an activity show up in the task list (overview screen). Possible values are listed in the following.
android:enabled	One of `true`, `false`. If false, the activity is disabled. Default is true.
android:excludeFromRecents	One of `true`, `false`. If true, the activity will not show up in the recents (overview) screen. Default is false.

(*continued*)

Table A-3. (*continued*)

Name	Description
android:exported	One of `true`, `false`. If true, the activity will be callable by other apps. Default is true.
android:finishOnTaskLaunch	One of `true`, `false`. If true, existing instances of the same activity will be shut down when the user launches the task by choosing it from the home screen. Default is false. If both this setting and `allowTaskReparenting` are true, a reparenting will not happen. Instead, the activity gets destroyed.
android:hardwareAccelerated	One of `true`, `false`. If true, enable graphics hardware acceleration. The memory consumption might be higher. Default is false.
android:icon	The resource ID of an icon to be used for the activity, for example, `@mipmap/activity1_icon`. If unset, use the app's icon instead.
android:immersive	Sets the immersive mode. An immersive activity wishes not to be interrupted by notifications. One of `true`, `false`.
android:label	The resource ID of a label string to be used for the activity, for example, `@string/activity1_label`. If unset, use the app's label instead.
android:launchMode	Specifies how the activity is to be started. Details are shown in Table A-4.
android:lockTaskMode	How the activity is represented in lock task mode. Since API level 23. See `https://developer.android.com/work/dpc/dedicated-devices/lock-task-mode`.
android:maxRecents	The maximum number of activities showing up in the task stack (overview screen). Default is 16, minimum is 1, and maximum is 50. If exceeded, the least recently used activity from the overview screen gets removed.

(*continued*)

Table A-3. (*continued*)

Name	Description
android:maxAspectRatio	Use this to specify the maximum aspect ratio. If exceeded on the device, the app gets letterboxed. A number greater than 1.0. On non-wearable devices greater than 1.33. Ignored if the attribute `resizeableActivity` is set to true.
android:multiprocess	One of `true`, `false`. If true, the activity can be launched into the process from where the activity got instantiated. You don't normally want that. The default value is false.
android:name	The fully qualified class name of the activity. If the package name is the same as the `package` attribute of the root element, you can omit it, but add a point in front of the name then.
android:noHistory	One of `true`, `false`. If the user navigates away from the activity and this flag is set to true, the activity will be removed from the task stack, and the activity gets finished with its `finish()` method called. Default is false.
android:parentActivityName	Use this to specify the parent activity's name when the user navigates up by tapping the *top* button. For API levels up to 16, also write an item like `<meta-data android:name = "android.support.PARENT_ACTIVITY" android:value = "com.example.app.MainActivity" />` inside the `<activity>` element.
android:persistableMode	For API level 21 or higher, defines whether an activity gets its state persisted if the device restarts. Use "persistRootOnly" if only the root of a task stack is to be preserved; this is also the default mode. Use "persistAcrossReboots" for activities above the root if you want their states also to be preserved. Use "persistNever" for no persisting. With persisting possible, you can use `onSaveInstanceState()` to do the persisting, and after reboot the `onCreate()` method gets a filled `PersistableBundle` object.

(*continued*)

Table A-3. (*continued*)

Name	Description
android:permission	The name of a permission the caller needs to be able to call the activity. If not set, use the `<application>` element's `permission` attribute. If both are not given, no restriction applies.
android:process	Normally an activity starts in the process of the app it is defined in. If you use this attribute, the process given by the value supplied here is used instead. If it starts with a ":", a new private process gets created for that aim. If it starts with a lowercase letter, a global process with that name will be used instead.
android:relinquishTaskIdentity	One of `true`, `false`. If true, an activity in the task stack transports its identity to the next activity on top of it once open. Default is false.
android:resizeableActivity	Added in API level 24. One of `true`, `false`. If set to true, the activity can participate in a multi-window mode, provided the device is capable of doing that. Otherwise, the activity uses the whole screen. Default value is true.
android:screenOrientation	Controls the screen orientation. Possible values are listed in Table A-5. Note that if you declare one of the portrait or landscape values there, it is considered a hard requirement of devices capable of providing that mode. So the app will not be installable on devices that cannot handle it. Consider using a `<uses-feature>` element instead – it will not prevent your app from being installed on devices with missing capabilities. See Chapter 17 for details about `<uses-feature>`.
android:showForAllUsers	Added in API level 23. One of `true`, `false`. If true, also show the activity to other users (those who haven't started it).

(*continued*)

Table A-3. (*continued*)

Name	Description
android:stateNotNeeded	One of `true`, `false`. If true, you express that in the process of killing and restarting the activity, a saving and restoring of the activity's state is not necessary. The method `OnSaveInstanceState()` is then possibly not called, and the `onCreate()` method will get a `null`-valued bundle as argument. Default is false.
android:supportsPictureInPicture	Added in API level 24. One of `true`, `false`. If true, a picture-in-picture display for Android TV will be possibly available to the activity. You then also must make sure the attribute `resizeableActivity` is set to true.
android:taskAffinity	Normally all activities of an app have the same affinity, which means they all go to the same task stack once active. Their affinity is then determined by the root activity's name. If you set an activity's `taskAffinity` though, you can express the activity to belong to another task stack, which takes effect once the activity is reparented or launched with the `FLAG_ACTIVITY_NEW_TASK` flag set. If unset, take the `application` element's affinity, and if that one is unset, too, take the package name.
android:theme	Points to a style resource to be used as the activity's style theme. If unset, take the `application` element's theme, and if this is unset, too, take the default system theme.
android:uiOptions	Extra UI options to use. One of "none" for nothing extra (default) and "splitActionBarWhenNarrow" to have an additional action bar at the bottom of the screen when horizontal space gets scarce.
android:windowSoftInputMode	Specifies how the soft keyboard interacts with the activity. See Table A-6 for details. You can combine a "state" and an "adjust" setting by using a "|" separator if necessary.

For the `android:configChanges` to be forwarded to the activity class, you can supply a list of the following values, separated by bars "|":

- **density** for the display density

- **fontScale** for the font scaling factor

- **keyboard** for the keyboard type

- **keyboardHidden** for the keyboard accessibility

- **layoutDirection** if changing from left-to-right to right-to-left or the other way round (only starting at API level 17)

- **locale** for the locale

- **mcc** for the mobile country code

- **mnc** for the mobile network code

- **navigation** for the navigation type

- **orientation** for the screen orientation

- **screenLayout** for the screen layout

- **screenSize** for the screen size

- **smallestScreenSize** for the physical screen size

- **touchscreen** if the touchscreen has changed

- **uiMode** if the user interface has changed, for example, if the device was placed in a dock

For the `documentLaunchMode` flag for controlling how to handle new document-related activities, you can provide one of the following:

- **intoExisting** to search for a matching (`ComponentName` and data URI) task and possibly restart it with the root activity receiving `onNewIntent()` calls

- **always** for the activity always creating a new task for a document

- **none** (this is the default value) to not create new tasks unless `FLAG_ACTIVITY_NEW_TASK` is set by the caller

- **never** to never create a new task.

If other than "none" and "never", the launchMode must have been set to "standard" for the setting to take effect.

Table A-4. *Launch Modes by the* launchMode *Setting*

Name	Description
standard	The default mode. A "standard" activity can be instantiated many times. Every time a new instance is created, it will show up as a new entry in the task list.
singleTop	Same as "standard", but with the difference that if an instance of the activity exists and is on top of the task's activity stack, this existing activity's onNewIntent() method gets called instead.
singleTask	There can only be one instance of this activity in the task stack. New activity launches of the same activity type will be routed to the onNewIntent() method of the existing activity. Other activities instantiated will pile up normally on top of this activity. Consider this for exceptional purposes only.
singleInstance	Same as "singleTask", except that other activities will not pile up here. So the task stack will only ever contain one element. Consider this for exceptional purposes only.
singleInstancePerTask	Always at the root of the activity task.

Table A-5. *Screen Orientation Modes*

Name	Description
unspecified	The default value. Here the Android OS chooses the orientation.
behind	Uses the same orientation as the activity underneath in the task stack.
landscape	Landscape orientation.
portrait	Portrait orientation.
reverseLandscape	Landscape orientation, but flipped.
reversePortrait	Portrait orientation, but flipped.
sensorLandscape	Like "landscape", but can be flipped based on the device sensor.
sensorPortrait	Like "portrait", but can be flipped based on the device sensor.
userLandscape	Like "sensorLandscape", but also influenced by the user preferences.
userPortrait	Like "sensorPortrait", but also influenced by the user preferences.
sensor	The orientation will be based on the device's orientation sensor.
fullSensor	Like "sensor", but also allows flipping.
nosensor	The orientation sensor will be disabled.
user	The orientation is based on the user preferences.
fullUser	Added in API level 18. Uses user preferences if the user has locked sensor-based rotation. Otherwise, same as "fullSensor".
locked	Locks to the current rotation.

Table A-6. *Soft Keyboard Input Modes*

Name	Description
stateUnspecified	The default setting. The Android OS decides how to present the soft keyboard.
stateUnchanged	Use the last state.
stateHidden	Hide the soft keyboard for forward navigation (the user affirmatively chooses the activity).
stateAlwaysHidden	Hide the soft keyboard when the activity has focus.
stateVisible	Show the soft keyboard for forward navigation (the user affirmatively chooses the activity).
stateAlwaysVisible	Show the soft keyboard when the activity has focus.
adjustUnspecified	The default adjustment. Android decides whether the activity's layout needs an adjustment to make space for the soft keyboard. The latter depends on the scrolling capability of the layout.
adjustResize	Force resizing the activity's layout to make space for the soft keyboard.
adjustPan	Does not force a resizing of the layout, but instead reduces its space and possibly pans the view on the layout to make sure the input widget is visible.

Intent Constituent Parts

This section of the online text companion describes various elements of Intents. Intents get used inside `<intent-filter>` elements inside the manifest file. For details see Chapter 3.

Intent Actions

Generic action attributes to be used inside `<action>` elements inside intent filters are specified by the constants whose names have `ACTION_*` inside class `android.content.Intent` and shown in Tables A-7 and A-8.

Table A-7. *Intent Actions for Activities*

Action	Description
ALL_APPS	List all available applications.
ANSWER	Handle an incoming phone call.
APPLICATION_PREFERENCES	An activity that provides a user interface for adjusting application preferences.
APP_ERROR	The user pressed the "Report" button in the crash/ANR dialog.
ASSIST	Perform assist action.
ATTACH_DATA	Used to indicate that some piece of data should be attached to some other place.
AUTO_REVOKE_PERMISSIONS	Launch UI to manage auto-revoke state.
BUG_REPORT	Show activity for reporting a bug.
CALL	Perform a call to someone specified by the data.
CALL_BUTTON	The user pressed the "call" button to go to the dialer or another appropriate UI for placing a call.
CARRIER_SETUP	Main entry point for carrier setup apps.
CHOOSER	Display an activity chooser, allowing the user to pick what they want to before proceeding.
CREATE_DOCUMENT	Allow the user to create a new document.
CREATE_REMINDER	Creates a reminder.
CREATE_SHORTCUT	Creates a shortcut.
DEFAULT	Synonym for VIEW, the "standard" action that is performed on a piece of data.
DEFINE	Allows for defining the meaning of selected words.
DELETE	Delete the given data from its container.
DIAL	Dial a number as specified by the data.
EDIT	Provide explicit editable access to the given data.

(*continued*)

Table A-7. (*continued*)

Action	Description
FACTORY_TEST	Main entry point for factory tests.
GET_CONTENT	Allow the user to select a particular kind of data and return it.
INSERT	Insert an empty item into the given container.
INSERT_OR_EDIT	Pick an existing item, or insert a new item, and then edit it.
INSTALL_FAILURE	Activity to handle split installation failures.
INSTALL_PACKAGE	Launch application installer.
MAIN	Start as a main entry point, does not expect to receive data.
MANAGE_NETWORK_USAGE	Show settings for managing network data usage of a specific application.
MANAGE_UNUSED_APPS	Launch UI to manage unused apps.
OPEN_DOCUMENT	Allow the user to select and return one or more existing documents.
OPEN_DOCUMENT_TREE	Allow the user to pick a directory subtree.
PASTE	Create a new item in the given container, initializing it from the current contents of the clipboard.
PICK	Pick an item from the data, returning what was selected.
PICK_ACTIVITY	Pick an activity given an Intent, returning the class selected.
POWER_USAGE_SUMMARY	Show power usage information to the user.
PROCESS_TEXT	Process a piece of text.
QUICK_VIEW	Quick-view the data.
RUN	Run the data, whatever that means.
SAFETY_CENTER	Starts UI to open the Safety Center.
SEARCH	Perform a search.
SEARCH_LONG_PRESS	Start action associated with long-pressing the search key.
SEND	Deliver some data to someone else.

(*continued*)

Table A-7. (*continued*)

Action	Description
SENDTO	Send a message to someone specified by the data.
SEND_MULTIPLE	Deliver multiple data to someone else.
SET_WALLPAPER	Show settings for choosing wallpaper.
SHOW_APP_INFO	Launch an activity showing the app information.
SHOW_WORK_APPS	Show the list of all work apps in the launcher.
SYNC	Perform a data synchronization.
SYSTEM_TUTORIAL	Start the platform-defined tutorial. The extra data SearchManager.QUERY (a String) is the text to search for.
TRANSLATE	Text translation.
UNINSTALL_PACKAGE	Launch application uninstaller.
VIEW	Display the data to the user.
VIEW_LOCUS	Display activity state associated with a Locus ID. Since API level 29.
VIEW_PERMISSION_USAGE	Launch UI to tell about usage of a given permission group.
VIEW_PERMISSION_USAGE_FOR_PERIOD	Launch UI to tell about usage of a given permission group for some period.
VOICE_COMMAND	Start voice command.
WEB_SEARCH	Perform a web search.

Table A-8. *Intent Actions for Broadcasts*

Action	Description
AIRPLANE_MODE_CHANGED	Device's airplane mode toggled.
APPLICATION_LOCALE_CHANGED	Application locale was changed.
APPLICATION_RESTRICTIONS_CHANGED	Application restrictions were changed.
BATTERY_CHANGED	A broadcast containing the charging state, level, and other information about the battery.
BATTERY_LOW	A low-battery condition occurs on the device.
BATTERY_OKAY	The battery is now okay after being low.
BOOT_COMPLETED	The device has finished booting.
CAMERA_BUTTON	The camera button was pressed.
CLOSE_SYSTEM_DIALOGS	Closing a temporary system dialog is pending.
CONFIGURATION_CHANGED	The current device configuration has changed, for example, orientation or locale.
DATE_CHANGED	The date has changed.
DEVICE_STORAGE_LOW	Defunct starting with API level 26. Apps should instead use `getCacheDir()` so the system can free up storage when needed.
DEVICE_STORAGE_OK	Defunct starting with API level 26. Apps should instead use `getCacheDir()` so the system can free up storage when needed.
DOCK_EVENT	A change in the physical docking state of the device occurred.
DREAMING_STARTED	The system started dreaming.
DREAMING_STOPPED	The system stopped dreaming.
EXTERNAL_APPLICATIONS_AVAILABLE	Resources for a set of packages (which were previously unavailable) are currently available since the media on which they exist is available.

(continued)

Table A-8. (*continued*)

Action	Description
EXTERNAL_APPLICATIONS_UNAVAILABLE	The media on which external apps exist is unavailable.
GET_RESTRICTION_ENTRIES	The system tells an app to query restrictions that are to be imposed on restricted users.
GTALK_SERVICE_CONNECTED	A GTalk connection has been established.
GTALK_SERVICE_DISCONNECTED	A GTalk connection has been disconnected.
HEADSET_PLUG	A wired headset has been plugged in or unplugged.
INPUT_METHOD_CHANGED	An input method has been changed.
LOCALE_CHANGED	The current device's locale has changed.
LOCKED_BOOT_COMPLETED	The device has finished booting, but is still in the "locked" state.
MANAGED_PROFILE_ADDED	A broadcast sent to the primary user when an associated managed profile is added.
MANAGED_PROFILE_AVAILABLE	A broadcast sent to the primary user when an associated managed profile has become available.
MANAGED_PROFILE_REMOVED	A broadcast sent to the primary user when an associated managed profile is removed.
MANAGED_PROFILE_UNAVAILABLE	A broadcast sent to the primary user when an associated managed profile has become unavailable.
MANAGED_PROFILE_UNLOCKED	A broadcast sent to the primary user when the credential-encrypted private storage for an associated managed profile is unlocked.
MANAGE_PACKAGE_STORAGE	The package management should be started after the user acknowledged a low-memory condition.
MEDIA_BAD_REMOVAL	An external medium was removed from the SD card slot without properly being unmounted.
MEDIA_BUTTON	The media button was pressed.

(*continued*)

Table A-8. (*continued*)

Action	Description
MEDIA_CHECKING	An external medium is present and being disk-checked. The path to the mount point of the checking media is contained in the `Intent.mData` field.
MEDIA_EJECT	The user has expressed the desire to remove the external storage medium.
MEDIA_MOUNTED	An external medium is present and mounted.
MEDIA_NOFS	An external medium is present, but it is using an incompatible file system. The path to the mount point is contained in the `Intent.mData` field.
MEDIA_REMOVED	An external medium has been removed.
MEDIA_SCANNER_FINISHED	The media scanner has finished scanning a directory.
MEDIA_SCANNER_SCAN_FILE	Request the media scanner to scan a file and add it to the media database.
MEDIA_SCANNER_STARTED	The media scanner has started scanning a directory.
MEDIA_SHARED	The external medium is unmounted because it is being shared as a USB mass storage.
MEDIA_UNMOUNTABLE	The external medium is present but cannot be mounted.
MEDIA_UNMOUNTED	An external medium is present, but not mounted.
MY_PACKAGE_REPLACED	A new version of your app has been installed, replacing an existing one.
NEW_OUTGOING_CALL	An outgoing call is about to be placed.
PACKAGES_SUSPENDED	Packages have been suspended.
PACKAGES_UNSUSPENDED	Packages have been unsuspended.
PACKAGE_ADDED	A new application package has been installed on the device.

(*continued*)

Table A-8. (*continued*)

Action	Description
PACKAGE_CHANGED	An existing app package has been changed, for example, it was enabled or disabled.
PACKAGE_DATA_CLEARED	The user has cleared the data of a package.
PACKAGE_FIRST_LAUNCH	Sent to the installer package of an application when that app is first launched.
PACKAGE_FULLY_REMOVED	An app has been completely removed from the device.
PACKAGE_INSTALL	Unused and deprecated since API level 14.
PACKAGE_NEEDS_VERIFICATION	Sent to the system package verifier when a package needs to be verified.
PACKAGE_REMOVED	An app has been removed from the device.
PACKAGE_REPLACED	A new version of an app has been installed, replacing an existing version.
PACKAGE_RESTARTED	The user has restarted a package, after all of its processes have been killed.
PACKAGE_VERIFIED	Sent to the system package verifier when a package is verified.
POWER_CONNECTED	External power has been connected to the device.
POWER_DISCONNECTED	External power has been removed from the device.
PROFILE_ACCESSIBLE	Sent to a user when an associated profile has been started and unlocked.
PROFILE_INACCESSIBLE	Sent to a user when an associated profile has stopped.
PROVIDER_CHANGED	Some content providers have parts of their namespace changed.
QUICK_CLOCK	Sent when the user taps the clock widget in the system's "quick settings" area.

(*continued*)

Table A-8. (*continued*)

Action	Description
REBOOT	Have the device reboot.
SCREEN_OFF	Sent when the device goes to sleep and becomes non-interactive.
SCREEN_ON	Sent when the device wakes up and becomes interactive.
SHUTDOWN	The device is shutting down.
TIMEZONE_CHANGED	The time zone has changed.
TIME_CHANGED	The time was set.
TIME_TICK	The current time has changed.
UID_REMOVED	A user ID has been removed from the system.
UMS_CONNECTED	Deprecated in API level 14. It is replaced by `android.os.storage.StorageEventListener`
UMS_DISCONNECTED	Deprecated in API level 14. It is replaced by `android.os.storage.StorageEventListener`.
USER_BACKGROUND	A user switch is happening, causing the process's user to be sent to the background.
USER_FOREGROUND	A user switch is happening, causing the process's user to be brought to the foreground.
USER_INITIALIZE	Sent the first time a user is starting.
USER_PRESENT	Sent when the user is present after device wakes up.
USER_UNLOCKED	Sent when the credential-encrypted private storage has become unlocked for the target user.
WALLPAPER_CHANGED	Deprecated in API level 16. Modern apps should instead use `WindowManager.LayoutParams.FLAG_SHOW_WALLPAPER` to have the wallpaper shown behind their UI.

667

To use generic actions, for the name attribute of the `<action>` element, prepend "android.intent.action." to the action name used from the table. For actions you defined yourself, prepend your package name.

Intent Categories

Generic category attributes to be used inside `<action>` elements inside intent filters are specified by the constants whose names have CATEGORY_* inside class `android.content.Intent` and shown in Table A-9.

Table A-9. *Intent Categories*

Category	Description
ACCESSIBILITY_ SHORTCUT_TARGET	Used to make an activity a shortcut target (accessibility).
ALTERNATIVE	Set if the activity should be considered as an alternative action to the data the user is currently viewing.
APP_BROWSER	Used with ACTION_MAIN to launch the browser application.
APP_CALCULATOR	Used with ACTION_MAIN to launch the calculator application.
APP_CALENDAR	Used with ACTION_MAIN to launch the calendar application.
APP_CONTACTS	Used with ACTION_MAIN to launch the contacts application.
APP_EMAIL	Used with ACTION_MAIN to launch the email application.
APP_FILES	Used with ACTION_MAIN to launch the files application.
APP_FITNESS	Used with ACTION_MAIN to launch the fitness application.
APP_GALLERY	Used with ACTION_MAIN to launch the gallery application.
APP_MAPS	Used with ACTION_MAIN to launch the maps application.
APP_MARKET	This activity allows the user to browse and download new applications.
APP_MESSAGING	Used with ACTION_MAIN to launch the messaging application.
APP_MUSIC	Used with ACTION_MAIN to launch the music application.
APP_WEATHER	Used with ACTION_MAIN to launch the weather application.

(*continued*)

Table A-9. (*continued*)

Category	Description
BROWSABLE	Activities that can be safely invoked from a browser must support this category.
CAR_DOCK	An activity to run when device is inserted into a car dock.
CAR_MODE	Used to indicate that the activity can be used in a car environment.
DEFAULT	Set if the activity should be an option for the default action (center press) to perform on a piece of data.
DESK_DOCK	An activity to run when device is inserted into a car dock.
DEVELOPMENT_ PREFERENCE	This activity is a development preference panel.
EMBED	Capable of running inside a parent activity container.
FRAMEWORK_ INSTRUMENTATION_ TEST	To be used as code under test for framework instrumentation tests.
HE_DESK_DOCK	An activity to run when device is inserted into a digital (high-end) dock.
HOME	This is the home activity, that is, the first activity that is displayed when the device boots.
INFO	Provides information about the package it is in; typically used if a package does not contain a LAUNCHER to provide a front door to the user without having to be shown in the all-apps list.
LAUNCHER	Should be displayed in the top-level launcher.
LEANBACK_LAUNCHER	Indicates an activity optimized for leanback mode and that it should be displayed in the leanback launcher.
LE_DESK_DOCK	An activity to run when device is inserted into an analog (low-end) dock.
MONKEY	This activity may be exercised by the monkey or other automated test tools.
OPENABLE	Used to indicate that an Intent only wants URIs that can be opened with `openFileDescriptor(Uri, String)`.

(*continued*)

Table A-9. (*continued*)

Category	Description
PREFERENCE	This activity is a preference panel.
SAMPLE_CODE	To be used as a code example (i.e., not part of the normal user experience).
SECONDARY_HOME	Home on secondary displays.
SELECTED_ALTERNATIVE	Set if the activity should be considered as an alternative selection action to the data the user has currently selected.
TAB	Intended to be used as a tab inside of a containing TabActivity.
TEST	To be used as a test (i.e., not part of the normal user experience).
TYPED_OPENABLE	Used to indicate that an intent filter can accept files that are not necessarily openable by openFileDescriptor(Uri, String), but at least streamable via openTypedAssetFileDescriptor(Uri, String, Bundle) using one of the stream types exposed via getStreamTypes(Uri, String).
UNIT_TEST	To be used as a unit test (e.g., run through the Test Harness).
VOICE	Categories for activities that can participate in voice interaction.
VR_HOME	An activity to use for the launcher when the device is placed in a VR headset viewer.

To use one of the categories from the table, for the name attribute of the <category> element, prepend "android.intent.category." to the category name from the table. For custom categories you defined yourself, prepend your package name.

Intent Extra Data

Note that the names in the following list are constant names from the android.content. Intent class, so, for example, write Intent.EXTRA_ALARM_COUNT as a key:

- **EXTRA_ALARM_COUNT**

  With the AlarmManager (`android.app.AlarmManager`) sending alarm events to registered broadcast receivers, this is an extra field that tells about the number of current and pending alarm events. Pending alarm events are events that, for example, couldn't be sent because the device was down.

- **EXTRA_BCC**

  When calling an emailer, a String[] array holding email addresses that should be blind carbon copied.

- **EXTRA_CC**

  When calling an emailer, a String[] array holding email addresses that should be carbon copied.

- **EXTRA_CHANGED_COMPONENT_NAME**

  An array of the components that have changed. Contains component class names or package names (treating the packages as super-components).

- **EXTRA_DATA_REMOVED**

  In ACTION_PACKAGE_REMOVED Intents, this Boolean extra field is set to `true` if the data is being removed as well.

- **EXTRA_DOCK_STATE**

  An int extra field in ACTION_DOCK_EVENT Intents telling about the dock state. Possible values are

  - **EXTRA_DOCK_STATE_HE_DESK**

    The device is in a digital (high-end) dock.

  - **EXTRA_DOCK_STATE_LE_DESK**

    The device is in an analog (low-end) dock.

  - **EXTRA_DOCK_STATE_CAR**

    The device is in a car dock.

- – **EXTRA_DOCK_STATE_DESK**

  The device is in a desk dock.

- – **EXTRA_DOCK_STATE_UNDOCKED**

  The device is not in any dock.

- **EXTRA_DONT_KILL_APP**

  For the action Intent ACTION_PACKAGE_REMOVED or ACTION_
  PACKAGE_CHANGED, setting this to true overrides the default
  action, hence signaling the application is not to be restarted.

- **EXTRA_EMAIL**

  When calling an emailer, a String[] array holding recipient email
  addresses.

- **EXTRA_INITIAL_INTENTS**

  With an action Intent ACTION_CHOOSER, a Parcelable[] array of
  intent or LabeledIntent objects of additional activities to place at
  the front of the list of choices presented to the user.

- **EXTRA_INTENT**

  For ACTION_PICK_ACTIVITY or ACTION_CHOOSER activities,
  this field must contain the string representation of the target
  Intent being issued.

- **EXTRA_KEY_EVENT**

  For Intents triggered by key events, this is the corresponding
  KeyEvent object.

- **EXTRA_ORIGINATING_URI**

  For actions ACTION_INSTALL_PACKAGE and ACTION_VIEW,
  this contains the originating URI of the installed APK.

- **EXTRA_PHONE_NUMBER**

  This is a string holding the phone number originally entered in
  action ACTION_NEW_OUTGOING_CALL or the actual number to
  call for an ACTION_CALL action.

- **EXTRA_REFERRER**

  A general-purpose field supplying information about who is launching an activity. This field contains a URI object (scheme "http:" or "https:", or also "android-app:" for native applications). However, to retrieve this value in a client, use `getReferrer()` instead. It is also valid for applications to instead supply EXTRA_REFERRER_NAME for cases where they can only create a string, not a URI (the field here, if supplied, will take precedence though).

- **EXTRA_REFERRER_NAME**

  A referrer as a string. See EXTRA_REFERRER earlier.

- **EXTRA_REMOTE_INTENT_TOKEN**

  A general-purpose field for remote Intents.

- **EXTRA_REPLACING**

  If this is set to `true`, the broadcast will immediately be followed by an "add" broadcast for a different version of the same package.

- **EXTRA_SHORTCUT_ICON**

  Deprecated in API level 26. Defines an icon of a shortcut. Instead, use `createShortcutResultIntent(ShortcutInfo)`.

- **EXTRA_SHORTCUT_ICON_RESOURCE**

  Deprecated in API level 26. Defines the resource ID of a shortcut icon. Replaced with createShortcutResultIntent(ShortcutInfo).

- **EXTRA_SHORTCUT_INTENT**

  Deprecated in API level 26. Defines the Intent of a shortcut. Replaced with `createShortcutResultIntent(ShortcutInfo)`.

- **EXTRA_STREAM**

  A "content:" URI holding a stream of data associated with the Intent, used with ACTION_SEND to supply the data being sent.

- **EXTRA_SHORTCUT_NAME**

Deprecated in API level 26. Defines the shortcut name. Replaced with `createShortcutResultIntent(ShortcutInfo)`.

- **EXTRA_SUBJECT**

  For emailers, a string holding the desired subject line of a message.

- **EXTRA_TEMPLATE**

  For content providers, the initial data to place in a newly created record. Use with ACTION_INSERT. The data here is a map containing the same fields as would be given to the underlying `ContentProvider.insert()` call.

- **EXTRA_TEXT**

  This is a CharSequence associated with the Intent, used with ACTION_SEND to supply the literal data to be sent. Note that this may be a styled CharSequence, so you must use `Bundle.getCharSequence()` to retrieve it.

- **EXTRA_TITLE**

  A CharSequence dialog title to provide to the user when used with a ACTION_CHOOSER.

- **EXTRA_UID**

  Used as an int extra field in ACTION_UID_REMOVED Intents to supply the UID the package had been assigned to. Also an optional extra value in ACTION_PACKAGE_REMOVED or ACTION_PACKAGE_CHANGED for the same purpose.

- **EXTRA_USER_INITIATED**

  Since API level 31. A Boolean extra field in ACTION_PACKAGE_REMOVED Intents. Signals that the application was removed by a user-initiated action.

Intent Flags

Tables A-10, A-11, and A-12 show the details for intent flags you can set inside your code.

Table A-10. *Activity Intent–Related Flags*

Name	Description
FLAG_ACTIVITY_BROUGHT_TO_FRONT	This flag is set by the system and corresponds to the singleTask mode, with only one instance of the activity in the task stack. New activity launches of the same activity type will be routed to the onNewIntent() method of the existing activity. Other activities instantiated will pile up normally on top of this activity.
FLAG_ACTIVITY_CLEAR_TASK	This flag will cause any existing task that would be associated with the activity to be cleared before the activity is started. That is, the activity becomes the new root of an otherwise empty task, and any old activities are finished. This can only be used in conjunction with FLAG_ACTIVITY_NEW_TASK.
FLAG_ACTIVITY_CLEAR_TOP	If set, and the activity being launched is already running in the current task, all of the other activities on top of it will be closed, and this Intent will be delivered by onNewIntent() to the (now on top) old activity as a new Intent.
FLAG_ACTIVITY_EXCLUDE_FROM_RECENTS	If set, the new activity is not kept in the list of recently launched activities.
FLAG_ACTIVITY_FORWARD_RESULT	Use this to have the reply target from an existing instance of the new activity forwarded to the newly built activity. This way the new activity can call setResult(int) and have that result sent back to the reply target of the original activity.
FLAG_ACTIVITY_LAUNCH_ADJACENT	Used only in split-screen multi-window mode and only in conjunction with FLAG_ACTIVITY_NEW_TASK. The new activity will be displayed adjacent to the one launching it. Note that setting FLAG_ACTIVITY_MULTIPLE_TASK is required if you want a new instance of an existing activity to be created.

(continued)

Table A-10. (*continued*)

Name	Description
FLAG_MATCH_EXTERNAL	If set while starting a new activity, this flag will attempt to launch an instant app if no full app on the device can already handle the intent.
FLAG_ACTIVITY_MULTIPLE_TASK is required if you want a new instance of an existing activity to be created.	
FLAG_ACTIVITY_NEW_DOCUMENT	This flag is used to open a document into a new task rooted at and on top of the activity launched by this Intent. If this flag is being used to create a new recents entry, then by default that entry will be removed once the activity is finished.
FLAG_ACTIVITY_NEW_TASK	If set, the activity starts a new task.
FLAG_ACTIVITY_NO_ANIMATION	This flag will prevent the system from applying an activity transition animation while going to the next activity state. An animation still can occur if the currently displayed activity has animation enabled.
FLAG_ACTIVITY_NO_HISTORY	Do not keep a new activity in the history stack.
FLAG_ACTIVITY_NO_USER_ACTION	This flag will prevent the normal onUserLeaveHint() callback from occurring on the current frontmost activity before it is paused as the newly started activity is brought to the front. If an activity is ever started via any non-user-driven events such as phone call receipt or an alarm handler, this flag should be passed to Context.startActivity(), ensuring that the pausing activity does not think the user has acknowledged its notification.
FLAG_ACTIVITY_PREVIOUS_IS_TOP	If set, the current activity will not be counted as the top activity for deciding whether the new Intent should be delivered to the top instead of starting a new instance. Instead, the penultimate activity will be used as the top.

(*continued*)

Table A-10. (*continued*)

Name	Description
FLAG_ACTIVITY_REORDER_TO_FRONT	Specify this if you want a previously existing activity of the same type to be brought to front first. Say you have a stack A, B, C, D. Now with this flag set and the Intent addressing B, the stack will become A, C, D, B. This flag has no effect if also FLAG_ACTIVITY_CLEAR_TOP is given.
FLAG_ACTIVITY_REQUIRE_DEFAULT	If starting an activity, the Intent only gets launched if it resolves to a single result.
FLAG_ACTIVITY_REQUIRE_NON_BROWSER	If starting an activity, the Intent only gets launched if it resolves to a single result that is not a browser.
FLAG_ACTIVITY_RESET_TASK_IF_NEEDED	If starting an activity, and in case the activity already exists in a different task, the activity gets moved to this task if this flag is set.
FLAG_ACTIVITY_RETAIN_IN_RECENTS	Usually a document created by FLAG_ACTIVITY_NEW_DOCUMENT will be removed from the recents list if the document gets closed. Use this flag if instead you want the document to remain in the recents list.
FLAG_ACTIVITY_SINGLE_TOP	If set, the activity will not be launched if it is already running at the top of the history stack.
FLAG_ACTIVITY_TASK_ON_HOME	This flag, only to be used in conjunction with FLAG_ACTIVITY_NEW_TASK, will cause a newly launching task to be placed on top of the current home activity task. This means pressing "back" from the task will always return the user to home.

Table A-11. *Broadcast Intent–Related Fags*

Name	Description
FLAG_RECEIVER_FOREGROUND	Set this if you want the recipient of a broadcast to be allowed to run at foreground priority (a shorter timeout interval applies). Not using this flag, during normal broadcasts, the receivers are not automatically hoisted out of the background priority class.
FLAG_RECEIVER_NO_ABORT	If this is an ordered broadcast, don't allow receivers to abort the broadcast. They can still propagate results through to later receivers, but they cannot prevent later receivers from seeing the broadcast.
FLAG_RECEIVER_REGISTERED_ONLY	Setting this to true will cause only registered receivers to be called if a broadcast happens. No BroadcastReceiver components will be launched.
FLAG_RECEIVER_REPLACE_PENDING	If set, when sending a broadcast, the new broadcast will replace any existing pending broadcast that matches it (defined by Intent.filterEquals(...) returning true).
FLAG_RECEIVER_VISIBLE_TO_ INSTANT_APPS	If set, the broadcast will be visible to receivers in instant apps. By default instant apps (see chapter 18) will not receive broadcasts. This flag has no effect when used by an instant app as a broadcast emitter.

Table A-12. *Other Intent Flags*

Name	Description
FLAG_DEBUG_LOG_RESOLUTION	This comes handy for debugging. When set, log messages will be printed during the resolution of this Intent to show you what has been found to create the final resolved list.
FLAG_DIRECT_BOOT_AUTO	Match Intents on their Direct Boot awareness.
FLAG_EXCLUDE_STOPPED_PACKAGES	If you want to disregard stopped packages while trying to match Intents, set this flag. Note that this is not the expected behavior of apps, but you can use it for corner cases.
FLAG_FROM_BACKGROUND	Use this to indicate the caller is running in background mode and is thus not part of a direct user interaction. Since background operations are more likely to be killed by the Android OS, checking this flag might be important for mission-critical broadcast receivers.
FLAG_GRANT_PERSISTABLE_URI_ PERMISSION	In conjunction with FLAG_GRANT_READ_URI_PERMISSION and/or FLAG_GRANT_WRITE_URI_PERMISSION, setting this flag indicates the URI permission grant to be persistable across device reboots until explicitly revoked with revokeUriPermission(Uri, Int). This flag only offers the grant for possible persisting – the receiving application must still call takePersistableUriPermis sion(Uri, Int) to actually persist.
FLAG_GRANT_PREFIX_URI_ PERMISSION	In conjunction with FLAG_GRANT_READ_URI_PERMISSION and/or FLAG_GRANT_WRITE_URI_PERMISSION, setting this flag indicates the URI permission grant applying to any URI that is a prefix match against the original granted URI. (Without this flag, the URI must match exactly for access to be granted.) Another URI is considered a prefix match only when scheme, authority, and all path segments defined by the prefix are an exact match.

(*continued*)

Table A-12. (*continued*)

Name	Description
FLAG_GRANT_READ_URI_PERMISSION	Use this if you want the recipient of this Intent to be granted permission to perform read operations on the URI in the Intent's data and any URIs specified in its `ClipData`.
FLAG_GRANT_WRITE_URI_ PERMISSION	Use this if you want the recipient of this Intent to be granted permission to perform write operations on the URI in the Intent's data and any URIs specified in its `ClipData`.
FLAG_INCLUDE_STOPPED_PACKAGES	Use this to override flag FLAG_EXCLUDE_STOPPED_ PACKAGES. If the flag FLAG_EXCLUDE_STOPPED_ PACKAGES is not given, you don't have to do anything, since including stopped packages is the default.

The Service Class

The API documentation of the `android.app.Service` class can be found here: `https://developer.android.com/reference/android/app/Service`.

Cursor Interface

The `android.database.Cursor` interface declares various methods for data retrieval from a database or content provider. The following is just an excerpt. The full API documentation can be found here: `https://developer.android.com/reference/android/database/Cursor`.

Administrative Methods

- **override fun close():Unit**

  Use this to close resources. The cursor object is not supposed to be usable any longer after this method call.

- **override fun isClosed(): Boolean**

  Return true if the cursor is closed and possibly unusable.

- **override fun deactivate(): Unit**

  This is deprecated; don't use it. Just make this a no-op. There is no need to do a deactivation, for a reactivation is deprecated too. See in the following. Clients should invoke `close()` instead. If you use it nevertheless, the cursor is supposed to be deactivated and possibly unusable after this call, maybe to temporarily free resources. A later `requery()` must reactivate the cursor.

- **override fun requery(): Boolean**

  This is deprecated; don't use it. Make this a no-op and let it return `true`. Clients can instead just request a new cursor. If you use it nevertheless, let it perform a requery of the same request that created the cursor object, possibly refreshing it. If the cursor was deactivated, it must be reactivated after this call. Supposed to return `true` if the requery was successful and otherwise `false`. If it returns `false`, the cursor may be invalid, that is, clients must not rely on its validity.

- **override fun setExtras(extras: Bundle?):Unit**

  Use this from inside your content provider if you want to provide any out-of-band values to clients. You should not normally use this for functional purposes, because it runs out of the contract and thus has a bad smell. You may use it for non-functional purposes though, for example, progress numbers when the cursor cannot yet provide real values, but a `requery()` is required to try again.

- **override fun getExtras(): Bundle**

  Clients may use this to get out-of-band data provided by your content provider. Must not return `null`; for empty sets return `Bundle.EMPTY` instead.

- **override fun respond(extras: Bundle?): Bundle**

  Clients may use this to communicate with the cursor in an out-of-band manner. For example, they may query the cursor state if the cursor does not yet provide actual values, but a `requery()` is needed. You should not normally use this for functional purposes, since this is the responsibility of the `ContentProvider` methods. Must not return `null`; for empty sets return `Bundle.EMPTY` instead. Other than suggested by the parameter signature, the `bundle` parameter should not be `null` by API contract, but surely it won't hurt to check that anyways.

Navigation

- **override fun getCount(): Int**

  Returns the numbers of rows in the cursor.

- **override fun moveToPosition(position: Int): Boolean**

  Move the cursor to an absolute position. `-1` is *before* the first row (you cannot retrieve columns there), `0` is the first row, `count-1` is the last row, and `count` is *past* the last row (you cannot retrieve columns there). Returns `true`, if the requested destination is reachable.

- **override fun moveToFirst(): Boolean**

  Move the cursor to the first row. Returns `true` if the first row exists.

- **override fun moveToLast(): Boolean**

  Move the cursor to the last row. Will return false if the cursor is empty.

- **override fun moveToPrevious(): Boolean**

  Move the cursor to the previous row. Returns `false` if the cursor is already before the first row.

- **override fun moveToNext(): Boolean**

  Move the cursor to the next row. Return false if the cursor is already past the last entry.

- **override fun move(offset: Int): Boolean**

  Move the cursor by a relative amount, forward (positive argument), or backward (negative argument), from the current position. Will be clamped to -1 or count. Returns true if the requested destination was reachable (implies false if clamped).

- **override fun getPosition(): Int**

  Returns the current position (zero based) of the cursor in the row set. Ranges from -1 to count, with the limits pointing to non-existing rows.

- **override fun isFirst(): Boolean**

  Returns whether the cursor is pointing to the first row.

- **override fun isLast(): Boolean**

  Returns whether the cursor is pointing to the last row.

- **override fun isBeforeFirst(): Boolean**

  Returns whether the cursor is pointing to the position before the first row (you cannot retrieve columns there).

- **override fun isAfterLast(): Boolean**

  Returns whether the cursor is pointing to the position after the last row (you cannot retrieve columns there).

Data Retrieval

- **override fun getColumnCount(): Int**

  Returns the number of columns.

- **override fun getColumnNames(): Array<String>**

  Returns the ordered string array with the names of all of the columns in the result set.

- **override fun getType(columnIndex: Int): Int**

The data type of the specified column (zero based). One of `FIELD_TYPE_NULL`, `FIELD_TYPE_INTEGER`, `FIELD_TYPE_FLOAT`, `FIELD_TYPE_STRING`, and `FIELD_TYPE_BLOB`.

- **override fun getColumnName(columnIndex: Int): String**

  Returns the column name at the given zero-based column index.

- **override fun getColumnIndex(columnName: String?): Int**

  Returns the zero-based index for the given column name or -1 if the column doesn't exist.

- **override fun getColumnIndexOrThrow(columnName: String?): Int**

  Returns the zero-based index for the given column name or throws an `IllegalArgumentException` if the column doesn't exist.

- **override fun isNull(columnIndex: Int): Boolean**

  The value of the requested column (zero based) is `null`.

- **override fun getInt(columnIndex: Int): Int**

  The value of the requested column (zero based) as an int.

- **override fun getShort(columnIndex: Int): Short**

  The value of the requested column (zero based) as a short int.

- **override fun getLong(columnIndex: Int): Long**

  The value of the requested column (zero based) as a long.

- **override fun getFloat(columnIndex: Int): Float**

  The value of the requested column (zero based) as a float.

- **override fun getDouble(columnIndex: Int): Double**

  The value of the requested column (zero based) as a double.

- **override fun getString(columnIndex: Int): String**

  The value of the requested column (zero based) as a string.

- **override fun copyStringToBuffer(columnIndex: Int, buffer: CharArrayBuffer?)**

Retrieves the requested column text (index zero based) and stores it in the buffer provided. Other than suggested by the argument signature, the buffer must not be null.

- **override fun getBlob(columnIndex: Int): ByteArray**

    Returns the value of the requested column (zero based) as a byte array.

What to do if for retrieving columns the types don't match and whether this method throws an exception when the column value is null are implementation defined. Usually you will add type converters where applicable.

Listeners

- **override fun setNotificationUri(cr: ContentResolver?, uri: Uri?**

    Clients use this to register to watch a content URI for changes. This can be the URI of a specific data row (e.g., "content:// my_provider_type/23") or a generic URI for a content type. The receiver of the changes is mediated by the `ContentResolver` parameter – the listener attached to this resolver will be notified.

- **override fun getNotificationUri(): Uri**

    Return the URI at which notifications of changes in this cursor's data will be delivered. Returns a URI that can be used with `ContentResolver.registerContentObserver()` to find out about changes to this cursor's data or `null` if no notification URI has been set.

- **override fun registerContentObserver(observer: ContentObserver?**

    Register an observer that is called when changes happen to the content backing this cursor.

- **override fun unregisterContentObserver(observer: ContentObserver?**

    Unregister an observer that has previously been registered with this cursor.

- **override fun registerDataSetObserver(observer: DataSetObserver?**

  Register an observer that is called when changes happen to the contents of this cursor's data set.

- **override fun unregisterDataSetObserver(observer: DataSetObserver?**

  Unregister an observer that has previously been registered.

Various

- **override fun getWantsAllOnMoveCalls(): Boolean**

  This sneaked into the interface from its base implementation `AbstractCursor`. The method `AbstractCursor.onMove()` will only be called across processes if this method returns true.

Features

Values for the `android:name` attribute of the `<uses-feature>` element inside the manifest. Adding such elements to `AndroidManifest.xml` expresses a requirement.

Hardware Features

Here we describe the hardware features supported by API level 26 or Android 8. For prior versions or the history of features, please consult the online documentation.

Audio Hardware Features

- **android.hardware.audio.low_latency**

  Use the low-latency audio pipeline for sound input or output, reducing lags and delays.

- **android.hardware.audio.output**

  The device must support some capability for output sound.

- **android.hardware.audio.pro**

  Expresses the requirement for the device to support high-end audio functionality.

- **android.hardware.microphone**

  The device must support some audio capture mechanism like a microphone.

Bluetooth Hardware Features

- **android.hardware.bluetooth**

  The device must support Bluetooth.

- **android.hardware.bluetooth_le**

  The device must support low-energy Bluetooth.

Camera Hardware Features

- **android.hardware.camera**

  The device must have a back-facing camera.

- **android.hardware.camera.any**

  The device must have any camera, including external cameras that can be connected to it.

- **android.hardware.camera.autofocus**

  The camera must have an auto-focus. Implies `android.hardware.camera` unless that one is declared with android:required="false".

- **android.hardware.camera.capability.manual_post_processing**

  The camera must have a MANUAL_POST_PROCESSING feature. Allow for the app to override the camera's auto white balance functionality. For that aim, in class `CaptureRequest` use `android.colorCorrection.transform`, `android.colorCorrection.gains`, and an `android.colorCorrection.mode` of TRANSFORM_MATRIX.

- **android.hardware.camera.capability.manual_sensor**

687

The camera must support the MANUAL_SENSOR feature, which implies auto-exposure locking. It must be possible to manually set a fixed exposure time and a fixed sensitivity.

- **android.hardware.camera.capability.raw**

The camera must be able to save raw image files, including the necessary DNG metadata.

- **android.hardware.camera.external**

The device provides a capability to communicate with externally connected cameras.

- **android.hardware.camera.flash**

The camera must have a flash. Implies `android.hardware.camera` unless that one is declared with android:required="false".

- **android.hardware.camera.front**

The device must have a front-facing camera. Implies `android.hardware.camera` unless that one is declared with android:required="false".

- **android.hardware.camera.level.full**

One of the cameras must have a FULL-level image-capturing support. This means burst-capture capabilities, per-frame control, and manual post-processing control.

Device UI Hardware Features

- **android.hardware.type.automotive**

The app expects to be shown inside a vehicle. This implies hard buttons, touch, rotary controllers, and mouse-like interfaces.

- **android.hardware.type.television**

Deprecated. Use `android.software.leanback` instead. The device is a television-like apparatus, the screen is big, and the user sits far away from it. That means a mouse or touch capabilities don't get used.

- **android.hardware.type.watch**

  The device is a wearable like a watch.

Fingerprint Hardware Features

- **android.hardware.fingerprint**

  The device has a fingerprint scanner.

Gamepad Hardware Features

- **android.hardware.gamepad**

  The device has a game controller or a gamepad input.

Infrared Hardware Features

- **android.hardware.consumerir**

  The device has an infrared sensor.

Location Hardware Features

- **android.hardware.location**

  The device provides for features for determining location – one of or a combination of GPS location, network location, and cell location.

- **android.hardware.location.gps**

  The device provides for features for determining precise location via GPS. Implies `android.hardware.location`, unless the latter got marked with android:required="false".

- **android.hardware.location.network**

  The device provides for features for determining coarse location via network. Implies `android.hardware.location`, unless the latter got marked with android:required="false".

NFC Hardware Features

- **android.hardware.nfc**

  The device has NFC capabilities.

- **android.hardware.nfc.hce**

  The device has NFC capabilities and uses card emulation hosted on the device.

OpenGL ES Hardware Features

- **android.hardware.opengles.aep**

  The device supports the OpenGL ES Android Extension Pack.

Sensor Hardware Features

- **android.hardware.sensor.accelerometer**

  The device has an accelerometer.

- **android.hardware.sensor.ambient_temperature**

  The device can detect the environmental temperature.

- **android.hardware.sensor.barometer**

  The device has a barometer.

- **android.hardware.sensor.compass**

  The device has a compass.

- **android.hardware.sensor.gyroscope**

  The device has a gyroscope to detect rotation and twist.

- **android.hardware.sensor.hifi_sensors**

  The device has high-fidelity (Hi-Fi) sensors.

- **android.hardware.sensor.heartrate**

  The device has a heart rate monitor.

- **android.hardware.sensor.heartrate.ecg**

The device has an electrocardiogram (ECG) heart rate sensor.

- **android.hardware.sensor.light**

  The device has a light sensor.

- **android.hardware.sensor.proximity**

  The device has a proximity sensor.

- **android.hardware.sensor.relative_humidity**

  The device has a relative humidity sensor.

- **android.hardware.sensor.stepcounter**

  The device has a step counter.

- **android.hardware.sensor.stepdetector**

  The device has a step detector.

Screen Hardware Features

- **android.hardware.screen.landscape**
- **android.hardware.screen.portrait**

  Specify that the device must be able to show the app in either landscape or portrait mode or both. If your app supports both orientations, then you don't need to declare either feature.

Telephony Hardware Features

- **android.hardware.telephony**

  The device can act as a phone.

- **android.hardware.telephony.cdma**

  The device provides a Code Division Multiple Access (CDMA) telephony radio system. Implies `android.hardware.telephony`, unless the latter is marked with android:required="false".

- **android.hardware.telephony.gsm**

The device provides a Global System for Mobile Communications (GSM) telephony radio system. Implies `android.hardware.telephony`, unless the latter is marked with android:required="false".

Touchscreen Hardware Features

- **android.hardware.faketouch**

  The device provides either real or fake touch features. Apps require that by default. The app uses basic touch interaction events, such as tapping and dragging, or their simulated counterpart.

- **android.hardware.faketouch.multitouch.distinct**

  The device provides for the capability to distinguish between two or more fingers. A device that provides a two-finger touch trackpad for cursor movement can support this feature.

- **android.hardware.faketouch.multitouch.jazzhand**

  The app tracks five or more distinct "fingers" on a fake touch interface. A device that provides a five-finger touch trackpad for cursor movement can support this feature.

- **android.hardware.touchscreen**

  The device must support more than basic touch events. If your app instead wants to allow for simulated touch events via fake touch, you must explicitly declare this element and add android:required="false"; otherwise, this feature is required by default.

- **android.hardware.touchscreen.multitouch**

  This is a superset of the android.hardware.touchscreen feature. The device must support basic two-point multitouch capabilities, but it needs not track touches independently.

- **android.hardware.touchscreen.multitouch.distinct**

  This is a superset of the android.hardware.touchscreen.multitouch. The device must allow to track multitouch gesture points independently.

- **android.hardware.touchscreen.multitouch.jazzhand**

  The device must allow for using five or more multitouch points independently.

USB Hardware Features

- **android.hardware.usb.accessory**

  The device must be able to connect to USB hosts.

- **android.hardware.usb.host**

  The device must be able to serve as a USB host.

Vulkan Hardware Features

- **android.hardware.vulkan.compute**

  The app requires the hardware-accelerated Vulkan implementation.

- **android.hardware.vulkan.level**

  Optional hardware features required.

- **android.hardware.vulkan.version**

  The minimum version of the Vulkan API support for the app.

Wi-Fi Hardware Features

- **android.hardware.wifi**

  The device must use 802.11 networking (Wi-Fi) features.

- **android.hardware.wifi.direct**

  The device must allow for Wi-Fi direct networking.

Software Features

The following paragraphs represent software features your app may declare to be required.

Communication Software Features

- **android.software.sip**

  The device must provide Session Initiation Protocol (SIP) services.

- **android.software.sip.voip**

  The device must support SIP-based Voice Over Internet Protocol (VoIP) services.

- **android.software.webview**

  The app wants to display content from the Internet.

Custom Input Software Features

- **android.software.input_methods**

  The app wants to define a new input method, as declared in an InputMethodService.

Device Management Software Features

- **android.software.backup**

  The app wants to use logic to handle backup and restore operations.

- **android.software.device_admin**

  The app wants to enforce a device policy in an administration workflow.

- **android.software.managed_users**

  The app supports secondary users and managed profiles.

- **android.software.securely_removes_users**

  The app wants to be able to permanently remove users and their associated data.

- **android.software.verified_boot**

  The app wants to handle results from the device's verified boot feature. This detects whether the device's configuration changes during a restart operation.

Media Software Features

- **android.software.midi**

  The app wants to address a MIDI interface to talk to connected instruments.

- **android.software.print**

  The app wants to use a printer.

- **android.software.leanback**

  The app needs a large screen, as, for example, a TV device.

- **android.software.live_tv**

  The app wants to stream live television programs.

Screen Interface Software Features

- **android.software.app_widgets**

  The app uses app widgets.

- **android.software.home_screen**

  The app provides a replacement to the device's home screen.

- **android.software.live_wallpaper**

  The app uses or provides animated wallpapers.

Permissions

Permissions get listed in Table A-13.

Table A-13. *Permissions*

Name	Description
ACCEPT_HANDOVER	Allows to continue a call that was started in another app.
ACCESS_BACKGROUND_LOCATION	Allows background access of the location.
ACCESS_BLOBS_ACROSS_USERS	Allows accessing data blobs across users.
ACCESS_CHECKIN_PROPERTIES	Allows read/write access to the "properties" table in the checkin database, to change values that get uploaded.
ACCESS_COARSE_LOCATION	Allows an app to access approximate location.
ACCESS_FINE_LOCATION	Allows an app to access precise location.
ACCESS_LOCATION_EXTRA_COMMANDS	Allows an application to access extra location provider commands.
ACCESS_MEDIA_LOCATION	Allows accessing location in a user's shared collection.
ACCESS_NETWORK_STATE	Allows applications to access information about networks.
ACCESS_NOTIFICATION_POLICY	Marker permission for applications that wish to access notification policy.
ACCESS_WIFI_STATE	Allows applications to access information about Wi-Fi networks.
ACCOUNT_MANAGER	Allows applications to call into AccountAuthenticators.
ACTIVITY_RECOGNITION	Allows recognizing physical activity.
ADD_VOICEMAIL	Allows an application to add voicemails into the system.
ANSWER_PHONE_CALLS	Allows the app to answer an incoming phone call.
BATTERY_STATS	Allows an application to collect battery statistics.
BIND_ACCESSIBILITY_SERVICE	Must be required by an AccessibilityService, to ensure that only the system can bind to it.

(continued)

Table A-13. (*continued*)

Name	Description
BIND_APPWIDGET	Allows an application to tell the AppWidget service which application can access AppWidget's data.
BIND_AUTOFILL_SERVICE	Must be required by an AutofillService, to ensure that only the system can bind to it.
BIND_CALL_REDIRECTION_SERVICE	Required for a `CallRedirectionService` to work. Protection level: signature|privileged.
BIND_CARRIER_MESSAGING_CLIENT_ SERVICE	Required for a `CarrierMessagingClientService`. Protection level: signature.
BIND_CARRIER_MESSAGING_SERVICE	This constant was deprecated in API level 23. Use BIND_CARRIER_SERVICES instead.
BIND_CARRIER_SERVICES	The system process that is allowed to bind to services in carrier apps will have this permission.
BIND_CHOOSER_TARGET_SERVICE	Must be required by a ChooserTargetService, to ensure that only the system can bind to it. Deprecated in API level 30.
BIND_COMPANION_DEVICE_SERVICE	Required for a `CompanionDeviceService` to work.
BIND_CONDITION_PROVIDER_SERVICE	Must be required by a ConditionProviderService, to ensure that only the system can bind to it.
BIND_CONTROLS	Required for `ControlsProviderService`.
BIND_DEVICE_ADMIN	Must be required by the device administration receiver, to ensure that only the system can interact with it.
BIND_DREAM_SERVICE	Must be required by a DreamService, to ensure that only the system can bind to it.
BIND_INCALL_SERVICE	Must be required by an InCallService, to ensure that only the system can bind to it.
BIND_INPUT_METHOD	Must be required by an InputMethodService, to ensure that only the system can bind to it.

(*continued*)

Table A-13. (*continued*)

Name	Description
BIND_MIDI_DEVICE_SERVICE	Must be required by a MidiDeviceService, to ensure that only the system can bind to it.
BIND_NFC_SERVICE	Must be required by a HostApduService or OffHostApduService, to ensure that only the system can bind to it.
BIND_NOTIFICATION_LISTENER_SERVICE	Must be required by a NotificationListenerService, to ensure that only the system can bind to it.
BIND_PRINT_SERVICE	Must be required by a PrintService, to ensure that only the system can bind to it.
BIND_QUICK_ACCESS_WALLET_SERVICE	Required for `QuickAccessWalletService` to work.
BIND_QUICK_SETTINGS_TILE	Allows an application to bind to third-party quick settings tiles.
BIND_REMOTEVIEWS	Must be required by a RemoteViewsService, to ensure that only the system can bind to it.
BIND_SCREENING_SERVICE	Must be required by a CallScreeningService, to ensure that only the system can bind to it.
BIND_TELECOM_CONNECTION_SERVICE	Must be required by a ConnectionService, to ensure that only the system can bind to it.
BIND_TEXT_SERVICE	Required by a TextService.
BIND_TV_INPUT	Must be required by a TvInputService, to ensure that only the system can bind to it.
BIND_TV_INTERACTIVE_APP	Required for a `TvInteractiveAppService`.
BIND_VISUAL_VOICEMAIL_SERVICE	Must be required by a link VisualVoicemailService, to ensure that only the system can bind to it.
BIND_VOICE_INTERACTION	Must be required by a VoiceInteractionService, to ensure that only the system can bind to it.

(*continued*)

Table A-13. (*continued*)

Name	Description
BIND_VPN_SERVICE	Must be required by a VpnService, to ensure that only the system can bind to it.
BIND_VR_LISTENER_SERVICE	Must be required by a VrListenerService, to ensure that only the system can bind to it.
BIND_WALLPAPER	Must be required by a WallpaperService, to ensure that only the system can bind to it.
BLUETOOTH	Allows applications to connect to paired Bluetooth devices.
BLUETOOTH_ADMIN	Allows applications to discover and pair Bluetooth devices.
BLUETOOTH_ADVERTISE	Required for advertising to nearby Bluetooth devices.
BLUETOOTH_CONNECT	Required for connecting to paired Bluetooth devices.
BLUETOOTH_PRIVILEGED	Allows applications to pair Bluetooth devices without user interaction and to allow or disallow phonebook access or message access.
BLUETOOTH_SCAN	Needed for nearby Bluetooth device discovery.
BODY_SENSORS	Required to access data from sensors that the user uses to measure what is happening inside their body, such as heart beat rate.
BODY_SENSORS_BACKGROUND	Required to access data, in background mode, from sensors that the user uses to measure what is happening inside their body, such as heart beat rate.
BROADCAST_PACKAGE_REMOVED	Allows an application to broadcast a notification that an application package has been removed.
BROADCAST_SMS	Allows an application to broadcast an SMS receipt notification.
BROADCAST_STICKY	Allows an application to broadcast sticky Intents.

(*continued*)

Table A-13. (*continued*)

Name	Description
BROADCAST_WAP_PUSH	Allows an application to broadcast a WAP Push receipt notification.
CALL_COMPANION_APP	Required to use the InCallService API.
CALL_PHONE	Allows an application to initiate a phone call without going through the dialer user interface for the user to confirm the call.
CALL_PRIVILEGED	Allows an application to call any phone number, including emergency numbers, without going through the dialer user interface for the user to confirm the call being placed.
CAMERA	Required to be able to access the camera device.
CAPTURE_AUDIO_OUTPUT	Allows an application to capture audio output.
CHANGE_COMPONENT_ENABLED_STATE	Allows an application to change whether an application component (other than its own) is enabled or not.
CHANGE_CONFIGURATION	Allows an application to modify the current configuration, such as locale.
CHANGE_NETWORK_STATE	Allows applications to change network connectivity state.
CHANGE_WIFI_MULTICAST_STATE	Allows applications to enter Wi-Fi multicast mode.
CHANGE_WIFI_STATE	Allows applications to change Wi-Fi connectivity state.
CLEAR_APP_CACHE	Allows an application to clear the caches of all installed applications on the device.
CONTROL_LOCATION_UPDATES	Allows enabling/disabling location update notifications from the radio.
DELETE_CACHE_FILES	Allows an application to delete cache files.
DELETE_PACKAGES	Allows an application to delete packages.

(*continued*)

Table A-13. (*continued*)

Name	Description
DELIVER_COMPANION_MESSAGES	Required for the delivery of companion messages to the system.
DIAGNOSTIC	Allows applications to RW to diagnostic resources.
DISABLE_KEYGUARD	Allows applications to disable the keyguard if it is not secure.
DUMP	Allows an application to retrieve state dump information from system services.
EXPAND_STATUS_BAR	Allows an application to expand or collapse the status bar.
FACTORY_TEST	Run as a manufacturer test application, running as the root user.
FOREGROUND_SERVICE	Required for using `Service.startForeground()`
GET_ACCOUNTS	Allows access to the list of accounts in the Accounts Service.
GET_ACCOUNTS_PRIVILEGED	Allows access to the list of accounts in the Accounts Service.
GET_PACKAGE_SIZE	Allows an application to find out the space used by any package.
GET_TASKS	This constant was deprecated in API level 21. No longer enforced.
GLOBAL_SEARCH	This permission can be used on content providers to allow the global search system to access their data.
HIDE_OVERLAY_WINDOWS	Enables an app to prevent other apps from drawing overlay windows on top of it.
HIGH_SAMPLING_RATE_SENSORS	Use this if you want to allow your app to fetch sensor data at a rate greater than 200 Hz.

(*continued*)

Table A-13. (*continued*)

Name	Description
INSTALL_LOCATION_PROVIDER	Allows an application to install a location provider into the Location Manager.
INSTALL_PACKAGES	Allows an application to install packages.
INSTALL_SHORTCUT	Allows an application to install a shortcut in Launcher.
INSTANT_APP_FOREGROUND_SERVICE	Allows an instant app to create foreground services.
INTERACT_ACROSS_PROFILES	Required to enable interaction across profiles.
INTERNET	Allows applications to open network sockets.
KILL_BACKGROUND_PROCESSES	Allows an application to call killBackgroundProcesses (String).
LAUNCH_MULTI_PANE_SETTINGS_DEEP_LINK	Needed for embedding deep links (settings app).
LOADER_USAGE_STATS	Used for reading a package's access logs (via data loader).
LOCATION_HARDWARE	Allows an application to use location features in hardware, such as the geofencing API.
MANAGE_DOCUMENTS	Allows an application to manage access to documents, usually as part of a document picker.
MANAGE_EXTERNAL_STORAGE	Required for extended access to an app's external storage.
MANAGE_MEDIA	Required for write access to an app's media files.
MANAGE_ONGOING_CALLS	Allows for managing ongoing calls.
MANAGE_OWN_CALLS	Allows a calling application that manages its own calls through the self-managed ConnectionService APIs.
MANAGE_WIFI_INTERFACES	Can only be sent by the system. Used for switching between WI-FI interfaces.

(*continued*)

Table A-13. (*continued*)

Name	Description
MANAGE_WIFI_NETWORK_SELECTION	Can only be sent by the system. Used for switching between WI-FI interfaces (access to privileged WI-FI API calls).
MASTER_CLEAR	Not for use by third-party applications.
MEDIA_CONTENT_CONTROL	Allows an application to know what content is playing and control its playback.
MODIFY_AUDIO_SETTINGS	Allows an application to modify global audio settings.
MODIFY_PHONE_STATE	Allows modification of the telephony state – power on, MMI, etc.
MOUNT_FORMAT_FILESYSTEMS	Allows formatting file systems for removable storage.
MOUNT_UNMOUNT_FILESYSTEMS	Allows mounting and unmounting file systems for removable storage.
NEARBY_WIFI_DEVICES	Required for advertising and connecting to WI-FI interfaces.
NFC	Allows applications to perform I/O operations over NFC.
NFC_PREFERRED_PAYMENT_INFO	Required to receive preferred payment service information.
NFC_TRANSACTION_EVENT	Required to receive NFC transaction events.
OVERRID_WIFI_CONFIG	Used by an app if you want to modify WI-FI configurations (all apps).
PACKAGE_USAGE_STATS	Allows an application to collect component usage statistics.
	Declaring the permission implies intention to use the API, and the user of the device can grant permission through the settings application.

(*continued*)

Table A-13. (*continued*)

Name	Description
PERSISTENT_ACTIVITY	This constant was deprecated in API level 9. This functionality will be removed in the future; please do not use. Allows an application to make its activities persistent.
POST_NOTIFICATIONS	Required for posting notifications.
PROCESS_OUTGOING_CALLS	Deprecated for API level 29 (use `CallRedirectionService`). Allows an application to see the number being dialed during an outgoing call with the option to redirect or abort the call.
QUERY_ALL_PACKAGES	Required to query any normal app on a device (regardless of the manifest declarations).
READ_ASSISTANT_APP_SEARCH_DATA	Used if, in ASSISTANT role, an AppSearch access to global data is needed.
READ_BASIC_PHONE_STATE	Required for read-only access to phone state.
READ_CALENDAR	Allows an application to read the user's calendar data.
READ_CALL_LOG	Allows an application to read the user's call log.
READ_CONTACTS	Allows an application to read the user's contacts data.
READ_EXTERNAL_STORAGE	Allows an application to read from external storage.
READ_HOME_APP_SEARCH_DATA	Used if, in HOME role, an AppSearch access to global data is needed.
READ_LOGS	Allows an application to read the low-level system log files.
READ_MEDIA_AUDIO	Required to read audio from external storage.
READ_MEDIA_IMAGES	Required to read images from external storage.
READ_MEDIA_VIDEO	Required to read videos from external storage.
READ_NEARBY_STREAMING_POLICY	Required to read nearby streaming policy (controls streaming of notifications and apps to nearby devices).

(*continued*)

Table A-13. (*continued*)

Name	Description
READ_PHONE_NUMBERS	Allows read access to the device's phone number(s).
READ_PHONE_STATE	Allows read-only access to phone state, including the phone number of the device, current cellular network information, the status of any ongoing calls, and a list of any PhoneAccounts registered on the device.
READ_PRECISE_PHONE_STATE	Needed for reading detailed phone state.
READ_SMS	Allows an application to read SMS messages.
READ_SYNC_SETTINGS	Allows applications to read the sync settings.
READ_SYNC_STATS	Allows applications to read the sync stats.
READ_VOICEMAIL	Allows an application to read voicemails in the system.
REBOOT	Required to be able to reboot the device.
RECEIVE_BOOT_COMPLETED	Allows an application to receive the ACTION_BOOT_ COMPLETED that is broadcast after the system finishes booting.
RECEIVE_MMS	Allows an application to monitor incoming MMS messages.
RECEIVE_SMS	Allows an application to receive SMS messages.
RECEIVE_WAP_PUSH	Allows an application to receive WAP Push messages.
RECORD_AUDIO	Allows an application to record audio.
REORDER_TASKS	Allows an application to change the Z-order of tasks.
REQUEST_COMPANION_PROFILE_APP_ STREAMING	Can only be sent by the system. Allows to request for associating virtual displays for streaming.
REQUEST_COMPANION_PROFILE_ AUTOMOTIVE_PROJECTION	Can only be sent by the system. Allows to request for associating head units with automotive projection.
REQUEST_COMPANION_PROFILE_ COMPUTER	Can only be sent by the system. Allows to request for associating with a computer.

(*continued*)

Table A-13. (*continued*)

Name	Description
REQUEST_COMPANION_PROFILE_WATCH	Can only be sent by the system. Allows to request for associating with a device as a watch.
REQUEST_COMPANION_RUN_IN_ BACKGROUND	Allows a companion app to run in the background.
REQUEST_COMPANION_SELF_MANAGED	Allows to create a self-managed association.
REQUEST_COMPANION_START_ FOREGROUND_SERVICES_FROM_ BACKGROUND	Needed in order for a companion app to start foreground services from the background.
REQUEST_COMPANION_USE_DATA_IN_ BACKGROUND	Allows a companion app to use data in the background.
REQUEST_DELETE_PACKAGES	Allows an application to request deleting packages.
REQUEST_IGNORE_BATTERY_ OPTIMIZATIONS	Permission an application must hold in order to use ACTION_REQUEST_IGNORE_BATTERY_OPTIMIZATIONS.
REQUEST_INSTALL_PACKAGES	Allows an application to request installing packages.
REQUEST_OBSERVE_COMPANION_ DEVICE_PRESENCE	Needed if you want to subscribe to notifications referring to status changes of an associated companion device.
REQUEST_PASSWORD_COMPLEXITY	Allows an application to request control over the screen lock complexity level.
SCHEDULE_EXACT_ALARM	Allows applications to use exact alarm APIs.
SEND_RESPOND_VIA_MESSAGE	Allows an application (phone) to send a request to other applications to handle the respond-via-message action during incoming calls.
SEND_SMS	Allows an application to send SMS messages.
SET_ALARM	Allows an application to broadcast an Intent to set an alarm for the user.

(*continued*)

Table A-13. (*continued*)

Name	Description
SET_ALWAYS_FINISH	Allows an application to control whether activities are immediately finished when put in the background.
SET_ANIMATION_SCALE	Modify the global animation scaling factor.
SET_DEBUG_APP	Configure an application for debugging.
SET_PROCESS_LIMIT	Allows an application to set the maximum number of (not needed) application processes that can be running.
SET_TIME	Allows applications to set the system time.
SET_TIME_ZONE	Allows applications to set the system time zone.
SET_WALLPAPER	Allows applications to set the wallpaper.
SET_WALLPAPER_HINTS	Allows applications to set the wallpaper hints.
SIGNAL_PERSISTENT_PROCESSES	Allow an application to request that a signal be sent to all persistent processes.
START_FOREGROUND_SERVICES_FROM_ BACKGROUND	Can only be sent by the system. Allows to start foreground services from the background.
START_VIEW_APP_FEATURES	Allows to start the screen with a list of app features.
START_VIEW_PERMISSION_USAGE	Allows to start the screen with the permission usage of an app.
STATUS_BAR	Allows an application to open, close, or disable the status bar and its icons.
SUBSCRIBE_TO_KEYGUARD_LOCKED_ STATE	Allows to subscribe to keyguard locked (showing) state.
SYSTEM_ALERT_WINDOW	Allows an app to create windows using the type TYPE_ APPLICATION_OVERLAY, shown on top of all other apps.
TRANSMIT_IR	Allows using the device's IR transmitter, if available.
UPDATE_DEVICE_STATS	Allows an application to update device statistics.
UPDATE_PACKAGES_WITHOUT_USER_ ACTION	Indicate that user approval is not needed for app updates.

(*continued*)

Table A-13. (*continued*)

Name	Description
USE_BIOMETRIC	Allows to use biometry for authentication.
USE_EXACT_ALARM	Required to use exact alarms.
USE_FULL_SCREEN_INTENT	Needed for notification full-screen Intents.
USE_ICC_AUTH_WITH_DEVICE_IDENTIFIER	Allows to read device identifiers and use ICC-based authentication.
USE_SIP	Allows an application to use SIP service.
UWB_RANGING	Needed for ranging to devices using ultra-wideband.
VIBRATE	Allows access to the vibrator.
WAKE_LOCK	Allows using PowerManager WakeLocks to keep processor from sleeping or screen from dimming.
WRITE_APN_SETTINGS	Allows applications to write the APN settings.
WRITE_CALENDAR	Allows an application to write the user's calendar data.
WRITE_CALL_LOG	Allows an application to write (but not read) the user's call log data.
WRITE_CONTACTS	Allows an application to write the user's contacts data.
WRITE_EXTERNAL_STORAGE	Allows an application to write to external storage.
WRITE_GSERVICES	Allows an application to modify the Google service map.
WRITE_SECURE_SETTINGS	Allows an application to read or write the secure system settings.
WRITE_SETTINGS	Allows an application to read or write the system settings.
WRITE_SYNC_SETTINGS	Allows applications to write the sync settings.
WRITE_VOICEMAIL	Allows an application to modify and remove existing voicemails in the system.

The System Intent Filters

The following (Tables A-14 through A-49) are the system intent filters. You can use them to launch activities and services of system apps – see Chapter 3, section "Intent Filters."

Unless otherwise noted, for all actions prepend "android.intent.action." and for all categories prepend "android.intent.category.".

Note These filters have been extracted by a script and with the help of "Apktool," which you can find on GitHub.

Table A-14. *"Browser2" Activity Intent Filters*

Action	Category	Data	Act
MAIN	LAUNCHER	-	1
VIEW	DEFAULT BROWSABLE	scheme:http scheme:https	(1)
VIEW	DEFAULT BROWSABLE	scheme:http scheme:https mimeType:text/html mimeType:text/plain mimeType:application/ xhtml+xml mimeType:application/ vnd.wap.xhtml+xml	(1)

(1) WebViewBrowserActivity

Table A-15. *"CalendarGooglePrebuilt" Activity Intent Filters*

Action	Category	Data	Act
MAIN	LAUNCHER	-	(1)
EDIT INSERT VIEW	DEFAULT	mimeType: vnd.android.cursor.item/event	(1)
EDIT INSERT	DEFAULT	mimeType: vnd.android.cursor.dir/event	(1)
VIEW	DEFAULT BROWSABLE	scheme:http scheme:https host:www.google.com pathPrefix:/calendar/event pathPattern: /calendar/hosted/.*/event	(1)
VIEW	DEFAULT BROWSABLE	scheme:http scheme:https host:calendar.google.com pathPrefix:/calendar/event pathPattern: /calendar/hosted/.*/event	(1)
EDIT VIEW	DEFAULT	host:calendar scheme:settings	(2)
SEARCH			(3)
VIEW	DEFAULT	scheme:http scheme:https scheme:content scheme:file scheme: host:* pathPattern:.*\.ics	(4)
VIEW	DEFAULT	scheme:http scheme:https scheme:content scheme:file scheme: host:* mimeType:text/calendar	(4)
VIEW	DEFAULT	scheme:http scheme:https scheme:content scheme:file scheme: host:* mimeType:application/ics	(4)

(continued)

Table A-15. (*continued*)

Action	Category	Data	Act
VIEW	DEFAULT	scheme:http scheme:https scheme:content scheme:file scheme: host:* mimeType: application/octet-stream pathPattern:.*\. ics	
MANAGE_ NETWORK_USAGE	DEFAULT		(5)
MAIN	DEFAULT NOTIFICATION_ PREFERENCES		(5)
MAIN	DEFAULT LAUNCHER APP_CALENDAR		(6)
VIEW	DEFAULT	mimeType:time/epoch host:com.android. calendar scheme:content	(6)
(7).EVENT_EDIT(7). EVENT_INSERT(7). EVENT_VIEW			(6)
(7).FIND_TIME	DEFAULT		(6)

(1) LaunchInfoActivity

(2) GoogleCalendarSettingsActivity

(3) SearchActivity

(4) ICalLauncher

(5) CalendarPublicPreferenceActvity

(6) AllInOneActivity

(7) com.google.android.calendar

Table A-16. *"Camera2" Activity Intent Filters*

Action	Category	Data	Act
(1).STILL_IMAGE_CAMERA	DEFAULT		(2)
MAIN	DEFAULT		(2)
(1).IMAGE_CAPTURE]	DEFAULT		(3)
(1).STILL_IMAGE_CAMERA_SECURE	DEFAULT		(4)
(1).IMAGE_CAPTURE_SECURE	DEFAULT		(4)
MAIN	DEFAULT LAUNCHER		(5)
(1).VIDEO_CAMERA	DEFAULT		(6)
(1).VIDEO_CAPTURE	DEFAULT		(6)

(1) android.media.action
(2) CameraActivity
(3) CaptureActivity
(4) SecureCameraActivity
(5) CameraLauncher
(6) VideoCamera

Table A-17. *"CaptivePortalLogin" Activity Intent Filters*

Action	Category	Data	Act
(1).CAPTIVE_PORTAL	DEFAULT		(2)

(1) android.net.conn
(2) CaptivePortalLoginActivity

Table A-18. *"CertInstaller" Activity Intent Filters*

Action	Category	Data	Act
(1).INSTALL	DEFAULT		(2)
VIEW	DEFAULT	mimeType: application/x-x509-ca-cert mimeType: application/x-x509-user-cert mimeType: application/x-x509-server-cert mimeType: application/x-pkcs12 mimeType: application/application/x-pem-file mimeType: application/pkix-cert mimeType: application/x-wifi-config	(2)
(1).INSTALL_AS_USER	DEFAULT		(3)

(1) android.credentials

(2) CertInstallerMain

(3) InstallCertAsUser

Table A-19. *"Chrome" Activity Intent Filters*

Action	Category	Data	Act
(8)	(9).DAYDREAM(9). CARDBOARD		(1)
(10).ADDBOOKMARK	DEFAULT		(2)
(11).ACTION_START_ WEBAPP	DEFAULT		(3)
SEND	DEFAULT	mimeType:text/plain	(4)
SEND	DEFAULT	mimeType:text/plain	(5)
(12).WEBVIEW_ LICENSE	DEFAULT		(6)

(continued)

Table A-16. (_continued_)

Action	Category	Data	Act
MAIN	DEFAULT LAUNCHER BROWSABLE APP_ BROWSER NOTIFICATION_ PREFERENCES		(7)
VIEW	DEFAULT BROWSABLE	scheme:googlechrome scheme:http scheme:https scheme:about scheme:javascript	(7)
VIEW	DEFAULT BROWSABLE	scheme:googlechrome scheme:http scheme:https scheme:about scheme:content scheme:javascript mimeType:text/html mimeType:text/ plain mimeType: application/xhtml+xml	(7)
VIEW	DEFAULT	scheme:file scheme:content mimeType: multipart/related	(7)
VIEW	DEFAULT BROWSABLE	scheme:file scheme:content host:* pathPattern:/.*\.mhtml pathPattern:/.*\.mht	(7)
VIEW	DEFAULT BROWSABLE	scheme:file scheme:content host:* mimeType:*/* pathPattern:/.*\.mhtml pathPattern:/.*\.mht	(7)
MEDIA_SEARCH	DEFAULT		(7)
(13).VOICE_SEARCH_ RESULTS	DEFAULT		(7)
(14).NDEF_ DISCOVERED	DEFAULT	scheme:httpscheme:https	(7)
SEARCH			(7)
(15).HOVER			(7)

(1) ChromeTabbedActivity

(2) BookmarkAddActivity

(3) WebappLauncherActivity

(4) PrintShareActivity

(5) PhysicalWebShareActivity

(6) LicenseActivity

(7) Main

(8) org.chromium.chrome.browser.dummy.action

(9) com.google.intent.category

(10) com.android.chrome

(11) com.google.android.apps.chrome.webapps.WebappManager

(12) android.settings

(13) android.speech.action

(14) android.nfc.action

(15) com.sec.android.airview

Table A-20. *"CompanionDeviceManager" Activity Intent Filters*

Action	Category	Data	Act
(1).START_DISCOVERY	DEFAULT		(2)

(1) android.companiondevice

(2) DeviceChooserActivity

Table A-21. *"CtsShimPrebuilt" Activity Intent Filters*

Action	Category	Data	Act
SEARCH	INFO		(1)
VIEW	BROWSABLE		(1)
SEND			(1)
SEND_MULTIPLE			(1)
SENDTO			(1)

(1) InstallPriority

Table A-22. *"CustomLocale (only virtual device!)" Activity Intent Filters*

Action	Category	Data	Act
MAIN	LAUNCHER		(1)

(1) CustomLocaleActivity

Table A-23. *"Development (only virtual device!)" Activity Intent Filters*

Action	Category	Data	Act
MAIN	LAUNCHER		Development
MAIN	TEST		PackageBrowser
MAIN	TEST		PointerLocation
MAIN	TEST		AccountsTester
MAIN	TEST		SyncAdapterDriver
MAIN	TEST		Connectivity
MAIN	TEST		InstrumentationList
MAIN	TEST		MediaScannerActivity
MAIN	TEST		RunningProcesses
VIEW	DEFAULT		ProcessInfo
VIEW	DEFAULT		AppHwPref
(1).VIEW_PERMISSION	DEFAULT		PermissionDetails
MAIN	TEST		BadBehaviorActivity
MAIN	TEST		CacheAbuser
MAIN	TEST		ConfigurationViewer

(1) com.android.development

Table A-24. *"DownloadProviderUi" Activity Intent Filters*

Action	Category	Data	Act
(1).MANAGE_ DOCUMENT	DEFAULT	scheme:contentmim eType:*/*host:com. android.providers. downloads.documents	(2)

(1) android.provider.action

(2) TrampolineActivity

Table A-25. *"Drive" Activity Intent Filters*

Action	Category	Data	Act
MAIN(30).SEARCH_ ACTION(31).SEARCH_ SHORTCUT_ACTION	LAUNCHER DEFAULT		(1)
VIEW			(2)
SEARCH			(2)
SENDSEND_MULTIPLE	DEFAULT	mimeType:*/*	(3)
SEND	DEFAULT	scheme:file	(3)
(32).WELCOME	DEFAULT		(4)
VIEW			(5)
BUG_REPORT			(6)
VIEW	DEFAULT		(7)
MAIN	PREFERENCE		(8)
(32).DRIVE_STORAGE	DEFAULT		(9)
VIEW			(10)

(continued)

Table A-25. (*continued*)

Action	Category	Data	Act
PICK	DEFAULT		(11)
SEND	DEFAULT	mimeType:text/plain	(12)
MAIN	NOTIFICATION_ PREFERENCES		(13)
(33).NOTIFICATION_ SETTINGS	DEFAULT		(14)
(33).NOTIFICATION_ HOME	DEFAULT		(15)
CREATE_SHORTCUT	DEFAULT		(16)
CREATE_SHORTCUT	DEFAULT		(17)
(34).APPWIDGET_ CONFIGURE			(18)
QUICK_VIEW	DEFAULT	scheme:projector-id	(19)
QUICK_VIEW	DEFAULT		(19)
QUICK_VIEW	DEFAULT	scheme:filescheme:contentschem e:http	(19)
QUICK_VIEW	DEFAULT	scheme:filescheme:contentschem e:httpmimeType:*/*	(19)
VIEW	DEFAULT BROWSABLE	scheme:filescheme:contentschem e:httpmimeType:application/pdf	(20)
VIEW	DEFAULT BROWSABLE	scheme:httppathPattern:.*\\. pdfhost:*	(20)
VIEW	DEFAULT	scheme:filepathPattern:.*\\.pdf	(20)
VIEW	DEFAULT	(43)	(21)

(*continued*)

Table A-25. (*continued*)

Action	Category	Data	Act
VIEW	DEFAULT	scheme:contentmimeType:(37). documenthost:(35)	(21)
VIEW	DEFAULT	scheme:contentmimeType:(37). presentationhost:(35)	(21)
VIEW	DEFAULT	scheme:contentmimeType:(37). spreadsheethost:(35)	(21)
VIEW			(22)
SEARCH			(22)
GET_CONTENT	DEFAULT OPENABLE	mimeType:*/*	(23)
PICK	DEFAULT		(24)
VIEW			(25)
VIEW	DEFAULT BROWSABLE	(40)	(26)
VIEW	DEFAULT BROWSABLE	(41)	(27)
VIEW	DEFAULT BROWSABLE	(42)	(27)
VIEW	DEFAULT BROWSABLE	(39)	(28)
VIEW(32).REQUEST_ ACCESS	DEFAULT BROWSABLE	s:http+ h:drive.google.com s:https+ h:drive.google.com s:http+ h:icing.drive.google.com s:https+ h:icing.drive.google.com	(29)
VIEW(32).REQUEST_ ACCESS	DEFAULT BROWSABLE	(38)	(29)

Inside "data": s = scheme, m = mimeType, h = host, pp = pathPattern

(1) NewMainProxyActivity

(2) DocumentOpenerActivity

(3) UploadMenuActivity

(4) WelcomeActivity

(5) DocumentOpenerActivityDelegate

(6) ErrorNotificationActivity

(7) LegacyPrintActivity

(8) DocsPreferencesActivity

(9) PaymentsActivity

(10) TestFragmentActivity

(11) PickEntryActivity

(12) SendTextToClipboardActivity

(13) NotificationPreferencesActivity

(14) ExportedNotificationPreferencesActivity

(15) ExportedNotificationHomeActivity

(16) CreateShortcutActivity

(17) CreateDocumentScanShortcutActivity

(18) WidgetConfigureActivity

(19) ProjectorActivity

(20) PdfViewerActivity

(21) OpenSafUrlActivity

(22) GlobalSearch

(23) GetContentActivity

(24) PickActivity

(25) DocumentOpenerActivityProxy

(26) PunchOpenUrlActivityAlias

(27) TrixOpenUrlActivityAlias

(28) KixOpenUrlActivityAlias

(29) DriveOpenUrlActivityAlias

(30) com.google.android.gms.actions

(31) com.google.android.apps.docs.actions

(32) com.google.android.apps.docs

(33) com.google.android.apps.docs.notification

(34) android.appwidget.action

(35) com.google.android.apps.docs.storage

(36) docs.google.com

(37) application/vnd.google-apps

(38) One of: pathPatten + scheme + host =

"" + http + docs.google.com

a/.*/ + http + docs.google.com

m + http + docs.google.com

a/.*/m + http + docs.google.com

folder.* + http + docs.google.com

a/.*/folder.* + http + docs.google.com

file/.* + http + docs.google.com

a/.*/file/.* + http + docs.google.com

open + http + docs.google.com

a/.*/open + http + docs.google.com

leaf + http + docs.google.com

a/.*/leaf + http + docs.google.com

uc + http + docs.google.com

a/.*/uc + http + docs.google.com

viewer + http + docs.google.com

a/.*/viewer + http + docs.google.com

"" + https + docs.google.com

a/.*/ + https + docs.google.com

m + https + docs.google.com

a/.*/m + https + docs.google.com

folder.* + https + docs.google.com

a/.*/folder.* + https + docs.google.com

file/.* + https + docs.google.com

a/.*/file/.* + https + docs.google.com

open + https + docs.google.com

a/.*/open + https + docs.google.com

leaf + https + docs.google.com

a/.*/leaf + https + docs.google.com

uc + https + docs.google.com

a/.*/uc + https + docs.google.com

viewer + https + docs.google.com

a/.*/viewer + https + docs.google.com

(39) One of: pathPatten + scheme + host =

/document/.* + http + docs.google.com

/a/.*/document/.* + http + docs.google.com

/Doc + http + docs.google.com

/a/.*/Doc + http + docs.google.com

/View + http + docs.google.com

/a/.*/View + http + docs.google.com

/document/.* + https + docs.google.com

/a/.*/document/.* + https + docs.google.com

/Doc + https + docs.google.com

/a/.*/Doc + https + docs.google.com

/View + https + docs.google.com

/a/.*/View + https + docs.google.com

(40) One of: pathPatten + scheme + host =

/present/.* + s:http + docs.google.com

/a/.*/present/.* + s:http + docs.google.com

presentation/.* + s:http + docs.google.com

/a/.*/presentation/.* + s:http + docs.google.com

/present/.* + s:https + docs.google.com

/a/.*/present/.* + s:https + docs.google.com

/presentation/.* + s:https + docs.google.com

/a/.*/presentation/.* + s:https + docs.google.com

(41) One of: pathPatten + scheme + host =

/spreadsheets/.* + s:http + docs.google.com

/spreadsheet/.* + s:http + docs.google.com

/a/.*/spreadsheet/.* + s:http + docs.google.com

/spreadsheets/d/.* + s:http + docs.google.com

/a/.*/spreadsheets/d/.* + s:http + docs.google.com

/spreadsheets/.* + s:https + docs.google.com

/spreadsheet/.* + s:https + docs.google.com

/a/.*/spreadsheet/.* + s:https + docs.google.com

/spreadsheets/d/.* + s:https + docs.google.com

/a/.*/spreadsheets/d/.* + s:https + docs.google.com

(42) One of: scheme + mimeType + host =

content + application/vnd.google-apps.drive-sdk.generic +

com.google.android.apps.docs.storage

content + application/vnd.google-apps.drawing +

com.google.android.apps.docs.storage

content + application/vnd.google-apps.form +

com.google.android.apps.docs.storage

content + application/vnd.google-apps.map +

com.google.android.apps.docs.storage

content + application/vnd.google-apps.site +

com.google.android.apps.docs.storage

content + application/vnd.google-apps.table +

com.google.android.apps.docs.storage

(43) One of: scheme + host =

http + spreadsheets.google.com

https + h:spreadsheets.google.com

Table A-26. *"Duo" Activity Intent Filters*

Action	Category	Data	Act
VIEW			RegistrationActivity
VIEW			VerificationActivity
MAIN	LAUNCHER		MainActivity
VIEW	DEFAULT BROWSABLE		TagManagerPreviewActivity

Table A-27. *"EasterEgg" Activity Intent Filters*

Action	Category	Data	Act
MAIN	DEFAULT(1).PLATLOGO		Ocquarium
(2).QS_TILE_PREFERENCESMAIN			NekoLand
MAIN	DEFAULT		NekoActivationActivity

(1) com.android.internal.category
(2) android.service.quicksettings.action

Table A-28. *"ExactCalculator" Activity Intent Filters*

Action	Category	Data	Act
MAIN	LAUNCHERAPP_ CALCULATOR		Calculator

Table A-29. *"GoogleHindiIME" Activity Intent Filters*

Action	Category	Data	Act
MAIN	LAUNCHER		LauncherActivity
MAIN	LEANBACK_LAUNCHER		LauncherActivity
MAIN			HinglishSpellCheckerSettingsActivity

Table A-30. *"GooglePinyinIME" Activity Intent Filters*

Action	Category	Data	Act
MAIN	LAUNCHER		LauncherActivity
MAIN	LEANBACK_LAUNCHER		LauncherActivity
(1).DEBUG_PRIMES_ EVENTS	DEFAULT		PrimesEventActivity

(1) com.google.android.primes.action

Table A-31. *"GoogleTTS" Activity Intent Filters*

Action	Category	Data	Act
(1).CHECK_TTS_DATA	DEFAULT		CheckVoiceData
(1).GET_SAMPLE_TEXT	DEFAULT		GetSampleText
(2).EngineSettings	DEFAULT		EngineSettings
(1).INSTALL_TTS_DATA	DEFAULT		VoiceDataInstallActivity

(1) android.speech.tts.engine
(2) com.google.android.tts.settings

Table A-32. *"HTMLViewer" Activity Intent Filters*

Action	Category	Data	Act
VIEW	DEFAULT	scheme:file scheme:content mimeType:text/html mimeType:text/plain mimeType:application/xhtml+xml mimeType:application/vnd.wap.xhtml+xml	(1)

(1) HTMLViewerActivity

Table A-33. *"KeyChain" Activity Intent Filters*

Action	Category	Data	Act
(1).CHOOSER	DEFAULT		KeyChainActivity

(1) com.android.keychain

Table A-34. *"LatinIMEGooglePrebuilt" Activity Intent Filters*

Action	Category	Data	Act
MAIN	LAUNCHER		LauncherActivity
MAIN			LatinSpellCheckerSettingsActivity
(1).DEBUG_PRIMES_ EVENTS	DEFAULT		PrimesEventActivity

(1) com.google.android.primes.action

Table A-35. *"LatinIMEGooglePrebuilt" Activity Intent Filters*

Action	Category	Data	Act
MAIN	LAUNCHER		LauncherActivity
MAIN			LatinSpellCheckerSettingsActivity
(1).DEBUG_PRIMES_ EVENTS	DEFAULT		PrimesEventActivity

(1) com.google.android.primes.action

Table A-36. *"LiveWallpapersPicker" Activity Intent Filters*

Action	Category	Data	Act
(1).LIVE_WALLPAPER_ CHOOSERSET_WALLPAPER	DEFAULT		LiveWallpaperActivity
(1).CHANGE_LIVE_WALLPAPER	DEFAULT		LiveWallpaperChange

(1) android.service.wallpaper

Table A-37. *"Maps" Activity Intent Filters*

Action	Category	Data	Act
VIEW	DEFAULT BROWSABLE	pathPrefix:/ oauth2redirectscheme:google.maps. taxi	(1)
VIEW	DEFAULT BROWSABLE	scheme:googlemapstaxihost:oauth2r edirect	(1)
MAIN	LAUNCHER APP_MAPS, DEFAULT		(2)
VIEW	DEFAULT BROWSABLE	scheme:peterparker	(2)
VIEW	DEFAULT	scheme:geo.replay	(2)
VIEW	DEFAULT BROWSABLE	scheme:google.navigation	(2)
VIEW	DEFAULT BROWSABLE	scheme:geo	(2)
VIEW	DEFAULT	scheme:google.maps	(2)
SENDSEND_MULTIPLE	DEFAULT	mimeType:application/vnd.google.pan orama360+jpgmimeType:image/*	(2)
VIEW	DEFAULT BROWSABLE	scheme:googlemapstaxihost:addpay ment	(2)
VIEW	DEFAULT BROWSABLE	scheme:httpscheme:httpspath:/ (13) (14)	(2)
VIEW	DEFAULT BROWSABLE	scheme:http scheme:https pathPrefix:/map/viewer host:mapsengine.google.com pathPrefix:/map/u/.*/viewer host:mapsengine.google.com	(2)
(15).NDEF_ DISCOVERED	DEFAULT	scheme:httpscheme:httpspath:/(14)	(2)

(continued)

Table A-37. (*continued*)

Action	Category	Data	Act
VIEW	DEFAULT BROWSABLE	scheme:http scheme:https path:/ maps path:/maps/preview (16) pathPattern:/maps/d/u/.*/viewer (17)	(2)
VIEW	DEFAULT BROWSABLE	scheme:httpscheme:httpspathPrefix:/ mapshost:goo.gl	(2)
(15).NDEF_ DISCOVERED	DEFAULT	scheme:google.navigation	(2)
VIEW	DEFAULT	mimeType:vnd.android.cursor.item/ postal-address_v2	(2)
MANAGE_NETWORK_ USAGE	DEFAULT		(2)
MAIN	NOTIFICATION_ PREFERENCES		(2)
VIEW	DEFAULT BROWSABLE	scheme:google.streetview	(2)
(18).SEARCH_ACTION	DEFAULT		(2)
(18).VIEW	DEFAULT	scheme:google.maps.timeline	(2)
VIEW	DEFAULT BROWSABLE	scheme:http scheme:https host:plus. codes (19)	(2)
CREATE_SHORTCUT	DEFAULT CAR_MODE		(3)
CREATE_SHORTCUT	DEFAULT		(4)
CREATE_SHORTCUT	DEFAULT		(5)
CREATE_SHORTCUT	DEFAULT		(6)
CREATE_SHORTCUT	DEFAULT		(7)
(20).PROJECTED_ FIRST_RUN	DEFAULT		(8)
(21).ACTION_ PREVIEW]	DEFAULT		(9)

(*continued*)

Table A-37. (*continued*)

Action	Category	Data	Act
MAIN			(10)
MAIN			(11)
VIEW	DEFAULT		(12)

(1) RedirectUriReceiverActivity

(2) MapsActivity

(3) CreateDirectionsShortcutActivity

(4) FreeNavCreateShortcutActivity

(5) TrafficHubCreateShortcutActivity

(6) LocationSharingCreateShortcutActivity

(7) SelectedPersonCreateShortcutActivity

(8) GmmProjectedFirstRunActivity

(9) PreviewActivity

(10) PlacesActivity

(11) DestinationActivity

(12) NavigationActivity

(13) One of pathPrefix: /locationhistory, /maps,

/maps/me, /localguides/signup

(14) All relevant Google Map hosts: e.g. host:maps.google.[...]

(15) android.nfc.action

(16) One of pathPrefix:

/locationhistory, /maps/timeline

/maps/contrib /local/guides/signup

/maps/@, /maps/place/

/maps/search/, /maps/dir/

/maps/offline, /maps/placelists/all

/maps/placelists/list/, /maps/preview/@

/maps/preview/place/, /maps/preview/search/

/maps/preview/dir/, /maps/d/viewer

/maps/me

(17) Alternate set of Google Map hosts: e.g. host:maps.google.[...]

(18) com.google.android.gms.actions

(19) One of pathPrefix: /2, /3, /4, /5, /6, /7, /8, /9, /C, /F, /G, /H, /J, /M

/P, /Q, /R, /V, /W, /X

(20) com.google.android.apps.maps.car

(21) com.google.android.gms.appinvite

Table A-38. *"Music2" Activity Intent Filters*

Action	Category	Data	Act
(1).PLAY	DEFAULT		(2)
(1).SHARED_PLAY	DEFAULT		(3)
VIEW	DEFAULT, BROWSABLE	pathPrefix:/music/playlist + scheme:https + host:play.google. com pathPrefix:/music/playlist + scheme:http + host:play.google.com	(3)
(1).MUSIC_SETTINGS	DEFAULT		(4)
MAIN	NOTIFICATION_ PREFERENCES		(4)
(1).LICENSES	DEFAULT		(5)
(1).SELECT_ACCOUNT	DEFAULT		(6)
(1).OPEN_WEAR_ SYNC_MANAGEMENT_ UI	DEFAULT		(7)
VIEW	DEFAULT BROWSABLE	scheme:file mimeType:audio/* mimeType:application/ogg mimeType:application/x-ogg mimeType:application/itunes	(8)

(continued)

Table A-38. (*continued*)

Action	Category	Data	Act
VIEW	DEFAULT BROWSABLE	scheme:http mimeType:audio/* mimeType:application/ogg mimeType:application/x-ogg mimeType:application/itunes	(8)
VIEW	DEFAULT BROWSABLE	scheme:https mimeType:audio/* mimeType:application/ogg mimeType:application/x-ogg mimeType:application/itunes	(8)
VIEW	DEFAULT BROWSABLE	scheme:content mimeType:audio/* mimeType:application/ogg mimeType:application/x-ogg mimeType:application/itunes	(8)
PICK	DEFAULT OPENABLE	mimeType:vnd.android. cursor.dir/audio	(9)
SEARCH	DEFAULT		(10)
VIEW	DEFAULT	mimeType:vnd.android. cursor.dir/vnd. google.music.playlist mimeType:vnd. android. cursor.dir/playlist	(11)
(1).shortcuts.START_IFL			(12)
(1).shortcuts.MY_ LIBRARY			(12)
(1).shortcuts.RECENT_ ACTIVITY			(12)
VIEW	DEFAULT BROWSABLE	scheme:googleplaymusic	(13)
VIEW	DEFAULT BROWSABLE	(24) or (25)	(13)

(*continued*)

Table A-38. (*continued*)

Action	Category	Data	Act
(22).MEDIA_PLAY_ FROM_SEARCH	DEFAULT		(14)
(1).DeviceManagement	DEFAULT		(15)
VIEW	DEFAULT	scheme:playmusichost:(1)	(16)
(23).ACTION_PREVIEW	DEFAULT		(17)
MAINMUSIC_PLAYER	DEFAULT LAUNCHER APP_MUSIC		(18)
(1).PLAYBACK_VIEWER	DEFAULT		(18)
VIEW	DEFAULT	mimeType:vnd.android. cursor.item/vnd. google.music.album mimeType:vnd. android. cursor.dir/artistalbum mimeType:vnd. android. cursor.dir/album mimeType:vnd. android. cursor.dir/vnd. google.music.album mimeType:vnd. android. cursor.dir/track	(18)
MANAGE_NETWORK_ USAGE	DEFAULT		(19)
CREATE_SHORTCUT	DEFAULT CAR_MODE		(20)
GET_CONTENT	DEFAULT OPENABLE	mimeType:audio/* mimeType:application/ogg mimeType:application/x-ogg	(21)

(1) com.google.android.music

(2) PlaySongsActivity

(3) SharedSongsActivity

(4) MusicSettingsActivity

(5) LicenseActivity

(6) TutorialSelectAccountActivity

(7) ManageWearDownloadsActivity

(8) AudioPreviewActivity

(9) MusicPickerActivity

(10) ClusteredSearchActivity

(11) TrackContainerActivity

(12) ShortcutTrampolineActivity

(13) MusicUrlHandlerActivity

(14) VoiceActionsActivity

(15) ManageDevicesActivity

(16) AppNavigationTrampolineActivity

(17) PreviewActivity

(18) TopLevelActivity

(19) NetworkUsage

(20) PlaylistShortcutActivity

(21) GetContent

(22) android.media.action

(23) com.google.android.gms.appinvite

(24) One of triplets pathPattern + scheme + host:

    /music/m/T.* + https + play.google.com

    /music/m/T.* + http + play.google.com

    /music/m/B.* + https + play.google.com

    /music/m/B.* + http + play.google.com

    /music/m/A.* + https + play.google.com

    /music/m/A.* + http + play.google.com

    /music/m/L.* + https + play.google.com

    /music/m/L.* + http + play.google.com

/music/m/I.* + https + play.google.com

/music/m/I.* + http + play.google.com

/music/m/D.* + https + play.google.com

/music/m/D.* + http + play.google.com

/music/m/N.* + https + play.google.com

/music/m/N.* + http + play.google.com

/music/r/m/T.* + https + play.google.com

/music/r/m/T.* + http + play.google.com

/music/r/m/B.* + https + play.google.com

/music/r/m/B.* + http + play.google.com

/music/r/m/A.* + https + play.google.com

/music/r/m/A.* + http + play.google.com

/music/r/m/L.* + https + play.google.com

/music/r/m/L.* + http + play.google.com

/music/r/playlist/A.* + https + play.google.com

/music/r/playlist/A.* + http + play.google.com

/music/gift + https + play.google.com

/music/gift + http + play.google.com

/music/podcasts + https + play.google.com

/music/podcasts + http + play.google.com

/music/topcharts + https + play.google.com

/music/topcharts + http + play.google.com

/music/newreleases + https + play.google.com

/music/newreleases + http + play.google.com

/music/settings + https + play.google.com

/music/settings + http + play.google.com

/music/settings/* + https + play.google.com

/music/settings/* + http + play.google.com

(25) One of scheme + path + host:

https + /music/listen + music.google.com

http + /music/listen + music.google.com

https + /music/uq + play.google.com

http + /music/uq + play.google.com

https + /music + play.google.com

http + /music + play.google.com

Table A-39. *"NetSpeed" Activity Intent Filters*

Action	Category	Data	Act
MAIN	DEFAULT		NetSpeedActivity

Table A-40. *"OpenWnn" Activity Intent Filters*

Action	Category	Data	Act
MAIN			OpenWnnControlPanelJAJP

Table A-41. *"Photos" Activity Intent Filters*

Action	Category	Data	Act
(1).CROP	DEFAULT ALTERNATIVE SELECTED_ALTERNATIVE	mimeType:image/*	(2)
EDIT	DEFAULT	mimeType:image/*	(2)
MAIN	DEFAULT LAUNCHER APP_GALLERYINFO		(3)
VIEW(1).REVIEW	DEFAULT BROWSABLE	scheme:"" scheme:http scheme:https scheme:content scheme:file mimeType:image/* mimeType:application/vnd. google.panorama360+jpg mimeType:video/ mpeg mimeType:video/mpeg4 mimeType:video/mp4 mimeType:video/3gp mimeType:video/3gpp mimeType:video/3gpp2 mimeType:video/webm mimeType:video/avi mimeType:video/x-matroska mimeType:video/ quicktime mimeType:application/sdp	(4)
VIEW	DEFAULT BROWSABLE	scheme:rtsp	(4)
VIEW(1).REVIEW	DEFAULT BROWSABLE	scheme:http scheme:https mimeType:audio/ x-mpegurl mimeType:audio/mpegurl mimeType:application/vnd. apple.mpegurl mimeType:application/x-mpegurl	(4)
VIEW	DEFAULT	mimeType:vnd. android.cursor.dir/image mimeType:vnd. android.cursor. dir/video	(4)
(6).edit	DEFAULT	mimeType:image/*	(5)
PICK	DEFAULT	mimeType:image/* mimeType:video/* mimeType:vnd.android.cursor. dir/image mimeType:vnd.android.cursor. dir/video	(7)

(continued)

Table A-41. (*continued*)

Action	Category	Data	Act
GET_CONTENT	OPENABLE DEFAULT	mimeType:image/* mimeType:video/* mimeType:vnd.android.cursor. dir/image	(7)
(21). NOTIFICATION_ SETTINGS	DEFAULT		(8)
ATTACH_DATA	DEFAULT	mimeType:image/*	(9)
SET_WALLPAPER	DEFAULT		(9)
SEND	DEFAULT	mimeType:application/vnd. google.panorama360+jpg mimeType:image/* mimeType:video/*	(10)
SEND_MULTIPLE	DEFAULT	mimeType:application/vnd. google.panorama360+jpg mimeType:image/* mimeType:video/*	(10)
VIEW	DEFAULT	scheme:gplus, path:/apiaryTrace, host:app	(11)
(13). USB_DEVICE_ ATTACHED			(2)
MAIN	DEFAULTNOTIFICATION_ PREFERENCES		(14)
EDIT	DEFAULT	mimeType:application/vnd. google.panorama360+jpg	(15)
(1).TRIM	DEFAULT	scheme:content scheme:file mimeType:video/*	(15)

(*continued*)

Table A-41. (*continued*)

Action	Category	Data	Act
VIEW	DEFAULT BROWSABLE	pathPattern:/share/.*+ scheme:http+ host:photos.google.com pathPattern:/share/.*+ scheme:https+ host:photos.google.com pathPattern:/u/.*/share/.*+ scheme:http+ host:photos.google.com pathPattern:/u/.*/ share/.*+ scheme:https+ host:photos.google. com pathPattern:/photos/.*+ scheme:http+ host:goo.gl pathPattern:/photos/.*+ scheme:https+ host:goo.gl	(16)
VIEW	DEFAULT BROWSABLE	pathPattern:/share/.*/inapp+ scheme:http+ host:photos.google.com pathPattern:/share/.*/ inapp+ scheme:https+ host:photos.google.com pathPattern:/u/.*/share/.*/inapp+ scheme:http+ host:photos.google.com pathPattern:/u/.*/ share/.*/inapp+ scheme:https+ host:photos. google.com]]]	(17)
VIEW	DEFAULT BROWSABLE	pathPattern:/assistant+ scheme:http+ host:photos.google.com pathPattern:/assistant+ scheme:https+ host:photos.google.com	(18)
(22).SEARCH_ ACTION	DEFAULT		(19)
VIEW	DEFAULT BROWSABLE	pathPattern:/search/.*+ scheme:http+ host:photos.google.com pathPattern:/search/.*+ scheme:https+ host:photos.google.com pathPattern:/u/.*/search/.*+ scheme:http+ host:photos.google.com pathPattern:/u/.*/ search/.*+ scheme:https+ host:photos.google. com	(19)
MAIN	DEFAULT NOTIFICATION_ PREFERENCES		(20)

(1) com.android.camera.action

(2) EditActivity

(3) HomeActivity

(4) HostPhotoPagerActivity

(5) ConsumerPhotoEditorActivity

(6) com.google.android.apps.photos.editor

(7) ExternalPickerActivity

(8) SettingsActivity

(9) SetWallpaperActivity

(10) UploadContentActivity

(11) TracingTokenQrCodeActivity

(12) IngestActivity

(13) android.hardware.usb.action

(14) NotificationSettingsActivity

(15) EditVideoActivity

(16) EnvelopeActivityAlias

(17) SharedAlbumPromoActivityAlias

(18) HomeActivityAlias

(19) SearchActivityAlias

(20) NotificationSettingsActivityAlias

(21) com.google.android.libraries.social.settings

(22) com.google.android.gms.actions

Table A-42. *"PrebuiltBugle" Activity Intent Filters*

Action	Category	Data	Act
VIEWSENDTO	DEFAULT BROWSABLE	scheme:smsscheme:smsto	(1)
VIEWSENDTO	DEFAULT BROWSABLE	scheme:mmsscheme:mmsto	(1)
MAIN	DEFAULT NOTIFICATION_ PREFERENCES		(2)
SEND	DEFAULT	mimeType:text/plain mimeType:text/x-vCard mimeType:text/x-vcard mimeType:image/* mimeType:audio/* mimeType:application/ogg	(3)
SEND_MULTIPLE	DEFAULT	mimeType:image/*	(3)
(7).APPWIDGET_ CONFIGURE			(4)
MAIN	LAUNCHER DEFAULT APP_ MESSAGING		(5)
SEND	DEFAULT	mimeType:video/*	(6)

(1) LaunchConversationActivity

(2) ApplicationSettingsActivity

(3) ShareIntentActivity

(4) WidgetPickConversationActivity

(5) ConversationListActivity

(6) VideoShareIntentActivity

(7) android.appwidget.action

Table A-43. *"PrebuiltDeskClockGoogle" Activity Intent Filters*

Action	Category	Data	Act
VIEW	DEFAULT	scheme:clock-apphost:com. google.android. deskclock	(1)
MAIN	DEFAULT LAUNCHER	(1)	
DISMISS_ALARMSHOW_ ALARMSSHOW_ TIMERSSNOOZE_ALARM	DEFAULT VOICE		(1)
SET_ALARMSET_TIMER	DEFAULT VOICE		(1)

(1) HandleUris
(2) DeskClock
(3) HandleApiCalls
(4) HandleSetAlarmApiCalls

Table A-44. *"PrebuiltGmail" Activity Intent Filters*

Action	Category	Data	Act
(1).FORCE_CREATE_ ACCOUNT(30).CREATE_NEW_ ACCOUNT	DEFAULT		(2)
MAIN			(2)
VIEW	DEFAULT	host:com.google.android. gm.email. ACCOUNT_ SETTINGSscheme:auth	(3)
VIEW	DEFAULT	host:com.google.android. gm.email. ACCOUNT_ SECURITYscheme:auth	(4)

(continued)

Table A-44. (*continued*)

Action	Category	Data	Act
SENDTOVIEW	DEFAULT BROWSABLE	scheme:mailto	(5)
(26).NDEF_DISCOVERED	DEFAULT	scheme:mailto	(5)
SEND	DEFAULT	pathPrefix:/ composescheme:contenthost:ui. email2.android.com	(5)
SEND	DEFAULT	host:gmail- lsscheme:gmail2from	(5)
SEND	DEFAULT(32).SELF_NOTE	mimeType:*/*	(5)
SEND_MULTIPLE	DEFAULT	mimeType:*/*	(5)
(27).LAUNCH_COMPOSE	DEFAULT		(6)
(27).LAUNCH_COMPOSE	DEFAULT	scheme:content	(6)
(27).GIG_ACTION_REPLY_ TO_ITEM_NOTIFICATION		scheme:content	(6)
(28).AUTO_SEND	DEFAULT	mimeType:*/*	(7)
(29).APPWIDGET_CONFIGURE			(8)
CREATE_SHORTCUT	DEFAULT		(9)
(30).ACCOUNT_MANAGER_ ENTRY_INTENT	DEFAULT		(10)
MANAGE_NETWORK_USAGE	DEFAULT		(10)
MAIN	DEFAULT NOTIFICATION_ PREFERENCES		(10)
VIEW	DEFAULT	host:gmailscheme:auth	(11)
VIEW	DEFAULT	scheme:contentmimeType:app lication/ gm-email-ls	(12)
VIEW	DEFAULT	host:com.android.gmail. uischeme:contentpath:/proxy	(13)

(*continued*)

Table A-44. (*continued*)

Action	Category	Data	Act
VIEW	DEFAULT	mimeType:message/rfc822mimeType:application/eml	(14)
(31).VIEW_PLID	DEFAULT		(15)
	DEFAULT		(16)
SEARCH	DEFAULT		(17)
MAIN	(33).EMAIL		(18)
MAIN	(33).FIRST_IMPRESSION		(18)
(29).APPWIDGET_CONFIGURE			(19)
CREATE_SHORTCUT	DEFAULT		(20)
EDIT, VIEW	DEFAULT	host:gmailscheme:setting	(21)
EDIT, VIEW	DEFAULT	host:com.google.android.gmscheme:feedback	(21)
EDIT, VIEW	DEFAULT	pathPrefix:/settingsscheme:contenthost:ui.email.android.com	(21)
VIEW	DEFAULT	scheme:contenthost:com.google.android.gmmimeType:vnd.android.cursor.item/vnd.com.google.android.gm.label	(22)
MAIN			(23)
MAIN	DEFAULT LAUNCHER BROWSABLE APP_EMAIL		(24)
VIEW	DEFAULT	host:gmail-lsscheme:contentmimeType:application/gmail-ls	(24)

(*continued*)

Table A-44. (*continued*)

Action	Category	Data	Act
VIEW	DEFAULT	scheme:contentmimeType:application/ gmail-ls	(24)
MAIN	DEFAULT LAUNCHER BROWSABLE APP_EMAIL		(25)
VIEW	DEFAULT	host:gmail-lsscheme:contentmimeType:application/ gmail-ls	(25)
VIEW	DEFAULT	scheme:contentmimeType:application/ gmail-ls	(25)

(1) com.google.android.gm.email

(2) AccountSetupFinalGmail

(3) HeadlessAccountSettingsLoader

(4) AccountSecurity

(5) ComposeActivityGmailExternal

(6) ComposeActivityGmail

(7) AutoSendActivity

(8) MailboxSelectionActivityGmail

(9) CreateShortcutActivityGmail

(10) PublicPreferenceActivity

(11) ReauthenticateActivity

(12) MailActivityGmail

(13) ViewProxyActivity

(14) EmlViewerActivityGmail

(15) TrampolineActivity

(16) OpenBrowserTrampolineActivity

(17) MailActivity

(18) AccountSetupFinalGmailSuggestions

(19) MailboxSelectionActivity

(20) CreateShortcutActivityGoogleMail

(21) Gmail2PreferenceActivity

(22) PublicGmailActivity

(23) GmailActivity

(24) ConversationListActivityGoogleMail

(25) ConversationListActivityGmail

(26) android.nfc.action

(27) com.android.mail.intent.action

(28) com.google.android.gm.action

(29) android.appwidget.action

(30) com.google.android.gm.email

(31) com.google.android.gm.intent

(32) com.google.android.voicesearch

(33) com.android.settings.suggested.category

Table A-45. *"PrintSpooler" Activity Intent Filters*

Action	Category	Data	Act
(1).PRINT_DIALOG	DEFAULT	pathPattern:*scheme:printjob	(2)

(1) android.print

(2) PrintActivity

Table A-46. *"Videos" Activity Intent Filters*

Action	Category	Data	Act
(1).VIEW	DEFAULT BROWSABLE	scheme:http scheme:https host:youtube.com host:*. youtube.com pathPrefix:/ watch pathPrefix:/show	(2)
VIEW(1).VIEW	DEFAULT BROWSABLE	scheme:httpscheme: httpshost:play.google. compathPrefix:/movies	(2)
MAIN	DEFAULT INFO		(2)
SEARCH	DEFAULT		(4)
(1).REDEEM	DEFAULT		(5)
(3).bugreport	DEFAULT		(6)
(11).VIEW	DEFAULT BROWSABLE	scheme:httpscheme:http shost:youtube.comhost:*. youtube.compathPrefix:/ watch	(7)
(12).VIEW	DEFAULT BROWSABLE	scheme:httpscheme: httpshost:play.google. compathPrefix:/trailers	(7)
(12).PLAY(12).PIN(12). UNPIN(12).PURCHASE	DEFAULT	scheme:httpscheme: httpshost:play.google. compathPrefix:/movies/ api	(8)
MAIN	DEFAULT LAUNCHER		(9)
MANAGE_NETWORK_ USAGE	DEFAULT		(10)

(1) com.google.android.videos.intent.action

(2) LauncherActivity

(3) com.google.android.youtube.videos.cast.action

(4) SearchActivity

(5) ChoosesEntryActivity

(6) LogCollectorActivity

(7) TrailerLauncherActivity

(8) ApiActivity

(9) EntryPoint

(10) ManageNetworkUsageActivity

(11) com.google.android.videos.intent.action.trailers

(12) com.google.android.videos.intent.action

Table A-47. *"WallpaperPickerGooglePrebuilt" Activity Intent Filters*

Action	Category	Data	Act
SET_WALLPAPER	DEFAULT		(1)
(4).CROP_AND_SET_WALLPAPER	DEFAULT	mimeType:image/*	(2)
MAIN	LAUNCHER		(3)

(1) TopLevelPickerActivity

(2) StandalonePreviewActivity

(3) CategoryPickerActivity

(4) android.service.wallpaper

Table A-48. *"WebViewStub" Activity Intent Filters*

Action	Category	Data	Act
(1).WEBVIEW_LICENSE	DEFAULT		LicenseActivity

(1) android.settings

Table A-49. *"YouTube" Activity Intent Filters*

Action	Category	Data	Act
SEARCH			(1)
(15).CLOSE_PLAYER	DEFAULT BROWSABLE		(1)
(15).FULL_SCREEN	DEFAULT BROWSABLE		(1)
(15).MINI_SCREEN	DEFAULT BROWSABLE		(1)
(15).NORMAL_SCREEN	DEFAULT BROWSABLE		(1)
(15).PAUSE	DEFAULT BROWSABLE		(1)
(15).PLAY	DEFAULT BROWSABLE		(1)
(15).STOP	DEFAULT BROWSABLE		(1)
(15).NEXT	DEFAULT BROWSABLE		(1)
(15).PREVIOUS	DEFAULT BROWSABLE		(1)
(15).SKIP_ADS	DEFAULT BROWSABLE		(1)
(16).CONNECT	DEFAULT BROWSABLE		(1)
(16).DISCONNECT	DEFAULT BROWSABLE		(1)
(15).PLAY_NTH_VIDEO	DEFAULT BROWSABLE		(1)
SEARCHMEDIA_SEARCH	DEFAULT		(2)
(17).UPLOAD	DEFAULT	mimeType:video/*	(3)
(17).INTERNAL_UPLOAD	DEFAULT	mimeType:video/*	(4)
(18).MEDIA_PLAY_FROM_ SEARCH	DEFAULT		(5)
MAIN	NOTIFICATION_PREFERENCES]		(6)
(17).CREATE_LIVE_STREAM	DEFAULT		(7)
(19).START	DEFAULT]		(8)
(20).PLAY_STORY	DEFAULT		(9)

(*continued*)

Table A-49. (*continued*)

Action	Category	Data	Act
(21).bugreport	DEFAULT		(10)
MAIN	DEFAULT LAUNCHER		(11)
(22).search	DEFAULT		(11)
(22).trending	DEFAULT		(11)
(22).subscriptions	DEFAULT		(11)
SENDSEND_MULTIPLE	ALTERNATIVE DEFAULT	mimeType:video/*	(12)
VIEW(23).MEDIA_PLAY_ FROM_SEARCH(24).NDEF_ DISCOVERED	DEFAULT BROWSABLE	scheme:httpscheme :httpshost:youtube. comhost:www.youtube. comhost:m.youtube. comhost:youtu. bepathPattern:.*	(13)
VIEW(23).MEDIA_PLAY_ FROM_SEARCH(24).NDEF_ DISCOVERED	DEFAULT BROWSABLE	scheme:vnd. youtubescheme:vnd. youtube.launch	(13)
MANAGE_NETWORK_USAGE	DEFAULT		(14)

(1) WatchWhileActivity

(2) Shell$ResultsActivity

(3) Shell$UploadActivity

(4) UploadActivity

(5) Shell$MediaSearchActivity

(6) Shell$SettingsActivity

(7) Shell$LiveCreationActivity

(8) StandalonePlayerActivity

(9) MoxieActivity

(10) LogCollectorActivity

(11) Shell$HomeActivity

(12) UploadIntentHandlingActivity

(13) UrlActivity

(14) ManageNetworkUsageActivity

(15) com.google.android.youtube.voice

(16) com.google.android.youtube.mdx.voice

(17) com.google.android.youtube.intent.action

(18) android.media.action

(19) com.google.android.youtube.api.StandalonePlayerActivity

(20) com.google.android.spotlightstories

(21) com.google.android.youtube.action

(22) com.google.android.youtube.action.open

(23) android.media.action

(24) android.nfc.action

System Broadcasts

This is an elaborate version of the list from SDK_INST_DIR/platforms/VERSION/data/ broadcast_actions.txt, describing all system broadcast actions. The version used is "android-32". Some entries that are missing there have been added. The string in the heading of each entry would be written in broadcast listener declarations inside AndroidManifest.xml; programmatically declared listeners should instead use the class field constants also shown.

Note   Deprecated entries usually are omitted. If needed, you can look them up in the documentation or in the sources (e.g., at https://cs.android.com/ android).

What broadcasts can be used and the broadcast methodology in general were described in depth in Chapter 5.

Many of those broadcasts have adjoint extra data – to fetch them all, you can use Intent.getExtras(). Listed are the keys – wherever feasible as class constants. Also have a look at the online API documentation of the class in question.

The section is split into parts as follows:

- User Account

- App Widgets

- Bluetooth

- USB

- Power Management

- Media

- Packages (Apps)

- Network

- Wi-Fi

- Notifications

- Telephony

- TV

- Audio

- Booting and Shutdown

- Security

- Various

User Account

- **android.accounts.LOGIN_ACCOUNTS_CHANGED**

  Constant LOGIN_ACCOUNTS_CHANGED_ACTION from class android.
  accounts.AccountManager. Deprecated in API level 26 (Android
  8.0). Use addOnAccountsUpdatedListener() instead. Fired when
  an account was added or removed or credentials were changed.

- **android.accounts.action.ACCOUNT_REMOVED**

Constant `ACTION_ACCOUNT_REMOVED` from class `android.accounts.AccountManager`. Fired when an account was removed or renamed. Extra data:

- **AccountManager.KEY_ACCOUNT_TYPE**: The type of the removed account (string)

- **AccountManager.KEY_ACCOUNT_NAME**: The name of the removed account (string)

- **android.app.action.ACTION_PASSWORD_CHANGED**

Constant `ACTION_PASSWORD_CHANGED` from class `android.app.admin.DeviceAdminReceiver`. Fired when the user changed their password.

- **android.app.action.ACTION_PASSWORD_EXPIRING**

Constant `ACTION_PASSWORD_EXPIRING` from class `android.app.admin.DeviceAdminReceiver`. Fired when the password is expiring.

- **android.app.action.ACTION_PASSWORD_FAILED**

Constant `ACTION_PASSWORD_FAILED` from class `android.app.admin.DeviceAdminReceiver`. The user failed to enter the correct password.

- **android.app.action.ACTION_PASSWORD_SUCCEEDED**

Constant `ACTION_PASSWORD_SUCCEEDED` from class `android.app.admin.DeviceAdminReceiver`. The user entered the correct password.

- **android.app.action.AFFILIATED_PROFILE_TRANSFER_OWNERSHIP_COMPLETE**

Constant `ACTION_AFFILIATED_PROFILE_TRANSFER_OWNERSHIP_COMPLETE` from class `android.app.admin.DeviceAdminReceiver`. The device owner whose ownership of one of its affiliated profiles is transferred.

- **android.app.action.COMPLIANCE_ACKNOWLEDGEMENT_REQUIRED**

Constant `ACTION_COMPLIANCE_ACKNOWLEDGEMENT_REQUIRED` from class `android.app.admin.DeviceAdminReceiver`. Notify the profile owner on an organization-owned device that it needs to acknowledge device compliance.

- **android.app.action.DATA_SHARING_RESTRICTION_APPLIED**

Constant `ACTION_DATA_SHARING_RESTRICTION_APPLIED` from class `android.app.admin.DevicePolicyManager`. Notify that the latest change to `UserManager.DISALLOW_SHARE_INTO_MANAGED_PROFILE` restriction has been successfully applied (cross-profile intent filters updated). Only used for CTS tests.

- **android.app.action.DEVICE_ADMIN_DISABLED**

Constant `ACTION_DEVICE_ADMIN_DISABLED` from class `android.app.admin.DeviceAdminReceiver`. Action sent to a device administrator when the user has disabled it.

- **android.app.action.DEVICE_ADMIN_DISABLE_REQUESTED**

Constant `ACTION_DEVICE_ADMIN_DISABLE_REQUESTED` from class `android.app.admin.DeviceAdminReceiver`. Action sent to a device administrator when the user has requested to disable it. Extra data:

  - **DeviceAdminReceiver.EXTRA_DISABLE_WARNING**: You can put a warning string here, which will then be shown to the user while disabling admin rights (string).

- **android.app.action.DEVICE_ADMIN_ENABLED**

Constant `ACTION_DEVICE_ADMIN_ENABLED` from class `android.app.admin.DeviceAdminReceiver`. The device is being enabled for administration.

- **android.app.action.DEVICE_OWNER_CHANGED**

Constant `ACTION_DEVICE_OWNER_CHANGED` from class `android.app.admin.DevicePolicyManager`. Device owner is set, changed, or cleared.

- **android.app.action.DEVICE_POLICY_CONSTANTS_CHANGED**

  Constant `ACTION_DEVICE_POLICY_CONSTANTS_CHANGED` from class `android.app.admin.DevicePolicyManager`. Notify that a value of `Settings.Global.DEVICE_POLICY_CONSTANTS` has been changed.

- **android.app.action.PROFILE_OWNER_CHANGED**

  Constant `ACTION_PROFILE_OWNER_CHANGED` from class `android.app.admin.DevicePolicyManager`. The profile owner is set, changed, or cleared. Only sent to the user managed by the new profile owner.

- **android.app.action.PROFILE_PROVISIONING_COMPLETE**

  Constant `ACTION_PROFILE_PROVISIONING_COMPLETE` from class `android.app.admin.DeviceAdminReceiver`. The provisioning of a managed profile or managed device has completed successfully.

- **android.app.action.SHOW_NEW_USER_DISCLAIMER**

  Constant `ACTION_SHOW_NEW_USER_DISCLAIMER` from class `android.app.admin.DevicePolicyManager`. A new Android user is added when the device is managed by a device owner, so receivers can show the proper disclaimer to the (human) user.

- **android.app.action.TRANSFER_OWNERSHIP_COMPLETE**

  Constant `ACTION_TRANSFER_OWNERSHIP_COMPLETE` from class `android.app.admin.DeviceAdminReceiver`. Notify the newly transferred administrator that the transfer from the original administrator was successful.

- **android.intent.action.UID_REMOVED**

  Constant `ACTION_UID_REMOVED` from class `android.content.Intent`. A user ID has been removed. Extra data:

  - **Intent.EXTRA_UID**: The UID (int)

- **android.intent.action.USER_PRESENT**

  Constant `ACTION_USER_PRESENT` from class `android.content.Intent`. Sent when the user is present after a device wakeup.

- **android.intent.action.USER_UNLOCKED**

  Constant `ACTION_USER_UNLOCKED` from class `android.content.Intent`. Sent when a user gets unlocked, now having access to the private encrypted data store.

- **android.app.action.USER_ADDED**

  Constant `ACTION_USER_ADDED` from class `android.app.admin.DeviceAdminReceiver`. Broadcast action: Notify the device owner that a user or profile has been added.

- **android.app.action.USER_REMOVED**

  Constant `ACTION_USER_REMOVED` from class `android.app.admin.DeviceAdminReceiver`. Broadcast action: Notify the device owner that a user or profile has been removed.

- **android.app.action.USER_STARTED**

  Constant `ACTION_USER_STARTED` from class `android.app.admin.DeviceAdminReceiver`. Broadcast action: Notify the device owner that a user or profile has been started.

- **android.app.action.USER_STOPPED**

  Constant `ACTION_USER_STOPPED` from class `android.app.admin.DeviceAdminReceiver`. Broadcast action: Notify the device owner that a user or profile has been stopped.

- **android.app.action.USER_SWITCHED**

  Constant `ACTION_USER_SWITCHED` from class `android.app.admin.DeviceAdminReceiver`. Broadcast action: Notify the device owner that a user or profile has been switched.

- **android.provider.action.SIM_ACCOUNTS_CHANGED**

  Constant `ACTION_` from class `android.provider.ContactsContract`. SIM accounts have changed. Call `getSimAccounts( ContentResolver )` to get the latest.

App Widgets

- **android.appwidget.action.APPWIDGET_DELETED**

  Constant `ACTION_APPWIDGET_DELETED` from class `android.appwidget.AppWidgetManager`. An instance of an AppWidget is deleted from its host.

- **android.appwidget.action.APPWIDGET_DISABLED**

  Constant `ACTION_APPWIDGET_DISABLED` from class `android.appwidget.AppWidgetManager`. The last AppWidget of this provider is removed from the last host.

- **android.appwidget.action.APPWIDGET_ENABLED**

  Constant `ACTION_APPWIDGET_ENABLED` from class `android.appwidget.AppWidgetManager`. An instance of an AppWidget is added to a host for the first time.

- **android.appwidget.action.APPWIDGET_HOST_RESTORED**

  Constant `ACTION_APPWIDGET_HOST_RESTORED` from class `android.appwidget.AppWidgetManager`. The AppWidget state related to the host has been restored from backup. Contains extra data:

  - **AppWidgetManager.EXTRA_APPWIDGET_OLD_IDS**: Old AppWidget IDs (int[])

  - **AppWidgetManager.EXTRA_APPWIDGET_IDS**: New AppWidget IDs (int[])

  - **AppWidgetManager.EXTRA_HOST_ID**: The host ID (int)

- **android.appwidget.action.APPWIDGET_RESTORED**

  Constant `ACTION_APPWIDGET_RESTORED` from class `android.appwidget.AppWidgetManager`. The AppWidget state related to that provider has been restored from backup. Extra data:

  - **AppWidgetManager.EXTRA_APPWIDGET_OLD_IDS**: Old restored AppWidget IDs (int[])

  - **AppWidgetManager.EXTRA_APPWIDGET_IDS**: New AppWidget IDs after restoring (int[])

- **android.appwidget.action.APPWIDGET_UPDATE**

  Constant `ACTION_APPWIDGET_UPDATE` from class `android.appwidget.AppWidgetManager`. Sent when it is time to update your AppWidget. Extra data:

  - **AppWidgetManager.EXTRA_APPWIDGET_IDS**: The AppWidget IDs to update

- **android.appwidget.action.APPWIDGET_UPDATE_OPTIONS**

  Constant `ACTION_APPWIDGET_OPTIONS_CHANGED` from class `android.appwidget.AppWidgetManager`. Sent when the custom extras for an AppWidget change.

Bluetooth

- android.bluetooth.a2dp.profile.action.CONNECTION_STATE_CHANGED

  Constant `ACTION_CONNECTION_STATE_CHANGED` from class `android.bluetooth.BluetoothA2dp`. A change in the connection state of the A2DP profile occurred. Contains extra data:

  - **android.bluetooth.BluetoothProfile.EXTRA_STATE**: The current state of the profile. One of

    android.bluetooth.BluetoothProfile.STATE_CONNECTED

    android.bluetooth.BluetoothProfile.STATE_DISCONNECTED

    android.bluetooth.BluetoothProfile.STATE_CONNECTING

    android.bluetooth.BluetoothProfile.STATE_DISCONNECTING

  - **android.bluetooth.BluetoothProfile.EXTRA_PREVIOUS_STATE**: The previous state of the profile. The possible values are the same as for `EXTRA_STATE`.

  - **android.bluetooth.BluetoothDevice.EXTRA_DEVICE**: The remote device (android.bluetooth.BluetoothDevice).

Requires permission "android.permission.BLUETOOTH".

- **android.bluetooth.a2dp.profile.action.ACTIVE_ DEVICE_CHANGED**

  Constant `ACTION_ACTIVE_DEVICE_CHANGED` from class `android. bluetooth.BluetoothA2dp`. Intent used to broadcast the selection of a connected device as active. Contains extra data:

  - **android.bluetooth.BluetoothDevice.EXTRA_DEVICE**: The remote device. It can be null if no device is active.

  Requires permission "android.permission.BLUETOOTH_ CONNECT".

- **android.bluetooth.a2dp.profile.action.AVRCP_CONNECTION_ STATE_CHANGED**

  Constant `ACTION_AVRCP_CONNECTION_STATE_CHANGED` from class `android.bluetooth.BluetoothA2dp`. Undocumented.

- **android.bluetooth.a2dp.profile.action.CODEC_ CONFIG_CHANGED**

  Constant `ACTION_CODEC_CONFIG_CHANGED` from class `android. bluetooth.BluetoothA2dp`. Intent used to broadcast the change in the Audio Codec state of the A2DP source profile. Contains extra data:

  - **android.bluetooth.BluetoothCodecStatus.EXTRA_CODEC_ STATUS**: The codec status.

  - **android.bluetooth.BluetoothCodecStatus.EXTRA_DEVICE**: The remote device if the device is currently connected. Otherwise, it is not included.

  Requires permission "android.permission.BLUETOOTH_ CONNECT".

- **android.bluetooth.a2dp.profile.action.PLAYING_ STATE_CHANGED**

Constant `ACTION_PLAYING_STATE_CHANGED` from class `android.bluetooth.BluetoothA2dp`. A change in the playing state of the A2DP profile occurred. Contains extra data:

- **android.bluetooth.BluetoothProfile.EXTRA_STATE**: The current state of the profile. One of

  android.bluetooth.BluetoothA2dp.STATE_PLAYING

  android.bluetooth.BluetoothA2dp.STATE_NOT_PLAYING

- **android.bluetooth.BluetoothProfile.EXTRA_PREVIOUS_STATE**: The previous state of the profile. The possible values are the same as for `EXTRA_STATE`.

- **android.bluetooth.BluetoothDevice.EXTRA_DEVICE**: The remote device (android.bluetooth.BluetoothDevice).

Requires permission "android.permission.BLUETOOTH".

- **android.bluetooth.action.LE_AUDIO_ACTIVE_DEVICE_CHANGED**

Constant `ACTION_LE_AUDIO_ACTIVE_DEVICE_CHANGED` from class `android.bluetooth.BluetoothLeAudio`. Intent used to broadcast the selection of a connected LE audio device as active. Extra data:

- **android.bluetooth.BluetoothDevice.EXTRA_DEVICE**: The remote device. It can be null if no device is active.

Requires permissions "android.permission.BLUETOOTH", "android.permission.BLUETOOTH_CONNECT", and "android.permission.BLUETOOTH_PRIVILEGED".

- **android.bluetooth.action.LE_AUDIO_CONNECTION_STATE_CHANGED**

Constant `ACTION_LE_AUDIO_CONNECTION_STATE_CHANGED` from class `android.bluetooth.BluetoothLeAudio`. Intent used to broadcast the change in connection state of the LeAudio profile. Extra data:

- **andoid.bluetooth.BluetoothProfile.EXTRA_STATE**: The current state of the profile

- **andoid.bluetooth.BluetoothProfile.EXTRA_PREVIOUS_STATE**: The previous state of the profile

- **andoid.bluetooth.BluetoothProfile.EXTRA_DEVICE**: The remote device

EXTRA_STATE or EXTRA_PREVIOUS_STATE can be any of (constants from `andoid.bluetooth.BluetoothProfile`) STATE_DISCONNECTED, STATE_CONNECTING, STATE_CONNECTED, and STATE_DISCONNECTING. Requires permissions "android.permission.BLUETOOTH" and "android.permission. BLUETOOTH_CONNECT".

- **android.bluetooth.action.TETHERING_STATE_CHANGED**

  Constant `ACTION_TETHERING_STATE_CHANGED` from class `android.bluetooth.BluetoothPan`. Intent used to broadcast the change in tethering state of the Pan profile. Extra data:

  - **android.bluetooth.BluetoothPan.EXTRA_TETHERING_STATE**: The current state of Bluetooth tethering. One of android.bluetooth.BluetoothPan.TETHERING_STATE_OFF and android.bluetooth.BluetoothPan.TETHERING_STATE_ON.

  Requires permission "android.permission.BLUETOOTH".

- **android.bluetooth.adapter.action.BLE_ACL_CONNECTED**

  Constant `ACTION_BLE_ACL_CONNECTED` from class `android.bluetooth.BluetoothAdapter`. ACL-connected event. This denotes GATT connection as Bluetooth LE is the only feature available in STATE_BLE_ON. Requires permission "android.permission.BLUETOOTH_CONNECT".

- **android.bluetooth.adapter.action.BLE_ACL_DISCONNECTED**

  Constant `ACTION_BLE_ACL_DISCONNECTED` from class `android.bluetooth.BluetoothAdapter`. ACL-disconnected event. This denotes GATT connection as Bluetooth LE is the only feature available in STATE_BLE_ON. Requires permission "android.permission.BLUETOOTH_CONNECT".

- **android.bluetooth.adapter.action.BLE_STATE_CHANGED**

  Constant `ACTION_BLE_STATE_CHANGED` from class `android.`
  `bluetooth.BluetoothAdapter`. The Bluetooth adapter state has
  changed in LE-only mode.

- **android.bluetooth.adapter.action.BLUETOOTH_
  ADDRESS_CHANGED**

  Constant `ACTION_BLUETOOTH_ADDRESS_CHANGED` from class
  `android.bluetooth.BluetoothAdapter`. Change in the Bluetooth
  address of the local Bluetooth adapter. Extra data:

  - **android.bluetooth.BluetoothAdapter.EXTRA_BLUETOOTH_
    ADDRESS**: The Bluetooth address

  Requires permission "android.permission.BLUETOOTH_
  CONNECT".

- **android.bluetooth.adapter.action.CONNECTION_
  STATE_CHANGED**

  Constant `ACTION_CONNECTION_STATE_CHANGED` from class
  `android.bluetooth.BluetoothAdapter`. A change in connection
  state of the local Bluetooth adapter to a profile of the remote
  device occurred. Contains extra data:

  - **android.bluetooth.BluetoothAdapter.EXTRA_CONNECTION_
    STATE**: The current state of the profile. One of

    android.bluetooth.BluetoothProfile.STATE_CONNECTED

    android.bluetooth.BluetoothProfile.STATE_DISCONNECTED

    android.bluetooth.BluetoothProfile.STATE_CONNECTING

    android.bluetooth.BluetoothProfile.STATE_
    DISCONNECTING

  - **android.bluetooth.BluetoothAdapter.EXTRA_PREVIOUS_
    CONNECTION_STATE**: The previous state of the profile. The
    possible values are the same as for `EXTRA_CONNECTION_STATE`.

  - **android.bluetooth.BluetoothDevice.EXTRA_DEVICE**: The
    remote device (android.bluetooth.BluetoothDevice).

Requires permission "android.permission.BLUETOOTH".

- **android.bluetooth.adapter.action.DISCOVERY_FINISHED**

Constant `ACTION_DISCOVERY_FINISHED` from class `android.bluetooth.BluetoothAdapter`. The local Bluetooth adapter has finished the device discovery process. Requires permission "android.permission.BLUETOOTH".

- **android.bluetooth.adapter.action.DISCOVERY_STARTED**

Constant `ACTION_DISCOVERY_STARTED` from class `android.bluetooth.BluetoothAdapter`. The local Bluetooth adapter has started the device discovery process. Requires permission "android.permission.BLUETOOTH".

- **android.bluetooth.adapter.action.LOCAL_NAME_CHANGED**

Constant `ACTION_LOCAL_NAME_CHANGED` from class `android.bluetooth.BluetoothAdapter`. The adapter has changed its externally visible Bluetooth name. Extra data:

    – **BluetoothAdapter.EXTRA_LOCAL_NAME**: The name (string)

Requires permission "android.permission.BLUETOOTH".

- **android.bluetooth.adapter.action.SCAN_MODE_CHANGED**

Constant `ACTION_SCAN_MODE_CHANGED` from class `android.bluetooth.BluetoothAdapter`. The Bluetooth scan mode of the local adapter has changed. Contains extra data:

    – **BluetoothAdapter.EXTRA_SCAN_MODE**: The new scan mode. Possible values are

    BluetoothAdapter.SCAN_MODE_NONE: Both inquiry and page scan disabled

    BluetoothAdapter.SCAN_MODE_CONNECTABLE: Inquiry scan disabled, page scan enabled

    BluetoothAdapter.SCAN_MODE_CONNECTABLE_DISCOVERABLE: Both inquiry and page scan enabled

- **BluetoothAdapter.EXTRA_PREVIOUS_SCAN_MODE**: The old scan mode. The possible values are the same as for EXTRA_SCAN_MODE.

Requires permission "android.permission.BLUETOOTH".

- **android.bluetooth.adapter.action.STATE_CHANGED**

Constant ACTION_STATE_CHANGED from class android.bluetooth. BluetoothAdapter. The state of the local Bluetooth adapter has been changed. Contains extra data:

- **BluetoothAdapter.EXTRA_STATE**: The new state. Possible values are

  BluetoothAdapter.STATE_OFF

  BluetoothAdapter.STATE_TURNING_ON

  BluetoothAdapter.STATE_ON

  BluetoothAdapter.STATE_TURNING_OFF

- **BluetoothAdapter.EXTRA_PREVIOUS_STATE**: The old state. The possible values are the same as for EXTRA_STATE.

Requires permission "android.permission.BLUETOOTH".

- **android.bluetooth.avrcp-controller.profile.action.CONNECTION_ STATE_CHANGED**

Constant ACTION_CONNECTION_STATE_CHANGED from class android.bluetooth.BluetoothAvrcpController. Used to broadcast the change in connection state of the AVRCP Controller profile. Extra data:

- **BluetoothAvrcpController.EXTRA_STATE**: The current state of the profile

- **BluetoothAvrcpController.EXTRA_PREVIOUS_STATE**: The previous state of the profile

- **BluetoothDevice.EXTRA_DEVICE**: The remote device (android. bluetooth.BluetoothDevice)

EXTRA_STATE or EXTRA_PREVIOUS_STATE can be any of (constants in BluetoothAvrcpController) STATE_ DISCONNECTED, STATE_CONNECTING, STATE_CONNECTED, and STATE_DISCONNECTING. Requires permissions "android.permission.BLUETOOTH" and "android.permission. BLUETOOTH_CONNECT".

- **android.bluetooth.avrcp-controller.profile.action. PLAYER_SETTING**

Constant `ACTION_PLAYER_SETTING` from class `android. bluetooth.BluetoothAvrcpController`. A change in player application setting state on AVRCP AG. Extra data:

- **BluetoothAvrcpController.EXTRA_PLAYER_SETTING**: The most recent player setting

Requires permission "android.permission.BLUETOOTH_ CONNECT".

- **android.bluetooth.device.action.ACL_CONNECTED**

Constant `ACTION_ACL_CONNECTED` from class `android.bluetooth. BluetoothDevice`. A low-level (ACL) connection has been established with a remote device. Contains extra data:

- **BluetoothDevice.EXTRA_DEVICE**: The remote device (android. bluetooth.BluetoothDevice)

Requires permission "android.permission.BLUETOOTH".

- **android.bluetooth.device.action.ACL_DISCONNECTED**

Constant `ACTION_ACL_DISCONNECTED` from class `android.bluetooth. BluetoothDevice`. A low-level (ACL) disconnection happened with a remote device. Contains extra data:

- **BluetoothDevice.EXTRA_DEVICE**: The remote device (android. bluetooth.BluetoothDevice)

Requires permission "android.permission.BLUETOOTH".

- **android.bluetooth.device.action.ACL_DISCONNECT_ REQUESTED**

Constant `ACTION_ACL_DISCONNECT_REQUESTED` from class `android.bluetooth.BluetoothDevice`. A low-level (ACL) disconnection with a remote device has been requested. Contains extra data:

- **BluetoothDevice.EXTRA_DEVICE**: The remote device (android. bluetooth.BluetoothDevice)

Requires permission "android.permission.BLUETOOTH".

- **android.bluetooth.device.action.ALIAS_CHANGED**
Constant `ACTION_ALIAS_CHANGED` from class `android.bluetooth. BluetoothDevice`. The alias of a remote device has been changed. Extra data:

- **BluetoothDevice.EXTRA_DEVICE**: The remote device (android. bluetooth.BluetoothDevice)

Requires permissions "android.permission.BLUETOOTH" and "android.permission.BLUETOOTH_CONNECT".

- **android.bluetooth.device.action.BATTERY_LEVEL_CHANGED**
Constant `ACTION_BATTERY_LEVEL_CHANGED` from class `android. bluetooth.BluetoothDevice`. The battery level of a remote device has been retrieved for the first time or changed since the last retrieval. Extra data:

- **BluetoothDevice.EXTRA_BATTERY_LEVEL**: The battery level

Requires permissions "android.permission.BLUETOOTH" and "android.permission.BLUETOOTH_CONNECT".

- **android.bluetooth.device.action.BOND_STATE_CHANGED**

Constant `ACTION_BOND_STATE_CHANGED` from class `android. bluetooth.BluetoothDevice`. A change in the bond state of a remote device happened. For example, a device is bonded (paired). Contains extra data:

- **BluetoothDevice.EXTRA_DEVICE**: The remote device (android. bluetooth.BluetoothDevice).

- **BluetoothDevice.EXTRA_BOND_STATE**: The new bond state. Possible values are

  BluetoothDevice.BOND_NONE

  BluetoothDevice.BOND_BONDING

  BluetoothDevice.BOND_BONDED

- **BluetoothDevice.EXTRA_PREVIOUS_BOND_STATE**: The previous bond state. The possible values are the same as for `EXTRA_BOND_STATE`.

• Requires permission "android.permission.BLUETOOTH".

• **android.bluetooth.device.action.CLASS_CHANGED**

Constant `ACTION_CLASS_CHANGED` from class `android.bluetooth.BluetoothDevice`. The Bluetooth class of a remote device has changed. Contains extra data:

- **BluetoothDevice.EXTRA_DEVICE**: The remote device (android.bluetooth.BluetoothDevice)

- **BluetoothDevice.EXTRA_CLASS**: The device class (android.bluetooth.BluetoothClass)

Requires permission "android.permission.BLUETOOTH".

• **android.bluetooth.device.action.CONNECTION_ACCESS_CANCEL**

Constant `ACTION_CONNECTION_ACCESS_CANCEL` from class `android.bluetooth.BluetoothDevice`. Used to broadcast CONNECTION ACCESS CANCEL. Requires permission "android.permission.BLUETOOTH_CONNECT".

• **android.bluetooth.device.action.CONNECTION_ACCESS_REPLY**

Constant `ACTION_CONNECTION_ACCESS_REPLY` from class `android.bluetooth.BluetoothDevice`. This action is the reply from ACTION_CONNECTION_ACCESS_REQUEST. Extra data:

- **BluetoothDevice.EXTRA_CONNECTION_ACCESS_RESULT**: Possible values: BluetoothDevice.CONNECTION_ACCESS_YES and BluetoothDevice.CONNECTION_ACCESS_NO.

- **BluetoothDevice.EXTRA_ALWAYS_ALLOWED**: A Boolean. Response is once for all so that next request will be granted without asking the user again.

Requires permission "android.permission.BLUETOOTH_ CONNECT".

- **android.bluetooth.device.action.CONNECTION_ ACCESS_REQUEST**

Constant ACTION_CONNECTION_ACCESS_REQUEST from class android.bluetooth.BluetoothDevice. This action will trigger a prompt for the user to accept or deny giving the permission for this device. Permissions can be specified. The reply will be an ACTION_CONNECTION_ACCESS_REPLY. Requires permission "android.permission.BLUETOOTH_CONNECT".

- **android.bluetooth.device.action.FOUND**

Constant ACTION_FOUND from class android.bluetooth. BluetoothDevice. A remote device has been discovered. Contains extra data:

- **BluetoothDevice.EXTRA_DEVICE**: The remote device (android. bluetooth.BluetoothDevice)

- **BluetoothDevice.EXTRA_CLASS**: The device class (android. bluetooth.BluetoothClass)

- **BluetoothDevice.EXTRA_NAME** (optional): The device friendly name (string)

- **BluetoothDevice.EXTRA_RSSI** (optional): The device signal strength RSSI (short int)

Requires permission "android.permission.BLUETOOTH".

- **android.bluetooth.device.action.MAS_INSTANCE**

Constant ACTION_MAS_INSTANCE from class android.bluetooth. BluetoothDevice. Undocumented.

- **android.bluetooth.device.action.NAME_CHANGED**

Constant `ACTION_NAME_CHANGED` from class `android.bluetooth.`
`BluetoothDevice`. The externally visible friendly name of a device
changed. Contains extra data:

- **BluetoothDevice.EXTRA_DEVICE**: The remote device (android.
  bluetooth.BluetoothDevice)

- **BluetoothDevice.EXTRA_NAME**: The device externalized
  friendly name (string)

Requires permission "android.permission.BLUETOOTH".

- **android.bluetooth.device.action.NAME_FAILED**

Constant `ACTION_NAME_FAILED` from class `android.bluetooth.`
`BluetoothDevice`. Indicates a failure to retrieve the name of a
remote device. Extra data:

- **BluetoothDevice.EXTRA_DEVICE**: The remote device (android.bluetooth.
  BluetoothDevice)

Requires permission "android.permission.BLUETOOTH_
CONNECT".

- **android.bluetooth.device.action.PAIRING_CANCEL**

Constant `ACTION_PAIRING_CANCEL` from class `android.`
`bluetooth.BluetoothDevice`. Used to broadcast PAIRING
CANCEL. Requires permission "android.permission.
BLUETOOTH_CONNECT".

- **android.bluetooth.device.action.PAIRING_REQUEST**

Constant `ACTION_PAIRING_REQUEST` from class `android.`
`bluetooth.BluetoothDevice`. Indicates a pairing request.
Requires permission "android.permission.BLUETOOTH".

- **android.bluetooth.device.action.SDP_RECORD**

Constant `ACTION_SDP_RECORD` from class `android.bluetooth.`
`BluetoothDevice`. Undocumented.

- **android.bluetooth.device.action.SILENCE_MODE_CHANGED**

  Constant ACTION_SILENCE_MODE_CHANGED from class android.bluetooth.BluetoothDevice. The silence mode changed.
  Extra data:

  - **BluetoothDevice.EXTRA_DEVICE**: The remote device (android.bluetooth.BluetoothDevice)

  Requires permission "android.permission.BLUETOOTH_CONNECT".

- **android.bluetooth.device.action.UUID**

  Constant ACTION_UUID from class android.bluetooth.BluetoothDevice. The UUID as a result of a service discovery has been fetched. Contains extra data:

  - **BluetoothDevice.EXTRA_DEVICE**: The remote device (android.bluetooth.BluetoothDevice)

  - **BluetoothDevice.EXTRA_UUID**: The UUID (android.os.ParcelUuid)

  Requires permission "android.permission.BLUETOOTH".

- **android.bluetooth.devicepicker.action.DEVICE_SELECTED**

  Fired when one BT device is selected from the BT device picker screen. Extra data:

  - **BluetoothDevice.EXTRA_DEVICE**: The remote device (android.bluetooth.BluetoothDevice)

  Requires permission "android.permission.BLUETOOTH".

- **android.bluetooth.devicepicker.action.LAUNCH**

  Someone wants to select one BT device from the devices list.
  Extra data:

  - **BluetoothDevice.EXTRA_NEED_AUTH**: Whether authentication is required (Boolean)

  - **BluetoothDevice.EXTRA_FILTER_TYPE**: The filter type (an int)

- **BluetoothDevice.EXTRA_LAUNCH_PACKAGE**: Where this Intent comes from (string)

- **BluetoothDevice.EXTRA_LAUNCH_CLASS**: The Intent's originating class (string)

- **android.bluetooth.headset.action.HF_INDICATORS_ VALUE_CHANGED**

  Constant `ACTION_HF_INDICATORS_VALUE_CHANGED` from class `android.bluetooth.BluetoothHeadset`. Intent used to broadcast the headset's indicator status. Extra data:

  - **BluetoothHeadset.EXTRA_HF_INDICATORS_IND_ID**: The assigned number of the headset indicator.

  - **BluetoothHeadset.EXTRA_HF_INDICATORS_IND_VALUE**: Updated value of the headset indicator.

  - **BluetoothHeadset.EXTRA_HF_INDICATORS_IND_ID**: Defined by Bluetooth SIG. Assigned number of the indicator:

    1 (Enhanced Safety): Valid values – 0, Disabled; 1, Enabled

    2 (Battery Level): Valid values – 0 100, remaining level of battery

  Requires permissions "android.permission.BLUETOOTH" and "android.permission.BLUETOOTH_CONNECT".

- **android.bluetooth.headset.action.VENDOR_SPECIFIC_ HEADSET_EVENT**

  Constant `ACTION_VENDOR_SPECIFIC_HEADSET_EVENT` from class `android.bluetooth.BluetoothHeadset`. The headset has posted a vendor-specific event. Extra data:

  - **android.bluetooth.BluetoothDevice.EXTRA_DEVICE**: The remote device (android.bluetooth.BluetoothDevice)

  - **BluetoothHeadset.EXTRA_VENDOR_SPECIFIC_HEADSET_ EVENT_CMD**: The vendor-specific command (string)

- **BluetoothHeadset.EXTRA_VENDOR_SPECIFIC_HEADSET_ EVENT_CMD_TYPE**: The AT command type. One of

  BluetoothHeadset.AT_CMD_TYPE_READ

  BluetoothHeadset.AT_CMD_TYPE_TEST

  BluetoothHeadset.AT_CMD_TYPE_SET

  BluetoothHeadset.AT_CMD_TYPE_BASIC

  BluetoothHeadset.AT_CMD_TYPE_ACTION

- **BluetoothHeadset.EXTRA_VENDOR_SPECIFIC_HEADSET_ EVENT_ARGS**: Command arguments (string array)

The Intent has a special category value: the Company ID of the vendor defining the vendor-specific command (int). Requires permission "android.permission.BLUETOOTH".

- **android.bluetooth.headset.profile.action.ACTIVE_ DEVICE_CHANGED**

Constant `ACTION_ACTIVE_DEVICE_CHANGED` from class `android. bluetooth.BluetoothHeadset`. The selection of a connected device as active. Extra data:

- **android.bluetooth.BluetoothDevice.EXTRA_DEVICE**: The remote device (android.bluetooth.BluetoothDevice). Can be null if no device is active.

Requires permissions "android.permission.BLUETOOTH" and "android.permission.BLUETOOTH_CONNECT".

- **android.bluetooth.headset.profile.action.AUDIO_ STATE_CHANGED**

Constant `ACTION_AUDIO_STATE_CHANGED` from class `android. bluetooth.BluetoothHeadset`. A change in the audio connection state of the A2DP profile occurred. Contains extra data:

- **android.bluetooth.BluetoothDevice.EXTRA_DEVICE**: The remote device (android.bluetooth.BluetoothDevice).

- **BluetoothHeadset.EXTRA_STATE**: The new state. Possible values are

  BluetoothHeadset.STATE_AUDIO_CONNECTED

  BluetoothHeadset.STATE_AUDIO_DISCONNECTED

- **BluetoothHeadset.EXTRA_PREVIOUS_STATE**: The old state. The possible values are the same as for EXTRA_STATE.

Requires permission "android.permission.BLUETOOTH".

- **android.bluetooth.headset.profile.action.CONNECTION_ STATE_CHANGED**

Constant ACTION_CONNECTION_STATE_CHANGED from class android.bluetooth.BluetoothHeadset. A change in connection state of the headset profile occurred. Contains extra data:

- **android.bluetooth.BluetoothDevice.EXTRA_DEVICE**: The remote device (android.bluetooth.BluetoothDevice).

- **BluetoothHeadset.EXTRA_STATE**: The new state. Possible values are

  BluetoothHeadset.STATE_CONNECTED

  BluetoothHeadset.STATE_DICONNECTED

  BluetoothHeadset.STATE_CONNECTING

  BluetoothHeadset.STATE_DICONNECTING

- **BluetoothHeadset.EXTRA_PREVIOUS_STATE**: The old state. The possible values are the same as for EXTRA_STATE.

Requires permission "android.permission.BLUETOOTH".

- **android.bluetooth.headsetclient.profile.action.AG_ CALL_CHANGED**

Constant ACTION_AG_CALL_CHANGED from class android.bluetooth. BluetoothHeadsetClient. The state of a call changes. Extra data:

- **BluetoothHeadsetClient.EXTRA_CALL**: Representing actual call state, with value of BluetoothHeadsetClientCall instance

Requires permission "android.permission.BLUETOOTH_ CONNECT".

- **android.bluetooth.headsetclient.profile.action.AG_EVENT**

Constant `ACTION_AG_EVENT` from class `android.bluetooth.BluetoothHeadsetClient`. Updates of the Audio Gateway state. Extra data (each extra is being sent only when the value it represents has been changed recently on AG):

- **BluetoothHeadsetClient.EXTRA_NETWORK_STATUS**: 0, network unavailable; 1, network available

- **BluetoothHeadsetClient.EXTRA_NETWORK_SIGNAL_ STRENGTH**: Integer representing signal strength

- **BluetoothHeadsetClient.EXTRA_NETWORK_ROAMING**: 0, no roaming; 1, active roaming

- **BluetoothHeadsetClient.EXTRA_BATTERY_LEVEL**: Integer representing battery level

- **BluetoothHeadsetClient.EXTRA_OPERATOR_NAME**: String representing operator name

- **BluetoothHeadsetClient.EXTRA_VOICE_RECOGNITION**: 0, voice recognition stopped; 1, voice recognition started

- **BluetoothHeadsetClient.EXTRA_IN_BAND_RING**: 0, in-band ringtone not supported; 1, in-band ringtone supported

Requires permission "android.permission.BLUETOOTH_ CONNECT".

- **android.bluetooth.headsetclient.profile.action.AUDIO_ STATE_CHANGED**

Constant `ACTION_AUDIO_STATE_CHANGED` from class `android.bluetooth.BluetoothHeadsetClient`. Sent whenever audio state changes. Extra data:

- **BluetoothProfile.EXTRA_STATE**: Values –
  BluetoothHeadsetClient.STATE_AUDIO_CONNECTING,
  BluetoothHeadsetClient.STATE_AUDIO_CONNECTED,
  BluetoothHeadsetClient.STATE_AUDIO_DISCONNECTED

- **BluetoothProfile.EXTRA_PREVIOUS_STATE**: Values like the
  preceding EXTRA_STATE

- When EXTRA_STATE is set to STATE_AUDIO_CONNECTED, it
  also includes BluetoothHeadsetClient.EXTRA_AUDIO_WBS
  indicating wide-band speech support.

Requires permission "android.permission.BLUETOOTH_
CONNECT".

- **android.bluetooth.headsetclient.profile.action.CONNECTION_
  STATE_CHANGED**

Constant ACTION_CONNECTION_STATE_CHANGED from class
android.bluetooth.BluetoothHeadsetClient. Signals a change
in connection state of the HFP Client profile. Extra data:

- **BluetoothHeadsetClient.EXTRA_STATE**: The current state of
  the profile

- **BluetoothHeadsetClient.EXTRA_PREVIOUS_STATE**: The
  previous state of the profile

- **BluetoothDevice.EXTRA_DEVICE**: The remote device

EXTRA_STATE or EXTRA_PREVIOUS_STATE can be any
of (constants from class BluetoothHeadsetClient) STATE_
DISCONNECTED, STATE_CONNECTING, STATE_CONNECTED,
and STATE_DISCONNECTING. Requires permissions "android.
permission.BLUETOOTH_CONNECT" and "android.permission.
BLUETOOTH_PRIVILEGED".

- **android.bluetooth.headsetclient.profile.action.LAST_VTAG**

Constant ACTION_LAST_VTAG from class android.bluetooth.
BluetoothHeadsetClient. Intent that notifies about the number
attached to the last voice tag. Extra data:

    – **BluetoothHeadsetClient.EXTRA_NUMBER**: String value repre-
      senting phone number

Requires permission "android.permission.BLUETOOTH_
CONNECT".

- **android.bluetooth.headsetclient.profile.action.RESULT**

Constant `ACTION_RESULT` from class `android.bluetooth.`
`BluetoothHeadsetClient`. Notifies about the result of the
last issued action. Requires permission "android.permission.
BLUETOOTH_CONNECT".

- **android.bluetooth.headsetclient.profile.action.VENDOR_
SPECIFIC_EVENT**

Constant `ACTION_VENDOR_SPECIFIC_EVENT` from class `android.`
`bluetooth.BluetoothHeadsetClient`. Vendor-specific event
arrival. Supported vendor events are of format "+eventCode" or
"+eventCode=xxxx" or "+eventCode:=xxxx". Vendor events can be
a response to a vendor-specific command or unsolicited. Requires
permission "android.permission.BLUETOOTH_CONNECT".

- **android.bluetooth.hearingaid.profile.action.ACTIVE_
DEVICE_CHANGED**

Constant `ACTION_ACTIVE_DEVICE_CHANGED` from class `android.`
`bluetooth.BluetoothHearingAid`. Broadcasts the selection of a
connected device as active. Extra data:

    – **BluetoothDevice.EXTRA_DEVICE**: The remote device. It can be
      null if no device is active.

Requires permissions "android.permission.BLUETOOTH" and
"android.permission.BLUETOOTH_CONNECT".

- **android.bluetooth.hearingaid.profile.action.CONNECTION_
STATE_CHANGED**

Constant `ACTION_CONNECTION_STATE_CHANGED` from class
`android.bluetooth.BluetoothHearingAid`. A change in
connection state of the Hearing Aid profile (possibly two different
LE devices for the left and right sides, if applicable). Extra data:

- **BluetoothHearingAid.EXTRA_STATE**: The current state of the profile.

- **BluetoothHearingAid.EXTRA_PREVIOUS_STATE**: The previous state of the profile.

- **BluetoothDevice.EXTRA_DEVICE**: The remote device. It can be null if no device is active.

EXTRA_STATE or EXTRA_PREVIOUS_STATE can be any of (constants from BluetoothHearingAid) STATE_DISCONNECTED, STATE_CONNECTING, STATE_CONNECTED, and STATE_ DISCONNECTING. Requires permissions "android.permission. BLUETOOTH" and "android.permission.BLUETOOTH_ CONNECT".

- **android.bluetooth.hiddevice.profile.action.CONNECTION_ STATE_CHANGED**

Constant `ACTION_CONNECTION_STATE_CHANGED` from class `android.bluetooth.BluetoothHidDevice`. The change in connection state of the Input Host profile. Extra data:

- **BluetoothHidDevice.EXTRA_STATE**: The current state of the profile.

- **BluetoothHidDevice.EXTRA_PREVIOUS_STATE**: The previous state of the profile.

- **BluetoothDevice.EXTRA_DEVICE**: The remote device. It can be null if no device is active.

EXTRA_STATE or EXTRA_PREVIOUS_STATE can be any of (constants from BluetoothHidDevice) STATE_DISCONNECTED, STATE_CONNECTING, STATE_CONNECTED, and STATE_ DISCONNECTING. Requires permissions "android.permission. BLUETOOTH" and "android.permission.BLUETOOTH_ CONNECT".

- **android.bluetooth.input.profile.action.CONNECTION_ STATE_CHANGED**

Constant `ACTION_CONNECTION_STATE_CHANGED` from class `android.bluetooth.BluetoothHidHost`. Used to broadcast the change in connection state of the input device profile. Extra data:

– **android.bluetooth.BluetoothProfile.EXTRA_STATE**: Current state. Possible values are

android.bluetooth.BluetoothProfile.STATE_CONNECTED

android.bluetooth.BluetoothProfile.STATE_DICONNECTED

android.bluetooth.BluetoothProfile.STATE_CONNECTING

android.bluetooth.BluetoothProfile.STATE_DICONNECTING

– **android.bluetooth.BluetoothProfile.EXTRA_PREVIOUS_STATE**: Previous state.

– **android.bluetooth.BluetoothProfile.EXTRA_DEVICE**: The device.

Requires permission "android.permission.BLUETOOTH".

- **android.bluetooth.input.profile.action.HANDSHAKE**

Constant `ACTION_HANDSHAKE` from class `android.bluetooth.BluetoothHidHost`. Undocumented. Requires permission "android.permission.BLUETOOTH_CONNECT".

- **android.bluetooth.input.profile.action.IDLE_TIME_CHANGED**

Constant `ACTION_IDLE_TIME_CHANGED` from class `android.bluetooth.BluetoothHidHost`. Undocumented. Requires permission "android.permission.BLUETOOTH".

- **android.bluetooth.input.profile.action.PROTOCOL_MODE_CHANGED**

Undocumented.

- **android.bluetooth.input.profile.action.REPORT**

Constant `ACTION_REPORT` from class `android.bluetooth.BluetoothHidHost`. Undocumented. Requires permission "android.permission.BLUETOOTH_CONNECT".

- **android.bluetooth.input.profile.action.VIRTUAL_UNPLUG_STATUS**

  Undocumented.

- **android.bluetooth.map.profile.action.CONNECTION_STATE_CHANGED**

  Constant `ACTION_CONNECTION_STATE_CHANGED` from class `android.bluetooth.BluetoothMap`. Undocumented. Requires permission "android.permission.BLUETOOTH_CONNECT".

- **android.bluetooth.mapmce.profile.action.CONNECTION_STATE_CHANGED**

  Constant `ACTION_CONNECTION_STATE_CHANGED` from class `android.bluetooth.BluetoothMapClient`. A change in connection state of the MAP Client profile. Extra data:

  - **BluetoothMapClient.EXTRA_STATE**: The current state of the profile

  - **BluetoothMapClient.EXTRA_PREVIOUS_STATE**: The previous state of the profile

  - **android.bluetooth.BluetoothProfile.EXTRA_DEVICE**: The device

  EXTRA_STATE or EXTRA_PREVIOUS_STATE can be any of (constants from BluetoothMapClient) STATE_DISCONNECTED, STATE_CONNECTING, STATE_CONNECTED, and STATE_DISCONNECTING.Requires permissions "android.permission.BLUETOOTH_CONNECT" and "android.permission.BLUETOOTH_PRIVILEGED".

- **android.bluetooth.mapmce.profile.action.MESSAGE_DELETED_STATUS_CHANGED**

  Constant `ACTION_MESSAGE_DELETED_STATUS_CHANGED` from class `android.bluetooth.BluetoothMapClient`. Deleted status changed. Requires permission "android.permission.BLUETOOTH_CONNECT".

- **android.bluetooth.mapmce.profile.action.MESSAGE_
  DELIVERED_SUCCESSFULLY**

  Constant `ACTION_MESSAGE_DELIVERED_SUCCESSFULLY` from class
  `android.bluetooth.BluetoothMapClient`. Undocumented.
  Requires permission "android.permission.BLUETOOTH_
  CONNECT".

- **android.bluetooth.mapmce.profile.action.MESSAGE_READ_
  STATUS_CHANGED**

  Constant `ACTION_MESSAGE_READ_STATUS_CHANGED` from class
  `android.bluetooth.BluetoothMapClient`. Read status changed.
  Requires permission "android.permission.BLUETOOTH_
  CONNECT".

- **android.bluetooth.mapmce.profile.action.MESSAGE_RECEIVED**

  Constant `ACTION_MESSAGE_RECEIVED` from class `android.
  bluetooth.BluetoothMapClient`. Undocumented. Requires
  permission "android.permission.RECEIVE_SMS".

- **android.bluetooth.mapmce.profile.action.MESSAGE_SENT_
  SUCCESSFULLY**

  Constant `ACTION_MESSAGE_SENT_SUCCESSFULLY` from class
  `android.bluetooth.BluetoothMapClient`. Undocumented.
  Requires permission "android.permission.BLUETOOTH_
  CONNECT".

- **android.bluetooth.pan.profile.action.CONNECTION_
  STATE_CHANGED**

  Constant `ACTION_CONNECTION_STATE_CHANGED` from class
  `android.bluetooth.BluetoothPan`. Intent used to broadcast the
  change in connection state of the Pan profile. Extra data:

  – **android.bluetooth.BluetoothPan.EXTRA_STATE**:Current
    state. One of

    BluetoothPan.STATE_DISCONNECTED

    BluetoothPan.STATE_CONNECTING

779

BluetoothPan.STATE_CONNECTED

BluetoothPan.STATE_DISCONNECTING

– **android.bluetooth.BluetoothPan.EXTRA_PREVIOUS_STATE**:
Previous state. One of

BluetoothPan.STATE_DISCONNECTED

BluetoothPan.STATE_CONNECTING

BluetoothPan.STATE_CONNECTED

BluetoothPan.STATE_DISCONNECTING

– **android.bluetooth.BluetoothDevice.EXTRA_DEVICE**:
The device

– **android.bluetooth.BluetoothPan.EXTRA_LOCAL_ROLE**: The
local role the remote device is bound to. One of

BluetoothPan.LOCAL_NAP_ROLE

BluetoothPan.LOCAL_PANU_ROLE

Requires the "android.Manifest.permission.BLUETOOTH"
permission.

• **android.bluetooth.pbap.profile.action.CONNECTION_
STATE_CHANGED**

Constant `ACTION_CONNECTION_STATE_CHANGED` from class
`android.bluetooth.BluetoothPbap`.

A change in connection state of the PBAP profile. Extra data:

– **BluetoothProfile.EXTRA_STATE**: The current state of the profile

– **BluetoothProfile.EXTRA_PREVIOUS_STATE**: The previous state
of the profile

– **BluetoothDevice.EXTRA_DEVICE**: The remote device

EXTRA_STATE or EXTRA_PREVIOUS_STATE can be any of (constants in BluetoothProfile) STATE_DISCONNECTED, STATE_CONNECTING, STATE_CONNECTED, and STATE_DISCONNECTING.Requires permission "android.permission.BLUETOOTH_CONNECT".

- **android.bluetooth.pbapclient.profile.action.CONNECTION_STATE_CHANGED**

  Constant `ACTION_CONNECTION_STATE_CHANGED` from class `android.bluetooth.BluetoothPbapClient`. A change in connection state of the PBAP client profile. Extra data:

  - **BluetoothPbapClient.EXTRA_STATE**: The current state of the profile

  - **BluetoothPbapClient.EXTRA_PREVIOUS_STATE**: The previous state of the profile

  - **BluetoothDevice.EXTRA_DEVICE**: The remote device

  EXTRA_STATE or EXTRA_PREVIOUS_STATE can be any of (constants in BluetoothPbapClient) STATE_DISCONNECTED, STATE_CONNECTING, STATE_CONNECTED, and STATE_DISCONNECTING.Requires permissions "android.permission.BLUETOOTH_CONNECT" and "android.permission.BLUETOOTH_PRIVILEGED".

- **android.bluetooth.sap.profile.action.CONNECTION_STATE_CHANGED**

  Constant `ACTION_CONNECTION_STATE_CHANGED` from class `android.bluetooth.BluetoothSap`. A change in connection state of the profile. Extra data:

  - **BluetoothSap.EXTRA_STATE**: The current state of the profile

  - **BluetoothSap.EXTRA_PREVIOUS_STATE**: The previous state of the profile

  - **BluetoothDevice.EXTRA_DEVICE**: The remote device

- Requires permissions "android.permission.BLUETOOTH" and "android.permission.BLUETOOTH_CONNECT".

USB

- **android.hardware.usb.action.USB_ACCESSORY_ATTACHED**

  Constant `ACTION_USB_ACCESSORY_ATTACHED` from class `android.hardware.usb.UsbManager`. The user attaches a USB accessory. Extra data:

  - **UsbManager.EXTRA_ACCESSORY**: Contains the UsbAccessory for the attached accessory (android.hardware.usb.UsbAccessory)

- **android.hardware.usb.action.USB_ACCESSORY_DETACHED**

  Constant `ACTION_USB_ACCESSORY_DETACHED` from class `android.hardware.usb.UsbManager`. The user detaches a USB accessory. Extra data:

  - **UsbManager.EXTRA_ACCESSORY**: Contains the UsbAccessory for the detached accessory (android.hardware.usb.UsbAccessory)

- **android.hardware.usb.action.USB_ACCESSORY_HANDSHAKE**

  Constant `ACTION_USB_ACCESSORY_HANDSHAKE` from class `android.hardware.usb.UsbManager`. Signals a handshake during a USB accessory connection attempt. Requires permission "android.permission.MANAGE_USB".

- **android.hardware.usb.action.USB_DEVICE_ATTACHED**

  Constant `USB_DEVICE_ATTACHED` from class `android.hardware.usb.UsbManager`. The user attaches a USB device. Extra data:

  - **UsbManager.EXTRA_DEVICE**: Contains the attached device (android.hardware.usb. UsbDevice)

- **android.hardware.usb.action.USB_DEVICE_DETACHED**

  Constant `USB_DEVICE_DETACHED` from class `android.hardware.usb.UsbManager`. The user detaches a USB device. Extra data:

  - **UsbManager.EXTRA_DEVICE**: Contains the detached device (android.hardware.usb. UsbDevice)

Power Management

- **android.intent.action.ACTION_POWER_CONNECTED**

  Constant `ACTION_POWER_CONNECTED` from class `android.content.Intent`. The device got the power connected.

- **android.intent.action.ACTION_POWER_DISCONNECTED**

  Constant `ACTION_POWER_DISCONNECTED` from class `android.content.Intent`. The device got the power disconnected.

- **android.intent.action.BATTERY_CHANGED**

  Constant `ACTION_BATTERY_CHANGED` from class `android.content.Intent`. Provide battery status changes. Extra data:

  - **android.os.BatteryManager.EXTRA_HEALTH**: An int containing the current health status. One of

    BatteryManager.BATTERY_HEALTH_COLD

    BatteryManager.BATTERY_HEALTH_DEAD

    BatteryManager.BATTERY_HEALTH_GOOD

    BatteryManager.BATTERY_HEALTH_OVERHEAT

    BatteryManager.BATTERY_HEALTH_OVER_VOLTAGE

    BatteryManager.BATTERY_HEALTH_UNKNOWN

    BatteryManager.BATTERY_HEALTH_UNSPECIFIED_FAILURE

  - **android.os.BatteryManager.EXTRA_ICON_SMALL**: A resource ID of an icon indicating the battery health state.

  - **android.os.BatteryManager.EXTRA_LEVEL**: An int containing the battery level, from 0 to BatteryManager.EXTRA_SCALE.

  - **android.os.BatteryManager.EXTRA_PLUGGED**: 0 means battery; other ints mean different types of power source.

  - **android.os.BatteryManager.EXTRA_PRESENT**: Boolean, whether a battery is present.

- **android.os.BatteryManager.EXTRA_SCALE**: An int containing the maximum battery level.

- **android.os.BatteryManager.EXTRA_STATUS**: One of

  BatteryManager.BATTERY_STATUS_CHARGING

  BatteryManager.BATTERY_STATUS_DISCHARGING

  BatteryManager.BATTERY_STATUS_FULL

  BatteryManager.BATTERY_STATUS_NOT_CHARGING

  BatteryManager.BATTERY_STATUS_UNKNOWN

- **android.os.BatteryManager.EXTRA_TECHNOLOGY**: A string describing the battery's technology.

- **android.os.BatteryManager.EXTRA_TEMPERATURE**: An int with the current battery temperature.

- **android.os.BatteryManager.EXTRA_VOLTAGE**: An int with the current battery voltage level.

- **android.intent.action.BATTERY_LOW**

  Constant `ACTION_BATTERY_LOW` from class `android.content.Intent`. Low-battery condition.

- **android.intent.action.BATTERY_OKAY**

  Constant `ACTION_BATTERY_OKAY` from class `android.content.Intent`. Battery now OK from formerly being low.

- **android.os.action.DEVICE_IDLE_MODE_CHANGED**

  Constant `ACTION_DEVICE_IDLE_MODE_CHANGED` from class `android.os.PowerManager`. Fired when the outcome of `PowerManager.isDeviceIdleMode()` changes.

- **android.os.action.ENHANCED_DISCHARGE_PREDICTION_CHANGED**

  Constant `ACTION_ENHANCED_DISCHARGE_PREDICTION_CHANGED` from class `android.os.PowerManager`. The enhanced battery discharge prediction changes. The new value can be retrieved via `getBatteryDischargePrediction()`.

- **android.os.action.LIGHT_DEVICE_IDLE_MODE_CHANGED**

  Constant `ACTION_LIGHT_DEVICE_IDLE_MODE_CHANGED` from class `android.os.PowerManager`. The state of `isDeviceLightIdleMode()` changes.

- **android.os.action.POWER_SAVE_MODE_CHANGED**

  Constant `ACTION_POWER_SAVE_MODE_CHANGED` from class `android.os.PowerManager`. Fired when the outcome of `PowerManager.isPowerSaveMode()` changes.

- **android.os.action.POWER_SAVE_MODE_CHANGED_INTERNAL**

  Constant `ACTION_POWER_SAVE_MODE_CHANGED_INTERNAL` from class `android.os.PowerManager`. The state of `isPowerSaveMode()` changes.

- **android.os.action.POWER_SAVE_TEMP_WHITELIST_CHANGED**

  Constant `ACTION_POWER_SAVE_TEMP_WHITELIST_CHANGED` from class `android.os.PowerManager`. The set of temporarily allowlisted apps has changed.

- **android.os.action.POWER_SAVE_WHITELIST_CHANGED**

  Constant `ACTION_POWER_SAVE_WHITELIST_CHANGED` from class `android.os.PowerManager`. The set of allowlisted apps has changed.

- **android.os.action.UPDATE_EMERGENCY_NUMBER_DB**

  Constant `ACTION_UPDATE_EMERGENCY_NUMBER_DB` from class `android.os.ConfigUpdate`. Emergency number database update. Extra data:

  - **ConfigUpdate.EXTRA_VERSION**: The numeric version of the database

  - **ConfigUpdate.EXTRA_REQUIRED_HASH**: Hash of the database, which is encoded by base-16 SHA512

Media

- **android.intent.action.MEDIA_BAD_REMOVAL**

  Constant `ACTION_MEDIA_BAD_REMOVAL` from class `android.`
  `content.Intent`. A medium (external SD card) was removed, but
  not previously unmounted properly.

- **android.intent.action.MEDIA_BUTTON**

  Constant `ACTION_MEDIA_BUTTON` from class `android.content.`
  `Intent`. The media button has been pressed. Contains extra data:

  - **intent.EXTRA_KEY_EVENT**: The corresponding key event
    (android.view.KeyEvent)

- **android.intent.action.MEDIA_CHECKING**

  Constant `ACTION_MEDIA_CHECKING` from class `android.content.`
  `Intent`. An external medium is present and is being disk-checked.

- **android.intent.action.MEDIA_EJECT**

  Constant `ACTION_MEDIA_EJECT` from class `android.content.`
  `Intent`. An external medium is *about* to be ejected – the app
  should now do a cleanup of its data. The mount point is contained
  in the `Intent.mData` field.

- **android.intent.action.MEDIA_MOUNTED**

  Constant `ACTION_MEDIA_MOUNTED` from class `android.content.`
  `Intent`. An external medium has been mounted. Extra data:

  - **"read-only"**: Whether the medium is mounted read-only
    (Boolean)

- **android.intent.action.MEDIA_NOFS**

  Constant `ACTION_MEDIA_NOFS` from class `android.content.`
  `Intent`. An external medium is present, but it does not contain a
  valid file system.

- **android.intent.action.MEDIA_REMOVED**

Constant `ACTION_MEDIA_REMOVED` from class `android.content.Intent`. An external medium has been removed. The mount point is contained in the `Intent.mData` field.

- **android.intent.action.MEDIA_SCANNER_FINISHED**

  Constant `ACTION_MEDIA_SCANNER_FINISHED` from class `android.content.Intent`. The media scanner has finished scanning a directory. The path is contained in the `Intent.mData` field.

- **android.intent.action.MEDIA_SCANNER_SCAN_FILE**

  Constant `ACTION_MEDIA_SCANNER_SCAN_FILE` from class `android.content.Intent`. Request the media scanner to scan a file and add it to its database. The file path must be entered in the `Intent.mData` field.

- **android.intent.action.MEDIA_SCANNER_STARTED**

  Constant `ACTION_MEDIA_SCANNER_STARTED` from class `android.content.Intent`. The media scanner has started scanning a directory. The path is contained in the `Intent.mData` field.

- **android.intent.action.MEDIA_SHARED**

  Constant `ACTION_MEDIA_SHARED` from class `android.content.Intent`. An external medium is unmounted because it is being shared via USB mass storage. The path to the mount point is contained in the `Intent.mData` field.

- **android.intent.action.MEDIA_UNMOUNTABLE**

  Constant `ACTION_MEDIA_UNMOUNTABLE` from class `android.content.Intent`. An external medium is present, but it cannot be mounted. The path to the requested mount point is contained in the `Intent.mData` field.

- **android.intent.action.MEDIA_UNMOUNTED**

  Constant `ACTION_MEDIA_UNMOUNTED` from class `android.content.Intent`. An external medium has been unmounted. The path to the mount point is contained in the `Intent.mData` field.

Packages (Apps)

- **android.intent.action.CANCEL_ENABLE_ROLLBACK**

  Constant `ACTION_CANCEL_ENABLE_ROLLBACK` from class `android.content.Intent`. The rollback for a certain package needs to be cancelled.

- **android.intent.action.DISTRACTING_PACKAGES_CHANGED**

  Constant `ACTION_DISTRACTING_PACKAGES_CHANGED` from class `android.content.Intent`. Distracting packages have been changed. Extra data:

  - **android.content.Intent.EXTRA_CHANGED_PACKAGE_LIST**: The set of packages that have been changed

  - **android.content.Intent.EXTRA_CHANGED_UID_LIST**: The set of UIDs that have been changed

  - **android.content.Intent.**EXTRA_DISTRACTION_RESTRICTIONS: The new restrictions set on these packages

- **android.intent.action.DOMAINS_NEED_VERIFICATION**

  Constant `ACTION_DOMAINS_NEED_VERIFICATION` from class `android.content.Intent`. An app's domains need to be verified. Can only be sent by the system. The data contains the domains' hosts to be verified against.

- **android.intent.action.MY_PACKAGE_REPLACED**

  Constant `ACTION_MY_PACKAGE_REPLACED` from class `android.content.Intent`. A new version of an app is replacing an existing one. Sent only to the app in question.

- **android.intent.action.MY_PACKAGE_SUSPENDED**

  Constant `ACTION_MY_PACKAGE_SUSPENDED` from class `android.content.Intent`. Sent to a package that has been suspended by the system. Can only be sent by the system. Sent whenever a package is put into a suspended state or any of its app extras change while in the suspended state. Extra data:

- **Intent.EXTRA_SUSPENDED_PACKAGE_EXTRAS**: A `Bundle` containing information for the app being suspended (optional)

- **android.intent.action.MY_PACKAGE_UNSUSPENDED**

  Constant `ACTION_MY_PACKAGE_UNSUSPENDED` from class `android.content.Intent`. Sent to a package that has been unsuspended. Can only be sent by the system.

- **android.intent.action.PACKAGES_SUSPENDED**

  Constant `ACTION_PACKAGES_SUSPENDED` from class `android.content.Intent`. Apps (packages) have been suspended. Extra data:

  - **Intent.EXTRA_CHANGED_PACKAGE_LIST**: The list of apps (string array)

- **android.intent.action.PACKAGES_SUSPENSION_CHANGED**

  Constant `ACTION_PACKAGES_SUSPENSION_CHANGED` from class `android.content.Intent`. One of the suspend conditions has been modified for the packages. Can only be sent by the system. Extra data:

  - **Intent.EXTRA_CHANGED_PACKAGE_LIST**: The set of packages that have been modified

  - **Intent.EXTRA_CHANGED_UID_LIST**: The set of UIDs that have been modified

- **android.intent.action.PACKAGES_UNSUSPENDED**

  Constant `ACTION_PACKAGES_UNSUSPENDED` from class `android.content.Intent`. Apps (packages) have been unsuspended. Extra data:

  - **Intent.EXTRA_CHANGED_PACKAGE_LIST**: The list of apps (string array)

- **android.intent.action.PACKAGE_ADDED**

  Constant `ACTION_PACKAGE_ADDED` from class `android.content.Intent`. An app was installed on the device. Extra data:

- **Intent.EXTRA_UID**: The UID of the app (int)

- **Intent.EXTRA_REPLACING**: If the app was replaced, follows an `ACTION_PACKAGE_REMOVED` (boolean)

- **android.intent.action.PACKAGE_CHANGED**

Constant `ACTION_PACKAGE_CHANGED` from class `android.content.Intent`. An existing app has been changed. Extra data:

- **Intent.EXTRA_UID**: The UID of the app (int)

- **Intent.EXTRA_CHANGED_COMPONENT_NAME_LIST**: A list of changed apps or components (string array)

- **android.intent.action.PACKAGE_DATA_CLEARED**

Constant `ACTION_PACKAGE_DATA_CLEARED` from class `android.content.Intent`. The data of an app has been cleared. Extra data:

- **Intent.EXTRA_UID**: The UID of the app, will be -1 if this is an *instant app* (int)

- **Intent.EXTRA_PACKAGE_NAME**: If the app is an *instant app*, the package name (string)

- **android.intent.action.PACKAGE_ENABLE_ROLLBACK**

Constant `ACTION_` from class `android.content.Intent`. Sent to the system rollback manager when a package needs to have rollback enabled. This broadcast is used internally by the system, and it can only be sent by the system.

- **android.intent.action.PACKAGE_FIRST_LAUNCH**

Constant `ACTION_PACKAGE_FIRST_LAUNCH` from class `android.content.Intent`. An app was launched the first time. The URI from `Intent.getData()` contains the package name.

- **android.intent.action.PACKAGE_FULLY_REMOVED**

Constant `ACTION_PACKAGE_FULLY_REMOVED` from class `android.content.Intent`. An app including its data has been removed from the system. Extra data:

- **Intent.EXTRA_UID**: The UID of the app (int)

- **android.intent.action.PACKAGE_INSTALL**

  Constant `ACTION_PACKAGE_INSTALL` from class `android.content.Intent`. Defunct – do not use.

- **android.intent.action.PACKAGE_NEEDS_INTEGRITY_VERIFICATION**

  Constant `ACTION_` from class `android.content.Intent`. Sent to the integrity component when a package needs to be verified. Can only be sent by the system.

- **android.intent.action.PACKAGE_NEEDS_VERIFICATION**

  Constant `ACTION_PACKAGE_NEEDS_VERIFICATION` from class `android.content.Intent`. Sent when a package needs to be verified. The URI from `Intent.getData()` contains the package name.

- **android.intent.action.PACKAGE_REMOVED**

  Constant `ACTION_PACKAGE_REMOVED` from class `android.content.Intent`. An existing app was removed. Extra data:

  - **Intent.EXTRA_UID**: The UID of the app (int)

  - **Intent.EXTRA_DATA_REMOVED**: Whether the data has been removed as well (Boolean)

  - **Intent.EXTRA_REPLACING**: Whether an `ACTION_PACKAGE_ADDED` for the same app will follow (Boolean)

- **android.intent.action.PACKAGE_REMOVED_INTERNAL**

  Constant `ACTION_PACKAGE_REMOVED_INTERNAL` from class `android.content.Intent`. An application package has been removed from the device. Used internally by the system and can only be sent by the system. The package that is being removed does *not* receive this Intent. Extra data:

  - **Intent.EXTRA_UID**: An integer UID previously assigned to the package

  - **Intent.EXTRA_DATA_REMOVED**: Set to true if the entire application (data and code) is being removed

- **Intent.EXTRA_REPLACING**: Set to true if this will be followed by a PACKAGE_ADDED for the same package

- **Intent.EXTRA_USER_INITIATED**: A Boolean field to signal that the application was removed by a user-initiated action

- **Intent.EXTRA_VISIBILITY_ALLOW_LIST**: An int array to indicate the visibility allow list

- **android.intent.action.PACKAGE_REPLACED**

  Constant `ACTION_PACKAGE_REPLACED` from class `android.content.Intent`. A new version of an existing app has been installed. The URI from `Intent.getData()` contains the package name. Extra data:

  - **Intent.EXTRA_UID** (optional): The UID of the app (int)

- **android.intent.action.PACKAGE_RESTARTED**

  Constant `ACTION_PACKAGE_RESTARTED` from class `android.content.Intent`. The user restarted an app. The URI from `Intent.getData()` contains the package name. Extra data:

  - **Intent.EXTRA_UID** (optional): The UID of the app (int)

- **android.intent.action.PACKAGE_UNSUSPENDED_MANUALLY**

  Details at `https://cs.android.com/android/platform/superproject/+/master:frameworks/base/core/java/android/content/Intent.java;l=2975?q=android.intent.action.PACKAGE_UNSUSPENDED_MANUALLY&sq=&ss=android%2Fplatform%2Fsuperproject`

- **android.intent.action.PACKAGE_VERIFIED**

  Constant `ACTION_PACKAGE_VERIFIED` from class `android.content.Intent`. An app has been verified. The URI from `Intent.getData()` contains the package name.

- **android.intent.action.QUERY_PACKAGE_RESTART**

Details at https://cs.android.com/android/platform/
superproject/+/master:frameworks/base/core/java/android/
content/Intent.java;l=2802?q=android.intent.action.
QUERY_PACKAGE_RESTART&sq=&ss=android%2Fplatform%2Fsu
perproject

- **android.intent.action.ROLLBACK_COMMITTED**

Details at https://cs.android.com/android/platform/
superproject/+/master:frameworks/base/core/java/android/
content/Intent.java;l=2786?q=android.intent.action.
ROLLBACK_COMMITTED&sq=&ss=android%2Fplatform%2Fsu
perproject

Network

- **android.app.action.NETWORK_LOGS_AVAILABLE**

Details at https://cs.android.com/android/platform/
superproject/+/master:frameworks/base/core/java/android/
app/admin/DeviceAdminReceiver.java;l=307?q=android.app.
action.NETWORK_LOGS_AVAILABLE&sq=&ss=android%2Fplatform%
2Fsuperproject

- **android.intent.action.PROXY_CHANGE**

Constant ACTION_PROXY_CHANGE from class android.net.Proxy. A
proxy has changed.

- **android.net.action.CLEAR_DNS_CACHE**

Details at https://cs.android.com/android/platform/
superproject/+/master:packages/modules/Connectivity/
framework/src/android/net/ConnectivityManager.
java;l=471?q=android.net.action.CLEAR_DNS_CACHE&sq=&ss=
android%2Fplatform%2Fsuperproject

- **android.net.conn.CAPTIVE_PORTAL_TEST_COMPLETED**

  Details at https://cs.android.com/android/platform/
  superproject/+/master:packages/modules/Connectivity/
  framework/src/android/net/ConnectivityManager.
  java;l=415?q=android.net.conn.CAPTIVE_PORTAL_TEST_COMPLE
  TED&sq=&ss=android%2Fplatform%2Fsuperproject

- **android.net.conn.CONNECTIVITY_CHANGE**

  Constant CONNECTIVITY_ACTION from class android.net.
  ConnectivityManager. Signals a change in the network
  connectivity. Contains extra data:

  - **ConnectivityManager.EXTRA_NETWORK_INFO**: Deprecated
    since API level 14 (android.net.NetworkInfo)

  - **ConnectivityManager.EXTRA_IS_FAILOVER** (optional): If this is
    a failover connection (Boolean)

  - **ConnectivityManager.EXTRA_NO_CONNECTIVITY** (optional):
    True if this is a disconnect event and there are no connected
    networks at all (Boolean)

- **android.net.conn.DATA_ACTIVITY_CHANGE**

  Details at https://cs.android.com/android/platform/
  superproject/+/master:packages/modules/Connectivity/
  framework/src/android/net/ConnectivityManager.
  java;l=306?q=android.net.conn.DATA_ACTIVITY_CHANGE&sq=&s
  s=android%2Fplatform%2Fsuperproject

- **android.net.conn.INET_CONDITION_ACTION**

  Details at https://cs.android.com/android/platform/
  superproject/+/master:packages/modules/Connectivity/
  framework/src/android/net/ConnectivityManager.
  java;l=358?q=android.net.conn.INET_CONDITION_ACTION&sq=&
  ss=android%2Fplatform%2Fsuperproject

- **android.net.conn.RESTRICT_BACKGROUND_CHANGED**

Constant `ACTION_RESTRICT_BACKGROUND_CHANGED` from class `ConnectivityManager`. A change in the background metered network activity restriction has occurred.

- **android.net.nsd.STATE_CHANGED**

Constant `ACTION_STATE_CHANGED` from class `android.net.nsd.NsdManager`. Indicate whether network service discovery is enabled or disabled. Extra data:

  - **NsdManager.EXTRA_NSD_STATE**: State information. One of

    NsdManager.NSD_STATE_DISABLED

    NsdManager.NSD_STATE_ENABLED

- **android.net.scoring.SCORER_CHANGED**

Constant `ACTION_SCORER_CHANGED` from class `android.net.NetworkScoreManager`. The active scorer has been changed. Extra data:

  - **NsdManager.EXTRA_NEW_SCORER**: The scorer package

    (string)

Requires the "android.Manifest.permission.SCORE_NETWORKS" permission.

- **android.net.scoring.SCORE_NETWORKS**

Constant `ACTION_SCORE_NETWORKS` from class `android.net.NetworkScoreManager`. New network scores are being requested. Extra data:

  - **NsdManager.EXTRA_NETWORKS_TO_SCORE**: Specifies the networks to score (android.net.NetworkKey array)

Requires the "android.Manifest.permission.SCORE_NETWORKS" permission.

- **android.net.sip.action.SIP_CALL_OPTION_CHANGED**

Constant `ACTION_SIP_CALL_OPTION_CHANGED` from class `android.net.sip.SipManager`. Sent when the SIP accounts or other configurations have changed.

- **android.net.sip.action.SIP_INCOMING_CALL**

  Constant `ACTION_SIP_INCOMING_CALL` from class `android.net. sip.SipManager`. There is a new incoming SIP call.

- **android.net.sip.action.SIP_REMOVE_PROFILE**

  Constant `ACTION_SIP_REMOVE_PROFILE` from class `android.net. sip.SipManager`. A SIP profile has been removed.

- **android.net.sip.action.SIP_SERVICE_UP**

  Constant `ACTION_SIP_SERVICE_UP` from class `android.net.sip. SipManager`. The SipManager becomes available.

- **android.net.sip.action.START_SIP**

  Constant `ACTION_START_SIP` from class `android.net.sip. SipManager`. Used by telephony to start the SIP service.

Wi-Fi

- **android.net.wifi.NETWORK_IDS_CHANGED**

  Constant `NETWORK_IDS_CHANGED_ACTION` from class `android.net. wifi.WifiManager`. Indicates a change of the IDs of the configured networks.

- **android.net.wifi.RSSI_CHANGED**

  Constant `RSSI_CHANGED_ACTION` from class `android.net.wifi. WifiManager`. The signal strength (RSSI) has changed. Extra data:

  - **WifiManager.EXTRA_NEW_RSSI**: The new RSSI in dBm (int)

- **android.net.wifi.SCAN_RESULTS**

  Constant `SCAN_RESULTS_AVAILABLE_ACTION` from class `android. net.wifi.WifiManager`.

  - **WifiManager.EXTRA_RESULTS_UPDATED** (optional): Whether the scan was successful (Boolean)

- **android.net.wifi.STATE_CHANGE**

Constant `NETWORK_STATE_CHANGED_ACTION` from class `android.net.wifi.WifiManager`. The state of Wi-Fi connectivity has changed. Contains extra data:

WifiManager.EXTRA_NETWORK_INFO: The `android.net.NetworkInfo` object

WifiManager.EXTRA_BSSID (optional): If the new state is CONNECTED, the BSSID of the access point (string)

WifiManager.EXTRA_WIFI_INFO (optional): If the new state is CONNECTED, the `android.net.wifi.WifiInfo` object

- **android.net.wifi.action.WIFI_NETWORK_SUGGESTION_POST_CONNECTION**

  Constant `ACTION_WIFI_NETWORK_SUGGESTION_POST_CONNECTION` from class `android.net.wifi.WifiManager`. The device has connected to one of the network suggestions provided. Extra data:

  - **WifiManager.EXTRA_NETWORK_SUGGESTION**: Holds an instance of `WifiNetworkSuggestion` corresponding to the connected network

  Permission required: "android.permission.ACCESS_FINE_LOCATION ACCESS_FINE_LOCATION"

- **android.net.wifi.action.WIFI_SCAN_AVAILABILITY_CHANGED**

  Constant `ACTION_WIFI_SCAN_AVAILABILITY_CHANGED` from class `android.net.wifi.WifiManager`. Indicates whether Wi-Fi scanning is currently available. Extra data:

  - **WifiManager.EXTRA_SCAN_AVAILABLE**: A Boolean

- **android.net.wifi.WIFI_STATE_CHANGED**

  Constant `STATE_CHANGED_ACTION` from class `android.net.wifi.WifiManager`. The Wi-Fi state has been changed. Contains extra data:

  - **WifiManager.EXTRA_WIFI_STATE**: The new state. One of

    WifiManager.WIFI_STATE_DISABLED

WifiManager.WIFI_STATE_DISABLING

WifiManager.WIFI_STATE_ENABLED

WifiManager.WIFI_STATE_ENABLING

WifiManager.WIFI_STATE_UNKNOWN

- **WifiManager.EXTRA_PREVIOUS_WIFI_STATE**: The previous state. The possible values are the same as for EXTRA_WIFI_STATE.

- **android.net.wifi.aware.action.WIFI_AWARE_STATE_CHANGED**

  Constant ACTION_WIFI_AWARE_STATE_CHANGED from class android.net.wifi.aware.WifiAwareManager. The state of Wi-Fi Aware availability has changed.

- **android.net.wifi.p2p.CONNECTION_STATE_CHANGE**

  Constant WIFI_P2P_CONNECTION_CHANGED_ACTION from class android.net.wifi.p2p.WifiP2pManager. The state of Wi-Fi p2p connectivity has changed. Extra data:

  - **WifiP2pManager.EXTRA_WIFI_P2P_INFO**: An android.net.wifi.p2p.WifiP2pInfo object

  - **WifiP2pManager.EXTRA_NETWORK_INFO**: An android.net.NetworkInfo object

  - **WifiP2pManager.EXTRA_WIFI_P2P_GROUP**: An android.net.wifi.p2p.WifiP2pGroup object

- **android.net.wifi.p2p.DISCOVERY_STATE_CHANGE**

  Constant WIFI_P2P_DISCOVERY_CHANGED_ACTION from class android.net.wifi.p2p.WifiP2pManager. Peer discovery has either started or stopped. Extra data:

  - **WifiP2pManager.EXTRA_DISCOVERY_STATE**: One of

    WifiP2pManager.WIFI_P2P_DISCOVERY_STARTED

    WifiP2pManager.WIFI_P2P_DISCOVERY_STOPPED

- **android.net.wifi.p2p.PEERS_CHANGED**

  Constant `WIFI_P2P_PEERS_CHANGED_ACTION` from class `android.net.wifi.p2p.WifiP2pManager`. The available peer list has changed. Extra data:

  - **WifiP2pManager.EXTRA_P2P_DEVICE_LIST**: The new peer list (android.net.wifi.p2p.WifiP2pDeviceList)

- **android.net.wifi.p2p.STATE_CHANGED**

  Constant `WIFI_P2P_STATE_CHANGED_ACTION` from class `android.net.wifi.p2p.WifiP2pManager`. Indicates whether Wi-Fi p2p is enabled or disabled. Extra data:

  - **WifiP2pManager.EXTRA_WIFI_STATE**: One of

    WifiP2pManager.WIFI_P2P_STATE_DISABLED

    WifiP2pManager.WIFI_P2P_STATE_ENABLED

- **android.net.wifi.p2p.THIS_DEVICE_CHANGED**

  Constant `WIFI_P2P_THIS_DEVICE_CHANGED_ACTION` from class `android.net.wifi.p2p.WifiP2pManager`. This Wi-Fi device's details have changed.

- **android.net.wifi.rtt.action.WIFI_RTT_STATE_CHANGED**

  Constant `ACTION_WIFI_RTT_STATE_CHANGED` from class `android.net.wifi.WifiManager`. The state of Wi-Fi RTT availability has changed (`isAvailable()` allows to query the current status). Note: Only delivered to programmatically registered receivers – no manifest-registered components will be launched.

- **android.net.wifi.supplicant.CONNECTION_CHANGE**

  Constant `SUPPLICANT_CONNECTION_CHANGE_ACTION` from class `android.net.wifi.WifiManager`. A connection to the supplicant has been established or lost. Extra data:

  - **WifiP2pManager.EXTRA_SUPPLICANT_CONNECTED**: True if connected (Boolean)

- **android.net.wifi.supplicant.STATE_CHANGE**

  Constant `SUPPLICANT_STATE_CHANGED_ACTION` from class `android.net.wifi.WifiManager`. The state of establishing a connection to an access point has changed. Extra data:

  - **WifiP2pManager.EXTRA_NEW_STATE**: An `android.net.wifi.SupplicantState` object describing the new state

Notifications

- **android.app.action.APP_BLOCK_STATE_CHANGED**

  Details at `https://cs.android.com/android/platform/superproject/+/master:frameworks/base/core/java/android/app/NotificationManager.java;l=118?q=android.app.action.APP_BLOCK_STATE_CHANGED&sq=&ss=android%2Fplatform%2Fsuperproject`

- **android.app.action.AUTOMATIC_ZEN_RULE_STATUS_CHANGED**

  Details at `https://cs.android.com/android/platform/superproject/+/master:frameworks/base/core/java/android/app/NotificationManager.java;l=259?q=android.app.action.AUTOMATIC_ZEN_RULE_STATUS_CHANGED&sq=&ss=android%2Fplatform%2Fsuperproject`

- **android.app.action.CLOSE_NOTIFICATION_HANDLER_PANEL**

  Details at `https://cs.android.com/android/platform/superproject/+/master:frameworks/base/core/java/android/app/NotificationManager.java;l=201?q=android.app.action.CLOSE_NOTIFICATION_HANDLER_PANEL&sq=&ss=android%2Fplatform%2Fsuperproject`

- **android.app.action.INTERRUPTION_FILTER_CHANGED**

  Constant `ACTION_INTERRUPTION_FILTER_CHANGED` from class `android.app.NotificationManager`. Fired when the state of `getCurrentInterruptionFilter()` changes.

- **android.app.action.INTERRUPTION_FILTER_CHANGED_INTERNAL**

  Details at `https://cs.android.com/android/platform/ superproject/+/master:frameworks/base/core/java/android/ app/NotificationManager.java;l=370?q=android.app.action. INTERRUPTION_FILTER_CHANGED_INTERNAL&sq=&ss=android%2Fpl atform%2Fsuperproject`

- **android.app.action.NOTIFICATION_POLICY_ACCESS_GRANTED_CHANGED**

  Constant `ACTION_NOTIFICATION_POLICY_ACCESS_ GRANTED_CHANGED` from class `android.app.NotificationManager`. Fired when the state of `isNotificationPolicyAccessGranted()` changes.

- **android.app.action.NOTIFICATION_POLICY_CHANGED**

  Constant `ACTION_NOTIFICATION_POLICY_CHANGED` from class `android.app.NotificationManager`. Broadcast when the state of `getNotificationPolicy()` changes.

- **android.app.action.NOTIFICATION_CHANNEL_BLOCK_STATE_CHANGED**

  Constant `ACTION_NOTIFICATION_CHANNEL_BLOCK_STATE_CHANGED` from class `android.app.NotificationManager`. Intent that is broadcast when a NotificationChannel is blocked.

- **android.app.action.NOTIFICATION_CHANNEL_GROUP_BLOCK_STATE_CHANGED**

  Constant `ACTION_NOTIFICATION_CHANNEL_GROUP_BLOCK_STATE_ CHANGED` from class `android.app.NotificationManager`. Intent that is broadcast when an application is blocked or unblocked..

- **android.app.action.NOTIFICATION_LISTENER_ENABLED_CHANGED**

  Constant `ACTION_NOTIFICATION_LISTENER_ENABLED_CHANGED` from class `android.app.NotificationManager`. Intent that is broadcast when the state of `hasEnabledNotificationListener(S tring, UserHandle)` changes.

- **android.os.action.ACTION_EFFECTS_SUPPRESSOR_CHANGED**

  Constant `ACTION_EFFECTS_SUPPRESSOR_CHANGED` from class `android.app.NotificationManager`. Broadcast when the state of `getEffectsSuppressor()` changes.

- **android.settings.ENABLE_MMS_DATA_REQUEST**

  Details at `https://cs.android.com/android/platform/superproject/+/master:frameworks/base/core/java/android/provider/Settings.java;l=2413?q=android.settings.ENABLE_MMS_DATA_REQUEST&sq=&ss=android%2Fplatform%2Fsuperproject`

Telephony

- **android.intent.action.CALL_DISCONNECT_CAUSE**

  Details at `https://cs.android.com/android/platform/superproject/+/master:frameworks/base/telephony/java/android/telephony/TelephonyManager.java;l=904?q=android.intent.action.CALL_DISCONNECT_CAUSE&sq=&ss=android%2Fplatform%2Fsuperproject`

- **android.intent.action.CONTENT_CHANGED**

  Constant `CONTENT_CHANGED_ACTION` from class `android.provider.Telephony.Mms.Intents`.

  The contents of specified URIs were changed.

- **android.intent.action.DATA_SMS_RECEIVED**

  Constant `DATA_SMS_RECEIVED_ACTION` from class `android.provider.Telephony.Sms.Intents`.

  The device received an SMS message. Extra data:

  - **"pdus"**: An object array of byte arrays containing the PDUs

Requires permission "android.permission.RECEIVE_SMS".

- **android.intent.action.DATA_STALL_DETECTED**

  Details at `https://cs.android.com/android/platform/`
  `superproject/+/master:frameworks/base/telephony/`
  `java/android/telephony/TelephonyManager.`
  `java;l=1493?q=android.intent.action.DATA_STALL_DETECTED&`
  `sq=&ss=android%2Fplatform%2Fsuperproject`

- **android.intent.action.EMERGENCY_CALLBACK_
  MODE_CHANGED**

  Details at `https://cs.android.com/android/platform/`
  `superproject/+/master:frameworks/base/telephony/`
  `java/android/telephony/TelephonyManager.`
  `java;l=1714?q=android.intent.action.EMERGENCY_CALLBACK_`
  `MODE_CHANGED&sq=&ss=android%2Fplatform%2Fsuperproject`

- **android.intent.action.EMERGENCY_CALL_STATE_CHANGED**

  Details at `https://cs.android.com/android/platform/`
  `superproject/+/master:frameworks/base/telephony/`
  `java/android/telephony/TelephonyManager.`
  `java;l=1902?q=android.intent.action.EMERGENCY_CALL_`
  `STATE_CHANGED&sq=&ss=android%2Fplatform%2Fsuperproject`

- **android.intent.action.NEW_OUTGOING_CALL**

  Constant `ACTION_NEW_OUTGOING_CALL` from class `android.`
  `content.Intent`.

  An outgoing call is being placed. Extra data:

  - **Intent.EXTRA_PHONE_NUMBER**: The original phone number
    being called (string)

  An app may replace the phone number by calling
  `BroadcastReceiver.setResultData(...)`. A receiver whose
  purpose is to prohibit phone calls should have a priority of 0
  (`setPriority()` in the intent filter), to ensure it will see the final
  phone number to be dialed. A receiver whose purpose is to rewrite

phone numbers to be called should have a positive priority. Negative priorities are reserved for the system; do not use them. Any BroadcastReceiver receiving this Intent must not abort the broadcast. Emergency calls cannot be intercepted, and other calls cannot be modified to call emergency numbers. If you want to redirect an outgoing call to your own service, set the resultData to null, `BroadcastReceiver.setResultData(null)`, and then start your own app to make the call.Requires permission "android. permission.PROCESS_OUTGOING_CALLS".

- **android.intent.action.PHONE_STATE**

Constant `ACTION_PHONE_STATE` from class `android.telephony. TelephonyManager`.

The call state on the device has changed. Extra data:

- **TelephonyManager.EXTRA_STATE**: The new state of the phone (string). One of

  TelephonyManager.EXTRA_STATE_IDLE: The phone is idle.

  TelephonyManager.EXTRA_STATE_RINGING: A new call arrived and is ringing or waiting.

  TelephonyManager.EXTRA_STATE_OFFHOOK: At least one call exists that is dialing, active, or on hold, and no calls are ringing or waiting.

- **TelephonyManager.EXTRA_INCOMING_NUMBER** (optional): If the state is RINGING, this field contains the number (string).

Requires permission "android.permission.READ_PHONE_STATE".

- **android.intent.action.SUB_DEFAULT_CHANGED**

Details at `https://cs.android.com/android/platform/ superproject/+/master:frameworks/base/telephony/ java/android/telephony/SubscriptionManager. java;l=1123?q=android.intent.action.SUB_DEFAULT_CHANGED& sq=&ss=android%2Fplatform%2Fsuperproject`

- **android.provider.action.SMS_MMS_DB_CREATED**

  Details at `https://cs.android.com/android/platform/`
  `superproject/+/master:frameworks/base/core/java/android/`
  `provider/Telephony.java;l=1323?q=android.provider.`
  `action.SMS_MMS_DB_CREATED&sq=&ss=android%2Fplatform%2Fsu`
  `perproject`

- **android.provider.action.SMS_MMS_DB_LOST**

  Details at `https://cs.android.com/android/platform/`
  `superproject/+/master:frameworks/base/core/java/android/`
  `provider/Telephony.java;l=1348?q=android.provider.`
  `action.SMS_MMS_DB_LOST&sq=&ss=android%2Fplatform%2Fsu`
  `perproject`

- **android.provider.Telephony.MMS_DOWNLOADED**

  Details at `https://cs.android.com/android/platform/`
  `superproject/+/master:frameworks/base/core/java/android/`
  `provider/Telephony.java;l=1258?q=android.provider.`
  `Telephony.MMS_DOWNLOADED&sq=&ss=android%2Fplatform%2Fsu`
  `perproject`

- **android.provider.Telephony.SIM_FULL**

  Constant `SIM_FULL_ACTION` from class `android.provider.`
  `Telephony`.

  The SIM storage for SMS messages is full.

- **android.provider.Telephony.SMS_CARRIER_PROVISION**

  Details at `https://cs.android.com/android/platform/`
  `superproject/+/master:frameworks/base/core/java/android/`
  `provider/Telephony.java;l=1172?q=android.provider.`
  `Telephony.SMS_CARRIER_PROVISION&sq=&ss=android%2Fplatfor`
  `m%2Fsuperproject`

- **android.provider.Telephony.SMS_CB_RECEIVED**

  Constant `SMS_CB_RECEIVED_ACTION` from class `android.`
  `provider.Telephony`.

A new Cell Broadcast message has been received. Extra data:

— **"message"**: A `android.telephony.SmsCbMessage` object containing the broadcast message

- **android.provider.Telephony.SMS_EMERGENCY_CB_RECEIVED**

Constant `SMS_EMERGENCY_CB_RECEIVED` from class `android.provider.Telephony`.

A new Emergency Broadcast message has been received. Extra data:

— **"message"**: A `android.telephony.SmsCbMessage` object containing the broadcast message, including ETWS or CMAS warning notification info if present

- **android.provider.Telephony.SMS_DELIVER**

Constant `SMS_DELIVER_ACTION` from class `android.provider.Telephony`.

An SMS has been received. This broadcast goes only to the default app. Extra data:

— **"pdus"**: An Object[] of byte[]s containing the PDUs

Requires permission "android.Manifest.permission.BROADCAST_SMS".

- **android.provider.Telephony.SMS_RECEIVED**

Constant `SMS_RECEIVED_ACTION` from class `android.provider.Telephony`.

A SMS has been received. Extra data:

— **"pdus"**: an Object[] of byte[]s containing the PDUs

- **android.provider.Telephony.SMS_REJECTED**

Constant `SMS_REJECTED_ACTION` from class `android.provider.Telephony`.

An SMS has been rejected by the telephony framework. Extra data:

- **"result"**: The reason for the rejection. One of

  Telephony.RESULT_SMS_GENERIC_ERROR: Generic error

  Telephony.RESULT_SMS_OUT_OF_MEMORY: Device out of memory

  Telephony.RESULT_SMS_UNSUPPORTED: Format or encoding not supported

  Telephony.RESULT_SMS_DUPLICATED: Message duplicated

- **android.provider.Telephony.SMS_SERVICE_CATEGORY_PROGRAM_DATA_RECEIVED**

  Constant `SMS_SERVICE_CATEGORY_PROGRAM_DATA_ RECEIVED_ ACTION` from class `android.provider.Telephony`.

  A new CDMA SMS has been received containing *Service Category Program Data*. Extra data:

  - **"operations"**: An array of `android.telephony.cdma. CdmaSmsCbProgramData` objects containing the service category operations (add/delete/clear) to perform

- **android.provider.Telephony.WAP_PUSH_DELIVER**

  Constant `WAP_PUSH_DELIVER_ACTION` from class `android. provider.Telephony`.

  A new WAP Push message has been received. This broadcast will only be delivered to the default SMS app. Extra data:

  - **"transactionId"**: The WAP transaction ID (int)

  - **"pduType"**: The WAP PDU type (int)

  - **"header"**: The message header (byte[])

  - **"data"**: The data payload (byte[])

  - **"contentTypeParameters"**: Parameters associated with the content type (Map<String,String>)

Requires the "android.Manifest.permission.BROADCAST_WAP_ PUSH" permission.

- **android.provider.Telephony.WAP_PUSH_RECEIVED**

Constant `WAP_PUSH_RECEIVED_ACTION` from class `android. provider.Telephony`.

A new WAP Push message has been received by the device. Extra data:

   - **"transactionId"**: The WAP transaction ID (int)

   - **"pduType"**: The WAP PDU type (int)

   - **"header"**: The message header (byte[])

   - **"data"**: The data payload (byte[])

   - **"contentTypeParameters"**: Parameters associated with the content type (Map<String,String>)

- **android.provider.action.DEFAULT_SMS_PACKAGE_CHANGED**

Constant `ACTION_DEFAULT_SMS_PACKAGE_CHANGED` from class `android.provider.Telephony`.

When this is the default SMS app, both the new and the previous package receive this broadcast. Extra data:

   - **Telephony.EXTRA_IS_DEFAULT_SMS_APP**: True if this is the new default SMS app (Boolean)

- **android.provider.action.EXTERNAL_PROVIDER_CHANGE**

Constant `ACTION_EXTERNAL_PROVIDER_CHANGE` from class `android.provider.Telephony`.

A change is made to the SmsProvider or MmsProvider by a process other than the default SMS application. The URI used for that can be read by `Intent.getData()`.

- **android.telephony.action.AREA_INFO_UPDATED**

Constant `ACTION_AREA_INFO_UPDATED` from class `android. telephony.CellBroadcastIntents`.

Area information has been updated. Also sent when the user turns off area info alerts. The information can be retrieved by `CellBroadcastService.getCellBroadcastAreaInfo()`. The associated SIM slot index of updated area information can be retrieved through the extra data supplied. Extra data:

- **SubscriptionManager.EXTRA_SLOT_INDEX**: SIM slot index (int)

- **android.telephony.action.CARRIER_SIGNAL_DEFAULT_NETWORK_AVAILABLE**

  Constant `ACTION_CARRIER_SIGNAL_DEFAULT_NETWORK_AVAILABLE` from class `android.telephony.TelephonyManager`.

  A protected Intent that can only be sent by the system. Sent when the availability of the system default network changes. Intended for carrier apps to set/reset carrier actions. It is only sent to the carrier apps specified in the carrier config for the subscription ID attached to this Intent. Extra data:

  - **TelephonyManager.EXTRA_DEFAULT_NETWORK_AVAILABLE**: The default network is now available (Boolean).

  - **SubscriptionManager.EXTRA_SUBSCRIPTION_INDEX**: The subscription ID on which the default network availability changed.

- **android.telephony.action.CARRIER_SIGNAL_PCO_VALUE**

  Constant `ACTION_CARRIER_SIGNAL_PCO_VALUE` from class `android.telephony.TelephonyManager`.

  Sent when a PCO value becomes available from the modem. This is a protected Intent that can only be sent by the system. Extra data:

  - **TelephonyManager.EXTRA_APN_TYPE**: An integer indicating the APN type

  - **TelephonyManager.EXTRA_APN_PROTOCOL**: An integer indicating the protocol of the APN connection

  - **TelephonyManager.EXTRA_PCO_ID**: An integer indicating the PCO ID for the data

- **TelephonyManager.EXTRA_PCO_VALUE**: A byte array of PCO data read from the modem

- **SubscriptionManager.EXTRA_SUBSCRIPTION_INDEX**: The subscription ID for which the PCO info was received

- **android.telephony.action.CARRIER_SIGNAL_REDIRECTED**

  Constant `ACTION_CARRIER_SIGNAL_REDIRECTED` from class `android.telephony.TelephonyManager`.

  A data connection is redirected with validation failure. This is a protected Intent that can only be sent by the system. Extra data:

  - **TelephonyManager.EXTRA_APN_TYPE**: An integer indicating the APN type

  - **TelephonyManager.EXTRA_REDIRECTION_URL**: A string indicating the redirection URL

  - **SubscriptionManager.EXTRA_SUBSCRIPTION_INDEX**: The subscription ID for which the PCO info was received

- **android.telephony.action.CARRIER_SIGNAL_REQUEST_ NETWORK_FAILED**

  Constant `ACTION_CARRIER_SIGNAL_REQUEST_NETWORK_FAILED` from class `android.telephony.TelephonyManager`.

  Sent when a data connection setup fails. This is a protected Intent that can only be sent by the system. Extra data:

  - **TelephonyManager.EXTRA_APN_TYPE**: An integer indicating the APN type

  - **TelephonyManager.EXTRA_DATA_FAIL_CAUSE**: An integer indicating the data fail cause

  - **SubscriptionManager.EXTRA_SUBSCRIPTION_INDEX**: The subscription ID for which the PCO info was received

- **android.telephony.action.CARRIER_SIGNAL_RESET**

  Constant `ACTION_CARRIER_SIGNAL_RESET` from class `android.telephony.TelephonyManager`.

Sent when carrier apps should reset their internal state (certain events such as turning on/off mobile data, removing the SIM, etc.). This is a protected Intent that can only be sent by the system. Extra data:

- **SubscriptionManager.EXTRA_SUBSCRIPTION_INDEX**: The subscription ID for which the PCO info was received

- **android.telephony.action.DEFAULT_SMS_SUBSCRIPTION_CHANGED**

  Constant `ACTION_DEFAULT_SMS_SUBSCRIPTION_CHANGED` from class `android.telephony.SubscriptionManager`.

  The default SMS subscription has changed. Extra data:

  - **SubscriptionManager.EXTRA_SUBSCRIPTION_INDEX**: Indicates which subscription has changed (int)

- **android.telephony.action.DEFAULT_SUBSCRIPTION_CHANGED**

  Constant `ACTION_DEFAULT_SUBSCRIPTION_CHANGED` from class `android.telephony.SubscriptionManager`.

  The default subscription has changed. Extra data:

  - **SubscriptionManager.EXTRA_SUBSCRIPTION_INDEX**: Indicates which subscription has changed (int)

- **android.telephony.action.PRIMARY_SUBSCRIPTION_ LIST_CHANGED**

  Constant `ACTION_PRIMARY_SUBSCRIPTION_LIST_CHANGED` from class `android.telephony.TelephonyManager`.

  The primary (non-opportunistic) subscription list has changed.

- **android.telephony.action.REFRESH_SUBSCRIPTION_PLANS**

  Constant `ACTION_REFRESH_SUBSCRIPTION_PLANS` from class `android.telephony.SubscriptionManager`.

  A refresh of the billing relationship plans between a carrier and a specific subscriber is requested. Extra data:

– **SubscriptionManager.EXTRA_SUBSCRIPTION_INDEX**: Indicates which subscription the user is interested in

- **android.telephony.action.SECRET_CODE**

Constant `ACTION_SECRET_CODE` from class `android.telephony.TelephonyManager`.

A debug code (*##<code>##; the intent has the data URI: `android_secret_code://<code>`)

- **android.telephony.action.SERVICE_PROVIDERS_UPDATED**

Constant `ACTION_SERVICE_PROVIDERS_UPDATED` from class `android.telephony.TelephonyManager`.

The Service Provider strings have been updated. Activities or services that use these strings should update their display. Can only be sent by the system. Extra data:

– **TelephonyManager.EXTRA_SHOW_PLMN**: Whether the PLMN should be shown (Boolean)

– **TelephonyManager.EXTRA_PLMN**: The operator name of the registered network (string)

– **TelephonyManager.EXTRA_SHOW_SPN**: Whether the SPN should be shown (Boolean)

– **TelephonyManager.EXTRA_SPN**: The service provider name (string)

– **TelephonyManager.EXTRA_DATA_SPN**: The service provider name for data service (string)

- **android.telephony.action.SIM_APPLICATION_STATE_CHANGED**

Constant `ACTION_SIM_APPLICATION_STATE_CHANGED` from class `android.telephony.TelephonyManager`.

The SIM application state has changed. Can only be sent by the system. Extra data:

- **TelephonyManager.EXTRA_SIM_STATE**: The SIM application state. One of (constants in TelephonyManager)

- **SIM_STATE_NOT_READY**

  SIM card applications not ready

- **SIM_STATE_PIN_REQUIRED**

  SIM card PIN locked

- **SIM_STATE_PUK_REQUIRED**

  SIM card PUK locked

- **SIM_STATE_NETWORK_LOCKED**

  SIM card network locked

- **SIM_STATE_PERM_DISABLED**

  SIM card permanently disabled due to PUK failures

- **SIM_STATE_LOADED**

  SIM card data loaded

Permission required: "android.permission.READ_PRIVILEGED_PHONE_STATE".

- **android.telephony.action.SIM_CARD_STATE_CHANGED**

  Constant ACTION_SIM_CARD_STATE_CHANGED from class android.telephony.TelephonyManager.

  The SIM card state has changed. Can only be sent by the system. Extra data:

  - **TelephonyManager.EXTRA_SIM_STATE**: The SIM card state. One of (constants in TelephonyManager)

  - **SIM_STATE_ABSENT**

    SIM card not found.

  - **SIM_STATE_CARD_IO_ERROR**

    SIM card IO error.

- **SIM_STATE_CARD_RESTRICTED**

  SIM card is restricted.

- **SIM_STATE_PRESENT**

  SIM card is present.

Permission required: "android.permission.READ_PRIVILEGED_
PHONE_STATE".

- **android.telephony.action.SIM_SLOT_STATUS_CHANGED**

Constant `ACTION_SIM_SLOT_STATUS_CHANGED` from class `android.`
`telephony.TelephonyManager`.

The status of the SIM slots on the device has changed (the status
can be queried using `getUiccSlotsInfo()`). Can only be sent by
the system. Permission required: "android.permission.READ_
PRIVILEGED_PHONE_STATE".

- **android.telephony.action.SUBSCRIPTION_CARRIER_
IDENTITY_CHANGED**

Constant `ACTION_` from class `android.telephony.`
`TelephonyManager`.

The subscription carrier identity has changed. Can only be sent by
the system. Extra data:

- **TelephonyManager.EXTRA_CARRIER_ID**: The up-to-date
  carrier ID of the current subscription ID

- **TelephonyManager.EXTRA_CARRIER_NAME**: The up-to-date
  carrier name of the current subscription

- **TelephonyManager.EXTRA_SUBSCRIPTION_ID**: The subscription ID associated with the changed carrier identity

Permission required: "android.permission.READ_PRIVILEGED_
PHONE_STATE".

- **android.telephony.action.SUBSCRIPTION_PLANS_CHANGED**

Constant `ACTION_SUBSCRIPTION_PLANS_CHANGED` from class
`android.telephony.SubscriptionManager`.

The billing relationship plans between a carrier and a specific subscriber have changed. Extra data:

- **SubscriptionManager.EXTRA_SUBSCRIPTION_INDEX**: Indicates which subscription changed

- **android.telephony.action.SUBSCRIPTION_SPECIFIC_CARRIER_ IDENTITY_CHANGED**

Constant `ACTION_SUBSCRIPTION_SPECIFIC_CARRIER_IDENTITY_ CHANGED` from class `android.telephony.TelephonyManager`.

The subscription-specific carrier identity (fine-grained carrier ID of the current subscription) has changed. Can only be sent by the system. The specific carrier ID would be used for configuration purposes, but apps wishing to know about the carrier itself should use the regular carrier ID returned by `getSimCarrierId()`. Extra data:

- **TelephonyManager.EXTRA_SPECIFIC_CARRIER_ID**: The up-to-date specific carrier ID of the current subscription

- **TelephonyManager.EXTRA_SPECIFIC_CARRIER_NAME**: The up-to-date name of the specific carrier ID

- **TelephonyManager.EXTRA_SUBSCRIPTION_ID**: The subscription ID associated with the changed carrier identity

- **android.telephony.euicc.action.NOTIFY_CARRIER_SETUP_ INCOMPLETE**

Constant `ACTION_NOTIFY_CARRIER_SETUP_INCOMPLETE` from class `android.telephony.euicc.EuiccManager`.

The carrier setup is not completed.

- **android.telephony.euicc.action.OTA_STATUS_CHANGED**

Constant `ACTION_OTA_STATUS_CHANGED` from class `android. telephony.euicc.EuiccManager`.

The eUICC OTA status is changed. Can only be sent by the system.

Permission required: "android.permission.WRITE_EMBEDDED_ SUBSCRIPTIONS".

- **android.telephony.ims.action.RCS_SINGLE_REGISTRATION_
CAPABILITY_UPDATE**

  Constant `ACTION_RCS_SINGLE_REGISTRATION_CAPABILITY_UPDATE`
  from class `android.telephony.ims.ProvisioningManager`.

  Provides the single registration capability of the device and the
  carrier. Extra data:

  - **ProvisioningManager.EXTRA_SUBSCRIPTION_ID**: The sub-
    scription index for which the intent is valid

  - **ProvisioningManager.EXTRA_STATUS**: The RCS VoLTE single
    registration status

  Permission required: "android.permission.PERFORM_IMS_
  SINGLE_REGISTRATION".

- **android.telephony.ims.action.WFC_IMS_REGISTRATION_ERROR**

  Constant `ACTION_WFC_IMS_REGISTRATION_ERROR` from class
  `android.telephony.ImsManager`.

  The IMS registration for Wi-Fi calling has resulted in an error.
  Extra data:

  - ImsManager.EXTRA_WFC_REGISTRATION_FAILURE_TITLE

  - ImsManager.EXTRA_WFC_REGISTRATION_FAILURE_MESSAGE

- **com.android.internal.intent.action.ACTION_FORBIDDEN_NO_
SERVICE_AUTHORIZATION**

  Details at `https://cs.android.com/android/platform/`
  `superproject/+/master:frameworks/base/telephony/java/`
  `android/telephony/ImsManager.java;l=57?q=com.android.`
  `internal.intent.action.ACTION_FORBIDDEN_NO_SERVICE_AUTHO`
  `RIZATION&sq=&ss=android%2Fplatform%2Fsuperproject`

- **com.android.internal.provider.action.VOICEMAIL_SMS_
RECEIVED**

Details at `https://cs.android.com/android/platform/`
`superproject/+/master:frameworks/base/core/java/android/`
`provider/VoicemailContract.java;l=119?q=com.android.`
`internal.provider.action.VOICEMAIL_SMS_RECEIVED&sq=&ss=a`
`ndroid%2Fplatform%2Fsuperproject`

TV

- **android.media.tv.action.CHANNEL_BROWSABLE_REQUESTED**

  Constant `ACTION_CHANNEL_BROWSABLE_REQUESTED` from class
  `android.media.tv.TvContract`.

- Sent when an application requests the system to make the given
  channel browsable. This is only relevant to channels with Channels.
  TYPE_PREVIEW type. Extra data:

  – **TvContract.EXTRA_CHANNEL_ID**: ID for the Channels.TYPE_
    PREVIEW channel (long)

  – **TvContract.EXTRA_PACKAGE_NAME**: The package name of the
    requesting application

- **android.media.tv.action.INITIALIZE_PROGRAMS**

  Constant `ACTION_INITIALIZE_PROGRAMS` from class `android.`
  `media.tv.TvContract`.

  Sent to the target TV input after it is first installed to notify the
  input to initialize its channels and programs to the system content
  provider.

- **android.media.tv.action.PREVIEW_PROGRAM_ADDED_TO_
  WATCH_NEXT**

  Constant `ACTION_PREVIEW_PROGRAM_ADDED_TO_ WATCH_NEXT` from
  class `android.media.tv.TvContract`.

  Sent by the system to tell the target TV that one of its existing
  preview programs is added to the "watch next" programs table.
  Extra data:

- **TvContract.EXTRA_PREVIEW_PROGRAM_ID**: The ID of the existing preview program (long)

- **TvContract.EXTRA_WATCH_NEXT_PROGRAM_ID**: The ID of the new "watch next" program (long)

- **android.media.tv.action.PREVIEW_PROGRAM_BROWSABLE_ DISABLED**

  Constant `ACTION_PREVIEW_PROGRAM_BROWSABLE_ DISABLED` from class `android.media.tv.TvContract`.

  Sent by the system to tell the target TV that one of its preview programs' browsable state is disabled. This means it will no longer be shown to users. Extra data:

  - **TvContract.EXTRA_PREVIEW_PROGRAM_ID**: The ID of the preview program (long)

- **android.media.tv.action.WATCH_NEXT_PROGRAM_ BROWSABLE_DISABLED**

  Constant `ACTION_WATCH_NEXT_PROGRAM_BROWSABLE_ DISABLED` from class `android.media.tv.TvContract`.

  Sent by the system to tell the target TV that one of its "watch next" programs' browsable state is disabled, that is, it will no longer be shown to users. Extra data:

  - **TvContract.EXTRA_WATCH_NEXT_PROGRAM_ID**: The disabled program ID (long)

Audio

- **android.intent.action.HEADSET_PLUG**

  Constant `ACTION_HEADSET_PLUG` from class `android.content.Intent`.

  Same as android.intent.action.HEADSET_PLUG for class `AudioManager` – see in the following.

- **android.intent.action.HEADSET_PLUG**

  Constant `ACTION_HEADSET_PLUG` from class `android.media.`
  `AudioManager`.

  A headset was plugged or unplugged. Extra data:

  - **"state"**: 0 for unplugged, 1 for plugged (int)
  - **"name"**: Human-readable name (string)
  - **"microphone"**: 1 if it has a microphone, 0 if not (int)

- **android.media.ACTION_SCO_AUDIO_STATE_UPDATED**

  Constant `ACTION_SCO_AUDIO_STATE_UPDATED` from class `android.`
  `media.AudioManager`.

  The bluetooth SCO audio connection state has been updated.
  Extra data:

  - **AudioManager.EXTRA_SCO_AUDIO_STATE**: The new SCO
    audio state. One of

    AudioManager.SCO_AUDIO_STATE_DISCONNECTED

    AudioManager.SCO_AUDIO_STATE_CONNECTING

    AudioManager.SCO_AUDIO_STATE_CONNECTED

  - **AudioManager.EXTRA_SCO_AUDIO_PREVIOUS_STATE**: The
    new SCO audio state. The possible values are the same as for
    `EXTRA_SCO_AUDIO_STATE`.

- **android.media.AUDIO_BECOMING_NOISY**

  Constant `ACTION_AUDIO_BECOMING_NOISY` from class `android.`
  `media.AudioManager`.

  A hint for applications that audio is about to become noisy.

- **android.media.INTERNAL_RINGER_MODE_CHANGED_ACTION**

  Constant `ACTION_INTERNAL_RINGER_MODE_CHANGED_ACTION` from
  class `android.media.AudioManager`.

Sticky broadcast intent action indicating that the internal ringer mode has changed. Extra data:

– **AudioManager.EXTRA_RINGER_MODE**: One of

AudioManager.RINGER_MODE_NORMAL

AudioManager.RINGER_MODE_SILENT

AudioManager.RINGER_MODE_VIBRATE

- **android.media.MASTER_MUTE_CHANGED_ACTION**

Constant `ACTION_MASTER_MUTE_CHANGED_ACTION` from class `android.media.AudioManager`.

Broadcast intent when the master mute state changes. Extra data:

– **AudioManager.EXTRA_MASTER_VOLUME_MUTED**: The new master volume mute state for the master mute changed Intent (Boolean)

- **android.media.RINGER_MODE_CHANGED**

Constant `RINGER_MODE_CHANGED_ACTION` from class `android.media.AudioManager`.

Indicates that the ringer mode has changed. Extra data:

– **AudioManager.EXTRA_RINGER_MODE**: One of

AudioManager.RINGER_MODE_NORMAL

AudioManager.RINGER_MODE_SILENT

AudioManager.RINGER_MODE_VIBRATE

- **android.media.STREAM_DEVICES_CHANGED_ACTION**

Constant `STREAM_DEVICES_CHANGED_ACTION` from class `android.media.AudioManager`.

Can only be sent by the system. Broadcast Intent when the devices for a particular stream type change. Extra data:

– AudioManager.EXTRA_VOLUME_STREAM_TYPE

– AudioManager.EXTRA_VOLUME_STREAM_DEVICES

  – AudioManager.EXTRA_PREV_VOLUME_STREAM_DEVICES

- **android.media.STREAM_MUTE_CHANGED_ACTION**

  Constant `STREAM_MUTE_CHANGED_ACTION` from class `android.media.AudioManager`.

  A stream mute state changes. Extra data:

  – **AudioManager.EXTRA_VOLUME_STREAM_TYPE**: The stream type for the volume changed intent

  – **AudioManager.EXTRA_STREAM_VOLUME_MUTED**: The new stream volume mute state for the stream mute changed intent (Boolean)

- **android.media.VOLUME_CHANGED_ACTION**

  Constant `VOLUME_CHANGED_ACTION` from class `android.media.AudioManager`.

  Can only be sent by the system. The volume for a particular stream type changes. Extra data:

  – EXTRA_VOLUME_STREAM_TYPE

  – EXTRA_VOLUME_STREAM_VALUE

  – EXTRA_PREV_VOLUME_STREAM_VALUE

- **android.media.action.CLOSE_AUDIO_EFFECT_ CONTROL_ SESSION**

  Constant `ACTION_CLOSE_AUDIO_EFFECT_CONTROL_ SESSION` from class `android.media.audiofx.AudioEffect`.

  Signals that an audio session is closed and that effects should not be applied anymore. Contains extra data:

  – **AudioEffect.EXTRA_PACKAGE_NAME**: Calling package (string)

  – **AudioEffect.EXTRA_AUDIO_SESSION**: The session ID (int)

- **android.media.action.HDMI_AUDIO_PLUG**

  Constant `ACTION_HDMI_AUDIO_PLUG` from class `android.media.AudioManager`.

821

An HDMI cable was plugged or unplugged. Extra data:

- **AudioManager.EXTRA_AUDIO_PLUG_STATE**: 1 = plugged in, 0 = unplugged (int)

- **AudioManager.EXTRA_MAX_CHANNEL_COUNT**: Maximum number of channels (int)

- **AudioManager.EXTRA_ENCODINGS**: The audio encodings supported by the connected HDMI device (int array). The values are as those fields in `android.media.AudioFormat` starting with "ENCODING_".

- **android.media.action.MICROPHONE_MUTE_CHANGED**

  Constant `ACTION_MICROPHONE_MUTE_CHANGED` from class `android.media.AudioManager`.

  The microphone muting state changed. The intent has no extra values; use `isMicrophoneMute()` to check whether the microphone is muted.

- **android.media.action.OPEN_AUDIO_EFFECT_CONTROL_ SESSION**

  Constant `ACTION_OPEN_AUDIO_EFFECT_CONTROL_ SESSION` from class `android.media.audiofx.AudioEffect`.

  Signals that an audio session is opened and that effects should be applied. Contains extra data:

  - **AudioEffect.EXTRA_PACKAGE_NAME**: Calling package (string)

  - **AudioEffect.EXTRA_AUDIO_SESSION**: The session ID (int)

- **android.media.action.SPEAKERPHONE_STATE_CHANGED**

  Constant `ACTION_` from class `android.media.AudioManager`.

  Speakerphone state changed. The intent has no extra values; use `isSpeakerphoneOn()` to check whether the speakerphone functionality is enabled or not.

Booting and Shutdown

- **android.intent.action.ACTION_SHUTDOWN**

  Constant `ACTION_SHUTDOWN` from class `android.content.Intent`.

  Device about to be shut down. May contain extra data:

  - **Intent.EXTRA_SHUTDOWN_USERSPACE_ONLY**: A boolean – true if this is only a shutdown of user processes. Default is false.

- **android.intent.action.BOOT_COMPLETED**

  Constant `ACTION_BOOT_COMPLETED` from class `android.content.Intent`.

  The device has finished booting. Requires permission "android.permission.RECEIVE_BOOT_COMPLETED".

- **android.intent.action.LOCKED_BOOT_COMPLETED**

  Constant `ACTION_LOCKED_BOOT_COMPLETED` from class `android.content.Intent`.

  The device has been booted, but is still locked. If you react to this broadcast, only the device-protected storage can be accessed if you need a data storage. Requires "android.permission.RECEIVE_BOOT_COMPLETED" permission.

- **android.intent.action.REBOOT**

  Constant `ACTION_REBOOT` from class `android.content.Intent`.

  Have the device do a reboot. Only system code; do not use.

- **android.scheduling.action.REBOOT_READY**

  Details at `https://cs.android.com/android/platform/superproject/+/master:packages/modules/Scheduling/framework/java/android/scheduling/RebootReadinessManager.java;l=80?q=android.scheduling.action.REBOOT_READY&sq=&ss=android%2Fplatform%2Fsuperproject`

Security

- **android.app.action.SECURITY_LOGS_AVAILABLE**

  Details at `https://cs.android.com/android/platform/` `superproject/+/master:frameworks/base/core/java/android/` `app/admin/DeviceAdminReceiver.java;l=297?q=android.app.` `action.SECURITY_LOGS_AVAILABLE&sq=&ss=android%2Fplatfor` `m%2Fsuperproject`

- **android.security.STORAGE_CHANGED**

  Constant `ACTION_STORAGE_CHANGED` from class `android.` `security.KeyChain`.

  Deprecated in API level 26. Instead use the more fine-grained events ACTION_KEYCHAIN_CHANGED, ACTION_TRUST_ STORE_CHANGED, and ACTION_KEY_ACCESS_CHANGED.

- **android.security.action.KEYCHAIN_CHANGED**

  Constant `ACTION_KEYCHAIN_CHANGED` from class `android.` `security.KeyChain`.

  The contents of the keychain have changed.

- **android.security.action.KEY_ACCESS_CHANGED**

  Constant `ACTION_KEY_ACCESS_CHANGED` from class `android.` `security.KeyChain`.

  The access permissions for a private key have changed.

- **android.security.action.TRUST_STORE_CHANGED**

  Constant `ACTION_TRUST_STORE_CHANGED` from class `android.` `security.KeyChain`.

  The contents of the trusted certificate store have changed. Fired when a preinstalled CA is disabled or re-enabled or a CA is added to or removed from the trusted store.

Various

- **android.app.action.APPLICATION_DELEGATION_
  SCOPES_CHANGED**

  Constant `ACTION_APPLICATION_DELEGATION_SCOPES_ CHANGED`
  from class `android.app.admin.DevicePolicyManager`.

  A broadcast sent after application delegation scopes are changed.
  The new scopes are listed in a string array from extra data with key
  `DevicePolicyManager.EXTRA_DELEGATION_SCOPES`.

- **android.app.action.LOCK_TASK_ENTERING**

  Constant `ACTION_LOCK_TASK_ENTERING` from class `android.app.
  admin.DeviceAdminReceiver`.

  The device is entering lock task mode. Extra data:

  - **DeviceAdminReceiver.EXTRA_LOCK_TASK_PACKAGE**: The
    name of the package using lock task mode (string)

- **android.app.action.LOCK_TASK_EXITING**

  Constant `ACTION_LOCK_TASK_EXITING` from class `android.app.
  admin.DeviceAdminReceiver`.

  The device is exiting from lock task mode.

- **android.app.action.NEXT_ALARM_CLOCK_CHANGED**

  Constant `ACTION_NEXT_ALARM_CLOCK_CHANGED` from class
  `android.app.AlarmManager`.

  Sent after the value returned by `getNextAlarmClock()` has
  changed.

- **android.app.action.NOTIFY_PENDING_SYSTEM_UPDATE**

  Details at `https://cs.android.com/android/platform/
  superproject/+/master:frameworks/base/core/java/android/
  app/admin/DeviceAdminReceiver.java;l=462?q=android.app.
  action.NOTIFY_PENDING_SYSTEM_UPDATE&sq=&ss=android%2Fpla
  tform%2Fsuperproject`

- **android.app.action.OPERATION_SAFETY_STATE_CHANGED**

  Details at `https://cs.android.com/android/platform/
  superproject/+/master:frameworks/base/core/java/android/
  app/admin/DeviceAdminReceiver.java;l=524?q=android.app.
  action.OPERATION_SAFETY_STATE_CHANGED&sq=&ss=android%2Fp
  latform%2Fsuperproject`

- **android.app.action.SCHEDULE_EXACT_ALARM_PERMISSION_
  STATE_CHANGED**

  Details at `https://cs.android.com/android/platform/
  superproject/+/master:frameworks/base/apex/
  jobscheduler/framework/java/android/app/AlarmManager.
  java;l=173?q=android.app.action.SCHEDULE_EXACT_ALARM_
  PERMISSION_STATE_CHANGED&sq=&ss=android%2Fplatform%2Fsu
  perproject`

- **android.app.action.SYSTEM_UPDATE_POLICY_CHANGED**

  Constant `ACTION_SYSTEM_UPDATE_POLICY_CHANGED` from class
  `android.app.admin.DevicePolicyManager`.

  A new local system update policy has been set by the
  device owner.

- **android.content.pm.action.SESSION_COMMITTED**

  Constant `ACTION_SESSION_COMMITTED` from class `android.
  content.pm.PackageInstaller`.

  Explicit broadcast sent to the last known default launcher when a
  session for a new install is committed. Contains extra data:

  – **EXTRA_SESSION**: The session (android.content.pm.
    PackageInstaller.SessionInfo)

  – **android.content.Intent.EXTRA_USER**: The user (android.os.
    UserHandle)

- **android.content.pm.action.SESSION_UPDATED**

Details at `https://cs.android.com/android/platform/`
`superproject/+/master:frameworks/base/core/java/android/`
`content/pm/PackageInstaller.java;l=166?q=android.`
`content.pm.action.SESSION_UPDATED&sq=&ss=android%2Fplatf`
`orm%2Fsuperproject`

- **android.hardware.action.NEW_PICTURE**

Constant `ACTION_NEW_PICTURE` from class `android.`
`hardware.Camera.`

Deprecated in API level 21. Brought back in API level 26. A new
picture is taken. Use `Intent.getData()` to get the URI of the picture.

- **android.hardware.action.NEW_VIDEO**

Constant `ACTION_NEW_VIDEO` from class `android.`
`hardware.Camera.`

Deprecated in API level 21. Brought back in API level 26. A new video
is recorded. Use `Intent.getData()` to get the URI of the video.

- **android.hardware.hdmi.action.OSD_MESSAGE**

Send when the HdmiControlManager service has a message to
display on screen for events that need the user's attention such as
ARC status change. Extra data:

  - **"android.hardware.hdmi.extra.MESSAGE_ID"**: The ID of the
    message to display on screen

Requires the "android.Manifest.permission.HDMI_CEC"
permission.

- **android.hardware.input.action.QUERY_KEYBOARD_LAYOUTS**

Constant `ACTION_QUERY_KEYBOARD_LAYOUTS` from class `android.`
`hardware.input.InputManager.`

The input manager service locates available keyboard layouts by
querying broadcast receivers that are registered for this action. For
details see the API documentation of `android.hardware.input.`
`InputManager.`

- **android.intent.action.ACTION_IDLE_MAINTENANCE_END**

  Details at `https://cs.android.com/android/platform/ superproject/+/master:frameworks/base/core/java/android/ content/Intent.java;l=3816?q=android.intent.action. ACTION_IDLE_MAINTENANCE_END&sq=&ss=android%2Fplatform%2F superproject`

- **android.intent.action.ACTION_IDLE_MAINTENANCE_START**

  Details at `https://cs.android.com/android/platform/ superproject/+/master:frameworks/base/core/java/android/ content/Intent.java;l=3787?q=android.intent.action. ACTION_IDLE_MAINTENANCE_START&sq=&ss=android%2Fplatform% 2Fsuperproject`

- **android.intent.action.ACTION_PREFERRED_ ACTIVITY_CHANGED**

  Details at `https://cs.android.com/android/platform/ superproject/+/master:frameworks/base/core/java/android/ content/Intent.java;l=3134?q=android.intent.action. ACTION_PREFERRED_ACTIVITY_CHANGED&sq=&ss=android%2Fplatf orm%2Fsuperproject`

- **android.intent.action.AIRPLANE_MODE**

  Constant `ACTION_AIRPLANE_MODE` from class `android. content.Intent`.

  The user toggled airplane mode. Contains extra data:

  – **"state"**: A boolean – true if airplane mode is on

- **android.intent.action.ALARM_CHANGED**

  Details at `https://cs.android.com/android/platform/ superproject/+/master:frameworks/base/core/java/android/ content/Intent.java;l=2546?q=android.intent.action. ALARM_CHANGED&sq=&ss=android%2Fplatform%2Fsuperproject`

- **android.intent.action.APPLICATION_RESTRICTIONS_CHANGED**

  Constant `ACTION_APPLICATION_RESTRICTIONS_CHANGED` from class `android.content.Intent`.

  Sent after application restrictions are changed.

- **android.intent.action.CAMERA_BUTTON**

  Constant `ACTION_CAMERA_BUTTON` from class `android.content.Intent`.

  The camera button was pressed. Extra data:

  - **Intent.EXTRA_KEY_EVENT**: The associated android.view. KeyEvent

- **android.intent.action.CLOSE_SYSTEM_DIALOGS**

  Constant `ACTION_CLOSE_SYSTEM_DIALOGS` from class `android.content.Intent`.

  A user action should request a temporary system dialog to dismiss.

- **android.intent.action.CONFIGURATION_CHANGED**

  Constant `ACTION_CONFIGURATION_CHANGED` from class `android.content.Intent`.

  The current device configuration (orientation, locale, etc.), represented by class `android.content.res.Configuration`, has changed.

- **android.intent.action.DATE_CHANGED**

  Constant `ACTION_DATE_CHANGED` from class `android.content.Intent`.

  The date has changed.

- **android.intent.action.DEVICE_STORAGE_FULL**

  Details at `https://cs.android.com/android/platform/superproject/+/master:frameworks/base/core/java/android/content/Intent.java;l=3404?q=android.intent.action.DEVICE_STORAGE_FULL&sq=&ss=android%2Fplatform%2Fsuperproject`

- **android.intent.action.DEVICE_STORAGE_LOW**

  Constant `ACTION_DEVICE_STORAGE_LOW` from class `android.content.Intent`.

  Defunct in API level 26 (Android 8.0).

- **android.intent.action.DEVICE_STORAGE_NOT_FULL**

  Details at `https://cs.android.com/android/platform/superproject/+/master:frameworks/base/core/java/android/content/Intent.java;l=3421?q=android.intent.action.DEVICE_STORAGE_NOT_FULL&sq=&ss=android%2Fplatform%2Fsuperproject`

- **android.intent.action.DEVICE_STORAGE_OK**

  Constant `ACTION_DEVICE_STORAGE_OK` from class `android.content.Intent`.

  Defunct in API level 26 (Android 8.0).

- **android.intent.action.DOCK_EVENT**

  Constant `ACTION_DOCK_EVENT` from class `android.content.Intent`.

  A change in the physical docking state occurred. Extra data:

  - **Intent.EXTRA_DOCK_STATE: the dock state**: Possible values are

    Intent.EXTRA_DOCK_STATE_UNDOCKED: Undocked

    Intent.EXTRA_DOCK_STATE_DESK: Desk dock

    Intent.EXTRA_DOCK_STATE_CAR: Car dock

    Intent.EXTRA_DOCK_STATE_LE_DESK: Low-performance (analog) dock

    Intent.EXTRA_DOCK_STATE_HE_DESK: High-performance (digital) dock

- **android.intent.action.DOWNLOAD_COMPLETE**

Constant `ACTION_DOWNLOAD_COMPLETE` from class `android.app.DownloadManager`.

A download completed.

- **android.intent.action.DOWNLOAD_NOTIFICATION_CLICKED**

Constant `ACTION_DOWNLOAD_NOTIFICATION_CLICKED` from class `android.app.DownloadManager`.

The user clicks a running download.

- **android.intent.action.DREAMING_STARTED**

Undocumented. See `android.service.dreams.DreamService` for a service approach to dreaming (custom interactive screensaver when the device is idle).

- **android.intent.action.DREAMING_STOPPED**

Undocumented. See `android.service.dreams.DreamService` for a service approach to dreaming (custom interactive screensaver when the device is idle).

- **android.intent.action.DROPBOX_ENTRY_ADDED**

Constant `ACTION_DROPBOX_ENTRY_ADDED` from class `android.os.DropBoxManager`.

A new entry is added in the dropbox. Requires "android.permission.READ_LOGS" permission.

- **android.intent.action.DYNAMIC_SENSOR_CHANGED**

Details at `https://cs.android.com/android/platform/superproject/+/master:frameworks/base/core/java/android/content/Intent.java;l=4340?q=android.intent.action.DYNAMIC_SENSOR_CHANGED&sq=&ss=android%2Fplatform%2Fsuperproject`

- **android.intent.action.EXTERNAL_APPLICATIONS_AVAILABLE**

Constant `ACTION_EXTERNAL_APPLICATIONS_AVAILABLE` from class `android.content.Intent`.

Previously unavailable apps are now available, for example, because a medium has been attached. Extra data:

- **Intent.EXTRA_CHANGED_PACKAGE_LIST**: List of new apps available (string array)

- **Intent.EXTRA_CHANGED_UID_LIST**: List of corresponding UIDs (int array)

- **android.intent.action.EXTERNAL_APPLICATIONS_ UNAVAILABLE**

Constant `ACTION_EXTERNAL_APPLICATIONS_UNAVAILABLE` from class `android.content.Intent`.

Previously available apps are now unavailable, for example, because a medium has been removed. Extra data:

- **Intent.EXTRA_CHANGED_PACKAGE_LIST**: List of new apps available (string array)

- **Intent.EXTRA_CHANGED_UID_LIST**: List of corresponding UIDs (int array)

- **android.intent.action.FACTORY_RESET**

Details at `https://cs.android.com/android/platform/ superproject/+/master:frameworks/base/core/java/android/ content/Intent.java;l=4387?q=android.intent.action. FACTORY_RESET&sq=&ss=android%2Fplatform%2Fsuperproject`

- **android.intent.action.FETCH_VOICEMAIL**

Constant `ACTION_FETCH_VOICEMAIL` from class `android. provider.VoicemailContract`.

Use this to request a voicemail source to fetch voicemail content from the remote server. The voicemail to fetch is specified by the data URI of the intent.

- **android.intent.action.GTALK_CONNECTED**

Constant `ACTION_GTALK_SERVICE_CONNECTED` from class `android. content.Intent`.

A GTalk connection has been established.

- **android.intent.action.GTALK_DISCONNECTED**

  Constant `ACTION_GTALK_SERVICE_DISCONNECTED` from class `android.content.Intent`.

  A GTalk connection has been closed.

- **android.intent.action.INPUT_METHOD_CHANGED**

  Constant `ACTION_INPUT_METHOD_CHANGED` from class `android.content.Intent`.

  An input method has been changed.

- **android.intent.action.LOCALE_CHANGED**

  Constant `LOCALE_CHANGED` from class `android.content.Intent`.

  The device's locale has been changed.

- **android.intent.action.MANAGE_PACKAGE_STORAGE**

  Constant `ACTION_MANAGE_PACKAGE_STORAGE` from class `android.content.Intent`.

  The low-memory condition notification acknowledged by the user and package management should be started.

  - **intent.EXTRA_USER**: The corresponding user (android.os.UserHandle)

- **android.intent.action.MASTER_CLEAR_NOTIFICATION**

  Details at `https://cs.android.com/android/platform/superproject/+/master:frameworks/base/core/java/android/content/Intent.java;l=4359?q=android.intent.action.MASTER_CLEAR_NOTIFICATION&sq=&ss=android%2Fplatform%2Fsuperproject`

- **android.intent.action.NEW_VOICEMAIL**

  Constant `ACTION_NEW_VOICEMAIL` from class `android.provider.VoicemailContract`.

  A new voicemail record was inserted.

- **android.intent.action.PROVIDER_CHANGED**

  Constant `ACTION_PROVIDER_CHANGED` from class `android.content.Intent`.

  A content provider signals a data change. The URI from `Intent.getData()` contains information about the change, and besides in the extra data, we have

  – **"count"**: The number of items in the data set (int)

- **android.intent.action.SCREEN_OFF**

  Constant `ACTION_SCREEN_OFF` from class `android.content.Intent`.

  The device goes to sleep and becomes non-interactive.

- **android.intent.action.SCREEN_ON**

  Constant `ACTION_SCREEN_ON` from class `android.content.Intent`.

  The device becomes interactive again after being non-interactive.

- **android.intent.action.SPLIT_CONFIGURATION_CHANGED**

  Details at `https://cs.android.com/android/platform/superproject/+/master:frameworks/base/core/java/android/content/Intent.java;l=3197?q=android.intent.action.SPLIT_CONFIGURATION_CHANGED&sq=&ss=android%2Fplatform%2Fsuperproject`

- **android.intent.action.TIMEZONE_CHANGED**

  Constant `ACTION_TIMEZONE_CHANGED` from class `android.content.Intent`.

  The time zone has changed. Extra data:

  – **"time-zone"**: The `java.util.TimeZone.getID()` value (string)

- **android.intent.action.TIME_SET**

  Constant `ACTION_TIME_CHANGED` from class `android.content.Intent`.

  The time was set.

- **android.intent.action.TIME_TICK**

  Constant `ACTION_TIME_TICK` from class `android.content.Intent`.

  The time has changed – sent every minute.

- **android.nfc.action.ADAPTER_STATE_CHANGED**

  Constant `ACTION_ADAPTER_STATE_CHANGED` from class `android.nfc.NfcAdapter`.

- The state of the local NFC adapter has been changed. Extra data:

  - **NfcAdapter.EXTRA_ADAPTER_STATE**: The new state. One of

    NfcAdapter.STATE_OFF

    NfcAdapter.STATE_TURNING_ON

    NfcAdapter.STATE_ON

    NfcAdapter.STATE_TURNING_OFF

- **android.nfc.action.PREFERRED_PAYMENT_CHANGED**
  Details at `https://cs.android.com/android/platform/superproject/+/master:frameworks/base/core/java/android/nfc/NfcAdapter.java;l=181?q=android.nfc.action.PREFERRED_PAYMENT_CHANGED&sq=&ss=android%2Fplatform%2Fsuperproject`

- **android.nfc.action.TRANSACTION_DETECTED**
  Details at `https://cs.android.com/android/platform/superproject/+/master:frameworks/base/core/java/android/nfc/NfcAdapter.java;l=169?q=android.nfc.action.TRANSACTION_DETECTED&sq=&ss=android%2Fplatform%2Fsuperproject`

- **android.location.MODE_CHANGED**
  Constant `MODE_CHANGED_ACTION` from class `android.location.LocationManager`.

  The device-location-enabled state changes. Extra data:

  - (Only for Android R and above) **LocationManager.EXTRA_LOCATION_ENABLED**: Whether enabled or not (Boolean)

- **android.location.PROVIDERS_CHANGED**
Constant `PROVIDERS_CHANGED_ACTION` from class `android.location.LocationManager`.

  The set of enabled location providers changes. Extra data:

  - **LocationManager.EXTRA_PROVIDER_NAME** (Android Q and above): Name of the provider

  - **LocationManager.EXTRA_PROVIDER_ENABLED** (Android R and above): Whether enabled or not (Boolean)

- **android.location.action.ADAS_GNSS_ENABLED_CHANGED**
Constant `ACTION_ADAS_GNSS_ENABLED_CHANGED` from class `android.location.LocationManager`.

- The ADAS (Advanced Driving Assistance Systems) GNSS location-enabled-state changes. This broadcast only has meaning on automotive devices. Extra data:

  - **LocationManager.EXTRA_ADAS_GNSS_ENABLED**: Enabled state of ADAS GNSS location

- **android.location.action.GNSS_CAPABILITIES_CHANGED**

  Constant from class `android.location.LocationManager`.

  GNSS capabilities change. This is most common at boot time as GNSS capabilities are queried from the chipset. Extra data:

  - **LocationManager.EXTRA_GNSS_CAPABILITIES**: The new `GnssCapabilities`

- **android.provider.action.SYNC_VOICEMAIL**

  Constant `ACTION_SYNC_VOICEMAIL` from class `android.provider.VoicemailContract`.

  Used to request all voicemail sources to perform a sync with the remote server.

- **android.speech.tts.TTS_QUEUE_PROCESSING_COMPLETED**

  Constant `ACTION_TTS_QUEUE_PROCESSING_COMPLETED` from class `android.speech.tts.TextToSpeech`.

The TextToSpeech synthesizer has completed processing all the text in the speech queue. Does not mean any sound has been generated yet.

- **android.speech.tts.engine.TTS_DATA_INSTALLED**

  Constant `ACTION_TTS_DATA_INSTALLED` from class `android.speech.tts.TextToSpeech.Engine`.

  Signals the change in the list of available languages or their features.

- **android.app.action.BUGREPORT_FAILED**

  Constant `ACTION_BUGREPORT_FAILED` from class `android.app.admin.DeviceAdminReceiver`.

  Action sent to a device administrator to notify that the collection of a bug report has failed.

- **android.app.action.BUGREPORT_SHARE**

  Constant `ACTION_BUGREPORT_SHARE` from class `android.app.admin.DeviceAdminReceiver`.

  Action sent to a device administrator to share the bug report.

- **android.app.action.BUGREPORT_SHARING_DECLINED**

  Constant `ACTION_BUGREPORT_SHARING_DECLINED` from class `android.app.admin.DeviceAdminReceiver`.

  Action sent to a device administrator to notify that the device user has declined sharing a bug report.

- **android.se.omapi.action.SECURE_ELEMENT_STATE_CHANGED**

  Details at `https://cs.android.com/android/platform/superproject/+/master:frameworks/base/omapi/java/android/se/omapi/SEService.java;l=82?q=android.se.omapi.action.SECURE_ELEMENT_STATE_CHANGED&sq=&ss=android%2Fplatform%2Fsuperproject`

- **android.service.controls.action.ADD_CONTROL**

  Undocumented

- **com.android.intent.action.DISMISS_KEYBOARD_SHORTCUTS**

  Details at `https://cs.android.com/android/platform/`
  `superproject/+/master:frameworks/base/core/java/android/`
  `content/Intent.java;l=1627?q=com.android.intent.action.`
  `DISMISS_KEYBOARD_SHORTCUTS&sq=&ss=android%2Fplatform%2Fs`
  `uperproject`

- **com.android.intent.action.SHOW_KEYBOARD_SHORTCUTS**

  Details at `https://cs.android.com/android/platform/`
  `superproject/+/master:frameworks/base/core/java/android/`
  `content/Intent.java;l=1617?q=com.android.intent.action.`
  `SHOW_KEYBOARD_SHORTCUTS&sq=&ss=android%2Fplatform%2Fsu`
  `perproject`

Index

A

B

BroadcastReceiver, 447, 448

connect(...) method, 461

connectDevice() method, 453, 454

connection socket, 459, 461

DeviceListActvity class, 446

device_list.xml, 444, 445

device_name.xml, 445

logging statement, 461

MainActivity class, 451

mState member, 461

onActivityResult() method, 454

onCreate() callback method, 448–452

onDestroy()/doDiscovery() methods, 450, 451

OnItemClickListener, 446, 447

private methods, 456, 457

public methods, 455, 456

rfComm/sendMessage() methods, 453

scanDevices() method, 452

testing, 462

Thread implementation, 458, 459

UUID, 461

write(...) method, 461

registerContentObserver(), 94

registerForContextMenu(), 340

Remote broadcast receivers, 52

Remote explicit broadcasts, 54

RemoteInput.getResultsFromIntent(), 182

Renderer, 307, 312

Reply notification, 179

replyTo parameter, 44

requestCode, 19

ResultReceiver class, 46, 235, 413–415

Reusable libraries

.aar file, 370

client, 371

creation, 368, 369

library modules, 368

publishing, 371

testing, 369, 370

Reverse geocoding, 232

revokeUriPermission(String, Uri, Int), 81

Room architecture

DAO/data access object, 146

database, 146

entity, 146

Runnable objects, 259

RxJava/RxKotlin, 158

S

saveRecentQuery() method, 219

sceneRoot, 292

Scoped storage methodology, 641

Scoping functions, 385, 386

Screen sizes, 265

SDK tools, 4, 615–618

ADB, 623, 624

build tools, 618–621

DEVICE_NAME argument, 624

platform-independent tools, 615

platform tools, 622, 623

SearchableActivity class, 212, 213, 218, 225

Searchable configuration, 211, 212

Search dialog, 211, 213, 214

Search framework

searchable activity, 212, 213

searchable configuration, 211, 212

search dialog, 213, 214

search facilities, 211

search suggestions

custom suggestions, 219–225

recent query suggestions, 217–219

search widget, 215, 216

user interface, 211

Search widget, 215, 216

855

Printed in the United States
by Baker & Taylor Publisher Services